Fodor's 07

ARIZONA & THE GRAND CANYON

Where to Stay and Eat for All Budgets

Must-See Sights and Local Secrets

Ratings You Can Trust

Fodor's Travel Publications   New York, Toronto, London, Sydney, Auckland
www.fodors.com

FODOR'S ARIZONA & THE GRAND CANYON 2007

Editor: Caroline Trefler

Editorial Production: Evangelos Vasilakis
Editorial Contributors: Rebecca I. Allen, Matt Baatz, Tom Carpenter, Janet Webb Farnsworth, Satu Hummasti, JoBeth Jamison, Denise Leto, Mara Levin
Maps: David Lindroth, *cartographer*; Bob Blake and Rebecca Baer, *map editors*
Design: Fabrizio La Rocca, *creative director*; Guido Caroti, *art director*; Melanie Marin, *senior picture editor*
Production/Manufacturing: Angela L. McLean
Cover Photo (Grand Canyon): *T. Gervis/Robert Harding World Imagery.*

ISBN-10: 1–4000–1706–8

ISBN-13: 978–1–4000–1706–5

ISSN: 1559–6230

SPECIAL SALES

This book is available for special discounts for bulk purchases for sales promotions or premiums. Special editions, including personalized covers, excerpts of existing books, and corporate imprints, can be created in large quantities for special needs. For more information, write to Special Markets/Premium Sales, 1745 Broadway, MD 6-2, New York, New York 10019, or e-mail specialmarkets@randomhouse.com.

AN IMPORTANT TIP & AN INVITATION

Although all prices, opening times, and other details in this book are based on information supplied to us at press time, changes occur all the time in the travel world, and Fodor's cannot accept responsibility for facts that become outdated or for inadvertent errors or omissions. So **always confirm information when it matters,** especially if you're making a detour to visit a specific place. Your experiences—positive and negative—matter to us. If we have missed or misstated something, **please write to us.** We follow up on all suggestions. Contact the Arizona editor at editors@fodors.com or c/o Fodor's at 1745 Broadway, New York, NY 10019.

PRINTED IN THE UNITED STATES OF AMERICA

10 9 8 7 6 5 4 3 2 1

Be a Fodor's Correspondent

Your opinion matters. It matters to us. It matters to your fellow Fodor's travelers, too. And we'd like to hear it. In fact, we *need* to hear it.

When you share your experiences and opinions, you become an active member of the Fodor's community. That means we'll not only use your feedback to make our books better, but we'll publish your names and comments whenever possible. Throughout our guides, look for "Word of Mouth," excerpts of your unvarnished feedback.

Here's how you can help improve Fodor's for all of us.

Tell us when we're right. We rely on local writers to give you an insider's perspective. But our writers and staff editors—who are the best in the business—depend on you. Your positive feedback is a vote to renew our recommendations for the next edition.

Tell us when we're wrong. We're proud that we update most of our guides every year. But we're not perfect. Things change. Hotels cut services. Museums change hours. Charming cafés lose charm. If our writer didn't quite capture the essence of a place, tell us how you'd do it differently. If any of our descriptions are inaccurate or inadequate, we'll incorporate your changes in the next edition and will correct factual errors at fodors.com *immediately.*

Tell us what to include. You probably have had fantastic travel experiences that aren't yet in Fodor's. Why not share them with a community of like-minded travelers? Maybe you chanced upon a beach or bistro or B&B that you don't want to keep to yourself. Tell us why we should include it. And share your discoveries and experiences with everyone directly at fodors.com. Your input may lead us to add a new listing or highlight a place we cover with a "Highly Recommended" star or with our highest rating, "Fodor's Choice."

Give us your opinion instantly at our feedback center at www.fodors.com/feedback. You may also e-mail editors@fodors.com with the subject line "Arizona Editor." Or send your nominations, comments, and complaints by mail to Arizona Editor, Fodor's, 1745 Broadway, New York, NY 10019.

You and travelers like you are the heart of the Fodor's community. Make our community richer by sharing your experiences. Be a Fodor's correspondent.

Happy Traveling!

Tim Jarrell, Publisher

CONTENTS

CLOSEUPS

MAPS & CHARTS

ABOUT THIS BOOK

Our Ratings

Sometimes you find terrific travel experiences and sometimes they just find you. But usually the burden is on you to select the right combination of experiences. That's where our ratings come in.

As travelers we've all discovered a place so wonderful that its worthiness is obvious. And sometimes that place is so experiential that superlatives don't do it justice: you just have to be there to know. These sights, properties, and experiences get our highest rating, **Fodor's Choice,** indicated by orange stars throughout this book.

Black stars highlight sights and properties we deem **Highly Recommended,** places that our writers, editors, and readers praise again and again for consistency and excellence.

By default, there's another category: any place we include in this book is by definition worth your time, unless we say otherwise. And we will.

Disagree with any of our choices? Care to nominate a place or suggest that we rate one more highly? Visit our feedback center at www.fodors.com/feedback.

Budget Well

Hotel and restaurant price categories from ¢ to $$$$ are defined in the opening pages of each chapter. For attractions, we always give standard adult admission fees; reductions are usually available for children, students, and senior citizens. Want to pay with plastic? **AE, D, DC, MC, V** following restaurant and hotel listings indicate if American Express, Discover, Diners Club, MasterCard, and Visa are accepted.

Restaurants

Unless we state otherwise, restaurants are open for lunch and dinner daily. We mention dress only when there's a specific requirement and reservations only when they're essential or not accepted—it's always best to book ahead.

Hotels

Hotels have private bath, phone, TV, and air-conditioning and operate on the European Plan (aka EP, meaning without meals), unless we specify that they use the Continental Plan (CP, with a Continental breakfast), Breakfast Plan (BP, with a full breakfast), or Modified American Plan (MAP, with breakfast and dinner) or are all-inclusive (including all meals and most activities). We always

list facilities but not whether you'll be charged an extra fee to use them, so when pricing accommodations, find out what's included.

Many Listings
- ★ Fodor's Choice
- ★ Highly recommended
- ⊠ Physical address
- ✛ Directions
- ⏍ Mailing address
- ☎ Telephone
- 🖶 Fax
- ⊕ On the Web
- ✉ E-mail
- 🖃 Admission fee
- ☉ Open/closed times
- ☞ Start of walk/itinerary
- Ⓜ Metro stations
- 🖃 Credit cards

Hotels & Restaurants
- 🏨 Hotel
- 🛏 Number of rooms
- ⚲ Facilities
- ⦿| Meal plans
- ✕ Restaurant
- ⚭ Reservations
- ⛿ Dress code
- ⤫ Smoking
- ⚏ BYOB
- ✕🏨 Hotel with restaurant that warrants a visit

Outdoors
- ⚑ Golf
- ⛺ Camping

Other
- ⚘ Family-friendly
- ☎ Contact information
- ⇨ See also
- ⊠ Branch address
- ☞ Take note

WHAT'S WHERE

PHOENIX, SCOTTSDALE, TEMPE & THE VALLEY OF THE SUN	Rising where the Sonoran Desert butts up against the Superstition Mountains, the Phoenix metropolitan area, known as the Valley of the Sun, is one of America's fastest growing cities. It includes Scottsdale, Tempe, and some 20 other communities surrounded by a landscape of stunning beauty. There are more than 200 golf courses here and outdoor enthusiasts find the nearby mountains delightful destinations for hiking, birding, and camping. The canal systems provide excellent biking and running trails along their banks. People come from around the world to enjoy the resorts and spas, and with competitive teams in all the major professional sports, there are always opportunities to watch well-paid athletes play ball.
THE GRAND CANYON	The Grand Canyon, one of nature's longest-running works in progress, both exalts and humbles the human spirit. You can view the spectacle from the South Rim, but the North Rim is the rim less traveled. Don't just peer over the edge—take the plunge into the canyon on a mule train, on foot, or on a raft trip.
NORTH-CENTRAL ARIZONA	The laid-back towns of north-central Arizona are as bewitching as the landscape they inhabit. Phoenicians flee the summertime heat of the Valley to cool off in the mountains and explore Prescott and Jerome, with an elevation range of 1,500 feet in its city limits, practically hangs like an oil painting from Cleopatra Hill. Today it's home to artists and craftsmen. The fracturing of the western edge of the Colorado Plateau created the red-rock buttes that loom over Sedona and this landscape has attracted artists and entrepreneurs from all over, as well as New Age followers who believe the area contains some of the Earth's most important vortices of energy. Flagstaff, surrounded by the Coconino National Forest and wrapped around the base of the tallest mountains in the state (the San Francisco Peaks at 12,643 feet), is a vibrant university town of outdoor enthusiasts, artists, and scientists.
THE NORTHEAST	Most residents of northeastern Arizona are Navajo and Hopi, and although computers are now part of their daily life traditions endure that predate the conquistadors. Wind and frost have created magical effects in stone, such as the petrified sand dunes in the sunset-hued Antelope Canyon. Monument Valley is the starkly beautiful landscape made popular by Ansel Adams and countless Hollywood Westerns. Along with the living Navajo and Hopi communities, the White House Ruin

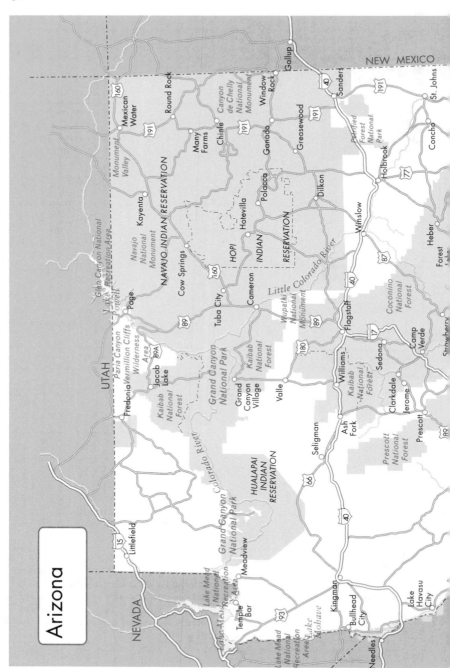

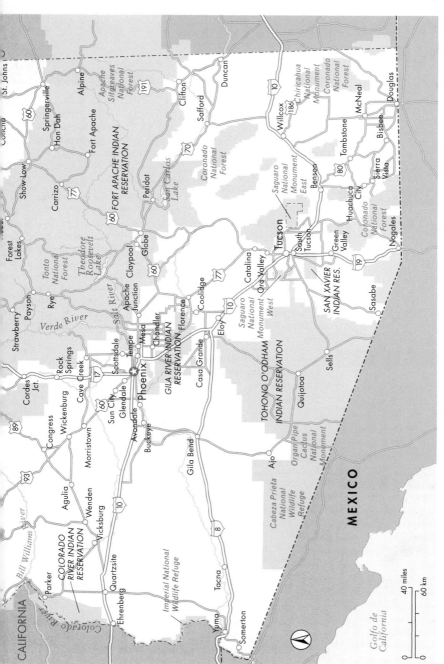

WHAT'S
WHERE

in breathtaking Canyon de Chelly and the ruins at Betatakin and Keet Seel in Navajo National Monument are eloquent reminders of how ancient peoples wrested shelter from this fierce land. At Lake Powell, Glen Canyon Dam inverted the equation here: humankind dominated nature, and the lake created is a spectacular meeting of earth and water.

EASTERN ARIZONA

Eastern Arizona is, by turns, verdant or stark and haunting. The White Mountains, northeast of Phoenix, contain the world's largest stand of ponderosa pines, as well as alpine meadows decked with wildflowers and some of the cleanest air you'll ever breathe. If you love the outdoor life, you may fall in love with this place. To the northeast, Homolovi Ruins State Park preserves five Hopi pueblos. The Painted Desert assumes hues from blood red to pink, then back again, as the sun rises, climbs, and sets. And Petrified Forest National Park protects a forest of trees that stood when dinosaurs walked the earth, the pieces of petrified logs looking deceptively like driftwood cast upon an oceanless beach.

TUCSON

The history of Arizona really begins here, where three cultures— Hispanic, Anglo, and Native America—began to become intertwined in the 17th century with the arrival of the Spanish explorers. Colonial Spain and Mexico left a strong imprint on Tucson's art, architecture, and culture—and residents of South 4th Avenue swear the best Mexican food north of the border is served here. Farther out, city slickers enjoy horseback rides at some of the region's many guest ranches, or luxury pampering at local spas.

SOUTHERN ARIZONA

Mountain and desert scenery in southern Arizona is as splendid as anywhere in the state. The 860,000-acre Cabeza Prieta Wildlife Refuge provides a protected habitat for bighorn sheep and other Sonoran Desert wildlife and the Organ Pipe Cactus National Monument is the largest habitat north of the border for organ pipe cacti. Enduring pockets of the Old West in the form of ghost towns are another draw. Once bigger than San Francisco thanks to silver mining in the area, Tombstone centers its fame on a single event: the Gunfight at the OK Corral. Yuma is the "Nile River Valley" of the state. The fertile soil and mild winter climate enable the agricultural industry here to produce 98% of the iceberg lettuce consumed in North America in winter. Kartchner Caverns, one of the most spectacular wet cave systems in the world is also in this area.

From pine-covered peaks to cacti-bedecked deserts, to the Colorado River and three enticing lakes, the under-explored northwest corner of Arizona is worth a closer look. Lake Havasu City offers a bit of Britannia in the form of London Bridge. Old-fashioned Americana reigns around Kingman, a hub on legendary Route 66. Chloride is, as one regular visitor put it, "not as commercial as Oatman," which means you can enjoy the shops and cafés without crowds and traffic. Take a quick jaunt into Nevada for a look at the monumental Hoover Dam and a hand or two of blackjack in a riverside casino at Laughlin.

QUINTESSENTIAL ARIZONA

Road Trips

Arizona is the place to take a road trip. Get in the car, pick a destination, and go take a look-see. For optimal enjoyment, avoid the Interstate highways and take the state routes instead. Stop at every roadside historic marker (well, OK, you can skip some if you want) and at any place with a sign that reads "pie." Go to Bisbee. Go to Jerome. Go to Oatman. Go to Greer. Travel AZ 260 from Payson to Show Low or historic Route 66 from Ash Fork to Topock; take AZ 60 through the Salt River Canyon, or U.S. Route 191 from Springerville to Clifton; take AZ 88, the Apache Trail, from Apache Junction to Roosevelt Dam. Wherever you go, roll down the windows, turn up the radio, inhale deeply, and enjoy the ride. Regardless of your destination, the wide-open spaces of Arizona entice and amaze anew with every bend in the road.

Chile Rellenos & Margaritas

You're in Arizona, so join the quest to find the world's most delicious stuffed chili. Most any restaurant touting Mexican cuisine has chile rellenos on the menu. The question is: will the chile be tough and tasteless, a mere vessel for the cheeses and other "secret" ingredients? Or will the chile come fresh from the fields, tender, succulent, and flavorful? Only taste will tell. The quest for the perfect chile relleno is frequently attended by the search for the world's greatest margarita. There's no guarantee that the two grails will be found in the same restaurant, but it's most efficient to order both.

The Night Sky

Away from the metropolitan areas of Phoenix and Tucson, where the by-products of urban life obscure the firmament, the night sky is clear and unpolluted by lights

Arizona is known for its magnificent natural landmarks, its rich history, and its captivating cuisine. Here are some easy ways to get to know the lay of the land and start thinking like an Arizonan.

or smog. In December, in the desert, the Milky Way stretches like a chiffon scarf across the celestial sphere. Lie on your back on the hood of your car at night, allow your eyes time to adjust to the darkness, and you'll see more stars than you could possibly have imagined. For a closer look, you can visit Lowell Observatory on Mars Hill, in Flagstaff, or the Kitt Peak National Observatory in Southwest Arizona (outside of Tucson) and look at celestial objects through large telescopes.

Rodeo

People take rodeo seriously out in Arizona, whether it's a holiday extravaganza like those in Prescott or Payson (which draw top cowboys from around the country), a bull-riding competition at Camp Verde, or a bunch of working cowboys gathered for a team-roping contest in Williams. These days, particularly with the emer-

gence of bull riding as a stand-alone event—and the crowds often cheer as much for the bulls as the cowboys—rodeos are no longer the hayseed and cowpoky events Arizona grandpas might have enjoyed. Rock and roll rodeo has arrived and there is frequently live music as well as roping. So, if you see a flyer posted in a shop window advertising a rodeo, take a walk on the wild side and check out the fine arts of riding and roping. You might be surprised how graceful it all is.

IF YOU LIKE

Hiking

The joke goes, when the Good Lord made the world, he practiced his geologic formations in Arizona. As a result, you can hike in and out, up and down, or just around beautiful and varied landscapes, into canyons, to a mountain summit; or just along a meandering trail through a desert or a forest. Wherever you go, make sure you're well-prepared with water, food, and a good hat.

- You could spend the rest of your life hiking the **Grand Canyon** and never cover all the trails. Bright Angel trail is the most famous, but it's tough: with an elevation change of more than 5,000 feet, don't try to hike it to the Colorado River and back in one day. Less strenuous is the 9 mi Rim Trail, a paved, generally horizontal walk. Other outstanding choices are the South Kaibab Trail and the Hermit Trail.

- **Havasu Canyon** is an 8 mi hike that descends 3,000 feet to a waterfall and turquoise pools of water.

- **Mount Humphreys,** the highest of the four peaks that comprise San Francisco Peaks, is the ultimate goal for hikers seeking the best view in the state. Timing an ascent can be tricky, though, as the snow doesn't melt until mid-July, and by then the summer rains and lightning come almost daily in the afternoon. Go early in the morning and pay attention to the sky.

- **Walnut Canyon National Monument** has a paved and stepped trail descending 185 feet into an island of stone where you can explore prehistoric cliff dwellings. There are steps and handrails but the climb out is strenuous.

Water Sports

You don't miss the water until it's not there, but Arizonians do their best to ensure the well doesn't go dry. Dams and canal systems help to fill vast reservoirs, and the resulting rivers and lakes provide all manner of water-sport recreation. You can have it easy, you can have it rough, or you can have it fast.

- Easy is a week on a houseboat on a lake. Houseboats are available for rent on major lakes along the Colorado River, as well as on Lake Powell, Lake Mead, and Lake Havasu. On smaller lakes motorized boats are prohibited, but kayaks and canoes make for an enjoyable excursion along the pine-covered shorelines. You can even take a rowboat out on Tempe Town Lake.

- Rough is a river raft trip. There are nearly two-dozen commercial rafting companies offering trips as short as three days or as long as three weeks through the Grand Canyon. Options include motorized rafts or dories rowed by Arizona's version of the California surfer—the Colorado River boatman. The Hualapai Tribe, through the Hualapai River Runners headquartered in Peach Springs, offers one-day river trips. Don't let the short duration fool you: the boatmen take you through several rapids, and thrills abound.

- Fast involves water skis or Jet Skis. Both are popular on major lakes and along the Colorado River. You can go from dam to dam along the Colorado, and on lakes the size of Powell and Mead you can ski until your legs give out.

Desert

Arizona has a desert for you; actually, it has more than one. The trouble is, any desert is inhospitable to life forms unaccustomed to its harsh realities. People die in the desert here every year, from thirst, exposure, and one inexplicable trait—stupidity. Assuming good sense, you can explore any stretch of desert in April and May and experience a landscape festooned with flowers and blooming cacti.

- To experience the desert without running the risk of leaving your bones to bleach in the sun, there are two exceptional alternatives: the **Desert Botanical Garden** in Scottsdale is a showcase of the ecology of the desert with more than 4,000 different species of desert flora sustained on 150 acres. A walk through here is wonderfully soothing. There's also the **Arizona-Sonora Desert Museum** in Tucson, which isn't really a museum but a zoo and a botanical garden featuring the animals and plants of the Sonoran Desert. If you want to see a diamondback rattlesnake without jumping out of your shoes, this is the place.

- And, of course, there are long drives in which you can see the wide expanses from the comfort of your car. Early spring brings the flaming-red blossoms of the ocotillo and the soft yellow-green branches of the palo verde, and the desert will be carpeted with ephemeral flowers of pink, blue, and yellow. Along U.S. Highway 93, south of Wikieup in northwest Arizona, is a good place to see the desert in its most abundant display, but there are countless others, as well.

Native American Culture

John Ford westerns and the enduring myths of the Wild West pale in comparison to the experience of seeing first-hand the Native American cultures that thrive in Arizona. You can stop at a trading post and see native artisans demonstrating their crafts, visit one of Arizona's spectacular Native American museums, or explore a Native American ruin.

- **Hubbell Trading Post** and **Cameron Trading Post** are on Navajo Reservations, while **Keam's Canyon Trading Post** is on the Hopi Reservation. The **Navajo Village Heritage Center** in Page offers an opportunity to understand life on the reservation.

- The **Heard Museum,** in Phoenix, houses an impressive array of Native American cultural exhibits. The **Museum of Northern Arizona,** in Flagstaff, has collections related to the natural and cultural history of the Colorado Plateau, an extensive collection of Navajo rugs, and an authentic Hopi kiva (men's ceremonial chamber). The **Colorado River Museum,** in Bullhead City, focuses on the history of the area and includes information and artifacts pertaining to the Mohave Indians. **Chiricahua Regional Museum and Research Center,** in Willcox, focuses on Apache culture.

- The **Montezuma Castle National Monument** is one of the best-preserved prehistoric ruins in North America. **Tuzigoot National Monument** is not as well preserved as Montezuma Castle, but more impressive in scope. The **Casa Grande National Monument** is a 35-foot-tall structure built by the Hohokam Indians who lived in the area.

GREAT ITINERARIES

HIGHLIGHTS & HIKES OF ARIZONA

Arizona is full of history, culture, and awe-inspiring natural landmarks. Here are some suggestions for mixing a road trip with some of the state's phenomenal hiking opportunities. Start or end with a few days in Phoenix.

Days 1–2: Wickenburg, Prescott & Sedona

From Phoenix, head northwest to Wickenburg and visit the Desert Caballeros Western Museum. Then proceed to Prescott, "Everyone's Hometown," with its old-fashioned town square, Victorian homes, and pine-covered foothills. In Jerome you'll find a vibrant artist's community. The red rocks of Sedona provide a stunning backdrop to a community famous for its chamber music and art galleries.

In Prescott you can take an extra day to visit the Sharlott Hall Museum and smell the roses in the garden, or hike the popular Thumb Butte Loop Trail. With an extra day in Sedona, a Pink Jeep tour among the towering red rocks is a hoot, and stunning vistas can be seen while hiking along the trails at Red Rock State Park.

Day 3: Flagstaff

In Flagstaff you can visit Lowell Observatory, the Museum of Northern Arizona, and the Arboretum. An evening stroll around the historic downtown district is less than a mile. If hiking and history are your desire, you can take the short drive out of town to Walnut Canyon National Monument with its preserved ancient Native American cliff dwellings. There are two trails to choose from—one easy, one more strenuous—but both are rewarding.

Day 4: The Grand Canyon

A hundred miles north of Flagstaff, the sight of the Grand Canyon's immense beauty has taken many a visitor's breath away. There are hiking and walking options aplenty, for all levels of fitness—if you prefer letting the mules do the trekking for you, book up to 6 months ahead. Whatever you do, though, make sure you catch a sunset or sunrise view of the canyon. A night, or even just dinner at the grand El Tovar Hotel won't disappoint, but again, book early.

Day 5: Navajo National Monument & Monument Valley

The landscape here is incredible, and even if you've seen it in the movies, up-close and personal is an unforgettable experience. There are self-guided driving tours of the area, but a tram tour led by Navajo guides takes you past the sandstone mesas and spires of Monument Valley, where private cars can't go. For those with an equine inclination, a guided horseback tour will probably be the trip of a lifetime.

Days 6–7: Canyon de Chelly

Canyon de Chelly is another of Arizona's unique and fascinating natural wonders. It's smaller than the Grand Canyon, but many say it's just as beautiful—and the archaeological sites and ruins make this a very spiritual sort of place. You can do a self-drive tour, or journey into this magical sandstone landscape on foot, on horseback, or in a guided four-wheel-drive vehicle.

Day 8: The Painted Desert & Petrified Forest

If rocks could talk, those in Petrified Forest National Park and the Painted Desert would tell how eons of wind and rain polished the remains of a primeval swamp into gem-color hills filled with fossils. While it's true that some visitors are underwhelmed, there's really nothing quite like the Petrified Forest anywhere else in the world.

Days 9–10: Coronado Trail & Scenic Byway

On the scenic Coronado Trail you can find treasure in abundance: aspen and fir trees, lakes stocked with trout, and a variety of wildlife. You'll never hear anybody lament having spent an extra day in the White Mountains, so if you have the time, you probably owe yourself an overnight stay in Greer, either in a fully furnished cabin or in a room at any of the lodges.

TIPS

❶ If your budget permits, renting a four-wheel-drive vehicle will allow you to take advantage of side trips to remote areas.

❷ Climate extremes, both heat and cold, make Arizona traveling hazardous so heed the advice of locals. If somebody tells you it's a "little warm" to be poking around in those hills, they're probably correct.

❸ Carry plenty of water and if your vehicle should break down, put the hood up and stay with the vehicle.

ON THE CALENDAR

	Arizona's top seasonal events are listed below, and any one of them could provide the stuff of lasting memories. Contact local tourism authorities for exact dates and further information.
WINTER Early December	For the three days of **Old Town Tempe Fall Festival of the Arts**, the downtown area closes to traffic for art exhibits, food booths, music, and other entertainment.
December	At the **Arizona Temple Gardens & Visitors Center Christmas Lighting**, in Mesa, more than 600,000 lights illuminate the walkways, reflection pool, trees, and plants.
	Near New Year's Tempe's nationally televised **Tostitos Fiesta Bowl Classic** kicks off the year with a match between two of the top college football teams in the nation.
January	**Lettuce Days** celebrates Yuma's title of "Winter Lettuce Capital of the World." Events include cabbage bowling and a lettuce boxcar derby.
Late January	At the **FBR Open Golf Tournament** (formerly the Phoenix Open) in Scottsdale, top players compete at the Tournament Players Club.
	The **Quartzsite Pow Wow Gem and Mineral Show** is a gigantic gem, mineral, and jewelry market, held the last Wednesday through Sunday of the month in Quartzsite, about 19 mi from the California border (take Interstate 10 west of Phoenix, then Exit 17 or 19 in Quartzsite).
February	The annual **Flagstaff Winterfest** celebrates winter in the high country with dozens of events from dogsled races to symphony performances.
	La Fiesta de los Vaqueros features the world's longest "nonmechanized" parade—horses pull floats and carry dignitaries—launching a five-day rodeo at the Tucson Rodeo Grounds.
	The huge **Tucson Annual Gem & Mineral Show** organized by the Tucson Gem and Mineral Society, attracts rock hounds—amateur and professional—from all over the world who come to buy, sell, and display their geological treasures and to attend lectures and competitive exhibits.
	History comes to life during **Wickenburg Gold Rush Days,** when the Old West town puts on a parade, rodeo, dances, gold-panning demonstrations, a mineral show, and other activities.
	The **World Championship Hoop Dance Contest** at the Heard Museum in Phoenix attracts superbly skilled native hoop dancers from across the United States and Canada to compete for a world champion title.

Mid-February	(President's Day Weekend) At **O'odham Tash** in Casa Grande, Native American tribes from around the country, and from Canada and Mexico, host parades, native dances, a rodeo, a powwow, costume displays, and food stands.
SPRING Early March	In Phoenix, the **Heard Museum Guild Indian Fair and Market** is a prestigious juried show of Native American arts and crafts. Visitors can also enjoy Native American foods, music, and dance.
February and March	The **Parada del Sol Rodeo and Parade,** a popular state attraction on Scottsdale Road in Scottsdale, features lots of dressed-up cowboys and cowgirls, plus horses and floats.
	Every year, Apache Junction hosts **Arizona's Annual Renaissance Festival**. This popular return to the Europe of the Renaissance is held on weekends.
Mid-March	The city of Chandler hosts the **Annual Ostrich Festival,** complete with ostrich races, carnival, parade, and lots of fun for all ages.
April	Yuma celebrates the diversity of the lower Colorado River with the **Yuma Birding & Nature Festival**. The event includes classes, hikes, field trips, and seminars covering a variety of subjects from astronomy to dutch-oven cooking.
Late April	Tucson hosts **International Mariachi Conference,** four days of mariachi-music workshops and performances, along with cultural and educational exhibits.
	Bisbee's **La Vuelta de Bisbee** is one of Arizona's largest bicycle races and attracts top racers from around the country to the hills of the historic mining town.
	Yaqui Easter is celebrated in old Pasqua Village (Tucson) with various activities taking place during the Palm Sunday and Easter weekends. Visitors are welcome to watch traditional Yaqui dances and ceremonies.
Early May	During the **Route 66 Fun Run Weekend** from Seligman to Topock, the longest drivable stretch of the historic road between Chicago and Los Angeles is feted with a Show-and-Shine car rally—anyone with a vehicle can join the ride—and various activities along the route, including entertainment, barbecues, and a Miss Route 66 beauty pageant.
Late May	During **Rendezvous Days,** the townspeople of Williams set up an interpretive village and reenact the lives of 1800s mountain traders. Events include a steak fry and a Buckskinners black powder shoot.

ON THE CALENDAR

Late May, early June	Experience the best of art, music, and poetry devoted to the cowboy culture at Flagstaff's annual **Trappings of the American West Exhibition** at the Coconino Center for the Arts.
SUMMER July–October	Flagstaff's Museum of Northern Arizona offers **Hispanic, Hopi, and Navajo, marketplaces** displaying the traditional and contemporary art of these significant Southwest cultures.
First week in July	**Prescott Frontier Days and Rodeo,** billed as the world's oldest rodeo, finds big crowds and an equally big party on downtown Whiskey Row.
Mid-July	The **Native American Arts & Crafts Festival** in Pinetop-Lakeside brings storytellers, dancers, musicians, and artists together for two days in the White Mountains east of Phoenix.
First weekend in August	Flagstaff's **SummerFest** is a gathering of painters, potters, musicians, and other artists from around the United States. They vie with carnival rides and food vendors for the crowd's attention.
Early August	The **Southwest Wings Birding Festival,** held throughout Cochise County and in Bisbee, includes field trips to local canyons and forests, lectures by recognized Audubon authorities, and other avian-oriented events.
Mid-August	The **Payson Rodeo,** known as the "World's Oldest Continuous Rodeo," draws top cowboys from around the country to compete in bull-riding and calf- and steer-roping contests.
FALL September	Each September the **Grand Canyon Chamber Music Festival** is held in the Shrine of the Ages auditorium at the South Rim. Call or write for schedule information and advance tickets.
Early September	The **Navajo Nation Annual Tribal Fair** is the world's largest Native American fair. Held in Window Rock, it includes a rodeo, traditional Navajo music and dances, food booths, and an intertribal powwow.
Late September	At the **Jazz on the Rocks Festival** in Sedona, four or five ensembles perform in a spectacular red-rock setting.
Early October	**Rex Allen Days** in Willcox honors the local cowboy film star and narrator for Walt Disney productions with a parade, country fair, concerts, rodeo, dances, and more.
Mid-October	**Andy Devine Days,** in Kingman, honors the film and television actor with a parade and rodeo.
	At **Tombstone's Helldorado Days,** this town relives the spirited Wyatt Earp era and the shoot-out at the OK Corral.

Mid–late October	A weeklong event, **London Bridge Days** includes a Renaissance festival, a parade, and British-theme contests in Lake Havasu City.
Late October	In late October, you can join the celebration of traditional Navajo culture at the **Western Navajo Fair** in Tuba City.
Late November	At 111 mi, **El Tour de Tucson** is the largest perimeter bicycling event in the world, attracting international celebrity cyclists.

WHEN TO GO

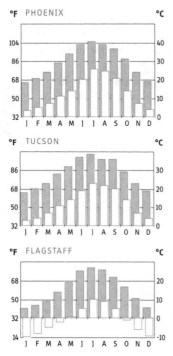

High season at the resorts of Phoenix and Tucson is winter, when the snowbirds fly south. Expect the best temperatures—and the highest prices—from December through March; the posh desert resorts drop their prices—sometimes by more than half—from June through September. The South Rim of the Grand Canyon is busy year-round, but least busy during the winter months.

Climate

Phoenix averages 300 sunny days and 7 inches of precipitation annually. The high mountains see about 25 inches of rain. The Grand Canyon is usually cool on the rim and about 20°F warmer on the floor. Approximately 6 to 12 inches of snow fall on the North Rim; the South Rim receives half that amount. Temperatures in valley areas like Phoenix and Tucson average about 60°F to 70°F in the daytime in winter and between 100°F and 115°F in summer. Flagstaff and Sedona stay much cooler, dropping into the 30s and 40s Fahrenheit in winter and leveling off at 80°F to 90°F in summer.

🅵 Forecasts **Weather Channel** (⊕ www.weather.com).

Phoenix, Scottsdale, Tempe & the Valley of the Sun

WORD OF MOUTH

"In Phoenix my top choices would be the Heard Museum—unique in all the world, I think. And the Frank Lloyd Wright school Taliesen West in northern Scottsdale. If you are interested in the ancient Indians of the valley, see the Pueblo Grande Museum, and if you're interested in the current ones, visit the Pima Indian Museum on the reservation just east of Scottsdale. There is also a branch of the Arizona history museum in Papago Park where Phoenix meets Scottsdale and Tempe."

—Vera

"I took the tour of Taliesen one day when it was 120 degrees. The bottom of my sneakers melted on the hot stones. Despite this, it was one of the highlights of my trip. I recommend it highly."

—BostonJay

Updated by
Rebecca I.
Allen

PHOENIX RISES in the shimmering heat of the great Sonoran Desert in central Arizona. Here are some of the oldest human dwellings in the Western Hemisphere along with the homes of contemporary Native American tribes and one of America's fastest-growing major urban centers: metropolitan Phoenix, a melding of 22 communities, with a population of more than 4 million people.

The Valley of the Sun, otherwise known as metro Phoenix, is named for its 325-plus days of sunshine each year. The Valley marks the northern tip of the Sonoran Desert, a prehistoric seabed that reaches from northwestern Mexico with a landscape offering much more than cacti. Palo verde and mesquite trees, creosote bushes, brittle bush, and agave dot the land, which is accustomed to being scorched by temperatures in excess of 100°F for weeks at a time. Late summer brings precious rain when monsoon storms illuminate the sky with lightning shows and the desert exudes the scent of creosote. Spring sets the Valley blooming, and the giant saguaros are crowned in white flowers for a short time in May—in the evening and cool early mornings—and masses of vibrant wildflowers fill desert crevices and span mountain landscapes.

As the Hohokam (the name comes from the Piman word for "people who have gone before") discovered 2,300 years ago, the miracle of water in the desert can be augmented by human hands. Having migrated from northwestern Mexico, Hohokam cultivated cotton, corn, and beans in tilled, rowed, and irrigated fields for about 1,700 years, establishing more than 300 mi of canals—an engineering miracle when you consider the limited technology available. They constructed a great town upon whose ruins modern Phoenix is built, and then vanished. Drought, long winters, and other causes are suggested for their disappearance.

From the time the Hohokam left until the Civil War, the once fertile Salt River valley lay forgotten, used only by occasional small bands of Pima and Maricopa Indians. Then, in 1865, the U.S. Army established Fort McDowell in the mountains to the east, where the Verde River flows into the Salt River. To feed the men and the horses stationed there, a former Confederate Army officer reopened the Hohokam canals in 1867. Within a year, fields bright with barley and pumpkins earned the area the name Pumpkinville. By 1870 the 300 residents had decided that their new city would arise from the ancient Hohokam ruins, just as the mythical phoenix rose from its own ashes.

Phoenix would rise indeed. Within 20 years, it had become large enough—its population was about 3,000—to wrest the title of territorial capital from Prescott. By 1912, when Arizona was admitted as the 48th state, the area, irrigated by the brand-new Roosevelt Dam and Salt River Project, had a burgeoning cotton industry. Copper and cattle were mined and raised elsewhere but were banked and traded in Phoenix, and the cattle were slaughtered and packed here in the largest stockyards outside of Chicago.

Meanwhile, the climate, so long a crippling liability, became an asset. Desert air was the prescribed therapy for the respiratory ills rampant in the sooty, factory-filled East; Scottsdale began in 1901 as "30-odd

GREAT ITINERARIES

IF YOU HAVE 3 DAYS

See the **Heard Museum** ⑫ for its internationally acclaimed collection of Native American artifacts, and swing by the **Burton Barr Central Library** ⑩ on your way downtown to the **Arizona Science Center** ❷ and **Phoenix Museum of History** ❸. On Day 2, rise early and begin your day at Frank Lloyd Wright's **Taliesin West** ㉙; then head south into Scottsdale for a day of gallery browsing and a walk through **Old Town Scottsdale** ㉔. On your final day visit the stunning **Desert Botanical Garden** ⑲, and take a detour on your way home across Lincoln Drive in northeast Phoenix. This scenic route provides the best views of the Valley's beauty, so be sure to head west as the sun descends and the sky absorbs dozens of colors, introducing the evening.

IF YOU HAVE 5 DAYS

Follow the tour above, and on the fourth day, consider some hiking: even inexperienced hikers will enjoy the walk up to **Papago Park's** ⑱ Hole-in-the-Rock or the 1¼-mi trip to the top of Piestewa (formerly Squaw) Peak, whereas the more experienced may choose to ascend Camelback Mountain. **South Mountain Park** ⑮ has many trails for hikers of all abilities. Spend the afternoon exploring the stark beauty of the surrounding desert on horseback, in a jeep, or by hot-air balloon. Or, hike Papago in the morning and then spend the afternoon hanging out in funky Tempe, checking out **Tempe Town Lake** ㉚. On your fifth day, drive the loop of the **Apache Trail** ㊷–㊽, enjoying breathtaking views of Fish Creek Canyon—or head north to take a tour of **Arcosanti** ㊴ or explore the Old West town of **Wickenburg** ㊳.

IF YOU HAVE 7 DAYS

Expand your drive of the **Apache Trail** ㊷–㊽ to include an overnight stay in 🏕 **Globe** ㊺. Along the way stop to enjoy the view of Weaver's Needle from the **Peralta Trail** ㊹, stroll through **Boyce Thompson Southwestern Arboretum** ㊻, or check out the ancient Hohokam ruins at **Casa Grande Ruins National Monument** ㊶ to the south of Phoenix.

If you'd like to plan your own driving tour, the Arizona Office of Tourism and *Arizona Highways* magazine have created a Web site ⊕ www.arizonascenicroads.com featuring 22 officially designated scenic routes.

---

tents and a half dozen adobe houses" put up by health-seekers. By 1930 travelers looking for warm winter recreation as well as rejuvenating aridity filled the elegant San Marcos Hotel and Arizona Biltmore, the first of the many luxury retreats for which the area is now known worldwide. The 1950s brought with them residential air-conditioning, an invention that made the summers bearable for the growing workforce of the burgeoning technology industry.

The Valley is very much a work still in progress. Historians are quick to point out that never in the world's history has a metropolis grown from "nothing" to attain the status of Phoenix in such a short period of time. But at the heart of all the bustle is a way of life that keeps its own pace: Phoenix is one of the world's largest small towns—where people dress informally and where the rugged, Old West spirit lives on in many of the Valley's nooks and crannies despite the sprawling growth. And if the summer heat can be overwhelming, at least it has the restorative effect of slowing things down to an enjoyable pace.

Although many come to Phoenix for the golf and the weather, the Valley has much to offer by way of shopping, outdoor activities, and nightlife. The best of the latter are in Scottsdale and the East Valley with a variety of hip dance clubs, old-time saloons, and upscale wine bars. Hiking in the Valley will open eyes to to the fascinating Arizona geology as well as stunning views, abundant wild flowers in the spring, and desert flora all year long.

Top 5 Experiences in the Phoenix Area

- **Eat well.** Enjoy a delectable dinner at one of Phoenix's excellent restaurants while you marvel at the red, orange, and purple colors of a sunset against the desert mountains and saguaros. Try the views from elements restaurant at Sanctuary Camelback Mountain in Paradise Valley or the Top of the Rock restaurant at the Wyndham Buttes Resort in Tempe.

- **Hike the hills.** Check out South Mountain Park, Camelback Mountain, or Papago Park and enjoy Arizona's cacti, wildflowers, and distinct geology. The parks offer a variety of hikes ranging from novice to difficult.

- **The Heard Museum.** Learn about Native American people, culture, art, and history at this fascinating, world-renowned museum.

- **Take a jeep tour.** Sign up with Desert Dog Hummer Adventures in Fountain Hills or Wild West Jeep Tours in Scottsdale to really get out there and see what the Sonoran desert looks like.

- **Golf.** Book a tee time and take your clubs to Troon North, The Phoenician, or the Tournament Players Club. They all boast spectacular views and world-class courses.

EXPLORING THE VALLEY OF THE SUN

Phoenix has grown around what was once a cluster of independent towns in Maricopa County. Gaps between communities that were open spaces of desert a few short years ago have begun to close in and blend the entire Valley into one large, sprawling community. If it were not for the WELCOME signs of various municipalities on roadways, you would be hard-pressed to tell where one community ends and another begins. First-time visitors are often surprised to discover that some of the area's finest restaurants and shops are tucked into hotels and strip malls. Metro Phoenix, which occupies a large valley surrounded by desert hills and mountains ranges, retains a strong Western heritage.

Getting around can be complex and exasperating unless you have a car. From Sky Harbor airport, the one-way cab fare to the Four Seasons Resort in North Scottsdale (about 32 mi) can easily cost more than the daily charge for a rental car. Public transit is here in varying degrees and is in-

IF YOU LIKE

GOLF
The Valley of the Sun is among the top U.S. golf destinations, thanks to warm temperatures, azure skies, the scenic desert backdrop, and more than 200 challenging courses. The burgeoning growth of the area has brought with it an explosion of golf courses, many of them world-class in both quality and price. However, there are equally exciting yet more affordable courses to satisfy all levels of play and most every pocketbook. November through April is peak season; in summer, golf fees are a fraction of the cost, and many resorts offer packages combining resort stays with golf. Each January, thousands of golf aficionados descend upon the Valley to attend the prestigious FBR Open at the Tournament Player's Club in Scottsdale.

MOUNTAINS
The mountains surrounding the Valley of the Sun are among its greatest assets. Outdoors enthusiasts have plenty of ground to cover within the city limits in pursuit of their passions—be it hiking, bird-watching, or mountain biking. Piestewa (formerly Squaw) Peak, north of downtown, is popular with hikers. Camelback Mountain and the Papago Peaks are landmarks between Phoenix and Scottsdale. South of the city are the much less lofty peaks of South Mountain Park, which separates the Valley from the rest of the Sonoran Desert. East of the city, beyond Tempe and Mesa, the peaks of the Superstition Mountains—named for their eerie way of seeming just a few miles away—are the first of a range that stretches all the way into New Mexico. To the west, past Glendale and Litchfield Park, the formidable White Tank Mountains separate the Valley from the lands that slope steadily downward to the Mojave Desert of California. Finally, just an hour north of the Valley, the slopes of the Mogollon (pronounced *muh*-gee-on) Rim, all green with piñon, juniper, and Ponderosa pines, serve as a cool refuge for Valley dwellers, where I–17 leads tens of thousands on exodus every weekend from May to September.

SPAS
How do you define pleasure? If you answered "pampering," this is the place for you. Treatments involving smooth warm stones soaked in aromatic waters placed strategically up and down your back or quiet massages outside amid the blooming Sonoran Desert are only two options. Maybe it's a seaweed wrap or warm mineral bath. Whatever your fancy, the Valley has some of the best facilities in the world, from destination spas where you can buy weeklong packages to day spas where both locals and visitors relax and retreat.

expensive, but services do not connect well within and between communities. A light-rail system connecting Mesa, Tempe, and Phoenix is scheduled to be completed in December 2008, but until then expect delays due to construction along the route (check ⊕ www.valleymetro.org/ for traffic restrictions) and around the Phoenix Convention Center expansion project so allow extra time when traveling to downtown Phoenix.

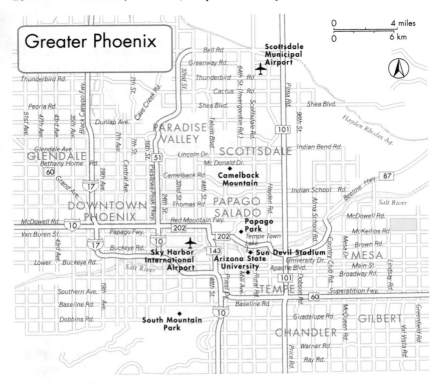

Getting Your Bearings

Phoenix is the center of the Valley, with other communities radiating out. The East Valley includes Scottsdale, Paradise Valley, Tempe, Mesa, Fountain Hills, and Apache Junction, and just beyond the last is the southern edge of the Superstition Mountains. To the southeast are Gilbert, Guadalupe, Queen Creek, Chandler, and Ahwatukee. The West Valley includes Glendale, Peoria, Sun City, Surprise, Waddell, Avondale, Goodyear, Buckeye, and Litchfield Park.

Central Avenue, which runs north and south through the heart of downtown Phoenix, is the city's east–west dividing line. Everything east of Central is considered the East Valley and everything west of Central is the West Valley. One block east and parallel to Central Avenue is 1st Street. Numbered avenues, drives, and lanes are on the west side of the Valley, and numbered streets, ways, and places are on the east side. Street numbers increase as you go farther from Central Avenue. Thus, 40th Street is 40 blocks east of Central, whereas 63rd Avenue is 63 blocks west of Central. North–south increments are taken from Washington Street in downtown Phoenix, so 4002 North 36th Street is 40 blocks north of Washington. Odd-numbered addresses are on the south and east sides of streets; even-numbered ones are on north and west sides.

Downtown Phoenix

Growth in the Valley over the past two decades has created new demands on the downtown area. More spaces for large conventions and trade shows, rapid growth brought on by new business development, creation of new apartments and lofts, and new cultural and sports facilities have helped create a more "real" downtown area. Downtown Phoenix is also known as Copper Square and is a mixture of Phoenix's past and present. Restored homes in Heritage Square, from the original town site, give you an idea of how far the city has come since its inception around the turn of the 20th century.

> ### BABY IT'S HOT OUT THERE
>
> Arizona can get pretty darn hot in summer—yes, it's a dry heat, but still! The Heard Museum is not only a must-see, it has the advantage of being indoors, while Taliesen and the Botanical Garden are both outdoors. The Phoenix Art Museum, also indoors, is near the Heard.

The light-rail construction and the expansion of the Phoenix Convention Center will tie up roads intermittently through 2008, so allow plenty of time to get to downtown destinations.

Downtown Phoenix has lots of parking options, they're listed on the free map provided by Downtown Phoenix Partnership and available in many local restaurants (⊕ www.coppersquare.com). Many downtown sites are served by DASH (Downtown Area Shuttle), a free bus service. You can use DASH to get around or to get back to your car when you're finished.

Numbers in the margin correspond to numbers on the What to See in Downtown Phoenix map.

What to See

❺ Arizona Center. Amid dramatic fountains, sunken gardens, and towering palm trees stands this two-tier, open-air structure, which is downtown's most attractive shopping venue. The center has about 50 shops and restaurants spread over two stories, open-air vendors, a large sports bar, and a multiplex cinema. If you stop for lunch at Mi Amigo's, ask for the guacamole "a la mesa" and the staff will mash the fresh ingredients together right at your table. ⊠ *Van Buren St. between 3rd and 5th Sts., Downtown Phoenix* ☎ *602/271–4000 or 480/949–4386* ⊕ *www.arizonacenter.com.*

★ ☾ ❷ Arizona Science Center. With more than 300 hands-on exhibits, this is the venue for science-related exploration. You can pilot a simulated airplane flight, travel through the human body, navigate your way through the solar system in the Dorrance Planetarium, and watch a movie in the giant, five-story film theater. ⊠ *600 E. Washington St., Downtown Phoenix* ☎ *602/716–2000* ⊕ *www.azscience.org* ▣ *Museum $9; combination museum, theater, and planetarium $19* ☉ *Daily 10–5.*

❾ Chase Field. Formerly known as Bank One Ballpark, the stadium is still affectionately referred to as BOB. The Valley's major-league ballpark is home to the Arizona Diamondbacks. A retractable roof, natural-grass

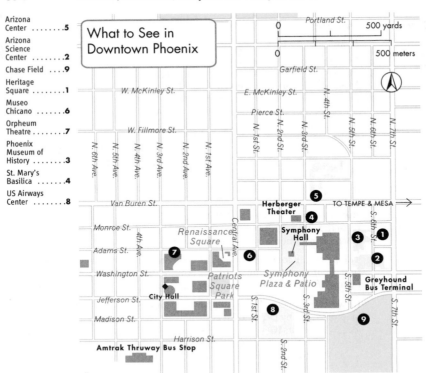

What to See in Downtown Phoenix

playing surface, family picnic area, and even a swimming pool (reserved for suite holders) let Phoenicians enjoy a day at the ballpark while escaping the summer heat. Tours are given Monday through Saturday but not on daytime game days. Given that most of the Valley is from somewhere else, home games at Chase Field see a mix of ball fans from across the nation. Be wary of wearing Yankees colors though, D-Backs fans are still smiling from winning the 2001 World Series, yet smarting from losing their star pitcher Randy Johnson to the Bronx Bombers. ⊠ *401 E. Jefferson St., between S. 4th and S. 7th Sts., Downtown Phoenix* ☎602/ 462–6000 *or* 888/177–4664, 602/462–6799 *tours* ⊕*www.diamondbacks. mlb.com* ⊡ *Tours $6* ☉ *Tours Mon.–Sat. 10:30, noon, 1:30, and 3; 10:30 and noon only on evening-game days.*

🐾 ❶ **Heritage Square.** In a parklike setting from 5th to 7th streets between Monroe and Adams streets, this city-owned block contains the only remaining houses from the original Phoenix town site. On the south side of the square, along Adams Street, stand several houses built between 1899 and 1901. The Teeter House contains a Victorian-style tearoom, and the Thomas House and Baird Machine Shop is now Pizzeria Bianco. The one-story brick Stevens House holds the **Arizona Doll and Toy Mu-**

seum (⊠ 602 E. Adams St., Downtown Phoenix ☎ 602/253–9337), which is open Tuesday through Saturday 10 to 4, Sunday noon to 4, and closed in August; admission is $3.

The queen of Heritage Square is the **Rosson House,** an 1895 Victorian in the Queen Anne style. Built by a physician who served a brief term as mayor, it's the sole survivor among fewer than two dozen Victorians erected in Phoenix. It was bought and restored by the city in 1974. ⊠ *6th and Monroe Sts., Downtown Phoenix* ☎ *602/262–5029* ⊠ *$4* ⊙ *Wed.–Sat. 10–4, Sun. noon–4.*

NEED A BREAK?
> The Victorian-style tearoom in the **Teeter House** (⊠ 622 E. Adams St., Downtown Phoenix ☎ 602/252–4682), which was built as a private home in 1899, serves authentic teatime fare; there are also heartier sandwiches and salads.

❻ **Museo Chicano.** Works of artists from the United States and Mexico are showcased here. Exhibits include art in many media from different periods, showing both classic and modern culture and making this site a premier center for enjoying Latin American art. ⊠ *147 E. Adams St., Downtown Phoenix* ☎ *602/257–5536* ⊕ *www.museochicano.com* ⊠ *$2* ⊙ *Tues.–Sat. 10–4.*

❼ **Orpheum Theatre.** The Spanish colonial–revival architecture and exterior reliefs of this 1929 movie palace have long been admired. The eclectic ornamental details of the interior were meticulously restored as part of a 12-year, $14 million renovation project. Today, the Orpheum is a venue for live performances, from Broadway shows to ballet to lectures. Call for details on free guided tours and upcoming events. ⊠ *203 W. Adams St., Downtown Phoenix* ☎ *602/534–9575* ⊙ *Tours by appointment only.*

❸ **Phoenix Museum of History.** This striking glass-and-steel museum offers exhibits on regional history from the 1860s (when Anglo settlement began) through the 1930s. Interactive exhibits are designed to help you appreciate the city's multicultural heritage as well as witness its growth. ⊠ *105 N. 5th St., Downtown Phoenix* ☎ *602/253–2734* ⊕ *www.pmoh.org* ⊠ *$6* ⊙ *Tues.–Sat. 10–5.*

❹ **St. Mary's Basilica.** The oldest church in Phoenix was erected in 1881. Inside the basilica there's a magnificent stained-glass window designed in Munich. Mass is held daily, but call for visiting hours. ⊠ *N. 3rd and Monroe Sts., Downtown Phoenix* ☎ *602/354–2100* ⊠ *Free* ⊙ *Hrs vary; call for opening times.*

❽ **US Airways Center.** This 20,000-seat venue, known locally as the Purple Palace, is home to the Phoenix Suns NBA team, the AFL Arizona Rattlers arena football team, and the Phoenix Mercury WNBA team. It's almost a mall in itself—with cafés and shops, it's interesting to see. Tour availability is determined by the day's schedule of events, and you must have a reservation. ⊠ *201 E. Jefferson St., at 2nd St., Downtown Phoenix* ☎ *602/379–2000, 602/379–7878 tour reservations only* ⊕ *www.americawestarena.com* ⊠ *Tours $3* ⊙ *Tours weekdays by appointment only.*

What to See in Greater Phoenix

Lookout Mountain Preserve

Piestewa Peak Recreational Area

PARADISE VALLEY

Camelback Mountain

TO BEAD MUSEUM

Viad Corporate Center

See What to See in Downtown Phoenix detail map

Sky Harbor International Airport

Salt River/Rio Salado

SOUTH PHOENIX

15th Ave.
7th St.
16th St.
Cave Creek Rd.
32nd St.
Tatum Blvd.
Bell Rd.
Greenway Rd.
40th St.
Thunderbird Rd.
Cactus Rd.
59th St.
Shea Blvd.
Doubletree
Lincoln Dr.
Camelback Rd.
Thunderbird Rd.
Cactus Rd.
Peoria Rd.
43rd Ave.
35th Ave.
Black Canyon Fwy.
Dunlap Ave.
Northern Ave.
19th Ave.
7th Ave.
Central Ave.
7th St.
16th St.
Glendale Ave.
Bethany Home Rd.
Grand Ave.
Camelback Rd.
Indian School Rd.
Thomas Rd.
Papago Fwy.
McDowell Rd.
Van Buren St.
35th Ave.
Buckeye Rd.
Lower Buckeye Rd.
19th Ave.
Broadway Rd.
Central Ave.
Southern Ave.
24th St.
35th Ave.
Baseline Rd.
Dobbins Rd.
24th St.
Piestewa Peak Pkwy.
32nd St.
44th St.
Camelback Rd.
Red Mountain Fwy.
McDowell
Thomas Rd.
48th St.
Priest Dr.
Cave Creek Rd.

1-9

10 **11** **12** **13** **14** **15** **16** **20**

The Cultural Center

The heart of Phoenix's downtown cultural center and renaissance is the Margaret T. Hance Park, also known as Deck Park. Built atop the I–10 "Deck Park" tunnel under Central Avenue, it spreads more than 1 mi from 3rd Avenue on the west to 3rd Street on the east, and ¼ mi from Portland Street north to Culver Street. It's the city's second-largest downtown park (the largest is half-century-old Encanto Park, 2 mi northwest). Deck Park is a good place from which to survey revitalized downtown neighborhoods and to appreciate the expansions and renovations of nearly all the area's museums.

Numbers in the text correspond to numbers in the margin and on the What to See in Greater Phoenix map.

What to See

⑩ Burton Barr Central Library. Architect Will Bruder's magnificent contribution to Phoenix has a copper exterior that evokes images of the mesas, buttes, and canyons of Monument Valley. Skylights, glass walls, and mirrors bathe the interior in natural light. The Crystal Canyon, a five-story glass atrium, is best appreciated on a swift ride in one of the glass elevators. On the top floor, a cable-suspended steel ceiling floats over the largest reading room in North America. Free one-hour tours are offered with advance reservations. Bring your laptop—the library has free Wi-Fi. ✉ *1221 N. Central Ave., Downtown Phoenix* ☎ *602/ 262–4636, 602/262–6582 tour reservations* ⊕ *www.phxlib.org* ☽ *Mon.–Thurs. 10–9, Fri. and Sat. 10–6, Sun. noon–6.*

NEED A BREAK?

Funky, friendly **Willow House** (✉ 149 W. McDowell Rd., at 3rd Ave., Downtown Phoenix ☎ 602/252–0272) is a place to people-watch from an armchair or sofa and to grab a sandwich, dessert, or coffee. Check out the artwork on display, as well as the kaleidoscopic fish painted on the restroom walls.

☾ ⑬ Encanto Park. Urban Encanto (Spanish for "enchanted") Park covers 222 acres at the heart of one of Phoenix's oldest residential neighborhoods. There are many attractions, including picnic areas, a lagoon where you can paddleboat and canoe, a municipal swimming pool, a nature trail, the Kiddieland–Enchanted Island amusement park, fishing in the park's lake, two public golf courses, and basketball and tennis courts. ✉ *15th Ave. and Encanto Blvd.* ☎ *602/ 261–8993* ▨ *Park free, Enchanted Island rides $1* ☽ *Park daily 6 AM–midnight; Enchanted Island Wed.–Fri. 10–4, weekends 7–4.*

☾ ⑫ Heard Museum. Pioneer settlers Dwight and Maie Heard built a Spanish colonial–revival building on their property to house their collection of Southwestern art. Today the staggering collection in-

Fodor's Choice
★

WORD OF MOUTH

"The Heard museum in Phoenix is not to be missed. It is one of the largest, most comprehensive collections of Native American art in the Southwest. There's even a large section of the museum which is targeted towards children and their interests (left side as you walk in)."   —mykidsherpa

cludes such exhibits as a Navajo hogan, an Apache wickie-up (a temporary Native American structure, similar to a lean-to, constructed from branches, twigs, and leaves, sometimes covered with hides), and rooms filled with art, pottery, jewelry, katsinas, and textiles. The Heard also actively supports and displays pieces by working Indian artists. An exciting new long-term exhibition entitled Home: Native People In the Southwest, opened in 2005. Annual events include the Guild Indian Fair & Market and the World Championship Hoop Dance Contest. Children enjoy the interactive art-making exhibits. The museum has an incredible gift shop with authentic, high-quality goods purchased directly from native artists. There's a museum satellite branch in Scottsdale that has rotating exhibits. ⊠ *2301 N. Central Ave., Downtown Phoenix* ☎ *602/252–8848 or 602/252–8840* ⊕ *www.heard.org* ⊠ *$10* ⊙ *Daily 9:30–5.*

⓫ **Phoenix Art Museum.** The green-quartz exterior of this modern museum is an eye-catching piece of architecture. The museum has 17,000 works of art from all over the world but is perhaps best known for its extensive and popular Western American Collection, which includes sculptures by Frederic Remington and paintings by Georgia O'-Keeffe, Thomas Moran, and Maxfield Parrish. Since the museum hosts more than 20 significant exhibitions annually, there's usually something special to see. Tours of the collection are given at 2 PM daily. ⊠ *1625 N. Central Ave., Downtown Phoenix* ☎ *602/257–1222* ⊕ *www.phxart.org* ⊠ *$9; free Thurs.* ⊙ *Tues., Wed., Fri., weekends 10–5, Thurs. 10–9.*

OFF THE BEATEN PATH

BEAD MUSEUM – In the historic district of downtown Glendale, this little museum attracts bead collectors from around the globe. Exhibits tell the intriguing story of international trade and intricate bead craft from 30,000 BC through today. There's a gift shop, and the 3,000-volume reference library can be perused by appointment. ⊠ *5754 W. Glenn Dr., northwest corner of Glenn Dr. and 58th Ave., Glendale* ☎ *623/931–2737* ⊕ *www.thebeadmuseum.com* ⊠ *$4, free Thurs. 5–8* ⊙ *Mon.–Wed., Fri., and Sat. 10–5, Thurs. 10–8, Sun. 11–4.*

South Phoenix

A mostly residential area and home to much of Phoenix's substantial Hispanic population, South Phoenix—the area south of Buckeye Road—is worth a visit for two reasons: its family-style restaurants and roadside stands offer some of the best Mexican food in the city, plus South Mountain Park and one of the more unusual sights in the Valley—the Mystery Castle.

A GOOD TOUR

From central Phoenix, take 7th Street south, past Baseline Road, to its junction with Mineral Road and **Mystery Castle** ⓮ ▶, a decidedly original home turned museum. After a tour, follow Mineral Road west for about ½ mi to Central Avenue and the entrance to **South Mountain Park** ⓯. Take any of several scenic drives through this 16,500-acre city-owned wilderness. Dobbins Lookout, 1,120 feet above Phoenix, has spectacular views of the city. Maps of all scenic drives as well as of hiking, mountain biking, and horseback trails are available at the Gatehouse Entrance just inside the park boundary.

TIMING Depending on how long you spend in the park, this tour can be a couple of hours or an entire day. Leave about a half hour each way for driving, an hour to 90 minutes at the castle, and anywhere from a quick 20-minute drive to an all-day hike in South Mountain.

What to See

▶ ★ ☙ ⑭ **Mystery Castle.** At the foot of South Mountain lies a curious dwelling built from desert rocks by Boyce Gulley, who came to Arizona to cure his tuberculosis. Boyce's daughter Mary Lou lives here now and leads tours on request. Full of fascinating oddities, the castle has 18 rooms with 13 fireplaces, a downstairs grotto tavern, and a roll-away bed with a mining railcar as its frame. The pump organ belonged to Elsie, the Widow of Tombstone, who buried six husbands under suspicious circumstances. ⊠ *800 E. Mineral Rd., South Phoenix* ☎ *602/268–1581* ⊡ *$5* ☉ *Oct.–June, Thurs.–Sun. 11–4.*

★ ☙ ⑮ **South Mountain Park.** This desert wonderland, the world's largest city park (almost 17,000 acres), offers a wilderness of mountain-desert trails for hikers, bikers, and horseback riders—and a great place to view sunsets. The Environmental Center has a model of the park as well as displays detailing its history, from the time of the ancient Hohokam people to gold-seekers. Roads climb past picnic ramadas (shaded, open-air shelters) constructed by the Civilian Conservation Corps, winding through desert flora to the trailheads. Look for ancient petroglyphs, try to spot a desert cottontail rabbit or chuckwalla lizard, or simply stroll among the desert vegetation. ⊠ *10919 S. Central Ave., South Phoenix* ☎ *602/ 495–0222* ⊡ *Free* ☉ *Daily 5:30 AM–10:30 PM; Environmental Center Mon.–Sat. 9–5, Sun. noon–5.*

NEED A BREAK?
Carolina's (⊠ 1202 E. Mohave St., South Phoenix ☎ 602/252–1503) makes the best flour tortillas for 100 mi, and the burritos are the best way to try them. You can eat at this small establishment or just pick up some carry-out, which you can enjoy as a picnic under one of the ramadas in South Mountain Park.

Papago Salado

The word Papago, meaning "bean eater," was a name given by 16th-century Spanish explorers to the Hohokam, a vanished native people of the Phoenix area. Farmers of the desert, the Hohokam lived in central Arizona from about AD 1 to 1450, at which point their civilization abandoned the Salt River (Rio Salado) valley, leaving behind the remnants of their villages and a complex system of irrigation canals. The Papago Salado region is between Phoenix and Tempe and includes the Pueblo Grande ruins, the Desert Botanical Garden, the Phoenix Zoo, and Papago Park, which are all popular family attractions. There's a lot to see here, so if you're spending the day, you may want to save the Desert Botanical Garden for last, as it stays open 8 AM to 8 PM year-round and is particularly lovely when lighted by the setting sun or by moonlight—but don't miss it, it's wonderful!

What to See

🔵 ⑲ **Desert Botanical Garden.** Opened in 1939 to conserve and showcase the
Fodor'sChoice ecology of the desert, these 150 acres contain more than 4,000 differ-
★ ent species of cacti, succulents, trees, and flowers. A stroll along the ½-
mi-long "Plants and People of the Sonoran Desert" trail is a fascinating
lesson in environmental adaptations; children will enjoy playing the self-
guiding game "Desert Detective." The Garden Shop is the place to purchase items associated with a green thumb. ⊠ *1201 N. Galvin Pkwy.,
Papago Salado* ☎ *480/941–1225* ⊕ *www.dbg.org* 🔖 *$9* ☉ *Oct.–Apr.,
daily 8–8; May–Sept., daily 7 AM–8 PM.*

**NEED A
BREAK?** If you're headed to the Papago Salado region from downtown Phoenix, stop in
Kohnie's Coffee (⊠ 4225 E. Camelback Rd., Camelback Corridor ☎ 602/952–
9948) for coffee, pastries, bagels, and scones. It's open at 7 AM (Sunday at 8
AM) and closed by 1 PM (noon on weekends and all day on Monday).

🔵 ⑳ **Hall of Flame.** Retired firefighters lead tours through more than 100 restored fire engines and tell harrowing tales of the "world's most dangerous profession." The museum has the world's largest collection of
firefighting equipment, and children can climb on a 1916 engine, operate alarm systems, and learn fire safety lessons from the pros. Helmets,
badges, and other firefighting-related articles are on display, dating
from as far back as 1725. ⊠ *6101 E. Van Buren St., Papago Salado*
☎ *602/275–3473* ⊕ *www.hallofflame.org* 🔖 *$6* ☉ *Mon.–Sat. 9–5,
Sun. noon–4.*

🔵 ⑱ **Papago Park.** An amalgam of hilly desert terrain, streams, and lagoons,
this park has picnic ramadas, a golf course, a playground, hiking and
biking trails, and even largemouth bass and trout fishing. (An urban fishing license is required for anglers age 15 and over.) The hike up to landmark **Hole-in-the-Rock** (a natural observatory used by the native
Hohokam to devise a calendar system) is steep and rocky and a much
easier climb up than down. **Governor Hunt's Tomb,** the white pyramid
at the top of Ramada 16, commemorates the former Arizona leader and
provides a lovely view. ⊠ *625 N. Galvin Pkwy., Papago Salado* ☎ *602/
256–3220* 🔖 *Free* ☉ *Daily 6 AM–10 PM.*

🔵 ⑰ **Phoenix Zoo.** Four designated trails wind through this 125-acre zoo, repli-
cating such habitats as an African savannah and a tropical rain forest.
Meerkats, warthogs, desert bighorn sheep, and the endangered Arabian
oryx are among the unusual sights. The Forest of Uco is home to the
endangered spectacled bear from South America. Harmony Farm on the
Discovery Trail introduces youngsters to small mammals, and a stop at
the big red barn provides a chance to groom a horse or milk a cow. Make
sure to save time to walk through the enchanting Butterfly Pavilion. The
30-minute narrated safari train tour costs $3 and provides a good ori-
entation to the park. In December the zoo stays open late (6–10) for the
popular "Zoo Lights" exhibit transforms the area into an enchanted forest of more than 225 million twinkling lights, many in the shape of the
zoo's residents. Starry Safari Friday Nights in the summer are fun and
prices are discounted. ⊠ *455 N. Galvin Pkwy., Papago Salado* ☎ *602/
273–1341* ⊕ *www.phoenixzoo.org* 🔖 *$14* ☉ *Jan.–May, daily 9–5;*

June–Sept., weekdays 7–2, weekends 7–4; Oct.–Nov. 11, daily 9–5; Nov. 12–Jan. 7, daily 9–4.

16 Pueblo Grande Museum and Cultural Park. Phoenix's only national landmark, this park was once the site of a 500-acre Hohokam village supporting about 1,000 people and containing homes, storage rooms, cemeteries, and ball courts. Three exhibition galleries hold displays on the Hohokam culture and archaeological methods. View the 10-minute orientation video before heading out on the ½-mi Ruin Trail past excavated mounds and ruins that give a hint of Hohokam savvy: there's a building whose corner doorway was perfectly placed to watch the summer-solstice sunrise. Children will particularly like the hands-on, interactive learning center. ⊠ *4619 E. Washington St., Papago Salado* ☎ *602/495–0901* ⊕ *www.pueblogrande.com* ☜ *$2, free Sun.* ☉ *Mon.–Sat. 9–4:45, Sun. 1–4:45.*

Scottsdale

Historic sites, nationally known art galleries, and souvenir shops fill downtown Scottsdale; a quick walking tour can easily turn into an all-day excursion if you browse. Old Town Scottsdale has the look of the Old West, and 5th Avenue is known for shopping and Native American jewelry and crafts stores. Cross onto Main Street and enter a world frequented by the international art set (Scottsdale has the third-largest artist community in the United States). Discover more galleries and interior-design shops along Marshall Way.

It's a short but very worthwhile side trip from downtown Scottsdale to **Taliesin West,** Frank Lloyd Wright's winter home. Drive 20-minutes north on the 101 Freeway to Frank Lloyd Wright Boulevard. The entrance to Taliesin West is at the corner of Frank Lloyd Wright Boulevard and Cactus Road.

Numbers in the margin correspond to numbers on the What to See in Scottsdale map.

TIMING You could easily spend a full day in downtown Scottsdale, browsing the countless galleries and shops. Most galleries on Main Street and Marshall Way are open Thursday evenings until 9. Although your tour of the downtown area can easily be completed on foot, a trolley runs through the area and out to several resorts: Ollie the Trolley charges $5 for an all-day pass, although service within downtown Scottsdale is free (☎ 480/970–8130 information). If you have limited time, spend a half-day in downtown Scottsdale and the rest of the day at Taliesin West.

> **WORD OF MOUTH**
>
> "A friend and I took advantage of cheap lodging and went to Scottsdale over July 4th last year . . . Yes it was hot during the day–drink lots of water!–but at night we'd sit on our balcony and marvel at how weightless the air felt. Also we had shops in old town Scottsdale almost entirely to ourselves!! Great deals and service."   –Vicky

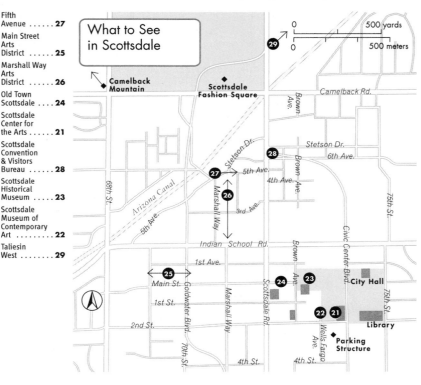

What to See

27 **5th Avenue.** Whether you seek handmade Native American Arts and Crafts, casual clothing or cacti, you'll find it here—at such landmark shops as Adolfos Espoza, Kactus Jock, and Gilbert Ortega—plus colorful store-fronts, friendly merchants, even an old "cigar-store" Indian. ⊠ *5th Ave. between Civic Center Rd. and Stetson Dr., Downtown Scottsdale.*

NEED A BREAK?
The **Sugar Bowl Ice Cream Parlor** (⊠ 4005 N. Scottsdale Rd., Downtown Scottsdale ☎ 480/946–0051) transports you back in time to a 1950s malt shop. Doing business in the same building since 1958, the Sugar Bowl serves great burgers and lots of yummy ice-cream confections. Valley resident Bil Keane, creator of the comic strip "Family Circus," has often used this spot as inspiration for his cartoons, many of which are on display here.

★ **25** **Main Street Arts District.** Gallery after gallery displays artwork of myriad styles—contemporary, Western realism, Native American, and traditional. Several antiques shops are also here; specialties include porcelains and china, jewelry, and Oriental rugs. ⊠ *Bounded by Main St. and 1st Ave., Scottsdale Rd. and 69th St., Downtown Scottsdale.*

㉖ Marshall Way Arts District. Galleries that exhibit predominantly contemporary art line the blocks of Marshall Way north of Indian School Road. Upscale gift and jewelry stores can be found here, too. Farther north on Marshall Way across 3rd Avenue, the street is filled with more art galleries and creative stores with a Southwestern flair. ⊠ *Marshall Way, from Indian School Rd. to 5th Ave., Downtown Scottsdale.*

㉔ Old Town Scottsdale. "The West's Most Western Town," this area has rustic storefronts and wooden sidewalks; it's touristy, but the closest you'll come to experiencing life here as it was 80 years ago. High-quality jewelry, pots, and Mexican imports are sold alongside kitschy souvenirs. ⊠ *Main St. from Scottsdale Rd. to Brown Ave., Downtown Scottsdale.*

㉘ Scottsdale Convention and Visitors Bureau. Pop inside to pick up some local maps, guidebooks, and brochures. Ask the helpful staff for a walking-tour map of Old Town Scottsdale's historic sites. ⊠ *4343 Scottsdale Rd., at Drinkwater Blvd., Suite 170, Downtown Scottsdale* ☎ *480/421–1004 or 800/782–1117* ⊕ *www.scottsdalecvb.com* 🎫 *Free* ⊙ *Weekdays 8:30–6, Sat. 9–1.*

㉑ Scottsdale Center for the Arts. Galleries within this cultural and entertainment complex rotate exhibits frequently, but they typically emphasize contemporary art and artists. The **Museum Store** (☎ 480/874–4464) stocks unusual jewelry and stationery, posters, and art books. ⊠ *7380 E. 2nd St., Downtown Scottsdale* ☎ *480/994–2787* ⊕ *www. scottsdalearts.org* 🎫 *Free* ⊙ *Mon.–Wed., Fri., and Sat. 10–5, Thurs. 10–8, Sun. noon–5; also during performance intermissions.*

㉓ Scottsdale Historical Museum. Scottsdale's first schoolhouse, this redbrick building houses a version of the 1910 schoolroom, as well as photographs, original furniture from the city's founding fathers, and displays of other treasures from Scottsdale's early days. ⊠ *7333 Scottsdale Mall, Downtown Scottsdale* ☎ *480/945–4499* ⊕ *www.scottsdalemuseum.com* 🎫 *Free* ⊙ *Sept.–June, Wed.–Sat. 10–5, Sun. noon–4.*

㉒ Scottsdale Museum of Contemporary Art. The spectacular Gerard L. Cafesjian Pavilion houses this museum. When you step through the immense glass entryway designed by artist James Fraser Carpenter and stroll through the spaces within the five galleries, you realize it's not just the spacious outdoor sculpture garden that makes this a "museum without walls." New installations are planned every few months, with an emphasis on contemporary art, architecture, and design. Free, docent-led tours are conducted on Thursday at 1:30. ⊠ *7374 E. 2nd St., Downtown Scottsdale* ☎ *480/994–2787* ⊕ *www.scottsdalearts.org* 🎫 *$7, free Thurs.* ⊙ *Sept.–May, Wed. noon–5, Thurs. 10–8, Fri. and Sat. 10–5, Sun. noon–5; June–Aug., Wed. 10–5, Thurs. 10–8, Fri. and Sat. 10–5, Sun. noon–5.*

㉙ Taliesin West. Ten years after visiting Arizona in 1927 to consult on designs for the Biltmore hotel, architect Frank Lloyd Wright chose 600 acres of rugged Sonoran Desert at the foothills of the McDowell Mountains as the site for his permanent winter residence. Today the site is a National Historic Landmark and still an active community of students and architects. Wright and apprentices constructed a desert camp here,

Fodor\$Choice
★

using organic architecture to integrate the buildings with their natural surroundings. In addition to the living quarters, drafting studio, and small apartments of the Apprentice Court, Taliesin West has two theaters, a music pavilion, and the Sun Trap—sleeping spaces surrounding an open patio and fireplace. Two guided tours cover different parts of the interior, and a guided desert walk winds through

the petroglyphs and landscape from which Wright drew his vision. Five guided tours are offered, ranging from a one-hour "panorama" tour to a three-hour behind-the-scenes tour, with other tours offered seasonally. In 2005, after a major renovation, Wright's living quarters were opened for the first time to the public. They include a living space and a private bedroom and work space. Times vary, so call ahead; all visitors must be accompanied by a guide. ✉ *12621 Frank Lloyd Wright Blvd., North Scottsdale* ☎ *480/860–2700* ⊕ *www.franklloydwright.org* ✉ *$18–$45* ⊙ *Sept.–June, daily 8:30–5:30; July and Aug., Thurs.–Mon. 8:30–5:30.*

Tempe

In 1860 Charles Trumbell Hayden arrived on the east end of the Salt River, where he built a flour mill, warehouses, and a ferry across the river. This settlement and trade center became known as Hayden's Ferry. Other settlers soon arrived, including an English lord who felt—upon approaching the town from Phoenix and seeing the buttes, river, and fields of green mesquite—that the name should be changed to Tempe after the Vale of Tempe in Greece.

Today Tempe is home of Arizona State University's main campus and a thriving student population. Tempe's new Arts Center is set to open in Fall 2006. A 20-minute drive from Phoenix, the tree- and brick-lined Mill Avenue (on which a flour mill at the site of Hayden's original still stands) is the main drag, lined with student hangouts, bookstores, boutiques, eateries, and a repertory movie house. There's always something to do or see—maybe an art festival or baseball spring training camp—and plenty of music venues and fun, casual dining spots. Twice a year (in early December and March–April), you can find the Tempe Festival of the Arts on Mill Avenue, with all sorts of interesting arts and crafts (⊕ www.tempefestivalofthearts.com).

The banks of the Rio Salado in Tempe are the site of a new commercial and entertainment district and Tempe Town Lake—a 2-mi-long waterway created by inflatable dams in a flood control channel—is open for boating. There are biking and jogging paths on the perimeter. It's a great place for a stroll.

Numbers in the text correspond to numbers on the What to See in Greater Phoenix map.

TIMING If you're planning to shop as well as tour the campus and museums, allow four or five hours for exploring. Stop by Town Lake for a break during the day for a boat ride or simply to soak up some sun.

What to See

③② **Arizona State University.** What began as the Tempe Normal School for Teachers—in 1886, a four-room redbrick building and 20-acre cow pasture—is now the 750-acre campus of ASU, the largest university in the Southwest. The **ASU Visitor Information Center** (✉ 826 E. Apache Blvd., at Rural Rd. ☎ 480/

> **TIPS FOR GETTING AROUND TEMPE**
>
> Street parking is hard to find, but you can park in the public garage at Hayden Square, just north of 5th Street and west of Mill Avenue. Get your ticket stamped by local merchants to avoid paying parking fees. The FLASH (Free Local Area Shuttle, ☎ 602/253–5000) does a loop around Arizona State University with stops at Mill Avenue and Sun Devil Stadium.

965–0100) has maps of a self-guided walking tour (it's a long walk from Mill Avenue, so you might opt for the short version suggested here). You'll wind past public art and innovative architecture—including a music building that bears a strong resemblance to a wedding cake (designed by Taliesin students to echo Frank Lloyd Wright's Gammage Auditorium) and a law library shaped like an open book—and end up at the 74,000-seat **Sun Devil Stadium** (✉ ASU Campus, 5th St. ☎ 866/800–2828), home to the school's Sun Devils. One of the most outstanding stadiums in the country it has a spectacular setting. It's literally carved out of a mountain and cradled between the Tempe buttes.

Heralded for its superior acoustics, the circular **Grady Gammage Auditorium** (✉ Mill Ave. at Apache Blvd. ☎ 480/965–4050) was the last public structure completed by architect Frank Lloyd Wright, who detached the rear wall from grand tier and balcony sections in an effort to surround every patron with sound. The stage can accommodate a full symphony orchestra, and there's a 2,909-pipe organ. Artwork is exhibited in the lobby and in two on-site galleries. Free half-hour tours are offered Monday between 1 and 3:30 during the school year.

While touring the west end of campus, stop into the **Arizona State University Art Museum** (✉ Mill Ave. and 10th St. ☎ 480/965–2787 ⊕ asuartmuseum.asu.edu ✉ Free ☉ School year: Tues. 10–9; summer, Tues. 10–5; year-round Wed.–Sat. 10–5). It's in the gray-purple stucco Nelson Fine Arts Center, just north of the Gammage Auditorium. For a relatively small museum, it has an extensive collection, including 19th- and 20th-century painting and sculpture by masters such as Winslow Homer, Edward Hopper, Georgia O'Keeffe, and Rockwell Kent. Works by faculty and student artists are also on display, and there's a gift shop.

A short walk east of the Nelson Fine Arts Center, just north of the Hayden Library, ASU's experimental gallery and collection of crockery and ceramics are in the **Matthews Center** (✉ Mill Ave. and 10th St. ☎ 480/965–2875 ✉ Free ☉ Sept.–May, Tues.–Sat. 10–5).

In Matthews Hall, the **Northlight Gallery** (✉ Matthews Hall, Mill Ave. and 10th St. ☎ 480/965–6517 ✆ Mon.–Thurs. 10:30–4:30) exhibits works by both renowned and emerging photographers. There's no admission charge.

The **Edna Vihel Center for the Arts** (✉ 3340 S. Rural Rd. ☎ 480/350–5287) is a short drive from downtown Tempe and a major arts venue, offering rotating exhibits of paintings and photography, as well as book signings, readings, and charity events. There's also a small theater for play and dance productions.

▌**NEED A BREAK?**

The outdoor patio of the **Coffee Plantation** (✉ 680 S. Mill Ave. ☎ 480/829–7878), a popular café near the ASU campus, is a lively scene—students cramming, local residents chatting over a cup of joe, and poets and musicians presenting their latest works.

③③ **Tempe Center for the Arts.** Set to open in Fall 2006, this new, publicly funded 88,000-square-foot arts center at the edge of Tempe Lake will be a showcase for visual art, music, theater, and dance, featuring local, regional, and international talent. ✉ *700 W. Rio Salada Pkwy.* ☎ *480/350–5287* 📠 *480/350–5161* ⊕ *www.tempe.gov/arts/tca.*

③① **Tempe City Hall.** Local architects Rolf Osland and Michael Goodwin constructed this inverted pyramid not just to win design awards (which they have) but also to shield city workers from the desert sun. The pyramid is built mainly of bronzed glass and stainless steel; the point disappears in a sunken courtyard lushly landscaped with jacaranda, ivy, and flowers, out of which the pyramid widens to the sky: stand underneath and gaze up for a weird fish-eye perspective. ✉ *31 E. 5th St., 1 block east of Mill Ave.* ☎ *480/967–2001* 📷 *Free.*

🐚 **③⓪** **Tempe Town Lake.** The Town Lake is the newest addition to the growth of Tempe and attracts college students and Valley residents of all ages. Little ones enjoy the Splash Playground, and fishermen appreciate the rainbow trout–stocked lake. **Rio Lago Cruises** rents boats and has a selection of short cruise options. ✉ *990 W. Rio Salado Pkwy., between Mill and Rural Aves. north of Arizona State University* ☎ *480/517–4050 Rio Lago Cruises* ⊕ *www.tempe.gov/lake or www.riolagocruise.com.*

WHERE TO EAT

Updated by
JoBeth Jamison

Generations of Arizona schoolchildren have learned the state's four Cs: copper, cattle, cotton, and climate. Today, a good argument could be made for adding a fifth in Phoenix: cuisine. New restaurants have proliferated in the Phoenix metropolitan area due to the Valley's rapid growth and the influence of adventurous chefs who have emigrated here. An influx of Thai, Peruvian, Vietnamese, and Japanese restaurants have created a culinary scene of sophistication and diversity. Contemporary menus feature touches of the creator's homeland or ethnicity mixed with local recipes and ingredients. Pacific Rim or Latino foods are fused with spices native to the Southwest, such as Mexican coriander, fragrant Mexican oregano, *canela* sticks (Mexican cinnamon), and, of course, chiles from mild to explosive. Italian, Spanish, and even French favorites served in Phoenix might have more "bite" than elsewhere.

Many of the best restaurants in the Valley are in resorts, camouflaged behind courtyard walls, or tucked away in shopping malls. Newer, upscale eateries are clustered along Camelback Corridor and in Scottsdale. Great Mexican food can be found throughout the Valley, but the most authentic spots are in the Hispanic neighborhoods of South Phoenix.

Restaurants change hours, locations, chefs, prices, and menus frequently, so it's best to call ahead to confirm. Show up without a reservation during tourist season, and you may have to head for a fast-food drive-through window to avoid a two-hour wait for a table. All listed restaurants are open for lunch and dinner unless otherwise specified.

Prices

	WHAT IT COSTS			
$$$$	**$$$**	**$$**	**$**	**¢**
AT DINNER	over $30	$21–$30	$13–$20	$8–$12	under $8

Prices are per person for a main course. The final tab will include sales tax of 8.1% in Phoenix, 7.7% in Scottsdale.

Downtown Phoenix

American

$$–$$$$ ✕ **Durant's Fine Foods.** Durant's has endured since 1950 in the same location, with the same menu, and even many of the original waitstaff, making it one of Phoenix's legendary eating establishments. Steaks, chops, and fresh seafood, including Florida stone crab, dominate here; when the restaurant once tried to update its menu, regulars protested so furiously the idea was shelved. Those in the know enter through the kitchen door and frequent the Rat Pack–style bar for jumbo martinis fit for ol' Blue Eyes himself. ⊠ *2611 N. Central Ave., at Virginia, Downtown Phoenix* ☎ *602/264–5967* ⊟ *AE, D, DC, MC, V.*

★ **$** ✕ **Pane Bianco.** Chef-owner Chris Bianco spends his evenings turning out some of the Valley's best pizza at his downtown pizzeria, and his days creating to-die-for focaccia sandwiches at this minimalist take-out sandwich shop. Order at the counter, pick up your brown-bagged meal (which always includes a piece of candy), and dine outside at an umbrella-shaded picnic table. The menu only has a handful of sandwich selections, but each work of art features wood-fire focaccia stuffed with farm-fresh ingredients. ⊠ *4404 N. Central Ave., Downtown Phoenix* ☎ *602/234–2100* ⊟ *AE, MC, V* ☉ *Closed Sun. and Mon. No dinner.*

¢–$ ✕ **MacAlpine's Soda Fountain.** Opened in 1928 as a Rexall Drug Store, this Norman Rockwell–like diner has the oldest operating soda fountain in the Southwest. Wooden booths, worn bar stools, and the vintage soda fountain and jukebox transport diners back to slower times. Traditional burgers, sandwiches, and salads are just like Grandma used to make. The decadent malts, sundaes, and ice-cream sodas are not to be missed. ⊠ *2303 N. 7th St., Downtown Phoenix* ☎ *602/262–5545*

🍴 *Reservations not accepted* 🞔 *AE, D, MC, V* ☾ *Closed Sun.*

¢–$ ✗ **Mrs. White's Golden Rule Café.** This downtown lunch spot is the best place in town for true Southern cooking. Every entrée—from fried chicken to pork chops—comes with corn bread, and the peach cobbler is legendary. Catfish, black-eyed peas, and collard greens are also on the menu. ✉ *808 E. Jefferson St., Downtown Phoenix* ☎ *602/262–9256* 🍴 *Reservations not accepted* 🞔 *No credit cards* ☾ *Closed Sat. and Sun. No dinner.*

¢–$ ✗ **Welcome Diner.** Sidle up to a bar stool in this tiny vintage 1930s diner for an all-day organic brunch menu, featuring hot dogs, hamburgers, tasty egg sandwiches, "a cup of sweet toast," and Nana's Ridiculous Oatmeal Chocolate Chip cookies. Recently purchased by Peter and Dafina Hearn, the Welcome Diner remains a welcoming downtown eatery. ✉ *924 E. Roosevelt, Downtown Phoenix* ☎ *602/495–1111* 🍴 *Reservations not accepted* 🞔 *No credit cards* ☾ *Closed Sun. No dinner.*

Chinese

¢–$$ ✗ **Gourmet House of Hong Kong.** Traditional Chinatown specialties, such as *chow fun* (thick rice noodles), are excellent here. Try the assorted-meat version, topped with chicken, shrimp, pork, and squid. Lobster with black-bean sauce is messy but tasty. Adventurous delights such as five-flavor frogs' legs, duck feet with greens, and beef tripe casserole are offered. ✉ *1438 E. McDowell Rd., Downtown Phoenix* ☎ *602/253–4859* 🞔 *AE, D, MC, V.*

Mexican

★ $$ ✗ **Barrio Cafe.** You won't find chips and salsa here; owners Wendy Gruber and Silvana Salcido Esparza have taken Mexican cuisine to a new level. Expect guacamole prepared tableside and modern Mexican specialties such as *cochinita pibil,* slow roasted pork with red achiote and sour orange; and *chiles en Nogada,* a delicious traditional dish from Central Mexico featuring a spicy poblano pepper stuffed with fruit, chicken, and raisins. The flavor-packed food consistently draws packs of people to this two-room restaurant but you can drink in the intimate atmosphere—and a specialty margarita—while you wait for a table. ✉ *2814 N. 16th St., Downtown Phoenix* ☎ *602/636–0240* 🍴 *Reservations not accepted* 🞔 *AE, MC, V* ☾ *Closed Mon.*

Native American

¢ ✗ **Fry Bread House.** Indian Fry bread, a specialty of the Native American culture, is a delicious treat—pillows of deep-fried dough topped with sweet or savory toppings and folded in half. Local fry bread fanatics get their fix via chef-owner Cecelia Miller of the Tohono O'odham Nation. Choose from culture-crossing combinations like savory shredded chili beef, with cheese, beans, green chiles, veggies, and sour cream, or try the sweeter synthesis of honey and sugar, or chocolate with butter. ✉ *4140 N. 7th Ave., Downtown Phoenix* ☎ *602/351–2345* 🞔 *D, MC, V* ☾ *Closed Sun.*

Pan Asian

$–$$ ✗ **Fate.** In an old house in the evolving downtown art district, this funky three-room eatery/art gallery/music salon/well-kept secret turns out some of the Valley's best Asian dishes. Hong Kong–born chef-owner

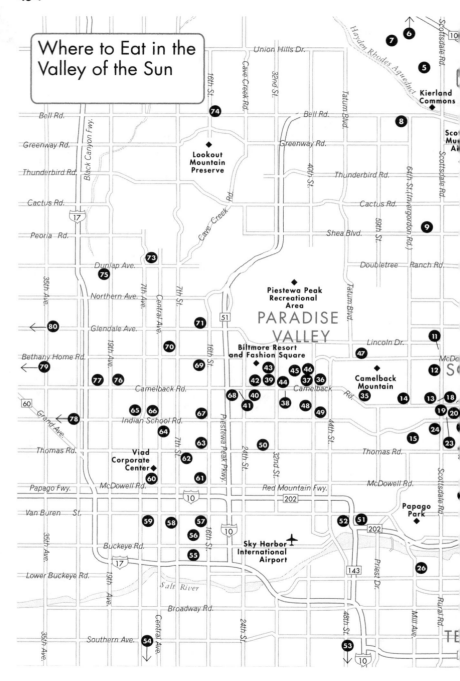

Where to Eat in the Valley of the Sun

Johnny Chu pairs simple fresh ingredients with fantastic sauces to create popular dishes such as House Dynamite, a spicy stir-fry of pineapple, fresh vegetables, and peanuts in a sweet and spicy sauce. Despite being one of the Valley's best "sleeper" establishments, Fate serves dinner until 3 AM on weekends accompanied by DJ-spun tunes. ⊠ *905 N. 4th St., Downtown Phoenix* ☎ *602/254–6424* ▤ *MC, V* ☺ *Closed Sun.*

Pizza

$ ✕ **Pizzeria Bianco.** Brooklyn native Chris Bianco makes pizza with a passion in this small establishment in Heritage Square. He uses a wood-fired brick oven imported from Italy and makes his own mozzarella cheese. Other toppings include homemade fennel sausage, wood-roasted cremini mushrooms, and the freshest herbs and spices. Bar Bianco next door is a good place to relax with a glass of wine or a soft drink while you wait for your table. Arrive a few minutes before they open at 5 PM to avoid the long wait, especially on Friday and Saturday nights. ⊠ *623 E. Adams St., Downtown Phoenix* ☎ *602/258–8300* ▤ *AE, MC, V* ☺ *Closed Sun. and Mon. No lunch.*

Fodor's Choice ★

Central Phoenix

Central Phoenix is bounded by Camelback Road on the north, Paradise Valley on the east, I–17 on the west, and Buckeye Road (excluding Papago Salado) on the south.

American–Casual

¢–$ ✕ **La Grande Orange.** A well-traveled and well-rounded couple, Craig and Kris DeMarco have come full-circle in central Phoenix. Their San Francisco–inspired store and eatery sells artisan cheeses, fruits, imported novelty and foody items, along with a formidable selection of wines, including a house label. Valley residents flock here to feast on mouthwatering sandwiches, pizzas, salads, and decadent breads and pastries baked fresh by the renowned MJ and Tammie Coe. The small tables inside fill up quickly at breakfast and lunch but there's also patio seating, and the connecting pizzeria helps accommodate the crowds. Try the Commuter Sandwich on a homemade English muffin or the delicious French pancakes with a Spanish latte that might be the most memorable cup of *jose* you'll ever have. ⊠ *4410 N. 40th St., Central Phoenix* ☎ *602/840–7777* ▤ *AE, MC, V.*

Fodor's Choice ★

Cajun

¢–$$ ✕ **Baby Kay's.** Named for the New Roads, Louisiana, native who brought her love and know-how for Creole creations to the Valley, Baby Kay's is one of the few Phoenix places that specializes in Cajun cuisine with authentic takes on red beans and rice, gumbo, jambalaya, po'boys, catfish, and the house specialty, crawfish *étouffée* (a spicy stew). Baby Kay sold the restaurant a few years ago but her spicy spirit rolls on in the able hands of her longtime chef (Lu Lu) and her loyal local following. Worthwhile extras include the deep-fried Baby Kay's sampler and green olive coleslaw. For the cholesterol conscious, Kay's grilled chicken with apricot habanero Tabasco sauce or the garden salad with creole vinaigrette will do in a pinch. ⊠ *2119 E. Camelback Rd., Town and Country Shopping Center, Central Phoenix* ☎ *602/955–0011* ▤ *AE, MC, V* ☺ *Closed Sun.*

Contemporary

$–$$$ ✕ **Chelsea's Kitchen.** For years, this former off-track betting bar with the splendid mountain views was visited only by sport and gaming fanatics but local foodie foursome Kris and Craig DeMarco and Ann and Bob Lynn bought and remodeled the charming canal-side adobe structure, betting that it would be the perfect location to realize their kind of restaurant vision. The gamble paid off; Chelsea's Kitchen is a casually sophisticated dining establishment with a friendly neighborhood feel. Executive chef Doug Robson insists on the freshest ingredients, used with equally fresh and flavorful ideas that complement the restaurants' cool but comfortable style. Specials change frequently but regulars love the short-rib hash, shrimp ceviche, and signature tacos with tortillas and corn chips made on-site. ✉ *5040 N. 40th St., Central Phoenix* ☎ *602/957–2555* ⊟ *AE, MC, V* ⊘ *No lunch.*

$–$$ ✕ **FEZ.** It's not a hat—but it does top the list of new restaurants in central Phoenix. From its upscale atmosphere and diverse clientele to its central location, right down to its affordable lunch, happy hour, dinner, and late-night menus, FEZ covers everything. The sleek interior has the feel of a martini bar, but the drink menu also revolves around specialty margaritas and wine. FEZ's Mediterranean/European/American inspired fare makes a bold culinary leap with items like the FEZ Burger (a ½ pound of meat with molasses BBQ sauce, cinnamon pears, feta, lemon garlic aioli, onions, and cilantro on a cibatta roll), lamb *kisra* (flatbread pizza), and the signature crispy rosemary pomegranate chicken—but it all lands safely on the taste buds. Head over for Uncorked Sundays when all bottles of wine are 50 percent off. You won't regret putting the money you save toward an order of cinnamon-dusted sweet potato FEZ fries or chicken phyllo packet appetizer. ✉ *3815 N. Central Ave., Central Phoenix* ☎ *602/287–8700* ⊟ *AE, MC, V* ⊘ *No lunch weekends.*

Fodor'sChoice
★

Italian

$$–$$$ ✕ **Avanti.** Owners Angelo Livi and Benito Mellino have been welcoming guests to this Italian restaurant since 1974. Candlelight, a piano bar, and a dance floor are perfect for a special celebration. For starters, try one of the house specialties, light potato gnocchi paired with spinach ravioli. The veal dishes, such as saltimbocca or osso buco, are particularly memorable. ✉ *2728 E. Thomas Rd., Central Phoenix* ☎ *602/956–0900* ⊟ *AE, D, DC, MC, V* ⊘ *No lunch weekends.*

$–$$ ✕ **La Fontanella.** Quality and value are a winning combination at this outstanding neighborhood restaurant. The interior is reminiscent of an Italian villa, with antiques, crisp table linens, fresh flowers, and windows dressed in lace curtains and chef-owner Isabelle Bertuccio turns out magnificent food, often using recipes from her Tuscan and Sicilian relatives. The escargot and herb-crusted rack of lamb top the list. Homemade pasta is served with Sicilian semolina bread and homemade sausages or meatballs. For dessert, Isabelle's husband, Berto, creates sumptuous gelato. ✉ *4231 E. Indian School Rd., Central Phoenix* ☎ *602/955–1213* ⊟ *AE, D, DC, MC, V* ⊘ *No lunch.*

Phoenix: Camelback Corridor

The Camelback Corridor, a veritable restaurant row, runs west to east from Phoenix to Scottsdale—the cities are divided by 64th Street.

American–Casual

¢–$ ✕ **Delux.** This small, hipster burger joint serves delicious salads, sandwiches, and burgers made with all-natural Harris Ranch beef (try the Delux Burger, with Maytag blue and Gruyere cheeses and caramelized onions), complemented by 40 international beers on tap. Suds lovers may want to partake in one of the "beer flights," a trio of 5-ounce tastes. Crispy fries (regular or sweet potato) arrive in a fun mini–shopping cart. Cool tones of blue and gray are accented by a granite-topped bar and a long candle-lit communal table in the center of the restaurant. Open every night until 2 AM, this is a great place to grab a late-night bite. ☒ 3146 E. Camelback Rd., Camelback Corridor ☎ 602/522–2288 ⊜ Reservations not accepted ⊟ AE, D, DC, MC, V.

Contemporary

$$–$$$ ✕ **Tarbell's.** Cutting-edge cuisine is the star at this sophisticated bistro. Grilled salmon served on a crispy potato cake and glazed with a molasses-lime sauce is a long-standing classic. The focaccia with red onion, Romano cheese, and roasted thyme with hummus is excellent and imaginative designer pizzas are cooked in a wood-burning oven. Your sweet tooth won't be disappointed by Tarbell's warm, rich, chocolate cake topped with pistachio ice cream. Hardwood floors, copper accents, and a curving cherrywood and maple bar create a sleek, cosmopolitan look. ☒ 3213 E. Camelback Rd., Camelback Corridor ☎ 602/955–8100 ⊜ Reservations essential ⊟ AE, D, DC, MC, V ☉ No lunch.

French

$$–$$$ ✕ **Bistro 24.** Smart and stylish, with impeccable service, the Ritz's Bistro 24 has a parquet floor, colorful murals, an elegant bar, and an outdoor patio. Take a break from shopping at nearby Biltmore Fashion Park and enjoy the largest Cobb salad in town and a cup of French-press coffee. For dinner, try classic French steak au poivre with frites or grilled fish. For $32, the Friday Night Grill lets you get your fill of Bistro signatures out on the patio. Happy hour is every day from 4 to 7, with half-price select martinis and appetizers. Sunday brunch is a local favorite. ☒ Ritz-Carlton Hotel, 2401 E. Camelback Rd., Camelback Corridor ☎ 602/952–2424 ⊟ AE, D, DC, MC, V.

$$–$$$ ✕ **Christopher's Fermier Brasserie & Paola's Wine Bar.** Chef Christopher Gross serves simple, delicious fare using the freshest ingredients and produce from local farmers. Foods are prepared in the brasserie tradition, and the salad with goat cheese, leek tart, lobster bisque, and the truffle-infused fillet are all of the highest order. Wine director Paola Gross offers more than 100 wines by the glass and stocks an excellent selection of cigars. Thursday to Saturday from 10 PM to midnight, Gross dishes out "Leftovers from the Kitchen" for $9.95. ☒ Biltmore Fashion Park, 2584 E. Camelback Rd., Camelback Corridor ☎ 602/522–2344 ⊟ AE, D, DC, MC, V.

Greek

$–$$$ ✕ **Greekfest.** This informal but elegant restaurant is lovingly decorated with arched whitewashed walls, hardwood floors, and Greek-imported artifacts. Search the menu's two pages of appetizers for *taramasalata* (caviar blended with lemon and olive oil) and *saganaki* (cheese flamed with brandy and extinguished with a squirt of lemon). The moussaka is wonderful, and don't forget dessert (try *galaktoboureko*, warm custard pie baked in phyllo). ⊠ *1940 E. Camelback Rd., Camelback Corridor* ☎ *602/265–2990* ▭ *AE, D, DC, MC, V* ⊘ *Closed Sun.*

Italian

$$–$$$$ ✕ **Tomaso's.** In a town where restaurants come and go overnight, Tomaso's has been a favorite since 1977, and for good reason. Chef Tomaso Maggiore learned to cook as a child at the family's restaurant in Palermo, Sicily, and honed his skills at the Culinary Institute of Rome. The result is authentic Italian cuisine that is consistently well prepared and delicious. The house specialty, *osso buco* (braised veal shank) is outstanding. Other notables include risotto and cannelloni. ⊠ *3225 E. Camelback Rd., Camelback Corridor* ☎ *602/956–0836* ▭ *AE, D, DC, MC, V* ⊘ *No lunch weekends* ⊠ *7341 N. Ray Rd., Chandler* ☎ *480/940–1200* ▭ *AE, D, DC, MC, V* ⊘ *No lunch weekends.*

$$–$$$ ✕ **Daniel's.** Once a year, chef-owner Daniel Malventano takes his cooking crew to Tuscany to train with some of Italy's top chefs and a visit to his richly romantic restaurant will make you feel like you've been to Italy, too. Enjoy their culinary travelogue while indulging in standout Northern Italian creations like veal scallopini with white truffle and porcini mushroom sauce or duck in wild cherry sauce. Finish the meal with *crostata* (Italian pastry filled with pastry cream and sautéed bananas). Specials change seasonally. ⊠ *4225 E. Camelback Rd., Camelback Corridor* ☎ *602/952–1522* ▭ *AE, MC, V* ⊘ *No lunch.*

Mediterranean

★ $$$–$$$$ ✕ **T. Cook's at the Royal Palms.** One of the finest restaurants in the Valley, T. Cook's oozes romance, from the floor-to-ceiling windows with dramatic views of Camelback Mountain to its 1930s-style Spanish-colonial architecture and decor. The Mediterranean-influenced menu includes seared duck breast with apples and winter root vegetables, and grilled beef tenderloin with celery root gratin, baby carrots, and Roquefort. Rotisserie specialties are prepared in the restaurant's signature lodge-style fireplace. Desserts and pastries are works of art. ⊠ *Royal Palms Resort & Spa, 5200 E. Camelback Rd., Camelback Corridor* ☎ *602/840–3610* ⌕ *Reservations essential* ▭ *AE, D, DC, MC, V.*

Southwestern

$$$–$$$$ ✕ **Vincent on Camelback.** Chef Guerithault is best known for creating French food with a Southwestern touch. You can make a meal of his famous appetizers: corn ravioli with white truffle oil, or shrimp beignets with lavender dressing. The dessert menu overflows with intoxicating soufflés. ⊠ *3930 E. Camelback Rd., Camelback Corridor* ☎ *602/224–0225* ⌲ *Reservations essential* ⊟ *AE, D, DC, MC, V* ☉ *Closed Sun. No lunch weekends.*

Sushi

$–$$$ ✕ **Zen 32.** In the ebb and flow of central Phoenix, Zen 32 has managed to stay afloat in a sea that has capsized just about every other sushi restaurant—and their consistently creative rolls, fresh sashimi, and a full kitchen menu make it easy to understand why. The soft-shell crab, rainbow and caterpillar rolls, and the succulent citrus yellowtail are favorites from the sushi menu while the grill produces plenty of tasty non-fish fare. Even though the covered patio faces the zoom and vroom of 32nd Street, the soothing mist and meditation music create a tranquil, yes, even Zen-like atmosphere, making it a popular outdoor dining destination. Try the perfectly steamed *edamame*, pot stickers, or vegetable tempura for starters. Happy hour includes drink and sushi specials. ⊠ *3160 E Camelback Rd., Camelback Corridor* ☎ *602/955–8700* ⊟ *AE, DC, MC, V* ☉ *No lunch weekends.*

> ## A TOUCH OF PROVENCE
>
> On Saturdays (except in summer) from 9 AM to 1 PM, some of the Valley's tastiest creations, from crepes to paella to *panini*, can be found in the parking lot of Vincent on Camelback, at the Touch of Provence market, where visitors have a tendency to believe that they've stumbled into the European vacation they've always dreamed of. Overseen by the restaurant, young Vincent protégés cook up custom orders. People are encouraged to "custom tip" into jars bearing creative causes such as "Saving for MIT" or "Honeymoon Fund." Touch of Provence also features a wine vendor and sellers of independent culinary curios like fresh pesto, honey, and jam.

North Central Phoenix

North Central Phoenix is the area north of Camelback Road between I–17 and Paradise Valley.

Contemporary

$$–$$$ ✕ **Convivo Bistro.** Nestled into the northwest side of the Squaw Peak Promenade shopping center, this restaurant is as close as the desert gets to a Manhattan dining experience: a dozen tables, a tiny kitchen, and a rotating new-American menu featuring fresh seasonal produce. American standards have an international flair, creating unexpected flavors in dishes such as the seared Muscovy duck breast with sweet and sour lime sauce. The wine list is thoughtful and not overpriced. Save room for delicious desserts like the lemon tart with Cointreau-soaked berries in a raspberry sauce. ⊠ *7000 N. 16th St., North Central Phoenix* ☎ *602/997–7676* ⊟ *AE, MC, V* ☉ *Closed Sun. year-round and Mon. May–Nov.*

1

French

$$–$$$$ ✗ **Coup Des Tartes.** Tables are scattered among three small rooms of an old house at this country French restaurant. It's BYOB, and there's an $8 corkage fee but all's forgiven when you taste the delicate cuisine prepared in the tiny kitchen. Chef-owner Natascha Ovando changes the menu weekly, sometimes daily. Offerings may include baked Brie, pineapple-caper *escolar* (a delicious, fattier version of sea bass), or herb-encrusted chicken with a creamy spinach sauce. Ovando's signature dessert, a banana brûlée tart, is delectable. ⊠ *4626 N. 16th St., North Central Phoenix* ☎ *602/212–1082* ⬟ *Reservations essential* ▭ *AE, D, MC, V* ⬡ *BYOB* ⊙ *Closed Sun. and Mon. No lunch.*

Indian

$–$$ ✗ **Taste of India.** This perennial favorite in the Valley specializes in northern Indian cuisine. Breads here—*bhatura, naan, paratha*—are superb, and vegetarians enjoy wonderful meatless specialties, including the eggplant-based *benghan bhartha*, and *bhindi masala*, a tempting okra dish. Just about every spice in the rack is used for the lamb and chicken dishes, so be prepared to guzzle extra water—or an English beer. If your server says an item is spicy, *trust them*. ⊠ *1609 E. Bell Rd., North Central Phoenix* ☎ *602/788–3190* ▭ *AE, MC, V.*

Italian

$–$$$ ✗ **Christo's Ristorante.** Cozy and unassuming in a Phoenix strip mall, Christo's keeps its tables filled with loyal customers. Attentive servers ensure your water glass never empties and folks rave about the roasted rack of lamb, the veal, and the tortellini alla papalina. Start with the delicious calamari. Dinner main courses come with soup and salad. ⊠ *6327 N. 7th St., North Central Phoenix* ☎ *602/264–1784* ▭ *AE, D, DC, MC, V* ⊙ *Closed Sun.*

Mediterranean

¢–$ ✗ **Mediterranean House.** The cuisine served here covers an area between Greece and the Middle East. The lentil soup is thick and spicy, and the Egyptian chicken—a huge plate of sliced chicken breast, battered and fried, is delicious. Vegetarians appreciate the combination plate piled with baba ghanoush, hummus, and falafel served with warm pita and tahini. ⊠ *1588 E. Bethany Home Rd., North Central Phoenix* ☎ *602/248–8460* ▭ *AE, MC, V* ⊙ *Closed Sun. No lunch Sat.*

Mexican

★
¢–$$ ✗ **Via Delosantos.** Finding real local flavor sometimes means remembering that you shouldn't judge a book by its cover. The family-owned Via Delosantos looks a little rough around the edges but it's what's inside that counts—and that includes an accommodating staff, a large menu with unique options, and one of the best-tasting and best-priced house margaritas in town. Before you fill up on the complimentary chips and salsa, remember that the entrées are ample and include more than just tired combinations of beef, beans, and cheese. Try the grilled pork tacos; the fajitas *calabacitas* with yellow and green squash, onions, and corn succotash; the delicious chicken *delosantos,* a rich, cheesy chicken breast and tortilla concoction; or the tasty *machaca* platter with beef, egg, and

chiles. You won't be the only one who finds this appealing, though; weekends are generally packed so expect to wait, either at the bar or outside, but also expect that the experience will be worth it. ✉ *9120 N. Central Ave., North Central Phoenix* ☎ *602/997–6239* ⌕ *Reservations not accepted* ☰ *AE, D, DC, MC, V.*

South Phoenix

South Phoenix is the area south of Buckeye Road, between 27th Avenue on the west and Tempe on the east.

American

$$–$$$$ ✕ **Stockyards Restaurant.** After a 50-year stint, Arizona's original steak house closed for a brief period and has reopened better than ever. If you're looking for a hearty meal, this is the place. Succulent prime rib, aged Midwestern corn-fed steaks, fresh seafood, and poultry are complemented by rib-sticking side dishes such as whiskey-sweet-potato mash and cowboy beans with chorizo and roasted corn. The handsome dining room has saloon-style heavy wood, etched glass, and pressed tin ceilings. A beautiful hand-carved mahogany bar and huge cut-glass chandelier adorn the 1889 Salon in back. ✉ *5009 E. Washington, South Phoenix* ☎ *602/273–7378* ☰ *AE, D, DC, MC, V* ☉ *No lunch weekends.*

Barbecue

¢–$ ✕ **Honey Bear's BBQ.** Honey Bear's motto—"You don't need no teeth to eat our meat"—may fall short on grammar, but this place isn't packed with folks looking to improve their language skills. This is Tennessee-style barbecue, which means smoky baby-back ribs basted in a zippy sauce with a wonderful orange tang. The sausage-enhanced "cowbro" beans and scallion-studded potato salad are great sides. ✉ *5012 E. Van Buren St., South Phoenix* ☎ *602/273–9148* ⌕ *Reservations not accepted* ✉ *2824 N. Central Ave., Phoenix* ☎ *602/279–7911* ✉ *7670 S. Priest Dr., Tempe* ☎ *480/222–2782* ☰ *AE, D, MC, V.*

Mexican

★ $–$$ ✕ **Los Dos Molinos.** In a hacienda that belonged to silent-era movie star Tom Mix, this fun restaurant focuses on New Mexican–style Mexican food. That means *hot.* New Mexico chiles form the backbone and fiery breath of the dishes, and the green-chile enchilada and beef taco are potentially lethal. The red salsa and enchiladas with egg on top are excellent. There's a funky courtyard where you can sip potent margaritas while waiting for a table. This is a must-do dining experience if you want authentic New Mexican–style food, but be prepared to swig lots of water. ✉ *8646 S. Central Ave., South Phoenix* ☎ *602/243–9113* ⌕ *Reservations not accepted* ☰ *AE, D, DC, MC, V* ☉ *Closed Sun. and Mon.*

★ ¢ ✕ **Carolina's.** This small, nondescript restaurant in South Phoenix makes the most delicious, thin-as-air, flour tortillas imaginable. In-the-know locals and downtown working folks have been lining up at Carolina's for years to partake of the homey, inexpensive Mexican food. Tacos, tamales, burritos, flautas, and enchiladas are served on paper plates. ✉ *1202 E. Mohave St., South Phoenix* ☎ *602/252–1503* ☰ *AE, D, DC, MC, V* ☉ *Closed Sun. Dinner on weekdays only until 7:30 PM and Sat. until 6 PM.*

1

Native American

$$$–$$$$ ✕ **Kai.** Kai (it means "seed" in the Pima language) features innovative southwestern cuisine that uses indigenous ingredients from local tribal farms. The seasonal menu reflects the restaurant's natural setting on the Gila River Indian Community. Standout appetizers include lobster tail on Indian fry bread and bacon-wrapped quail. Entrées like seared duck breast with pheasant sausage and the Cheyenne River buffalo tenderloin are excellent. The restaurant is adorned with Native American artifacts and has huge windows that showcase gorgeous mountain and desert views. ⊠ *Sheraton Wild Horse Pass Resort & Spa, 5594 W. Wild Horse Pass Blvd., Chandler* ☎ *602/225–0100* ⌖ *Reservations essential* ⊟ *AE, D, DC, MC, V* ⊗ *Closed Sun. and Mon.*

Paradise Valley

Paradise Valley is a town that has been absorbed into the greater Phoenix area; it's bordered by McDonald Drive to the south, Scottsdale Road to the east, Shea Boulevard to the north, and the Phoenix Mountain Preserve to the west.

Contemporary

$$$ ✕ **elements.** Perched on the side of Camelback Mountain at the Sanctuary Resort, this stylish, modern restaurant offers breathtaking desert-
Fodor$Choice sunset and city-light views. There's a cordial community table where you
★ can sit and order such appetizers as the trilogy of duck, wild escargot won tons, and fried calamari with miso-scallion vinaigrette. Entrées are excellent; among the best is the bacon-wrapped fillet of beef with Maytag blue cheese and merlot demi-glace. ⊠ *Sanctuary on Camelback Mountain, 5700 E. McDonald Dr., Paradise Valley* ☎ *480/607–2300* ⌖ *Reservations essential* ⊟ *AE, D, DC, MC, V.*

$$$ ✕ **Lon's at the Hermosa.** In an adobe hacienda hand-built by cowboy artist
Fodor$Choice Lon Megargee, this romantic spot has sweeping vistas of Camelback
★ Mountain and the perfect patio for after-dinner drinks under the stars. Megargee's art and cowboy memorabilia decorate the dining room. The menu changes seasonally but includes appetizers like rock shrimp with roasted-corn sauce and juniper-smoked wild Chinook salmon. Wood-grilled, melt-in-your-mouth filet mignon over Gorgonzola-mashed potatoes and more exotic dishes like pecan-grilled antelope are main course options. Phoenicians love the Sunday brunch. ⊠ *Hermosa Inn, 5532 N. Palo Cristi Dr., Paradise Valley* ☎ *602/955–7878* ⊟ *AE, D, DC, MC, V* ⊗ *No lunch Sat. and Sun.*

Scottsdale

Fast-growing Scottsdale can be broken down into roughly three neighborhoods. Downtown encompasses the small area bordered by Highland Avenue to the north, 56th Street to the west, Thomas Road to the south, and Scottsdale Road to the east; North Scottsdale includes everything north of Shea Boulevard; and Central Scottsdale is everything between Downtown and North Scottsdale. The Camelback Corridor restaurant row runs west–east from Phoenix to Scottsdale, with 64th Street the border between the two.

American

$$$–$$$$ ✕ **The Grill.** In the Tournament Players Club golf course clubhouse, the Grill promises a hole-in-one for the palette. You don't have to be Tiger Woods to enjoy the upscale atmosphere and incredible eats like "melt-in-your-mouth" steak and an impressive selection of fresh multicoast fish like salmon and halibut flown in daily. ⊠ *TPC Golf Course, 17020 N. Hayden Rd., North Scottsdale, Scottsdale* ☎ *480/585–4848 for Fairmont Scottsdale Princess Resort* ⊟ *AE, D, DC, MC, V.*

American–Casual

$–$$$ ✕ **Bandera.** For a tasty dinner before a night out on the town, try this casual, high-volume spot. The rotisserie chicken is wonderfully moist and meaty; you'll see the birds spinning in the window before you even walk through the door. Salads, fresh fish, prime rib, and meat loaf are also on the menu. The mashed potatoes and grilled artichoke are divine. If you get here during prime eating hours, especially on weekends, be prepared to wait. ⊠ *3821 N. Scottsdale Rd., Central Scottsdale* ☎ *480/994–3524* ⌖ *Reservations not accepted* ⊟ *AE, D, DC, MC, V* ⊘ *No lunch.*

¢–$ ✕ **AZ 88.** A great spot for people-watching, this sleek, glassed-in restaurant serves some of the Valley's best cocktails and food at affordable prices. Large portions of tasty salads, sandwiches, sumptuous burgers (try the Au Poivre II), and perfectly poured cosmopolitans never fail to satisfy. If you're seeking quiet, dine outside on the beautiful patio overlooking Scottsdale Mall. ⊠ *7353 E. Scottsdale Mall, Central Scottsdale* ☎ *480/994–5576* ⊟ *AE, D, DC, MC, V* ⊘ *No lunch weekends.*

¢–$ ✕ **Kashman's Place.** Brooklyn transplants Nancy and Steve Kashman serve sumptuous omelets with crisp home fries, creatively blended salads, and piled-high sandwiches to a large following of locals. Everything is deliciously fresh and portions are generous. New York bagels are done the authentic way—boiled and baked on premises using filtered water they've duplicated from NYC water samples. Expect lines on weekends. ⊠ *32531 N. Scottsdale Rd., at Ashler Hills, North Scottsdale* ☎ *480/ 488–5274* ⊟ *AE, D, DC, MC, V* ⊘ *No dinner.*

¢–$ ✕ **Original Pancake House.** The flapjacks here inspire worship from locals, who wait patiently for a table on weekends. The signature apple pancake is made from homemade batter poured over sautéed apples, then baked to crispy perfection and glazed with cinnamon sugar. Other varieties, such as the Dutch Baby, an oven-baked confection served with whipped butter and powdered sugar, are also worth braving the crowds. Everything is made from scratch. ⊠ *6840 E. Camelback Rd., Central Scottsdale* ☎ *480/946–4902* ⊟ *No credit cards* ⊘ *No dinner.*

Contemporary

$$$–$$$$ ✕ **Acacia.** Worth the drive into the foothills of Pinnacle Peak, this restaurant is in the Four Seasons Hotel in far North Scottsdale. The menu includes some exotic offerings like wild boar bacon-wrapped buffalo tenderloin, but most folks come for the steaks (try the 18-ounce bone-in rib eye). Seafood is excellent, too, and the Chilled Seafood Pinnacle (Alaskan king crab legs, jumbo shrimp, seasonal oysters, Maine lobster, and tuna) is great to share. ⊠ *Four Seasons Scottsdale at Troon North,*

10600 E. Crescent Moon Dr., North Scottsdale ☎ *480/513–5086* ⌂ *Reservations essential* ▤ *AE, D, DC, MC, V* ⊘ *No lunch.*

$$–$$$$ ✕ **Cowboy Ciao.** Looking for a culinary kick? This kitchen weds Southwestern fare and Italian flair, and it's no shotgun wedding. Main dishes, such as the espresso-rubbed filet mignon and the elk strip loin with hazelnut pesto are creative favorites. The pineapple coconut bread pudding with rum praline sauce and rum-spiked pineapple brown sugar ice cream is a must-try. The wine list represents more than 40 countries and features 225 grape varietals. Too much to choose from? Ask for the *Nifty Fifty*, a one-page list of guest favorites. ✉ *7133 E. Stetson Dr., Central Scottsdale* ☎ *480/946–3111* ▤ *AE, D, DC, MC, V.*

$$–$$$$ ✕ **Michael's at the Citadel.** One of this town's best-looking places has a two-story sandstone waterfall, several fireplaces, outdoor seating, and lush desert landscaping. The contemporary American fare changes seasonally. Sunday brunch showcases offerings like orange-ricotta cheese blintzes with lingonberry and cinnamon syrup. For a special occasion, reserve the chef's table in the kitchen (it accommodates 6 to 10 people) and watch the chefs work their magic. ✉ *8700 E. Pinnacle Peak Rd., North Scottsdale* ☎ *480/515–2575* ⌂ *Reservations essential* ▤ *AE, D, DC, MC, V* ⊘ *No lunch weekends.*

★ **$$–$$$$** ✕ **Roaring Fork.** Elk-antler chandeliers, earth-tone fabrics and leathers, barbed-wire accessories, and a buffalo skull above the bar add up to a comfortable, rustic restaurant named after the river that winds past Aspen in Colorado. Chef Robert McGrath's creations include a pork porterhouse steak and fork-barbecued gulf shrimp on lobster, alongside such mouthwatering side dishes as stone-ground chile cheese grits and green-chile macaroni. The reasonably priced saloon menu is served in the bar from 4 to 7 PM Monday to Saturday. ✉ *Finova Building, 4800 N. Scottsdale Rd., Central Scottsdale* ☎ *480/947–0795* ⌂ *Reservations essential* ▤ *AE, D, DC, MC, V* ⊘ *No lunch.*

$$–$$$ ✕ **Rancho Pinot Grill.** The attention to quality paid by the husband-and-wife proprietors here—he manages, she cooks—has made this one of the town's top dining spots. The inventive menu changes daily, depending on what's fresh. If you're lucky, you might come on a day when the kitchen has made *posole*, a mouthwatering broth with hominy, salt pork, and cabbage. Entrées might include quail with soba noodles, rosemary-infused chicken with Italian sausage, or grilled sea bass atop basmati rice. ✉ *6208 N. Scottsdale Rd., Central Scottsdale* ☎ *480/367–8030* ▤ *AE, D, DC, MC, V* ⊘ *Closed Sun. and Mon. mid-May–Nov. No lunch.*

$$–$$$ ✕ **Razz's Restaurant and Bar.** There's no telling what part of the globe chef-proprietor Erasmo "Razz" Kamnitzer will use for culinary inspiration but his creations give dormant taste buds a wake-up call: black-bean paella is a twist on a Spanish theme; South American bouillabaisse is a fragrant fish stew, stocked with veggies; and *bah mie goreng* teams noodles with fish, meat, and vegetables, perked up with dried cranberries and almonds. Count on it—Razz'll dazzle. ✉ *10315 N. Scottsdale Rd., North Scottsdale* ☎ *480/905–1308* ▤ *AE, D, DC, MC, V* ⊘ *Closed Sun. and Mon. No lunch. Closed June–Aug.*

$$ ✕ **L'Ecole.** You won't regret putting yourself in the talented hands of the student chefs at the Valley's premier cooking academy. Choose from an extensive list of French-inspired entrées or the six-course prix-fixe menu, available for lunch ($26) and dinner ($33). The menu changes seasonally but expect inventive appetizers such as roasted chicken and Brie ravioli, and entrées such as filet mignon. ✉ *Scottsdale Culinary Institute, 8100 E. Camelback Rd., Central Scottsdale* ☎ *480/425–3111* ✍ *Reservations essential* ▤ *AE, D, DC, MC, V* ☉ *Closed weekends.*

French

$$$$ ✕ **Mary Elaine's.** Formal and elegant, this is the Valley's finest high-end
Fodor'sChoice   dining experience. The austerity of Mary Elaine's (in the Phoenician Hotel)
★   is a perfect backdrop for dramatic city-light views of Scottsdale from every table. Choose from a seasonally changing three- or six-course prix-fixe or an à la carte menu and indulge in modern French-inspired offerings such as fricassee of lobster or foie gras drizzled with maple syrup and 100-year-old balsamic vinegar. Desserts like the warm chocolate-soufflé tart are breathtaking. An extensive wine cellar, impeccable service, a pleasant jazz vocalist, and new, view-studded patio seating make this an exceptional dining experience. ✉ *The Phoenician, 6000 E. Camelback Rd., Camelback Corridor* ☎ *480/423–2530* ✍ *Reservations essential* ▤ *AE, D, DC, MC, V* ☉ *Closed Sun. and Mon. No lunch.*

$–$$$ ✕ **Zinc Bistro.** No detail was overlooked at this replica of a Parisian bistro, from the zinc-top bar and linen-lined tables topped with butcher paper to the sidewalk café seating and mirrored walls. A Valley local, chef-owner Matt Carter prepares traditional French cuisine almost as if he were a native Frenchman. Bistro classics such as the flatiron steak, cassoulet with duck confit, and the omelet piled high with pommes frites are excellent. Also recommended are the roasted Dungeness crab and mushroom crepes, and the onion soup. The wine list offers a good selection of reasonably priced French wines. ✉ *15034 N. Scottsdale Rd., Kierland Commons, North Scottsdale* ☎ *480/603–0922* ✍ *Reservations not accepted* ▤ *AE, DC, MC, V.*

Japanese

$–$$$$ ✕ **Sushi on Shea.** You may be in the middle of the desert, but the sushi here will make you think you're at the ocean's edge. Fresh yellowtail, toro, shrimp, scallops, freshwater eel, and even monkfish liver pâté are among the long list of delights. *Nabemono* (hot pot or meals-in-a-bowl) are prepared at your table. The best dish? Maybe it's the *una-ju* (broiled freshwater eel with a sublime smoky scent), served over sweet rice. The fact that some people believe eel is an aphrodisiac only adds to its charm. ✉ *7000 E. Shea Blvd., North Scottsdale* ☎ *480/483–7799* ▤ *AE, D, DC, MC, V* ☉ *No lunch Sun. and Mon.*

$$–$$$ ✕ **Sea Saw.** Chef Nobu Fukada is creating some of the Valley's most in-
Fodor'sChoice   teresting food at this small, simple eatery. "Tapanese" cuisine—small
★   plates of Japanese tapas such as baked black cod marinated in miso, allow you to sample lots of different items. Other delights include the white fish carpaccio (served warm) and the sushi foie gras. If you're feeling really adventurous, try the "Omakase Menu," a 10-course dinner created from what's fresh that day. The few tables and bar seats fill up quickly so if you don't have a reservation, do as the locals do—indulge in a glass of wine next door at Kazmierz wine bar while you wait. ✉ *7133 E. Stet-*

On the Mexican Menu

CLOSE UP

1

ALTHOUGH YOU'LL FIND the largest concentration of good Mexican restaurants in Tucson, Phoenix has its fair share as well.

Some menus are in Spanish only, so it's helpful to know the key words.

The predominant cuisine is Sonoran, which is often accented with chiles, tamarind, cilantro, lime, and fresh native produce.

Aguas frescas: A fresh-fruit drink, sort of a smoothie

Albondigas: Meatball soup

Almendrado: An almond dessert, often the colors of the Mexican flag

Atole: A sweet drink made with corn masa, milk, and crushed fruit

Birria: Traditionally stewed goat, but often made with beef

Caldo de queso: Cheese-and-potato soup

Carne asada: Grilled marinated beef

Carne seca: Sun-dried, marinated beef

Carnitas: Stewed pork

Cazuela: *Machaca* soup

Chorizo: Spicy pork or pork-and-beef sausage

Enchiladas: Soft corn tortillas filled with meat or cheese, covered with sauce

Flautas: Rolled, deep-fried tacos

Horchata: Rice-milk and cinnamon drink

Machaca: Dried beef cooked with tomatoes, onions, chiles, and often egg

Mariscos: Shellfish

Menudo: Hominy-and-tripe stew

Mole: A sauce made from chiles, spices, crushed seeds, and flavored with chocolate

Posole: Hominy-and-pork stew

Sopa Azteca: Soup, made with chicken, avocados, and tortillas in broth

Tacos: Tortillas, briefly heated, filled and wrapped into thin cylinders

Tamales: Pockets of corn dough, with savory fillings, which are wrapped in corn husks and steamed.

Tortas: Sandwich on a white bun

Tostadas: Lightly fried, open tortillas topped with meat, lettuce, etc.

Tripitas de leche: Tripe (the stomach) of a cow

---

son Dr., Central Scottsdale ☎ 480/481–9463 ⌲ Reservations essential ▤ AE, D, DC, MC, V ☉ No lunch.

Latin

$–$$$ ✕ **Havana Patio Cafe.** Tapas are marvelous here, particularly the shrimp pancakes, ham and chicken croquettes, and Cuban tamales. There's an intoxicating choice of entrées including paella heaped with a whole Maine lobster. And there's even something for vegetarians: *cho cho*, a fresh chayote squash stuffed with loads of veggies and topped with a Jamaican curry sauce. ⊠ 6245 E. Bell Rd., North Scottsdale ☎ 480/991–1496 ⊠ 4225 E. Camelback Rd., Camelback Corridor, Phoenix ☎ 602/952–1991 ▤ AE, D, DC, MC, V ☉ No lunch Sun.

Mediterranean

$$$$ ✕ **Marquesa.** Polished marble, antiques, and floor-to-ceiling oil paintings adorn this Spanish colonial–style dining room in the Fairmont Scottsdale Princess Resort. Herbs and flavors indigenous to coastal Spain, France, and Italy season such appetizers as Spanish pequillo peppers stuffed with crab and cheese, baked in picada sauce. Main courses include expertly prepared seafood, meats, and poultry—but the real triumph is the paella, bursting with lobster, chicken, shrimp, escargots, pork, and mussels. A wonderful market-style Sunday brunch can be enjoyed on the garden patio. ⊠ *Fairmont Scottsdale Princess Resort, 7575 E. Princess Dr., North Scottsdale* ☎ *480/585–4848* ⌚ *Reservations essential* ▭ *AE, D, DC, MC, V* ⊗ *Closed Mon. and Tues. Brunch only Sun. No lunch.*

Mexican

★ **$$$–$$$$** ✕ **La Hacienda.** La Hacienda is widely considered to be among the finest Mexican restaurants in North America. To ensure authentic cuisine, executive chef Reed Groban took tasting tours through Mexican villages and towns. You'll find no burritos or tacos here, just appetizers like the crab enchilada with creamy pumpkin-seed sauce and La Hacienda's signature dish—spit-roasted suckling pig marinated in tamarind and bitter orange, carved tableside. The restaurant is on the grounds of the Fairmont Scottsdale Princess Resort. ⊠ *Fairmont Scottsdale Princess Resort, 7575 E. Princess Dr., North Scottsdale* ☎ *480/585–4848* ▭ *AE, D, DC, MC, V* ⌚ *Reservations essential* ⊗ *Closed Wed. No lunch.*

$–$$ ✕ **Carlsbad Tavern.** This busy New Mexico–style eatery serves big portions of such tasty dishes as a half-pound habanero cheeseburger, green-chile mashed potatoes, chipotle barbecue baby back ribs, and *carne adovada*, a spicy, slow-roasted pork specialty. They'll custom-mix your margarita with fresh lime and lemon juice and blend it with your choice of some 35 tequilas. There's a late-night menu for the after 10 PM crowd. ⊠ *3313 N. Hayden Rd., Central Scottsdale* ☎ *480/970–8164* ▭ *AE, D, MC, V.*

$–$$ ✕ **Los Sombreros Mexican Cantina.** Los Sombreros is in a converted brick home with lovely patio seating and serves dishes not found in typical Mexican restaurants. Start with the smoked salmon tostada, a crisp corn tortilla spread with cream cheese and chipotle chile, then topped with smoked salmon. Entrées include lamb *adobo*, a shank braised in a piquant sauce of ancho chiles, garlic, and cinnamon. Ice creams are housemade, and the *tamal de chocolate* is made with Mexican chocolate, sugar, and ground almonds. Los Sombreros also serves the best flan you'll find this side of Mexico City. ⊠ *2534 N. Scottsdale Rd., Downtown Scottsdale* ☎ *480/994–1799* ⌚ *Reservations not accepted* ▭ *AE, D, DC, MC, V* ⊗ *Closed Mon. No lunch.*

Pizza

¢–$$ ✕ **Nello's.** Leave it to two brothers from Chicago to come up with some of the best pizza in the Valley. The motto is "In Crust We Trust," and Nello's excels in both thin-crust and deep-dish pies. Try traditional varieties heaped with homemade sausage and mushrooms, or go vegetarian with the spinach pie. Pasta entrées are very good, and the family-style salads are inventive and fresh. ⊠ *8658 E. Shea Blvd., North Scottsdale* ☎ *480/922–5335* ⊗ *Closed Mon.* ⊠ *2950 S. Alma School Dr., Mesa* ☎ *480/820–5995* ⊗ *Closed Mon.* ⊠ *1806 E. South-*

ern Ave., Tempe ☎ 480/897–2060 ◎ Closed Mon. No lunch on Sun.
✉ 4710 E. Warner Rd., Ahwatukee, Phoenix ☎ 480/893–8930
◎ Closed Mon. No lunch on Sun. ⊟ AE, MC, V.

Seafood

$$–$$$ ✕ **Salt Cellar.** It's rare to find a restaurant in a cellar, especially in the desert. Originally an Arizona State University–frequented hamburger joint with concrete walls and floors, the space has been transformed with crisp linen tablecloths and nautical decor. The kitchen dishes out straightforward, fresh seafood. For starters try Chesapeake Bay crab cakes, oysters Rockefeller, or turtle soup. Move on to entrées such as Idaho trout, Yakimono Hawaiian ahi, or charcoal-broiled king salmon. If you're really hungry, splurge on the 5-pound Maine lobster. ✉ 550 N. Hayden Rd., South Scottsdale ☎ 480/947–1963 ⊟ AE, MC, V ◎ No lunch.

Southwestern

$–$$$ ✕ **Old Town Tortilla Factory.** Aside from the tasty Sonoran cuisine and the best homemade tortillas in Scottsdale, the draw here is the location: a historic adobe home in Old Town Scottsdale. Pecan trees shade the large flagstone patio, which is the spot for alfresco dining or for sipping a margarita made with premium tequila. Dishes include ancho raspberry-encrusted pork chops and Shawnee sea bass with a cheese and rock shrimp quesadilla, topped with shoestring sweet potatoes. The banana crisp wrapped in a sweet tortilla with blackberry compote is out of this world. ✉ 6910 E. Main St., Downtown Scottsdale ☎ 480/945–4567 ⊟ AE, D, DC, MC, V ◎ No lunch.

Steak

$$–$$$$ ✕ **Don & Charlie's.** A favorite with major-leaguers in town for spring training, this venerable chophouse specializes in prime-grade steak and baseball memorabilia—the walls are covered with pictures, autographs, and uniforms. The New York sirloin, prime rib, and double-thick lamb chops are a hit; sides include au gratin potatoes and creamed spinach. ✉ 7501 E. Camelback Rd., Central Scottsdale ☎ 480/990–0900 ⊟ AE, D, DC, MC, V ◎ No lunch.

$$–$$$$ ✕ **Morton's of Chicago.** The Windy City chain is famous for exceptional service, immense steaks, and entertaining tableside presentations, but most of all for consistency. If you've been hankerin' for a great aged prime steak, you won't go wrong here. The monstrous 24-ounce porterhouse or 14-ounce double-cut fillet can satisfy the hungriest cowpoke. The seafood is excellent, too, but plays second fiddle to the beef. ✉ 15233 N. Kierland Blvd., North Scottsdale ☎ 480/951–4440 ⌲ Reservations essential ⊟ AE, D, DC, MC, V ◎ No lunch ✉ 2501 E. Camelback Rd., Camelback Corridor Phoenix ☎ 602/955–9577 ⌲ Reservations essential ⊟ AE, D, DC, MC, V ◎ No lunch.

Thai

$–$$ ✕ **Malee's on Main.** This fashionable, casual eatery in the heart of Scottsdale's Main Street Arts District serves sophisticated, Thai-inspired fare. Try the best-selling crispy *pla*, flash-fried whitefish fillets with fresh cilantro and sweet jalapeño garlic sauce. The spicy garlic sautéed spinach is a must, along with curries, made to order with tofu, chicken, beef, pork, or seafood. You specify the spiciness—from mild to flaming. But even the "mild" dishes have a bite. ✉ *7131 E. Main St., Downtown Scottsdale* ☎ *480/947–6042* ⊕ *www.maleesonmain.com* ⚲ *Reservations essential* ⊟ *AE, DC, MC, V* ✉ *Desert Ridge Mall, Tatum Blvd. and 101, North Scottsdale* ☎ *480/342–9220* ⊟ *AE, DC, MC, V.*

East Valley: Tempe, Mesa, Chandler

American

$–$$$ ✕ **Landmark.** In a 1908 building that was originally a Mormon church, this family-run restaurant serves all-American home cooking. The traditional dining room is decorated with lace curtains, chandeliers, and white linens, and the food is straightforward and comfy—roast turkey, prime rib, chicken-fried chicken and steak, and seafood dishes. The real draw, though, is the salad *room,* probably the largest salad bar you'll ever see, featuring nearly 100 items that include soups, breads, salad fixings, and hot dishes. Save room for landmark ice-cream pie. ✉ *809 W. Main St., Mesa* ☎ *480/962–4652* ⊟ *AE, D, MC, V.*

Chinese

$–$$ ✕ **C-Fu Gourmet.** This is serious Chinese food, the kind you'd expect to find on Mott Street in New York City's Chinatown or Grant Avenue in San Francisco. C-Fu's specialty is fish, and you can see several species in big holding tanks. Shrimp are fished out of the tank, steamed, and bathed in a potent garlic sauce. Clams in black-bean sauce and tilapia in a ginger-scallion sauce also hit all the right buttons. If you don't find what you're looking for on the menu, tell them what you want and they'll make it. There's a daily dim sum brunch, too. ✉ *2051 W. Warner Rd., Chandler* ☎ *480/899–3888* ⊟ *AE, D, DC, MC, V.*

Contemporary

$$–$$$ ✕ **House of Tricks.** There's nothing up the sleeves of Robert and Robin Trick, who work magic on their eclectic menu emphasizing the freshest available seafood, poultry, and fine meats, as well as vegetarian selections. One of the Valley's most unique dining venues, the restaurant encompasses a 1920s home and a separate brick- and adobe-style house originally built in 1903, adjoined by an intimate wooden deck and outdoor patio shaded by a canopy of grapevines and trees. At lunch you can't go wrong with the quiche of the day. ✉ *114 E. 7th St., Tempe* ☎ *480/968–1114* ⊟ *AE, D, MC, V* ☉ *Closed Sun.*

$$ ✕ **98 South Wine Bar & Kitchen.** This cool and relaxing wine bar in the historic San Marcos Plaza is the place to sip primo *prosecco* (Italian sparkling wine) and pinots while enjoying live music from a comfy couch or dining on the fine culinary creations of chef P.T. Barnum at the bar or at a table. Appetizers like the cheese plate, the roasted

CHANDLER

The rural residential town of Chandler, south of Tempe, isn't really on the way to anywhere in the Valley but its days as a destination location are coming around. With improved freeway access, the new Chandler Fashion Square megamall, and hip new restaurants like 98 South, Chandler is making its way onto the Phoenix area maps.

vegetables and hummus, and the skirt steak starters make for a meal on their own, but the dinner and lunch menus feature a full range of delicious entrées with wines to match. If you have trouble finding it, remember the name is also the address. ⊠ *98 South San Marcos Pl., Chandler* ☎ *480/814–9800* ⊟ *AE, D, DC, MC, V* ⊗ *Closed Sun.*

French

$$–$$$ ✕**Citrus Cafe.** Elegant yet casual, this small restaurant does everything right, from the romantic candlelight dining room to a daily menu featuring what's freshest from the market. For starters, try the baked Brie with almonds and apples or the superb leek-and-potato soup. Main dishes are pure French comfort food: veal kidneys, sweetbreads, leg of lamb, roast pork, and occasionally rabbit. ⊠ *2330 N. Alma School Rd., Chandler* ☎ *480/899–0502* ⊟*AE, D, DC, MC, V* ⊗ *Closed Mon. No lunch.*

Italian

¢–$$ ✕**Oregano's.** Huge portions are an understatement at this casual Chicago-theme eatery. Come hungry and feast on fresh salads, tasty baked sandwiches, pizza (deep-dish, thin crust, or stuffed), and pasta dishes. The young, friendly staff and kitchsy 1950s decor create a fun and comfortable, family-friendly vibe. Save room for the famous pizza cookie, a half pound of chocolate chip or white chocolate macadamia nut cookie dough, baked on a 6-inch pizza pan and topped with three scoops of vanilla-bean ice cream. ⊠ *523 W. University Dr., Tempe* ☎ *480/858–0501* ⌂ *Reservations not accepted* ⊠ *3622 N. Scottsdale Rd., Downtown Scottsdale* ☎ *480/970–1860* ⊠ *7215 E. Shea Blvd., North Scottsdale* ☎ *480/348–0500* ⊠ *1008 E. Camelback Rd., Central Phoenix* ☎ *602/241–0707* ⊠ *1130 S. Dobson Rd., Mesa* ☎ *480/962–0036* ⊟ *AE, D, DC, MC, V.*

Mexican

¢–$ ✕**Rosa's Mexican Grill.** This festive, family-friendly restaurant summons up images of a Baja beach taqueria. The tacos are Rosa's true glory: beef, pork, and chicken are marinated in fruit juices and herbs for 12 hours, slowly oven-baked for another 10, then shredded and charbroiled. The fish taco is in a class by itself. Spoon on one of Rosa's five fresh homemade salsas but beware the fiery habanero version—it can strip the enamel right off your teeth. ⊠ *328 E. University Dr., Mesa* ☎ *480/964–5451* ⊟ *AE, D, DC, MC, V* ⊗ *Closed Sun.*

Middle Eastern

¢ ✕**Haji Baba.** This casual Tempe treasure is a local favorite that serves hummus, *labni* (fresh cheese made from yogurt), falafel, and kebab plates. The adjoining store stocks delicious cured olives and hard-to-find Middle Eastern ingredients. ⊠ *1513 E. Apache Blvd., Tempe* ☎ *480/894–1905* ⌂ *Reservations not accepted* ⊟ *AE, D, MC, V* ⊗ *Take-out only on Sun.*

Vietnamese

$–$$ ✕ **Cyclo.** It's always exciting to find an outstanding one-of-a-kind restaurant in a town filled with corporate-chain establishments. Cyclo is just that. Friendly and gracious owner Justina Dwong is as much a draw as the well-prepared Vietnamese food. Try the *bánh xéo,* a crispy, turmeric-yellow crepe filled with juicy bites of pork and shrimp, or crispy *cha gío,* a spicy lemongrass chicken. A French-inspired, jasmine-scented crème brûlée provides a perfect ending to the meal. ⊠ *1919 W. Chandler Blvd., Chandler* ☎ *480/963–4490* 🖃 *MC, V* ⊗ *Closed Sun.*

West Valley: West Phoenix, Glendale, Litchfield Park

Chinese

$ ✕ **Silver Dragon.** This is one of the best Chinese restaurants in town—if you order properly. Insist on sitting in the big room to the left as you walk in the door, and ask for the Chinese menu (it has brief English descriptions). Your boldness will be rewarded with some of the best Hong Kong–style Chinese fare to be found between New York and California. Crispy Hong Kong–Style Chicken is a plump whole bird steamed, flash-fried, and cut into bite-size pieces. Other standouts include the hot-pot dishes, noodles, fish, and vegetarian dishes—the Buddhist-style rolls are outstanding. ⊠ *8946 N. 19th Ave., West Phoenix* ☎ *602/674–0151* 🖃 *AE, MC, V* ⊗ *Closed Wed. No lunch Sat.*

German

$–$$$ ✕ **Haus Murphy's.** On weekends, kick back with the accordionist at this charming storefront restaurant. Schnitzel is a specialty, especially the spicy paprika version, teamed with crispy chunks of fried potatoes and green beans. Sauerbraten, paired with tart red cabbage and two huge potato dumplings, is not for the faint of appetite. Wash everything down with a German beer—there are eight on tap—and save room for the homemade apple strudel and Black Forest torte. ⊠ *5739 W. Glendale Ave., Glendale* ☎ *623/939–2480* 🖃 *AE, D, MC, V* ⊗ *Closed Mon.*

Mexican

¢–$ ✕ **Lily's Cafe.** Friendly mom-and-pop proprietors, a jukebox with south-of-the-border hits, and low-price, fresh Mexican fare have kept patrons coming here for almost 50 years. Beef is the featured ingredient. The chimichanga is stuffed with tender beef and covered with cheese, guacamole, and sour cream. Fragrant tamales, spunky red-chile beef, and chiles rellenos right out of the fryer also shine. ⊠ *6706 N. 58th Dr., Glendale* ☎ *623/937–7755* 🖎 *Reservations not accepted* 🖃 *No credit cards* ⊗ *Closed Mon., Tues., and Aug.*

¢–$ ✕ **Pepe's Taco Villa.** The neighborhood's not fancy, and neither is this restaurant. But in a town filled with gringo-ized, south-of-the-border fare, this is the real friendly real deal. Tacos *rancheros*—spicy, shredded pork pungently lathered with adobo paste—are a dream. So are the green-corn tamales, authentic imported *machacado* (air-dried beef), and chiles rellenos that are perfect with a margarita from their full bar. Don't leave without trying the sensational mole, a rich, exotic sauce fashioned from chiles and chocolate. ⊠ *2108 W. Camelback Rd., West Phoenix* ☎ *602/242–0379* 🖃 *AE, D, MC, V* ⊗ *Closed Tues.*

Southwestern

$$–$$$$ ✕ **Arizona Kitchen.** With the help of a historian of Native American foods, the chef has put together a bold Southwestern menu. Appetizers such as duck tamales and braised pork relleno give you an indication of what's to come. Entrées include braised duck breast and Colorado rack of lamb. For dessert, try the chile-spiked ice cream in the striking turquoise "bowl" of hardened sugar. It's worth the 20-minute drive from downtown Phoenix to the Wigwam Resort. ⊠ *Wigwam Resort, 300 E. Wig-wam Blvd., Litchfield Park* ☎ *623/935–3811* ▤ *AE, D, DC, MC, V.*

Vietnamese

¢–$$ ✕ **Pho Bang.** What makes this little hole-in-the-wall restaurant so appealing—aside from price—is the simplicity and freshness of the food. The house specialty is *tom va bo nuong vi* (#35 on the menu): the server brings three plates, one with transparently thin slices of marinated beef and raw shrimp; another with piles of mint, lettuce, cilantro, pickled leeks, cucumber, and carrot; and the last with rice paper. You fire up the portable grill and cook the beef and shrimp. When they're done, combine with the veggies, fold into rice paper, and start dunking. ⊠ *1702 W. Camelback Rd., West Phoenix* ☎ *602/433–9440* ▤ *MC, V.*

WHERE TO STAY

Updated by
JoBeth Jamison

The Valley of the Sun has long been the domain of resorts and historic places to stay, including the Arizona Biltmore, Camelback Inn, and Royal Palms—all in Phoenix and Paradise Valley—are still among the Valley's most popular getaways. Most others are in the neighboring, tourist-friendly city of Scottsdale.

Competition among the newest megaresorts is fierce and properties vie for family and leisure business with immaculately manicured golf courses and incredible water features—the Valley of the Sun is carpeted with green and, surprisingly, filled with water so rivers, waterfalls, lakes, slides, pools, and even canals replete with gondolas put the humble hotel pool to shame. The resorts come in all shapes and sizes; some properties consist of a large main hotel, but others are spread out in casitas (little houses) surrounding the golf courses.

Most downtown Phoenix properties are business and family hotels, closer to the heart of the city—and to the average vacationer's budget. Many properties here cater to corporate travelers during the week but lower their rates on weekends to entice leisure travelers, so ask about weekend specials when making reservations. With more than 55,000 hotel rooms in the metro area, you can take your pick of anything from a luxurious resort to a guest ranch to an extended-stay hotel. For a true Western experience, guest-ranch territory is 60 mi northwest, in the town of Wickenburg.

Many people flee snow and ice to bask in the warmth of the Valley so winter is the high season, peaking in January through March. Summer season—mid-May through the end of September—is giveaway time, when a night at a resort often goes for half of the winter price.

WHAT IT COSTS				
$$$$	**$$$**	**$$**	**$**	**¢**
FOR 2 PEOPLE over $250	$176–$250	$121–$175	$70–$120	under $70

Prices are for a standard double in high season.

Where to Stay in the
Valley of the Sun

Downtown Phoenix

$$–$$$$ ▦ **Hyatt Regency Phoenix.** This convention-oriented hotel efficiently handles the arrival and departure of hundreds of business travelers each day. The seven-story atrium has huge sculptures, colorful tapestries, potted plants, and comfortable seating areas. Rooms are spacious, but the atrium roof blocks east views on floors 8 through 10. There's a revolving restaurant with panoramic views of the Phoenix area. ⊠ *122 N. 2nd St., Downtown Phoenix, 85004* ☎ *602/252–1234* 🖷 *602/254–9472* ⊕ *www.hyatt.com* ⟿ *712 rooms, 25 suites* ⚿ *4 restaurants, cable TV with movies, in-room data ports, pool, wading pool, gym, outdoor hot tub, 2 bars, concierge, business services, meeting rooms, car rental, parking (fee), no-smoking rooms* ▭ *AE, D, DC, MC, V.*

$–$$$$ ▦ **Wyndham Phoenix.** When Wyndham took over this former Crowne Plaza, the chain invested $6 million to create an appealing mix of classic comfort and modern metro accommodations. Ideally situated for all things downtown (but little else) the hotel stands, with very little competition, in the center of bustling Copper Square within 1 mi of Heritage and Science Parks, America West Arena, Bank One Ballpark, and the Arizona Center. It's also near the light rail and downtown renovation construction, which, although tedious, gives it a more appealing price tag. Spacious rooms with subtle southwestern tones are designed for the business traveler, relatively quiet (in spite of construction), and well-lighted with large desks, and ergonomic desk chairs, but they're also kid-friendly, comfortable, and convenient for pro baseball and basketball fans, as well as theater, symphony, convention, and celebrity concertgoers. ⊠ *50 E. Adams St., Downtown Phoenix, 85004* ☎ *602/333–0000* ⊕ *www.wyndham.com* ⟿ *532 rooms, 108 suites* ⚿ *Restaurant, room service, some refrigerators, cable TV with movies, in-room data ports, in-room broadband, Wi-Fi, pool, gym, sauna, bar, shop, laundry service, business services, car rental, parking (fee), no-smoking rooms* ▭ *AE, D, DC, MC, V.*

$–$$$ ▦ **Hotel San Carlos.** Built in 1927 in an Italian Renaissance design, the seven-story San Carlos is the only historic hotel still operating in downtown Phoenix. Among other distinctions, the San Carlos was the Southwest's first air-conditioned hotel, and suites bear the names of such movie-star guests as Marilyn Monroe and Spencer Tracy. Big-band music, wall tapestries, Austrian crystal chandeliers, shiny copper elevators, and an accommodating staff transport you to a more genteel era. The rooms are snug by modern standards but have attractive period furnishings and coffeemakers. ⊠ *202 N. Central Ave., Downtown Phoenix, 85004* ☎ *602/253–4121 or 800/678–8946* 🖷 *602/253–6668* ⊕ *www. hotelsancarlos.com* ⟿ *109 rooms, 12 suites* ⚿ *Cable TV with movies, in-room data ports, pool, dry cleaning, laundry service, meeting rooms, parking (fee), no-smoking rooms* ▭ *AE, D, DC, MC, V.*

Central Phoenix

$$–$$$ ▦ **Embassy Suites Phoenix Airport West.** Just minutes from downtown, this four-story all-suites hotel is very family friendly and features a charming courtyard oasis of palm and olive trees surrounding bubbling

Top Spas

THE VALLEY OF THE SUN is all about relaxation and there's no better place for it than at one of Phoenix's rejuvenating resort spas. Many feature Native American–inspired treatments and use indigenous ingredients such as agave, desert clay, and neroli oil (derived from orange blossoms). Spa lovers should plan to enjoy not only the treatments that include pools, whirlpools, eucalyptus steam rooms, and relaxation areas with outdoor fireplaces. Some of our top picks are as follows. Contact information for the properties can be found in the Where to Stay section.

Aji Spa at the Sheraton Wild Horse Pass Resort & Spa. A gem on the grounds of the Gila River Indian community, Aji incorporates its Native American surroundings into every aspect of the light-filled spa, from the name ("Aji" is Pima for sanctuary) to its contemporary Sonoran design and treatments. The Blue Coyote Wrap ($185 for 80 minutes) begins with a dry brush exfoliation and an application of Azulene mud, and culminates with a cedar–sage oil massage. A 50-minute massage starts at $125.

Alvadora at the Royal Palms Resort & Spa. At this Mediterranean-style villa treatments incorporate herbs, flowers, oils, and minerals indigenous to the Mediterranean. One signature treatment is the Orange Blossom Body Buff, a full body scrub that uses neroli oil. A 60-minute massage starts at $125. Spa use for nonresort guests is limited to Sun.–Thurs. and requires purchase of a spa package.

The Spa at JW Marriott's Camelback Inn. This is one of the Valley's most popular spas. Aches and pains will melt away with the 60-minute Native Hot Stone Massage (starts at $125) incorporating the Native American art of massaging the body with heated basalt stones. A 60-minute massage starts at $100. The men's spa lounge, with comfy leather chairs and a large television, will make even the most hesitant spa-goer feel at home.

Sanctuary Spa at Sanctuary on Camelback Mountain. This sleek Zen-like spa has 11 Asian-inspired indoor–outdoor treatment rooms nestled against Camelback Mountain. Try a transporting 30-minute Thai foot massage (starts at $85) or a Bamboo Lemongrass Scrub (30 minutes is $85). A 60-minute massage starts at $135. Spa use is restricted to resort guests only.

Willow Stream Spa at the Fairmont Scottsdale Princess. This is one of the Valley's most elaborate spas. Inspired by "Havasupai," a hidden oasis in the Grand Canyon, there's water everywhere—from the glamorous rooftop pool to streams that flow throughout the grounds. Amid this luxury, you might want to splurge for the two-hour Havasupai Body Treatment ($309) in which aches and pains are kneaded away under three waterfalls of varying pressure. It includes a eucalyptus foot massage, a body scrub, a soak in a private tub, and a body, face, and scalp massage. A 60-minute massage starts at about $140.

fountains and a sunken pool in its enclosed atrium. Complimentary breakfast (cooked to order) and an evening social hour are offered in the lounge. Also pet friendly, the apartment-style suites are comfortable and tastefully modern with wet bars and refrigerators. ☒ *2333 E. Thomas Rd., Central Phoenix, 85016* ☎ *602/957–1910* 🖷 *602/955–2861* ⊕ *www. embassy-suites.com* ⇨ *183 suites* ♿ *Restaurant, cable TV, in-room broadband, Wi-Fi, pool, gym, hot tub, lounge, laundry service, airport shuttle, free parking, no-smoking rooms* ⊟ *AE, D, DC, MC, V* ⦶ *BP.*

$$–$$$ ⊡ **Hilton Suites.** This practical hotel is a model of excellent design within tight limits. It sits off Central Avenue, 2 mi north of downtown amid the Central Corridor cluster of office towers. The marble-floor, pillared lobby opens into an 11-story atrium containing palm trees, natural boulder fountains, glass elevators, and a lantern-lighted café. Each suite has a large walk-through bathroom between the living room and bedroom. The hotel offers a full breakfast and if you're up for more than a drink at the inviting lounge bar or dinner at the on-site chain restaurant, you can take the free shuttle service to other area eats and attractions. ☒ *10 E. Thomas Rd., Central Phoenix, 85012* ☎ *602/222–1111* 🖷 *602/265–4841* ⊕ *www.hilton.com* ⇨ *226 suites* ♿ *Restaurant, room service, cable TV with movies and video games, in-room VCRs, in-room data ports, indoor pool, gym, hot tub, sauna, bar, shop, laundry facilities, laundry service, concierge, business services, parking (fee), some pets allowed, no-smoking rooms* ⊟ *AE, D, DC, MC, V* ⦶ *BP.*

$ ⊡ **Best Western Inn Suites Hotel & Suites.** Just north of the Pointe Squaw Peak, this affordable all-suites hotel is often overlooked as an option for the north central neighborhood but it has the same proximity to everything that the Hilton does: great recreation areas, including Dreamy Draw Park, Piestewa Peak Mountain Preserve; great dining, including Richardsons, the Rokerij, Gallaghers, Convivo, and the Coffee Plantation; and is less than 1 mi from State Route 51, which offers quick and easy access to major freeways, Valley shopping, and Sky Harbor airport. Decor is dated but the price is right, especially for the area. ☒ *1615 E. Northern Ave., Central Phoenix, 85004* ☎ *602/997–6285* ⊕ *www.bestwestern. com* ⇨ *77 rooms, 32 2-room suites* ♿ *Cable TV with movies, in-room data ports, in-room broadband, gym, pool, hot tub, dry cleaning, laundry service, business services, meeting rooms, parking (fee), no-smoking rooms, some pets allowed* ⊟ *AE, D, DC, MC, V.*

Phoenix: Camelback Corridor

$$$$ ⊡ **Arizona Biltmore.** Designed by Frank Lloyd Wright's colleague Albert
Fodor's Choice Chase McArthur, the Biltmore has been Phoenix's premier resort since
★ it opened in 1929. The lobby, with its stained-glass skylights, wrought-iron pilasters, and cozy sitting alcoves, fills with piano music each evening. Guest rooms are spacious, with Southwestern-print fabrics and Mission-style furniture. Accommodating staff are unobtrusive. The Biltmore sits on 39 impeccably manicured acres of cool fountains, open walkways, and colorful flower beds. ☒ *2400 E. Missouri Ave., Camelback Corridor, 85016* ☎ *602/955–6600 or 800/950–0086* 🖷 *602/381–7600* ⊕ *www.arizonabiltmore.com* ⇨ *739 rooms, 72 villas* ♿ *4 restaurants, in-room safes, minibars, cable TV with movies, in-room broad-*

band, some Wi-Fi, golf privileges, miniature golf, putting green, 7 tennis courts, 8 pools, gym, 3 outdoor hot tubs, sauna, spa, bicycles, lobby lounge, children's programs (ages 6–12), laundry service, concierge, business services, car rental, free parking, no-smoking rooms ▤ AE, D, DC, MC, V.

$$$$ ▦ **Ritz-Carlton.** The sand-color facade hides a graceful luxury hotel well known for impeccable service. The lobby and spacious public rooms are elegantly inviting, decorated with 18th- and 19th-century European paintings and a handsome china collection. Guest rooms and suites are spacious enclaves of luxury with premium mattresses and pillows, 800-thread-count sheets, and downy duvets that are even more inviting after the nightly turn-down service, complete with fine chocolate. A conscientious and attentive staff offers impeccable service while the central location means both upscale and casual dining, shopping, and entertainment are within strolling distance. Summer packages are creative, fun, and very affordable. Mountain and city vistas can be appreciated from the rooftop terrace, where there is also a heated pool. ✉ 2401 E. Camelback Rd., Camelback Corridor, Phoenix 85016 ☎ 602/468–0700 or 800/241–3333 🖨 602/468–0793 ⊕ www.ritzcarlton.com ⇲ 269 rooms, 12 suites ⟐ Restaurant, room service, in-room safes, refrigerators, cable TV, in-room boadband, Wi-Fi, pool, gym, 2 saunas, bicycle, 3 bars, shop, laundry service, concierge floor, business services, meeting rooms, parking (fee), no-smoking rooms ▤ AE, D, DC, MC, V.

$$$$ ▦ **Royal Palms Resort & Spa.** Once the home of Cunard Steamship executive Delos T. Cooke, this Mediterranean-style resort has a stately row of the namesake palms at its entrance, courtyards with fountains, and individually designed rooms. Deluxe casitas are all different, though they follow one of three elegant styles—trompe l'oeil, romantic retreat, Spanish colonial. The restaurant, T. Cook's ($3–$4), is renowned and the open-air Alvadora Spa seems like it has every imaginable amenity, including an outdoor rain shower. ✉ 5200 E. Camelback Rd., Camelback Corridor, 85018 ☎ 602/840–3610 or 800/672–6011 🖨 602/840–6927 ⊕ www.royalpalmshotel.com ⇲ 34 rooms, 34 suites, 44 casitas ⟐ Restaurant, room service, in-room safes, refrigerators, cable TV, in-room broadband, Wi-Fi, golf privileges, pool, gym, spa, hiking, bar, laundry service, business services, meeting rooms, parking (fee), no-smoking rooms ▤ AE, D, DC, MC, V.

FodorśChoice
★

$$$ ▦ **Phoenix Inn Suites.** The Phoenix representative of this Arizona chain is a bargain, considering the amenities. Local calls and high-speed Internet access are free, and several rooms have corner jetted tubs. The four-story hotel is a block off Camelback Road. ✉ 2310 E. Highland Ave., Camelback Corridor, 85016 ☎ 602/956–5221 or 800/956–5221 🖨 602/468–7220 ⊕ www.phoenixinnsuites.com ⇲ 120 suites ⟐ Some in-room hot tubs, microwaves, refrigerators, cable TV with movies, in-room data ports, Wi-Fi, pool, gym, hot tub, shop, laundry facilities, no-smoking rooms ▤ AE, D, DC, MC, V ⌾ CP.

$$–$$$ ▦ **Courtyard Phoenix Camelback.** Public areas in this four-story hotel are mostly glass and tile, filled with greenery. A lap pool and Jacuzzi await in the landscaped courtyard. There's a small café on premises that serves breakfast, lunch, and dinner or, if you prefer, there are more than 50

restaurants within a 1½-mi radius. ⊠ *2101 E. Camelback Rd., Camelback Corridor, 85016* ☎ *602/955–5200 or 800/321–2211* ☒ *602/955–1101* ⊕ *www.courtyard.com* ↩ *155 rooms, 12 suites* ↺ *Restaurant, some microwaves, some refrigerators, cable TV with movies, in-room data ports, pool, gym, hot tub, laundry facilities, laundry service, meeting rooms, free parking* ☰ *AE, D, DC, MC, V.*

$–$$$ ⊞ **Homewood Suites Phoenix-Biltmore.** This all-suites chain is a major value, especially considering its location in the heart of the upscale Biltmore District. Suites have a spacious living and working area with a sleeper-sofa and one or two separate bedrooms; each has a full kitchen. From Monday to Thursday evening there's a "Welcome Home" reception— a minifeast featuring anything from a taco bar to baked potatoes with all the trimmings. Guests also get free passes to a nearby fitness club, free breakfast, and transportation within a 5-mi radius of the hotel. ⊠ *2001 E. Highland Ave., Camelback Corridor, 85016* ☎ *602/508–0937* ☒ *602/508–0854* ⊕ *www.homewood-suites.com* ↩ *124 rooms* ↺ *Kitchens, cable TV with movies, in-room data ports, Wi-Fi, pool, gym, laundry facilities, laundry service, no-smoking rooms* ☰ *AE, D, DC, MC, V* ⑩ *BP.*

North Phoenix

☾ $$$$ ⊞ **JW Marriott Desert Ridge Resort & Spa.** Arizona's largest resort has an immense entryway with floor-to-ceiling windows that allow the sandstone lobby, the Sonoran Desert, and the resort's amazing water features to meld together in a single prospect. Four acres of water fun include the "lazy river," where you can flop on an inner tube and float the day away, and there are two golf courses. Rooms have balconies or patios. Southwestern celebrity chef Mark Miller's Blue Sage ($$–$$$$) is just one of many convenient restaurants on the property. ⊠ *5350 E. Marriott Dr., North Central Phoenix, 85054* ☎ *480/293–5000 or 800/835–6206* ☒ *480/293–3600* ⊕ *www.marriott.com* ↩ *869 rooms, 81 suites* ↺ *9 restaurants, coffee shop, room service, in-room safes, mini-bars, some refrigerators, cable TV with movies, in-room data ports, in-room broadband, some Wi-Fi, 2 18-hole golf courses, 8 tennis courts, 5 pools, hair salon, spa, bicycle, 2 lounges, shops, babysitting, children's programs (ages 4–12), business services, meeting rooms, no-smoking rooms* ☰ *AE, D, DC, MC, V.*

☾ $$$–$$$$ ⊞ **Pointe Hilton at Squaw Peak.** The highlight of Squaw Peak, the more family-oriented of the two Pointe Hiltons in Phoenix, is the 9-acre recreation area *Hole-in-the-Wall River Ranch.* It has swimming pools with waterfalls, a 130-foot water slide, and a 1,000-foot "river" that winds past a miniature golf course, tennis courts, and artificial buttes with stunning mountain vistas. Accommodations in the pink-stucco buildings vary from standard two-room suites to a grand three-bedroom house; all have balconies and TVs. The resort is adjacent to the Phoenix Mountain Preserve, making it an ideal base for hiking and biking trips. ⊠ *7677 N. 16th St., North Central Phoenix, 85020* ☎ *602/997–2626 or 800/876–4683* ☒ *602/997–2391* ⊕ *www.pointehilton.com* ↩ *431 suites, 130 casitas, 1 house* ↺ *3 restaurants, some kitchens, minibars, cable TV, golf privileges, miniature golf, 3 tennis courts, 7 pools, gym, spa, mountain* *bikes, hiking, 2 lounges, shops, children's programs (ages 6–12), meeting rooms, parking, no-smoking rooms* = *AE, D, DC, MC, V.*

Near Sky Harbor Airport

$$$ ⊞ **Phoenix Doubletree Guest Suites.** In the Gateway Center, just 1½ mi north of the airport, this honeycomb of six-story towers is the best choice for anyone who just wants to get off the plane and into a comfortable, central hotel. Bedroom furnishings cater to the corporate crowd that travels light—two-drawer credenzas serve as bureaus, and dinky wardrobes function as closets. ⊠ *320 N. 44th St., Airport, 85008* ☎ *602/225–0500* 📠 *602/225–0957* ⊕ *www.doubletree.com* ⇥ *242 suites* ♨ *Restaurant, room service, microwaves, refrigerators, cable TV with movies, in-room data ports, in-room broadband, pool, gym, sauna, bar, laundry facilities, laundry service, meeting rooms, airport shuttle, free parking, no-smoking rooms* = *AE, D, DC, MC, V* ⫟⦿⫠ *BP.*

$–$$ ⊞ **Hampton Inn & Suites Phoenix-Airport Tempe.** More affordable than many other airport options, this four-story hotel is 5 mi from downtown and 2½ mi from the airport. Guest rooms are moderate in size with handsome armoires and bright-color prints. Free Continental breakfast is available in the lobby. Take advantage of free local calls and the 24-hour hotel airport shuttle. ⊠ *4234 S. 48th St., Phoenix 85040* ☎ *602/438–8688 or 800/426–7866* 📠 *602/431–8339* ⊕ *www.phoenixhampton.com* ⇥ *78 rooms, 29 suites* ♨ *Restaurant, refrigerators, cable TV with movies, in-room VCRs, Wi-Fi, pool, gym, hot tub, bar, shop, laundry facilities, laundry service, meeting rooms, free parking, no-smoking rooms* = *AE, D, DC, MC, V* ⫟⦿⫠ *CP.*

South Phoenix

☼ $$$–$$$$ ⊞ **Crowne Plaza San Marcos Golf Resort.** When it opened in 1912, the San Marcos was the first golf resort in Arizona and it still one of the state's most treasured landmarks. Now a part of the Crowne Plaza family, the palm-studded, mission-style San Marcos has undergone luxury upgrades to keep it on par with its boomtown competition, while maintaining its historic beauty, architectural integrity, and charm. Improvements include the Images day spa and restyled rooms with pillow top mattresses, high thread-count sheets, down-filled duvets. Each room and suite has either a balcony or patio and the quiet, single-level golf course casitas offer patios with *"Fore!-*star" views. The resort operates an on-site Starbucks and there is great nearby shopping and dining. ⊠ *One San Marcos Pl., Chandler 85225* ☎ *480/812–0900* 📠 *480/899–5441* ⊕ *www.sanmarcosresort.com* ⇥ *238 rooms, 45 casitas, 12 suites* ♨ *2 restaurants, 2 bars, spa, golf, room service, cable TV with movies and video games, in-room broadband, in-room data ports, 2 outdoor pools, free parking; no-smoking rooms.* = *AE, D, DC, MC, V.*

☼ $$$–$$$$ ⊞ **Pointe South Mountain Resort.** This all-suites resort next to South Mountain Park has a golf course and the largest water park in Arizona—guests can tube down a river, splash in the wave pool, or zoom down the nation's tallest water slide. There's a four-story sports center, golf, tennis, horseback riding, and mountain biking. Each suite has two TVs and a sofa bed. ⊠ *7777 S. Pointe Pkwy., South Phoenix, 85044* ☎ *602/*

438–9000 or 877/800–4888 🖷 *602/431–6535* ⊕ *www.pointesouthmtn. com* ⟿ *642 suites* ♻ *6 restaurants, room service, minibars, in-room data ports, 18-hole golf course, 10 tennis courts, pro shop, 6 pools, health club, sauna, mountain bikes, hiking, horseback riding, laundry facilities, meeting rooms, parking* ⊟ *AE, D, DC, MC, V.*

$$$–$$$$ 🏨 **Sheraton Wild Horse Pass Resort & Spa.** On the grounds of the Gila River Indian community, 11 mi south of Sky Harbor Airport, the culture and heritage of the Pima and Maricopa tribes are reflected in every aspect of this property. Guest rooms are detailed with Native art and textiles, and Kai (Pima for "seed") Restaurant ($$$–$$$$) combines Southwestern- and Native-culinary traditions. A 2½-mi replica of the Gila River meanders through the property; you can take a boat to the Whirlwind Golf Clubhouse or nearby Wild Horse Pass Casino. Keep your eyes open for the wild horses for which the resort is named. ⊠ *5594 W. Wild Horse Pass Blvd., Chandler 85226* 🕾 *602/225–0100 or 800/325–3535* 🖷 *602/225–0300* ⊕ *www.wildhorsepassresort.com* ⟿ *474 rooms, 26 suites* ♻ *4 restaurants, in-room safes, minibars, cable TV with movies, in-room data ports, Wi-Fi, 2 18-hole golf courses, 2 tennis courts, 4 pools, gym, spa, boating, hiking, horseback riding, 2 lounges, casino, children's programs (ages 5–12), laundry service, business services, free parking, no-smoking rooms* ⊟ *AE, D, DC, MC, V.*

Paradise Valley

★ $$$$ 🏨 **JW Marriott's Camelback Inn Resort, Golf Club & Spa.** This historic resort is a swank spot for relaxation in the gorgeous valley between Camelback and Mummy mountains. Built on 125 acres in the mid-1930s, the latilla (peeled log) beam buildings ooze Southwestern charm; the grounds are adorned with stunning cacti and desert flowers. Rooms are spacious, and seven suites have private swimming pools. Visit one of 32 treatment rooms in the spa for a para-joba body wrap or an adobe-mud purification treatment. ⊠ *5402 E. Lincoln Dr., Paradise Valley 85253* 🕾 *480/948–1700 or 800/242–2635* 🖷 *480/951–8469* ⊕ *www. camelbackinn.com* ⟿ *453 rooms, 27 suites* ♻ *6 restaurants, coffee shop, in-room faxes, some kitchenettes, cable TV with movies, in-room broadband, 2 18-hole golf courses, 6 tennis courts, 3 pools, hot tub, sauna, spa, hiking, lounge, shops, children's programs (ages 5–12), business services, free parking, no-smoking rooms* ⊟ *AE, D, DC, MC, V.*

$$$$ 🏨 **Sanctuary on Camelback Mountain.** This luxurious boutique hotel is
Fodor'sChoice the only resort on the north slope of Camelback Mountain. Secluded
★ mountain casitas are painted in desert hues and feature breathtaking views of Paradise Valley. Chic spa casitas surround the pool and are outfitted with contemporary furnishings and private patios. Bathrooms are travertine marble with elegant sinks and roomy tubs. For those who enjoy going *eau* and even *au naturale* some suites have outdoor tubs. An infinity-edge pool, Zen meditation garden, and Asian-inspired Sanctuary Spa make this a haven for relaxation. The hotel's restaurant, elements ($$$), is the hotspot for a martini at sunset. ⊠ *5700 E. McDonald Dr., Paradise Valley 85253* 🕾 *480/948–2100 or 800/245–2051* 🖷 *480/483–7314* ⊕ *www.sanctuaryaz.com* ⟿ *98 casitas* ♻ *Restaurant, room service, some kitchenettes, minibars, cable TV, in-room data ports, 6 tennis courts, 4*

1

pools, gym, massage, spa, bar, shop, business services, meeting rooms, free parking, no-smoking rooms ⊟ *AE, D, DC, MC, V.*

$$$–$$$$ ⬛ **Hermosa Inn.** The ranch-style lodge at the heart of this small resort
Fodor's Choice was the home and studio of cowboy artist Lon Megargee in the 1930s;
★ today the adobe structure houses Lon's at the Hermosa, justly popular for its new American cuisine. Villas as big as private homes and individually decorated casitas hold an enviable collection of art. The Hermosa, on 6 acres of lushly landscaped desert, is a blessedly peaceful alternative to some of the larger resorts. ⊠ *5532 N. Palo Cristi Rd. Paradise Valley, 85253* ☎ *602/955–8614 or 800/241–1210* ☐ *602/955–8299* ⊕ *www.hermosainn.com* ⇆ *4 villas, 3 haciendas, 11 casitas, 17 ranchos* ⚿ *Restaurant, some kitchenettes, minibars, cable TV, in-room data ports, 3 tennis courts, pool, 2 hot tubs, massage, bar, free parking; no smoking* ⊟ *AE, D, DC, MC, V* ⍾⃝ *CP.*

Scottsdale

★ ⚘ **$$$$** ⬛ **Fairmont Scottsdale Princess.** Home of the TPC Stadium golf course, this resort covers 450 breathtakingly landscaped acres of desert. Willow Stream Spa, one of the top spots in the country, has a dramatic rooftop pool. Kids love the fishing pond and water slides. Rooms are Southwestern in style, with tile showers and huge closets. Service is what you'd expect at a resort of this caliber: excellent and unobtrusive. Even pets get the royal treatment: a specially designated pet room comes with treats and turn-down service. ⊠ *7575 E. Princess Dr., North Scottsdale, 85255* ☎ *480/585–4848 or 800/344–4758* ☐ *480/585–0091* ⊕ *www.fairmont.com* ⇆ *458 rooms, 119 casitas, 72 villas, 2 suites* ⚿ *5 restaurants, in-room safes, minibars, cable TV with movies and video games, some in-room data ports, 2 18-hole golf courses, 7 tennis courts, pro shop, 5 pools, health club, spa, racquetball, squash, 3 bars, 4 shops, children's programs (ages 6–12), business services, some pets allowed, free parking, no-smoking rooms* ⊟ *AE, D, DC, MC, V.*

★ **$$$$** ⬛ **Four Seasons Scottsdale at Troon North.** This is a logical choice for serious golfers as it's adjacent to two Troon North premier courses where guests receive preferential tee times and free shuttle service. The resort is tucked in the shadows of Pinnacle Peak, near the Pinnacle Peak hiking trail. Large, casita-style rooms have separate sitting and sleeping areas as well as outdoor garden showers, fireplaces, and balconies or patios. Suites come with telescopes and star charts. Acacia ($$$–$$$$), the hotel's main restaurant, is elegant and accommodating. ⊠ *10600 E. Crescent Moon Dr., North Scottsdale, 85255* ☎ *480/515–5700 or 888/207–9696* ⊠ *480/515–5599* ⊕ *www.fourseasons.com* ↬ *210 rooms, 22 suites* ♨ *3 restaurants, in-room safes, minibars, cable TV, in-room data ports, golf privileges, 2 tennis courts, 2 pools, gym, sauna, spa, steam room, bicycles, hiking, 2 lounges, shops, children's programs (ages 5–12), laundry service, business services, meeting rooms, parking (fee), no-smoking rooms* ▤ *AE, D, DC, MC, V.*

☙ **$$$$** ▦ **Hyatt Regency Scottsdale at Gainey Ranch.** When you stay here, it's easy to imagine that you're relaxing at an oceanside resort instead of the desert. Shaded by towering palms, with manicured gardens and paths, the property has water everywhere—a large pool area has waterfalls, a lagoon, and you can take a ride in a *sandolo* (small gondola). The two-story lobby, filled with Native American art, opens to outdoor conversation areas where cozy fires burn in stone fireplaces on cool nights. Large rooms have balconies or patios. Three golf courses at nearby Gainey Ranch Golf Club will suit any duffer's fancy. ⊠ *7500 E. Doubletree Ranch Rd., North Scottsdale, 85258* ☎ *480/991–3388 or 800/233–1234* ⊠ *480/483–5550* ⊕ *www.hyatt.com* ↬ *461 rooms, 7 casitas, 22 suites* ♨ *4 restaurants, cable TV with movies, in-room data ports, 3 9-hole golf courses, 4 tennis courts, 10 pools, health club, sauna, spa, bicycles, bars, children's programs (ages 6–12), concierge floor, business services, free parking, no-smoking rooms* ▤ *AE, D, DC, MC, V.*

$$$$ ▦ **The Phoenician.** In a town where luxurious, expensive resorts are the
Fodor'sChoice rule, the Phoenician still stands apart, primarily in the realm of service.
★ The gilded, marbled lobby with towering fountains is the backdrop for the $8 million collection of authentic Dutch masterworks. Large rooms, in both the main building and outer-lying casitas, are decorated with rattan furniture and have private patios and oversize marble bathrooms. There's a secluded tennis garden and 27 holes of premier golf. The Center for Well Being Spa has a meditation atrium and a pool lined with mother of pearl tiles. Mary Elaine's ($$$$) is one of the finest (and most expensive) restaurants in the state. ⊠ *6000 E. Camelback Rd., Camelback Corridor, 85251* ☎ *480/941–8200 or 800/888–8234* ⊠ *480/947–4311* ⊕ *www.thephoenician.com* ↬ *572 rooms, 73 suites* ♨ *10 restaurants, room service, in-room safes, minibars, cable TV, in-room data ports, 3 9-hole golf course, 12 tennis courts, pro shop, 9 pools, health club, sauna, steam room, archery, badminton, basketball, children's programs (ages 5–12), business services, meeting rooms, some free parking, no-smoking rooms* ▤ *AE, D, DC, MC, V.*

$$$$ ▦ **Westin Kierland Resort & Spa.** Original artwork by Arizona artists is displayed throughout the Westin Kierland. Spacious rooms all have balconies or patios with views of the mountains or the resort's waterpark and tubing river. Kierland Commons, within walking distance, is a planned village of upscale specialty boutiques and restaurants. Of the eight restaurants, Deseo ($$$–$$$$) is the star, presided over by well-known chef Douglas Rodriguez, regarded as the inventor of Nuevo Latino cuisine. ⊠ *6902 E. Greenway Pkwy., North Scottsdale, 85254* ☎ *480/624–1000* ⊠ *480/624–1001* ⊕ *www.westin.com* ↬ *732 rooms, 63 suites, 32 casitas* ♨ *8 restaurants, minibars, cable TV with movies and video games, in-room data ports, 3 9-hole golf courses, 2 tennis courts,* *pro shop, 2 pools, gym, hot tub, sauna, spa, hiking, lounge, recreation room, children's programs (ages 4–12), business services, meeting rooms, free parking, no-smoking rooms* ☰ *AE, D, DC, MC, V.*

$$$–$$$$ 🏨 **Gainey Suites Hotel.** In the posh Gainey Ranch area, this independently owned boutique hotel is a rare find in both amenities and price. Floorplans vary from studio suites to two-bedroom suites that sleep eight, all with fully equipped kitchens. Cozy conversation areas in the lobby and an evening hors d'oeuvres reception create a warm atmosphere. The hotel is directly adjacent to the Gainey Village development, which encompasses boutique shopping and upscale dining, as well as a spa. Golfers are not forgotten; the hotel can book tee times at more than 60 courses in the area. ⊠ *7300 East Gainey Suites Dr., North Scottsdale, 85258* ☎ *480/922–6969 or 800/970–4666* 🖷 *480/922–1689* ⊕ *www. gaineysuiteshotel.com* ↪ *162 suites* ⚺ *Kitchens, microwaves, refrigerators, cable TV with movies and video games, in-room data ports, in-room broadband, Wi-Fi, golf privileges, pool, outdoor hot tub, laundry facilities, no-smoking rooms* ☰ *AE, D, MC, V* ⦿ *CP.*

★
☾ **$–$$$$**
🏨 **Caleo Resort & Spa.** New to the Scottsdale resort and spa block, this branch of the Kimpton family tree boasts a different approach to hospitality. The company, whose founder believed that a hotel should "relieve travelers of their insecurity and loneliness," prides itself on intimate and eco- and family-friendly boutique environments. An attentive staff focus on even the smallest details—personal and professional—to anticipate and alleviate worries guests might not even know they have. Caleo's spa, Jurlique, offers massages and treatments the muscles will fondly remember. Luxury rooms with patios have crisp linens, cozy bathrobes, and brand-name bath amenities. Free wine is offered to guests nightly from 5 PM to 6 PM. As if all of that weren't enough to soothe the soul, Caleo also soothes the soles with their sand-bottom pool. Parents traveling with children can also relax during Club Caleo when kids play games and enjoy pool time and snacks with certified staff members. Kids of all ages will love the large, plasma screen TVs, and the simple fun of Caleo's "S'more Kits," which can be cooked over the outdoor fire pits. ⊠ *4925 N. Scottsdale Rd. Dr., Scottsdale, 85251* ☎ *480/945–7666 or 800/528–7867* 🖷 *480/946–4056* ⊕ *www.caleoresort.com* ↪ *196 rooms, 8 suites, 1 presidential suite* ⚺ *Restaurant, minibars, cable TVs, Web TV, Wi-Fi, no-smoking rooms* ☰ *AE, D, DC, MC, V.*

$$$ 🏨 **Hotel Valley Ho.** One of Scottsdale's newest hotels is actually one of its oldest. Originally opened in 1956, it was a hangout for celebrities including Natalie Wood, Robert Wagner, and Tony Curtis. After closing in the 1980s, the hotel has been restored to its former '50s fabulousness—complete with Trader Vic's ($$–$$$), the hotel's original restaurant. A large pool is at the heart of this Frank Lloyd Wright–inspired hotel, surrounded by a two-story, U-shaped building of guest rooms, lush landscaping, and an outdoor grill and dining area. A 6,000-square-foot spa, a fitness center, and 10,000 square feet of meeting space have been added. ⊠ *6850 E. Main St., Downtown Scottsdale, 85251* ☎ *480/248–2000* 🖷 *480/248–2002* ⊕ *www.hotelvalleyho.com* ↪ *194 rooms* ⚺ *Restaurant, cable TV, pool, gym, hot tub, spa, meeting rooms, in-room data ports, Wi-Fi, no-smoking rooms* ☰ *AE, D, DC, MC, V.*

☺ **$$–$$$** ⚏ **Hotel Waterfront Ivy.** Near downtown shopping and attractions, the Ivy is a boutique extended-stay hotel geared to budget-oriented business travelers and families with reasonably priced suites. The studio guest rooms are a bit snug, but have mini-refrigerators and microwaves. One- and two-bedroom suites have full kitchens. Freebies include a full breakfast buffet; an evening social hour with beer, wine, and munchies (available Monday–Thursday); and fresh-baked cookies at night. The pools are a bit small, but kids will enjoy them as well as the soon-to-be-renovated outdoor play area and in-room TV video games. ⊠ *7445 E. Chaparral Rd., Central Scottsdale, 85250* ☎ *480/994–5282 or 877/284–3489* 🖷 *480/994–5625* ⊕ *www.hotelwaterfrontivy.com* ⇄ *25 studios, 80 suites* △ *In-room safes, some kitchens, some microwaves, some refrigerators, cable TV with movies and video games, in-room data ports, 2 tennis courts, 5 pools, gym, hot tub, bicycles, laundry facilities, meeting rooms* ⊟ *AE, D, DC, MC, V* ⍑❘ *BP.*

$$ ⚏ **Comfort Inn.** This may be one of the nicest Comfort Inns you ever lay eyes on, and it's in a quiet, upscale North Scottsdale neighborhood along the Scottsdale Road corridor. The three-story glass entryway is as welcoming as the enthusiastic staff inside. Rooms are utilitarian but clean and have free HBO. There are trendy restaurants and shopping opportunities within easy walking distance. It's a comfortable, affordable, and family-friendly alternative in a town filled with expensive resorts. ⊠ *7350 E. Gold Dust Rd., at Scottsdale Rd., North Scottsdale, 85258* ☎ *480/596–6559 or 888/296–9776* 🖷 *480/596–0554* ⊕ *www.comfortinn.com* ⇄ *123 rooms, 3 suites* △ *Refrigerators, cable TV with movies, in-room data ports, pool, gym, hot tub, business services, Internet room, free parking, no-smoking rooms* ⊟ *AE, D, DC, MC, V* ⍑❘ *CP.*

☺ **$$** ⚏ **Hampton Inn & Suites.** The Hampton Inn is within easy walking distance of restaurants and shops; plus there's complimentary shuttle service within 5 mi of the hotel. Despite their slightly outdated mauve and dark green decor, the straightforward rooms have either balconies or patios and furnishings that meet every basic need—perfectly suited for families attending the PGA's FBR Open. ⊠ *16620 N. Scottsdale Rd., North Scottsdale, 85254* ☎ *480/348–9280* 🖷 *480/348–9281* ⊕ *www.hamptoninn.com* ⇄ *123 rooms, 40 suites* △ *BBQs, microwaves, refrigerators, cable TV with movies, in-room data ports, Wi-Fi, 2 pools, gym, hot tub, shop, laundry facilities, business services, free parking, no-smoking rooms* ⊟ *AE, D, DC, MC, V* ⍑❘ *CP.*

☺ **$–$$** ⚏ **Country Inn & Suites.** The reasonable price and prime location within one block of shops and restaurants make this chain outpost a great bargain. The cozy lobby has comfortable seating around a flagstone fireplace. Standard rooms have two queen beds and suites all have a bedroom, living room, two TVs, two phones, and an activity table. Several specialty suites offer fireplaces and whirlpool baths. ⊠ *10801 N. 89th Pl., North Scottsdale, 85260* ☎ *480/314–1200 or 800/456–4000* 🖷 *480/314–7367* ⊕ *www.countryinns.com* ⇄ *163 rooms* △ *BBQs, mini-bars, microwaves, refrigerators, cable TV with movies and video games, in-room data ports, 2 pools, gym, hot tub, free parking, some pets allowed, no-smoking rooms* ⊟ *AE, D, DC, MC, V* ⍑❘ *CP.*

$ 🏨 **Ramada Limited Scottsdale.** There are two attractive things about this exterior-corridor, three-story motel: the location, which is within walking distance of Scottsdale's Old Town, and the price, which includes complimentary Continental breakfast. The simple but clean rooms have standard, serviceable furnishings. ⊠ *6935 E. 5th Ave., Downtown Scottsdale, 85251* ☎ *480/994–9461 or 800/528–7396* 🖷 *480/947–1695* ⊕ *www.ramada.com* ⌨ *92 rooms* ♿ *Some microwaves, refrigerators, cable TV, pool, gym, laundry facilities, free parking, no-smoking rooms* ▤ *AE, D, DC, MC, V* ❚◎❙ *CP.*

¢–$ 🏨 **Motel 6 Scottsdale.** The best bargain in downtown Scottsdale has a small sign and is set back from the road, so it can be easy to miss. It's worth the hunt, however, because it's close to the specialty shops of 5th Avenue and Scottsdale's Civic Plaza Mall. Rooms are small and spare with few amenities, but the price is remarkable for the area. Anyway, how many Motel 6 properties have a pool surrounded by palms and rooms with a view of Camelback Mountain? ⊠ *6848 E. Camelback Rd., Downtown Scottsdale, 85251* ☎ *480/946–2280 or 800/466–8356* 🖷 *480/949–7583* ⊕ *www.motel6.com* ⌨ *122 rooms* ♿ *Cable TV, in-room data ports, pool, hot tub, free parking, some pets allowed, no-smoking rooms* ▤ *AE, D, DC, MC, V.*

Fountain Hills

$$$$ 🏨 **CopperWynd Resort and Club.** Nestled high on a mountain ridge above Scottsdale and Fountain Hills, this secluded resort offers breathtaking views of the Sonoran Desert and mountain vistas. Luxurious guest rooms have imported handmade furniture, granite counters, fireplaces, custom linens, and a private terrace overlooking serene desert vistas. The expansive two- and three-bedroom villas are equipped with kitchens, washers and dryers, and private garages. The Spa at CopperWynd rivals many of the Valley's top spas, and Alchemy, the resort's restaurant ($$$–$$$$), is perfect for a romantic evening. ⊠ *13225 N. Eagle Ridge Dr., Fountain Hills 85268* ☎ *480/333–1900 or 877/707–7760* 🖷 *480/333–1901* ⊕ *www.copperwynd.com* ⌨ *32 rooms, 8 villas* ♿ *Restaurant, cable TV, in-room data ports, 9 tennis courts, pro shop, 2 pools, gym, hot tub, spa, no-smoking rooms* ▤ *AE, D, DC, MC, V.*

East Valley: Tempe

$–$$$$ 🏨 **Tempe Mission Palms Hotel.** A handsome, casual lobby and an energetic young staff set the tone at this three-story courtyard hotel. Rooms are Southwestern in style, and comfortable. Between the Arizona State University campus and Old Town Tempe, this is a particularly convenient place to stay if you're attending ASU sports and pro-football Cardinals events (the stadium is virtually next door). Harry's Bar becomes a lively sports lounge at game time. ⊠ *60 E. 5th St., Tempe 85281* ☎ *480/894–1400 or 800/547–8705* 🖷 *480/968–7677* ⊕ *www.missionpalms.com* ⌨ *303 rooms* ♿ *Restaurant, room service, 3 tennis courts, pool, hot tub, gym, bar, business services, meeting rooms, airport shuttle, free parking, no-smoking rooms* ▤ *AE, D, DC, MC, V.*

$$–$$$ 🏨 **The Buttes Marriott Resort.** Two miles east of Sky Harbor airport, nestled in desert buttes at I–10 and AZ 60, this hotel joins dramatic architecture (the lobby's back wall is the volcanic rock itself) and classic Southwest design (pine and saguaro-rib furniture, works by major regional artists) with stunning Valley views. Recently purchased by Marriott, the Buttes is set to become a top relaxation destination with its "Revive" spa facility. "Radial" rooms are largest, with the widest views; inside rooms face the huge free-form pools, with waterfall, hot tubs, and poolside cantina. The elegant Top of the Rock restaurant is a definite plus. ⊠ *2000 Westcourt Way, Tempe 85282* ☎ *602/225–9000 or 800/843–1986* ⊟ *602/438–8622* ⊕ *www.wyndham.com* ⤳ *353 rooms* �ひ *2 restaurants, minibars, cable TV with movies, in-room data ports, 4 tennis courts, 2 pools, gym, 4 hot tubs, massage, sauna, spa, bicycles, hiking, 3 bars, shop, laundry service, concierge floor, business services, meeting rooms, free parking, some pets allowed (fee), no-smoking rooms* ⊟ *AE, D, DC, MC, V.*

$$–$$$ 🏨 **Courtyard by Marriott.** This three-story, business-oriented hotel offers amenities that also make it a good place for visiting families. Conveniently located ½ mi from Arizona State University and Sun Devil Stadium, and ¼ mi from Tempe Town Lake, this hotel has spacious guest rooms with comfortable sitting areas, large work desks, and dual phones with data ports; some rooms have sleeper sofas. ⊠ *601 S. Ash Ave., Tempe 85281* ☎ *480/966–2800 or 800/321–2211* ⊟ *480/829–8446* ⊕ *www.courtyard.com* ⤳ *155 rooms, 5 suites* ひ *Cable TV with movies, in-room data ports, pool, gym, hot tub, bar, business services, meeting rooms, free parking, airport shuttle, no-smoking rooms* ⊟ *AE, D, DC, MC, V.*

$$–$$$ 🏨 **Twin Palms Hotel.** Across from ASU's Gammage Auditorium and minutes from shopping, dining, and entertainment venues, this seven-story high-rise has a domed-window facade. Faux finishes creatively mask dated, textured walls in the rooms, and corner basins create more space in cramped bathrooms. Hotel guests receive free admission to facilities at the nearby ASU Recreation Complex, with three Olympic-size pools, badminton and squash courts, and aerobics classes. ⊠ *225 E. Apache Blvd., Tempe 85281* ☎ *480/967–9431 or 800/367–0835* ⊟ *480/968–1877* ⊕ *www.twinpalmshotel.com* ⤳ *139 rooms, 1 suite* ひ *Restaurant, room service, cable TV with movies, in-room broadband, in-room data ports, pool, basketball, bar, laundry facilities, laundry service, airport shuttle, free parking, no-smoking rooms* ⊟ *AE, D, DC, MC, V.*

West Valley: Litchfield Park

$$$$ 🏨 **Wigwam Resort.** Built in 1918 as a retreat for executives of the Goodyear Company, the Wigwam has the pleasing feel of an upscale lodge. Casita-style rooms, situated along paths overflowing with cacti, palms, and huge bougainvillea, are decorated in a Southwestern style: distressed-wood furniture, iron lamps, pastel walls, and brightly patterned spreads. Local art adorns the walls, and all rooms have patios. This isolated world of graciousness inspires a fierce loyalty in its guests, some of whom have been returning for more than 50 years. ⊠ *300 Wigwam Blvd., Litchfield Park 85340* ☎ *623/935–3811 or 800/327–0396* ⊟ *623/935–3737* ⊕ *www.wigwamresort.com* ⤳ *261 rooms, 70 suites* ひ *2 restaurants, cable TV, 3 18-hole golf courses, 9 tennis courts, pro shop, 2 pools, gym, spa, 2 hot tubs, 2 bars, children's programs (ages 6–12), business services, meeting rooms, free parking* ⊟ *AE, D, DC, MC, V.*

NIGHTLIFE & THE ARTS

The Arts

For weekly listings of theater, arts, and music, check out "The Rep Entertainment Guide" in Thursday's *Arizona Republic*; pick up a free issue of the independent weekly *New Times,* the weekly *Get Out* in Thursday's *East Valley Tribune* or free on newsstands, or check out *Where Phoenix/Scottsdale Magazine,* available free in most hotels. A good online source of information on events in the Valley is **Digital City** (⊕ www. digitalcity.com). The online arm of the *Arizona Republic* (⊕ www. azcentral.com) has extensive nightlife and arts listings.

TICKETS **Arizona State University Public Events Box Office** (☎ 480/965–6447 ⊕ www. herbergercollege.asu.edu) sells tickets for events performed at ASU through the Herberger College of Fine Arts. **Tickets.com** (⊕ www.tickets. com) sells tickets for ASU Public Events at Grady Gammage Auditorium, Kerr Theatre, and the Maricopa County Events Center, formerly the ASU Sundome. **Ticketmaster** (☎ 480/784–4444 ⊕ www.ticketmaster.com) sells tickets for nearly every event in the Valley and has outlets at all Robinsons-May department stores, Fry's, Wherehouse, and Tower Records stores.

Classical Music

Arizona Opera (✉ 4600 N. 12th St., Downtown Phoenix ☎ 602/266–7464 ⊕ www.azopera.com) stages an opera season, primarily classical, in both Tucson and Phoenix. The Phoenix season runs from October to March at Symphony Hall.

Phoenix Symphony Orchestra (Box Office ✉ Arizona Center, 455 N. 3rd St., Suite 390, Downtown Phoenix ☎ 602/495–1999 ⊕ www. phoenixsymphony.org) is the resident company at Symphony Hall. Its season, which runs September through May, includes orchestral works from classical and contemporary literature, a chamber series, composer festivals, and outdoor Pops concerts.

Dance

Ballet Arizona (✉ 3645 E. Indian School Rd., Central Phoenix ☎ 602/ 381–1096 ⊕ www.balletaz.org), the state's professional ballet company, presents a full season of classical and contemporary works (including pieces commissioned for the company) in Tucson and Phoenix, where it performs at the Orpheum Theater. The season runs from October through May. The box office is open weekdays 9 AM to 4:30 PM.

Film

Farrelli's Cinema Supper Club (✉ 14202 N. Scottsdale Rd., North Scottsdale Scottsdale ☎ 480/905–7200 ⊕ www.cinemasupperclub.com) offers dinner and a movie. Watch new releases on a big screen while dining on contemporary American cuisine.

Theater

Actors Theatre of Phoenix (✉ Box 1924, Phoenix 85001 ☎ 602/253–6701 ⊕ www.atphx.org) is the resident theater troupe at the Herberger Theater Center. The theater presents a full season of drama, comedy, and musical productions; it runs from September through May.

Arizona Theatre Company (⊠ 808 N. 1st St. ☎ 602/252–8497 ⊕ www. aztheatreco.org) is the only resident company in the country with a two-city (Tucson and Phoenix) operation. Productions, held from September through June, range from classic dramas to musicals and new works by emerging playwrights.

Black Theater Troupe (⊠ 333 E. Portland St., Downtown Phoenix ☎ 602/258–8128) performs at its own house, the Helen K. Mason Center, a half-block from the city's Performing Arts Building on Deck Park. It presents original and contemporary dramas and musical revues, as well as adventurous adaptations, between September and May.

🅒 **Childsplay** (⊡ Box 517, Tempe 85280 ☎ 480/350–8101 ⊕ www. childsplayaz.org) is the state's theater company for young audiences and families, which runs during the school year. Rotating through many a venue these players deliver high-energy performances.

🅒 **Great Arizona Puppet Theatre** (⊠ 302 W. Latham St., Downtown Phoenix ☎ 602/262–2050 ⊕ www.azpuppets.org), which performs in a historic building featuring lots of theater and exhibit space, mounts a year-long cycle of inventive puppet productions that change frequently.

Phoenix Theatre (⊠ 100 E. McDowell Rd., Downtown Phoenix ☎ 602/254–2151 ⊕ www.phxtheatre.org), across the courtyard from the Phoenix Art Museum, stages musical and dramatic performances as well as productions for children by the Cookie Company.

DINNER THEATER   **Broadway Palm Dinner Theatre** (⊠ 5247 E. Brown Rd., Mesa ☎ 480/325–6700 or 888/504–7256 ⊕ www.broadwaypalmwest.com) offers a buffet dinner followed by a live, full-length Broadway-style musical in its 500-seat theater.

Arizona Broadway Theatre (⊠ 7710 Paradise La., Peoria ☎ 623/776–8400 ⊕ www.azbroadwaytheatre.com) opened its doors in January 2006. They stage full-scale musicals and have table service.

WILD WEST   **Rawhide at the Wildhorse Pass**
SHOWS   (⊠ 5700 West North Loop Rd., Gila River Indian Community, Chandler 85226 ☎ 480/502–5600 ⊕ www.rawhide.com) After moving from Scottsdale in 2006, Rawhide now calls the 2,400-acre master-planned Wild Horse Pass Development in the Gila River Indian Community, home. Large portions of the original Rawhide were moved to the new site, including the legendary steakhouse and saloon, Main Street and all of its retail shops, and the Six Gun Theater. Exciting additions will include canal rides along the Gila River Riverwalk, train rides, and a Native American village honoring the history and culture of the Akimel O'otham and Pee Posh Tribes.

> ## EXPERIENCE THE WILD WEST
>
> With the exception of the state and county fairs, and some seasonal shows, there are two Valley locales to experience the Wild West: Rawhide at Wild Horse Pass and the Pioneer Living History Village. Rawhide offers regular "gun fight" performances in a more commercial and kid friendly venue with burro, stagecoach, and train rides, as well as a petting ranch and game gallery. Pioneer is more sedate with an emphasis on the authentic historic buildings and reenactments of territorial life.

☽ **Rockin' R Ranch** (✉ 6136 E. Baseline Rd., Mesa ☎ 480/832–1539
⊕ www.rockinr.net) includes a petting zoo, a reenactment of a wild shoot-
out, and—the main attraction—a nightly cookout with a Western stage
show. Pan for gold or take a wagon ride until the "vittles" are served,
followed by music and entertainment.

Nightlife

From brewpubs, sports bars, and coffeehouses to dance clubs, mega-
concerts, and country venues, the Valley of the Sun offers nightlife of
all types. Nightclubs, comedy clubs, upscale lounges, and wine bars
abound in downtown Phoenix; along Camelback Road in north–central Phoenix; and in Scottsdale and Tempe, as well as other suburbs.

Among music and dancing styles, country-and-western has the longest
tradition here. Jazz venues, rock clubs, and hotel lounges are also numerous and varied. Phoenix is getting hipper and more cosmopolitan:
cigar lovers and martini sippers will find plenty of places to indulge. There
are also more than 30 gay and lesbian bars, primarily on 7th Avenue,
7th Street, and the stretch of Camelback Road between the two.

You can find listings and reviews in the *New Times* free weekly news-
paper, distributed Wednesday, "The Rep Entertainment Guide" of the
Arizona Republic, or the entertainment weekly *Get Out* in Thursday's
East Valley Tribune or free on newsstands (⊕ www.getoutaz.com).
PHX Downtown, a free monthly available in downtown establish-
ments, has an extensive calendar for events from art exhibits and po-
etry readings to professional sports. The local gay scene is covered in
Echo Magazine, which you can pick up all over town.

Bars & Lounges

Casey Moore's Oyster House (✉ 850 S. Ash Ave., Tempe ☎ 480/968–9935)
is a laid-back institution where rockers, hippies, and families come together in a 1910 house rumored to be haunted by ghosts. Enjoy 28 beers
on tap and fresh oysters at this Irish pub-style favorite.

Dos Gringos Trailer Park (✉ 1001 E. 8th St., Tempe ☎ 480/968–7879
✉ 4209 N. Craftsman Ct., Central Scottsdale, Scottsdale ☎ 480/423–
3800) is a kitschy indoor–outdoor cantina that will remind you of trips
over the Mexican border, or at least spring break. Crowds (mostly college students and twentysomethings) swig margaritas and beer amid a
multilevel courtyard, TVs, and limestone fountains.

Fox Sports Bar (✉ 16203 N. Scottsdale Rd., North Scottsdale, Scottsdale ☎ 480/368–0369) is where trendy, stylish sports fans (and those
looking to meet one) gather to watch live Fox Sports broadcasts on sleek
flat-screen TVs, play pool, and socialize in the sleek VIP room.

J Bar (✉ 7353 E. Indian School Rd., James Hotel, Central Scottsdale,
Scottsdale ☎ 480/308–1100) is the swanky spot where the Valley's
elite sip perfectly crafted, albeit pricey, cocktails.

★ **Jade Bar** (✉ 5700 E. McDonald Dr., Sanctuary on Camelback Resort,
Paradise Valley ☎ 480/948–2100) has spectacular views of Paradise Valley and Camelback Mountain, an upscale modern bar lined with windows, and a relaxing fire-lighted patio.

Enter **Kazimierz World Wine Bar** (✉ 7137 E. Stetson Dr., Central Scottsdale, Scottsdale ☎ 480/946–3004) through the door with the sign THE TRUTH IS INSIDE and discover a dark, cavelike wine bar filled with comfy chairs, and good music.

Majerle's Sports Grill (✉ 24 N. 2nd St., Downtown Phoenix, Phoenix ☎ 602/253–9004), operated by former Suns basketball player Dan Majerle, is within striking distance of the major sports facilities and offers a comprehensive menu for pre- and postgame celebrations.

The Monastery (✉ 4114 N. 28th St., Central Phoenix, Phoenix ☎ 602/ 840–7510 ✉ 4810 E. McKellips, Mesa ☎ 480/474–4477) is a casual beer and wine pub where you grill your own burgers and nosh picnic food. Relax with friends over a game of horseshoes, chess, or volleyball.

Postino Winebar (✉ 3939 E. Campbell Ave., Central Phoenix, Phoenix ☎ 602/852–3939) occupies a former post office in the Arcadia neighborhood. More than 40 wines are poured by the glass. Order a few grazing items off the appetizer menu and settle in, or carry out a bottle of wine, hunk of cheese, and loaf of bread for a twilight picnic.

The Salty Senorita (✉ 336 N. Scottsdale Rd.,,, Central Scottsdale, Scottsdale ☎ 480/946–7258) is known more for an extensive margarita selection and lively patio crowd than for its food. The restaurant-bar touts 51 different margaritas—with some recipes so secret they won't tell you what goes in them—try the El Presidente or the Chupacabra.

Seamus McCaffrey's Irish Pub (✉ 18 W. Monroe St., Downtown Phoenix ☎ 602/253–6081) is a fun and friendly place to enjoy one of the dozen European brews on draft. A small kitchen turns out traditional Irish fare.

Six Lounge and Restaurant (✉ 7316 E. Stetson Dr., Central Scottsdale, Scottsdale ☎ 480/663–6620) is a crowded see-and-be-seen hotspot attracting the Valley's designer-clad jetsetters who groove to the tunes of a DJ.

Blues & Jazz

Char's Has the Blues (✉ 4631 N. 7th Ave., Central Phoenix ☎ 602/230– 0205) is one of the Valley's top blues club, with nightly bands.

Remington's Lounge (✉ Scottsdale Plaza Resort, 7200 N. Scottsdale Rd., North Scottsdale, Scottsdale ☎480/948–5000) has a popular piano player, Danny Long, who delivers jazz standards as well as ballads to a very appreciative following from Tuesday to Saturday night.

★ **Rhythm Room** (✉ 1019 E. Indian School Rd., Central Phoenix ☎ 602/ 265–4842) attracts excellent local and national blues artists seven nights a week. The perfect sidekick, Rack Shack Blues BBQ, in the parking lot, cooks up some good barbecue Wednesday through Saturday evenings.

Sugar Daddy's Blues (✉ 3102 N. Scottsdale Rd., North Scottsdale, Scottsdale ☎ 480/970–6556) serves rhythm, blues, and eclectic Cajun-meets-Southwestern food nightly until 2 AM. A gratis graffiti-clad limo will pick you up anywhere within a 7-mi radius of the bar.

Casinos

Casino Arizona at Indian Bend (✉ 9700 E. Indian Bend Rd., North Scottsdale, Scottsdale ☎ 480/850–8642) draws locals for blackjack, poker, keno, more than 200 slot machines, and an off-track betting room that has wide-screen TVs.

Casino Arizona at Salt River (✉ Loop 101 and McKellips Rd., South Scottsdale, Scottsdale ☎ 480/850–7777, 480/850–7790 for free transportation ⊕ www.casinoaz.com) is the largest casino in the area, with five restaurants, four lounges, a sports bar, a 250-seat theater featuring live performances, two large blackjack rooms, and a keno parlor. There's live music and dancing most nights.

Fort McDowell Casino (✉ AZ 87 at Fort McDowell Rd., Fountain Hills ☎ 602/843–3678 or 800/843–3678) is popular with the resort crowd. In addition to the cards, slot machines, bingo hall, and keno games, off-track greyhound wagering takes place in a classy mahogany room with 18 giant video screens. One slot room is designated as smoke free. Take advantage of the free Valley-wide shuttle.

Gila River Casino (✉ 5550 W. Wildhorse Pass, Chandler ☎ 480/796–7777 or 800/946–4452) near Wildhorse Pass Resort & Spa includes 500 slots, live poker, blackjack, keno, and complimentary soft drinks.

PHOENIX CASINOS

Arizona has 22 casinos on Indian Reservations across the state, offering a variety slots, poker, blackjack, off-track betting, keno, and bingo. Six casinos, three with hotels, are located around the Valley of the Sun and, compared with Las Vegas, they offer smaller venues with low-key atmosphere. The casinos follow Arizona gaming law, such as no betting cash—chips only. Some have their own rules for certain games. While playing blackjack at Ft. McDowell you can split aces once, whereas at Casino Arizona and the Sheraton Wild Horse Pass Resort you can split aces up to four times. Unlike Vegas, dealers keep their own tips instead of pooling with others, and while gamers can get gratis soda and coffee, alcoholic drinks are not free.

Coffeehouses

Gold Bar Espresso (✉ 3141 S. McClintock Dr., Suite 6, Tempe ☎ 480/839–3082) is an inviting coffeehouse, decorated with funky antiques. The coffee is first-rate, and there's live jazz on weekends.

★ **Lux** (✉ 4404 N. Central, Downtown Phoenix ☎ 602/266–6469), with local art and retro furniture, provides an eclectic gathering place for artists, architects, and downtown businesspeople to enjoy excellent classic European espresso drinks.

Paisley Violin European Cafe (✉ 128 E. Roosevelt St., Downtown Phoenix ☎ 602/254–7843) is an offbeat, beatnik coffeehouse–café with live local music Wednesday through Saturday nights. Nosh on Mediterranean food and sip a cappuccino amid local art and mismatched furniture.

Willow House (✉ 149 W. McDowell Rd., Downtown Phoenix ☎ 602/252–0272) is a uniquely fun and funky spot in a city not overflowing with great coffeehouses. Thursday-night poetry readings are a big draw. The espresso flows until midnight on weeknights, 1 AM on weekends.

Comedy

The **Comedy Spot** (✉ 7117 E. 3rd Ave., Downtown Scottsdale, Scottsdale ☎ 480/945–4422 ⊕ www.thecomedyspot.net) is Scottsdale's only comedy venue featuring local and national stand-up talent. They also offer classes to wanna-be comedians on Sunday.

Rascal's (✉ 100 N. 1st St., Wyndham Hotel, Downtown Phoenix ☎ 602/254–0999) is part of a chain featuring headline comics. Sunday is open-mike night.

The **Tempe Improv** (✉ 930 E. University Dr., Tempe ☎ 480/921–9877), part of a national chain, showcases better-known headliners from Thursday to Sunday. Get there early for good seats.

Theater 168 (✉ 7117 E. McDowell Rd., Central Scottsdale, Scottsdale ☎ 480/423–0120) has clean, family-friendly comedy shows, performed by Jester'Z Improvisational Troupe on Thursday, Friday, and Saturday nights at 8 PM.

Country & Western

★ **Greasewood Flats** (✉ 27500 N. Alma School Pkwy., North Scottsdale, Scottsdale ☎ 480/585–7277) isn't fancy; in fact, it's downright ramshackle, but the burgers are delicious and the crowds friendly. There's a dance floor with live music from Thursday through Sunday. In winter, wear jeans and a jacket, since everything is outside; to keep warm, folks congregate around fires burning in halved oil drums.

Handlebar-J (✉ 7116 E. Becker La., Central Scottsdale, Scottsdale ☎ 480/948–0110) is a lively restaurant and bar with a Western line-dancing, 10-gallon-hat–wearing crowd.

Dance Clubs

Andserson's Fifth Estate (✉ 4224 N. Craftsman Ct., Scottsdale ☎ 480/941–9333) two DJs and two dance floors make this is one hot night spot. There's live music some Fridays and a retro-dance party aired live on a local radio on Saturday.

★ **Axis and Radius** (✉ 7340 E. Indian Plaza Rd., Central Scottsdale, Scottsdale ☎ 480/970–1112) is the dress-to-impress locale where you can party at side-by-side clubs connected by a glass catwalk.

Myst (✉ 7340 E. Shoeman La., North Scottsdale, Scottsdale ☎ 480/970–5000) is an ultraswanky dance club where you can sip cocktails in a sunken lounge or hang out at the white-hot Milk Bar adorned with white leather seating, stools, and an all-white bar. Upstairs is the private VIP lounge, complete with sky boxes overlooking the dance floor.

Scorch (✉ Desert Ridge Marketplace, 21001 N. Tatum Blvd., North Phoenix ☎ 480/513–7211) is a subterranean dance club and bar, L.A.-style. Dancers behind a translucent screen entertain the crowd with their shadowy forms. Plush booths, lava lights, and a small dance floor complete the scene. Only open on Friday and Saturday nights.

Gay & Lesbian Bars

Ain't Nobody's Bizness (✉ 3031 E. Indian School Rd., Central Phoenix ☎ 602/224–9977) is the most popular lesbian bar in town; you'll also find a few gay men at this male-friendly establishment, well known as one of the most fun in town.

★ **Amsterdam** (✉ 718 N. Central Ave., Downtown Phoenix ☎ 602/258–6122) attracts a young crowd that wants to see and be seen; it's where Phoenix's beautiful (gay) people hang out.

B. S. West (✉ 7125 E. 5th Ave., Downtown Scottsdale, Scottsdale ☎ 480/945–9028) is tucked behind a shopping center on Scottsdale's main shopping drag and draws a stylish, well-heeled crowd.

Charlie's (✉ 727 W. Camelback Rd., West Phoenix ☎ 602/265–0224), a longtime favorite of local gay men, has a country-western look (cowboy hats are the accessory of choice) and friendly staff.

Microbreweries

★ **Four Peaks Brewing Company** (✉ 1340 E. 8th St., Tempe ☎ 480/303–9967) is the former redbrick home of Bordens Creamery. Ten different brews are on tap. Pub grub, pizza, and burgers fill the menu.

Rio Salado Brewing Company (✉ 1520 W. Mineral Rd., Tempe ☎ 480/755–1590) brews excellent German-style beers, with at least six on tap regularly. The low-key Tap Room is a great place to relax, shoot darts, or play pool. Complimentary tours of the brewery are available Saturday afternoon.

Rock Bottom Brewery (✉ 8668 E. Shea Blvd., North Scottsdale, Scottsdale ☎ 480/998–7777 ✉ 21001 N. Tatum Blvd., Desert Ridge Mall, North Phoenix, Phoenix ☎ 480/513–9125 ✉ 14205 S. 50th St., Ahwatukee, Phoenix ☎ 480/598–1300) has tasty pub grub (start with the giant soft pretzels served with spicy spinach dip) and beer brewed on the premises. Watch out: the bill tends to rack up quickly.

Zona Brewing Company (✉ 20751 N. Pima Rd., DC Ranch, North Scottsdale, Scottsdale ☎ 480/502–5557) has a bar and a beer garden patio where you can sample handcrafted beers and good pub grub.

Rock

Bash on Ash (✉ 230 W. 5th St., Tempe ☎ 480/966–8200) plays alternative and indie rock for a college crowd.

Marquee Theatre (✉ 730 N. Mill Ave., Tempe ☎ 480/829–0607) hosts mainly headlining rock-and-roll entertainers.

Mason Jar (✉ 2303 E. Indian School Rd., Phoenix ☎ 602/954–0455) draws a mixed crowd to nightly shows, mostly hard rock, in a dark, black-lighted basement.

Old Brickhouse Grill (✉ 1 E. Jackson St., Downtown Phoenix, Phoenix ☎ 602/258–7888) is the place to be if you're looking for hip-hop, rap, rock, and the occasional poetry slam.

SPORTS & THE OUTDOORS

Central Arizona's dry desert heat imposes particular restraints on outdoor endeavors—even in winter, hikers and cyclists should wear lightweight opaque clothing, a hat or visor, and high-UV-rated sunglasses and should carry a quart of water for each hour of activity. The intensity of the sun makes strong sunscreen (SPF 15 or higher) a must, and don't forget to apply it to your hands and feet. From May 1 to October 1, you shouldn't jog or hike from one hour after sunrise until a half hour before sunset. During those times, the air is so hot and dry that your body will lose moisture at a dangerous, potentially lethal rate. Don't head out to desert areas at night to jog or hike in summer; that's when rattlesnakes and scorpions are on the prowl. Tickets for most sporting events can be purchased from **Ticketmaster** (☎ 480/784–4444 ⊕ www.ticketmaster.com).

Baseball's Three Seasons

FOR DYED-IN-THE-WOOL BASEBALL FANS, there's no better place than the Valley of the Sun. Baseball has become nearly a year-round activity in the Phoenix area, beginning with spring training in late February and continuing through the Arizona Fall League championships in mid-November.

Professional baseball sunk its roots in the warm Sonoran Desert more than a half-century ago, in 1947, when Bill Veeck brought his Cleveland Indians to Tucson and Horace Stoneham brought the New York Giants to Phoenix for spring training. Before 1947, only a few exhibition games had been played in Arizona; most spring-training games took place in the Florida Grapefruit League, as they had since 1914. Some teams trained in California in the 1930s, and a few teams played in such places as San Antonio, Savannah, Puerto Rico, and even Havana, Cuba. In 1951 baseball fans in Arizona watched Joe DiMaggio and rookie Mickey Mantle train and play at the Phoenix Municipal Stadium, when the New York Yankees came over from Florida for a year, brought by owner—and Phoenix resident—Del Webb.

SPRING

Today, the Cactus League consists of 12 major league teams (9 in the Valley and 3 in Tucson). Ticket prices are reasonable, around $7 to $8 for bleacher seats to $15 for reserved seats. Many stadiums have lawn-seating areas in the outfield, where you can spread a blanket and bring a picnic. Cactus League stadiums are more intimate than big-league parks, and players often come right up to the stands to say hello and to sign autographs. Special events such as fireworks nights, bat and T-shirt giveaway nights, and visits from sports mascots add to the festive feeling during spring training.

Tickets for some teams go on sale as early as December. Brochures listing game schedules and ticket information are available by calling the Arizona teams' venues or checking the Cactus League's Web site.

SUMMER

During the regular major-league season, the hometown Arizona Diamondbacks play on natural grass at Chase Field, formerly Bank One Ballpark (BOB), in the heart of Phoenix's Copper Square (the team does spring training in Tucson). The stadium is a technological wonder; if the weather's a little too warm outside, they close the roof, turn on the gigantic air-conditioners, and keep you cool while you enjoy the game. You can tour the stadium, except on afternoon-game days and holidays.

FALL

At the conclusion of the regular season, the Arizona Fall League runs until the week before Thanksgiving. Each major league team sends six of their most talented young prospects to compete with other young promising players—180 players in all. There are six teams in the league, broken down into two divisions. It's a great way to see future Hall of Famers in their early years. Tickets for Fall League games are $5 for adults, $4 for kids and seniors, or you can get season tickets.

Bob and Gloria Willis

Baseball

Take one step outside during March and you'll realize why many of the major-league baseball teams choose Phoenix for spring training. The weather can't get much better. The 12 teams of the **Cactus League** (⊕ www.cactus-league.com) start playing in late February and reside in the Valley through March. You can get information on teams on the Web site of **Major League Baseball** (⊕ www.mlb.com), where you can also buy tickets to games. Additionally, the Arizona Diamondbacks major-league team is based in Phoenix and holds spring training games at Tucson's Electric Park.

LOCAL TEAMS   The **Arizona Diamondbacks** (⊠ Chase Field, 401 E. Jefferson St., between S. 4th and S. 7th Sts., Downtown Phoenix ☎ 602/462–6000 team offices, 602/514–8400 tickets ⊕ www.azdiamondbacks.com) play at the 48,500-seat former Bank One Ballpark, which has a slew of restaurants, luxury boxes, and party suites. Their Cactus League spring training takes place in **Tucson's Electric Park** (⊠ 2500 E. Ajo Way, Tucson ☎ 520/434–1111).

SPRING   **Anaheim Angels** (⊠ Tempe Diablo Stadium, Tempe ☎ 480/784–4444
TRAINING TEAMS   tickets ⊕ www.angelsbaseball.com).
Chicago Cubs (⊠ HoHoKam Stadium, Mesa ☎ 480/964–4467, 800/905–3315 tickets ⊕ www.cubspringtraining.com).
Kansas City Royals (⊠ Surprise Stadium, Surprise ☎ 623/594–5600, 816/504–4040 tickets ⊕ www.kcroyals.com).
Milwaukee Brewers (⊠ Maryvale Baseball Park, West Phoenix ☎ 800/933–7890 tickets ⊕ www.milwaukeebrewers.com).
Oakland A's (⊠ Phoenix Municipal Stadium, Downtown Phoenix ☎ 602/392–0217, 800/352–0212 tickets ⊕ www.oaklandathletics.com).
San Diego Padres (⊠ Peoria Sports Complex, Peoria ☎ 800/409–1511 ⊕ www.padres.com).
San Francisco Giants (⊠ Scottsdale Stadium, Downtown Scottsdale, Scottsdale ☎ 480/990–7972 ⊕ www.sfgiants.com).
Seattle Mariners (⊠ Peoria Sports Complex, Peoria ☎ 800/409–1511 ⊕ www.seattlemariners.com).
Texas Rangers (⊠ Surprise Stadium, Surprise ☎ 623/594–5600 ⊕ www.texasrangers.com).

Basketball

Phoenix Mercury (⊠ America West Arena, 201 E. Jefferson St., at 2nd St., Downtown Phoenix ☎ 602/379–7867 team offices, 602/379–2000 US Airways Center Ticket Office ⊕ www.wnba.com/mercury) draw among the top crowds in the Women's NBA (WNBA).
Phoenix Suns (⊠ America West Arena, 201 E. Jefferson St., at 2nd St., Downtown Phoenix ☎ 602/379–7867 team offices, 602/379–2000 US Airways Ticket Office ⊕ www.suns.com) often fill all 19,000 spectator seats in the US Airways Center on game nights, and they remain the Valley's marquee pro team.

Bicycling

Tempe Town Lake (southwest corner of Mill Avenue and Washington Street) has 5 mi of paths for skating, running, bicycling, and walking. **Scottsdale's Indian Bend Wash** (along Hayden Road, from Shea Boulevard south to Indian School Road) has paths suitable for bikes winding among its golf courses and ponds. **Pinnacle Peak,** about 25 mi northeast of downtown Phoenix, is a popular place to take bikes for the ride north to Carefree and Cave Creek, or east and south over the mountain pass and down to the Verde River, toward Fountain Hills. Mountain bikers will want to check

> **BIKE TIPS**
>
> The desert climate can be tough on cyclists, so make sure you're prepared with lots of water. Riding in the streets isn't recommended as there are few adequate bike lanes in the city.

out the **Trail 100,** which runs throughout the Phoenix Mountain preserve (enter at Dreamy Draw park, just east of the intersection of Northern Avenue and 16th Street). **South Mountain Park** is the prime site for mountain bikers, with its 40-plus mi of trails—some of them with challenging ascents and all of them quiet and scenic. **Phoenix Parks and Recreation** (☎ 602/262–6861 ⊕ www.ci.phoenix.az.us/parks) has detailed maps of Valley bike paths.

ABC/Desert Biking Adventures (☎ 602/320–4602 or 888/249–2453 ⊕ www.desertbikingadventures.com) provides transportation from Scottsdale hotels and offers two-, three-, and four-hour mountain-biking excursions through the McDowell Mountains and the Sonoran Desert. **Wheels N' Gear** (✉ 16447 N. 91st St., North Scottsdale, Scottsdale ☎ 480/945–2881) rents bikes by the day or the week.

Four-Wheeling

Taking a jeep or a wide-track Humvee through the backcountry has become a popular way to experience the desert terrain's saguaro-covered mountains and curious rock formations.

Arrowhead Desert Jeep Tours (✉ 841 E. Paradise La., North Phoenix ☎ 602/942–3361 or 800/514–9063 ⊕ www.azdeserttours.com) offers gold-panning on a private claim, cookouts, cattle drives, river crossings, and Native American–dance demonstrations.
Desert Dog Hummer Adventures (⌂ 17212 E. Shea Blvd., Fountain Hills ☎ 480/837–3966) heads out on half- and full-day Hummer tours to the Four Peaks Wilderness Area in Tonto National Forest and the Sonoran Desert. U-Drive desert cars and ATV tours are also available.
Desert Storm Hummer Tours (✉ 15525 N. 83rd Way, No. 8, Scottsdale 85260 ☎ 480/922–0020 or 866/374–8637 ⊕ www.dshummer.com) conducts four-hour nature tours for $100 per person (children 12 and under are $80), climbing 4,000 feet up the rugged trails of Tonto National Forest via Hummer.
Wayward Wind Tours (✉ 2418 E. Danbury St., Phoenix, Phoenix ☎ 602/867–7825 ⊕ www.waywardwindtours.com) ventures down to the Verde River on its own trail and offers wilderness cookouts for large groups.
Wild West Jeep Tours (✉ 7127 E. Becker La., Suite #74, Scottsdale ☎ 480/922–0144 ⊕ www.wildwestjeeptours.com) has special permits that allow it to conduct four-wheeler excursions in the Tonto National Forest and to visit thousand-year-old Indian ruins listed on the National Register of Historic Places.

Football

The **Arizona Cardinals** (✉ Maryland and 91st Aves., Glendale ☎ 602/ 379–0101 ⊕ www.azcardinals.com), the area's professional football team, is set to kick off the 2006 NFL season in their new state-of-the-art, $450-million stadium in Glendale, complete with 63,000 seats and a roll-out natural grass field and a retractable roof. This will also be home to the 2008 Super Bowl and the Tostitos Fiesta Bowl.

Golf

Arizona has more golf courses per capita than any other state west of the Mississippi River, making it one of the most popular golf destinations in the United States. It's also one of Arizona's major industries, as greens fees can run from $35 at a public course to more than $500 at some of Arizona's premier golfing spots. New courses seem to pop up monthly: there are more than 200 in the Valley (some lighted at night), and the PGA's Southwest section has its headquarters here. Call well ahead for tee times during the cooler months. During the summer, fees drop dramatically and it's not uncommon to schedule a round before dawn. Check course Web sites for discounts before making your reservations. Also, package deals abound at resorts as well as through booking agencies like **Arizona Golf Adventures** (☎ 877/841–6570 ⊕ www. azteetimes.com), who will plan and schedule a nonstop golf holiday for you. For a copy of the *Arizona Golf Guide*, contact the **Arizona Golf Association** (✉ 7226 N. 16th St., Phoenix 85020 ☎ 602/944–3035 or 800/458–8484 ⊕ www.azgolf.org).

Arizona Biltmore Country Club (✉ Arizona Biltmore Resort & Spa, 24th St. and Missouri Ave., Camelback Corridor ☎ 602/955–9655 ⊕ www. arizonabiltmore.com), the granddaddy of Valley golf courses, has two 18-hole PGA championship courses, lessons, and clinics. Greens fees range from $130 to $175.

Fodor'sChoice ★ **ASU Karsten Golf Course** (✉ 1125 E. Rio Salado Pkwy., Tempe ☎ 480/ 921–8070 ⊕ www.asukarsten.com) is the Arizona State University 18-hole golf course where NCAA champions train. Greens fees are between $75 and $89.

Encanto Park (✉ 2775 N. 15th Ave., West Phoenix ☎ 602/253–3963 ⊕ www.phoenix.gov) has an attractive, affordable public course with 9- and 18-hole courses. Greens fees range from $29 to $38.

Fodor'sChoice ★ **Gold Canyon Golf Club** (✉ 6100 S. King's Ranch Rd., Gold Canyon ☎ 480/982–9449 ⊕ www.gcgr.com), near Apache Junction in the East Valley, offers fantastic views of the Superstition Mountains and challenging golf. Greens fees range from $102 to $187.

★ **Grayhawk Country Club** (✉ 8620 E. Thompson Peak Pkwy., North Scottsdale, Scottsdale ☎ 480/502–1800 ⊕ www.grayhawk.com), a 36-hole course has beautiful mountain views. The cost for 18 holes ranges from $230 to $245; 36 holes is $375. **Hillcrest Golf Club** (✉ 20002 Star Ridge Dr., Sun City West ☎ 623/ 584–1500 ⊕ www.hillcrestgolfclub.

> **DUFFERS TIP**
>
> Some golf courses offer a discounted twilight rate—and the weather is often much more amenable at this time of day.

com) is the best course in the Sun Cities development, with 18 holes on 179 acres of well-designed turf. Greens fees range from $36 to $65.

Lookout Mountain Golf Club (✉ Pointe Hilton at Tapatio Cliffs, 1111 N. 7th St., North-Central Phoenix ☎ 602/866–6356 ⊕ www.pointehilton. com) has one 18-hole, par-72 course. Greens fees range from $129 to $144.

Marriott's Camelback Golf Club (✉ Marriott's Camelback Inn, 7847 N. Mockingbird La., Paradise Valley ☎ 480/596–7050 ⊕ www.camelbackinn. com) has two 18-hole courses. Greens fees range from $125 to $170.

Ocotillo Golf Resort (✉ 3751 S. Clubhouse Dr., Chandler ☎ 480/917–6660 ⊕ www.ocotillogolf.com) is designed around 95 acres of man-made lakes; there's water in play on nearly all 27 holes. Greens fees are $155.

Papago Golf Course (✉ 5595 E. Moreland St., North-Central Phoenix ☎ 602/275–8428) is a low-priced 18 holes and Phoenix's best municipal course. Greens fees are $45.

★ The **Phoenician Golf Club** (✉ The Phoenician, 6000 E. Camelback Rd., Camelback Corridor ☎ 480/423–2449 ⊕ www.thephoenician.com) has a 27-hole course. Greens fees are $110 to $180.

Raven Golf Club at South Mountain (✉ 3636 E. Baseline Rd., South Phoenix ☎ 602/243–3636 ⊕ www.ravenatsouthmountain.com) has thousands of Aleppo pines and Lombardy poplars, making it a cool, shady 18-hole haven for summertime golfers. Eighteen holes are $159.

SunRidge Canyon (✉ 13100 N. SunRidge Dr., Fountain Hills ☎ 480/837–5100 ⊕ www.sunridgegolf.com), east of Scottsdale, is a great 18-hole course for both the low handicapper and those who score above 100. The incredible mountain views are almost distracting. Greens fees are $165 to $190.

★ **Tournament Players Club of Scottsdale** (✉ Fairmont Scottsdale Princess Resort, 17020 N. Hayden Rd., North Scottsdale, Scottsdale ☎ 480/585–3600 ⊕ www.fairmont.com), a 36-hole course by Tom Weiskopf and Jay Morrish, is the site of the PGA FBR. Open each January. Greens fees are $228.

Fodor's Choice **Troon North** (✉ 10320 E. Dynamite Blvd., North Scottsdale, Scottsdale
★ ☎ 480/585–5300 ⊕ www.troonnorthgolf.com) is a challenge for the length alone (7,008 yards). The million-dollar views add to the experience at this perfectly maintained 36-hole course. Greens fees are $245 to $295.

Wigwam Golf and Country Club (✉ Wigwam Resort, 300 Wigwam Blvd., Litchfield Park ☎ 623/935–3811 ⊕ www.wigwamresort.com) is the home of the famous Gold Course, as well as two other 18-hole courses. Greens fees are $120.

Hiking

One of the best ways to see the beauty of the Valley of the Sun is from above. Hikers of all calibers seek a better vantage point in the mountains surrounding the flat Valley. No matter the season, be sure to bring sunscreen, a hat, plenty of water, and a camera to capture a dazzling sunset. When hiking in

> **WORD OF MOUTH**
>
> "You should hike up Camelback for an amazing 360 degree look at the Valley of the Sun. Even if you only climb a short way up you can get a great view south over the Phoenician Hotel and much of Phoenix. If you are in good shape and aren't afraid of heights, climbing to the top is a blast. "   –amwosu

Arizona it's a good idea to tell someone where you'll be and when you plan to return. The city's **Phoenix Mountain Preserve System** (⌂ Phoenix Mountain Preservation Council, Box 26121, Phoenix 85068 ☎ 602/262–6861 ⊕ www.phoenixmountains.org) administers the mountainous regions that surround the city and has its own park rangers who can help plan your hikes. It also publishes a book, *Day Hikes and Trail Rides in and around Phoenix.*

★ At **Camelback Mountain and Echo Canyon Recreation Area** (✉ Tatum Blvd. and McDonald Dr., Paradise Valley ☎ 602/256–3220 Phoenix Parks & Recreation Dept.), there are intermediate to difficult hikes up the Valley's most outstanding landmark.

☾ The **Papago Peaks** (✉ Van Buren St. and Galvin Pkwy., Central Scottsdale, Scottsdale ☎ 602/256–3220 Phoenix Parks & Recreation Dept. Eastern and Central District) were sacred sites for the Tohono O'odham. The soft-sandstone peaks contain accessible caves, some petroglyphs, and splendid views of much of the Valley. This is a good spot for family hikes.

Pinnacle Peak Trail (✉ 26802 N. 102nd Way, 1 mi south of Dynamite and Alma School Rds., North Scottsdale, Scottsdale ☎ 480/312–0990). This well-maintained trail offers a moderately challenging 3½-mi round-trip hike or horseback experience. Interpretive programs and trail signs along the way describe the geology, flora, fauna, and cultural history of the area.

★ **South Mountain Park** (✉ 10919 S. Central Ave., South Phoenix ☎ 602/261–8457) is the jewel of the city's Mountain Park Preserves. Its mountains and arroyos contain more than 60 mi of marked and maintained trails—all open to hikers, horseback riders, and mountain bikers. It also has three auto-accessible lookout points, with 65-mi sight lines. Rangers can help you plan hikes to view some of the 200 petroglyph sites.

☾ **Waterfall Trail** (✉ 13025 N. White Tank Mountain Rd., Waddell ☎ 623/935–2505). This short and easy trail, part of the 25 mi of trails available at the White Tanks Regional Park, is kid-friendly, and strollers and wheelchairs roll along easily. Stop at the visitor center to view desert reptiles such as the king snake and a gopher snake in the aquariums. The barrier-free ⁵⁄₁₀-mi trail leads to Petroglyph Plaza, which boasts 1,500-year-old boulder-carvings—dozens are in clear view from the trail. The waterfall, only a trickle during the summer and fall, turns into a rushing torrent during winter rains.

Hockey
The **Phoenix Coyotes** (☎ 623/463–8800 team offices ⊕ www.phoenixcoyotes.com) are the local NHL team. They skate in the $180 million **Glendale Arena** (✉ Loop 101 and Glendale Ave. ☎ 23/772–3200 general information, 480/563–7825 tickets ⊕ www.glendalearenaaz.com).

Horseback Riding
More than two dozen stables and equestrian tour outfitters in the Valley attest to the saddle's enduring importance in Arizona—even in this auto-dominated metropolis. Stables offer rides for an hour, a whole day, and even some overnight adventures.

Cowboy College (✉ 30208 N. 152nd St., North Scottsdale, Scottsdale ☎ 480/471–3151 or 888/330–8070 ⊕ www.cowboycollege.com) has wranglers who will teach you everything you need to know about ridin', ropin', and ranchin'.

MacDonald's Ranch (✉ 26540 N. Scottsdale Rd., North Scottsdale, Scottsdale ☎ 480/585–0239 ⊕ www.macdonaldsranch.com) offers one- and two-hour trail rides and guided breakfast, lunch, and dinner rides through desert foothills above Scottsdale.

★ **OK Corral & Stable** (✉ 2655 E. Whiteley St., Apache Junction ☎ 480/982–4040 ⊕ www.okcorrals.com) offers one-, two-, and four-hour horseback trail rides and steak cookouts as well as one- to five-day horse-packing trips. Ron Feldman, an authority on the history and secrets of the Lost Dutchman Mine, is the guide for historical pack trips through the Superstition Mountains.

Ballooning

A sunrise or sunset hot-air-balloon ascent is a remarkable desert sight-seeing experience. The average fee—there are more than three dozen Valley companies to choose from—is $135 per person, and hotel pickup is usually included. Since flight paths and landing sites vary with wind speeds and directions, a roving land crew follows each balloon in flight. Time in the air is generally between 1 and 1½ hours, but allow 3 hours for the total excursion.

> **HOW COOL IS IT UP THERE?**
>
> Balloon trips are an awe-inspiring way to see the desert. Be prepared for changing temperatures as the sun rises or sets, but the altitude shouldn't have much effect on how cold it is.

Adventures Out West (☎ 602/996–6100 or 800/755–0935 ⊕ www.adventuresoutwest.com) has horseback riding, jeep tours, and hot-air-balloon flights. You can get a video of your flight taped from the balloon.

The Hot Air Balloon Company (☎ 602/482–6030 or 800/843–5987 ⊕ www.arizonaballooning.com) offers private and group sunrise and sunset flights with sparkling beverages and fresh pastries served on touchdown.

Hot Air Expeditions (☎ 480/502–6999 or 800/831–7610 ⊕ www.hotairexpeditions.com) is the best ballooning in Phoenix. Flights are long, the staff is charming, and the snacks are out of this world.

Unicorn Balloon Company (☎ 480/991–3666 or 800/468–2478 ⊕ www.unicornballoon.com), operating since 1978, concludes the balloon ride with complimentary champagne and a flight certificate.

Sailplaning–Soaring

Arizona Soaring Inc. (✉ Maricopa ☎ 480/821–2903 or 800/861–2318 ⊕ www.azsoaring.com), at the Estrella Sailport in Maricopa, 35 mi south of Phoenix, off I–10, gives sailplane rides in a basic trainer or high-performance plane. The adventuresome can opt for a wild 15-minute acrobatic flight.

Tennis

With all of the blue sky and sunshine in the Valley, it's a perfect place to play tennis or to watch the pros. The Fairmont Scottsdale Princess hosts several national championships, including the annual Franklin Templeton Men's Classic and the State Farm Women's Tennis Championship. Major resorts, such as the Radisson, Phoenician, Wigwam, Fairmont Princess, and J W Marriott Desert Ridge (and many smaller properties), have tennis courts. Tennis plays second fiddle to golf here; however, many of the larger resorts offer package deals for tennis as well. If you're not staying at a resort, there are more than 60 public facilities in the area.

Camelback Village Racquet & Health Club (✉ 4444 E. Camelback Rd., Camelback Corridor ☎ 602/840–6412 ⊕ www.dmbclubs.com ✉ 7477 E. Doubletree Ranch Rd., Scottsdale ☎ 602/609–6979) is a private tennis facility, health club, and spa featuring lighted courts, ball-machine clinics, and lessons. Visitors can enjoy club amenities for $25 a day.
Kiwanis Park Recreation Center (✉ 6111 S. All America Way, Tempe ☎ 480/350–5201) has 15 lighted premier-surface courts (all for same-day or one-day-advance reserve).
Phoenix Tennis Center (✉ 6330 N. 21st Ave., West Phoenix ☎ 602/249–3712) is a city facility with 22 lighted hard courts.
Scottsdale Ranch Park (✉ 10400 E. Via Linda, North Scottsdale, Scottsdale ☎ 480/312–7774) is a city facility with 12 lighted courts. Lessons are available here, too.

Tubing

The Valley may not be known for its wealth of water, but locals manage to make the most of whatever they can. A popular summer stop is the northeast side of the Salt River, where sun worshippers can rent an inner tube and float down the river for an afternoon. Tubing season runs from May to September. Several Valley outfitters rent tubes. Make sure you bring lots of sunscreen, a hat, water—and a rope to attach your cooler to a tube. **Salt River Recreation** (✉ Usery Pass and Power Rds., Mesa ☎ 480/984–3305 ⊕ www.saltrivertubing.com), offering shuttle-bus service to and from your starting point, rents tubes for $13 (cash only) for the day.

SHOPPING

Updated by
JoBeth Jamison

Since its resorts began multiplying in the 1930s and 1940s, Phoenix has acquired many high-fashion clothiers and leisure-wear boutiques. But long before that, Western clothes dominated fashion here—jeans and boots, cotton shirts and dresses, 10-gallon hats, and bola ties (the state's official neckwear). In many places around town, they still do.

On the scene as well were the arts of the Southwest's true natives—Navajo weavers, sand painters, and silversmiths; Hopi weavers and katsina-doll carvers; Pima and Tohono O'odham (Papago) basket makers and potters; and many more. Inspired by the region's rich cultural traditions, contemporary artists have flourished here, making Phoenix—particularly Scottsdale, a city with more art galleries than gas stations—one of the Southwest's largest art centers (alongside Santa Fe, New Mexico).

Today's shoppers find the best of the old and the new—all presented with Southwestern style. Upscale stores, one-of-a-kind shops, and outlet malls sell the latest fashions, cowboy collectibles, hand-woven rugs, traditional Mexican folk art, and contemporary turquoise jewelry.

Most of the Valley's power shopping is concentrated in central Phoenix, downtown Scottsdale, and the Kierland area in North Scottsdale but auctions and antiques shops cluster in odd places—and as treasure hunters know, you've always got to keep your eyes open.

Shopping Centers

Arizona Mills (⊠ 5000 Arizona Mills Circle, I-10 and Baseline Road, Tempe ☎ 480/491–9700), the leader in the local discount-shopping competition, is a mammoth center featuring almost 200 outlet stores, including Off 5th–Saks Fifth Avenue, Kenneth Cole, and Neiman Marcus Last Call. When you tire of bargain hunting relax in the food court, cinemas, or faux rain forest.

★ **Biltmore Fashion Park** (⊠ 24th St. and Camelback Rd., Camelback Corridor ☎ 602/955–8400), across Camelback Road from the Ritz-Carlton, has posh shops and 12 restaurants in a parklike setting. Macy's and Saks Fifth Avenue are the anchors for more than 70 stores and upscale shops, such as Betsey Johnson and Cartier.

The **Borgata** (⊠ 6166 N. Scottsdale Rd., Central Scottsdale, Scottsdale), an outdoor re-creation of the Italian village of San Gimignano with courtyards, stone walls, turrets, and fountains, is a lovely setting for browsing upscale boutiques or merely sitting at an outdoor café.

Cofco Chinese Cultural Center (⊠ 668 N. 44th St., Phoenix ☎ 602/275–8578) is adorned by replicas of pagodas, statues, and traditional Chinese gardens. It's the place to find Asian restaurants, gift shops, and the *99 Market*, a huge Asian grocery store. Take a stroll through the market's fish department—you'll forget you're in the desert.

✿ **Desert Ridge Marketplace** (⊠ Tatum Blvd. and Loop 101, North Phoenix ☎ 480/513–7586), an outdoor megamall, has more than 1 million square feet of shops and restaurants, but it's also a family entertainment destination. The District area of the mall has an 18-theater cineplex, bowling alley, rock-climbing wall, and Dave & Buster's, a multivenue entertainment center with a virtual-reality game room and dance club.

★ **Kierland Commons** (⊠ Greenway Pkwy. at Scottsdale Rd., North Scottsdale, Scottsdale ☎ 480/348–1577), next to the Westin Kierland Resort, is one of the city's newest shopping areas. "Urban village" is the catchphrase for this outdoor pedestrian mall with restaurants and upscale chain retailers, among them Crate & Barrel, J. Crew, and Tommy Bahama.

★ **Mill Avenue Shops** (⊠ Mill Avenue, between Rio Salado Pkwy and University Dr., Downtown, Tempe ☎ 480/967–4877), increasingly commercial, this area, named for the landmark Hayden Flour Mill, still makes for a fun-filled walk-and-shop experience. Directly west of the Arizona State University campus, Mill Avenue is an active melting pot of students, artists, residents, and tourists. Shops include Borders, Urban

Outfitters, Z Gallerie, a few remaining locally owned clothing and curio stores, and countless bars and restaurants. Once notorious for its Rocky Horror Picture Show screenings, the recently renovated Valley Art theater is a Mill Avenue institution and Tempe's place for indie cinema. Twice a year (in early December and March/April), the Mill Avenue area is the place to find indie arts and crafts when it hosts the Tempe Festival of the Arts (⊕ www.tempefestivalofthearts.com).

★ **Old Town Scottsdale** (⊠ Between Goldwater Blvd., Brown Ave., 5th Ave. and 3rd Street Dr., Downtown, Scottsdale ☎ 800/737–0008) is the place to go for authentic southwest inspired gifts, clothing, art, and artifacts. Despite its massive modern neighbors, this area and its merchants have long respected and maintained the single-level brick storefronts that embody Scottsdale's upscale cowtown charm. More than 100 businesses are open to meet just about any aesthetic want or need, including Gilbert Ortega, one of the premiere places for fine Indian jewelry and art. Some of the Scottsdale's best restaurants are also tucked in this pleasing maze of merchants.

★ **Scottsdale Fashion Square** (⊠ Scottsdale and Camelback Rds., Central Scottsdale, Scottsdale ☎ 480/941–2140) has a retractable roof and many specialty shops unique to Arizona. There are also Nordstrom, Dillard's, Neiman Marcus, Macy's, Juicy Couture, Anthropologie, Z Gallerie, Louis Vuitton, Tiffany, and Arizona's only Gucci store. A huge food court, sit-down restaurants, and a cineplex complete the picture.

★ **The Shops at Gainey Village** (⊠ 8787 N. Scottsdale Rd., North Scottsdale, Scottsdale ☎ 480/458–8064) flows from the neighboring historic Gainey Ranch. This new addition makes for stiff shopping competition in the area. Composed primarily of upscale boutiques this stylish strip mall also features fine dining at hot spots like Bloom and Thai Foon and nosh spots like Paradise Bakery, the Coffee Bean, and Pei Wei Asian Café.

Open-Air Markets

Two of metropolitan Phoenix's best markets can be found in the tiny town of Guadalupe, which is tucked around I–10, Baseline Road, and Warner Road, almost entirely surrounded by Tempe. Take I–10 south to Baseline Road, go east ½ mi, and turn south on Avenida del Yaqui to find open-air vegetable stalls, roadside fruit stands, and tidy houses covered in flowering vines. Other than these, the fast pace of Phoenix development has made it difficult for many markets to stay in one place. The changing seasons and variety of vendors are also a factor. To find the fresh wares of a Valley farmers market, visit ⊕ www.farmersmarketsaz.blogspot.com, a comprehensive calendar listing started and maintained by longtime market coordinators Denise and John Logan.

Guadalupe Farmer's Market (⊠ 9210 S. Ave. del Yaqui, Guadalupe ☎ 480/730–1945) has all the fresh ingredients you'd find in a rural Mexican market—tomatillos, varieties of chile peppers (fresh and dried), fresh-ground *masa* (cornmeal) for tortillas, spices like cumin and cilantro, and on and on. It's open every day year-round: from 9 AM to 6 PM in fall, winter, and spring; to 7 PM in summer; and to 5 PM Sunday.

Mercado Mexico (✉ 8212 S. Ave. del Yaqui, Guadalupe ☎ 480/831–5925) carries ceramics, paper, tin, and lacquerware, all at unbeatable prices. Stock up from 10 AM to 6 PM daily, year-round.

Specialty Shops

Antiques & Collectibles

The central Phoenix corridor, between 7th Street and 7th Avenue, has many antiques stores. Most shops sit north of Thomas and south of Camelback. Prices, though reasonable, are firm at most shops. A surprise to many visitors is the old-town district of suburban Glendale, with more than 80 antiques and collectible shops nestled around Historic Old Towne and Catlin Court, which are listed on the National Register of Historic Places.

Antique Centre (✉ 2012 N. Scottsdale Rd., Central Scottsdale, Scottsdale ☎ 480/675–9500) has a hodgepodge of collectibles and trinkets.
Antique Gallery (✉ 5037 N. Central Ave., Uptown Plaza, Camelback Corridor ☎ 602/241–1174) is one of the best places in the Valley to find fine china and silver and high-end antiques.
Central Antiques (✉ 36 E. Camelback Ave., Uptown Plaza, Camelback Corridor ☎ 602/241–1636) is in the same shopping center as Antique Gallery, but around the corner, Central Antiques is also a top spot for high-end antiques and interior decor.
Glendale Old Towne & Catlin Court (✉ 59th and Glendale Aves., Glendale) antiques district has more than 80 shops and restaurants in colorful, century-old bungalows. Stop in at antiques-filled Aunt Pittypat's Kitchen for breakfast or lunch or have a cup of tea at the Spicery, which is in an 1895 Victorian home.

Arts & Crafts

Check out the work of Downtown Phoenix artists at **Art Link's First & Third Fridays** when local galleries stay open late for the large crowds that converge on the normally empty-after-dark streets to view the work of emerging and established artists, listen to live music, and view impromptu street performances. For a map of locations, visit the Art Link Web site. ✉ *Various locations throughout Downtown Phoenix* ☎ 602/ 256–7539 ⊕ *www.artlinkphoenix.com.*

★ **Art Walk** (✉ Main St., Downtown Scottsdale, Scottsdale ☎ 480/990– 3939) is the best option, if you're interested in touring Scottsdale's galleries. It's held from 7 PM to 9 PM every Thursday year-round (except Thanksgiving). Main Street and Marshall Way, the two major gallery strips, take on a party atmosphere during the evening hours when tourists and locals are browsing.
Art One (✉ 4120 N. Marshall Way, Central Scottsdale, Scottsdale ☎ 480/946–5076) carries works by students as well as local and emerging artists.
Cosanti Originals (✉ 6433 Doubletree Ranch Rd., Paradise Valley, Scottsdale ☎ 480/948–6145) is the studio where architect Paolo Soleri's famous bronze and ceramic wind chimes are made and sold. You can watch the craftspeople at work, then pick out your own—prices are surprisingly reasonable.

Drumbeat Indian Arts (✉ 4143 N. 16th St., Central Phoenix ☎ 602/266–4823) is a small, interesting shop specializing in Native American music, movies, books, drums, and crafts supplies. If you're lucky, you might find a Native American selling homemade fry bread and Navajo tacos in the parking lot on weekends.

★ The **Heard Museum Shop** (✉ 2301 N. Central Ave., Downtown Phoenix ☎ 602/252–8344) is hands-down the best place in town for Southwestern Native American and other crafts, both traditional and modern. Prices tend to be high, but quality is assured, with many one-of-a-kind items among the collection of rugs, katsina dolls, pottery, and other crafts; there's also a wide selection of lower-priced gifts.

Trailside Galleries (✉ 7330 Scottsdale Mall, Downtown Scottsdale, Scottsdale ☎ 480/945–7751) has been showcasing works by members of the Cowboy Artists of America for more than 40 years and specializes in traditional American paintings and sculptures.

Xanadu Gallery (✉ Shops at Gainey Village, 8977 N. Scottsdale Rd., North Scottsdale, Scottsdale ☎ 480/368–9929) specializes in paintings and sculptures of desert scenes, children, and flower gardens.

Books

The major U.S. chains—Barnes & Noble, B. Dalton, Borders, and Waldenbooks—are all represented in the Valley.

Bookstar (✉ 2073 E. Camelback Rd., Camelback Corridor ☎ 602/957–2001 ✉ 12863 N. Tatum Blvd., North Central Phoenix ☎ 602/953–8066 ✉ 8919 E. Indian Bend., Scottsdale ☎ 480/443–4909). Now a part of Barnes and Noble, Bookstar is still a good place for discounts on popular books.

Borders Books and Music (✉ 2402 E. Camelback Rd., Biltmore Fashion Park, Camelback Corridor ☎ 602/957–6660 ✉ 4555 E. Cactus Rd., North Central Phoenix ☎ 602/953–9699 ✉ 7135 E. Camelback Rd., Scottsdale Fashion Square ☎ 480/423–0700 ✉ 699 South Mill Ave., Tempe ☎ 480/921–8659) is the popular chain. It has a good music selection.

Brentano's Bookstore (✉ Scottsdale Fashion Square South, 7014–590 E. Camelback Rd., Camelback Corridor ☎ 480/423–8717) is a small bookstore with an assortment of stationery and cards.

Changing Hands Bookstore (✉ 6428 S. McClintock Dr., Tempe ☎ 480/730–0205) has a large selection of new and used books.

Gifts Anonymous (✉ 4524 N. 7th St., Central Phoenix ☎ 602/277–5256) carries books and gifts exclusively for those in 12-step, recovery, and life issue programs.

Guidon (✉ 7117 W. Main St., Downtown Scottsdale, Scottsdale ☎ 480/945–8811), a small, independent bookshop in Scottsdale's art district, specializes in out-of-print and hard-to-find Western fiction and nonfiction titles.

The **Poisoned Pen** (✉ 4014 N. Goldwater Blvd., Central Scottsdale, Scottsdale ☎ 480/947–2974) specializes in mysteries.

Those Were the Days (✉ 516 S. Mill Ave., Tempe ☎ 480/967–4729) sells used and rare books.

Food Shops

★ **AJ's Fine Foods** (✉ 5017 N. Central Ave., Phoenix ☎ 602/230–7015 ✉ 4430 E. Camelback Rd., Phoenix ☎ 602/522–0956 ✉ 7141 E.

Lincoln Dr., Scottsdale ☎ 480/998–0052 ✉ 7131 W. Ray Rd., Chandler ☎ 480/705–0011 ✉ 20050 N. 67th Ave., Glendale ☎ 623/537–2310 ✉ 23251 N. Pima Rd., North Scottsdale ☎ 480/563–5070) is the Valley's grandest upscale grocery store and a great place to fill your basket with exclusive local creations ranging from Goldwater's salsas and sauces (created by the daughters of the late senator Barry Goldwater), to Sada's Pepper Melody and Rene's Desert Rub spice mixes, Berto's Gelato, and creative gift items like handbags, high-end bath products, greeting cards, books, decorative stoneware, and festive southwestern wear. The spirits department is renowned for its selection of hard to find wines, beers, and liquors (which include some of Arizona's own first-rate fermentations). It's possible to spend hours here, and it's also possible to spend far more money than you would at an average grocery store, but the vast inventory of unique items not found together anywhere else and the first class, one-stop shopping experience make it all worthwhile. Be sure to partake of the fresh, chef-prepared food offerings, like homemade soups, salad, pizza, specialty sandwiches, and gourmet take-out entrées from the bistro. Finish off with fresh baked cookies, pastry, chocolates, and cappuccino from the boulangerie.

Vintage Clothing, Furniture & Collectibles

In certain parts of the Valley, "old" is the new "new." The Melrose District, on 7th Avenue between Indian School and Camelback Roads in central Phoenix, is banking on its old Phoenix charm in a slow but steady race to become the next hip historic neighborhood. New faces on old buildings are the perfect welcome mat for progress with forthcoming lofts, condos, eateries, and big plans for public art, but the overall charm is anchored by its variety of vintage stores. Some shops are closed on Monday.

7th Heaven Vintage & More (✉ 4200 N. 7th Ave., Melrose District, Phoenix ☎ 602/277–4405 ☉ Mon.–Sat. 10–6, Sun. noon–5) could be considered chicken soup for the collector's soul. Offering an eclectic mix of 1940s through 1970s furniture and accessories, 7th Heaven encourages customers to "let their homes envelope them in the comfort time provides."

Figs (✉ 4501 N. 7th Ave., Melrose District, Phoenix ☎ 602/279–1443 ☉ Tues.–Sat. 10–5:30, Sun 11–4:30) carries a wealth of stylish interior, architectural, and garden elements (including shabby chic). Owner John Douglas prides himself on being a direct importer of eastern Asian furniture, antiques, and accessories.

Garden Party and Vintage Solutions (✉ 4302 N. 7th Ave., Melrose District, Phoenix ☎ 602/604–1831 ☉ Tues.–Sun. 11–6) is the place for sweet deals on deco and mid-century furniture, collectibles, and accessories that stand the test of time. A local newspaper recently called the owners and operators of Garden Party "eagle-eye tchotchke aficionados who know a good deal when they see one, and aren't above passing their savings on to you."

Home Again (✉ 4955 N. 7th Ave., Melrose District, Phoenix ☎ 602/424–0488 ☉ Tues.–Sun. 11–5 (Mon. "by chance") is a down-home store that buys and sells vintage and modern home furnishings and antiques. A registered antique dealer, Home Again welcomes dealers.

La Dolce Vintage (✉ 702 W. Montecito Ave., Melrose District, Phoenix ☎ 602/277–0819 ☾ Tues.–Sun. 11–7) is dwarfed by a massive billboard on one side and a strip of larger stores on the other, so don't blink when looking for this gem of a vintage clothing and accessories store. It's easily overlooked, but this needle is worth digging through the haystack. The selection might seem slim, but the cup cool, quality pieces are handpicked by the owner. La Dolce also sells restored vintage bicycles.

Melrose Vintage (✉ 4238 N. 7th Ave., Melrose District, Phoenix ☎ 602/636–0300 ☾ Wed.–Sat. 10–5:30) has a cheerful, dollhouse-like yellow exterior and that's not the only thing that makes it memorable. The no-nonsense staff knows its stuff, which includes tasteful and fun low- to high-end shabby chic furnishings: everything from ribbon to armoires.

Phoenix Metro Retro (✉ 708 W. Montecito Ave., Melrose District, Phoenix ☎ 602/636–0300 ☾ Wed.–Sun. 11–6), is it a hip New York loft? No, it's a vintage, mid-century and modern furniture store. Cool and inviting, Metro Retro aptly exhibits the talent and time it takes for people like owner Carl Reese to find those "perfect" pieces for your purchasing pleasure. It's closed Monday and Tuesday.

Retro Redux (✉ 4303 N. 7th Ave., Melrose District, Phoenix ☎ 602/234–0120 ☾ Tues.–Sun. 11–6) has a selection of vintage clothing, costume jewelry, period pictures, furnishings, and accessories that's as fun and funky as its name.

SIDE TRIPS NEAR PHOENIX

The following sights are within a 1- to 1½-hour drive of Phoenix. To the north, the thriving artist communities of Carefree and Cave Creek are popular Western attractions. Arcosanti and Wickenburg are half- or full-day trips from Phoenix. Stop along the way to visit the petroglyphs of Deer Valley Rock Art Center and the reenactments of Arizona territorial life at the Pioneer Living History Village. You also might consider Lake Pleasant, Arcosanti, and Wickenburg as stopovers on the way to or from Flagstaff, Prescott, or Sedona.

South of Phoenix, an hour's drive takes you back to prehistoric times and the site of Arizona's first known civilization at Casa Grande Ruins National Monument, a vivid reminder of the Hohokam who began farming this area more than 1,500 years ago. The nearby town of Florence, one of central Arizona's first cities, is filled with territorial architecture.

Deer Valley Rock Art Center

㉞ *15 mi north of downtown Phoenix on I–17. Exit at W. Deer Valley Rd. and drive 2 mi west.*

On the lower slopes of the Hedgepeth Hills, Deer Valley Rock Art Center has the largest concentration of ancient petroglyphs in the metro-

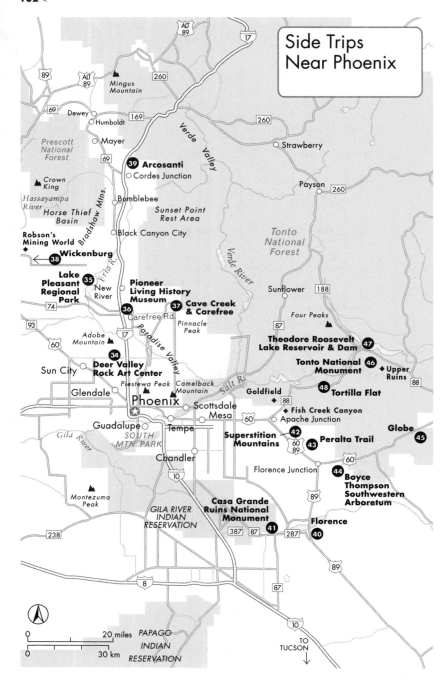

Side Trips Near Phoenix

politan Phoenix area. Some 1,500 of the cryptic symbols are here, left behind by Native American cultures that lived in the Valley (or passed through) during the last 1,000 years. After watching a video about the petroglyphs, pick up a pair of binoculars ($1) and an informative trail map and set out on the ¼-mi path. Telescopes point to some of the most well-formed petroglyphs, but you'll soon be picking them out everywhere; they range from human and animal forms to more abstract figures. For more information about petroglyphs, *see* The Writing on the Wall CloseUp box *in Chapter 5.* ⊠ *3711 W. Deer Valley Rd., North Phoenix* ☎ *623/582–8007* ⊕ *www.asu.edu/clas/shesc/dvrac* ⊠ *$5* ☉ *May–Sept., Tues.–Fri. 8–2, Sat. 9–5, Sun. noon–5; Oct.–Apr., Tues.–Sat. 9–5, Sun. noon–5.*

Lake Pleasant Regional Park

🐚 ❸❺ *From central Phoenix, take 1–17 north to Carefree Hwy. (AZ 74). Turn west and drive 15 mi to Castle Hot Springs Rd. Travel north to park entrance.*

This northwest valley park is one of the most scenic water recreational areas in the Valley of the Sun. Recreational opportunities include camping, boating, fishing, hiking, swimming, picnicking, and wildlife viewing. At the visitor center you can learn the history of the area and view the lake and Waddell Dam. The park provides 148 sites for RV and tent camping, and private shoreline camping is possible for most of the year depending on the water level. With the city lights of Phoenix in the distance, this is a great place for stargazing. ⊠ *41835 N. Castle Hot Springs Rd., Morristown* ☎ *928/501–1710* ⊕ *www. maricopa.gov/parks/lake_pleasant* ⊠ *$5 per car entrance fee; lakeside tent camping $5; tent camping with facilities $10; RV camping with hookup $18.*

Pioneer Living History Village

🐚 ❸❻ *25 mi north of downtown Phoenix on I–17 (Exit 225, Pioneer Rd.), just north of Carefree Hwy. (AZ 74).*

The Pioneer Arizona Living History Museum contains 28 original and reconstructed buildings from throughout territorial Arizona. Costumed guides filter through the bank, schoolhouse, and print shop, as well as the Pioneer Opera House, where classic melodramas are performed daily. It's popular with the grade-school field-trip set, and it's your lucky day if you can tag along for their tour of the site—particularly when John the Blacksmith forges, smelts, and answers sixth-graders' questions that adults are too know-it-all to ask. For an extra $5 per adult, tour the grounds via a reproduction Conestoga wagon. ⊠ *3901 W. Pioneer Rd., North Phoenix, Phoenix* ☎ *623/465–1052* ⊕ *www.pioneer-arizona.com* ⊠ *$7* ☉ *Oct.–May, Wed.–Sun. 9–5; June–Sept., Wed.–Sun. 9–5.*

Cave Creek & Carefree

❸❼ *15 mi north of downtown Phoenix on I–17. Exit at Carefree Hwy. (AZ 74) and turn right, then go 12 mi. Turn left onto Cave Creek Rd. and go 3 mi to downtown Cave Creek then another 4 mi on Cave Creek Rd. to Carefree.*

Some 30 mi north of Phoenix, resting high in the Sonoran Desert at an elevation of 2,500 feet, the towns of Cave Creek and Carefree look back to a lifestyle far different from that of their more populous neighbors to the south.

Cave Creek got its start with the discovery of gold in the region. When the mines and claims "played out," the cattlemen arrived, and the sounds of horse hooves and lowing cattle replaced those of miners' picks. The area grew slowly and independently from Phoenix to the south, until a paved road connected the two in 1952. Today the mile-long main stretch of town on Cave Creek Road is a great spot to have some hot chili and cold beer, try on Western duds, or learn the two-step in a "cowboy" bar. You're likely to run into folks dressed in cowboy hats, boots, and bold belt buckles. Horseriders and horse-drawn wagons have the right of way here and the 25-mph speed limit is strictly enforced by county deputies. You can amble up the hill and rent a horse for a trip into the Tonto National Forest in search of some long-forgotten native petroglyphs, or take a jeep tour out to the forest. Some tours include a stop at the world's largest saguaro: the 46-foot "Grand One," with a base circumference of 7 feet, 10 inches, was partially burned during the 2005 Cave Creek Complex Fire.

Just about the time the dirt road–era ended in Cave Creek, planners were sketching out a new community, which became neighboring Carefree. The world's largest sundial, at the town's center, is surrounded by crafts shops, galleries, artists' workshops, and cafés. Today Cave Creek and Carefree sit cheek by jowl—but the one has beans, beef, biscuits, and beer, while the other discreetly orders up a notch or two.

Pick up maps and information about the area at the **Carefree-Cave Creek Chamber of Commerce.** ⊠ *748 Easy St., No. 9, Carefree 85377* ☎ *480/488-3381* ⊕ *www.carefree-cavecreek.com* ⊙ *Weekdays 8–4.*

Exhibits at the **Cave Creek Museum** depict pioneer living, mining, and ranching. There's a restored 1920s tuberculosis cabin and a collection of Indian artifacts from the Hohokam and Yavapai tribes. ⊠ *6140 E. Skyline Dr., Cave Creek* ☎ *480/488-2764* ⊕ *www.cavecreekmuseum. org* 🖃 *$3* ⊙ *Oct.–May, Wed.–Sun. 1–4:30.*

Pseudo-Western **Frontier Town** (⊠ *6245 E. Cave Creek Rd., Cave Creek*) has wooden sidewalks, ramshackle buildings, and souvenir shops. Grab a sandwich and a bottle of Cave Creek Chile Beer (with a real chile pep-

---

WORD OF MOUTH

"If you are looking for different, try Carefree and Cave Creek in Northern Phoenix. Carefree is beautiful desert. It usually blooms in April. There are hiking trails in Cave Creek and you can also climb a trail winding around Pinnacle Peak. Cave Creek is a small cowboy town with a funky hotel. There are lots of Mexican, Southwest, and western shops and also great cowboy restaurants. Carefree is artsy . . . It is very friendly and relaxed."

–Skooger

per in each bottle) at **Crazy Ed's Satisfied Frog** (✉ 6245 E. Cave Creek Rd., Cave Creek ☎ 480/488–3317).

The **Heard Museum North,** a satellite of the big Heard in downtown Phoenix, has one gallery with its own small, permanent collection of Native American art; it also hosts two rotating exhibits during the year. The gift shop is well stocked with expensive, high-quality items. ✉ *El Pedregal Shopping Mall, 34505 N. Scottsdale Rd., at Carefree Hwy., Carefree* ☎ *480/488–9817* ⊕ *www.heard.org* ☎ *$3* ☉ *Mon.–Sat. 10–5:30, Sun. noon–5.*

NEED A BREAK?

Bakery Café at el Pedregal Marketplace (✉ 34505 N. Scottsdale Rd., at Carefree Hwy., Carefree ☎ 480/488–4100). Near the Heard Museum North, this is a good place to pick up a breakfast or lunch of fresh-baked goods or to take a shopping break with a sandwich and a cool drink.

Sports & the Outdoors

GOLF The **Boulders Resort Golf Club** (✉ The Boulders, 34631 N. Tom Darlington Dr., Carefree ☎ 480/488—9028 or 866/397–6520 ⊕ www.theboulders.com) has two championship 18-hole, par-72 courses and a tennis garden.

HORSEBACK RIDING **Spur Cross Stable** (✉ 44029 Spur Cross Rd., Cave Creek ☎ 480/488–9117 or 800/758–9530 ⊕ www.horsebackarizona.com) has well-cared-for horses that will take you on one- to seven-hour rides to the high Sonoran Desert of the Spur Cross Preserve and the Tonto National Forest. Longer rides include visits to petroglyph sites and a saddlebag lunch.

Where to Stay & Eat

$$–$$$ ✕ **Tonto Bar & Grill at Rancho Manana.** Old West ambience oozes from every corner of the Tonto Bar & Grill, from the hand-carved beams of the ceiling to the latilla (stick)-covered patios with views of the pristine Sonoran Desert. Try the cowboy Cobb salad or the Tonto burger piled with fried onions and Tillamook cheddar for lunch; lamb chops with leek fondue or grilled grouper with orange-tomato salsa are good choices at dinner. ✉ *5736 E. Rancho Manana Blvd., Cave Creek* ☎ *480/488–0698* ▤ *AE, D, DC, MC, V.*

$–$$$ ✕ **Horny Toad Restaurant.** The Horny Toad is a rustic spot for barbecued pork ribs and steak, but the real star is the crispy fried chicken. There's a chapel out back in case you feel like "making it legal." ✉ *6738 E. Cave Creek Rd., Cave Creek* ☎ *480/488–9542* ▤ *AE, D, DC, MC, V.*

$$$$ ▦ **The Boulders Resort and Golden Door Spa.** One of the country's top resorts hides amid hill-size, 12-million-year-old granite boulders and the lush Sonoran Desert. Casitas snuggled against the rocks have exposed log-beam ceilings and curved, pueblo-style half-walls. Each has a patio with a view, a wood-burning fireplace, and a spacious bathroom with deep soaking tub. El Pedregal Market Place, an upscale mall, adjoins the resort, and there are two golf courses. The Golden Door spa is one of the best in the state. ✉ *34631 N. Tom Darlington Dr., Carefree 85377* ☎ *480/488–9009 or 800/553–1717* ▤ *480/488–4118* ⊕ *www.theboulders.com* ⬎ *160 casitas, 46 patio homes* ♦ *5 restaurants, room*

Fodor's Choice
★

service, in-room safes, some kitchens, minibars, cable TV, in-room data ports, 2 18-hole golf courses, 6 tennis courts, 2 pools, gym, hair salon, spa, hiking, horseback riding, concierge, business services, meeting rooms, car rental, free parking ☒ *AE, D, DC, MC, V.*

$–$$ 🏨 **Cave Creek Tumbleweed Hotel.** Innkeepers Gary and Jeri Rust have kept the 1950s flavor of Cave Creek's only hotel intact. There's a fireplace in the lobby and a quiet pool outside. Red and tan rooms have Southwestern and cowboy accents. The hotel is a short walk from restaurants and shops in town. ☒ *6333 E. Cave Creek Rd., Cave Creek 85327* ☎ *480/488–3668* ⊕ *www.tumbleweedhotel.com* ☞ *32 rooms, 8 casitas* ☼ *Picnic area, BBQs, some kitchenettes, cable TV, some in-room broadband, pool, hot tub, shop, no-smoking rooms* ☒ *AE, MC, V.*

Nightlife

Watch real cowboys and cowgirls doing the two-step to live music at **Buffalo Chip Saloon** (☒ 6811 E. Cave Creek Rd., Cave Creek ☎ 480/488–9118). Chow down on mesquite grilled chicken and buffalo chips (hot, homemade potato chips). Reservations are suggested for the all-you-can-eat Friday night fish fry that draws crowds. There's live music and dancing Thursdays through Saturdays. Sing along with Jack "Fast Fingers" Fairclough as he plays the honky-tonk piano at **Crazy Ed's Satisfied Frog Restaurant and Goatsucker Saloon** (☒ 6245 E. Cave Creek Rd., Cave Creek ☎ 480/488–3317). **Harold's Cave Creek Corral** (☒ 6895 E. Cave Creek Rd., Cave Creek ☎ 480/488–1906 ⊕ www.haroldscorral. com) is just across the dirt parking lot from the Buffalo Chip Saloon. Harold's has two full bars, a restaurant (serving some of the best ribs in the Valley), a huge dance floor with live bands on weekends, a game room, and 15 TVs. If you're a Steelers fan, this is the place to be on Sunday during football season.

Shopping

Cave Creek and Carefree have a thriving arts community with hundreds of artists and dozens of galleries. **el Pedregal Festival Marketplace** (☒ Scottsdale Rd. and Carefree Hwy., Carefree ☎ 480/488–1072) is a two-tier shopping plaza at the foot of a 250-foot boulder formation. In spring and summer there are open-air Thursday-night concerts in the courtyard amphitheater. In addition to its posh boutiques and specialty stores, el Pedregal contains the Heard Museum North, a satellite of the downtown Heard with its own gift shop. **Spanish Village** (☒ Ho and Hum Rds., Carefree ☎ 480/488–0350), an outdoor shopping area, comes complete with bell tower, fountains, courtyards, and winding alleyways. While away an afternoon browsing 30 shops and contemplating dinner at one of several casual restaurants.

Wickenburg

③ *70 mi from Phoenix. Follow I–17 north for about 25 mins to Carefree Hwy. (AZ 74) junction. About 30 mi west on AZ 74, take U.S. 89/93 north and go another 10 mi to Wickenburg.*

This town, land of guest ranches and tall tales, is named for Henry Wickenburg, whose nearby Vulture Mine was the richest gold strike in the

Arizona Territory. By the late 1800s, Wickenburg was a booming mining town on the banks of the Hassayampa River with a seemingly endless supply of gold, copper, and silver. Resident miners developed a reputation for waxing overenthusiastic about the area's potential wealth, helping to coin the term "Hassayamper" for tellers-of-tales throughout the Old West. Legend has it that a drink from the Hassayampa River will cause one to fib forevermore—a tough claim to test, since for most of the river's 100-mi course it flows underground. Nowadays, Wickenburg's Old West history attracts visitors to its sleepy downtown and Western museum. There's a group of good antiques shops, most of which are on Tegner and Frontier streets. On the northeast corner of Wickenburg Way and Tegner Street, check out the **Jail Tree,** to which prisoners were chained, the desert heat sometimes finishing them off before their sentences were served. Maps for self-guided walking tours of the town's historic buildings are available at the **Wickenburg Chamber of Commerce** (✉ 216 N. Frontier St. ☎ 928/684–5479 ∰ www.wickenburgchamber. com), in the city's old Santa Fe Depot.

☼ The **Desert Caballeros Western Museum** has one of the best collections of Western art in the nation with paintings and sculpture by Remington, Bierstadt, Joe Beeler (founder of the Cowboy Artists of America), and others. Kids will enjoy the re-creation of a turn-of-the-20th-century Main Street that includes a general store, period clothing, and a large collection of cowboy gear. ✉ *21 N. Frontier St.* ☎ *928/684–2272* ∰ *www.westernmuseum.org* ✑ *$7.50* ☽ *Mon.–Sat. 10–5, Sun. noon–4.*

The self-guided trails of **Hassayampa River Preserve** wind through lush cottonwood-willow forests, mesquite trees, and around a 4-acre, spring-fed pond and marsh habitat. Waterfowl, herons, and Arizona's rarest raptors shelter here. ✉ *3 mi southeast of Wickenburg on U.S. 60* ☎ *928/ 684–2272* ✑ *$5* ☽ *Mid-Sept.–mid-May, Wed.–Sun. 8–5; mid-May–mid-Sept., Fri.–Sun. 7–11 AM.*

☼ **Robson's Mining World** is a replica of a 19th-century mining town that has the world's largest collection of antique mining equipment, the Nellie Meda gold mine, more than 30 buildings, a restaurant, a saloon, and a general store. Visitors can stay at the old mining hotel ($) which has 26 rooms and space for RVs. Attractions include hanging out in town, panning for gold, or hiking in the desert or the nearby Harcuvar Mountains. The restaurant serves juicy prime rib and a miner's pie filled with meat, potatoes, and vegetables, baked in pastry. ✉ *29 mi west of Wickenburg on US Rte. 60 to AZ Rte. 71, Box 3465, Wickenburg* ☎ *928/685–2609* 🖷 *928/685–4164* ∰ *www. robsonsminingworld.com* ✑ *$5* ☽ *Sat. and Sun. 9–5, Mon.–Fri. 10–4* ☽ *Closed May–Sept.*

The **Vulture Mine** was once the largest producing gold mine in Arizona, though its vein has long since run out. A small town originally grew up around the mine, but the only thing left today are a few storage buildings and a home where caretakers live. The self-guided tour through this "ghost town" wanders past mining memorabilia (still in place on the grounds); old buildings including bunkhouses, the jail, and a black-smith shop; the mine shaft itself; and the infamous hanging tree where more than a dozen ore thieves (high graders) were hanged. Raw ore was crushed in the Hassayampa River, about 10 mi away, and the town of Wickenburg sprung up to provide services to miners working at the Vulture operation. Head west from Wickenburg on U.S. 60 for about 6 mi; then turn left onto Vulture Mine Road and travel 12 mi to the mine at the end of the pavement. ⊠ *Vulture Mine Rd., Vulture Mine* ☎ *602/859–2743* 🎫 *$7* ☉ *Open daily 9–4* ☉ *Closed June–Aug.*

Where to Stay & Eat

¢–$$ ✕ **Anita's Cocina.** Reliable Tex-Mex fare is served at Anita's. Fresh tamales are tasty, for either lunch or dinner. Try a fruit burrito for dessert. ⊠ *57 N. Valentine St.* ☎ *928/684–5777* 🍴 *MC, V.*

$$$$ 🏨 **Kay El Bar Ranch.** On the National Register of Historic Places, this personable, low-key, and remote guest ranch only accepts 24 guests at one time. Some of the biggest mesquite trees in Arizona shade the lodge, a family cottage with private patio (built in 1914), two separate casitas, and charming adobe cookhouse. In the evening everyone gathers in the living room by the stone fireplace for cocktails and homemade hors d'oeu-vres. ⊠ *37500 S. Rincon Rd.* 📪 *Box 2480, 85358* ☎ *928/684–7593 or 800/684–7583* ⊕ *www.kayelbar.com* 🛏 *8 rooms, 1 house, 2 casitas* ⟡ *Dining room, golf privileges, pool, hot tub, horseback riding, hik-ing, library; no room phones, no room TVs* 🍴 *MC, V* ☉ *Closed May–mid-Oct.* ⦿*FAP.*

☾ $$$$ 🏨 **Rancho de los Caballeros.** This 20,000-acre property combines the guest-ranch experience with first-class amenities. Meals are served in the lodge's bright, festive dining room, and everyone is asked to dress for each night's sit-down dinner. Rooms are spacious, done in low-key Southwestern style. Some contain two queen-size beds and can be creatively configured—through a system of adjoining doors—to annex separate living rooms or sleeping quarters for children. The Los Ca-balleros Golf Club course is considered one of the country's top re-sort courses. ⊠ *1551 S. Vulture Mine Rd., 85390* ☎ *928/684–5484 or 800/684–5030* 🖷 *928/684–2267* ⊕ *www.guestranches.com/ caballeros* 🛏 *79 rooms* ⟡ *Dining room, driving range, 18-hole golf course, 4 tennis courts, pool, massage, bicycles, horseback riding, lounge, children's programs (ages 5–12)* 🍴 *No credit cards* ☉ *Closed mid-May–early Oct.*

Nightlife

The **Rancher Bar** (⊠ 910 W. Wickenburg Way ☎ 928/684–5957) is a modern-day saloon where real live wranglers and cowboys meet up to shoot some pool, and the breeze, after a hard day's work.

Arcosanti

➌➒ *65 mi north of Phoenix on I–17, near exit for Cordes Junction (AZ 69).*

Two miles down a partly paved road northeast from the gas stations and cafés, the evolving complex and community of Arcosanti was mas-terminded by Italian architect Paolo Soleri to be a self-sustaining habitat in which architecture and ecology function in symbiosis. Arcosanti is a bit tired-looking these days and hasn't quite achieved Soleri's original vision. However, it's still worth a stop to take a tour, have a bite at the café, and purchase one of the hand-cast bronze wind-bells made at the site. The town is off I–17 at Cordes Junction, near the town of Mayer. ☎ 928/632–7135 ⊕ *www.arcosanti.org* ✍ *Tour $8* ☉ *Daily 9–5; tours hourly 10–noon, 1–4.*

Florence

40 *Take U.S. 60 east (Superstition Freeway) to Florence Junction (U.S. 60 and AZ 89) and head south 16 mi on AZ 89 to Florence.*

A Victorian courthouse and more than 150 other sites listed on the National Register of Historic Places distinguish this Old West town southeast of Phoenix. It was once a tough place where saloons outnumbered churches by 28 to 1 and even women robbed stagecoaches. You may recognize Florence as the location where *Murphy's Romance* was filmed. The **Pinal County Visitor's Center** (✉ 330 W. Butte St. ☎ 520/868–4331 ⊕ www.co.pinal.az. us/visitorcenter) answers questions and provides brochures September through May, weekdays 8 to 3, and June–August, weekdays 9 to 2.

The **Pinal County Historical Society** (✉ 715 S. Main St. ☎ 520/868–4382), a free museum open Tuesday through Saturday 11 to 4 and Sunday noon to 4, displays furnishings from 1900s houses and Native American crafts and tools. There's also a collection of nooses from actual executions.

Open Thursday through Monday 8 to 5, **McFarland State Historic Park** (✉ Main and Ruggles Sts. ☎ 520/868–5216 ⊕ www.azparks.gov/ Parks/parkhtml/mcfarland.html) houses memorabilia of former governor and U.S. senator Ernest W. McFarland in the circa-1878 Pinal County Courthouse.

Where to Eat

¢–$$ ✗ **Old Pueblo Restaurant.** Of the down-home Mexican and American fare served in this simple restaurant, the steak fajita burros, chimichangas, and *carne asada* (grilled beefsteak) are favorites. ✉ *505 S. Main St.* ☎ *520/ 868–4784* ▭ *AE, D, DC, MC, V* ☉ *Closed Sat.*

Casa Grande Ruins National Monument

41 *9 mi west of Florence on AZ 287 or, from I–10, 16 mi east on AZ 387 and AZ 87. Note: follow signs to ruins, not to town of Casa Grande. When leaving the ruins, take AZ 87 north 35 mi back to U.S. 60.*

The ruins of Casa Grande were unknown to European explorers until Father Kino, a Jesuit missionary, first recorded their existence in 1694. The ruins were set aside as federal land in 1892 and named a national monument in 1918. Allow an hour to explore the site, longer if park rangers are giving a talk or leading a tour.

Start at the visitor center, where a small museum displays artifacts and information on the Hohokam, who lived here and farmed irrigated fields until they vanished mysteriously in about AD 1450. Begin your self-guided tour with an inspection of the 35-foot-tall (that's four stories) Casa Grande (Big House), the tallest Hohokam building known, built in the early 14th century. Today it sits underneath a modern roof erected on posts to protect it from sun and wind. Neighboring structures are much smaller, and only a bit of the 7-foot wall around the compound is still in evidence. The original purpose of Casa Grande still eludes archaeologists; some think it was an ancient astronomical observatory or a center of government, religion, trade, or education. On your way out, cross the parking lot by the covered picnic grounds and climb the platform for a view of a ball court and two platform mounds, said to date from the 1100s. Although only a few prehistoric sites can be viewed, more than 60 are included in the monument area. ⊠ *AZ 87, Coolidge* ☎ *520/723–3172* ⊕ *www.nps.gov/cagr* ⊠ *$5* ⊙ *Daily 8–5.*

THE APACHE TRAIL

Fodor'sChoice ★ President Roosevelt called this 150-mi drive "the most awe-inspiring and most sublimely beautiful panorama nature ever created." A stretch of winding highway, the AZ 88 portion of the Apache Trail closely follows the route forged through wilderness in 1906 to move construction supplies to build Roosevelt Dam, which lies at the northernmost part of the loop. Take a day to drive the trail, which makes a large loop east of Phoenix, drink in the vistas, and stop to explore along the way.

From the town of Apache Junction, you can choose to drive the trail in either direction; there are advantages to both. If you begin the loop going clockwise—heading eastward on AZ 88—your drive may be more relaxing; you'll be on the farthest side of this narrow dirt road some refer to as the "white-knuckle route," with its switchbacks and drop-offs straight down into spectacular Fish Creek Canyon—this 42-mi-long drive is not for someone who is afraid of heights. But if you follow the route counterclockwise—continuing on U.S. 60 past the town of Apache Junction—you'll be able to appreciate each attraction better.

The tour below follows the route counterclockwise. Although the drive itself can be completed in one day, it's advisable to spend a night in Globe and continuing the loop back to Phoenix the following day.

Superstition Mountains

42 *From Phoenix, take I–10 and then U.S. 60 (the Superstition Freeway) east through suburbs of Tempe, Mesa, and Apache Junction.*

As the Phoenix metro area gives way to cactus- and creosote-dotted desert, the massive escarpment of the Superstition Mountains heaves into view and slides by to the north. The Superstitions are supposedly where the legendary Lost Dutchman Mine is, the location—not to mention the existence—of which has been hotly debated since pioneer days (⇨ The Lost Dutchman Mine CloseUp). The best place to learn about the "Dutchman" Jacob Waltz and the Lost Dutchman Mine is at **Superstition**

The Lost Dutchman Mine

1

NOT MUCH IS KNOWN ABOUT JACOB "THE DUTCHMAN" WALTZ, except that he was born around 1808 in Germany (he was "Deutsch," not "Dutch") and emigrated to the United States, where he spent several years at mining camps in the Southeast, in the West, and finally in Arizona. There's documentation that he indeed did have access to a large quantity of gold, though he never registered a claim for the mine that was attributed to him.

In 1868 Waltz appeared in the newly developing community of Pumpkinville, soon to become Phoenix. He kept to himself on his 160-acre homestead on the banks of the Salt River. From time to time, he would disappear for a few weeks and return with enough high-quality ore to keep him in a wonderful fashion. Soon word was out that "Crazy Jake" had a vast gold mine in the Superstition Mountains, east of the city near the Apache Trail.

Stories were also circulating at that time about a wealthy gold mine discovered by the Peralta family of Mexico. Local Apaches raided the mine, which was near their sacred Thunder Mountain. The Peraltas and more than 100 people working for them at the mine were killed. Rumors soon spread that Waltz had saved the life of a young Mexican who was part of Peralta's group—one of few who had escaped—and was shown the Peralta's mine as a reward.

As the legend of the Dutchman's mine grew, many opportunists attempted to follow Waltz into the Superstition Mountains. A crack marksman, Waltz quickly discouraged several who tried to track him. The flow of gold continued for several years.

In 1891 the Salt River flooded, badly damaging Waltz's home. When the floodwaters receded, neighbors found Waltz there in a weakened condition. He was taken to the nearby home and boarding house of Julia Thomas, who nursed the Dutchman for months. When his death was imminent, he reportedly gave Julia the directions to his mine.

Julia and another boarder searched for the mine fruitlessly. In her later years, she sold maps to the treasure, based upon her recollections of Waltz's description. Thousands have searched for the lost mine; many losing their lives in the process. More than a century later, gold seekers are still trying to connect the pieces of the puzzle.

There's no doubt that the Dutchman had a source of extremely rich gold ore. Was it in the Superstition Mountains, or the nearby Goldfields, or even in the Four Peaks region? The source of the Dutchman's gold remains hidden somewhere in the parched desert surrounding Phoenix. Perhaps the best-researched books on the subject are T. E. Glover's *The Lost Dutchman Mine of Jacob Waltz* and the companion book, *The Holmes Manuscript*. Ron Feldman of OK Corral (☏ 480/982-4040 ⊕ www.okcorrals. com) in Apache Junction has become an expert on the subject during his 30-plus years in the region. He leads adventurers on pack trips into the mysterious mountains to relive the lore and legends.

Bob and Gloria Willis

Mountain Museum (⊠ 4087 N. Apache Trail, AZ 88, Apache Junction 85217 ☏ 480/983–4888 ⊕ www.superstitionmountainmuseum.org ☜ $4 ⊙ Daily 9–4). The museum exhibits include a collection of mining tools, historical maps, and artifacts relating to the "gold" age of the Superstition Mountains.

Goldfield became an instant city of about 4,000 residents after a gold strike in 1892. The town dried up five years later when the gold mine flooded. Today, **Goldfield Ghost Town** (⊠ 4650 N. Mammoth Mine Rd., 4 mi northeast of Apache Junction on AZ 88, Goldfield ☏ 480/983–0333 ⊕ www.goldfieldghosttown.com) is an interesting place to grab a cool drink, pan for gold, go for a mine tour, or take a desert jeep ride or horseback tour of the area. The ghost town's shops are open daily 10 to 5, the saloon daily 10 to 8.

Peralta Trail

㊽ *About 11½ mi southeast of Apache Junction, off U.S. 60, take Peralta Trail Rd., just past King's Ranch Rd., an 8-mi, rough gravel road that leads to the start of the Peralta Trail.*

The 4-mi round-trip Peralta Trail winds 1,400 feet up a small valley for a spectacular view of **Weaver's Needle**, a monolithic rock formation that is one of Arizona's more famous sights. Allow a few hours for this rugged and challenging hike, bring plenty of water, sunscreen, a hat, and a snack or lunch, and don't hike it in the middle of the day in summer.

Boyce Thompson Southwestern Arboretum

★ **㊹** *12 mi east of Florence Junction (U.S. 60 and AZ 89).*

At the foot of Picketpost Mountain in Superior, the Boyce Thompson Arboretum is often called an oasis in the desert: rocky open desert gives way to lush riparian glades home to 3,200 different desert plants and more than 230 bird and 72 terrestrial species. The arboretum offers a living album of the plants of the world's deserts and semiarid regions including exotic species such as Canary Islands date palms and Australian eucalyptus. You can spend hours on the trails enjoying breathtaking scenery in the gardens and the exhibits. The signs, guides, and maps for this living museum are extremely well thought out. Benches with built-in misters offer relief from the heat. Bring along a picnic and enjoy the beauty. ⊠ 37615 U.S. 60, Superior ☏ 520/689–2811 ⊕ www.ag.arizona.edu/bta ☜ $7.50 ⊙ May–Aug., daily 6 AM–3 PM; Sept.–Apr., daily 8–5.

EN ROUTE A few miles past the arboretum, **Superior** is the first of several modest mining towns and the launching point for a dramatic winding ascent through the Mescals to a 4,195-foot pass that affords panoramic views of this copper-rich range and its huge, dormant, open-pit mines. Collectors will want to watch for antiques shops through these hills, but be forewarned that quality varies considerably. A gradual descent will take you into **Miami** and **Claypool**, once-thriving boomtowns that have carried on quietly since major-corporation mining ground to a halt in

1

the 1970s. Working-class buildings are dwarfed by the mountainous piles of copper tailings to the north. At a stoplight in Claypool, AZ 88 splits off northward to the Apache Trail, but continue on U.S. 60 another 3 mi to make the stop in the city of Globe.

Globe

45 *U.S. 60, 51 mi east of Apache Junction, 25 mi east of Superior, and 3 mi east of Claypool's AZ 88 turnoff.*

In the southern reaches of Tonto National Forest, Globe is the most cosmopolitan of the area's mining towns. Initially, it was gold and silver that brought miners here—the city allegedly got its name from a large, circular boulder of silver, with lines like continents, found by prospectors—although the region is now known for North America's richest copper deposits. If you're driving the Apache Trail loop; stop in Globe to fill up the tank, as it's the last chance to gas up until looping all the way back to U.S. 60 at Apache Junction. But Globe is worth more than a quick pit stop; its charm is its lack of prestige—and, in some cases, modernity. At the **Globe Chamber of Commerce** (⊠ 1360 N. Broad St., Globe, 1¼ mi north of downtown on U.S. 60 ☎ 928/425–4495 or 800/804–5623 ⊕ www.globemiamichamber.com), open weekdays 9–5, you can pick up brochures detailing the self-guided Historic Downtown Walking Tour.

A good place to begin a visit to Globe is the **Gila County Historical Museum** (⊠ 1330 N. Broad St. ☎ 928/425–7385) to see the collection of memorabilia from the area's mining days. The museum, which is free, is open weekdays 9 to 5. The restored late-19th-century Gila County Courthouse houses the **Cobre Valley Center for the Arts** (⊠ 101 N. Broad St. ☎ 928/425–0884), showcasing works by local artists. Also visit the ladies and their looms in the basement Weaver's Studio, open Thursday through Saturday 10 to 3.

For a step 800 years back in time, tour the 2 acres of excavated Salado Indian ruins on the southeastern side of town at the **Besh-Ba-Gowah Archaeological Park.** After a trip through the small museum and a video introduction, enter the area full of remnants of more than 200 rooms occupied here by the Salado during the 13th and 14th centuries. Public areas include the central plaza (also the principal burial ground; archaeologists have uncovered more than 150 burials), roasting pits, and open patios. Besh-Ba-Gowah is a name given by the Apaches, who, arriving in the 17th century, found the pueblo abandoned and moved in. Loosely translated, the name means "metal camp," as remains left on the site point to it as part of an extensive commerce and trading network. ⊠ *150 N. Pine St.* ☎ *928/425–0320 or 800/804–5623* ⊕ *www.jqjacobs.net/southwest/besh_ba_gowah.html* 🎫 *$3* ☉ *Daily 9–5.*

Where to Stay & Eat

¢–$ ✕ **Chalo's.** This roadside spot offers top-notch Mexican and Tex-Mex food. Try the savory stuffed sopaipillas, filled with pork and beef, beans, and red or green chiles. ⊠ *902 E. Ash St.* ☎ *928/425–0515* ▭ *MC, V.*

¢–$ 🏠 **Noftsger Hill Inn.** Built in 1907, this B&B was originally the North Globe Schoolhouse; now classrooms serve as guest rooms, filled with mining-era antiques and affording fantastic views of the Pinal Mountains and historic Old Dominion Mine. All rooms have private baths; one has air-conditioning, and the rest have evaporative coolers, which work well at this cooler elevation. You'll enjoy walking off "miner-size" breakfasts with a hike through the scenic Copper Hills behind the old school. ✉ *425 North St., 85501* ☎ *928/425–2260 or 877/780–2479* ⊕ *www.noftsgerhillinn.com* ⌁ *6 rooms* ⌂ *Some in-room VCRs; no a/c in some rooms, no TV in some rooms, no smoking* ⊟ *MC, V* ¶⊙¶ *BP.*

¢   🏠 **El Rey Motel.** Hosts Rebecca and Ricardo Bernal operate this quintessential roadside motel, where wagon wheels and potted plants pepper the grounds. This vintage motor court offers small, immaculate rooms; covered parking spaces; and a shared central picnic and barbecue area. ✉ *1201 E. Ash St., 85501* ☎ *928/425–4427* 📠 *928/402–9147* ⌁ *23 rooms* ⌂ *Picnic area, BBQ, cable TV* ⊟ *AE, D, MC, V.*

Nightlife

Run by the San Carlos Apache tribe, **Apache Gold** (✉ U.S. 70, 5 mi east of Globe ☎ 928/425–7800 or 800/272–2433 ⊕ www.apachegoldcasinoresort.com) has more than 500 slots, blackjack, keno, bingo, and video and live poker. Call about the free shuttle from most of Globe's hotels and motels. The Apache Grill Restaurant offers gourmet dishes and the Wickiup Buffet serves authentic Apache and Southwestern cuisine.

Shopping

Broad Street, Globe's main drag, is lined with antiques and gift shops. On Ash, between Hill and South East streets, **Copper City Rock Shop** (✉ 566 Ash St. ☎ 928/425–7885) specializes in mineral products, many from Arizona. **Past Times** (✉ 1068 Adonis Ave. ☎ 928/473–3791) carries antiques. **Simply Sarah** (✉ 294 N. Broad St. ☎ 928/425–2248), with its ornately carved stone arch, has upscale ladies' clothing in predominantly natural fibers and high-quality accessories. **True Blue Jewelry** (✉ 200 N. Willow St., Globe ☎ 928/425–8361) carries high-quality jewelry made with turquoise supplied by Globe's Sleeping Beauty Mine. Ask to watch the five-minute video about turquoise mining and preparing it for use. Try **Turquoise Ladies** (✉ 996 N. Broad St. ☎ 928/425–6288) for owner June Stratton's collection of uniquely Globe souvenirs and stories.

EN ROUTE   At the stoplight 3 mi south of Globe on U.S. 60, AZ 88 splits off to the northwest. About 25 mi later on AZ 88, heading toward the Tonto National Monument, you'll see towering quartzite cliffs about 2 mi in the distance—look up and to the left for glimpses of the 40-room **Upper Ruins,** 14th-century condos left behind by the Salado people. They can't be seen from within the national monument, so make sure you've got binoculars.

Tonto National Monument

46 *30 mi northeast of the intersection of U.S. 60 and AZ 88.*

This well-preserved complex of 13th-century Salado cliff dwellings is worth a stop. There's a self-guided walking tour of the Lower Cliff Dwellings, but if you can, take a ranger-led tour of the 40-room Upper Cliff Dwellings, offered on selected mornings from November to April. Tour reservations are required and should be made as far as a month in advance. ⊠ *AZ 88, Roosevelt* ⬛ *HC 02, Box 4602, 85545* ☎ *928/467–2241* ⊕ *www.nps.gov/tont* ⬛ *$3* ☉ *Daily 8–5; Nov.–Apr., tours Thurs. and weekends at 9:30 AM; May–Oct., tours Tues., Thurs., and weekends at 9:30 AM.*

Theodore Roosevelt Lake Reservoir & Dam

47 *5 mi northwest of Tonto National Monument on AZ 88.*

Flanked by the desolate Mazatzal and Sierra Anchas mountain ranges, this aquatic recreational area is a favorite with bass anglers, water-skiers, and boaters. This is the largest masonry dam on the planet, and the massive bridge is the longest two-lane, single-span, steel-arch bridge in the nation.

EN ROUTE Past the reservoir, AZ 88 turns west and becomes a meandering dirt road, eventually winding its way back to Apache Junction via the magnificent, bronze-hue volcanic cliff walls of **Fish Creek Canyon,** with views of the sparkling lakes, towering saguaros, and, in the springtime, vast fields of wildflowers.

Tortilla Flat

48 *AZ 88, 38 mi southwest of Roosevelt Dam; 18 mi northeast of Apache Junction.*

Close to the end of the Apache Trail, this old-time restaurant and country store are what is left of an authentic stagecoach stop. This is a fun place to stop for a well-earned rest and refreshment—miner- and cowboy-style grub, of course—before heading back the last 18 mi to civilization. Enjoy a hearty bowl of killer chili and some prickly-pear-cactus ice cream while sitting at the counter on a saddle barstool.

VALLEY OF THE SUN ESSENTIALS

To research prices, get advice from other travelers, and book travel arrangements, visit ⊕ *www.fodors.com.*

Transportation

BY AIR

Phoenix Sky Harbor International Airport (PHX) is served by most major airlines; it's a major hub for both America West and Southwest, and it's just 3 mi east of downtown Phoenix, surrounded by freeways linking it to almost every part of the metro area. The new "Stage & Go Lot," west of the Terminal 2 parking garage, allows drivers to wait in their cars free of charge as an alternative to circling the terminals. The new "pet park" with restroom facilities and water for Fido is outside the west end baggage claim level at Terminal 4.

It's easy to get from Sky Harbor to downtown Phoenix (3 mi west) and Tempe (3 mi east). The airport is also only about 30 minutes by freeway from Glendale (to the west) and Mesa (to the east). Scottsdale (to the northeast) can be reached by AZ 101; depending on your destination, expect the trip to take anywhere from 25 minutes to downtown Scottsdale to an hour to North Scottsdale.

Valley Metro buses can get you directly from Terminal 2, 3, or 4 to the bus terminal downtown (at 1st and Washington streets) or to Tempe (Mill and University avenues). With free transfers, the bus can take you from the airport to most other Valley cities (Glendale, Sun City, Scottsdale, etc.), but the trip is likely to be slow unless you take an express.

The Red Line runs westbound to Phoenix every half hour from about 6 AM until after 9 PM weekdays. Saturday, take Bus 13 and transfer at Central Avenue to Bus 0 north. The Red Line runs eastbound to Tempe every half hour from 3:30 AM to 7 PM; 25 minutes later, it goes to downtown Mesa. Fares range from $.60 to $1.75.

The blue vans of SuperShuttle cruise Sky Harbor, each taking up to seven passengers to their individual destinations, with no luggage fee or airport surcharge. Wheelchair vans are also available. Drivers accept credit cards and expect tips. Fares are $6 to downtown Phoenix, around $16 to most places in Scottsdale, and $18 to $35 to places in far north Scottsdale or Carefree.

Only a few taxi firms (Checker/Yellow Cab and Courier Cab are good options) are licensed to pick up at Sky Harbor's commercial terminals. All add a $1 surcharge for airport pickups, don't charge for luggage, and are available 24 hours a day. A trip to downtown Phoenix can cost from $8 to $12. The fare to downtown Scottsdale averages about $18. If you're headed to the East Valley, expect to shell out more than $20.

A few limousine firms cruise Sky Harbor, and many more provide airport pickups by reservation. Scottsdale Limousine requires reservations but offers a toll-free number; rates start at $65 (plus tip).

🚐 **Scottsdale Limousine** ☎ 480/946-8446 or 800/747-8234. **Sky Harbor International Airport (PHX)** ☎ 602/273-3300 ⊕ www.phxskyharbor.com. **SuperShuttle** ☎ 602/244-9000 or 800/258-3826 ⊕ www.supershuttle.com. **Valley Metro buses** ☎ 602/253-5000.

BY BUS

Greyhound Lines has statewide and national routes from its main terminal near Sky Harbor airport.

Valley Metro routes service most of the Valley suburbs, but these routes are not really suitable for vacationers and offer limited service evenings and weekends. Phoenix also runs a free Downtown Area Shuttle (DASH), with purple minibuses circling the area between the Arizona Center and the state capitol at 15-minute intervals from 6:30 AM to 11 PM weekdays and from 11 AM to 11 PM weekends; this system also serves major thoroughfares in several suburbs—Glendale, Scottsdale, Tempe, Mesa, and Chandler. The city of Tempe operates the Free Local Area Shuttle (FLASH), which serves the downtown Tempe and Arizona State University area from 7 AM until 8 PM. Check the Valley Metro Web site for all public transit options (including DASH and FLASH) in the Valley.

🚌 **Greyhound Lines** ✉ 2115 E. Buckeye Rd., Phoenix ☎ 602/389-4200 or 800/229-9424 ⊕ www.greyhound.com. **Valley Metro** ☎ 602/262-7433 ⊕ www.valleymetro.org.

BY CAR

To get around Phoenix, *you will need to rent a car.* Only the major downtown areas (Phoenix, Scottsdale, Tempe, and Glendale) are pedestrian-friendly. There's no mass transit beyond a commuter-bus system. At the airport most rental companies offer shuttle services to their lots. Don't expect to nab a car without a reservation, however, especially in the high season, from January to April.

If you're coming to Phoenix from the west, you'll probably come in on I–10. The trip from the Los Angeles basin, via Palm Springs, takes six to seven hours, depending on where you start. From San Diego, I–8 slices across the low desert to Yuma and on toward the Valley on what the Spanish called El Camino del Diablo (the Devil's Highway); at Gila Bend, take AZ 85 up to I–10. The trip takes a total of six to seven hours. From the east, I–10 takes you from El Paso, across southern New Mexico, and through Chiricahua Apache country into Tucson, then north to Phoenix (a total of about six to seven hours).

From the northwest, I–40 crosses over from California and runs along old Route 66 to Flagstaff. East of Kingman, however, U.S. 93 branches off diagonally to the southeast, becoming U.S. 60 at Wickenburg and continuing into Phoenix.

The northeastern route, I–40 from Albuquerque, crosses Hopi and Navajo historic lands to Flagstaff, where I–17 takes you south to Phoenix—an eight-hour journey. For a scenic shortcut, take AZ 377 south at Holbrook to Heber and the pines of the Mogollon Rim; then take AZ 260 down the 2,000-foot drop to Payson and AZ 87 through the forests of saguaro cactus into Phoenix.

Around downtown Phoenix, AZ 202 (Papago Freeway), AZ 143 (Hohokam Freeway), and I–10 (Maricopa Freeway) make an elongated east–west loop, encompassing the state capitol area to the west and Tempe to the east. At mid-loop, AZ 51 (Piestewa—formerly Squaw—Peak Parkway) runs north into Phoenix. From AZ 202 east, the AZ 101 runs north to Scottsdale and makes a loop west through Glendale, Peoria, Sun City, and Avondale and connects to I–10. And from the loop's east end, I–10 runs south to Tucson, 100 mi away (although it's still referred to as I–10 East, as it's eventually headed that way); U.S. 60 (Superstition Freeway) branches east to Tempe and Mesa.

Roads in Phoenix and its suburbs are laid out on a single, 800-square-mi grid. Even the freeways run predominantly north–south and east–west. (Grand Avenue, running about 20 mi from northwest downtown to Sun City, is the *only* diagonal.)

Central Avenue is the main north–south grid axis: all roads parallel to and west of Central are numbered *avenues*; all roads parallel to and east of Central are numbered *streets*. The numbering begins at Central and increases in each direction.

RULES OF THE ROAD Camera devices are mounted on several streetlights to catch speeders and red-light runners, and their locations are constantly changing. You may think you've gotten away with a few miles over the limit and return home only to find a ticket waiting for you.

Many accidents in the Valley are created as a result of confusion in the left-turn lanes. Each individual jurisdiction varies. In some jurisdictions, the left-turn arrow precedes the green light and in other jurisdictions it follows the green light. As well, the yellow lights tend to be shorter than most drivers are accustomed to so be prepared for sudden stops and watch intersections for yellow-light runners. Weekdays 6 AM to 9 AM and 4 PM to 6 PM, the center or left-turn lanes on the major surface arteries of 7th Street and 7th Avenue become one-way traffic-flow lanes between McDowell Road and Dunlap Avenue. These specially marked lanes are dedicated mornings to north–south traffic (into downtown) and afternoons to south–north traffic (out of downtown).

BY TAXI

Taxi fares are unregulated in Phoenix, except at the airport. The 800-square-mi metro area is so large that one-way fares in excess of $50 are not uncommon; you might want to ask what the damages will be before you get in, since it will often be cheaper to rent a car, even if you are renting for only a day. Except within a compact area, such as central Phoenix, travel by taxi is not recommended.

Taxis charge about $3 for the first mile and $1.50 per mile thereafter (not including tips).

🚖 **Checker/Yellow Cab** ☎ 602/252–5252. **Courier Cab** ☎ 602/232–2222.

BY TRAIN

Amtrak provides train service in Arizona with bus transfers to Phoenix. Eastbound train passengers will stop in Flagstaff, where Amtrak buses depart daily for Phoenix each morning. Westbound train travelers will likely make the transfer in Tucson, where Amtrak-run buses have limited service to Phoenix on Sunday, Tuesday, and Thursday nights. What used to be Phoenix's downtown train terminal is now the Amtrak Thruway Bus Stop.

🚆 **Amtrak** ✉ 4th Ave. and Harrison St. ☎ 602/253–0121 or 800/872–7245 🌐 www.amtrak.com.

Contacts & Resources

EMERGENCIES

🛂 Emergencies **Ambulance, Fire, and Police Emergencies** ☎ 911.

🛂 Hospitals **Maricopa County Medical Center** ✉ 2601 E. Roosevelt St., Central Phoenix ☎ 602/344–5011. **Scottsdale Memorial Hospital** ✉ 7400 E. Osborn Rd., Central Scottsdale, Scottsdale ☎ 480/481–4000 or 480/860–3000. **Doctor Referral** ☎ 602/252–2844.

🛂 Pharmacies **Osco Drug** ✉ 3320 N. 7th Ave., Central Phoenix ☎ 602/266–5501 ✉ 35th and Glendale Aves., West Phoenix ☎ 602/841–7861 ✉ Scottsdale and Shea Rds., North Scottsdale, Scottsdale ☎ 480/998–3500 ✉ 1836 W. Baseline Rd., Mesa ☎ 480/831–0212. **Walgreens** ✉ 4114 N. 24th St., Central Phoenix ☎ 602/381–0275 ✉ 3605 E. Thomas Rd., Central Phoenix ☎ 602/267–0648 ✉ 1120 S. 16th St., South Phoenix ☎ 602/252–8758 ✉ 4006 E. Bell Rd., North-Central Phoenix ☎ 602/971–1096 ✉ 8449 E. MacDonald Dr., Paradise Valley ☎ 480/483–0628 ✉ 3420 N. Scottsdale Rd., Central Scottsdale, Scottsdale ☎ 480/941–0525.

TOUR OPTIONS

Reservations for tours are a must all year, with seats often filling up quickly in the busy season, October through April. All tours provide pickup services at area resorts, but some offer lower prices if you drive to the tour's point of origin.

FLOAT TRIPS Cimarron Adventures and River Co. arranges half-day float trips down the Salt and Verde rivers. Trips cost about $35 per person.

ORIENTATION Gray Line Tours gives seasonal, three-hour narrated tours including down-
TOURS town Phoenix, the Arizona Biltmore hotel, Camelback Mountain, mansions in Paradise Valley, Arizona State University, Papago Park, and Scottsdale's Old Town; the price is about $40.

Open Road Tours offers excursions to Sedona and the Grand Canyon, Phoenix city tours, and Native American–culture trips to the Salt River Pima–Maricopa Indian Reservation.

For $38, Vaughan's Southwest Custom Tours gives a 4½-hour city tour for 11 or fewer passengers in custom vans, stopping at the Pueblo Grande Museum, the Arizona Biltmore, and the state capitol. Vaughan's will also take you east of Phoenix on the Apache Trail. The tour is offered on Tuesday, Friday, and Saturday; the cost is $75.

🛂 **Cimarron Adventures and River Co.** ✉ 7901 E. Pierce St., Scottsdale ☎ 480/994–1199 ⊕ www.thetent.com/arcadia/az/azcr_cimarron.htm. **Gray Line Tours** 🖃 Box 21126, Phoenix 85036 ☎ 602/495–9100 or 800/732–0327 ⊕ www.graylinearizona.com. **Open Road Tours** ✉ 522 E. Dunlap Ave., No. 2, Phoenix 85020 ☎ 602/997–6474 or 800/766–7117 ⊕ www.openroadtours.com. **Vaughan's Southwest Custom Tours** 🖃 Box 31250, Phoenix 85046 ☎ 602/971–1381 or 800/513–1381 ⊕ www.southwesttours.com.

VISITOR INFORMATION

The Arizona Office of Tourism is open weekdays 8 to 5. The Native American Tourism Center aids in arranging tourist visits to reservation lands; it can't afford to send information packets, but you can call or stop in weekdays 8 to 5. You can find more information at the Greater Phoenix

Convention and Visitors Bureau and at the Phoenix Chamber of Commerce. The Scottsdale Convention and Visitors Bureau is open weekdays 8:30 to 6:30, Saturday 10 to 5, and Sunday 11 to 5.

🚩 Before You Leave **Arizona Office of Tourism** ✉ 1110 W. Washington, Suite 155, Phoenix 85007 ☎ 602/364-3730 or 888/520-3444 ⊕ www.arizonaguide.com. **Native American Tourism Center** ☎ 480/945-0771 🖷 480/945-0264.

🚩 In Phoenix & Central Arizona **Greater Phoenix Convention and Visitors Bureau** ☎ 602/254-6500 ⊕ www.phoenixcvb.com. **Scottsdale Convention and Visitors Bureau** ☎ 480/421-1004 or 800/782-1117 ⊕ www.scottsdalecvb.com.

The Grand Canyon

INCLUDING HAVASU CANYON & GRAND CANYON WEST

WORD OF MOUTH

"I went to the south rim in the summer. People complain about the crowds, but I didn't think it was too bad. North Rim supposedly doesn't have the crowds, but in my opinion the views are better on the south rim. Just stay away from the crowded overlooks like Mather Point and Yavapai Observation station and go to Hermits Rest and/or Desert View."

—asdaven

"Even if you don't do much hiking, there's a lot to do and see at the Grand Canyon . . . you could spend one day taking the free shuttle bus to Hermit's Rest and maybe walking along the rim between some of the stops . . . Sunrises and sunsets are worth being at the rim for."

—utahtea

www.fodors.com/forums

Updated by
Janet
Farnsworth

THE GRAND CANYON IS FAR MORE than an experience, it's an emotion—ask anyone who's visited, hiked, worked, or lived here. Many think it deserves a greater superlative than just "Grand." Although it's easy to list the statistics of the canyon—both geological and historical—that all becomes immaterial as you lose your breath when standing at the edge for the first sunrise or the thousandth sunset.

As you gaze out from the rim, you're viewing 2 billion years of geologic history, exposed for all to see in the canyon's rock walls. There's more Paleozoic and Pre-Cambrian Earth history on view here than anywhere else on the planet.

Far below the rim, the Colorado River continues its timeless carving process. It's been estimated that, prior to the completion of the Glen Canyon Dam, an average of 400,000 tons of silt was carried away every day. That equates to 80,000 5-ton dump-truck loads—one per second, nonstop.

If you were to travel from one end of the Grand Canyon to the other, you would journey just under 280 mi from Lees Ferry near the junction of the Paria and Colorado rivers in northern Arizona to the western border shared by Arizona and Nevada. At its deepest point, the canyon is nearly 6,000 feet. From the North Rim to the South Rim, the distance across varies from 18 mi to less than ½ mi. However, to travel between rims by car requires a journey of 200 mi. Hiking steep and arduous trails from rim to rim is a strenuous trek of at least 21 mi. A rim-to-rim hike for the very fit is well worth the effort, though. You'll travel through four of the seven life zones—that is, regions sharing the same climate and plant and animal life—found in North America. To otherwise witness this, you'd need to travel south to north from the Mexican desert to the Canadian woods.

There is ample evidence of early habitation from ruins that are between 8,000 and 10,000 years old in some of the highest, most inaccessible areas of the canyon. The Paleo-Indians were nomadic peoples known as Elephant Hunters, whose existence depended upon hunting large prehistoric elephants, mastodons, and mammoths. Then, about 1,500 years ago, the Puebloan people more popularly known as the Anasazi (a name that means both "ancient ones" and "enemy ancestors") arrived on the scene. More than 2,000 of their sites have been found, including Tusayan Pueblo, some 3 mi west of Desert View in the South Rim. The last of the Native Americans to occupy the region were the Navajo, who came into the area some 600 years ago.

The first Europeans to view the canyon were Spanish Conquistadors, who were more interested in finding the fabled Cibola, the Seven Cities of Gold. Don Garcia Lopez de Cardenas's band spent four days vainly searching for a path to the bottom of the canyon. They were not able to reach the Colorado River to obtain the water they so desperately needed and left uninspired and disappointed.

The first recorded Americans to visit the region were an army survey party seeking an alternate southern supply route to Utah. They, too, left in despair and recorded that the canyon was of dubious value. Then, in

1869, John Wesley Powell undertook a famous voyage down the Colorado that created the first everlasting interest in the Grand Canyon. In 1908 the area was declared a national monument, and in 1919 Congress passed legislation making it a national park.

Today, more than 5 million people each year stand in awe at the canyon and leave with the realization that they have witnessed nature at her finest. "Leave it as it is," President Teddy Roosevelt proclaimed. "You cannot improve on it. Keep it for your children, your children's children, and for all who come after you as the one great sight which every American should see."

Top 5 Experiences At & Around the Grand Canyon

- **Float your way through the Grand Canyon:** From the stomach-sinking ride over Lava Falls to the eerie silence of the Inner Gorge, this once-in-a-lifetime ride is frequently rated one of the top adventure trips in the nation.

- **Take a mule trek:** Hop on a mule and experience the interior of the canyon without *you* doing the hiking.

- **Enjoy the views and relative solitude of the North Rim:** Open only from mid-May to mid-October because of snow, the high-country park is especially spectacular in the fall when aspen leaves turn golden.

> ### WORD OF MOUTH
>
> "I did a 100-mile, 8-day, oar-powered rafting trip through the Grand Canyon starting from Phantom Ranch. We hiked the 10 miles down to the river and helicoptered out. It was an amazing experience. Some of the rapids were towering-over-our-heads enormous but I was never afraid, especially since all I had to do was hold on."
>
> –Migs

- **Take a helicopter tour:** Appreciate the massive scale of the Grand Canyon on a helicopter fly-over. Grand Canyon West is the only spot where helicopters can fly down into the canyon and land along the river.

- **Admire the color and mood of the Canyon at sunrise or sunset:** On the South Rim, Hopi Point is the place for the outdoor experience; and if you want to enjoy the view in comfort, head to the Arizona Room at Bright Angel Lodge.

Exploring the Grand Canyon

Although the average length of stay for the South Rim is about a half-day, you'll need to spend several days to appreciate this special place. Two words of caution, though: *plan ahead*. Each year, fewer than 30,000 can be accommodated on rafting trips, and mule rides into the canyon require at least a six-month advance reservation.

Because the North Rim is less crowded than its southern counterpart, a trip here allows you to explore the Grand Canyon in a more leisurely way. Lodgings are available but your best bet is to pack your camping gear and hiking boots and take several days to explore the lush Kaibab Forest and the highest, most dramatic rim views.

GREAT ITINERARIES

IF YOU HAVE 1 DAY

Although Grand Canyon National Park covers more than 1,900 square mi, you can see all of the primary sights at the South Rim in one full day. Start early, pack a picnic lunch, then take the shuttle to **Canyon View Information Plaza** ❷ just north of the South Entrance, where you can pick up information about the canyon and see your first incredible view at **Mather Point** ❶. Continue east along Desert View Drive for about 2 mi to **Yaki Point** ❾, your first stop. Then, continue 7 mi east to **Grandview Point** ❿, where you can get a good view of Krishna Shrine and Vishnu Temple, among other buttes. Four miles east is another good spot for a view, **Moran Point** ⓫. Then, take the shuttle 3 mi to the **Tusayan Ruin and Museum** ⓬, with a small display area devoted to preserving the history of the Ancestral Puebloans who inhabited the region 800 years ago. After the museum, continue another mile east to **Lipan Point** ⓭, one of the best angles in the park from which to view the Colorado River and some of its white-water rapids. **Navajo Point** ⓮, the highest elevation on the South Rim, is less than a mile farther. **Desert View and the Watchtower** ⓯ are the final stops along the shuttle route, again less than a mile beyond Navajo Point. Climb the stairs to the third-floor roof of the stone-and-mortar Watchtower for views of the Painted Desert to the east, the Vermilion Cliffs to the north, and the Colorado River below. Have your lunch at one of the picnic tables below.

After lunch, return to Grand Canyon Village and take a walk on the paved Rim Trail to **Maricopa Point** ⓱. Along the way, stop in at the historic **El Tovar Hotel** ❹, where you can make reservations for dinner. Before your walk or afterward, you can go souvenir shopping in the village.

If you have time in the late afternoon before dinner, take the shuttle on Hermit Road to **Hermits Rest** ㉓, 8 mi one-way. Stop at the **Powell Memorial** ⓲, a tribute to the explorer who measured, charted, and named many of the creeks and small canyons in the park; **Hopi Point** ⓳, where you can see Zoroaster Temple and the thin line of the Colorado River below; **The Abyss** ㉑, perhaps the most awesome stop on the route, which reveals a sheer drop of 3,000 feet to the Tonto Plateau; and Hermits Rest, the westernmost viewpoint on the South Rim and a good place to watch the sunset.

IF YOU HAVE 2 DAYS

You'll need at least two days to fully explore **Grand Canyon West** ㉖. Start early on your first day with Grand Canyon West Tours, a narrated bus ride to Quarter Master, Eagle Point, and Guano Point. Extend your afternoon with a Hummer Tour along the rim or a helicopter ride into the canyon paired with a 20-minute pontoon ride up the Colorado River. On the second day, get geared up for a day on the rapids. A bus ride down Diamond Creek road to the river will introduce you to the canyon's geology before you hop onboard a raft for a thrilling rush along Class III and IV rapids, a box lunch, and a side hike to

2

Travertine Falls. After a helicopter lift out of the canyon and a narrated bus ride through the pine forest, you'll end back up at the Hualapai Lodge, where you can fill up on a Hualapai taco at the Diamond Creek Restaurant before heading home.

If you're more adventurous and a hardy hiker, you might consider going to 🖼 **Havasu Canyon** ㉗. Hike 8 mi down into the canyon to the small village of Supai and the Havasupai Lodge. It's a healthy drive to the trailhead, and you'll need a Havasupai tribal permit to hike here; but it's unforgettable. Reservations are required to stay at the lodge and are highly recommended for the backpacker's campground. You'll need plenty of time and water for your rigorous climb back to the rim. You might even consider returning to the top by mule.

IF YOU HAVE 3 DAYS

At the South Rim, three days will allow you to experience Grand Canyon National Park more fully. On your first day, follow the one-day itinerary above, but spend more time exploring the sights on Desert View Drive, and take a leisurely picnic or luncheon in Grand Canyon Village. Leave Hermit Road for your second morning, riding the shuttle as described in the one-day itinerary, or drive to Grand Canyon Airport for a small plane or helicopter tour of the area. Have lunch in **Tusayan** ㉕, and cool off in the IMAX theater while you watch a short but big film on the Grand Canyon that may reenact your flightseeing trip. Return to Grand Canyon Village, and join one of the free educational programs led by park rangers.

On your third day, hike on **Bright Angel Trail** ⑨, or plan a longer hike into the canyon. Remember, it will take twice as long to hike back up as it does to hike down, so plan accordingly. Pick up trail maps at **Canyon View Information Plaza** ② and bring plenty of water.

IF YOU HAVE 6 DAYS

Stay six days between May and October and you can visit the North and South Rim. First, follow the three-day South Rim itinerary. On the morning of your fourth day, start out on the long but rewarding drive to the North Rim: from Grand Canyon Village, take Route 64 east out of the park for 55 mi. Turn left onto U.S. 89 and head north over the Painted Desert. You can see thousands of square miles of mesas and windswept plains. At Bitter Springs, bear left onto U.S. 89A, and drive 14 mi west to the Navajo Bridge, hanging 500 feet above the Colorado River. Once used for car traffic, the narrow steel bridge is now pedestrian-only. A newer bridge beside it carries cars across the river. At **Jacob Lake** ㉛, 55 mi past Marble Canyon, turn left and drive south on Route 67. The remaining 45 mi to the North Rim of the Grand Canyon lie ahead. Along Route 67, you'll drive over the summit of the 9,000-foot Kaibab Plateau. Spend the night at **Grand Canyon Lodge** ㉜ on the North Rim.

Spend the next day hiking around the area. The most popular trails are Transept Trail, which starts near the **Grand Canyon Lodge** ㉜, and Cliff Springs Trail, which starts near **Cape Royal** ㉟. If you're not too car-weary, drive out Cape Royal Road 11 mi to **Point Imperial** ㉞. At 8,803 feet, it's the highest vista on either rim. Spend a second night at **Grand Canyon Lodge** ㉜ before beginning the long drive back on your sixth day.

About the Restaurants

Throughout the Grand Canyon region, restaurants that offer fast food, standard American fare, and Native American specialties at reasonable prices prevail. One exception is El Tovar, the oldest existing hotel in the canyon and a pleasant surprise for anyone expecting traditional National Park Service dining. Dress is casual but you might want to don your best jeans.

About the Hotels

Reservations at Grand Canyon National Park are a must, especially during the busy summer season when rooms on both rims book up fast. You might find a last-minute cancellation, but you shouldn't count on it. If you can't find accommodations on the South Rim or in Tusayan (the development of hotels and restaurants 7 mi south of Grand Canyon Village), you may find available lodging 60 mi south in Williams or 80 mi southeast in Flagstaff. Although lodging in Tusayan and at the South Rim will keep you close to the action, the frenetic activity and crowded facilities are off-putting to some people. If you don't mind the hour-long jaunt to and from Williams, the cozy mountain town can give you a respite from the multitudes at the South Rim and also a break on prices for food and lodging. Even though the North Rim is dramatically less crowded than the South Rim, the number of rooms is severely limited. With short notice, the best time to find a room on the South Rim is in winter (the North Rim is closed from mid-October through mid-May). The snow only increases the canyon's sublime beauty, which makes up for the chance of encountering icy roads and chilly winds.

WHAT IT COSTS					
	$$$$	**$$$**	**$$**	**$**	**¢**
RESTAURANTS	over $30	$21–$30	$13–$20	$8–$12	under $8
HOTELS	over $250	$176–$250	$121–$175	$70–$120	under $70

Restaurant prices are per person for a main course at dinner. Hotel prices are for a standard double in high season, excluding taxes and service charges.

Timing

There's not a bad time to visit the canyon, though summer and spring-break season are the busiest times. Spring heralds colorful blankets of wildflowers. In summer, afternoon thunderstorms paint the canyon walls, darkening the colorful strata. Autumn color on the canyon oaks and snow-capped stone create images of change and peace in the fall and winter months. March is the month with the best chance for snow at the South Rim. Since the North Rim gets considerable snowfall, the highways and facilities are closed from mid-October until mid-May. The South Rim, open year-round, is an exposed high-desert region, where the weather changes on a whim. Thanksgiving, Christmas, and New Year's can also get quite busy.

The Grand Canyon covers 1,900 square mi on the Colorado Plateau; elevations range from 1,200 to 9,100 feet, which means climatic con-

IF YOU LIKE

2

BICYCLING

Rangers say the best bet for mountain bikers is the Rainbow Rim Trail, which goes along the North Rim of the canyon through a ponderosa-pine forest and up and down through side canyons, aspen groves, and pristine meadows. Mountain bikers heading to the North Rim will enjoy testing the many dirt access roads found in this remote area—including the 17-mi trek to Point Sublime. It's a rarity to spot other people on these primitive roads. On the other hand, bikers wanting to see the South Rim of the Grand Canyon on two wheels might be disappointed by the experience, because of narrow shoulders on park roads and the heavy traffic. Bicycles are prohibited on park trails with the exception of the Greenway System, which is currently under development on the South Rim, so the opportunities for off-road biking are also limited here. Mountain bikers visiting the South Rim may be better off meandering through the ponderosa-pine forest on the Tusayan Bike Trail.

HIKING

Hikers can choose from a plethora of canyon trails including everything from an easy rim hike to a strenuous trek into the depths of this massive gorge. Even though an immense network of trails winds through the Grand Canyon, the popular corridor trails are recommended for the first overnight trip in the canyon for hikers new to the region. Although permits are not required for day hikes, you must have a backcountry permit for longer trips. Some of the more popular paths and trails are listed in this chapter, and more detailed information and maps can be obtained from the Backcountry Information Center.

RAFTING

Those who have taken a white-water raft trip down the Colorado River often list it as one of their most memorable life experiences. Trips begin at Lees Ferry, a few miles below the Glen Canyon Dam near Page. There are tranquil half- and full-day float trips from the Glen Canyon Dam to Lees Ferry as well as raft trips that run from three days to three weeks. Many of these voyages end at Phantom Ranch at the bottom of the Grand Canyon at river mile 87. You'll encounter some good white water along the way, including Lava Falls, considered by many to be the wildest navigable rapids on the continent.

ditions vary immensely. Rainfall, for example, is more than 25 inches annually at the North Rim, while the South Rim collects but 16 inches in a typical year. The North Rim accumulates considerably more snow— about 130 inches per year—compared to less than half of that at the South Rim. Temperatures vary widely, too. In summer, the canyon floor may easily reach 115°F. At the South Rim temperatures rarely exceed 90°F. It's seldom more than 80°F at the North Rim.

Numbers in the margin correspond to numbers on the Grand Canyon South Rim and Grand Canyon North Rim maps.

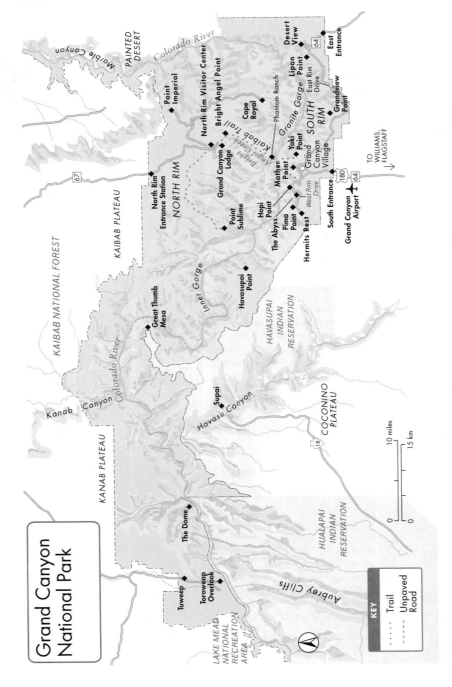

Grand Canyon National Park

PAINTED DESERT

Marble Canyon

Colorado River

KAIBAB NATIONAL FOREST

KAIBAB PLATEAU

67

North Rim Entrance Station

NORTH RIM

Point Imperial

North Rim Visitor Center

Bright Angel Point

Grand Canyon Lodge

Cape Royal

Point Sublime

Phantom Ranch

Granite Gorge

Desert View

64

East Entrance

Lipan Point

East Rim Drive

Grandview Point

SOUTH RIM

Yaki Point

Mather Point

Grand Canyon Village

Hopi Point

The Abyss

Pima Point

Hermits Rest

West Rim Drive

South Entrance

180

64

Grand Canyon Airport

TO WILLIAMS, FLAGSTAFF

Inner Gorge

Colorado River

Great Thumb Mesa

Havasupai Point

HAVASUPAI INDIAN RESERVATION

KANAB PLATEAU

Kanab Canyon

Supai

Havasu Canyon

COCONINO PLATEAU

18

The Dome

Tuweep

Toroweap Overlook

Aubrey Cliffs

HUALAPAI INDIAN RESERVATION

LAKE MEAD NATIONAL RECREATION AREA

KEY

...... Trail

– – – Unpaved Road

0   10 miles

0   15 km

THE BEST TIME OF DAY TO SEE THE GRAND CANYON

The canyon is at its best before 10 AM and after 2 PM, when the angle of the sun brings out the colors of the rocks, and clouds and shadows add dimension. "It is never the same, even from day to day, or even from hour to hour. Every passing cloud, every change in the position of the sun, recasts the whole," gushed Clarence Dutton of the U.S. Geological Survey in 1882.

GRAND CANYON NATIONAL PARK: SOUTH RIM

Out of the roughly 5 million people who visit the Grand Canyon each year, 4 million throng the South Rim's lodges, restaurants, and breathtaking viewpoints. Visiting during peak summer weekends and holidays requires patience and a tolerance for crowds. Even while they are jostling for a spot at the most popular viewpoints, most visitors are enthralled by the sheer scope of the deepest, most stunning canyon on the planet. The canyon offers a more intimate experience in the off-season, including winter, when snow mantles the landscape and contrasts with the reds, oranges, yellows, blues, and purples of the canyon.

Most people don't give the canyon enough time, flitting quickly from viewpoint to viewpoint near the main lodge in a fit of drive-by sightseeing. Many drive to the main visitors center, then take the 25-mi Desert View Drive, which follows the rim and offers frequent viewpoints. But even during the peak times you can find some solitude from the pressing crowds. A bus shuttles passengers to the less-visited and less-crowded viewpoints to the west of the main lodge. You can also walk down several different trails from various viewpoints, although the steep climb and the high elevation can pose problems for people who aren't in shape or have heart or respiratory problems.

Another option is to start from the main lodge and stroll along the mostly paved Rim Trail. Crowds drop off sharply as soon as you start walking, even during the busy seasons. Try to arrange your schedule to take in at least one sunrise or sunset. The light of midday flattens even the Grand Canyon, but early and late light makes the sandstone cliffs glow and fills the canyon's depths with shadow. The drama of the canyon is enhanced with a glimpse of one of the endangered California condors, which were reintroduced to their historical canyon habitat in 1996. The condors often visit the South Rim, although watchful biologists try to shoo them away to prevent them from getting used to human beings.

WORD OF MOUTH

"I love the South Rim. [I] saw the most beautiful sunset I've ever seen. Even more so than the ones I've seen in Hawaii (and that's saying something)."

–chasechow

HOURS   The South Rim is open year-round. The entrance gates are open 24 hours but are generally staffed from about 7 AM to 7 PM. If you arrive when there's no one at the gate, you may enter legally without paying.

ADMISSION FEES   A fee of $20 per vehicle (regardless of the number of passengers) is collected at the East Entrance near Cameron and at the South Entrance near Tusayan; pedestrians and cyclists pay $10 per person. In all cases, this fee is for one week's access. If you plan to visit the canyon more than once, consider purchasing a Grand Canyon Pass: for $40 you get unlimited access to the park for 12 months from the purchase date. Another option is the National Park Pass ($50), which waives the entrance fees for a passenger vehicle entering any national park. The pass is good for one year from date of purchase. **National Park Foundation** (☎ 888/467–2757 ⊕ www.nationalparks.org).

Grand Canyon Village

Most of the services at the South Rim are in Grand Canyon Village, where you'll find accommodations and dining as well as many attractions. Grand Canyon Village and the Village Rim can be explored on foot via a paved footpath that runs along the rim, about 1 mi round-trip. You can leave your car at the El Tovar parking lot, but it's often full, so try parking along the railroad tracks below the historic hotel. Free buses shuttle visitors between lodges and popular view points.

❼ Bright Angel Lodge was built in 1935 from Oregon pine logs and native stone; rustic cabins are set off from the main building. The rocks used to make the "geologic" fireplace are arranged in the order in which they are layered in the Grand Canyon, and the history room displays memorabilia from the South Rim's early years. Although not luxurious, these rooms are about half the price of El Tovar and just steps away from the canyon.

★ **❽ Bright Angel Trailhead** is the starting point for one of America's most famous hiking trails. It began as a path used by bighorn sheep, later used by the Havasupai, and was improved and widened in the late 1800s for prospectors. It's now a path for foot and mule traffic but during the last few years, the trail has been deteriorating and has been closed several times for repairs. Before you start your trek to the bottom, keep in mind that the trail descends 5,510 feet to the Colorado River. Be certain to have an adequate supply of water, food, and sunscreen before you begin. Rangers discourage hikers from attempting to make it to Phantom Ranch on the river and back up to the South Rim as a day hike. Permits are required for overnight hikes.

★ **❷ Canyon View Information Plaza,** near Mather Point, cannot be reached by private vehicle. It's a short walk from Mather Point, or you can take one of the free shuttle buses from anywhere in the village area. Here park rangers can answer questions and assist in planning your excursions. The new, roomy information building has plenty of rangers available to answer questions. Check here for a schedule of ranger-led hikes and lectures, study the exhibits, or find out about upcoming activities. ⊠ *East side of Grand Canyon Village, about 2 mi east of El Tovar Hotel*

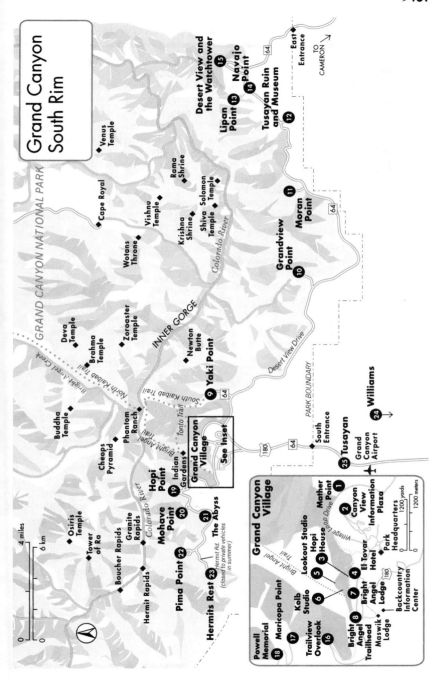

Grand Canyon South Rim

GRAND CANYON NATIONAL PARK

Venus Temple

Cape Royal

Rama Shrine

Vishnu Temple

Krishna Shrine

Shiva Temple

Solomon Temple

Wotans Throne

Deva Temple

Zoroaster Temple

Brahma Temple

Buddha Temple

Osiris Temple

Tower of Ra

Boucher Rapids

Hermit Rapids

Granite Rapids

Cheops Pyramid

Colorado River

Bright Angel Creek

North Kaibab Trail

Bright Angel Trail

Phantom Ranch

INNER GORGE

Newton Butte

9 Yaki Point

South Kaibab Trail

Tonto Trail

Colorado River

Desert View and the Watchtower

15
14 Navajo Point
13 Lipan Point
12 Tusayan Ruin and Museum

East Entrance
TO CAMERON

64

64

11

10 Grandview Point
Moran Point

Desert View Drive

PARK BOUNDARY

South Entrance

180

64

25 Tusayan
Grand Canyon Airport

24 Williams

19 Indian Gardens
Hopi Point

Grand Canyon Village

See Inset

Mohave Point **20**
21 The Abyss

Pima Point **22**
23 Hermits Rest
Hermit Rd (closed to private vehicles in summer)

Maricopa Point **17**
Powell Memorial **18**

Trailview Overlook **16**

4 miles
6 km

Grand Canyon Village

Mather Point **1**

2 Canyon View Information Plaza

Village Loop Drive

Hopi House **3**
Lookout Studio
5
El Tovar Hotel
4

Park Headquarters

180

Kolb Studio
6
7 Bright Angel Lodge
Backcountry Information Center

Bright Angel Trailhead **8**
Maswik Lodge

Bright Angel Trail

0   1200 yards
0   1200 meters

CLOSE UP

Tips for Avoiding Canyon Crowds

IT'S HARD TO COMMUNE WITH NATURE while you're searching for a parking place, dodging video cams, and stepping away from strollers but this scenario is only likely to occur during the peak months of mid-May through mid-October. One option is to bypass Grand Canyon National Park altogether and head to the West Rim of the canyon, tribal land of the Hualapai and Havasupai. If only the park itself will do, the following tips will help you to keep your distance and your cool.

PLAN AHEAD
In peak season, get an early start to avoid the noon inbound rush at the South Rim. Make your reservations well in advance for lodgings in the park and for a mule trek.

TAKE ANOTHER ROUTE
Choose a different route to the South Rim, foregoing the traditional highways AZ 64 and U.S. 180 from Flagstaff. Take U.S. 89 north from Flagstaff instead, passing near the Sunset Crater and Wupatki national monuments. You can take a break, or stay overnight at the Cameron Trading Post at the junction with AZ 64. It's a good place to shop for Native American artifacts, souvenirs, and the usual postcards, dream-catchers, recordings, and T-shirts. There are also high-quality Navajo rugs, jewelry, and other authentic handicrafts. Try the Navajo tacos before heading out. Take U.S. 64 west directly into the park at the East Entrance; the scenery along the Little Colorado River Gorge en route is eye-popping. It's 25 mi from the Grand Canyon East Entrance to the visitor center at Canyon View Information Plaza.

BYPASS THE SOUTH RIM ALTOGETHER
Although the North Rim is 10 mi across from the South Rim, getting there is a five-hour drive of about 215 mi. It might not sound worth it, but the payoff is huge. Along the way you'll travel through some of the prettiest parts of the state. Those who make the North Rim trip usually insist it has the most beautiful scenic views and the best hiking. To get to the North Rim from Flagstaff, take U.S. 89 north past Cameron, turning left onto U.S. 89A at Bitter Springs. You'll pass the area known as Vermilion Cliffs. At Jacob Lake, take AZ 67 directly to the Grand Canyon North Rim. The road to the North Rim closes in mid-October because of snow, but in summer and early fall, it's a wonderful way to beat the crowds at the South Rim.

TAKE THE GRAND CANYON RAILWAY
Skip the hassle of other drivers, twisting rim roads, jaywalking pedestrians, and jammed parking lots. Instead, sit back and relax in the comfy train cars of the Grand Canyon Railway. Live music and storytelling enliven the trip as you journey past the unfolding landscape. The train departs from the depot every morning at 9:30 sharp and makes the 65-mi journey in $2\frac{1}{4}$ hours. You can do the round-trip in a single day but you might choose to stay overnight at the South Rim and return to Williams the following afternoon.

☎ *928/638–7888* ▭ *Free after $20 per vehicle park admission*
⊙ *Mar.–Nov., daily 8 AM–5 PM; Dec.–Feb., daily 9 AM–5 PM.*

★ ❹ **El Tovar Hotel** has been the man-made focal point of a visit to the South Rim since it opened in 1905 and was recognized as the most elegant hotel west of the Mississippi. Built of Oregon pine at a cost of $250,000, it was designed as a cross between a Swiss chalet and a Norwegian villa. When the weather gets chilly, grab a seat by the rustic lobby's stone fireplace for some good people-watching. The rooms are updated to modern convenience, but the place still has the feel of a grand old hotel.

❸ **Hopi House,** a multistory structure of rock and mortar, was modeled after buildings found in the Hopi village of Oraibi, Arizona, one of the oldest continuously inhabited communities in the United States. An attempt by the Fred Harvey Company to encourage Southwest Native American crafts at the turn of the 20th century, Hopi House was one of the first gift shops to open in the Grand Canyon, where it catered to the desires of early westbound rail passengers. Today the shop—especially the upstairs gallery—is an excellent place for high-quality native art.

❻ **Kolb Studio,** built in 1904, was the Grand Canyon's first photo studio. The Kolb brothers, Ellsworth and Emery, bought a photo studio in Flagstaff and moved the equipment to the canyon. They photographed people departing on mule trips into the canyon. There was no water available at the rim so the Kolbs would then travel 4½ mi to the Indian Garden (visible from the studio window), where they set up a lab with the available water to process the film and prints, returning to the rim to sell the finished images to the mule riders. Emery operated the studio until his death in 1976 at age 95. The gallery displays photography, paintings, and crafts exhibits year-round, and has a bookstore.

★ ❺ **Lookout Studio** was built in 1914 to compete with the Kolbs' photographic studio. Architect Mary Jane Colter designed it to blend into the surrounding landscape. A paved trail at the rim leads here from El Tovar Hotel. From the upstairs loft you are eye-to-eye with the birds riding the canyon's air currents. Stand outside and you might get to see the endangered California condors that seem to enjoy people watching here.

★ ❶ **Mather Point,** about 4 mi north of the South Entrance, gives you the first glimpse of the canyon from one of the most impressive and accessible vista points on the rim—you can see nearly one-quarter of the Grand Canyon. Undulating side canyons and chiseled buttes with variegated colors demonstrate the immensity of the canyon. This overlook, named for the National Park Service's first director, Stephen Mather, yields extraordinary views of the Inner Gorge and the numerous buttes that rise out of the eroded chasm: Wotan's Throne, Brahma Temple, Zoroaster Temple, and many others. It can be very busy—to the point of overcrowding—at peak periods. The Grand Canyon Lodge, on the North Rim, is almost directly north from Mather Point and only 10 mi away—but you'd have to drive nearly 210 mi to get from one to the other.

Sports & the Outdoors

HIKING It's important to remember that there are large elevation changes and, in summer, extreme temperature ranges in the Grand Canyon. **Carry plenty of water** and energy foods. Each year there are scores of unnecessary rescues simply because hikers underestimate the enormous size of the canyon, hike beyond their ability, or do not take with them sufficient quantities of food and water. Overnight hikes into the canyon require a backcountry permit (*see* the Grand Canyon Essentials section at the end of this chapter).

The well-maintained **Bright Angel Trail** is one of the most scenic hiking paths from the South Rim to the bottom of the canyon (9 mi). Rest houses are equipped with water at the 1½- and 3-mi points from May through September and at Indian Garden (4 mi) year-round. Water is also available at Bright Angel Campground, 9¼ mi below the trailhead. Plateau Point, about 1½ mi below Indian Garden, is as far

WORD OF MOUTH

"Don't miss going to the Grand Canyon and hiking down at least a portion of the Bright Angel trail. It'll give you a whole new perspective. You don't have to go far, but try to go down an hour or so."

–Malesherbes

as you should attempt to go on a day hike. Bright Angel Trail is the easiest of the footpaths into the canyon, but because the climb out from the bottom is an ascent of 5,510 feet, the trip should be attempted only by those in good physical condition and should be avoided in midsummer due to extreme heat. The top of the trail, a tight set of switchbacks called Jacob's Ladder, can be icy in winter. Note that you will be sharing the trail with mule trains, which have the right-of-way and sometimes leave unpleasant surprises in your path.

If you've been driving too long and want some exercise along with great views of the canyon, it's an easy mile-long hike from the **Information Plaza to El Tovar Hotel.** The path runs through a quiet wooded area for about ½ mi, and then along the rim for another ¾ mi.

The most popular walking path at the South Rim is 9-mi (one-way) **Rim Trail,** which runs along the edge of the canyon from Mather Point to Hermits Rest. This walk, which is paved to Maricopa Point, allows visits to several of the South Rim's historic landmarks. The Rim Trail is an ideal day hike as it only varies a few hundred feet in elevation from Mather Point (7,120 feet) to the trailhead at Hermits Rest (6,640 feet). The trail can also be accessed from the major viewpoints along Hermit Road, which you can reach by shuttle bus during the busy summer months.

MULE TOURS Nearly as well known as the canyon itself, mule trips, run by **Xanterra ★ Parks & Resorts** (✉ 6312 S. Fiddlers Green Circle, Suite 600, N. Greenwood Village, CO 80111 ☎ 303/297–2757 or 888/297–2757 🖷 303/297–3175 ⊕ www.grandcanyonlodges.com), go down the precipitous trails to the Inner Gorge of the Grand Canyon. It's hard to get reservations unless you make them months in advance: reservations are usually accepted up to 13 months in advance, or you can check the waiting list for last-minute cancellations. These trips have been conducted since the early 1900s. A very comforting fact to know as you ride the narrows trail: no one's ever been killed while riding a mule that fell off a cliff. Nevertheless, the treks are not for the faint of heart or people in questionable health. Riders must be at least 4 feet 7 inches tall, weigh less than 200 pounds, and understand English. Pregnant women are not allowed to ride, and adults must accompany children under 15. The all-day ride to Plateau Point is $136.35 (lunch included). An overnight with a stay at Phantom Ranch at the bottom of the canyon is $366.38 ($651.80 for two) for one night. Two nights at Phantom Ranch, an option available from November through March, cost $513.58 ($865.23 for two). Meals are included.

> **WORD OF MOUTH**
>
> "The wrangler told us that the mules have a tendency to walk along the edge. He says they train them like that so that we can get a better view of the canyon. Everybody laughs nervously . . . And off we headed down the Bright Angel Trail. And yes, the mules do walk close to the edge, but what a view . . . We continued farther down into the canyon and I caught my first glimpse of the Colorado River—a beautiful emerald green . . . Overall, the trip was a fantastic experience . . . the Grand Canyon is spectacular beyond words, but the mules were the best part of it!"   —Gilbert

SKIING   Although you can't schuss down into the Grand Canyon, you can cross-country ski in the woods near the rim when there's enough snow. The best season for cross-country skiing is mid-December though early March. Trails, suitable for beginner and intermediate skiers, begin $3/10$ mi north of the Grandview Lookout and travel through the Kaibab National Forest. Contact the **Tusayan Ranger District** (⊕ Box 3088, Grand Canyon 86023 ☎ 928/638–2443 ⊕ www.fs.fed.us/r3/kai) for details.

Where to Stay & Eat

If you want to get your first choice (especially at Bright Angel Lodge or El Tovar), make reservations as far in advance as possible although sometimes lodging is available at the last minute.

$–$$$ ✕ **Arizona Room.** The canyon views from this casual Southwestern-style steak house are the best of any restaurant at the South Rim, a fact reflected in the prices on the menu, which includes chicken, steak, and seafood. It's open for lunch 11:30–3 and for dinner starting at 4:30; arrive early to avoid the crowds. ⊠ *Bright Angel Lodge, West Rim Dr., Grand Canyon Village* ☎ *928/638–2631* ⚊ *Reservations not accepted* ☱ *AE, D, DC, MC, V* ☉ *Closed Jan.–mid-Feb.*

$–$$$ ✕ **El Tovar Dining Room.** Modeled after a European hunting lodge, this
Fodor'sChoice   rustic 19th-century dining room built of hand-hewn logs is worth a visit
★   in itself. Breakfast, lunch, and dinner are served beneath the beamed ceiling. The cuisine is modern Southwestern, and the menu includes such dishes as sautéed rainbow trout served with a wild rice salad and grilled New York strip steak with buttermilk-cornmeal onion rings and pep-

per jack au gratin potatoes. You can even order blackened trout for breakfast. ⊠ *El Tovar Hotel, West Rim Dr., Grand Canyon Village* ☎ *928/638–2631* ⌂ *Reservations essential* ⊟ *AE, D, DC, MC, V.*

¢ ✗ **Yavapai Canyon Café.** Families favor the home-style food at Yavapai Lodge, which offers dining on a budget. Fast-food favorites here include pastries, burgers, and pizza. Open for breakfast, lunch, and dinner, the cafeteria also serves specials, chicken potpie, fried catfish, and fried chicken. ⊠ *Grand Canyon Village* ☎ *928/638–2631* ⌂ *Reservations not accepted* ⊟ *AE, D, DC, MC, V* ⊗ *Closed mid-Dec.–Feb.*

★ **$$–$$$$** ⊡ **El Tovar Hotel.** A registered National Historic Landmark, El Tovar was built in 1905 of Oregon pine logs and native stone. The hotel's proximity to all of the canyon's facilities, its European hunting-lodge atmosphere, and its renowned dining room make it the best place to stay on the South Rim. It's usually booked well in advance (up to nine months ahead), though it's easier to get a room during winter months. Only three suites have canyon views and these are usually booked two years in advance, but you can enjoy the view anytime from the cocktail-lounge back porch. ⊠ *West Rim Dr., Grand Canyon Village* ⌂ *Box 699, Grand Canyon 86023* ☎ *303/297–2757, 888/297–2757 reservations only, 928/638–2631 direct to hotel, no reservations* ⊟ *303/297–3175 reservations only, 928/638–2855 direct to hotel, no reservations* ⊕ *www.grandcanyonlodges.com* ⇆ *70 rooms, 8 suites* ⌂ *Restaurant, room service, some in-room hot tubs, some refrigerators, cable TV, bar; no a/c in some rooms, no smoking* ⊟ *AE, D, DC, MC, V.*

$$ ⊡ **Kachina Lodge.** Located on the rim half-way between El Tovar and Bright Angel Lodge, this motel-style lodge has many rooms with a partial canyon view ($10 extra). Although lacking the historical charm of the neighboring lodges, these rooms are a good bet for families and are within easy walking distance of dining facilities at El Tovar and Bright Angel Lodge. There are also several rooms for people with physical disabilities. There's no air-conditioning, but swamp coolers keep the heat at bay. Check in at El Tovar Hotel to the east. ⊠ *West Rim Dr., Grand Canyon Village* ⌂ *Box 699, Grand Canyon 86023* ☎ *303/297–2757, 888/297–2757 reservations only, 928/638–2631 direct to hotel, no reservations* ⊟ *303/297–3175 reservations only* ⊕ *www.grandcanyonlodges.com* ⇆ *50 rooms* ⌂ *Refrigerators, cable TV, in-room data ports, no-smoking rooms; no a/c* ⊟ *AE, D, DC, MC, V.*

$$ ⊡ **Thunderbird Lodge.** A favorite with families, this motel with comfortable, no-nonsense rooms is next to Bright Angel Lodge in Grand Canyon Village. For $10 extra, you can get a room with a partial view of the canyon. Rooms have either two queen beds or one king. Check in at Bright Angel Lodge, the next hotel to the west. ⊠ *West Rim Dr., Grand Canyon Village* ⌂ *Box 699, Grand Canyon 86023* ☎ *303/297–2757, 888/297–2757 reservations only, 928/638–2631 direct to hotel, no reservations* ⊟ *303/297–3175 reservations only* ⊕ *www.grandcanyonlodges.com* ⇆ *55 rooms* ⌂ *Refrigerators, some in-room data ports, no-smoking rooms; no a/c in some rooms, no TV in some rooms* ⊟ *AE, D, DC, MC, V.*

$–$$ ⊡ **Maswik Lodge.** The lodge, named for a Hopi Kachina who is said to guard the canyon, is ¼ mi from the rim. Accommodations, nestled in the ponderosa pine forest, range from rustic cabins to more modern rooms, refurbished in 2006. The cabins are the cheapest option but are available only spring through fall. Some rooms have air-conditioning and the rest have ceiling fans. Maswik Cafeteria has sandwiches, salads, snack foods, and a choice of several hot meals. Teenagers like the lounge, where they can shoot pool, throw darts, or watch the big-screen TV. Kids under 16 stay free. ⊠ *Grand Canyon Village* ✆ *Box 699, Grand Canyon 86023* ☎ *303/297–2757, 888/297–2757 reservations only, 928/638–2631 direct to hotel, no reservations* 🖷 *303/297–3175 reservations only* ⊕ *www. grandcanyonlodges.com* ➴ *250 rooms, 28 cabins* ⌂ *Cafeteria, sports bar, shop, no-smoking rooms, Internet room; no a/c in some rooms* ⊟ *AE, D, DC, MC, V.*

$ ⊡ **Yavapai Lodge.** The largest motel-style lodge in the park is tucked in a piñon and juniper forest at the eastern end of Grand Canyon Village, near the RV park. The basic rooms are near the park's general store, the visitor center (½ mi), and the rim (¼ mi). The cafeteria, open for breakfast, lunch, and dinner, serves standard park service food. Reservations are accepted 12 months in advance. ⊠ *Grand Canyon Village* ✆ *Box 699, Grand Canyon 86023* ☎ *303/297–2757, 888/297–2757 reservations only, 928/638–2631 direct to hotel, no reservations* 🖷 *303/ 297–3175 reservations only* ⊕ *www.grandcanyonlodges.com* ➴ *358 rooms* ⌂ *Cafeteria, fans, shop, Internet room, no-smoking rooms; no a/c in some rooms* ⊟ *AE, D, DC, MC, V* ⊗ *Closed Jan. and Feb.*

↻ ¢–$ ⊡ **Bright Angel Lodge.** Famed architect Mary Jane Colter designed this
Fodor'sChoice   1935 log-and-stone structure, which sits within a few yards of the
★   canyon rim and blends superbly with the canyon walls. It has a similar location to El Tovar for about half the price. Accommodations are in motel-style rooms or cabins. Lodge rooms don't have TVs and some rooms do not have private bathrooms. Cabins, some with fireplaces, are scattered among the pines and do have TVs and private baths. Expect historic charm but not luxury. The Bright Angel Dining Room serves family-style meals all day, and a Warm Apple Grunt dessert that's large enough to share. The Arizona Room serves dinner only. There is an ice-cream parlor, a gift shop, and a small history museum with exhibits on Fred Harvey and Mary Jane Colter. ⊠ *West Rim Dr., Grand Canyon Village* ✆ *Box 699, Grand Canyon 86023* ☎ *303/297–2757, 888/ 297–2757 reservations only, 928/638–2631 direct to hotel, no reservations* 🖷 *303/297–3175 reservations only, 928/638–2876 direct to hotel, no reservations* ⊕ *www.grandcanyonlodges.com* ➴ *30 rooms, 6 with shared bath; 42 cabins* ⌂ *Restaurant, coffee shop, bar, Internet room, shop; no a/c, no TV in some rooms* ⊟ *AE, D, DC, MC, V.*

¢–$ ⊡ **Phantom Ranch.** In a grove of cottonwood trees on the canyon floor, Phantom Ranch is accessible only to hikers, mule trekkers, or rafters. The wood-and-stone buildings were originally a hunting camp built in 1922. There are 40 dormitory beds and 14 beds in cabins, all with shared baths. Seven additional cabins are reserved for mule riders, who buy their trips as a package. The restaurant, probably the most remote eating establishment in the United States, serves family-style meals, with breakfast, dinner, and box lunches available. Food and lodging reservations should be made 9 to 11 months ahead. ⊠ *On canyon floor at intersection of Bright Angel and Kaibab trails* ☎ *303/297–2757 reservations only, no direct phone* 🖷 *303/297–3175 reservations only* ⊕ *www.*

grandcanyonlodges.com ⟟ *4 dormitories, 2 cabins for hikers, 7 cabins with outside showers for mule riders* ⚭ *Dining room; no a/c, no room phones, no room TVs* ▤ *AE, D, DC, MC, V.*

CAMPING   **Bright Angel Campground.** This free campground is near Phantom Ranch
¢   on the South and North Kaibab trails, at the bottom of the canyon. There are toilet facilities and running water but no showers. A backcountry permit, which serves as your reservation, is required to stay here. ⊠ *Intersection of South and North Kaibab trails, Grand Canyon* ⊕ *Backcountry Office, Box 129, Grand Canyon 86023* ☎ *928/638–7875* 📠 *928/638–2125* ✍ *Free* ⟟ *32 tent sites* ⚭ *Flush toilets, drinking water, picnic tables* ⚭ *Reservations essential* ⊙ *Open year-round.*

¢   **Indian Garden.** Halfway down the canyon is this free campground, en route to Phantom Ranch on the Bright Angel Trail. Running water and toilet facilities are available, but not showers. A backcountry permit, which serves as a reservation, is required. ⊠ *Bright Angel Trail, Grand Canyon* ⊕ *Backcountry Office, Box 129, Grand Canyon 86023* ☎ *928/638–7875* 📠 *928/638–2125* ✍ *Free* ⟟ *15 tent sites* ⚭ *Pit toilets, drinking water, picnic tables* ⊙ *Open year-round.*

¢   **Mather Campground.** Mather has RV and tent sites but no hookups. No reservations are accepted from December to March, but the rest of the year they're a good idea, especially during the busy spring and summer seasons. Reservations can be made up to five months in advance. Ask at the campground entrance for daily availability. ⊠ *Off Village Loop Dr., Grand Canyon Village* ⊕ *National Park Reservation Service, Box 1600, Cumberland, MD 21501* ☎ *800/365–2267* ⊕ *reservations. nps.gov/index.cfm* ✍ *$15–$18* ⟟ *97 RV sites, 190 tent sites* ⚭ *Flush toilets, drinking water, guest laundry, showers, fire grates, picnic tables* ⊙ *Open year-round.*

¢   **Trailer Village.** This campground in Grand Canyon Village has RV sites—no tent camping sites—with full hookups and bathroom facilities, though the bathrooms are ½ mi from the campground. The fee is good for two people; it's an extra $2 for each additional person over 16. The facility is busy in spring and summer, so make reservations ahead of time. No reservations are accepted from December through March. The dump station is closed in winter. ⊠ *Off Village Loop Dr., Grand Canyon Village* ☎ *303/297–2757, 888/297–2757 reservations only, 928/638–2631 direct to village, no reservations* 📠 *303/297–3175 reservations only* ⊕ *www.xanterra.com* ✍ *$25* ⟟ *78 RV sites* ⚭ *Flush toilets, full hookups, dump station, drinking water, guest laundry, showers, fire grates* ⊙ *Open year-round.*

Nightlife & the Arts

Nightlife in these parts consists of watching a full moon above the soaring buttes of the Grand Canyon, crawling into your bedroll beside some lonely canyon trail, or attending a free evening program on area lore. The following Grand Canyon properties have cocktail lounges: **Bright Angel Lodge** (occasional live entertainment), **El Tovar Hotel** (casual relaxation), and **Maswik Lodge** (sports bar).

★   The **Grand Canyon Chamber Music Festival** (☎ 928/638–9215 or 800/997–8285 ⊕ www.grandcanyonmusicfest.org) is held for three weeks each

September at the Shrine of Ages amphitheater and stages nearly a dozen concerts. In the early 1980s, music aficionados Robert Bonfiglio and Clare Hoffman hiked through the Grand Canyon and decided the stunning spectacle should be accompanied by the strains of a symphony. One of the park rangers agreed, and the wandering musicians performed an impromptu concert. Encouraged by the experience, Bonfiglio and Hoffman started the Grand Canyon Music Festival.

Shopping

Nearly every lodging facility and retail store at the South Rim stocks Native American arts and crafts and Grand Canyon books and souvenirs. Prices are comparable to other souvenir outlets, though you may find some better deals in Williams. However, a portion of the proceeds from items purchased at Hopi House, Desert Watchtower, and the visitor center go to the Grand Canyon Association. **El Tovar Hotel Gift Shop** (⊠ West Rim Dr., Grand Canyon Village ☎ 928/638–2631) carries Native American jewelry, rather expensive casual wear, and souvenir gifts. **Hopi House** (⊠ West Rim Dr., east of El Tovar Hotel, Grand Canyon Village ☎ 928/638–2631) has the widest selection of Native American handicrafts in the vicinity. **Verkamp's** (⊠ West Rim Dr., across from El Tovar Hotel, Grand Canyon Village ☎ 928/638–2242 or 888/817–0806 ⊕ www.verkamps.com) is the best place on the South Rim to buy inexpensive souvenirs of your Grand Canyon adventure.

Desert View Drive

The breathtaking Desert View Drive proceeds east for about 25 mi along the South Rim from Grand Canyon Village to Desert View. Before beginning the drive, consider stopping to see the exhibits and attend the free lectures offered by park naturalists at Yavapai Observation Station. There are four marked picnic areas along the route and restrooms at Tusayan Museum and Desert View. This is the road you come into the park on if you enter at the East Entrance.

Enjoy the view without worrying the traffic. **Xanterra Motorcoach Tours** (☎ 928/638–2631) offers year-round bus tours along Desert View ($30, 3¾ hours) or Hermits Rest ($17.75, 2 hours) and a Sunrise or Sunset Tour ($13.50, 1½ hours). You can combine any two of the tours for a special trip ($38).

★ ☺ ⓯ **Desert View and the Watchtower** make for a climactic final stop if you are driving Desert View Drive from Grand Canyon Village, or a dramatic beginning if you enter the park through the East Entrance. From the top of the 70-foot stone-and-mortar Watchtower even the muted hues of the distant Painted Desert to the east and the 3,000-foot-high Vermilion Cliffs rising from a high plateau near the Utah border are visible. In the chasm below, angling to the north toward Marble Canyon, you can see an imposing stretch of the Colorado River. The Watchtower houses a glass-enclosed observatory with powerful telescopes. Desert View originally served as a trading post; now the building is a small museum and information center. ⊠ *Desert View Dr., Grand Canyon* ☎ *928/638–2736, 928/638–2360 trading post* ▣ *Free* ☉ *June–Aug., daily 8–7 or 8–8 in summer; Sept.–May, daily 9–5.*

⑩ Grandview Point (✉ Desert View Dr., Grand Canyon), at an altitude of 7,496 feet, has large stands of ponderosa pine, piñon pine, oak, and juniper. The view from here is one of the finest in the canyon. To the northeast is a group of dominant buttes, including Krishna Shrine, Vishnu Temple, Rama Shrine, and Shiva Temple. A short stretch of the Colorado River is also visible. Directly below the point and accessible by the rugged Grandview Trail is Horseshoe Mesa, where you can see ruins of the Last Chance Copper Mine. Grandview Point was also the site of the Grandview Hotel, constructed in the late 1890s but closed in 1908; logs salvaged from the hotel were used for the Kiva Room of the Desert View and the Watchtower.

⑬ Lipan Point (✉ Desert View Dr., Grand Canyon), 1 mi northeast of Tusayan Ruin, is the canyon's widest point. From here you can get an astonishing visual profile of the gorge's geologic history, with a view of every eroded layer of the canyon. You can also see Unkar Delta, where a wide creek joins the Colorado to form powerful rapids and a broad beach. Ancestral Puebloan farmers worked the Unkar Delta for hundreds of years, growing corn, beans, squash, and melons.

> ## TOP SPOTS FOR A PICNIC
>
> Bring your picnic basket and enjoy dining alfresco surrounded by some of the most beautiful backdrops in the country.
>
> - **Buggeln:** 15 mi east of Grand Canyon Village on Desert View Drive, this spot has some secluded, shady spots, and is wheelchair accessible.
>
> - **Desert View:** This large popular spot along Desert View Drive, 23 mi east of the Village, is wheelchair accessible but offers little shade.
>
> - **Grandview Point:** As the name implies, the views are wonderful. The picnic tables are nicely spaced apart as well. It's 12 mi east of the Village on Desert View Drive.
>
> - **South Kaibab Trailhead:** The closest picnic spot to Grand Canyon Village is often filled with hikers' cars. It's 1 mi east of the Village on Desert View Drive.

⑪ Moran Point (✉ Desert View Dr., Grand Canyon), about 5 mi east of Grandview Point, was named for American landscape artist Thomas Moran, who painted Grand Canyon scenes from many points on the rim but was especially fond of the play of light and shadows from this location. He first visited the canyon with John Wesley Powell in 1873, and his vivid canvases helped persuade Congress to create a national park at the Grand Canyon. "Thomas Moran's name, more than any other, with the possible exception of Major Powell's, is to be associated with the Grand Canyon," wrote the noted canyon photographer Ellsworth Kolb. Moran Point continues to be a favorite spot for painters, and photographers as well.

⑭ Navajo Point (✉ Desert View Dr., Grand Canyon) is just over 1 mi east of Lipan Point at 7,461 feet. This is probably the spot where the first Spaniards descended into the canyon in 1540. Just west of Navajo Point—the highest natural elevation on the South Rim, at 7,498 feet—is the head of the unmaintained Tanner Trail, a rugged route once favored by prospectors, rustlers (it's also called Horsethief Trail), and bootleggers.

⑫ Tusayan Ruin and Museum is 3 mi east of Moran Point on the south side
Fodor'sChoice of the highway. This easy-to-reach archaeological site contains evidence
★ of early habitation in the Grand Canyon, and the accompanying museum provides plenty of information about ancestral Puebloan people who once lived here. *Tusayan* comes from a Hopi phrase meaning "country of isolated buttes," which certainly describes the scenery. The partially intact rock dwellings here were occupied for roughly 20 years around AD 1200 by 30 or so Native American hunters, farmers, and gatherers. They eventually moved on like so many others, perhaps pressured by drought and depletion of natural resources. The museum displays artifacts, models of the dwellings, and exhibits on modern tribes of the region. Free 30-minute guided tours—as many as five in summer, fewer in winter—are given daily. ⊠ *Desert View Dr., 3 mi east of Moran Point, Grand Canyon* ☎ *928/638–2305* ⚐ *Free* ☉ *Daily 9–5.*

⑨ Yaki Point (⊠ Desert View Dr., Grand Canyon), east of Grand Canyon Village on AZ 64, has an exceptional view of Wotan's Throne, a majestic flat-top butte named by François Matthes, a U.S. Geological Survey scientist who developed the first topographical map of the Grand Canyon. Due north is Buddha Temple, capped by limestone. Newton Butte, with its flat top of red sandstone, lies to the east. At Yaki Point the popular South Kaibab Trail starts the descent to Inner Gorge, crosses the Colorado over a steel suspension bridge, and wends its way to Phantom Ranch, the only lodging facility at the bottom of the canyon. If you plan to go more than a mile, carry water. If you encounter a mule train, the animals have the right-of-way. Move to the inside of the trail and wait as they pass. Yaki Point is accessible only by the park shuttle bus most of the year. Sometimes, during winter months when visitation is low, the road is open to private vehicles.

Sports & the Outdoors

HIKING Accessible from the parking area at Grandview Point, the trailhead for **Grandview Trail** is at 7,400 feet. The path heads down into the canyon for 4⁸/₁₀ mi to the junction at East Horseshoe Mesa Trail. Classified as a wilderness trail, the route is aggressive and not as heavily traveled as some of the more well-known trails, such as Bright Angel and Hermit. There is no water available along the trail and it follows a steep descent to 4,800 feet at Horseshoe Mesa, where Hopi Indians once collected mineral paints.

The **New Hance Trail** was blazed in the late 1800s by canyon guide and storyteller John Hance. The strenuous hike begins at 7,000 feet and descends 8 mi to the Colorado River at 2,600 feet. The trailhead is 1 mi south of Moran Point. This wilderness trail is occasionally blocked by small rock slides or washouts, making for a more interesting and difficult hike than the regularly maintained trails. Make sure to take plenty of water and don't attempt to hike down to the river and back in one day. As Hance once remarked, "You can't imagine how hot it is [in the canyon]. Why I'll give my word, I've been down there when it was so hot it melted the wings off the flies."

GRAND CANYON NATIONAL PARK: TOP PICKS HIKING TRAILS

	Grade	Miles (one way)	Beginning Elevation	Ending Elevation	Mules	Campground Open Info*	Water	Shuttle Access	Ranger Station	Toilet/Restroom	Emergency Telephone	Hiking Level	Trail Conditions?
South Rim													
Bright Angel Trail South	Steep	9.6 mi	6785 ft	2480 ft (Colorado River)	Y	Y Y/R	(Seasonal)	Y	Y	Y	Y	Intermediate-Experienced	Maintained
Grandview Trail	Very Steep	3.2 mi	7400 ft	4800 ft (Horseshoe Mesa)	Y	Y/R		Y		Y		Experienced	Maintained
Hermit Trail	Steep	9.3 mi	6640 ft	2400 ft (Colorado River)		Y/R	(Untreated)	Y		Y (Trailhead)	Y (Trailhead)	Experienced	Unmaintained
New Hance Trail	Steep	8 mi	7000 ft	2600 ft (Colorado River)		Y/R						Experienced	Unmaintained
Rim Trail	Level	9 mi	6640 ft (Hermits Rest)	7120 ft (Mather Point)		Y/R	Y	Y		Y	Y	Beginner-Experienced	Maintained
South Kaibab Trail	Steep	7.1 mi	7100 ft	2546 ft (Phantom Ranch)	Y	Y Y/R	Y (Trailhead)	Y	Y	Y	Y	Experienced	Unmaintained
North Rim													
Ken Patrick Trail	Level/Incline	10 mi	8250 ft	8803 ft (Point Imperial)		mid-May–mid-Oct.		Y				Beginner-Experienced	Unmaintained
North Kaibab Trail	Steep	7.1 mi	8255 ft	2400 ft (Colorado River)	Y	Y mid-May–mid-Oct.	Y	Y		Y	Y	Intermediate-Experienced	Maintained
Transept Trail	Level	1.5 mi	8255 ft	8200 ft (Campground)		mid-May–mid-Oct.				Y	Y	Beginner	Maintained
Uncle Jim Trail	Level	2.5 mi	8300 ft	8244 ft (Uncle Jim Point)	Y	mid-May–mid-Oct.						Beginner-Experienced	Maintained
Widforss Trail	Level/Incline	4.9 mi	8080 ft	7900 ft (Widforss Point)		mid-May–mid-Oct.						Beginner-Experienced	Unmaintained

*(South Rim trails occasionally close due to weather or trail conditions)

Y/R = year-round

CLOSE UP

Freebies at the Canyon

WHILE YOU'RE HERE, take advantage of the freebies offered at Grand Canyon National Park. The most useful is the system of free shuttle buses at the South Rim that will ease the road-weary with three routes winding through the park—Hermits Rest Route, Village Route, and Kaibab Trail Route. The Hermits Rest Route runs only from March through November; the other two run year-round, and the Kaibab Trail Route provides the only access to Yaki Point. Hikers coming or going from the Kaibab Trailhead can catch the Hikers Express, which departs three times each morning from the Bright Angel Lodge, makes a quick stop at the Backcountry Office, and then heads out to the South Kaibab Trailhead.

Ranger-led programs are free and offered year-round, though more are scheduled in spring and summer.

These might include such activities as stargazing and topics such as geology and the cultural history of prehistoric peoples. Some programs are held during the day and others in the evening. Some of the more in-depth programs include a fossil walk and a condor talk. Also make sure to check with the visitor center for seasonal programs including wildflower walks and fire ecology.

Kids ages 4 to 14 can get involved with the park's Junior Ranger program, with activities including a ranger-led rim hike and hands-on experiments detailing how the Grand Canyon was formed.

As the rangers will tell you, though, the best free activity in the canyon is watching the magnificent splashes of color on the canyon walls during sunrise and sunset.

2

The **South Kaibab Trail,** starting near Yaki Point on Desert View Drive near Grand Canyon Village, connects at the bottom of the canyon (after the Kaibab Bridge across the Colorado River) with the **North Kaibab Trail.** Plan on two to three days if you want to hike the gorge from rim to rim (it's easier to descend from the North Rim, as it's more than 1,000 feet higher than the South Rim). The South Kaibab Trail is steep, descending from the trailhead at 7,260 feet to 2,480 feet at the Colorado River. Along the trail there's no water and very little shade, and there are no campgrounds, though there are portable toilets at Cedar Ridge (6,320 feet), 1½ mi from the trailhead. Toilets and an emergency phone are also at the Tipoff, 4½ mi down the trail (3 mi past Cedar Ridge). The trail corkscrews down through some spectacular geology, closely following the 300-million-year-old Supai and Redwall formations. Look for (but don't remove) fossils in the limestone when you take your frequent water breaks. If you're going back up to the South Rim, ascend **Bright Angel Trail.** Accommodations along the way include the backcountry campgrounds at Indian Garden and Phantom Ranch (reservations are required far in advance for the latter). Don't forget—hikers traveling down the canyon are required to yield to mules and to hikers going uphill. Overnight hikes into the canyon require a backcountry permit (see the Essentials section at the end of this chapter).

Where to Stay

CAMPING   🛃 **Desert View Campground.** Popular for spectacular views of the
¢ canyon at nearby Watchtower, this campground books up fast in summer. Fifty RV (without hookups) and tent sites are available on a
first-come, first-served basis. 🛋 *Grills, flush toilets, drinking water,
picnic tables* → *50 campsites* ⌂ *Desert View Dr., 23 mi east of Grand
Canyon Village off AZ 64* 📬 *Box 129, Grand Canyon 86023* ☎ *928/
638–7875* 🖶 *928/638–2125* ⌂ *$10* ⌂ *Reservations not accepted*
☉ *Mid-May–mid-Oct.*

Shopping

Desert View Trading Post (⌂ Desert View Dr., near Watchtower at Desert
View, Grand Canyon ☎ 928/638–2360) sells a mix of traditional Southwestern souvenirs and authentic Native American arts and crafts.

Hermit Road

The Santa Fe Company built Hermit Road, formerly known as West
Rim Drive, in 1912 as a scenic tour route. There are 10 scenic overlooks along this 8-mi stretch, each worth a visit. Hermit Road is filled
with hairpin turns; be certain to adhere to posted speed limits. Hermit Road is usually closed to private auto traffic from March through
November because of congestion; during this period, a free shuttle bus
can carry you to all the overlooks. To ride the bus round-trip without
getting off at any of the viewpoints takes 75 minutes, as the return
trip only stops at Mohaveand Hopi points. Make sure to take plenty
of water with you for the ride—the only water along the way is at Hermits Rest.

❶1 The Abyss (⌂ Hermit Rd., Grand Canyon), at an elevation of 6,720 feet,
is one of the most awesome stops on Hermit Road, revealing a sheer
drop of 3,000 feet to the Tonto Platform. From the Abyss you'll also
see several isolated sandstone columns, the largest of which is called
the Monument.

★ **❷3 Hermits Rest** (⌂ Hermit Rd., Grand Canyon), the westernmost viewpoint,
and the Hermit Trail that descends from it were named for the "her-
mit" Louis Boucher, a 19th-century French-Canadian prospector who
had a number of mining claims and a roughly built home down in the
canyon. The indigenous-looking building, called Hermits Rest, is another
of architect Mary Colter's Grand Canyon creations. Designed to look
like it was built by a mountain man, it opened in 1914 as a terminal
point for Hermit Road. The focal point is the fireplace; Colter had the
stones covered with soot so they appeared to be old and well used. Canyon
views from here include Hermit Rapids and the towering cliffs of the
Supai and Redwall formations. The
stone building at Hermits Rest sells
curios and refreshments and—more
important—has the only restrooms
on Hermit Road.

❳9 Hopi Point (⌂ Hermit Rd., Grand
Canyon) is at an elevation of 7,071

> **WORD OF MOUTH**
>
> "Hopi Point is a favorite sunset
> point and crowds will form there
> long before sunset."   –utahtea

feet, and a large section of the Colorado River is visible from here; although it appears as a thin line, the river is nearly 350 feet wide below this overlook. Across the canyon to the east is Zoroaster Temple. Directly below Hopi Point lies Dana Butte, named for a prominent 19th-century geologist. In 1919 an entrepreneur proposed connecting Hopi Point, Dana Butte, and the Tower of Set across the river with an aerial tramway, a technically feasible plan that, fortunately, has not been realized.

⑰ Maricopa Point (⊠ Hermit Rd., Grand Canyon) merits a stop for its arresting scenery and a view of the Colorado River below. On your left as you face the canyon are the Orphan Mine and (below) a mine shaft and cable lines leading up to the rim. The Orphan Mine was operated briefly as a copper mine around the beginning of the 20th century. In the 1950s it was reopened as a uranium mine and closed again in the late '60s. It was one of the few profitable mines in the region.

⑳ Mohave Point (⊠ Hermit Rd., Grand Canyon) also has striking views of the Colorado River and of 5,401-foot Cheops Pyramid, the grayish rock formation behind Dana Butte. You can also see Granite and Salt Creek rapids from this spot.

㉒ Pima Point (⊠ Hermit Rd., Grand Canyon) provides a bird's-eye view of the Tonto Platform and the Tonto Trail, which wends its way through the canyon for more than 70 mi. Also to the west, two dark cone-shape mountains—Mount Trumbull and Mount Logan—are visible on clear days. They rise in stark contrast to the surrounding flat-top mesas and buttes. From here you can see the scars from Hermit Camp, which can be seen up close if you hike the Hermit Trail.

★ ⑱ The Powell Memorial (⊠ Hermit Rd., Grand Canyon), a large, granite monument, stands as a tribute to the first man to ride the wild rapids of the Colorado River through the canyon in 1869. John Wesley Powell measured, charted, and named many of the canyons and creeks along the river. It was here that the dedication ceremony for Grand Canyon National Park took place on April 3, 1920. The canyon layers are especially clear from this viewpoint, plus you can spot the Colorado River far below in Granite Gorge.

⑯ Trailview Overlook (⊠ Hermit Rd., Grand Canyon) provides a dramatic view of the Bright Angel and Plateau Point trails as they zigzag down the canyon. Across the canyon, in the deep gorge to the north, flows Bright Angel Creek, one of the permanent tributary streams of the Colorado River in the region. Toward the south is an unobstructed view of the distant San Francisco Peaks, Arizona's highest mountains (the tallest is 12,633 feet), as well as of Bill Williams Mountain (on the horizon) and Red Butte (about 15 mi south of the canyon rim).

Sports & the Outdoors

HIKING   The steep, 9-mi **Hermit Trail** beginning just west of Hermits Rest (8 mi west of Grand Canyon Village) is recommended for experienced long-distance hikers only. The trail descends from the trailhead at 6,640 feet to the Colorado River at 2,400 feet.

The route leads down to the Colorado River and has inspiring views of Hermit Gorge and the Redwall and Supai formations. Six miles from the trailhead are the ruins of Hermit Camp, which the Santa Fe Railroad ran as a tourist camp from 1911 until 1930. Hiking here requires a backcountry permit (see the Essentials section at the end of this chapter).

> **CAUTION**
>
> Day hikers on the Hermit Trail should not go past Santa Maria Springs at 4,880 feet. Also, for much of the year, no water is available along the way; ask a park ranger about the availability of water at Santa Maria Springs and Hermit Creek before you set out, but all water from these sources should be treated before drinking.

APPROACHING THE SOUTH RIM: WILLIAMS & TUSAYAN

As a result of the tremendous popularity of the Grand Canyon as a destination in itself, few visitors to this remote part of Arizona realize that there are other places to rest their heads than at the lodgings within the park boundaries. However, it can be much more relaxing to retreat to either Tusayan or Williams than it is to fight the crowds at the Canyon for lodging and dining facilities. Once purchased, the park pass is valid for seven days, and it allows you to bypass the regular traffic lines approaching the Grand Canyon on return visits. Tusayan offers less selection and style than the historic town of Williams, which sits on the shoulders of the Mother Road—Historic Route 66.

Williams

㉔ *30 mi west of Flagstaff on Interstate 40 and AZ 64. 55 mi south of Grand Canyon Village.*

At the turn of the 20th century, Williams was a rough-and-tumble town replete with saloons and bordellos. Today, it reflects a much milder side of the Wild West, with 2,900 residents and some 1,400 motel rooms. Wander along main street, named—like the town—after mountain man Bill Williams, and indulge in Route 66 nostalgia. There are antiques shops, cozy eateries, and the ever-present souvenir and T-shirt stores.

The town sits at 6,700 feet in the world's largest stand of ponderosa pines. Often considered just a jumping-off point for the Grand Canyon (it's only an hour away from the South Rim by car and a little more than two hours by train), Williams is temperate in summer, offers skiing in the winter, and is within minutes of seven mountain lakes.

 Children enjoy the **Grand Canyon Deer Farm,** a petting zoo with pygmy goats and deer, including fawns born every June, July, and August. Buffalo, pot-bellied pigs, pronghorn antelope, reindeer, and exotic birds are also in residence. ⊠ *6752 E. Deer Farm Rd., 8 mi east of Williams off I–40, Exit 171* ☎ *928/635–4073 or 800/926–3337* ⊕ *www.deerfarm.com*

Adults $7.50; ages 3–13 $4.25 ☉ *Mar.–May, Sept., and Oct., daily 9–6; June–Aug., daily 8–7; Nov.–Feb., daily 10–5, weather permitting.*

In 1989 service on the **Grand Canyon Railway** was reinaugurated along a route first established in 1901. The 65-mi trek from Williams Depot to the South Rim (2¼ hours each way) takes the vintage train through prairie, ranch, and national park land to the log-cabin train station in Grand Canyon Village. You won't see the Grand Canyon from the train, but you can walk or catch the shuttle at the Grand Canyon Railway Station. The ride includes refreshments, commentary, and corny but fun onboard entertainment by Wild West characters from the Cataract Creek Gang. Passengers ride in restored 1923 cars. Club Class, with its fully stocked mahogany bar and complimentary morning pastries and coffee, costs an additional $20. A First-Class ($60 upgrade), Deluxe Observation Dome, or Luxury Parlor Car ($85–$95 upgrade) ticket gets you Continental breakfast and complimentary afternoon champagne and snacks. Both Coach and Club Classes provide the basics, with padded benches to sit on and ceiling fans to keep you cool; the other three classes provide much more comfortable seating and air-conditioning. Your pet can stay at the Pet Resort while you ride the train.

Even if you don't take the train, it's worth visiting the **Williams Depot,** where the trains depart. It was built in 1908 to replace the terminal where the Williams Visitor Center now resides. Attractions at the depot include a passenger car and the locomotive of a turn-of-the-20th-century steam train, a gift shop where you can find bizarre souvenirs such as a tie that plays "I've Been Working on the Railroad," and Max and Thelma's, a full-service restaurant. A small **Railroad Museum** is next to the depot in the original dining room of the former Harvey House hotel. The museum holds a collection of old railroad and Harvey-girl photographs and is a good place to learn about the history of the Grand Canyon Railway, which once carried American presidents, Franklin D. Roosevelt among them, on their whistle-stop campaigns through the West. ⊠ *Williams Depot, 233 N. Grand Canyon Blvd. at Fray Marcos Blvd.* ☎ *800/843–8724 railway reservations and information* ⊕ *www.thetrain. com* ☞ *$60–$155 round-trip and $8 national park entrance fee* ☉ *Departs daily from Williams at 10 AM, from South Rim at 3:30 PM.*

Planes of Fame Museum. At the junction of U.S. Highway 180 and State Route 64 in Valle, thirty miles north of Williams, this satellite of the Air Museum Planes of Fame in Chino, California, is a good stop for those interested in airplanes. It chronicles the history of aviation with an array of historic and modern aircraft. One of the featured pieces is a C-121A Constellation "Bataan," the personal aircraft of General MacArthur used during the Korean War. Since the planes are in flying condition, visitors are not allowed inside the cockpits. ⊠ *755 Mustang Way, Valle* ☎ *928/635–1000* ⊕ *www.planesoffame.org* ☞ *$5.95* ☉ *Daily 9–5.*

The **Williams Visitor Center,** also housing the Williams–Grand Canyon Chamber of Commerce and National Forest Service office, is the former passenger-train depot, built in 1901. Its brick walls still show graffiti scrawled by early railroad workers and hobos. A small bookstore offers a selection of regional materials and an interactive exhibit on the history of the town and Route 66. ✉ *200 W. Railroad Ave., at Grand Canyon Blvd.* ☎ *928/635–1418 or 800/863–0546* ⊕ *www. williamschamber.com* ☼ *Daily 8–5 except June–Aug., daily 8–6:30.*

Sports & the Outdoors

BICYCLING Cyclists can enjoy the scenery along the abandoned sections of Route 66 on the Historic Route 66 Mountain Bike Tour. Maps of the tour, which include the 6-mi Ash Fork Hill Trail and the 5-mi Devil Dog Trail, are available at the Williams Visitor Center. You can rent a bike from **RIM to RIM Cyclery** (✉ 326 W. Rte. 66 ☎ 928/635–1117).

FISHING Fish for trout, crappie, catfish, and smallmouth bass at a number of lakes surrounding Williams. Anglers age 14 and older are required to obtain a fishing license from the **Arizona Game and Fish Department** (🖰 3500 S. Lake Mary Rd., Flagstaff 86001 ☎ 928/774–5045 or 866/462–0433 ⊕ www.gf.state.az.us) to fish on public land.

SKIING **Elk Ridge Ski and Outdoor Recreation** (✉ Off I–40 🖰 7596 Buckridge Dr., ☾ 86046 ☎ 928/234–6587 ⊕ www.elkridgeski.com) is usually open from mid-December through much of March, weather permitting. There are four groomed runs (including one for beginners), areas suitable for cross-country skiing, and a hill set aside for tubing. The lodge rents skis, snowboards, and inner tubes. From Williams, take South 4th Street for 2 mi, and then turn right at the sign and go another 1½ mi.

Where to Stay & Eat

★ $–$$ ✕ **Pancho McGillicuddy's.** Established in 1893 as the Cabinet Saloon, this restaurant is on the National Register of Historic Places. Gone are the spittoons and pipes—the smoke-free dining area now has Mexican-inspired decor and such specialties as "armadillo eggs," the local name for deep-fried jalapeños stuffed with cheese. Other favorites are the fish tacos, buzzard wings—better known as hot wings—and the pollo verde (chicken breasts smothered in a sauce of cheese, sour cream, and green chiles). The bar—on the smoking side of the restaurant—has TVs tuned to sporting events and pours more than 30 tequilas. ✉ *141 Railroad Ave.* ☎ *928/635–4150* ▭ *AE, D, MC, V.*

$–$$ ✕ **Rod's Steak House.** You can't miss this steak house with the plastic Angus cow out front. The emphasis here is on meat—sizzling mesquite-broiled steaks, prime rib, and the like. The local favorite is Rod's special steak, a hefty sirloin dipped in sugar and grilled over mesquite. Other specialties include chicken, ribs, and seafood. ✉ *301 E. Rte. 66* ☎ *928/635–2671* ▭ *D, MC, V* ☼ *Closed Sun.*

¢–$$ ✕ **Cruisers Café 66.** Talk about nostalgia. Imagine your favorite 1950s-style, high school hangout—with cocktail service. Good burgers, salads, and malts are family-priced, but a choice steak is available, too, for $30. The large mural of the town's heydey along the "Mother Road," stuffed buffalo, and historic cars out front make this a Route 66 favorite. Kids especially enjoy the relaxed atmosphere and the jukebox tunes. ✉ *233 W. Rte. 66* ☎ *928/635–2445* ▭ *AE, DC, MC, V.*

FodorsChoice ★

¢–$ ✕ **Pine Country Restaurant.** This spotless restaurant is across from the Grand Canyon Railway Depot. Owner Dee Seehorn serves home-

2

made pies and hearty meals such as country-fried steak and hamburgers. The crafts that make most of the decor are handmade by local artists and for sale. Try the fabulous fudge, in flavors from maple nut to vanilla chocolate caramel. Open daily at 5:30 AM, the restaurant serves breakfast, lunch, and dinner; for an extra 15%, they will deliver to any hotel in town. ⊠ *107 N. Grand Canyon Blvd.* ☎ *928/635–9718* ⊟ *AE, D, MC, V.*

¢ ✕ **Grand Canyon Coffee Café.** You'll find good espresso drinks here, along with wonderful sandwiches on homemade focaccia. The mountain man sandwich is piled-high roast beef with cheddar cheese and onions on Italian bread, or try the English-style fish and chips. ⊠ *125 W. Rte. 66* ☎ *928/635–1255* ⊟ *AE, MC, V* ✪ *Closed Jan. and Feb.*

¢ ✕ **Twisters.** Get your kicks on Route 66 at this old-fashioned soda fountain and gift shop. Dine on hamburgers and hot dogs, or get a famous Twisters sundae, a Route 66 Beer Float, or a cherry phosphate—all to the sounds of hip-shaking 1950s tunes. The adjoining gift shop is a blast from the past with Route 66 merchandise, classic Coca-Cola memorabilia, and fanciful items celebrating the careers of such characters as Betty Boop, James Dean, Elvis, and Marilyn Monroe. ⊠ *417 E. Rte. 66* ☎ *928/635–0266* ⊕ *www.route66place.com* ⊟ *AE, D, MC, V.*

★ $$–$$$ 🏨 **Sheridan House Inn.** Nestled among 2 acres of pine trees near Route 66, this B&B has outside decks looking to the tall ponderosa pines and a flagstone patio with a hot tub. Average-size bedrooms all have king beds and marble bathrooms. The game room has puzzles, board games, and VCRs, and the entertainment room has a pool table and piano. Hearty breakfasts that include scrambled eggs, fruit plates, bacon, sausage, and breakfast potatoes plus a specialty item such as eggs Benedict or buttermilk pancakes will ready you for the hour-long drive to the canyon. K. C. and Mary Seidner are gracious hosts who will gladly help guests plan itineraries. ⊠ *460 E. Sheridan Ave., 86046* ☎ *928/635–9441 or 888/635–9345* ⟿ *6 rooms, 2 suites* ♦ *Dining room, cable TV, Wi-Fi, in-room VCRs, hot tub, hiking; no a/c* ⊟ *AE, D, MC, V* ⎮◯⎮ *BP.*

★ $–$$$ 🏨 **Grand Canyon Railway Hotel.** This hotel was designed to resemble the train depot's original Fray Marcos lodge. Neoclassical Greek columns flank the grand entrance leading into a lobby with maple-wood balustrades, an enormous flagstone fireplace, and oil paintings of the Grand Canyon by local artist Kenneth McKenna. Original bronzes by Frederic Remington, from the private collection of hotel owners Max and Thelma Biegert, also adorn the lobby. The pleasant Southwestern-style accommodations have large bathrooms. Adjacent to the lobby is Spenser's, a pub with an ornate 19th-century hand-carved bar. ⊠ *235 N. Grand Canyon Blvd., 86046* ☎ *928/635–4010 or 800/843–8724* ⊕ *www.thetrain.com* ⟿ *287 rooms, 10 suites* ♦ *Cable TV, indoor pool, gym, hot tub, bar, meeting room, no-smoking rooms* ⊟ *AE, D, MC, V.*

$–$$ 🏨 **Mountainside Inn Gateway to the Grand Canyon.** At the east entrance to town, this basic motel has comfortable rooms, a good American restaurant called Miss Kitty's Steakhouse, and country-and-western bands in summer. ⊠ *642 E. Rte. 66, 86046* ☎ *928/635–4431 or 800/462–9381* ⊞ *928/635–2292* ⇨ *95 rooms, 1 suite* ♿ *Restaurant, cable TV, pool, hot tub* ⊟ *AE, D, MC, V.*

$–$$ 🏨 **Red Garter.** This restored 1897 saloon and bordello is now a small, antique-filled B&B. Guest rooms are on the second floor; the Best Gal's room has its own sitting room overlooking the train tracks. All four rooms (two are interior, with skylights but no windows) are very quiet, as the only train traffic is the Grand Canyon Railway, with one daily arrival and departure. Even if you don't stay here, the fresh pastries served in the first-floor coffee shop are worth a stop. ⊠ *137 W. Railroad Ave., 86046* ☎ *928/635–1484 or 800/328–1484* ⊕ *www.redgarter.com* ⇨ *4 rooms* ♿ *Coffee shop, Wi-Fi, in-room data ports; no kids under 8, no smoking* ⊟ *D, MC, V* ⟏⟍ *CP* ☉ *Closed Dec.–mid-Feb.*

⟁ $ 🏨 **Canyon Motel.** Rail cars, cabooses, and cottages make up this 13-acre property on the outskirts of Williams. The best room is the 1929 Santa Fe red caboose: it's family-friendly with two sides separated by a bathroom, giving parents a litle privacy. The original wooden floor and tool equipment add to the authenticity. The other caboose looks much like a standard hotel room inside, as do the flagstone cottage rooms built from the local sandstone known for its variegated colors. A Pullman passenger car holds three rooms (rail-car suites), each with its own bathroom. The motel also has a few dry (no water available) campsites and a 47-space RV park with full hookups, opened in 2006. ⊠ *1900 E. Rodeo Rd., 86046* ☎ *928/635–9371 or 800/482–3955* ⊞ *928/635–4138* ⊕ *www.thecanyonmotel.com* ⇨ *18 rooms, 5 rail-car suites* ♿ *BBQs, microwaves, refrigerators, cable TV, some in-room VCRs, indoor pool, hiking, horseshoes, playground; no a/c in some rooms, no room phones* ⊟ *D, MC, V* ⟏⟍ *CP.*

⟁ $ 🏨 **Quality Inn Mountain Ranch & Resort.** Seven miles east of town, off Exit 171, the warm lights and friendly staff of this motel beckon. Rooms are basic but include a full breakfast in the coffee shop, which has views of the San Francisco Peaks. In season, kick back on evening hay rides, with singing cowboys, staged gunfights, and a cookout. Horseback riding is available at **Mountain Ranch Stables** (928/635–0706). One hour is $30, two hours is $50, and half-day rides are $90. ⊠ *6701 E. Mountain Ranch Rd., 86046* ☎ *928/635–2693 or 866/687–2624* ⊞ *928/635–4188* ⊕ *www.mountainranchresort.com* ⇨ *73 rooms* ♿ *Restaurant, coffee shop, microwaves, refrigerators, cable TV, in-room VCRs, putting green, 2 tennis courts, pool, hot tub, horseback riding, horseshoes, volleyball, bar, some pets allowed (fee), no-smoking rooms* ⊟ *AE, D, MC, V* ☉ *Closed Nov.–Mar.* ⟏⟍ *BP.*

CAMPING Both developed and undeveloped campsites are available on a first-come, first-served basis in the **Kaibab National Forest** (☎ 928/635–4061 or 800/863–0546 ⊕ www.fs.fed.us/r3/kai), which surrounds Williams and extends to the Grand Canyon encompassing Cataract Lake, Kaibab Lake, Dogtown Lake, and White Horse Lake.

Shopping

Whether you're looking for Grand Canyon souvenirs, Western kitsch, or the best in Native American art and jewelry, you'll likely find it in

GRAND CANYON CAMPGROUNDS

	Total # of sites	# of RV sites	# of hook-ups	Drive-to sites	Hike-to sites	Flush toilets	Pit toilets	Drinking water	Showers	Fire grates/pits	Swimming	Boat access	Playground	Dump Station	Ranger Station	Public telephone	Reservation possible	Daily fee per site	Dates open
Inside the Park																			
Bright Angel	33	0	0		Y	Y		Y										Free	Y/R
Desert View	50	50	0	Y		Y		Y		Y					Y		Y	$12	mid-May–mid-Oct.
Indian Garden	15	0	0		Y		Y	Y								Y	Y	Free	Y/R
Mather	319	319	0	Y		Y		Y	Y	Y				Y	Y	Y	Y	$18	May–Oct.
North Rim	83	83	0	Y		Y		Y	Y	Y				Y	Y	Y	Y	$15–$20	May–Oct.
Near the Park																			
Demotte	46	46	0	Y			Y	Y	Y	Y					Y			$15–$20	May–Oct.
Grand Canyon Camper Village	250	200	200	Y		Y		Y	Y	Y			Y	Y	Y	Y	Y	$3	Y/R
Jacob Lake Campground	53	0	0	Y		Y		Y	Y	Y					Y		Y	$10–$20	Y/R
Kaibab Lodge Camper Village	130	80	70	Y			Y	Y	Y	Y				Y	Y		Y	$10–$20	May–Nov.
Ten X Campground	70	0	0	Y			Y	Y		Y								$10–$20	mid-Apr.–Sep.

Y/R = year-round

the shops on Historic Route 66. **The Pueblo Indian Gallery** (✉ 202 W. Rte. 66 ☎ 928/635–4966 ⊕ www.puebloindiangallery.com) is an upscale gallery that offers authentic Native American jewelry as well as Indian arts. The cheery **Rustic Raspberry** (✉ 309 W. Rte. 66 ☎ 928/635–3024) has a homey, spicy smell along with country crafts for sale.

Tusayan

㉕ *48 mi north of Williams on AZ 64/U.S. 180, 7 mi south of Grand Canyon Village*

Tusayan, the gateway to the South Entrance of the national park, is 7 mi from Grand Canyon Village on the South Rim. Here you'll find basic amenities, including restaurants and motels, several stores, and an airport that serves as a starting point for airplane and helicopter tours of the canyon.

☺ At the **National Geographic Visitor Center Grand Canyon** you can watch river runners battle rapids, experience the Grand Canyon from the air, and discover the canyon's natural history in the half-hour film *Grand Canyon—The Hidden Secrets*, on a screen that stands six stories high. At the theater, you'll also find an **Arizona Tourist Information Center**, where you can schedule and purchase air tours and daily Colorado River trips. You can save time by purchasing a pass to Grand Canyon National Park here; it will grant access to the park by special entry lanes. ✉ *AZ 64/U.S. 180* ☎ *928/638–2203 or 928/638–2468* ⊕ *www.explorethecanyon.com* ☞ *$10* ☉ *Mar.–Oct., daily 8:30–8:30; Nov.–Feb., daily 10:30–6:30; shows every hr on the ½ hr.*

> If the kids—or you—can't live without fast food you better stop here, in Tusayan. None of the fast food chains have restaurants in Grand Canyon National Park.

Sports & the Outdoors

BICYCLING Pedal the depths of the Kaibab National Forest on the **Tusayan Bike Trail** (✉ Tusayan Ranger District, Tusayan ☎ 928/638–2443). Following linked loop trails at an elevation of 6,750 feet, you can bike as few as 3 mi or as many as 32 mi round-trip along old logging roads, through ponderosa pine forest. Keep an eye out for elk, mule deer, hawks, eagles, pronghorn antelope, turkeys, coyote, and porcupines. Open for biking from March through October, the trail is accessed on the west side of AZ 64 between Tusayan and the Moqui Lodge.

HORSEBACK RIDING You can rent horses at the **Apache Stables** (✉ AZ 64/U.S. 180 ☎ 928/638–2891 ⊕ www.apachestables.com) for $30.50 an hour or $55.50 for a two-hour guided tour of the Kaibab National Forest. A four-hour ride through Long Jim Canyon ($95.50) will take you through rugged canyon country to the viewpoint on the rim. The stables open in March, and rides are offered, weather permitting, through November.

Where to Stay & Eat

$$–$$$ ✕ **Canyon Star.** Relax in the rustic dining room at the Grand Hotel for breakfast, lunch, or dinner. The dinner menu includes prime rib, steak, and salmon, and some evenings there's live entertainment or Indian dance

performances. In the summer, be sure to reserve a table. ⊠ *AZ 64/U.S. 180* ☎ *928/638–3333* ⊟ *AE, DC, MC, V.*

$$–$$$ ✕ **The Coronado Room.** When pizza and burgers just won't do, the restaurant at the Best Western Grand Canyon Squire Inn is the best upscale choice in Tusayan. The menu encompasses everything from escargots to elk steak. Even though the Coronado Room takes pride in its fine-dining atmosphere, dress is casual and comfortable. Reservations are usually a good idea, particularly in the busy season. ⊠ *AZ 64/U.S. 180* ☎ *928/638–2681* ⊟ *AE, D, DC, MC, V* ⊘ *No lunch.*

¢–$$ ✕ **Café Tusayan.** Homemade pies and local microbrews from Sedona, Flagstaff, and Tucson brighten the menu of standard fare—salads, burgers, pastas, and prime rib—at this basic restaurant. Locals swear by the Café Tusayan omelet with pine nuts. ⊠ *AZ 64/U.S. 180* ☎ *928/638–2151* ⊟ *MC, V.*

★ $$ ▦ **The Grand Hotel.** At the south end of Tusayan, this popular hotel has bright, clean rooms decorated in Southwestern colors. The lobby has a stone-and-timber design, and cozy seating areas. Good steaks, Mexican fare, and barbecue are on the restaurant's menu, and a Starbucks in the lobby is a bonus. At the bar, you can sit on a saddle that was once used for the canyon mule trips. Don't miss the well-stocked, reasonably priced gift shop, and keep in mind that most of the photos displayed in the lobby are for sale. ⊠ *AZ 64/U.S. 180* ☎ *Box 3319, Grand Canyon 86023* ☎ *928/638–3333* ☒ *928/638–3131* ⊕ *www.grandcanyongrandhotel.com* ⇌ *119 rooms, 2 suites* ☖ *Restaurant, cable TV, in-room broadband, Wi-Fi, indoor pool, gym, hot tub, laundry facilities, bar, meeting rooms, some pets allowed (fee), no-smoking rooms* ⊟ *AE, DC, MC, V.*

$$ ▦ **Red Feather Lodge.** This motel and adjacent hotel are a good value, with an outdoor pool and seasonal hot tub. All rooms were remodeled in 2005, with a Southwestern theme in the large rooms. The lodge's Café Tusayan serves standard American food. The motel portion of the lodge is closed January through March, except to guests with pets and smokers. ⊠ *AZ 64/U.S. 180* ☎ *Box 1460, Grand Canyon 86023* ☎ *928/638–2414 or 800/538–2345* ☒ *928/638–9216* ⊕ *www.redfeatherlodge.com* ⇌ *212 rooms, 1 suite* ☖ *Restaurant, cable TV with movies and video games, pool, gym, hot tub, Internet room, pets (fee), no-smoking rooms* ⊟ *AE, D, DC, MC, V* ⊙ *CP.*

★ ☺ $–$$ ▦ **Best Western Grand Canyon Squire Inn.** About 2 mi south of the park's South Entrance, this motel lacks the historic charm of the older lodges at the canyon rim, but has more amenities, including a small cowboy museum in the lobby and an upscale gift shop. Children enjoy the bowling alley, arcade, and outdoor swimming pool. Rooms are spacious and furnished in Southwestern style. Those in the rear have a view of the woods. The Coronado Dining Room has an adventurous menu and good service. ⊠ *AZ 64/U.S. 180* ☎ *Box 130, Grand Canyon 86023* ☎ *928/638–2681 or 800/622–6966* ☒ *928/638–2782* ⊕ *www.grandcanyonsquire.com* ⇌ *250 rooms, 4 suites* ☖ *Restaurant, coffee shop, cable TV, pool, gym, hair salon, hot tub, sauna, billiards, bowling, bar, some in-room broadband, some in-room data ports, some*

Wi-Fi, video game room, laundry facilities, concierge, meeting rooms, travel services, no-smoking rooms ⊟ *AE, D, DC, MC, V.*

☾ **$–$$** ⊞ **Holiday Inn Express Hotel and Suites.** The main building of this hotel at the south end of Tusayan has most of the rooms, which are modern but plain and lower priced. The more expensive and more comfortable rooms are the Arizona Rooms, an adjacent all-suites annex, which has Western-theme suites with separate sitting rooms, coffeemakers, and VCRs. Kids Suites cater to families, with bunk beds and PlayStation games. ⊠ *AZ 64/U.S. 180* ✆ *Box 3251, Grand Canyon 86023* ☎ *928/638-3000 or 888/538-5353* 🖷*928/638-0123* ⊕*www.grandcanyon.hiexpress. com* ☞ *164 rooms, 30 suites* ᗑ *Some microwaves, some refrigerators, cable TV, some in-room VCRs, in-room broadband, indoor pool, hot tub, business services* ⊟ *AE, MC, V.*

CAMPING ᗒ **Grand Canyon Camper Village and RV Park.** More a city than a village, this popular RV park and campground has 200 utility hookups
¢ and 50 tent sites. Hookups run $39 for electric, $46 for water and electric, and $50 for full. Tent sites are $22. Reservations are a good idea during the busy spring and summer seasons. ⊠ *Off AZ 64/U.S. 180, Grand Canyon* ✆ *Box 490, 86023* ☎ *928/638-2887* ▧ *$18–$26* ☞ *200 full hookups, 50 tent sites* ᗑ *Flush toilets, full hookups, dump station, drinking water, showers, picnic tables, general store, play area* ☉ *Open Mar.–Nov.*

¢ ᗒ **Ten X Campground.** Two miles south of Tusayan, this campground offers 70 sites with water and pit toilets but no electrical hookups or showers. Campsites are first-come, first served with no reservations. Reservations are required for the two large groups sites. Unlike campgrounds in the Grand Canyon National Park itself, campfires are allowed. Learn about the surrounding ponderosa pine forest on a self-guided nature trail or check out one of the evening, ranger-led weekend programs. ⊠ *Kaibab National Forest, 9 mi south of Grand Canyon National Park east of AZ 64/U.S. 180* ✆ *Tusayan Ranger District, Box 3088, Grand Canyon 86023* ☎ *928/638-2443* ⊕ *www. fs.fed.us/r3/kai* ▧ *$10* ☞ *70 tent sites, 2 group sites* ᗑ *Grills, pit toilets, drinking water, fire pits, picnic tables* ᗒ *Reservations not accepted* ☉ *Open mid-Apr.–Sept.*

GRAND CANYON: THE WEST RIM

West of Grand Canyon National Park, the tribal lands of the Hualapai and the Havasupai lie on the West Rim of the Canyon.

The Hualapai tribe has been attempting to foster tourism to the little known West Rim, where a road travels through their reservation lands down to the Colorado River. This is a launch point for the region's river runners but because few others know about the road, traffic is a rarity.

Some 12,000 people a year hike, ride, or fly deep into the Grand Canyon to visit the more well-known Havasupai, the "people of the blue green waters." Dubbed the "Shangri-la of the Grand Canyon," the remote, inaccessible Indian reservation includes some of the world's most beautiful and famous waterfalls, together with streams and pools tinted a mystical blue green by dissolved travertine.

The Hualapai Tribe & Grand Canyon West

㉖ *78 mi west of Williams via Interstate 40 and AZ 66.*

The Hualapai Tribe is expanding its tourism offerings on the West Rim, but you still won't be shoulder to shoulder with other visitors. Hualapai guides add Native American perspective to a canyon trip that you won't find on North and South Rim tours. **Diamond Creek Road,** directly north of the Hualapai Lodge in Peach Springs, is the access point for adventures in this developing section of the Grand Canyon, and winds past Diamond Peak to the Colorado River above Diamond Creek Rapid. The road is at river mile 226, which is 138 mi downstream from Phantom Ranch (as the crow flies the distance is about half of that). Diamond Creek Road can be braved by high clearance passenger vehicles, but your best bet is four-wheel-drive, especially in summer when storms are common.

The Hualapai Tribe requires visitors to obtain permits to travel on tribal lands. No permit is required to drive to the West Rim if you take a tour while there. ⊠ *Hualapai Tourist Information, Peach Springs 86434* ☎ *928/769–2230 or 888/255–9550* ⊕ *www.grandcanyonresort. com* ⊠ *$15–$17* ☉ *Daily.*

Sports & the Outdoors

TOURS Shuttle bus, helicopter, boat trips, and food are available at the West Rim, but there's no hotel since all water has to be trucked in. Visitors aren't allowed to travel in their own vehicles once they reach the West Rim, but must purchase tour packages on **Grand Canyon West Tours** (⊠ 887 Rte. 66, Peach Springs 86434 ☎ 928/769–2230 or 888/255–9550 ⊕ www. grandcanyonresort.com) shuttle buses ($29–$109). For an extra $149 you can add a helicopter trip into the canyon or a boat trip on the Colorado. Depending on the package you purchase, Hualapai guides will take you to canyon viewpoints (Quarter Master, Eagle Point, and Guano Point) and Hualapai Ranch (western town) or the Indian Village. The tour includes a barbecue lunch.

> ### COMING FROM VEGAS
>
> Perhaps the easiest way to visit the West Rim from Vegas is with a tour. The 14-mi, dirt access road is rough, and high-clearance vehicles are a necessity, but **Bighorn Wild West Tours** (702/385-4676 or 888/385-4676) will pick you up in a Hummer at your Las Vegas hotel for an all-day trip that includes the $49 shuttle-bus package and lunch. Trips cost $239.

RAFTING One-day river trips are offered by the Hualapai tribe through the **Hualapai River Runners** (⊠ 887 Rte. 66, Peach Springs 86434 ☎ 928/769–2230 or 888/255–9550 ⊕ www.grandcanyonresort.com) from March through October. The trips, which cost $290 (plus 7% tax) paid in advance, leave from the Hualapai Lodge at 8 AM and return between 6:30 and 8:30

PM. Lunch, snacks, and beverages are provided. Children must be eight or older to take the trip, which runs several rapids with the most difficult rated as Class V or VI, depending on the river flow.

Where to Stay & Eat

¢–$ ✕⊡ **Hualapai Lodge.** Located at Peach Springs, the hotel has a comfortable lobby with a large fireplace that is welcoming on chilly nights. The rooms are clean, but basic. The Diamond Creek Café offers standard American fare, including hamburgers and sandwiches along with specialties such as Hualapai tacos, which are worth a stop on their own. ⊠ *900 Rte. 66, Peach Springs 86434* ☎ *928/769–2230 or 888/255–9550* ⊕ *www.grandcanyonresort.com* ⟿ *55 rooms* ⚭ *Restaurant, cable TV, saltwater pool, gym, spa, shop, laundry facilities, no-smoking rooms* ⊟ *AE, D, MC, V.*

CAMPING The Hualapai permit camping on their tribal lands at Diamond Creek. An overnight camping permit is $20 per person per night and can be purchased at the **Hualapai Lodge** (⊠ 900 Rte. 66, Peach Springs 86434 ☎ 928/769–2230 or 888/255–9550). Camping on the beach of the Colorado is accessed by Diamond Creek Road. The camping area is primitive with only a picnic table and pit toilets. No fires are allowed but grills may be used.

The Havasupai Tribe & Havasu Canyon

➋⓻ *141 mi from Williams (to head of Hualapai Trail), west on Interstate 40 and AZ 66, north on Indian Hwy. 18. Note: last gas is at junction of AZ 66 and Indian Hwy. 18.*

Havasu Canyon, south of the middle part of the national park and away from the crowds, is the home of the Havasupai, a tribe that has lived in this isolated area for centuries. Their name means "people of the blue green waters," and you'll know why when you see the canyon's waterfalls, as high as 200 feet, cascading over red cliffs into travertine pools surrounded by thick foliage and sheltering trees.

The striking falls, plunging into deep turquoise pools, seem like something from Hawaii or Shangri La. The travertine in the water coats the walls and lines the pools with bizarre, drip-castle rock formations. Centuries of accumulated travertine formations in some of the most popular pools were washed out in massive flooding decades ago, de-

WORD OF MOUTH

"Havasu Falls is without a doubt one of the most breathtaking sights I've experienced. The turquoise colored water, which is warm year round, cascading over the travertine walls is otherworldly. Sometimes the ponies (I don't know if they are wild or not) will come up to the pool at the base of the falls to drink. The pool is the perfect swimming hole. The ribbon that is Mooney Falls is almost as breath-taking. Climbing down through the travertine cave to get to the bottom of Mooney Falls is scary and exciting at the same time."   –KEITH

stroying some of the otherworldly scenes pictured in older photos but the place is still magical.

The 500 tribal members now live in the village of Supai, accessible only down the 8-mi-long **Hualapai Trail,** which drops 3,000 feet. The quiet and private Havasupai mostly remain apart from the modest flow of tourists, which nevertheless plays a vital role in the tribal economy.

To reach Havasu's waterfalls, you must hike downstream from the village of Supai. The first fall, 1½ mi from Supai, is the 75-foot-high **Navajo Falls,** named after a 19th-century Havasupai chief who was abducted as a child and raised by the Navajo until he eventually discovered his origin and returned to his tribe as an adult. Navajo Falls rushes over red-wall limestone and collects in a beautiful blue-green pool perfect for swimming. Not much farther downstream, the striking **Havasu Falls** dashes over a ledge into another pool of refreshing 70°F water. The last of the enchanting waterfalls is **Mooney Falls,** 2 mi down from Navajo Falls. Mooney Falls, named after a prospector who fell to his death here in 1880, plummets 196 feet down a sheer travertine cliff. The hike down to the pool below is a steep descent down slippery rocks with only the assistance of chains suspended along a series of iron stakes.

The Havasupai restrict the number of visitors to the canyon; you must have reservations. They ask that hikers call ahead before taking the trek into the canyon. Hualapai Trail leaves from Hualapai Hilltop, 63 mi north on Indian Route 18 from Route 66. From an elevation of 5,200 feet, the trail travels down a moderate grade to Supai village at 3,200 feet. Bring plenty of water and avoid hiking during the middle of the day, when canyon temperatures can reach into the 100s. If you'd rather ride, you can rent a horse for the trip down for $150 round-trip, or $75 one-way. Riders must be able to mount and dismount by themselves; be at least 4 feet, 7 inches; and weigh less than 250 pounds. Reservations must be made at least six weeks in advance with Havasupai Tourist Enterprise, which requires a 50% deposit. You'll need to spend the night if you're hiking or riding.

Another option is a helicopter ride into the canyon with **Air West Helicopters** (☎ 623/516–2790). Flights leave from Hualapai Hilltop and cost $85 per person each way. They do not accept reservations.

There's a $30 entrance fee for visiting the Havasupai tribal lands. You're expected to respect the land and its people. The tribe does not allow alcohol, drugs, pets, or weapons. ⊠ *Havasupai Tourist Enterprise, Supai 86435* ☎ *928/448–2141 general information, 928/448–2111 lodging reservations* ⊕ *www.havasupaitribe.com.*

Where to Stay & Eat

$$ ✕▥ **Havasupai Lodge.** These are fairly spartan accommodations, but you won't notice it too much when you see all of the natural beauty surrounding you. The lodge and restaurant are at the bottom of Havasu Canyon and are operated by the Havasupai tribe. The restaurant serves three meals a day, mostly sandwiches and fast-food-type fare, and a daily special. In addition to the room rate, there's a $30 per-person tribal entry

fee. ⊠ *Supai 86435* ☎ *928/448–2111 or 928/448–2201* ⊕ *www.
havasupaitribe.com* ↩ *24 rooms* ⚲ *Restaurant; no room phones, no
room TVs, no smoking* ⊟ *MC, V.*

CAMPING   For information about camping in Havasu Canyon, call the **Havasupai
Tourist Enterprise** (☎ 928/448–2141). You can stay in the primitive campgrounds for $12 (plus 8% tax) per person per night, in addition to the
$30 entry fee.

GRAND CANYON NATIONAL PARK: THE NORTH RIM

The North Rim, within the 14,000-square-mi Arizona Strip, draws only
about 10% of the Grand Canyon's visitors but is, many believe, more
gorgeous than the South Rim. At 1,000 feet higher than the South Rim,
the northern edge offers a more stretched out view of the buttes and
ridges scattered though the wide expanse cut by the Colorado River
millions of years ago. Because of its remote location, the North Rim
provides a more intimate and unhurried experience than the South Rim.
However, the North Rim is closed during the long, hard winter. The
8,000-foot elevation, which keeps things cool in summer, is arduous
in winter.

Author Edward Abbey once wrote: "I find that in contemplating the
natural world my pleasure is greater if there are not too many others
contemplating it with me, at the same time." The North Rim will give
you that opportunity.

HOURS   The North Rim is open mid-May through mid-October, depending on
the weather. AZ 67 from Jacob Lake is often closed due to snowfall from
mid-October to mid-May, and during these times all facilities at the North
Rim are closed.

The entrance gates are open 24 hours but are generally staffed from about
7 AM to 7 PM. If you arrive when there's no one at the gate, you may
enter legally without paying.

ADMISSION FEES   A fee of $20 per vehicle (regardless of the number of passengers) is col-
lected as you enter the North Entrance. Those on foot, bicycle, or mo-
torcycle pay $10 per person. In all cases, this fee is for one week's
access to the entire park.

The North Rim

Fodor's Choice   *44 mi south of Jacob Lake on AZ 67.*
★

Unlike the tourist-driven South Rim, the north side only offers one historic lodge and restaurant and a single campground. The easily accessible Bright Angel Point offers a wonderful view of the canyon. In the
fall, the aspens turn a beautiful gold adding even more color to an already magnificent scene. You can drive to three different, developed viewpoints. Point Imperial and Cape Royal await at the end of a winding,
scenic drive—with several stops along the way, the trip can easily con-

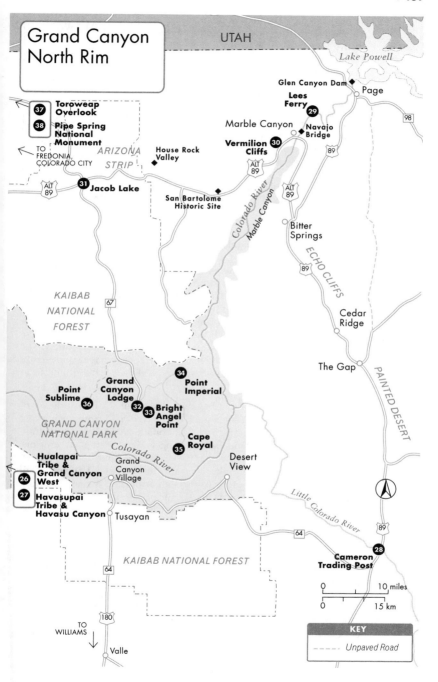

Grand Canyon North Rim

UTAH

Lake Powell

Glen Canyon Dam ◆ Page

Lees Ferry

Marble Canyon

29

Navajo Bridge

98

37 **Toroweap Overlook**

38 **Pipe Spring National Monument**

Vermilion Cliffs **30**

ALT 89

ARIZONA

House Rock Valley

TO FREDONIA, COLORADO CITY

STRIP

ALT 89

Colorado River

Marble Canyon

ALT 89

31 **Jacob Lake**

San Bartolome Historic Site

Bitter Springs

89

ECHO CLIFFS

KAIBAB NATIONAL FOREST

67

Cedar Ridge

The Gap

PAINTED DESERT

34

Point Imperial

Point Sublime 36

Grand Canyon Lodge

32 33 **Bright Angel Point**

GRAND CANYON NATIONAL PARK

Cape Royal

35

Colorado River

Desert View

Hualapai Tribe & Grand Canyon West

26

27

Havasupai Tribe & Havasu Canyon

Grand Canyon Village

Little Colorado River

89

Tusayan

KAIBAB NATIONAL FOREST

64

64

Cameron Trading Post 28

0 ——— 10 miles

0 ——— 15 km

180

TO WILLIAMS

Valle

KEY
- - - - *Unpaved Road*

sume half a day. The highest point on the North Rim at 8,800 feet, Point Imperial overlooks the Painted Desert to the east and dramatic views of the Grand Canyon. Cape Royal, a popular sunset destination, showcases the jagged landscape within the canyon. At this viewpoint, you'll also get a glimpse of the Colorado River, which is framed by a natural stone arch whimsically called the Angels Window. The third developed viewpoint, Point Sublime, requires four-wheel drive and half a day of effort, but in return has some of the best views in the canyon.

★ ㉝ The trail to **Bright Angel Point** (⊠ North Rim Dr., Grand Canyon), one of the most awe-inspiring overlooks on either rim,

---

MORE TOP SPOTS FOR A PICNIC

- **Point Imperial:** This picnic area offers both shade and some privacy and is 11 mi northeast of the North Rim Visitor Center.

- **Cape Royal:** Because of its panoramic views, this area 23 mi south of the North Rim Visitor Center is the most popular designated picnic area on the North Rim.

- **North Rim Visitor Center:** Often crowded with tourists who have just arrived at the park, this area is at the end of Rte. 67, 10 mi south of the North Entrance.

---

starts on the grounds of the Grand Canyon Lodge and runs along the crest of a point of rocks that juts into the canyon for several hundred yards. The walk is only ½ mi round-trip, but it's an exciting trek accented by sheer drops on each side of the trail. In a few spots where the route is extremely narrow, metal railings ensure visitors' safety. The temptation to clamber out to precarious perches to have your picture taken could get you killed. Every year several people die from falls at the Grand Canyon.

★ ㉟ **Cape Royal** (⊠ AZ 67, Grand Canyon) is about 23 mi southeast of Grand Canyon Lodge. A short walk on a paved road from the parking lot leads to this southernmost viewpoint on the North Rim. In addition to a large slice of the Grand Canyon, Angels Window, a giant, erosion-formed hole, can be seen through the projecting ridge of Cape Royal. At Angels Window Overlook, ⅓ mi north of here, **Cliff Springs Trail** starts its 1-mi route (round-trip) through a forested ravine. The trail, narrow and precarious in spots, passes ancient dwellings, winds beneath a limestone overhang, and terminates at Cliff Springs, where the forest opens on another impressive view of the canyon walls.

㉜ **Grand Canyon Lodge** (⊠ AZ 67, Grand Canyon) is literally at the end of the road. Built in 1928 by the Union Pacific Railroad, the massive stone structure is listed on the National Register of Historic Places. Its huge sunroom has hardwood floors, high-beam ceilings, and a marvelous view of the canyon through plate-glass windows. On warm days visitors sit in the sun and drink in the surrounding beauty at a spacious outdoor viewing deck, where National Park Service employees deliver free lectures on geology and history. Lunch, dinner, or a snack in the lodge's rock-and-log dining room is an integral part of

2

the North Rim experience; the food is good and reasonably priced. If you don't want a full meal, just buy a soda at Pizza Place or a drink at the saloon and sit out on the west veranda to watch the sun set over the canyon.

The **Transept Trail** (⊠ AZ 67, Grand Canyon) begins near the corner of the Grand Canyon Lodge's east patio. This 3-mi (round-trip) trail stays near the rim before plunging into the forest, ending at the North Rim Campground and General Store, 1½ mi from the lodge. The trail is well maintained and easy walking. Check the posted schedules to find the time for the "Ranger Talk" along this trail.

Eleven miles northeast of Grand Canyon Lodge is one of the North Rim's most popular lookouts, **Point Imperial** (⊠ AZ 67, Grand Canyon), the highest vista point (elevation 8,803 feet) at either rim, offering magnificent views of both the canyon and the distant country: the Vermilion Cliffs to the north, the 10,000-foot Navajo Mountain to the northeast in Utah, the Painted Desert to the east, and the Little Colorado River canyon to the southeast.

Fodor'sChoice
★

Talk about solitude. There's plenty at **Point Sublime** (⊠ North Rim Dr., Grand Canyon), where you can camp within feet of the canyon's edge. Sunrises and sunsets are spectacular. The winding road, through gorgeous high country, to Point Sublime is only 17 mi, but it will take at least an hour. It's intended only for vehicles with high-road clearance (pickups and four-wheel-drive vehicles) that are properly equipped for wilderness road travel. Check with a park ranger or at the information desk at Grand Canyon Lodge before taking this journey. You need a permit from the Backcountry Office at the park-ranger station to camp here.

Sports & the Outdoors

BICYCLING   The **Rainbow Rim Trail** (☎ 928/635–4061 or 800/863–0546 ⊕ www. fs.fed.us/r3/kai) is an 18-mi, one-way trail that begins at Parissawamitts. It travels past four other fantastic viewpoints—Fence, Locust, North Timp, and Timp—winding through a ponderosa pine forest and up and down through side canyons, aspen groves, and pristine meadows. The trail's elevation of 7,550 feet doesn't vary more than 200 feet along the way. The Rainbow Rim Trail is in the **Kaibab National Forest.**

HIKING   **Cliff Springs Trail** is an easy 1-mi North Rim walk near Cape Royal. The trailhead begins across from Angels Window Overlook and descends through a forested ravine. Narrow and precarious in spots, the trail passes ancient dwellings, winds beneath a limestone overhang, and terminates at the boulder-protected Cliff Springs.

Ken Patrick Trail begins at a trailhead on the east side of the North Kaibab trailhead parking lot. It travels 10 mi from the trailhead at 8,250 feet to Point Imperial at 8,803 feet. There's no water on this primitive trail, which crosses drainages and occasionally detours around fallen trees. But the trip is worth it—with the views at the highest point on either rim at the end of the road.

The trailhead to **North Kaibab Trail** is about 2 mi north of the Grand Canyon Lodge. Only open from May through October, the trail begins at 8,250 feet and travels down to the Colorado River at 2,400 feet. This is a long, steep hike that drops 5,850 feet over a distance of 14½ mi and is recommended for experienced hikers only. The National Park Service recommends that day hikers not go any farther than Roaring Springs (5,020 feet) before turning to hike back up out of the canyon. Cottonwood Campground (4,080 feet) has drinking water in summer, restrooms, shade trees, and a ranger. Like Bright Angel and South Kaibab trails, this one also leads to Phantom Ranch.

Transept Trail is a popular 1½-mi trail that starts near Grand Canyon Lodge, ducks through dense forests, and emerges on the rim to a dramatic view of a large stream through Bright Angel Canyon. The trail has little elevation change. The well-marked route leads to a side canyon called Transept Canyon, which geologist Clarence Dutton named in 1882—announcing that it was "far grander than Yosemite."

Uncle Jim Trail is a 5-mi loop trail that starts at the Ken Patrick trailhead and winds south through the forest past Roaring Springs Canyon and Bright Angel Canyon. The highlight of this easy rim hike is Uncle Jim Point, which overlooks the upper sections of the North Kaibab Trail.

Round-trip, **Widforss Trail** is 9⁹⁄₁₀ mi with an elevation change of 200 feet, unusually great for a rim hike. The trailhead, at 8,100 feet, is across from the North Kaibab Trail parking lot. The trail passes through shady forests of pine, spruce, fir, and aspen on its way to Widforss Point, at 7,900 feet. You're likely to see wildflowers in summer, and this is the best trail on the North Rim for viewing fall foliage. It is named in honor of Gunnar M. Widforss, an artist renowned for his paintings of National Park landscapes.

MULE RIDES **Canyon Trail Rides** (☎ 435/679–8665 ⊕ www.canyonrides.com) conducts short mule rides suitable for children on the easier trails along the North Rim. A one-hour ride, available to those seven and older, runs about $30. Half-day trips on the rim or into the canyon (minimum age 10) cost $55; full-day trips (minimum age 12), which include lunch and water, go for $105. These excursions are popular, so make reservations in advance. Rides are available daily from May 15 to October 15.

Where to Stay & Eat

$–$$ ✕⌂ **Grand Canyon Lodge.** This historic property, constructed mainly in
Fodor'sChoice the 1920s and '30s, is the premier lodging facility in the North Rim area.
★ The main building has limestone walls and timbered ceilings. Lodging options include small, rustic cabins; larger cabins (some with a canyon view and some with two bedrooms); and newer, traditional motel rooms. You might find marinated pork kebabs or linguine with cilantro on the dining room's dinner menu ($$). Dining room reservations are essential and should be made as far in advance as possible. ⊠ *AZ 67, North Rim, Grand Canyon National Park 86052* ☎ *303/297–2757 reserva-*

2

tions only, 928/638–2611 direct to hotel, no reservations ⌨ 303/297–3175 reservations only ⊕ www.grandcanyonnorthrim.com ⬅ 44 rooms, 157 cabins ♿ Cafeteria, dining room, bar, shop, laundry facilities; no a/c, no room TVs, no smoking ▭ AE, D, MC, V ⊘ Closed mid-Oct.–mid-May.

CAMPING

¢ **North Rim Campground.** The only designated campground at the North Rim of Grand Canyon National Park, 3 mi north of the rim, has 83 RV and tent sites (no hookups) for $15 per day. You can reserve a site up to five months in advance. *⊠ AZ 67, Grand Canyon ⬁ National Park Reservation Service, Box 1600, Cumberland, MD 21501 ☎ 800/365–2267 ⊕ reservations.nps.gov/index.cfm ⬈ $18–$25 Golden Age or Golden Access pay ½ price ⬅ 83 campsites ♿ Flush toilets, dump station, drinking water, guest laundry, showers, fire grates, picnic tables, general store ⬀ Reservations essential ⊘ Open mid-May–mid-Oct.*

APPROACHING THE NORTH RIM: LEES FERRY & JACOB LAKE

John Wesley Powell, the one-armed Civil War veteran who first explored the depths of the Grand Canyon on the Colorado River, wrote: "Mountains of music swell in the river, hills of music billow in the creek . . . while other melodies are heard in the gorges of the lateral canyons. The Grand Canyon is a land of song."

This land of song has one vital crossing point—Lees Ferry. There isn't another crossing point until you reach river mile 226 at Diamond Creek on the West Rim. Lees Ferry, the junction of several canyons just 15 mi below Glen Canyon dam, has for thousands of years offered one of the best places to cross the deep gash of the Grand Canyon. Today, the town, the Lonely Dell Ranch Historic District, a small, sad cemetery, and a scattering of historic buildings offer a glimpse of frontier life. But most people journey to Lees Ferry to get onto the river. Commercial raft trips take off from the boat ramps, and fly-fishing guides regularly shuttle people upstream to the base of Glen Canyon dam.

The tiny town of Jacob Lake, nestled high in pine country at an elevation of 7,925 feet, was named after the Mormon explorer Jacob Hamblin, who was also known as the "Buckskin Missionary." Jacob Lake is mostly just an en route point for visitors heading to the North Rim, but the lush mountain countryside is worth a day or two of exploration.

Cameron Trading Post

28 *53 mi north of Flagstaff on U.S. 89, 57 mi east of Grand Canyon Village on AZ 64.*

If you're heading to the Eastern Entrance on the South Rim or to the North Rim via U.S. 89 from Flagstaff and points south, **Cameron Trading Post** on the Navajo Indian Reservation is a worthwhile stop along the way. Most of the jewelry, rugs, baskets, and pottery sold here are made by Navajo and Hopi artisans, but some are created by New Mexico's Zuni and Pueblo Indians. Come armed with knowledge of Native American artisanship if you're looking at high-ticket items, some of which are sold at a separate gallery. Also at the post are a restaurant, cafeteria, grocery store, butcher shop, and post office. An outlet of the **Navajo Arts and Crafts Enterprises** (⊠ AZ 64/U.S. 89 ☎ 928/679–2244) stocks authentic Navajo products.

> ### WORD OF MOUTH
>
> "We left Grand Canyon via the east exit and headed into [the] Painted Desert. Stopped at Cameron Trading post for lunch and shopping. Excellent value. Try the Navajo taco. I loved it. [I am]now a big fan of Navajo fry bread."
>
> –teegeezfun

Where to Stay & Eat

$$$ ✕🖼 **Cameron Trading Post.** Fifty-four miles north of Flagstaff, this trad-
Fodor'sChoice ing post dates back to 1916. Southwestern-style rooms have carved-oak
★ furniture, tile baths, and balconies overlooking the Colorado River. Native-stone landscaping—including fossilized dinosaur tracks—and a small, well-kept garden are pleasant. Make your reservations far in advance for high season. The dining room's (¢–$$) delicious homemade green chili and fry bread, Navajo tacos, and hamburgers are alone worth the stop. ⊠ *U.S. 89* ⓓ *Box 339, Cameron 86020* ☎ *928/679–2231, 800/338–7385 Ext. 414* 🖶 *928/679–2350* ⊕ *www.camerontradingpost.com* ➪ *62 rooms, 4 suites* ⌂ *Restaurant, cafeteria, grocery, cable TV* ▤ *AE, DC, MC, V.*

¢ ⚠ **Cameron RV Park.** This park, open year-round, is adjacent to the Cameron Trading Post. There are 60 spaces with hookups for $15 a day. However, there are no public restrooms or showers. No reservations accepted. ⊠ *U.S. 89* ⓓ *Box 339, Cameron 86020* ☎ *928/679–2231 or 800/338–7385* 🖶 *928/679–2350* ⊕ *www.camerontradingpost.com* 🖼 *$15* ➪ *60 RV sites* ⌂ *Full hookups, dump station, drinking water, food service, general store* ☺ *Open year-round.*

▌ **EN ROUTE** The route north from Cameron Trading Post on U.S. 89 offers a stunning view of the **Painted Desert** to the right. The desert, which covers thousands of square miles and stretches to the south and east, is a vision of subtle, almost harsh beauty, with windswept plains and mesas, isolated buttes, and barren valleys in pastel patterns. The sparse vegetation is mostly desert scrub, which provides sustenance for only the hardiest wildlife. Most of the undulating hills belong to the 200-million-year-old Chinle formation, the depository of countless fossil records.

About 30 mi north of Cameron Trading Post, the Painted Desert country gives way to sandstone cliffs that run for miles to the right. Brilliantly hued and ranging in color from light pink to deep orange, the **Echo Cliffs** rise to more than 1,000 feet in many places. They are essentially devoid of vegetation, but in a few places high up, thick patches of tall cotton-

CLOSE UP

Rafting Basics

SO, YOU'RE READY TO TACKLE the churning white water of the Colorado River as it rumbles and hisses its way through the Grand Canyon? Well, you're in good company: The crafty, one-armed Civil War veteran John Wesley Powell first charted these dangerous rapids during the summer of 1869. It wasn't until 1938, though, that the first commercial river trip made its way down this fearsome corridor, and running the river has come a long way since then—and since Norman Neville made the first trip by kayak, in 1941, in a craft he built out of scrap lumber that he salvaged from an outhouse and a run-down barn.

White-water rafting still offers all of the excitement of the early days—without the danger and the discomfort. Professional river runners take rafters on everything from relaxing motorized three-day trips to adventurous 14-day oar excursions. Seats fill up fast due to the restricted number of visitors allowed on the river each season by the National Park Service. Many book their trips for the peak periods of the summer: June through August. If you're flexible, though, and can take advantage of the Arizona weather, May to early June and September are ideal rafting times for the Grand Canyon.

Once you've secured your seat, all that's left is for you to pack your bags and to get geared up for an experience of a lifetime. Lifejackets, beverages, tents, sheets, tarps, sleeping bags, wet bags, first aid, and food are provided—but you'll just need to pack clothes, a hat, sunscreen, toiletries, and other sundries.

wood and poplar trees, nurtured by springs and water seepage from the rock escarpment, manage to thrive.

At Bitter Springs, 60 mi north of Cameron, U.S. 89A branches off U.S. 89, running north and providing views of **Marble Canyon,** the geographical beginning of the Grand Canyon. Like the Grand Canyon, Marble Canyon was formed by the Colorado River. Traversing a gorge nearly 500 feet deep is **Navajo Bridge,** a narrow steel span built in 1929 and listed on the National Register of Historic Places. Formerly used for car traffic, it now functions only as a pedestrian overpass. The visitor center is informational and handy.

Lees Ferry Area

76 mi north of Cameron Trading Post, U.S. 89 to U.S. 89A.

★ ㉙ A turnoff at Marble Canyon Lodge, about 1 mi past Navajo Bridge in the small town of Marble Canyon, leads to historic **Lees Ferry,** 3 mi away. On a sharp bend in the Colorado River where Echo Cliffs and Vermilion Cliffs intersect, Lees Ferry is considered "mile zero" of the river—the point from which all distances on the rivers system in the Grand Canyon are measured.

This spot, one of the last areas in the mainland United States to be completely charted, was first visited by non–Native Americans in 1776, when Spanish priests Fray Francisco Atanasio Domínguez and Fray Silvestre Velez de Escalante tried, but failed, to cross the Colorado. In March 1864, Mormon frontiersman and missionary Jacob Hamblin made the first crossing by raft. Efforts by the Mormons to establish colonies in the area generated high ferry traffic in the 1870s through the 1890s. It became part of the Honeymoon Trail, a gateway to Utah for young couples who wanted their civil marriages in Arizona sanctified at the Latter-day Saints temple in St. George. The ferry also became a crossing and a supply point for miners and other pioneers who shaped the American West. Its most infamous ferryman was John Doyle Lee, who tended the crossing for years before he was arrested and finally executed in connection with the Mountain Meadows massacre in Utah. The ferry was operational until 1928, when a bridge was finally built to span the river.

Lees Ferry retains vestiges of the mining era, but it's now primarily known as the spot where most of the Grand Canyon river rafts put into the water. Huge trout lurk in the river near here, so there are several places to pick up angling gear and a guide.

★ ⑳   West from the town of Marble Canyon are the spectacular **Vermilion Cliffs,** in many places more than 3,000 feet high. Keep an eye out for condors; the giant endangered birds were reintroduced into the area in the winter of 1996–97. Reports suggest that the birds, once in captivity, are surviving well in the wilderness.

Sports & the Outdoors

FISHING This stretch of ice-cold, crystal-clear water provides arguably the best trout fishing in the Southwest. Many rafters and fishermen stay the night in a campground near the river or in nearby Marble Canyon before hitting the river at dawn. Marble Canyon Lodge sells Arizona fishing licenses. **Lees Ferry Anglers** (✉ Milepost 547, N. U.S. 89A, Marble Canyon ☎ 928/355–2261, 800/962–9755 outside Arizona ⊕ www.leesferry. com) operates guided fishing trips, starting from $300 per day; it practices year-round catch and release.

RAFTING **Arizona Raft Adventures** (✉ 4050 E. Huntington Rd., Flagstaff, 86004 ☎ 928/526–8200 or 800/786–7238 🖷 928/526–8246 ⊕ www.azraft. com) organizes 6- to 14-day combination paddle-and-motor trips, all paddle, and all motor trips for all skill levels. Trips, which run $1,600 to $3,320, depart from May through October. With a reputation for high quality and a roster of 3- to 13-day trips, **Canyoneers** (✆ Box 2997, Flagstaff, 86003 ☎ 928/526–0924 or 800/525–0924 🖷 928/527–9398 ⊕ www.canyoneers.com) is popular with those who want to include some hiking as well. The five-day "Best of the Grand" includes a hike down to Phantom Ranch. Their 3- to 12-day trips, available April through September, cost between $705 and $2,700. Owned and operated by a mother-and-daughters team, **Diamond River Adventures** (✆ Box 1300, Page, 86040 ☎ 928/645–8866 or 800/343–3121 🖷 928/645–9536 ⊕ www.diamondriver.com) offers both oar-powered and motorized river trips from 4 to 14 days from May through September. Prices range from $800 to $2,500. Expert and long-established **Grand Canyon Expeditions** (🏠 Box O, Kanab, UT 84741 ☎435/644–2691 or 800/544–2691 🖷 435/644–2699 ⊕ www.gcex.com) has guided the likes of the Smithsonian Institution along the Colorado River. You can count on them to take you down the river safely and in style: they limit the number of people on each boat to 14, and evening meals might include filet mignon, pork chops, or shrimp. The April through October trips cost $2,145 to $3,500 for 8 to 16 days.

Where to Stay & Eat

★ ¢–$$ ✕▦ **Marble Canyon Lodge.** This Arizona Strip lodge opened in 1929 on the same day the Navajo Bridge was dedicated. Three types of accommodations are available: rooms in the original building; standard motel rooms in the newer building; and two-bedroom apartments. You can sit on the porch swing of the native-rock lodge and look out on Vermilion Cliffs and the desert or play the 1920s piano. Zane Grey and Gary Cooper are among the well-known past guests. The restaurant ($–$$$) serves steaks, seafood, pasta, and sandwiches. ⊠ *¼ mi west of Navajo Bridge on U.S. 89A* 🏠 *Box 6001, Marble Canyon 86036* ☎ *928/355–2225 or 800/726–1789* 🖷 *928/355–2227* 🛏 *52 units* ⚫ *Restaurant, lounge, shop, laundry facilities, meeting room, airstrip, some pets allowed* ▭ *AE, D, MC, V.*

¢–$ ✕▦ **Lees Ferry Lodge.** Geared to the Lees Ferry trout-fishing trade, this lodge will outfit you, guide you, and freeze your catch. At the end of the day you can sit out on one of the garden patios of this rustic 1929 building. Rooms are charming, if a bit quirky in their plumbing. The hotel's Vermilion Cliffs Bar and Grill ($–$$$) is a popular gathering spot for river raft guides, and serves good American fare—especially steaks and ribs—in an authentic Western setting. The bar has an extensive beer collection: more than 100 types. ⊠ *4 mi west of Navajo Bridge on U.S. 89A* 🏠 *HC 67, Box 1, Marble Canyon 86036* ☎ *928/355–2231 or 800/ 451–2231* ⊕ *www.leesferrylodge.com* 🛏 *10 rooms, 2 5-person trailers* ⚫ *Restaurant, beer garden; no room phones, no TV in some rooms* ▭ *AE, MC, V.*

¢–$ ▦ **Cliff Dwellers Lodge.** Built in 1949, this dining and lodging complex sits at the foot of Vermilion Cliffs. Rooms in the modern motel building are attractive and clean. **Lees Ferry Anglers** (☎ 928/355–2261 or 800/962–9755 ⊕ www.leesferry.com) is headquartered at this lodge, adding to the convenience of a fly-fishing trip on the Colorado River. ⊠ *U.S. 89A, 9 mi west of Navajo Bridge* 🏠 *HC 67, Box 30, Marble Canyon 86036* ☎ *928/355–2228 or 800/433–2543* 🖷 *928/355–2229* 🛏 *22 rooms* ⚫ *Restaurant, cable TV, fishing, bar, shops, some pets allowed (fee)* ▭ *AE, D, MC, V.*

EN ROUTE As you continue the journey to the North Rim, the immense blue-green bulk of the Kaibab Plateau stretches out before you. About 18 mi past Navajo Bridge, a sign directs you to the **San Bartolome Historic Site,** an overlook with plaques that tell the story of the Domínguez-Escalante expedition of 1776. At **House Rock Valley,** a large road sign announces the House Rock Buffalo Ranch, operated by the Arizona Game and Fish Department. A 23-mi dirt road leads to the home of one of the largest herds of American bison in the Southwest. You can drive out to the ranch, but you might not see any buffalo—the expanse of their range is so great that they frequently cannot be spotted from a car.

As it nears its junction with AZ 67, U.S. 89A starts climbing to the top of the **Kaibab Plateau,** heavily forested, filled with animals and birds, and more than 9,000 feet at its highest point. The rapid change from barren desert to lush forest is dramatic.

Jacob Lake

㉛ *25 mi west of town of Marble Canyon on U.S. 89A, at AZ 67.*

Jacob Lake junction is a good base camp for exploring the beautiful Kaibab Plateau, often described as an "island in the sky." The Kaibab squirrel—a tassel-eared squirrel found nowhere else in the world—is one of the many species of wildlife encountered here. The U.S. Forest Service's **Kaibab Plateau Visitor's Center** (⊠ U.S. 89A/AZ 67 ☎ 928/643–7298) is open May–mid-October and has several interpretive displays, books, and educational gifts. Gas and groceries are also available in the area.

Where to Stay & Eat

¢–$$ ✕⌑ **Jacob Lake Inn.** The bustling lodge at Jacob Lake Inn is a popular stop for those heading to the North Rim; it has a grocery store, coffee shop, restaurant (¢–$), and gift shop. Even if you don't stay here, stop for one of their famous malts or milk shakes. The 5-acre complex in Kaibab National Forest has basic cabins and standard motel rooms that overlook the highways. Twenty-five rooms added in 2006 have TVs, phones, Wi-Fi, and in-room broadband. ⊠ *AZ 67/U.S. 89A, 86022* ☎ *928/643–7232* ⊕ *www.jacoblake.com* ⤴ *39 rooms, 22 cabins* ⚐ *Restaurant, café, grocery, some room phones, some room TVs, some Wi-Fi, some in-room data ports; no a/c in some rooms* ▭ *AE, D, MC, V.*

CAMPING ⚠ **Jacob Lake Campground.** Fifty-three family and group RV and tent
¢ sites (no hookups) are available at this U.S. Forest Service campground. On summer evenings, rangers present interpretive programs. Reservations are accepted only for groups of 10 or more. ⊠ *U.S. 89A/AZ 67* ⌖ *North Kaibab Ranger District, Box 248, Fredonia 86022* ☎ *928/ 643–7395* ▱ *$14* ⤴ *53 campsites* ⚐ *Grills, flush toilets, fire pits, picnic tables* ⚑ *Reservations not accepted* ☉ *Open May–Oct.*

¢ ⚠ **Kaibab Camper Village.** Fire pits and more than 70 picnic tables are spread out in this wooded spot, which is near a gas station, store, and restaurant. Reservations are accepted by the Canyoneers outfitter and are recommended, particularly during the height of the busy summer season. There are 50 tent sites ($13 for two people) and 60 RV and trailer sites ($27 for a pull-through with full hookup, $13 without hookup). ⊠ *AZ 67, ¼ mi south of U.S. 89A* ⌖ *Box 3331, Flagstaff 86003* ☎ *928/643–7804 in season, 928/526–0924, 800/525–0924 outside AZ in winter* ▤ *928/527–9398* ⊕ *www.canyoneers.com* ▱ *$13–$27* ⤴ *60 full hookups, 50 tent sites* ⚐ *Portable toilets, full hookups, drinking water, showers, fire pits, picnic tables* ☉ *Open mid-May–mid-Oct.*

CLOSE UP

Grand Canyon Flora and Fauna

2

ALMOST 2 BILLION YEARS WORTH of Earth's history is written between the colored layers of sedimentary rock that are stacked from the river bottom to the top of the plateau. The South Rim's Coconino Plateau is fairly flat, at an elevation of about 7,000 feet, and covered with stands of piñon and ponderosa pine, juniper, and Gambel's oak. On the Kaibab Plateau on the North Rim, Douglas fir, spruce, quaking aspen, and more ponderosa-pine trees prevail. In spring, you're likely to see asters, sunflowers, and lupine in bloom at both rims.

Eighty-eight mammal species inhabit the park, as well as 300 species of birds, 24 kinds of lizard, and 24 kinds of snake. The rare Kaibab squirrel is found only on the North Rim—you can

recognize them by their all-white tails and the long tufts of white hair on their ears. The pink Grand Canyon rattlesnake lives at lower elevations within the canyon. Hawks and ravens are visible year-round, usually coasting on the wind above the canyon. The endangered California condor has been reintroduced to the canyon. Park rangers give daily talks on the magnificent birds, whose wingspan measures nine feet. In spring, summer, and fall, mule deer—recognizable by their large antlers—are abundant at the South Rim, even aggressive. Don't be tempted to feed them; it's illegal, and it will disrupt their natural habits and increase your risk of being bitten.

EN
ROUTE

AZ 67 runs south from U.S. 89A to the North Rim; the route passes through one of the thickest stands of ponderosa pine in the United States. You'll see mule deer and Kaibab squirrels. Keep an eye out for mountain lions, elk, and black bear . . . they're here, but seeing them is rare. You're more likely to see wild turkeys.

Elsewhere in the Arizona Strip

The Arizona Strip—the part of the state directly north of Grand Canyon National Park—is sometimes called the American Tibet because of its isolation; it has only two small towns, Fredonia and Colorado City. The combined population of these two towns is less than 7,000, and fewer than 700 permanent residents—including 150 members of the Kaibab-Paiute tribe—live in the rest of the strip. Services are extremely limited; top off your tank when you find a gas station, and keep an ample supply of drinking water in your car. Away from the paved highways in this region, roads tend to be rough and may be impassable when wet.

㊳ **Pipe Spring National Monument,** 90 mi from the North Rim and 14 mi

Fodor'sChoice from Fredonia, has one of the few reliable sources of water in the Ari-

★ zona Strip. The park contains a restored rock fort and ranch, with exhibits of Southwestern frontier life. In summer there are living-history demonstrations of ranching operations or weaving. The fort was intended to fend off Native American attacks (which never came because a peace treaty was signed before the fort was finished). It ended up functioning mainly as headquarters for a dairy and ranching operation and in 1871 became the first telegraph station in the Arizona Territory. About ½ mi north of the monument is a campground and picnic area operated by the Kaibab-Paiute tribe. Check out the museum and visitor center, which is operated jointly by the tribe and the National Park Service. ⊠ *401 N. Pipe Spring Rd.* ⌂ *HC 65, Box 5, Fredonia 86022* ☎ *928/643–7105* ⊕ *www.nps.gov/pisp* ⊠ *$4* ⊙ *Historic structures daily 8:30–4:30, visitor center and museum Sept.–May, daily 8–5; June–Aug., daily 7–5.*

Six miles back toward Fredonia from Pipe Spring on AZ 389, a dirt road leads 50 mi south through starkly beautiful, uninhabited country to **Toroweap Overlook,** a lonely and awesome viewpoint over one of the narrowest stretches of the Grand Canyon (less than 1 mi across). The overlook has the deepest sheer cliff (more than 3,000 feet straight down) in the Grand Canyon. From this vantage point, you can see upstream to sedimentary ledges, cliffs, and talus slopes. Looking downstream, you can see miles of the lava flow that forms steep deltas, some of which look like black waterfalls frozen on the cliff. Be sure you have plenty of gas, drinking water, good tires, and a reliable car; a high-clearance vehicle is best for this trip. It's a rough drive, especially the last 3 mi over slickrock. Allow up to three hours to drive from the highway to the overlook. Don't try to go in wet weather, when the dirt road is likely to be washed out. There's a ranger station near the rim as well as a primitive campground, which has 11 first-come, first-served tent sites, picnic tables, grates, and compost toilets. If you plan to return the same day, make motel reservations in advance at an Arizona Strip motel.

THE GRAND CANYON ESSENTIALS

To research prices, get advice from other travelers, and book travel arrangements, visit ⊕ *www.fodors.com.*

Transportation

BY AIR
Several carriers fly to the Grand Canyon Airport from Las Vegas, including Air Vegas, Scenic Airlines, and Vision Air.

North Las Vegas Airport in Las Vegas is the primary air hub for flights to Grand Canyon Airport. You can also make connections into the Grand Canyon from Sky Harbor International Airport in Phoenix.

Xanterra Transportation Company offers 24-hour taxi service at Grand Canyon Airport, Grand Canyon Village, and the nearby village of Tusayan. Taxis also make trips to other destinations in and around Grand Canyon National Park.

🔒 **Air Vegas** ☎ 800/940-2550 ⊕ www.airvegas.com. **Grand Canyon National Parks Airport** ☎ 928/638-2446. **North Las Vegas Airport** ☎ 702/261-3806. **Phoenix Sky Har-**

bor International Airport (PHX) ☎ 602/273-3300. **Scenic Airlines** ☎ 800/634-6801 ⊕ www.scenic.com. **Vision Air** ☎ 702/261-3850 ⊕ www.visionholidays.com. **Xanterra Transportation Company** ☎ 928/638-2822.

BY BUS

There's no public bus transportation to the Grand Canyon. Greyhound Lines provides bus service to Williams, Flagstaff, and Kingman. Schedules change frequently; call or check the Web site for information.

Within the park, there are three free shuttle routes. Hermits Rest Route operates from March through November between Grand Canyon Village and Hermits Rest; it runs every 15 to 30 minutes one hour before sunrise until one hour after sunset, depending on the season. The Village Route operates year-round in the village area from one hour before sunrise until after dark; it is the easiest access to the Canyon View Information Center. The Kaibab Trail Route travels from Canyon View Information Center to Yaki Point, including a stop at the South Kaibab Trailhead.

From mid-May to late October, the Trans Canyon Shuttle leaves Bright Angel Lodge at 1:30 PM and arrives at the North Rim's Grand Canyon Lodge about 6 PM. The return trip leaves the North Rim each morning at 7 AM, arriving at the South Rim at about noon. One-way fare is $65, round-trip $120. A 50% deposit is required two weeks in advance. 🔒 **Greyhound Lines** ☎ 800/231-2222 ⊕ www.greyhound.com. **Trans Canyon Shuttle** ☎ 928/638-2820.

BY CAR

Most of Arizona's scenic highlights are many miles apart, and a car is essential for touring the state. However, you won't really need one if you're planning to visit only the Grand Canyon's most popular area, the South Rim. Some people choose to fly to the Grand Canyon and then hike, catch a shuttle or taxi, or sign on for bus tours or mule rides.

If you're driving to Arizona from the east, or coming up from the southern part of the state, the best access to the Grand Canyon is from Flagstaff. You can take U.S. 180 northwest (81 mi) to Grand Canyon Village on the South Rim. Or, for a scenic route with stopping points along the canyon rim, drive north on U.S. 89 from Flagstaff, turn left at the junction of AZ 64 (52 mi north of Flagstaff), which merges with U.S. 180 at Valle, and proceed north and west for an additional 57 mi until you reach Grand Canyon Village on the South Rim.

To visit the North Rim of the canyon, proceed north from Flagstaff on U.S. 89 to Bitter Springs. Then take U.S. 89A to the junction of AZ 67. Travel south on AZ 67 for approximately 40 mi to the North Rim, which is 210 mi from Flagstaff.

If you're crossing Arizona on Interstate 40 from the west, your most direct route to the South Rim is on AZ 64 (U.S. 180), which runs north from Williams for 58 mi to Grand Canyon Village.

GASOLINE The only gas station inside the national park on the South Rim is at Desert View, and this station operates only from March 31 to September 30 depending on snowfall. Gas is available year-round near the South Entrance at Moqui Lodge (though the lodge itself is now closed), in Tusayan, and at Cameron, to the east.

At the South Rim, in Grand Canyon Village, the Public Garage is a fully equipped AAA garage that provides auto repair daily 8 to noon and 1 to 5 as well as 24-hour emergency service. This is a garage for repairs only and does not sell gasoline.

At the North Rim, the Chevron service station, which repairs autos, is inside the park on the access road leading to the North Rim Campground. No diesel fuel is available at the North Rim.

ROAD
CONDITIONS   When driving off major highways in low-lying areas, watch for rain clouds. Flash floods from sudden summer rains can be deadly.

The South Rim stays open to auto traffic year-round, although access to Hermits Rest is limited to shuttle buses in summer because of congestion. Roads leading to the South Rim near Grand Canyon Village and the parking areas along the rim are congested in summer as well. If you visit from October through April, you can experience only light to moderate traffic and have no problem with parking.

Reaching elevations of 8,000 feet, the more remote North Rim has no services available from late October through mid-May. AZ 67 south of Jacob Lake is closed by the first heavy snowfall in November or December and remains closed until early to mid-May.

To check on Arizona road conditions, call the Arizona Department of Transportation's recorded hotline.

🚩 **Arizona Department of Transportation** ☎ 888/411-7623 ⊕ www.dot.state.az.us. **Chevron** ☎ 928/638-2611. **Public Garage** ☎ 928/638-2225.

Contacts & Resources

EMERGENCIES
There are no pharmacies at the North or South Rim. Prescriptions can be delivered daily to the South Rim Clinic from Flagstaff.

🚩 **Emergency services** ☎ 911, 9-911 in park lodgings. **Grand Canyon Walk-in Clinic** ⊠ Grand Canyon Village ☎ 928/638-2551.

BANKS
There's a 24-hour teller machine at the Bank One South Rim office in Market Plaza near the General Store and at the Maswik Lodge. There are also ATM machines at several hotels and stores in Tusayan. There are no banking facilities at the North Rim.

🚩 **Bank One** ☎ 928/638-2437.

CAMPING SUPPLIES
The Canyon Village Marketplace has three locations in the South Rim: at Grand Canyon Village, in nearby Tusayan, and at Desert View near the park's east entrance. The main store, in Grand Canyon Village, is a department store selling a full line of camping, hiking, and backpack-

2

ing supplies, in addition to groceries. The store also rents hiking supplies including backpacks, tents, and walking sticks.

The North Rim General Store, inside the park at the North Rim Campground, carries groceries, some clothing, and travelers' supplies.
⚑ **Canyon Village Marketplace** ✉ Grand Canyon Village ☎ 928/638-2262 ✉ Tusayan ☎ 928/638-2854 ✉ Desert View ☎ 928/638-2393. **North Rim General Store** ✉ North Rim Campground, Grand Canyon North Rim ☎ 928/638-2611.

FEES
It costs $20 per motorized vehicle to enter the park. Individuals arriving by bicycle or foot pay $10. In all cases, this fee is for one week's access. Backcountry permits are $10 plus $5 per person per night.

HOURS
The South Rim is open year-round. The North Rim is open mid-May through mid-October. AZ 67 from Jacob Lake is often closed due to snowfall from mid-October to mid-May, and during these times all facilities at the North Rim are closed.

The entrance gates are open 24 hours but are generally staffed from about 7 AM to 7 PM. If you arrive when there's no one at the gate, you may enter legally without paying.

LOST & FOUND
Report lost or stolen items or turn in found items at Canyon View Information Plaza or Yavapai Observation Station at 928/638–7798 from Tuesday to Friday, 8 AM to 5 PM. For items lost or found at a dining or lodging establishment, call 928/638–2631.

MAIL & SHIPPING
There's a U.S. Post Office in the Market Plaza shopping center near Yavapai Lodge. It's open weekdays 9 to 4:30 and Saturday 11 to 3.

PETS
Pets are allowed in Grand Canyon National Park; however, they must be on a leash at all times. Pets are not allowed below the rim or on the park buses, with the exception of service animals. There's a kennel, near the Maswik Lodge, which houses cats and dogs. It's open daily from 7:30 AM to 5 PM. Reservations are highly recommended.
⚑ Grand Canyon Kennel ☎ 928/638-0534.

TOURS
AIR TOURS Flights by plane and helicopter over the canyon are offered by a number of companies, departing for the Grand Canyon Airport at the south end of Tusayan. Prices and lengths of tours vary, but you can expect to pay about $75–$100 per adult for short plane trips and approximately $100–$150 for a brief helicopter tour.

WORD OF MOUTH

"A helicopter tour over the Grand Canyon is money well spent . . . what a panoramic view!"

–rxtennis

🔝 **Air Grand Canyon** ✉ Grand Canyon Airport, Tusayan ☎ 928/638-2686 ⊕ www. airgrandcanyon.com. **AirStar Helicopters/Airlines** ✉ Grand Canyon Airport, Tusayan ☎ 928/638-2622 or 800/962-3869 ⊕ www.airstar.com. **Grand Canyon Airlines** ✉ Grand Canyon Airport, Tusayan ☎ 928/638-2463 or 866/235-9422 ⊕ www. grandcanyonairlines.com. **Grand Canyon Helicopters** ✉ Grand Canyon Airport, Tusayan ☎ 928/638-2764 or 800/541-4537 ⊕ www.grandcanyonhelicoptersaz.com. **Papillon Helicopters** ✉ Grand Canyon Airport, Tusayan ☎ 928/638-2419 or 800/528-2418 ⊕ www. papillon.com.

BUS TOURS 🔝 **Xanterra Motorcoach Tours** ✉ Grand Canyon Village ☎ 928/638-2631 or 928/638-3283.

HIKING TOURS The Grand Canyon Field Institute leads a full program of educational guided hikes around the canyon year-round. Topics include everything from archaeology and backcountry medicine to photography and natural history. Reservations are essential and cost from $85 to $1,200. For a personalized tour of the Grand Canyon and surrounding sacred sites, contact Marvelous Marv, whose knowledge of the area is as extensive as his repertoire of local legends. 🔝 The **Grand Canyon Field Institute** ✆ Box 399, Grand Canyon 86023 ☎ 928/638-2485 or 866/471-4435 ⊕ www.grandcanyon.org/fieldinstitute. **Marvelous Marv** ✆ Box 544, Williams 86046 ☎ 928/635-4948 ⊕ www.marvelousmarv.com.

JEEP TOURS If you'd like to get off the pavement and see parts of the park that are accessible only by dirt road, a jeep tour can be just the ticket. Rides can be rough; if you have had back injuries, check with your doctor before taking a jeep tour. From March through October, Grand Canyon Outback Jeep Tours leads daily 1½- to 4½-hour off-road tours within the park, as well as in Kaibab National Forest. Expect to pay from $40 to $94, and reservations are essential. 🔝 **Grand Canyon Outback Jeep Tours** ✆ Box 1772, Grand Canyon 86023 ☎ 928/638-5337 or 800/320-5337 🖨 928/638-5337 ⊕ www.grandcanyonjeeptours.com.

RAFTING TOURS Nearly two dozen companies currently offer excursions, but reservations for raft trips (excluding smooth-water, one-day cruises) often need to be made more than six months in advance. A complete list of concessionaires offering trips on the Colorado River is available on the Grand Canyon National Park Web site. National Park Service white-water concessionaires include Arizona River Runners, Canyoneers, Diamond River Adventures, Grand Canyon Expeditions, and Tour West. For a smooth-water, one-day trip check out Wilderness River Adventures. Prices for river-raft trips vary greatly, depending on type and length. Half-day trips on smooth water run as low as $54 per person. Trips that negotiate the entire length of the canyon and take as long as 12 days can cost more than $2,000. 🔝 **Arizona River Runners** ☎ 602/867-4866 or 800/477-7238 ⊕ www.raftarizona.com. **Canyoneers, Inc.** ☎ 928/526-0924, 800/525-0924 outside Arizona ⊕ www.canyoneers. com. **Diamond River Adventures, Inc.** ☎ 928/645-8866 or 800/343-3121 ⊕ www. diamondriver.com. **Grand Canyon Expeditions** ☎ 435/644-2691 or 800/544-2691 ⊕ www.gcex.com. **Tour West, Inc.** ☎ 801/225-0755 or 800/453-9107 ⊕ www.twriver. com. **Wilderness River Adventures** ☎ 928/645-3279 or 800/992-8022 ⊕ www. riveradventures.com.

SPECIAL
INTEREST TOURS

The National Park Service sponsors all sorts of free Ranger Prog at both the South and the North rims. These orientation activitie clude daily guided hikes and talks. The focus may be on any aspect of the canyon—from geology, flora, and fauna to history and early inhabitants. Programs change seasonally. For schedules, go to Canyon View Information Plaza on the South Rim or the Grand Canyon Lodge on the North Rim.

Several of the free programs are designed especially for children. Children ages 9 to 11 use field guides, binoculars, magnifying glasses, and other exploration tools on the one-hour Junior Ranger Discovery Pack Program. Park rangers also coordinate Way Cool for Kids, free, hourlong introductions to the park for ages 7 to 11. Kids and rangers walk around the Village Rim area and talk about local plants and animals, history, or archaeology. These two programs are only offered in the summer; check for times at the Canyon View Information Plaza.

Ranger Programs Box 129, Grand Canyon 86023 928/638-7888 www.nps. gov/grca.

VISITOR INFORMATION

Every person arriving at the South or North Rim is given a detailed map of the area. Centers at both rims also publish a free newspaper, the *Guide,* which contains a detailed area map; it's available at the visitor center, entrance stations, and many of the lodging facilities and stores. The park also distributes *Accessibility Guide,* a free newsletter that details the facilities accessible to travelers with disabilities. Grand Canyon National Park is the contact for general information. Write ahead for a complimentary *Trip Planner,* updated regularly by the National Park Service.

Several Web sites are useful for trip-planning information, including the National Park Service's Web site, which has information on fees and permits. Try thecanyon.com, a commercial site where you'll find information on lodging, dining, and general park information. You can use the Xanterra Parks & Resorts Grand Canyon Web site to make reservations for park lodging, mule rides, bus tours, and some smooth-water rafting trips. The park service allows camping reservations to be made online as well, through the campground reservation vendor.

In summer, transportation-services desks are maintained at El Tovar, Bright Angel, Maswik Lodge, and Yavapai Lodge in Grand Canyon Village; in winter, the one at Yavapai is closed. The desks provide information and handle bookings, sightseeing tours, taxi and bus services, mule and horseback rides, and accommodations at Phantom Ranch (at the bottom of the Grand Canyon). The concierge at El Tovar can also arrange most tours, with the exception of mule rides and lodging at Phantom Ranch.

Grand Canyon Lodge has general information about local services available in summer when the North Rim is open.

The Williams and Forest Service Visitor Center, run by the U.S. Forest Service and the Williams Chamber of Commerce, offers information on the Kaibab National Forest and the entire Grand Canyon region.

Grand Canyon Contacts **Grand Canyon Lodge** 📞 928/638-2611 direct to hotel, 303/297-2757 in winter off-season. **Grand Canyon National Park** 📞 928/638-7888 recorded message 📠 928/638-7797 🌐 www.nps.gov/grca. **Grand Canyon National Park Lodges** 📞 303/297-2757 📠 303/297-3175 🌐 www.grandcanyonlodges.com. **North and South Rim Camping** 📞 800/365-2267 🌐 http://reservations.nps.gov/index.cfm. **thecanyon.com** 🌐 www.thecanyon.com. **Williams and Forest Service Visitor Center** 📞 928/635-4061.

North-Central Arizona

WORD OF MOUTH

"Sedona is a magical, romantic place to visit, with wonderful sights, great places to hike, and good sightseeing day trips."

—MikePinTucson

"Prescott is beautiful . . . But if you do go, you have to go to Sedona, it's not that far from Prescott . . . Also, if you are going to go you should also check out Flagstaff. Prescott, Sedona, and Flagstaff are pretty close to each other and the drive is wonderful. That whole area is full of great scenic hiking and it is so peaceful and gorgeous."

—jb1923

Updated by
Matt Baatz

RED-ROCK BUTTES ABLAZE in the slanting light of late afternoon, the San Francisco peaks tipped with white from a fresh snowfall, pine forests clad in dark green needles—north-central Arizona is rich in natural attractions, a landscape of vast plateaus punctuated by steep ridges and canyons. To the north of Flagstaff, a string of tall volcanic mountains, the San Francisco Peaks, rises above 12,000 feet, tapering to the 9,000-foot Mount Elden and a scattering of diminutive cinder cones. To the south, a seemingly endless stand of ponderosa pines covers this part of the Colorado Plateau before the terrain plunges dramatically into Oak Creek Canyon. The canyon then opens up to reveal red buttes and mesas in the high-desert areas surrounding Sedona. The desert gradually descends to the Verde Valley, crossing the Verde River before reaching the 7,000-foot Black Range, over which lies the Prescott Valley.

Flagstaff, the hub of this part of Arizona, was historically a way station en route to southern California. First the railroads, then Route 66 carried westbound traffic right through the center of town—today the roads are filled with vacationers on their way north to the Grand Canyon, students at Northern Arizona University, and Phoenix weekenders fleeing the heat of the valley. Many of those who were just "passing through" have stayed and built a community, revitalizing downtown with cafés, an activity-filled square, eclectic shops, and festivals. The town's large network of bike paths and parks abuts hundreds of miles of trails and forest roads, an irresistible lure for outdoors enthusiasts. There's a long backlog of future projects, proposing new trails and bike paths for years to come. Not surprisingly, the typical resident of Flagstaff is outdoorsy, young, and has a large, friendly dog in tow.

Down AZ 89A in Sedona, the average age and income rises considerably. This was once a hidden hamlet used by Western filmmakers but New Age enthusiasts flocked to the region in the 1980s believing it was the center of spiritual powers. Well-off retirees followed soon after, populating clusters of mazelike cul-de-sacs all along the two highways through Sedona. Sophisticated restaurants, upscale shops, luxe accommodations, and New Age entrepreneurs cater to both these populations, and to the tourist trade, which brings close to 5 million visitors a year to the area. It can be difficult, though not impossible, to find a moment of serenity, even in wilderness areas. A hike into apparently remote territory is often disturbed by a tour plane buzzing above or a gonzo mountain biker who brakes for no one. Despite these quibbles, the beauty here is unsurpassed. For this reason, Sedona and much of north-central Arizona attracts more than its share of artists and galleries.

Pioneers and miners are now part of north-central Arizona's past, but the wild and woolly days of the Old West are not forgotten. The preserved fort at Camp Verde recalls frontier life, and the decrepit facades of the funky former mining town of Jerome have an infectious charm. Jerome's hillside streets are blessed with a sublime panorama from the red-rock buttes to the snowcapped peaks of the San Francisco range. The many Victorian houses in temperate Prescott attest to the attempt to bring "civilization" to Arizona's territorial capital.

GREAT ITINERARIES

A short stay can give you a little taste of this rich part of the state, but at least five days are necessary for the full flavor. Linger longer if you want to savor the region's history and landscape or enjoy outdoor activities. The following itineraries assume you'll start in Phoenix and head north.

IF YOU HAVE 3 DAYS

Spend the first two nights in 📷 **Sedona** ⓑ ⌐ - ㉓. Take a jeep tour or a hike in **Red Rock State Park** ㉓, and then explore the town's shops and sights. On the next day, visit the ghost town of **Jerome** ㉛. On your third day, drive through scenic **Oak Creek Canyon** ㉔ to 📷 **Flagstaff** ❶ - ❽, where you can visit the **Riordan State Historic Park** ❹ or the **Museum of Northern Arizona** ❼ in the afternoon and the **Lowell Observatory** ❸ at night.

IF YOU HAVE 5 DAYS

Expand your time in 📷 **Sedona** ⓑ ⌐ - ㉓ by exploring **Oak Creek Canyon** ㉔ and **Red Rock State Park** ㉓ on the first day and shopping or exploring the town on the second. Enjoy a good part of the third day in **Jerome** ㉛; then

continue on to 📷 **Prescott** ㉜ - ㊱, where you can spend the night in one of the many Victorian-era lodgings. Next day, poke around the town's antiques shops and **Sharlot Hall Museum** ㉞ and in the late afternoon drive up to 📷 **Flagstaff** ❶ - ❽. Then make excursions to the adjacent **Sunset Crater Volcano National Monument** ⓭ and **Wupatki** ⓮ national monuments, where Native American artifacts may be explored in an inactive volcanic field.

IF YOU HAVE 7 DAYS

Take your time driving up from Phoenix to Sedona, spending the morning of the first day at **Fort Verde State Historic Park** ㉖ ⌐ and **Montezuma Castle National Monument** ㉗. In the afternoon, ride the **Verde Canyon Railroad** and spend the night in 📷 **Jerome** ㉛. Continue on to 📷 **Prescott** ㉜ - ㊱ for a day or two before heading over to 📷 **Flagstaff** ❶ - ❽, where you can ski in winter or view the entire San Francisco Peaks region from the Agassiz ski lift in summer. Conclude your trip in 📷 **Sedona** ⓑ - ㉓ for a very satisfying circle of the area.

North-central Arizona is also rich in artifacts from its earliest inhabitants: several national and state parks—among them Walnut Canyon, Wupatki, Montezuma Castle, and Tuzigoot national monuments—hold well-preserved evidence of the architectural accomplishments of Native American Sinagua and other ancestral Puebloans who made their homes in the Verde Valley and the region near the San Francisco Peaks.

Top 5 Experiences in North Central Arizona

- **Cleopatra Hill:** After a day browsing art galleries and antiquing, stroll the sidewalks of the precipitous hill that Jerome was built on and look out at the red buttes rising from the white desert. The oft-snowcapped San Francisco Peaks are a stark blue silhouette in the distance.

- **Overnight at a Sedona resort or hotel:** You can really relax in Sedona; stay overnight and indulge your senses amid the warm glow of the red buttes, as the wind rustles the manzanita trees.

- **Sinagua ruins:** Visit the well-preserved ruins of these Native Americans who lived here before Columbus "discovered" America. You can learn their history in the excellent National Monument visitor centers.

- **Hike the red rocks:** Walking through the Mars-scape around Sedona and watching the rock go ablaze in the sunlight will rejuvenate you whether you believe in the vortex lore or not.

- **Stargaze in the high desert:** With the nearest major city more than 100 mi away from the high elevation deserts of Northern Arizona, you'll log shooting stars on both sets of fingers and peer farther into the Milky Way than you ever thought possible.

Exploring North-Central Arizona

Avoid the Interstates as much as possible; the back ways are sometimes the most direct and usually provide the best vantage points from which to view the stunning contrasts of the landscape. It's wise, especially if you're an outdoors enthusiast, to start in the relatively lowland areas of Prescott and the Verde Valley, climbing gradually into Sedona and Flagstaff—it can take several days to grow accustomed to high elevation in Flagstaff. If you can, plan to be in Sedona midweek, when the perennial weekend crowds aren't around to crowd the streets.

About the Restaurants

Sedona and Flagstaff have the largest number of good, multiethnic restaurants in the region. Prescott and Jerome have their share of good cafés, but beyond the main streets of these towns, restaurants tend toward standard American and Mexican road food, some of which is homey and delicious.

About the Hotels

Flagstaff has many comfortable motels (most of the familiar U.S. chains are represented) and pleasant bed-and-breakfasts, but no real luxury. There's a nearly continuous string of motels lining Route 66 once you're within the city limits, and if you aren't too particular about accommodations and rumbling trains, you can usually book a room on the fly. Otherwise, it's good to make reservations, if only a day or two ahead of arrival. Stunning settings and outstanding amenities abound in Sedona, but there are few bargains. Book rooms well ahead in the busy spring and fall seasons; you might find some relative bargains in winter and summer, when tourism in the area isn't quite as brisk. Sedona has springlike temperatures even in January, when it's sure to be snowing in Flagstaff, but summer temperatures above 100°F are common. Many of Prescott's hotels have fabled pasts. Little Jerome has a few B&Bs, but call ahead if you think you might want to spend the night here.

IF YOU LIKE

CAMPING

The Prescott and Coconino national forests cover a large part of north-central Arizona. Campgrounds close to Sedona often fill up in summer, especially those along Oak Creek in Oak Creek Canyon; if you want to camp near the red rocks, two good places to try are Manzanita and Banjo Bill. In Coconino National Forest near Flagstaff, the campgrounds near Mormon Lake and Lake Mary—including Pinegrove, Lakeview, Forked Pine, Double Springs, and Dairy Springs—are popular to the point of overcrowding in summer. Sites near Prescott and Jerome in the Prescott National Forest are generally less visited; Potato Patch and Granite Basin are both scenic, and sleeping out on top of Mingus Mountain is unforgettable.

HIKING

Ancient seas, colliding land masses, spewing volcanoes, and other geological forces have cast and recast northern Arizona into a sprawling sculpture of incredible contrasts. Hikes along the canyon rims often look out among red rock monoliths, and treks to the barren crests of the San Francisco Peaks overlook verdant pine forests stretching to the edge of the Grand Canyon to the north and the Mogollon Rim to the south. You can hike through thickly wooded areas in the Verde Valley and the Prescott National Forest in the state's highest alpine region (and even ascend a volcano), and among the rock formations around Sedona. National Forest Service offices in Camp Verde, Prescott, Sedona, and Flagstaff direct trekkers to the best trails.

NATIVE AMERICAN CULTURE

The achievements of the Sinagua people, who lived in north-central Arizona from the 8th through the 15th centuries, reached their height in the 12th and 13th centuries, when related groups occupied most of the San Francisco Volcanic Field and a large portion of the upper and middle Verde Valley. The Sinagua sites around modern-day Camp Verde, Clarkdale, and Flagstaff provide a window onto this remarkable culture. Some of the best examples of surviving Sinagua architecture can be found at Wupatki National Monument, northeast of Flagstaff.

WHAT IT COSTS				
$$$$	**$$$**	**$$**	**$**	**¢**
RESTAURANTS over $30	$21–$30	$13–$20	$8–$12	under $8
HOTELS over $250	$176–$250	$121–$175	$70–$120	under $70

Restaurant prices are per person for a main course at dinner. Hotel prices are for a standard double in high season, excluding taxes and service charges.

Timing

Autumn, when the wet season ends, the stifling desert temperatures moderate, and the mountain aspens reach their full golden splendor, is a great

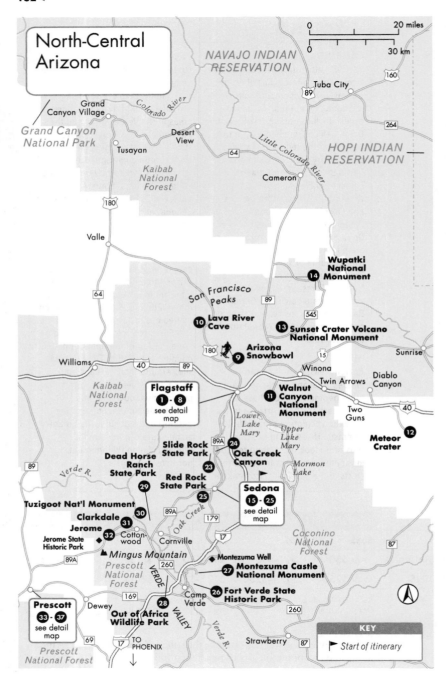

North-Central Arizona

NAVAJO INDIAN RESERVATION

0 — 20 miles
0 — 30 km

160

Tuba City
89

264

Grand Canyon Village
Grand Canyon National Park

Colorado River

Desert View

Tusayan

HOPI INDIAN RESERVATION

64

Little Colorado River

Cameron

Kaibab National Forest

180

Valle

64

Wupatki National Monument 14

San Francisco Peaks

89

545

Lava River Cave 10

Sunset Crater Volcano National Monument 13

Sunrise

180

Arizona Snowbowl 9

15

Williams

40   89

Kaibab National Forest

Flagstaff 1 - 8 see detail map

Walnut Canyon National Monument 11

Winona   Twin Arrows

Diablo Canyon

Two Guns

40

Meteor Crater 12

Lower Lake Mary

Upper Lake Mary

89

Verde R.

Dead Horse Ranch State Park

Slide Rock State Park

89A   24

Oak Creek Canyon 23

Mormon Lake

Red Rock State Park 29   25

Sedona 15 - 25 see detail map

Tuzigoot Nat'l Monument

Clarkdale 31   30

Jerome

32   Cottonwood

Oak Creek

89A   179

Coconino National Forest

87

Jerome State Historic Park

89A

Cornville

17

Montezuma Well

Mingus Mountain

Prescott National Forest

VERDE   260

Montezuma Castle National Monument 27

Prescott 33 - 37 see detail map

Dewey

169

Out of Africa Wildlife Park 28

Camp Verde

Fort Verde State Historic Park 26

260

69   17   TO PHOENIX

VALLEY

Verde R.

Strawberry   87

Prescott National Forest

KEY

► Start of itinerary

time to visit. Hotel rooms in Prescott and Flagstaff are less expensive in winter, but mountain temperatures dip below zero, and snowstorms often occur weekly, especially near Flagstaff. Prescott and Flagstaff hold most of their festivals and cultural events in summer. Sedona's biggest event, the Jazz on the Rocks Festival, takes place in September.

FLAGSTAFF

146 mi northwest of Phoenix, 27 mi north of Sedona via Oak Creek Canyon.

Few travelers slow down long enough to explore Flagstaff, a town of 54,000, known locally as "Flag." Most stop only to spend the night at one of the town's many motels before making the last leg of the trip to the Grand Canyon, 80 mi north. Flag makes a good base for day trips to Native American ruins and the Navajo and Hopi reservations, as well as to the Petrified Forest National Park and the Painted Desert, but the city is a worthwhile destination in its own right. Set against a lovely backdrop of pine forests and the snowcapped San Francisco Peaks, downtown Flagstaff retains a frontier flavor.

Flagstaff has more fast-food outlets than most cities, no doubt because of the incredible demand for them: two major interstate highways meet just south of downtown; thousands of tourists drive through; thousands of students attending Northern Arizona University reside here; and many Native Americans come in from nearby reservations. In summer, Phoenix residents head here, seeking relief from the desert heat since at any time of the year, temperatures in Flagstaff are about 20°F cooler than in Phoenix.

Phoenicians also come to Flagstaff in winter to ski at the small Arizona Snowbowl, about 15 mi northeast of town among the San Francisco Peaks. Flagstaff has many accommodations (although no major hotels or resorts), but you should make reservations, especially in summer.

Exploring Flagstaff

TIMING You can see most of Flagstaff's attractions in a day—easier if you visit the Lowell Observatory or the Northern Arizona University Observatory in the evening—which is also when the Museum Club is best experienced. Consult the schedule of tour times if you want to visit the Riordan State Historic Park. Plan on devoting at least an hour to the excellent Museum of Northern Arizona. The Historic Railroad District is a good place to have lunch. If you're a skier, you might spend part of a winter's day at Arizona Snowbowl; in summer you can spend a couple of hours on the sky ride and scenic trails at the top. Take your time enjoying the trails on Mount Elden, and remember to pace yourself in the higher elevations; allow a full day if you decide to hike these trails. The Lava River Cave is an easy—if dark—hike that can be comfortably completed in an hour.

Numbers in the margin correspond to numbers on the Flagstaff, North-Central Arizona, Sedona, and Prescott maps.

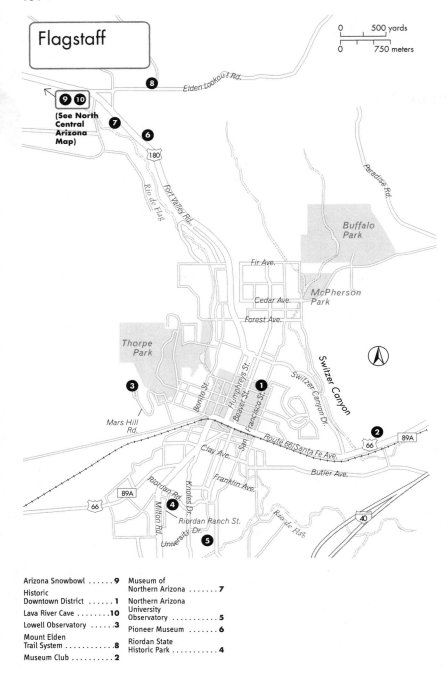

Flagstaff

0   500 yards
0   750 meters

Elden Lookout Rd.

9 10
(See North
Central
Arizona
Map)

8

7

6

180

Paradise Rd.

Rio de Flag

Fort Valley Rd.

Buffalo
Park

Fir Ave.

Cedar Ave.

McPherson
Park

Forest Ave.

Thorpe
Park

Bonito St.

Humphreys St.

Beaver St.

San Francisco St.

Switzer Canyon

Switzer Canyon Dr.

1

Mars Hill
Rd.

Clay Ave.

Route 66/Santa Fe Ave.

2   89A

66

Butler Ave.

Riordan Rd.

Knoles Dr.

Franklin Ave.

89A

66

Milton Rd.

4

Riordan Ranch St.
Dr.

University

5

Route de Flag

40

What to See

9 Arizona Snowbowl. One of Flagstaff's most popular winter attractions also lures patrons in summer, when the Agassiz ski lift, which climbs to a height of 11,500 feet in 25 minutes, doubles as a sky ride through the Coconino National Forest. From this vantage point, you can see up to 70 mi; views may even include the North Rim of the Grand Canyon. There's a lodge at the base with a restaurant and bar. To reach the ski area, take U.S. 180 north from Flagstaff; it's 7 mi from the Snowbowl exit to the skyride entrance. ☒ *Snowbowl Rd., North Flagstaff* ☎ *928/779–1951* ⊕ *www.arizonasnowbowl.com* ☒ *Skyride $10* ☉ *Skyride Memorial Day–early Sept., daily 10–4; early Sept.–mid-Oct., Fri.–Sun. 10–4, weather permitting.*

1 Historic Downtown District. Storied Route 66 runs right through the heart of downtown Flagstaff. The late Victorian, Tudor Revival, and early-art-deco architecture in this district recalls the town's heyday as a logging and railroad center. A walking-tour map of the area is available at the visitor center in the Tudor Revival–style **Santa Fe Depot** (☒ 1 E. Rte. 66, Downtown), an excellent place to begin sightseeing.

Highlights include the 1927 **Hotel Monte Vista** (☒ 100 N. San Francisco St., Downtown), built after a community drive raised $200,000 in 60 days. The construction was promoted as a way to bolster the burgeoning tourism in the region, and the hotel was held publicly until the early 1960s. The 1888 **Babbitt Brothers Building** (☒ 12 E. Aspen Ave., Downtown) was constructed as a building-supply store and then turned into a department store by David Babbitt, the mastermind of the Babbitt empire. The Babbitts are one of Flagstaff's wealthiest founding families. Bruce Babbitt, the most recent member of the family to wield power and influence, was the governor of Arizona from 1978 through 1987 and secretary of the Interior under President Clinton (1993–2001). Most of the area's first businesses were saloons catering to railroad construction workers, which was the case with the 1888 **Vail Building** (☒ 5 N. San Francisco St., Downtown), a brick art deco–influenced structure covered with stucco in 1939. It now houses Crystal Magic, a New Age shop. ☒ *Downtown Historic District, Rte. 66 north to Birch Ave., and Beaver St. east to Agassiz St.*

NEED A BREAK

The town's most interesting shops are concentrated downtown, and there are a couple of brewpubs and some spots where you can grab a quick bite. Students, skiers, new and aging hippies, and just about everyone else who likes good coffee jam into **Macy's European Coffee House and Bakery** (☒ 14 S. Beaver St., Downtown ☎ 928/774–2243) for the best cup in town. The **Black Bean** (☒ 12 E. Rte. 66, Downtown ☎ 928/779–9905) is the place for do-it-yourself burritos, as healthful or as guacamole-smothered as you like.

10 Lava River Cave. Subterranean lava flow formed this mile-long cave roughly 700,000 years ago. Once you descend into its boulder-strewn maw, the cave is spacious, with 40-foot ceilings. But claustrophobes take heed: about halfway through the cave tapers to a 4-foot-high squeeze that can be a bit unnerving. Pack an extra flashlight and warm clothing. A yearlong 40°F chill pervades the cave. To reach the turnoff for the cave, go approximately 14 mi north of Flagstaff on U.S. 180, then turn west onto FR 245. Turn left at the intersection of FR 171 and look for the sign to the cave. Although the cave is on National Forest Service property, the only thing here is an interpretive sign, so it's definitely something you tackle at your own risk. ⊠ *FR 171B.*

⟲ ❸ **Lowell Observatory.** In 1894, Boston businessman, author, and scientist Percival Lowell founded this observatory from which he studied Mars. His theories of the existence of a ninth planet sowed the seeds for the discovery of Pluto at Lowell in 1930 by Clyde Tombaugh. V. M. Slipher's observations here between 1912 and 1920 led to the theory of the expanding universe. The 6,500-square-foot Steele Visitor Center hosts exhibits and lectures and has a gift shop. Several interactive exhibits—among them Pluto Walk, a scaled-down version of the solar system—will interest children. Some evenings the public is invited to

> **WORD OF MOUTH**
>
> "The Lowell Observatory in Flagstaff . . . we found the daytime tour very interesting, very worthwhile; would highly recommend! Too bad we didn't get to see it at night. "   –susan4

peer through the 24-inch Clark telescope or through a more up-to-date 16-inch reflecting telescope. Viewings all week are offered from June through August; call ahead for a schedule. The observatory dome is open and unheated, so dress for the outdoors. To reach the observatory, less than 2 mi from downtown, drive west on Route 66, which resumes its former name, Santa Fe Avenue, before it merges into Mars Hill Road. ⊠ *1400 W. Mars Hill Rd., West Flagstaff* ☎ *928/774-3358* ⊕ *www. lowell.edu* ☜ *$5* ☾ *Visitor center and night viewing hrs change seasonally; call ahead.*

❽ **Mount Elden Trail System.** Most trails in the 35-mi-long Mount Elden Trail System lead to views from the dormant volcanic field, across the vast ponderosa pine forest, all the way to Sedona. The most challenging trail in the Mount Elden system, which happens to be the route with the most rewarding views, is along the steep switchbacks of the **Elden Lookout Trail** (⊠ Off U.S. 89, 3 mi east of downtown Flagstaff). If you traverse the full 3 mi to the top, keep your focus on the landscape rather than the tangle of antennae and satellite dishes that greet you at the top. The 4-mi-long **Sunset Trail** (⊠ Off U.S. 180, 3 mi north of downtown Flagstaff, then 6 mi east on FR 420 [Schultz Pass Rd.]) proceeds with a gradual pitch through the pine forest, emerging onto a narrow ridge nicknamed the Catwalk. By all means take pictures of the stunning valley views, but make sure your feet are well placed. The access road to this trail is closed in winter.

❷ **Museum Club.** For real Route 66 color, don't miss this local institution fondly known as the Zoo because the building housed an extensive taxidermy collection in the 1930s. Most of the stuffed animals—including the one-eyed sheep—are gone, but some owls still perch above the dance floor of what is now a popular country-and-western club. Even if you don't like crowds or country music, it's worth coming to see this gigantic log cabin constructed around five trees; the entryway consists of a huge wishbone-shape pine. ⊠ *3404 E. Rte. 66, Downtown* ☎ *928/ 526–9434* ⊕ *www.museumclub.com* ▨ *Free* ☉ *Daily 11* AM*–2* AM.

★ ☾ ❼ **Museum of Northern Arizona.** A visit is worthwhile, if only to see the striking native-stone building in a cool, tree-shaded site. The institution, founded in 1928, is respected worldwide for its research and its collections centering on the natural and cultural history of the Colorado Plateau. Among the permanent exhibitions are an extensive collection of Navajo rugs and a Hopi kiva (men's ceremonial chamber).

A gallery devoted to area geology is usually a hit with children: it includes a life-size model dilophosaurus, a carnivorous dinosaur that once roamed northern Arizona. Outdoors, a life-zone exhibit shows the changing vegetation from the bottom of the Grand Canyon to the highest peak in Flagstaff. A nature trail, open only in summer, heads down across a small stream into a canyon and up into an aspen grove. In summer the museum hosts exhibits and the works of Native American artists, whose wares are also sold in the museum gift shop. The museum's education department sponsors excellent tours of the area and as far away as New Mexico and Utah. ⊠ *3101 N. Fort Valley Rd., North Flagstaff* ☎ *928/774–5213* ⊕ *www.musnaz.org* ▨ *$5* ☉ *Daily 9–5.*

❺ **Northern Arizona University Observatory.** The observatory, with its 24-inch telescope, was built in 1952 by Dr. Arthur Adel, a scientist at Lowell Observatory until he joined the college faculty as a professor of mathematics. His work on infrared astronomy pioneered research into molecules that absorb light passing through the Earth's atmosphere. Today's studies of Earth's shrinking ozone layer rely on some of Dr. Adel's early work. Visitors to the observatory—which houses one of the largest telescopes that the public is allowed to move and manipulate—are usually hosted by friendly students and faculty members of the university's Department of Physics and Astronomy. ⊠ *Bldg. 47, Northern Arizona Campus Observatory, Dept. of Physics and Astronomy, S. San Francisco St., just north of Walkup Skydome, University* ☎ *928/523–8121 weekdays, 928/523–7170 Fri. night* ▨ *Free* ☉ *Viewings Fri. 7:30–10* PM*, weather permitting.*

❻ **Pioneer Museum.** The Arizona Historical Society operates this museum in a volcanic-rock building constructed in 1908. The structure was Coconino County's first hospital for the poor, and the current displays include one of the depressingly small nurses' rooms, an old iron lung, and a reconstructed doctor's office. Most of the exhibits, however, touch on more cheerful aspects of Flagstaff history—like road signs and children's toys. The museum holds a folk-crafts festival on July 4, with blacksmiths, weavers, spinners, quilters, and candle makers. Their crafts, and those of other local artisans, are sold in the museum's gift shop. The museum is part of the Fort Valley Park complex, in a wooded residential section at the northwest end of town. ⊠ *2340 N. Fort Valley Rd., North Flagstaff* ☎ *928/774–6272* ▨ *$3* ☉ *Mon.–Sat. 9–5.*

❹ Riordan State Historic Park. This must-see artifact of Flagstaff's logging

FodorśChoice heyday is near Northern Arizona University. Its centerpiece is a man-

★ sion built in 1904 for Michael and Timothy Riordan, lumber-baron brothers who married two sisters. The 13,300-square-foot, 40-room
log-and-stone structure—designed by Charles Whittlesley, who was
also responsible for the El Tovar Hotel at the Grand Canyon—contains
furniture by Gustav Stickley, father of the American Arts and Crafts–design movement. One room holds "Paul Bunyan's shoes," a 2-foot-long
pair of boots made by Timothy in his workshop. Everything on display
is original to the house. The mansion may be explored on a guided tour
only. ⊠ *409 W. Riordan Rd., University* ☎ *928/779–4395* ⊕ *www.pr.
state.az.us* ✑ *$6* ☉ *May–Oct., daily 8:30–5, with tours on the hr 9–4;
Nov.–Apr., daily 10:30–5, with tours on the hr 11–4.*

Sports & the Outdoors

Camping

Contact the **Coconino National Forest** (⊠ Peaks Ranger Station, 5075 N.
U.S. 89, North Flagstaff ☎ 928/526–0866 ⊕ www.fs.fed.us/r3/co-
conino) for information on campgrounds in the area.

Hiking & Rock Climbing

You can explore Arizona's alpine tundra in the San Francisco Peaks, where
more than 80 species of plants grow on the upper elevations. The habitat is fragile, so hikers are asked to stay on established trails (there are
lots of them). The altitude here will make even the hardiest hikers
breathe a little harder, so individuals with cardiac or respiratory problems should be cautious about overexertion. Flatlanders should give themselves at least a day or two to adjust to the altitude.

The rangers of the **Coconino National Forest** (⊠ 1824 S. Thompson St.,
North Flagstaff ☎ 928/527–3600 ⊕ www.fs.fed.us/r3/coconino)
maintain many of the region's trails and can provide you with details
on hiking in the area; the forest's main office is open weekdays 7:30
to 4:30.

Flagstaff is in the **Peaks District** (⊠ Peaks Ranger Station, 5075 N. U.S.
89, East Flagstaff ☎ 928/526–0866) of the Coconino National Forest,
and there are many trails to explore. The **Humphreys Peak Trail** (⊠ Trailhead: Snowbowl Rd., 7 mi north of U.S. 180) is 9-mi round-trip, with
a vertical climb of 3,843 feet to the summit of Arizona's highest mountain (12,643 feet). Those who don't want a long hike can do just the
first mile of the adjacent, 5-mi-long **Kachina Trail** (⊠ Trailhead: Snowbowl Rd., 7 mi north of U.S. 180); gently rolling, this route is surrounded
by huge stands of aspen and offers fantastic vistas. In fall, changing leaves
paint the landscape shades of yellow, russet, and amber.

Flagstaff Mountain Guides (☎ 928/635–0145) organizes rock-climbing
trips around town or as far away as Sedona. If you'd prefer to hone
your skills first, **Vertical Relief Rock Gym** (⊠ 205 S. San Francisco St.,
Downtown ☎ 928/556–9909) provides the tallest indoor climbing
walls in the Southwest.

Horseback Riding

The wranglers at **Hitchin' Post Stables** (⊠ 4848 Lake Mary Rd., South Flagstaff ☎ 928/774–1719) lead rides into Walnut Canyon and operate horseback or horse-drawn wagon rides with sunset barbecues. In winter they'll take you through Coconino National Forest on a sleigh.

Mountain Biking

With more than 30 mi of challenging trails a short ride from town, it was inevitable that one of Flagstaff's best-kept secrets would leak out. The mountain biking on Mount Elden is on par with that of more celebrated trails in Colorado and Utah.

The **Coconino National Forest** (⇨ Hiking & Rock Climbing) holds some of the best trails in the region. A good place to start is the **Lower Oldham Trail** (⊠ Trailhead: Cedar St.), which originates on the north end of Buffalo Park in Flagstaff; there's a large meadow with picnic areas and an exercise path. The terrain rolls, climbing about 800 feet in 3 mi, and the trail is technical in spots but easy enough to test your tolerance of the elevation. Many fun trails spur off this one. They're all hemmed in by roads and cabins so it's difficult to get too lost.

The very popular **Schultz Creek Trail** (⊠ Trailhead: Schultz Pass Rd., near intersection with U.S. 180) is fun and suitable for strong beginners, though seasoned experts will be thrilled as well. Most opt to start at the top of the 600-foot-high hill and swoop down the smooth, twisting path through groves of wildflowers and stands of ponderosa pines and aspens and end at the trailhead four giddy miles later.

The **Sunset Trail** (⊠ Trailhead: Elden Lookout Rd., 7 mi from intersection with Schultz Pass Rd.), near the summit of Mount Elden, affords amazing views off the ridge rendered barren by a 1977 fire. The trail narrows into the aptly nicknamed Catwalk, with precipitous drops a few feet on either side. ⚠ **Vertigo, either from the 9,000-foot elevation or the sheer exposure, is not an option. You need to be an at least moderately experienced mountain biker to attempt this trail.** When combined with Elden Lookout Road and Schultz Creek Trail, the usual loop, the trail totals 15 mi and climbs almost 2,000 feet. You can avoid the slog up Mount Elden by parking one vehicle at the top of Elden Lookout Road, at the trailhead, and a friend's vehicle at the bottom.

You can rent mountain bikes, garner good advice, and purchase trail maps at **Absolute Bikes** (⊠ 18 N. San Francisco St., Downtown ☎ 928/779–5969). From mid-June through mid-October, the **Flagstaff Nordic Center** (⊠ U.S. 180, 16 mi north of Flagstaff, North Flagstaff ☎ 928/220–0550) opens its cross-country trails to mountain bikers, gratis if you bring your own wheels; rentals are available. **Mountain Sports** (⊠ 24 N. San Francisco St., Downtown ☎ 928/226–2885 or 800/286–5156) offers competitive rates for bike rentals. A map of the **Urban Trails System** (⊠ 1 E. Rte. 66, Downtown ☎ 928/774–9541 or 800/842–7293), available at the Flagstaff Visitor Center, details biking options in town.

Skiing & Snowboarding

The ski season usually starts in mid-December and ends in mid-April but the recent addition of snowmaking will lengthen the season. The

Arizona Snowbowl (✉ Snowbowl Rd., North Flagstaff ☎ 928/779–1951, 928/779–4577 snow report ⊕ www.arizonasnowbowl.com), 7 mi north of Flagstaff off U.S. 180, has 32 downhill runs (37% beginner, 42% intermediate, and 21% advanced), four chairlifts, and a vertical drop of 2,300 feet. There are a couple of good bump runs, but it's better for beginners or those with moderate skill serious area skiers take a road trip to Teluride. Still, it's a fun place to spend the day. Snowboarders share trails with downhill skiers. The Hart Prairie Lodge has an equipment-rental shop and a SKIwee center for ages 4 to 8. All-day adult lift tickets are $44. Half-day discounts are available, and group-lesson packages (including two hours of instruction, an all-day lift ticket, and equipment rental) are a good buy at $66. A children's program (which includes lunch, progress card, and full supervision 9–3:30) runs $65. Many Flagstaff motels offer ski packages, including transportation to Snowbowl.

The **Flagstaff Nordic Center** (✉ U.S. 180, 16 mi north of Flagstaff, North Flagstaff ☎ 928/220–0550 ⊕ www.flagstaffnordiccenter.com) is 9 mi north of Snowbowl Road. There are 25 mi of well-groomed cross-country trails here that are open Thursday through Sunday and holidays. Coffee, hot chocolate, and snacks are served at the lodge. You can also rent sleds for a nearby run called Crowley Pit. A day pass for skiing costs $10. An instruction package costs $40 including equipment. To rent equipment by itself costs $15.

Where to Stay & Eat

★ **$$$–$$$$** ✕ **Cottage Place.** An elegant spot in a town known for fast food and drive-through service, this restaurant in a 50-year-old cottage has intimate dining rooms and an extensive wine list. The menu strays slightly from Continental to include some classic American dishes, such as charbroiled lamb chops. Try the artichoke chicken breast or chateaubriand for two. Dinner includes soup and salad, but save room for Chocolate Decadence and other desserts. ✉ *126 W. Cottage Ave., Downtown* ☎ *928/774–8431* ▭ *AE, MC, V* ☉ *Closed Mon. No lunch.*

$$–$$$ ✕ **Black Bart's Steakhouse Saloon & Old West Theater.** The Wild West decor at this rollicking, brightly lighted barn of a restaurant is somewhat cornball, but the barbecued chicken is tender and flavorful. Don't expect to see vegetables on your plate unless they're deep-fried. Northern Arizona University music students entertain while they wait on tables, so don't be surprised if your server suddenly jumps onstage to belt out a couple of show tunes. ✉ *2760 E. Butler Ave., Downtown* ☎ *928/779–3142* ⌖ *Reservations not accepted* ▭ *AE, MC, V* ☉ *No lunch.*

$$–$$$ ✕ **Sakura Restaurant.** The excellent fish at this Japanese restaurant in the Radisson is flown in every other day from the West Coast. If sushi doesn't entice you, dine at a large grill table where the well-seasoned, large portions of steak or seafood with vegetables are flipped in front of you. ✉ *Radisson Woodlands*

SMOKING?

It's good to note that by city ordinance, all restaurants in Flagstaff forbid smoking.

3

Plaza Hotel, 1175 Rte. 66, University ☎ 928/773–9118 ⊟ *AE, D, DC, MC, V* ⊘ *No lunch Sun.*

$$ ✕ **Pasto.** This downtown Italian restaurant—two intimate dining rooms in adjacent historic buildings—is popular with for good food at reasonable prices. Such southern Italian standards as lasagna and spaghetti with meatballs appear on the menu along with more innovative fare, such as artichoke orzo and salmon Caesar salad. A courtyard in the back, tucked among higher buildings, has a romantic urban feel. ⊠ *19 E. Aspen St., Downtown* ☎ 928/779–1937 ⊟ *MC, V.*

$–$$ ✕ **Buster's Restaurant.** At lunchtime, families and students from nearby Northern Arizona University settle into comfortable booths to enjoy fresh seafood, homemade soups, salads, giant burgers, and mesquite-grilled steaks. Try the *lahvosh* appetizer—a huge cracker heaped with toppings ranging from smoked salmon to mushrooms—or the Caesar salad with grilled Cajun chicken. At night, single professionals and skiers crowd the bar and work through its impressive beer selection. ⊠ *1800 S. Milton Rd., University* ☎ 928/774–5155 ⊟ *AE, D, DC, MC, V.*

$ ✕ **Beaver Street Brewery and Whistle Stop Cafe.** Popular among the wood-fired pizzas is the Enchanted Forest, with Brie, portobello mushrooms, roasted red peppers, spinach, and artichoke pesto. Whichever pie you order, expect serious amounts of garlic. Sandwiches, such as the Southwestern chicken with three types of cheese, come with a hefty portion of tasty fries. You won't regret ordering one of the down-home desserts, such as the super-gooey chocolate bread pudding. Among the excellent microbrews usually on tap, the raspberry ale is a local favorite. An outdoor beer garden opens in summer. ⊠ *11 S. Beaver St., Downtown* ☎ 928/ 779–0079 ⊟ *AE, D, DC, MC, V.*

¢–$ ✕ **Café Espress.** The menu is largely vegetarian at this natural-foods restaurant. Stir-fried vegetables, pasta dishes, Mediterranean salads, tempeh burgers, pita pizzas, fish or chicken specials, and wonderful baked goods made on the premises all come at prices that will make you feel good, too. This is an artsy and hip place (the work of local artists hangs on the walls) but friendly, and it's open for breakfast every day at 7. ⊠ *16 N. San Francisco St., Downtown* ☎ 928/774–0541 ⊟ *MC, V.*

¢–$ ✕ **Salsa Brava.** This cheerful Mexican restaurant, with light-wood booths and colorful designs, eschews heavy Sonoran-style fare in favor of the grilled dishes found in Guadalajara. It's considered the best Mexican food in town—but there's not much competition. The fish tacos are particularly good. On weekends come for a huevos rancheros breakfast. ⊠ *2220 E. Rte. 66, East* ☎ 928/779–5293 ⊟ *AE, MC, V.*

★ ¢ ✕ **La Bellavia.** At this favorite bohemian breakfast nook, the trout and eggs platter is the standard—two eggs served with Idaho trout flavored with a hint of lemon and rounded off by a buttermilk pancake. Other options include Swedish oat pancakes, seven-grain French toast, and nine varieties of eggs Benedict. A palette of creative sandwiches and familiar salads makes this a worthwhile lunch stop as well. The café doubles as a gallery for local artists whose artwork hangs on the walls. ⊠ *18 S. Beaver St., Downtown* ☎ 928/774–8301 ⊟ *MC, V* ⊘ *No dinner.*

¢ ✕ **Bun Huggers.** The best burger in town is flipped over a mesquite-fired grill. Also try the tasty, if decadent, deep-fried zucchini served with shredded cheddar cheese and ranch dressing. There's a small salad bar here, but it seems like an afterthought, existing only to heal guilty consciences. ⊠ *901 S. Milton Rd., University* ☎ *928/779–3743* ▤ *AE, D, MC, V.*

★ $$–$$$ ▦ **Inn at 410.** An inviting alternative to the chain motels in Flagstaff, this B&B has a convenient but quiet downtown location. All the accommodations in the beautifully restored 1907 residence are suites with private baths. Some have private entrances and fireplaces; all have coffeemakers. Monet's Garden is a lovely Jacuzzi suite with fireplace. Pancakes with blue cornmeal and piñon nuts, and curried cornbread pudding with pumpkin sauce highlight a tantalizing breakfast menu. No kids in some rooms. ⊠ *410 N. Leroux St., Downtown, 86001* ☎ *928/774–0088 or 800/774–2008* 🖷 *928/774–6354* ⊕ *www.inn410.com* ⬩ *9 suites* ⌂ *Some in-room hot tubs, refrigerators, in-room DVD/VCR; no room phones, no smoking* ▤ *MC, V* ▥ *BP.*

★ $–$$ ▦ **Little America of Flagstaff.** The biggest hotel in town is deservedly popular. It's far from the roar of the trains, the grounds are surrounded by evergreen forests, and it's one of the few places in Flagstaff with room service. Plush rooms have comfortable sitting areas with French provincial–style furniture and stereo TVs. Other pluses are courtesy van service to the airport and the Amtrak station, and a gift shop with great Southwestern stuff. Don't miss the famous Sunday Brunch with breakfast fare alongside prime rib, seafood, and European-style pastries. ⊠ *2515 E. Butler Ave., Downtown, 86004* ☎ *928/779–2741 or 800/352–4386* 🖷 *928/779–7983* ⊕ *www.flagstaff.littleamerica.com* ⬩ *248 rooms* ⌂ *Restaurant, coffee shop, room service, kitchenettes, refrigerators, cable TV with movies and video games, pool, gym, hair salon, croquet, hiking, horseshoes, bar, playground, laundry facilities, laundry service, meeting rooms* ▤ *AE, D, DC, MC, V.*

$–$$ ▦ **Sled Dog Inn.** This inn is on 4 acres, but its grounds seem vastly larger, since the land borders the immense Coconino National Forest. A big draw here is, as the name implies, the owners' Siberian huskies, which are lovingly cared for. Sometimes in winter you can accompany the owners on a dog-sled run, but they no longer offer regular rides to guests. Rooms are contemporary rustic. ⊠ *10155 Mountainaire Rd., South Flagstaff, 86001* ☎ *928/525–6212 or 800/754–0064* ⊕ *www.sleddoginn. com* ⬩ *8 rooms, 2 suites* ⌂ *Hot tub, sauna; no room TVs, no kids under 6, no smoking* ▤ *AE, MC, V* ▥ *CP.*

$–$$ ▦ **Starlight Pines Bed and Breakfast.** If you prefer the clean lines of 1920s design to Victorian froufrou, consider staying at this stylish B&B. Rooms in this residence on the city's east side are all beautifully appointed with art deco pieces; one room has a private porch, another a fireplace. ⊠ *3380 E. Lockett Rd., East Flagstaff, 86004* ☎ *928/527–1912 or 800/752–1912* ⊕ *www.jeanettesbb.com* ⬩ *4 rooms* ⌂ *No room TVs, no smoking* ▤ *D, MC, V* ▥ *BP.*

¢–$ ▦ **Hotel Monte Vista.** Over the years many Hollywood stars, including Bob Hope and Spencer Tracy, have stayed at this downtown hotel. It's a quirky and fun place, but renovations have not yet restored it to its heyday. Funky room designs are inspired by the famous guests: golden cherubs descend from an azure ceiling in the Air Supply Room, and framed antique postcards of Western novel book covers hang on the walls of the Zane Grey Room. ⊠ *100 N. San Francisco St., Downtown, 86001*

☎ *928/779–6971 or 800/545–3068* 🖷 *928/779–2904* 🌐 *www. hotelmontevista.com* 🛏 *48 rooms* ⚲ *Restaurant, cable TV, bar, laundry service, some pets allowed (fee)* ▭ *AE, D, MC, V.*

¢ 🎬 **Hotel Weatherford.** With a columned veranda, this hotel, built in 1897, is a dramatic presence at the hub of town. Imbued with a creaky charm, the rooms are spartan and a bit worn around the edges but comfortable. Forgo TV and a telephone for a taste of the Old West. The Exchange Pub downstairs has a bustling nightlife scene. ⊠ *23 N. Leroux St., Downtown, 86001* ☎ *928/779–1919* 🖷 *928/773–8951* 🌐 *www. weatherfordhotel.com* 🛏 *8 rooms, 5 with bath* ⚲ *Restaurant, 2 bars; no a/c, no room phones, no room TVs* ▭ *AE, D, DC, MC, V.*

Nightlife & the Arts

THE ARTS There is also no shortage of cultural entertainment in Flagstaff, not to mention summer festivals.

The **Flagstaff Symphony Orchestra** (☎ 928/774–5107) has year-round musical events. The 1917 **Orpheum Theater** (⊠ 15 W. Aspen St., Downtown ☎ 928/556–1580) features music acts, films, lectures and plays. **Theatrikos Theatre Company** (⊠ 11 W. Cherry Ave., Downtown ☎ 928/774–1662) is highly regarded with an eclectic lineup of plays.

A Celebration of Native American Art (⊠ 3101 N. Fort Valley Rd., North Flagstaff ☎ 928/774–5211), featuring exhibits of work by Zuni, Hopi, and Navajo artists, is held at the Museum of Northern Arizona from late May through September. In August the **Flagstaff Festival of the Arts** (☎ 928/774–7750 or 800/266–7740) fills the air with classical music and pops performances, many by world-renowned artists. **Flagstaff SummerFest** (⊠ Fort Tuthill Coconino County Park, S. AZ 89A, South Flagstaff ☎ 928/774–5130), held the first weekend in August, includes an arts-and-crafts fair. Flagstaff's observatories help make September's **Festival of Science** (☎ 800/842–7293) a stellar attraction.

NIGHTLIFE Flagstaff's large college contingent has plenty of places to gather after dark, most in historic downtown and most charge little or no cover. It's easy to walk from one rowdy spot to the next. For information on what's going on, pick up the free *Flagstaff Live.*

The **Hotel Weatherford** (⊠ 23 N. Leroux St., Downtown ☎ 928/779–1919) has a double bill, with Charly's, which hosts late-night jazz and blues bands, and the Exchange Pub, which tends to attract folksy ensembles. The **Mogollon Brewing Company** (⊠ 15 N. Agassiz St., Downtown ☎ 928/773–8950) rolls out live music and hardy stout. The **Monte Vista Lounge** (⊠ 100 N. San Francisco St., Downtown ☎ 928/774–2403) packs them in with nightly live blues, jazz, classic rock, punk, and an open mike on Wednesday. **San Felipe's Coastal Cantina** (⊠ 103 N. Leroux, Downtown ☎ 928/774–6000) is the place for tequila, fish tacos, dancing, and a raucous Spring Break atmosphere.

Shopping

Flagstaff's prime shopping area is downtown. Even if you're not looking for anything in particular, it's fun to stroll along San Francisco

Street and Route 66. The **Flagstaff Mall** (✉ 4650 N. U.S. 89, East Flagstaff ☎ 928/526–4827) is just east of town off Interstate 40 at Exit 201. It has the greatest number of department and specialty stores in the area, including Dillard's, Sears Roebuck, and JCPenney. There's also a food court and a two-screen cinema.

For fine arts and crafts—everything from ceramics and stained glass to weaving and painting—visit the **Artists Gallery** (✉ 17 N. San Francisco St., Downtown ☎ 928/773–0958), a local artists' cooperative. You can pick up sporting goods at **Babbit's Backcountry Outfitters** (✉ 12 E. Aspen Ave., Downtown ☎ 928/774–4775). The **Black Hound Gallerie** (✉ 120 N. Leroux St., Downtown ☎ 928/774–2323) specializes in posters, prints, and funky kitsch of all kinds. **Bookman's** (✉ 1520 S. Riordan Ranch Rd., University ☎ 928/774–0005) is packed solid with used books on every topic. Coffee, a cybercafé, and live folk music occupy a corner of the store. The 20-odd vendors at **Carriage House Antique and Gift Mall** (✉ 413 N. San Francisco St., Downtown ☎ 928/774–1337) sell vintage clothing and jewelry, furniture, fine china, and other collectibles. The **Museum of Northern Arizona Gift Shop** (✉ 3101 N. Fort Valley Rd., University ☎ 928/774–5213) carries high-quality jewelry and crafts. **Winter Sun Trading Company** (✉ 107 N. San Francisco St., Downtown ☎ 928/774–2884) sells medicinal herbs, jewelry, and crafts. **Zani** (✉ 111-C S. San Francisco St., Downtown ☎ 928/774–9409) stocks hip home furnishings and greeting cards in addition to futons.

SIDE TRIPS NEAR FLAGSTAFF

Travelers who head straight through town bound for the Grand Canyon often neglect the area north and east of Flagstaff but a detour has its rewards. If you don't have enough time to do everything, take a quick drive to Walnut Canyon—only about 15 minutes out of town.

East of Flagstaff

★ ⓫ **Walnut Canyon National Monument** consists of a group of cliff dwellings constructed by the Sinagua people, who lived and farmed in and around the canyon starting around AD 700. The more than 300 dwellings here were built between 1080 and 1250 and abandoned, like those at so many other settlements in Arizona and New Mexico, around 1300. The Sinagua traded far and wide with other Native Americans, including people at Wupatki. Even macaw feathers, which would have come from tribes in what is now Mexico, have been excavated in the canyon. Early Flagstaff settlers looted the site for pots and "treasure," and Woodrow Wilson declared the site a national monument in 1915, which began a 30-year process of stabilizing the ruins.

Part of the fascination of Walnut Canyon is the opportunity to enter the dwellings, stepping back in time to an ancient way of life. Some of the Sinagua homes are in near-perfect condition, in spite of all the looting, because of the dry, hot climate and the protection of overhanging cliffs. You can reach them by descending 185 feet on the 1-mi stepped **Island Trail,** which starts at the visitor center. As you follow the trail, look across the canyon for other dwellings not accessible on the path.

Island Trail takes about an hour to complete at a normal pace. Those with health concerns should opt for the easier ½-mi **Rim Trail,** which has overlooks from which dwellings, as well as an excavated, reconstructed pit house, can be viewed. Picnic areas dot the grounds and line the roads leading to the park. Guides conduct tours on Wednesday, Saturday, and Sunday

from late May through early September. ⊠ *Walnut Canyon Rd., 3 mi south of Interstate 40, Exit 204, Winona* ☎ *928/526–3367* ⊕ *www. nps.gov/waca* ⊠ *$5* ☉ *Mar.–May, and Sept.–Nov., daily 8–5; June–Aug., daily 8–6; Dec.–Feb., daily 9–5.*

 Meteor Crater, a natural phenomenon in a privately owned park 43 mi east of Flagstaff, is impressive if for no other reason than its sheer size. A hole in the ground 600 feet deep, nearly 1 mi across, and more than 3 mi in circumference, Meteor Crater is large enough to accommodate the Washington Monument or 20 football fields. It was created when a meteorite crashed here 49,000 years ago. The area looks so much like the surface of the moon that NASA made it one of the official training sites for the Project Apollo astronauts. You can't descend into the crater because of the efforts of its owners to maintain its condition—scientists consider this to be the best-preserved crater on Earth—but guided rim tours, given every hour on the hour from 9 to 3, give useful background information. There's a small snack bar, and the Rock Shop sells specimens from the area and jewelry made from native stones. Take Interstate 40 east of Flagstaff to Exit 233, then 6 mi south on Meteor Crater Road. ⊠ *Meteor Crater Rd., 43 mi east of Flagstaff* ☎ *800/289–5898* ⊕ *www.meteorcrater.com* ⊠ *$12* ☉ *Memorial Day–Labor Day, daily 7–7; Labor Day–Memorial Day, daily 8–5.*

San Francisco Volcanic Field

The San Francisco Volcanic Field north of Flagstaff encompasses 2,000 square mi of fascinating geological phenomena—ancient volcanoes, cinder cones, valleys carved by water and ice, and the San Francisco Peaks themselves, some of which soar to almost 13,000 feet—as well as some of the most extensive Native American ruins in the Southwest: don't miss Sunset Crater and Wupatki. These national monuments can be explored in relative solitude during much of the year. The area is short on services, so fill up on gas and consider taking a picnic. A good source for hiking and camping information in the San Francisco Volcanic Field area are the rangers of **Coconino National Forest** (⊠ Peaks Ranger Station, 5075 N. U.S. 89, North Flagstaff ☎ 928/526–0866 ⊕ www.fs.fed.us/r3/coconino). If you camp, do not pitch your tent in a low-lying area, where flash floods can literally wipe you out.

★ **Sunset Crater Volcano National Monument** lies 14 mi northeast of Flagstaff off U.S. 89. Sunset Crater, a cinder cone that rises 1,000 feet, was an active volcano 900 years ago. The final eruption contained iron and sulfur, which gives the rim of the crater its glow and thus its name. You can walk around the base, but you can't descend into the huge, fragile cone. The **Lava Flow Trail**, a half-hour, mile-long, self-guided walk, provides a good view of the evidence of the volcano's fiery power: lava formations and holes in the rock where volcanic gases vented to the surface.

> ## WHAT IS A PUEBLO?
>
> A pueblo is an ancient village consisting of stone structures several stories high centered around a main plaza. The largest pueblo, located in Wupatki, near Flagstaff, housed close to 100 people who relied on agriculture to survive.

If you're interested in hiking a volcano, head to **Lenox Crater,** about 1 mi east of the visitor center, and climb the 280 feet to the top of the cinder cone. The cinder is soft and crumbly so wear closed, sturdy shoes. From **O'Leary Peak,** 5 mi from the visitor center on Forest Route 545A, great views can be had of the San Francisco Peaks, the Painted Desert, and beyond. The road is unpaved and rutted, however, so it's advisable to take only high-clearance vehicles, especially in winter. In addition, there's a gate, about halfway along the route, which is usually closed. This will mean a steep 2½-mi hike to the top on foot. To get to the area from Flagstaff, take Santa Fe Avenue east to U.S. 89, and head north for 12 mi; turn right onto the road marked Sunset Crater and go another 2 mi to the visitor center. ⊠ *Sunset Crater–Wupatki Loop Rd., 14 mi northeast of Flagstaff* ☎ *928/556–0502* ⊕ *www.nps.gov/sucr* ⌦ *$5, including Wupatki National Monument and Doney Mountain* ⊙ *Mar.–May and Sept.–Nov., daily 8–5; June–Aug., daily 8–6; Dec.–Feb., daily 9–5.*

 FodorsChoice ★

Families from the Sinagua and other ancestral Puebloans are believed to have lived together in harmony on the site that is now **Wupatki National Monument,** farming and trading with one another and with those who passed through. The eruption of Sunset Crater may have caused migration to this area a century after the event, as freshly laid volcanic cinders held in moisture needed for crops—and may have disrupted the settlement more than once around AD 1064. Although there's evidence of earlier habitation, most of the settlers moved here around 1100 and left the pueblo by about 1250. The 2,700 identified sites contain archaeological evidence of a Native American settlement.

> ## WORD OF MOUTH
>
> "Wupatki/Sunset Crater are nice in that you can go into some of the ruins. There are 3-4 different sites spread out over the park that you can visit. Visit all of them. Be sure to go all the way down to the ball court and blowhole at the largest ruins (Wupatki)."   –bigtyke

The site for which the national monument was named, the Wupatki (meaning "tall house" in Hopi), was originally three stories

Vortex Tour

WHAT IS A VORTEX? The word "vortex" comes from the Latin *vertere*, which means "to turn or whirl." In Sedona, a vortex is a funnel created by the motion of spiraling energy. Sedona has long been believed to be a center for spiritual power because of the vortices of subtle energy in the area. This energy isn't described as electricity or magnetism, though it's said to leave a slight residual magnetism in the places where it's strongest.

New Agers believe there are four major vortices in Sedona: Airport, Red Rock Crossing/Cathedral Rock, Boynton Canyon, and Bell Rock. Each manifests a different kind of energy, and this energy interacts with the individual in its presence. People come from all over the world to experience these energy forms, hoping for guidance in spiritual matters, health, and relationships.

Juniper trees, which are all over the Sedona area, are said to respond to vortex energy in a way that reveals where this energy is strongest. The stronger the energy, the more axial twist the junipers bear in their branches.

Airport Vortex is said to strengthen one's "masculine" side, aiding in self-confidence and focus. Red Rock Crossing/Cathedral Rock Vortex nurtures one's "feminine" aspects, such as patience and kindness. You'll be directed to Boynton Canyon Vortex if you're seeking balance between the masculine and feminine. And finally, Bell Rock Vortex, the most powerful of all, strengthens all three aspects: masculine, feminine, and balance.

These energy centers are easily accessed, and vortex maps are available at crystal shops all over Sedona.

---

high, built above an unexplored system of underground fissures. The structure had almost 100 rooms and an open ball court—evidence of Southwestern trade with Mesoamerican tribes for whom ball games were a central ritual. Next to the ball court is a blowhole, a geologic phenomenon in which air is forced upward by underground pressure.

Other ruins to visit are Wukoki, Lomaki, and the Citadel, a pueblo on a knoll above a limestone sink. Although the largest remnants of Native American settlements at Wupatki National Monument are open to the public, other sites are off-limits. If you're interested in an in-depth tour, consider a ranger-led overnight hike to the **Crack-in-Rock Ruin.** The 14-mi (round-trip) trek covers areas marked by ancient petroglyphs and dotted with well-preserved ruins. The trips are conducted in April and October; call by February or August if you'd like to take part in the lottery for one of the 100 available places on these $25 hikes. Between the Wupatki and Citadel ruins, the **Doney Mountain** affords 360-degree views of the Painted Desert and the San Francisco Volcanic Field. It's a perfect spot for a sunset picnic. In summer, rangers give lectures. ⊠ *Sunset Crater–Wupatki Loop Rd., 19 mi north of Sunset Crater visitor center* ☎ *928/679–2365* ⊕ *www.nps.gov/wupa* ✑ *$5, including Wupatki National Monument and Doney Mountain*

🕑 *Mar.–May and Sept.–Nov., daily 8–5; June–Aug., daily 8–6; Dec.–Feb., daily 9–5.*

SEDONA & OAK CREEK CANYON

119 mi north of Phoenix, Interstate 17 to AZ 179 to AZ 89A; 60 mi northeast of Prescott, U.S. 89 to AZ 89A; 27 mi south of Flagstaff on AZ 89A.

It's easy to see what draws so many people to Sedona. Red-rock buttes—Cathedral Rock, Bear Mountain, Courthouse Rock, and Bell Rock, among others—reach up into an almost always blue sky, both colors intensified by dark-green pine forests. Surrealist Max Ernst, writer Zane Grey, and many filmmakers drew inspiration from these vistas (more than 80 Westerns were shot in the area in the 1940s and '50s alone).

These days, Sedona lures enterprising restaurateurs and gallery owners from the East and West coasts. New Age followers, who believe that the area contains some of the Earth's more important vortices (energy centers), also come in great numbers in the belief that the area's "vibe" confers a sense of balance and well-being and enhances creativity.

Expansion since the early 1980s has been rapid, and lack of planning has taken its toll in unattractive developments and increased traffic. The town has been chosen to take part in the federally sponsored Main Street program, which means, among other things, that a number of Red Rock Territorial–style buildings in the Uptown section will be preserved and that a separate parking district will be built. A widening project in the works on AZ 179 should help alleviate some of the traffic, and finally put to rest the proposal to build a bridge over Oak Creek, which would have impinged on the natural glory of Red Rock Crossing, one of the town's most-photographed vistas.

The town itself is young and there are few historic sites. The main downtown activity is shopping, mostly for Southwestern-style paintings, clothing, rugs, jewelry, and Native American artifacts. Just beyond the shops and restaurants, however, canyons, creeks, Indian ruins, and the red rocks beckon. The area is easy to hike or you can take a jeep tour. During warmer months visit air-conditioned shops at midday and do hiking and jeep tours in the early morning or late afternoon, when the light is softer and the heat less oppressive.

Any whimsical turn off the main drag of Sedona is almost certain to lead to somewhere worthwhile. The following excursions will divert you for a hastily spent hour to a full day. Those with their own wheels might want to take the drive out to **Boynton Canyon,** sacred to the Yavapai Apache, who believe it was their ancient birthplace. It's where you'll find the Enchantment Resort, where all are welcome to hike the canyon and stop in for lunch or a late-afternoon drink. Weather permitting, the bumpy **Schnebly Hill Scenic Drive** is an option too rocky for anything but all-terrain vehicles. The vistas of Sedona from **Airport Mesa** at sunset can't be beat. The **Upper Red Rock Loop** will likely consume a roll or two of film. Many of the most memorable spots in Sedona are considered en-

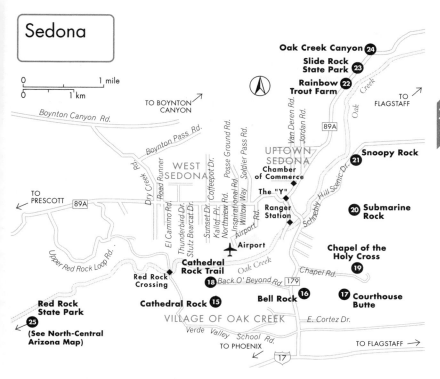

ergy centers; vortex maps of the area are available at most of Sedona's New Age stores.

Exploring Sedona

TIMING   Arrange your time in Sedona for midweek, if possible. The notorious crowds clog AZ 179 to near gridlock on the weekends, and finding a place to park, both in town and by the trails, is a chore. Remember that a Red Rock Pass is required to park in the Coconino National Forest. If driving, you can tour all of the famous buttes in a day with time to linger. Otherwise, allow several days to enjoy the full palate of outdoor activities. You can spend mornings hiking, mountain biking, or jeep touring, and afternoons swimming in Oak Creek.

What to See

16 Bell Rock. With its distinctive shape right out of your favorite Western film and its proximity to the main drag ensuring a steady flow of admirers, you may want to arrive early to see this popular butte. The parking lot next to the Bell Rock Pathway often fills by mid-morning even in the middle of the week. The views from the parking lot are good, but an easy and fairly accessible path follows mostly gentle terrain for 1 mi to the base of the butte. Mountain bikers, parents with all-terrain baby

Red Rock Geology

IT'S HARD TO IMAGINE that the landlocked desert surrounding Sedona was, for much of prehistoric time, an area of dunes and swamps on the shore of an ancient sea. The ebb and flow of this sea shaped the land. When the sea rose, it planed the dunes before dropping more sediment on top. The process continued for a few hundred million years. Eventually the sediment hardened into gray layers of limestone on top of the red sandstone. When North America collided with another continental plate, the land buckled and lifted, forming the Rocky Mountains and raising northern Arizona thousands of feet. Volcanoes erupted in the area, capping some of the rock with erosion-resistant basalt.

Oak Creek started flowing at this time, eroding through the layers of

sandstone and limestone. Along with other forces of erosion, the creek carved out the canyons and shaped the buttes. Sedona's buttes stayed intact because a resilient layer of lava had hardened on top and slowed the erosion process considerably. As iron minerals in the sandstone were gradually exposed to the elements, they turned red in a process similar to rusting. The iron minerals, in turn, stained the surrounding colorless quartz and grains of sand—it only takes a couple of percent of red iron materials to give the sandstone it's red color.

Like the rings of a tree, the striations in the rock document the passage of time and the events, limestone marking the rise of the sea, sandstone when the region was coastline.

strollers, and not-so-avid hikers should have little problem getting there. No official paths climb the rock itself, but many forge their own routes (at their own risk). ⊠ *AZ 179, several hundred yards north of Bell Rock Blvd., Village of Oak Creek.*

⑮ Cathedral Rock. It's almost impossible not to be drawn to this butte's towering, variegated spires. The approximately 1,200-foot-high Cathedral Rock looms dramatically over town. When you emerge from the narrow gorge of Oak Creek Canyon, this is the first recognizable formation you'll spot. The butte is best seen toward dusk from a distance. Hikers may want to drive to the Airport Mesa and then hike the rugged but generally flat path that loops around the airfield. The trail is a ½ mi up Airport Road off AZ 89A in West Sedona. The reward is a panoramic view of Cathedral Rock without the crowds. Those not hiking should drive through the Village of Oak Creek, and 5 mi west on Verde Valley School Road to its end, to a small park called **Red Rock Crossing** and a picnic area on the other side of the creek named Crescent Moon Park, where you can view the butte from a beautiful streamside vantage point and take a dip in Oak Creek if you wish. ⊠ *5 mi to end of Verde Valley School Rd., west off AZ 179, Village of Oak Creek.*

⑱ Cathedral Rock Trail. A vigorous but nontechnical 1½-mi scramble up the slickrock, this path leads to a nearly 360-degree view of red-rock country. Follow the cairns (rock piles marking the trail) and look for the footholds in the rock. Carry plenty of water: though short, the trail offers little shade and the pitch is steep. You can see the Verde Valley and Mingus Mountain in the distance. Look for the barely discernible "J" etched on the hillside marking the former ghost town of Jerome 30 mi distant. ✉ *Trailhead: About ½ mi down Back O' Beyond Rd. off AZ 179, 3 mi south of Sedona.*

⑲ Chapel of the Holy Cross. You needn't be religious to be inspired by the setting and the architecture here. Built in 1956 by Marguerite Brunwige Staude, a disciple of Frank Lloyd Wright, this modern landmark, with a huge cross on the facade, rises between two red-rock peaks. Vistas of the town and the surrounding area are spectacular. There are no regular services, but anyone is welcome for quiet meditation. A small gift shop sells religious artifacts and books. A trail east of the chapel leads you—after a 20-minute walk over occasional loose-rock surfaces—to a seat surrounded by voluptuous red-limestone walls, worlds away from the bustle and commerce around the chapel. ✉ *Chapel Rd., off AZ 179, Village of Oak Creek* ☎ *928/282–4069* ✍ *Free* ☼ *Daily 9–5.*

⑰ Courthouse Butte. The red sandstone seems to catch on fire toward sunset when the large monolith is free of shadow. From the highway, it sits in back of Bell Rock and can be viewed without any additional hiking or driving. ✉ *AZ 179, Village of Oak Creek.*

㉔ Oak Creek Canyon. Whether you want to swim, hike, picnic, or enjoy
Fodor'sChoice beautiful scenery framed through a car window, head north through the
★ wooded Oak Creek Canyon. It's the most scenic route to Flagstaff and the Grand Canyon, and worth a drive-through even if you're not heading north. The road winds through a steep-walled canyon, where you crane your neck for views of the dramatic rock formations above. Although the forest is primarily evergreen, the fall foliage is glorious. Oak Creek, which runs along the bottom, is lined with tent

campgrounds, fishing camps, cabins, motels, and restaurants. ✉ *AZ 89A, beginning 1 mi north of Sedona, Oak Creek Canyon.*

㉒ Rainbow Trout Farm. Anglers young and old always enjoy a sure catch and you can rent a cane pole here with a hook and bait for $1. There's no charge if your catch is under 8 inches; above that it's $2.85 to $5.85, depending on the length. The real bargain is that the staff will clean and pack your fish for 50¢ each. ✉ *3500 N. AZ 89A, 3 mi north of Sedona, Oak Creek Canyon* ☎ *928/282–3379* ✍ *$1* ☼ *Daily 9–5.*

㉕ Red Rock State Park. Two miles west of Sedona via AZ 89A is the turnoff for this 286-acre state park, a less-crowded alternative to Slide Rock State Park, though without the possibility for swimming. The 5 mi of interconnected park trails are well marked and provide beautiful vistas. There are daily ranger-guided nature walks, bird-watching excursions on Wednesday and Saturday, and a guided hike to Eagle's Nest scenic overlook—the highest point in the park—every Saturday. Call ahead for times, which change with the season. ⊠ *4050 Red Rock Loop Rd., West* ☎ *928/282–6907* ⊕ *www.pr. state.az.us* ✉ *$6 per car* ⊙ *Oct.–Mar. 8–5* PM, *Apr. 8–6* PM, *May–Aug. 8–8* PM, *Sept. 8–6* PM.

WORD OF MOUTH

"If your kids are young enough the Sliding Rock Park in Oak Creek will be fun. A hint: do your sliding in clothing (jeans type) that won't come off as you go down!"
                                   –John_T_Cuttino

🌀 ㉓ **Slide Rock State Park.** A good place for a picnic, Slide Rock is 7 mi north of Sedona. On a hot day you can plunge down a natural rock slide into a swimming hole (bring an extra pair of jeans or a sturdy bathing suit and river shoes to wear on the slide). The site started as an early-20th-century apple orchard and the natural beauty attracted later Hollywood, with a number of John Wayne and Jimmy Stewart, flicks being filmed here. A few easy hikes run along the rim of the gorge. Fly-fishing for trout is possible when it's too cold for swimming. One downside is the traffic, particularly on summer weekends; you might have to wait to get in. Also, the popularity of the stream has led to the occasional midsummer closing due to e. coli–bacteria infestations. ⊠ *6871 N. AZ 89A, Oak Creek Canyon* ☎ *928/282–3034* ⊕ *www.pr.state.az. us* ✉ *$10 per vehicle for up to 4 persons* ⊙ *Labor Day–Memorial Day, daily 8–5; Memorial Day–Labor Day, daily 8–7.*

㉑ **Snoopy Rock.** When you look almost directly to the east, this butte looks like the famed Peanuts beagle laying atop red rock instead of his doghouse. You can distinguish the formation from several places around town including the mall in Uptown Sedona, but to get a clear view, venture up Schnebly Hill Road. Park by the trailhead on the left immediately before the paved road deteriorates to dirt. Marg's Draw, one of several trails originating here, is worthwhile, gently meandering 100 feet down-canyon, through the tortured desert flora to Morgan Road. Backtrack to the parking lot for close to a 3-mi hike. Always carry plenty of water, no matter how easy the hike appears. ⊠ *Schnebly Hill Rd., off AZ 179, Central.*

㉚ **Submarine Rock.** This elongated vessel of a rock has an interesting shape, but is not as photogenic as the others. Nestled in the canyon and colored in beige tones, it doesn't catch the sunlight in the same way. But getting to Submarine Rock is perhaps more interesting than seeing the rock itself. You can drive up FR 179F, a very technical jeep trail that should be attempted only by highly skilled off-road-vehicle drivers, or you can take a jeep tour offered in town. For experienced mountain bikers, Broken Arrow Trail, used heavily by cyclists and hikers, rolls across washes, red clay, and large mounds of slickrock. The 2-mi hike is moderate but best done in the early morning in summer. Note that Submarine Rock is not the best retreat for serenity seekers: the rock abuts the jeep trail, which is clogged with tour jeeps revving over the rugged terrain. ⊠ *End of Morgan Rd., off AZ 179, Central.*

Sports & the Outdoors

A Red Rock Pass is required to park in the Coconino National Forest from Oak Creek Canyon through Sedona and the Village of Oak Creek.

Golf

The **Oak Creek Country Club** (⊠ 690 Bell Rock Blvd., Village of Oak Creek ☏ 928/284–1660) is a good semiprivate course. The 18-hole **Sedona Golf Resort** (⊠ 7260 AZ 179, Village of Oak Creek ☏ 928/284–9355) was designed by Gary Panks to take advantage of the many changes in elevation and scenery. The 10th hole has a sweeping view of the Sedona Valley's red rocks.

Hiking & Backpacking

For free detailed maps, hiking advice, and information on campgrounds, contact the rangers of the **Coconino National Forest** (⊠ Sedona Ranger District, 250 Brewer Rd., West, 86339 ☏ 928/282–4119 ⊕ www.fs.fed.us/r3/coconino ☉ Weekdays 8–4:30). Ask here or at your hotel for directions to trailheads for Doe's Mountain (an easy ascent, with many switchbacks), Loy Canyon, Devil's Kitchen, and Long Canyon.

> **WORD OF MOUTH**
>
> "Sedona has lots of excellent hiking, from very basic to much more advanced; tons of shopping; and good restaurants. We had never hiked before and really enjoyed that. "   −tdoubrava

Among the paths in Coconino National Forest, the popular **West Fork Trail** (⊠ Trailhead: AZ 89A, 9½ mi north of Sedona) traverses the Oak Creek Canyon for a 3-mi hike. A walk through the woods in the midst of sheer red-rock walls and a dip in the stream make a great summer combination. The trailhead is about 3 mi north of Slide Rock State Park.

Any backpacking trip in the **Secret Mountain Wilderness** near Sedona guarantees stunning vistas, otherworldly rock formations, zenlike serenity, but little water, so pack a good supply. ▮ TIP→ **Plan your trip for the spring or fall: summer brings 100°F heat and sudden thunderstorms that flood canyons without warning.** Most individual trails in the wilderness are too short for anything but an overnighter, but several trails can be linked up to form a memorable multiday trip. Contact the Sedona Ranger District for full details.

Horseback Riding

Among the tour options at **Trail Horse Adventures** (⊠ 85 Five J La., Lower Red Rock Loop Rd., West ☏ 800/723–3538) are a midday picnic, an Oak Creek swim, and a full-moon ride with a campfire cookout.

Mountain Biking

Given the red-rock splendor, challenging terrain, miles of single track, and mild weather, you might think Sedona would be a mountain-biking destination on the order of Moab or Durango. Inexplicably, you won't find the lycra-clad throngs patronizing pasta bars or throwing back microbrews on the Uptown mall, but all the better for you: the mountain-biking culture remains fervent but low-key. A few strategically located, excellent bike shops can outfit you and give advice.

As a general rule, mountain bikes are allowed on all trails and jeep paths unless designated as wilderness or private property. The rolling terrain, which switches between serpentine trails of buff red clay and mounds of slickrock, has few sustained climbs but ⚠ **be careful of blind drop-offs that often step down several feet in unexpected places.** The thorny trailside flora makes carrying extra inner tubes a must, and an inner tube sealant is a good idea. If you plan to ride for several hours, pack close to a gallon of water and start early in the morning on hot days. Shade is rare, and with the nonpotable exception of Oak Creek, water is nonexistent.

For the casual rider, **Bell Rock Pathway** (✉ Trailhead: 5 mi south of Sedona on AZ 179) is a scenic and easy ride traveling 3 mi through some of the most breathtaking scenery in red-rock country. Several single-track trails spur off this one making it a good starting point for many other rides in Sedona. **Submarine Rock Loop** is perhaps the most popular single-track loop in the area, and for good reason. The 10-mi trail is a heady mixture of prime terrain and scenery following slickrock and twisty trails up to Chicken Point, a sandstone terrace overlooking colorful buttes. The trail continues as a bumpy romp through washes almost all downhill. Be wary of blind drop-offs in this section. It wouldn't be overly cautious to scout any parts of the trail that look sketchy.

A few hundred yards south of Bell Rock Pathway, **Bike and Bean** (✉ 6020 AZ 179, Village of Oak Creek ☎ 928/284–0210) offers rentals, tours, and their own blend of coffee.

Where to Stay & Eat

Some Sedona restaurants close in January and February, so call before you go; make reservations in high season (April to October). Sedona is roughly divided into three neighborhoods: Uptown, which is a walkable shopping district; West Sedona, which is a 4-mi-long commercial strip; and Central Sedona, which encompasses everything south of the "Y" where AZ 179 and AZ 89A intersect.

★ $$$–$$$$ ✕ **L'Auberge.** The most formal dining room in Sedona promises a quiet, civilized evening of indulgence. Chef Frank Brunacci finds inventive ways to mix seasonal ingredients creating such specialties as duck *percik* (a spicy Malay sauce) with date and kumquat chutney, cumin polenta, and orange-carrot reduction. The restaurant has one of the best (and priciest) wine lists in Arizona and will match a wine to each course for you. Don't miss the lavish Sunday brunch. ✉ *L'Auberge de Sedona, 241 AZ 89A, Uptown* ☎ *928/282–4200* ▱ *AE, D, DC, MC, V.*

$$–$$$$ ✕ **Cowboy Club.** At this upscale restaurant, you can hang out in the casual Cowboy Club or dine in the more formal Silver Saddle Room, where suede booths are situated amid cowboy art and a pair of large cow horns. High-quality cuts of beef are the specialty, but the fried chicken served with cumin-mashed potatoes is good, too. ✉ *241 AZ 89A, Uptown* ☎ *928/282–4200* ▱ *AE, D, DC, MC, V.*

$$–$$$$ ✕ **Sasaki.** Somewhat off the tourist path, this understated restaurant serves a limited selection of impeccably fresh sushi and sashimi. There's a full Japanese menu, too. Pork *katsu* (lightly battered and fried cutlets of pork) and *ten-zura* (cold buckwheat noodles with tempura) are good cooked options. The service couldn't be friendlier. ✉ *65 Bell Rock Blvd., Village of Oak Creek* ☎ *928/284–1757* ⊟ *AE, MC, V* ☺ *No lunch.*

$$$ ✕ **Shugrue's Hillside.** Almost everything is good, which has made this one of the most popular restaurants in Sedona, but the salads and meats are particularly noteworthy. The Caesar salad is refreshingly traditional and the inventive ginger-walnut chicken salad is large enough to share. Rack of lamb and filet mignon are prepared and presented simply. There's a small, well-priced wine list. Shugrue's Hillside is not owned by the same folks who own Shugrue's West, a less appealing restaurant. ✉ *671 AZ 179, Central* ☎ *928/282–5300* ⊟ *AE, DC, MC, V.*

★ **$$–$$$** ✕ **Dahl & DiLuca.** A husband-and-wife team—Andrea DiLuca and Lisa Dahl—has created one of the most popular Italian restaurants in town. Renaissance reproductions and café seating give the impression of having been transported to a Roman plaza. Andrea runs the kitchen, and Lisa meets and greets diners. Lisa also slips into the kitchen every day to make delicious homemade soups like white bean with ham and hearty minestrone. ✉ *2321 W. AZ 89A, West* ☎ *928/282–5219* ⊟ *AE, D, MC, V* ☺ *No lunch.*

★ **$$–$$$** ✕ **Heartline Café.** Fresh flowers and innovative, modern Southwestern cuisine are this attractive café's hallmarks. The oak-grilled salmon is marinated in tequila and lime, and the chicken breast has a prickly pear sauce. Appealing vegetarian plates are also on the menu and the rosebush-lined terrace is delightful. Desserts include a phenomenal crème brûlée, as well as homemade truffles at the chef's whim. ✉ *1610 W. AZ 89A, West* ☎ *928/282–0785* ⊟ *AE, D, MC, V* ☺ *No lunch Tues.–Thurs. and Sun.*

$$–$$$ ✕ **Pietro's.** Good northern Italian cuisine plus a friendly and attentive staff have made this lively and casual dining spot one of Sedona's most popular. Don't miss anything made with the buffalo mozzarella from Naples. Homemade soups are always fabulous. ✉ *2445 W. AZ 89A, West* ☎ *928/282–2525* ⊟ *AE, D, DC, MC, V* ☺ *No lunch.*

$$–$$$ ✕ **René at Tlaquepaque.** Ease into the plush banquettes of this lace-curtained restaurant for classic Continental dishes. Recommended starters include French-onion soup and the salade Walter—baby-spinach leaves and sautéed mushrooms in a hazelnut vinaigrette. Rack of lamb is the house specialty, and the Dover sole is a real find, far from the white cliffs. Crêpes suzette for two, prepared table-side, is an impressive dessert. There's a well-selected wine list, too. Service is formal but casual attire is acceptable. ✉ *Tlaquepaque Arts & Crafts Village, Unit B–117, AZ 179, Central* ☎ *928/282–9225* ⊟ *AE, MC, V.*

★ **$$–$$$** ✕ **Robert's.** A long-standing favorite on the banks of Oak Creek gained notoriety when Regis Philbin breezed through town and fell in love with the restaurant's peach cobbler. It's quite good, as are the grilled polenta, baby back ribs, and prime rib. Nightly specials, such as fresh mako shark, are always intriguing, and stellar views of the buttes from the patio make for a sublime dining experience. ✉ *251 AZ 179, Central* ☎ *928/282–3671* ⊟ *AE, MC, V.*

$$–$$$ ✕ **Takashi.** Those seeking serenity and a respite from heavy meals will enjoy this Japanese restaurant, which provides aesthetic pleasure in everything from tea (with little bits of floating popcorn and brown rice) to dessert (sweet ginger or red-bean ice cream). Salads include spicy sushi tuna with Japanese mayonnaise on a bed of cabbage and fresh vegetables. Combination dinners such as sashimi with tempura or teriyaki let you sample a bit of everything. ✉ *465 Jordan Rd., Uptown* ☎ *928/282–2334* 🖃 *AE, DC, MC, V* ⊗ *Closed Mon. No lunch weekends.*

$–$$ ✕ **Oaxaca Restaurant.** Tasty standards complement some of the best uptown canyon vistas at this modern Mexican restaurant with a lovely balcony. The smoky kick of the salsa, along with the old-world Mexican decor and sun-kissed scenery may transport you south of the border, but dishes are prepared under the auspices of a dietitian who shuns the traditional use of lard and cholesterol-containing oils in favor of healthier options—with delicious results. ✉ *321 N. AZ 89 A, Uptown* ☎ *928/282–4179* 🖃 *AE, DC, MC, V.*

$ ✕ **Thai Spices.** This small restaurant has a loyal following of vegetarians and health-food enthusiasts, though not everything is meatless. The curries, especially red curry with tempeh, are delicious and can be prepared at the spice level of your choice. Traditional pad thai with chicken is satisfyingly homey and the spicy beef salad will make your hair stand on end. ✉ *2986 W. AZ 89A, West* ☎ *928/282–0599* 🖃 *MC, V.*

FodorśChoice
★

¢–$ ✕ **Coffee Pot Restaurant.** Locals and tourists alike swarm to this spacious diner for scrumptious food served by a brisk and friendly waitstaff. One hundred and one omelet options are the stars of the show, and include such concoctions as the quirky peanut butter and jelly or the basic ham and cheese. The warm homemade biscuits hit the spot. An extensive lunch menu that includes Mexican dishes round out the offerings. ✉ *2050 W. 89 A, West* ☎ *928/282–6626* 🖃 *MC, V* ⊗ *No dinner.*

¢–$ ✕ **Mesquite Tree Barbecue.** Although it offers limited indoor seating, this Uptown hideaway behind a long row of tourist shops is worth a visit. Follow your nose to the mesquite-burning grill, where you can watch your dinner get cooked. The sauce has a slight kick, and the homemade french fries are fabulous. ✉ *250 Jordan Rd., No. 9, Uptown* ☎ *928/282–6533* 🖃 *MC, V.*

¢ ✕ **Sedona Coffee Roasters.** Not only does this café serve the best coffee in town by a mile, but the lunch sandwiches are perfect fare before or after a red-rock hike. Daily specials might include a healthful chicken salad with sprouts or a more decadent jumbo-beef Polish hot dog. You can also choose your own sandwich fixings from a list of fresh ingredients. ✉ *2155 W. AZ 89A, West* ☎ *928/282–0282* 🖃 *No credit cards.*

★ **$$$$** 🏨 **L'Auberge de Sedona.** This hillside resort consists of a central lodge building; a creekside lodge a four-bedroom home with a living room, dining room, and kitchen, and—the major attraction—cabins in the woods along Oak Creek. Rooms in the lodge are decorated in lush Country European style and the cabins have wood-burning fireplaces. Phoenix couples flock to this country-French hideaway and dine in the hotel's French restaurant, one of the most romantic eateries in Arizona (⇨ *see* Where to Eat). ✉ *301 L'Auberge La., Uptown* ✆ *Box B, 86336* ☎ *928/*

282–1661 or 800/272–6777 🖶 *928/282–2885* ⊕ *www.lauberge.com*
⟳ *21 rooms, 33 cottages* ⚹ *2 restaurants, minibars, refrigerators, cable TV, pool, hot tub, shop* ⊟ *AE, D, DC, MC, V.*

$$$$
Fodor'sChoice
★

🏨 **Enchantment Resort.** Southwest-style rooms and suites at this resort are tucked into pueblo-style buildings in serene Boynton Canyon. Accommodations come in many configurations, some with kitchens, separate living and dining areas, and multiple bedrooms, which can be joined to create large, elaborate suites. All have beehive gas fireplaces and superb views. The Yavapai Room serves excellent Southwestern cuisine. The resort's full-service spa, Mi Amo, offers treatments like hot stone massage and myo-facial release. ⊠ *525 Boynton Canyon Rd., West, 86336* ☎ *928/282–2900 or 800/826–4180* 🖶 *928/282–9249* ⊕ *www. enchantmentresort.com* ⟳ *107 rooms, 115 suites* ⚹ *2 restaurants, in-room safes, some kitchens, some kitchenettes, putting green, 12 tennis courts, pro shop, 4 pools, health club, spa, mountain bikes, hiking, bar, children's programs (ages 4–12)* ⊟ *AE, D, MC, V.*

★ **$$$$**

🏨 **El Portal Sedona.** This stunning hacienda is one of the most beautifully designed hotels in the Southwest. Decor accents include authentic Tiffany and Roycroft pieces, French doors leading to balconies or a grassy central courtyard, stained-glass windows and ceiling panels, river-rock or tile fireplaces, and huge custom-designed beds. All rooms have flat-screen TVs with DVD players, and guests can enjoy gym, spa, and pool privileges next door at Los Abrigados Resort. Wine and hors d'oeuvres are served in the afternoon, and the inn also presents prix-fixe ($45 per person) dinners on Saturday night, to the sounds of classical guitar. ⊠ *95 Portal La., Central, 86336* ☎ *928/203–9405 or 800/313–0017* 🖶 *928/ 203–9401* ⊕ *www.innsedona.com* ⟳ *11 rooms, 1 suite* ⚹ *Some in-room hot tubs, refrigerators, cable TV with DVDs, Wi-Fi; no smoking* ⊟ *AE, D, MC, V* ⫟❍⫞ *BP.*

$$$–$$$$
Fodor'sChoice
★

🏨 **Briar Patch Inn.** This B&B in a verdant canyon with a rushing creek has rooms in wooden cabins, some with decks overlooking Oak Creek. On summer mornings you can sit outside and enjoy home-baked breads and fresh egg dishes while listening to live classical music. New Age and crafts workshops are sometimes held on the premises. Winter is equally beautiful; request a cabin with a fireplace and wake to see icicles hanging from the trees. ⊠ *3190 N. AZ 89A, Oak Creek Canyon, 86336* ☎ *928/282–2342* 🖶 *928/282–2399 or 888/809–3030* ⊕ *www. briarpatchinn.com* ⟳ *13 two-person cabins, 4 four-person cabins* ⚹ *Fans, some kitchenettes, massage, fishing, library, meeting room; no room TVs, no smoking* ⊟ *AE, MC, V* ⫟❍⫞ *BP.*

★ **$$$–$$$$**

🏨 **Graham Inn and Adobe Village.** Some of the rooms at this inn south of Sedona have Jacuzzi tubs and balconies that look out onto the red rocks. Each of the four individually decorated casitas on the lot next door has a gas fireplace that opens into both the sitting area and the bathroom area, which is outfitted with a two-person Jacuzzi tub. What makes this place special, though, is the impeccable yet casual service, and the French chef makes breakfasts worth the price of admission. The owners are committed to always having at least one room under $200. ⊠ *150 Canyon Circle Dr., Village of Oak Creek, 86351* ☎ *928/284– 1425 or 800/228–1425* 🖶 *928/284–0767* ⊕ *www.sedonasfinest.com* ⟳ *6*

3

rooms, 1 suite, 4 private villas ☆ Some in-room hot tubs, some kitch-enettes, some refrigerators, cable TV, in-room VCRs, pool, hot tub, mountain bikes, library, Internet room; no smoking ⊟ D, MC, V ⦿ BP.

★ **$$–$$$$** ⊞ **Alma de Sedona.** Under new management, the Alma de Sedona continues to be one of Sedona's most enchanting B&Bs. It has large rooms with spectacular views and ultracomfortable beds. The inn was built well off the main drag and in the shadow of the buttes for views and privacy. Understated, elegant, and inviting rooms all have private entrances and patios; bath salts and candles await in the bathrooms. ⊠ *50 Hozoni Dr., West, 86336* ☎ *928/282–2737 or 800/923–2282* 🖷 *928/203–4141* ⊕ *www.almadesedona.com* ⥂ *12 rooms ☆ Some in-room hot tubs, cable TV, pool, meeting room; no smoking ⊟ AE, MC, V ⦿ BP.*

$$–$$$$ ⊞ **Junipine Creekside Retreat.** These one- and two-bedroom cabins—here called creek houses—nestled in a juniper and pine forest (hence the name) are spacious and airy, with vaulted ceilings and fireplaces. An excellent value for groups of four or more, some of the cabins sleep six. Junipine's most enchanting feature is the sound of Oak Creek roaring below, lulling you to sleep by the fire. ⊠ *8351 N. AZ 89A, Oak Creek Canyon, 86336* ☎ *928/282–3375* 🖷 *928/282–7402* ⊕ *www.junipine.com* ⥂ *50 suites ☆ Restaurant, kitchens, outdoor hot tub, no-smoking rooms; no TV in some rooms ⊟ AE, D, MC, V.*

$$$ ⊞ **Amara Resort.** You might not expect to find such an urbane boutique hotel in small, outdoorsy Sedona, but Amara fits right in with its ochre-and-tan–sandstone exterior and secluded setting adjacent to gurgling Oak Creek. Sleek rooms deviate from the usual Sedona look, with low-slung beds and work desks with ergonomic seating. Other cushy extras include in-room DVD players, free high-speed Internet, and Aveda bath products. Step out onto your room's private balcony or terrace to take in expansive red-rock views. On property, the Amara Grille serves globally inspired contemporary victuals. ⊠ *310 N. AZ 89, Village of Oak Creek, 86336* ☎ *928/282–4828 or 866/455–6610* 🖷 *928/282–4825* ⊕ *www.amararesort.com* ⥂ *92 rooms, 8 suites ☆ Restaurant, some in-room hot tubs, minibars, cable TV, in-room data ports, lounge, concierge, meeting rooms, no-smoking rooms ⊟ AE, D, DC, MC, V.*

$$$ ⊞ **Garland's Oak Creek Lodge.** In the heart of Oak Creek Canyon, this 1930s lodge and its 16 comfortably furnished cabins—some with fireplaces and pullout beds—are owned by Gary and Mary Garland. This mile-high, 17-acre spread has its own apple orchard, and accommodations look out over the rugged cliffs of the canyon or the creek. Excellent daily breakfast and dinner are included in the room price, along with afternoon tea. It's often booked solid a year in advance, but it's worth a call to check for vacancies. ⊠ *AZ 89A, 8 mi north of Uptown, Oak Creek Canyon* ✉ *Box 152, 86339* ☎ *928/282–3343* ⊕ *www.garlandslodge.com* ⥂ *16 cabins ☆ Restaurant, tennis court, fishing, croquet, volleyball; no room phones, no room TVs, no smoking ⊟ MC, V* ☉ *Closed late Nov.–Mar.* ⦿ *MAP.*

$$–$$$ ⊞ **Apple Orchard Inn.** Within walking distance of Uptown, nestled among pine and juniper trees, Apple Orchard Inn is an affordable choice

and the inn can provide you with a personal guide to the are can just relax in the massage room. ⊠ *656 Jordan Rd., Uptor* ☎ *928/282–5328 or 800/663–6968* ⎙ *928/204–0044 appleorchardbb.com* ⟿ *7 rooms* ⚐ *Refrigerators, cable TV VCRs, pool; no smoking* ⊟ *AE, MC, V* ❘⊙❘ *BP.*

$$–$$$ ⊞ **Boots & Saddles.** Irith and Sam are the worldly and consummate hosts at this quiet inn tucked behind the main street in West Sedona. The rooms are decorated in an upscale Western motif, complete with genuine cowboy artifacts, and the Gentleman Cowboy room has un-paralleled red-rock views and a telescope for stargazing. ⊠ *2900 Hopi Dr., West, 86336* ☎ *928/282–1944 or 800/201–1944* ⊕ *www.oldwestbb. com* ⟿ *4 rooms* ⚐ *BBQ, refrigerators, in-room VCRs, hot tub, shop; no smoking* ⊟ *AE, D, MC, V* ❘⊙❘ *BP.*

$$–$$$ ⊞ **Lodge at Sedona.** Rooms in this rambling wood-and-stone house are Mission-style; some have fireplaces, redwood decks, or hot tubs. For solitude, walk the seven-path classic labyrinth (made of local rock) and through the gardens. A chef prepares a five-course breakfast each morn-ing. ⊠ *125 Kallof Pl., West, 86336* ☎ *928/204–1942 or 800/619– 4467* ⎙ *928/204–2128* ⊕ *www.lodgeatsedona.com* ⟿ *6 rooms, 8 suites* ⚐ *Dining room, some in-room hot tubs, some in-room VCRs, pool, gym, massage, library, concierge, meeting room; no room phones, no TV in some rooms, no smoking* ⊟ *D, MC, V* ❘⊙❘ *BP.*

★ $$ ⊞ **The Canyon Wren.** The best value in the Oak Creek Canyon area, this small B&B has free-standing cabins with views of the canyon walls. Milena and Mike (she's Slovenian, he's Floridian) regard guests' privacy first and foremost. It's likely that their two lovable dogs, Nasa and Stubby, will greet you on arrival. Cabins have private decks and fireplaces. Breakfast is a selection of delicious baked goods from Milena's kitchen. ⊠ *6425 N. AZ 89A, Oak Creek Canyon, 86336* ☎ *928/282–6900 or 800/437–9736* ⎙ *928/282–6978* ⊕ *www.canyonwrencabins.com* ⟿ *4 cabins* ⚐ *In-room hot tubs, kitchens; no room phones, no room TVs, no smoking* ⊟ *AE, D, MC, V* ❘⊙❘ *CP.*

$–$$ ⊞ **Sky Ranch Lodge.** There may be no better vantage point in town from which to view Sedona's red-rock canyons than the private patios and balconies at Sky Ranch Lodge, near the top of Airport Mesa. Some rooms have stone fireplaces and some have kitchenettes; a few are a bit worn, but all are very clean. Paths on the grounds wind around fountains and, in summer, through colorful flower gardens. This is an excellent value, primarily because of the views. ⊠ *Airport Rd., West, 86339* ☎ *928/ 282–6400* ⎙ *928/282–7682* ⊕ *www.skyranchlodge.com* ⟿ *92 rooms, 2 cottages* ⚐ *Some kitchenettes, some refrigerators, cable TV, pool, hot tub, no-smoking rooms* ⊟ *AE, MC, V.*

$ ⊞ **Desert Quail Inn.** Close to a lion's share of the trailheads, but out of the main flow of tourist traffic, this is a good base for outdoor ad-ventures. The front desk is well stocked with maps and advice. Rooms are spacious and bright. ⊠ *6626 AZ 179, Village of Oak Creek, 86351* ☎ *928/284–1433 or 800/385–0927* ⎙ *928/284–0487* ⊕ *www. desertquailinn.com* ⟿ *41 rooms* ⚐ *Some in-room hot tubs, some microwaves, refrigerators, cable TV, pool, laundry facilities* ⊟ *AE, D, DC, MC, V.*

$ ▦ **Sedona Motel.** Built on a terrace removed from the highway in order to afford it the same expansive red-rock views as the pricier resorts, this motel is pretty typical in all other respects. It's within easy reach of most of Sedona's attractions, and the rooms are well kept. ✉ *218 AZ 179, Central, 86336* ☎ *928/282–7187* ⌃ *16 rooms* ⚭ *Microwaves, refrigerators, cable TV* ▭ *D, MC, V.*

CAMPING ⚠ **Cave Springs and Pine Flat Campgrounds.** Try to arrive midweek to
¢ secure one of the popular national-forest campsites in Oak Creek Canyon. These neighboring campgrounds are the only two in the canyon to accept RVs as well as tents, but there are no hookups. The sites are near or next to Oak Creek, and at 5,500 feet in elevation, the summer nights are pleasantly cool. ✉ *AZ 89A, 12 mi north of Sedona* ⌂ *Red Rock Ranger District, Box 300, Sedona, 86336* ☎ *877/444–6777 reservations only, 928/282–4119 information* ⊕ *www.reserveusa.com* ◈ *$16* ⌃ *136 sites* ⚭ *Grills, pit toilets, drinking water, showers, picnic tables* ⊘ *Closed late Sept.–mid-Apr.*

Nightlife & the Arts

Find out about cultural events in Sedona at the **Book Loft** (✉ 175 AZ 179, just south of the "Y," Central ☎ 928/282–5173), which often hosts poetry readings, theatrical readings, book signings, and lectures. The Sedona **Jazz on the Rocks Festival** (☎ 928/282–1985 ⊕ www.sedonajazz. com), held every September, always attracts a sellout crowd that fills the town to capacity. The **Sedona Arts Center** (✉ N. AZ 89A and Art Barn Rd., Uptown ☎ 928/282–3809) sponsors events ranging from classical concerts to plays; there's an innovative and growing film festival every March. The **Sedona Heritage Day Festival** (☎ 928/282–7038), a family-oriented event in early October, includes pioneer storytellers, square-dance exhibitions, music, and a barbecue.

Nightlife in Sedona tends to be sedate. On high-season weekends, there's usually live music at the Enchantment Resort. Shugrue's Hillside also regularly presents local musicians. Offerings vary from jazz to rock and pop; in all cases, call ahead. **Casa Rincon** (✉ 2620 W. AZ 89A, West ☎ 928/282–4849) hosts a dance party with local bands and open-mike nights. The closest thing to a rollicking cowboy bar in Sedona is **Rainbow's End** (✉ 3235 W. AZ 89A, West ☎ 928/282–1593), a steak house with a dance floor and country-and-western bands on weekends.

> ## WORD OF MOUTH
>
> "Be forewarned, Sedona is dead, dead, dead by 8:30 PM, which may be okay if you are dead tired from hiking."   –amwosu

Shopping

Shopping Areas & Malls

Most stores in what is known as the **Uptown** area, north of the "Y," running along AZ 89A to the east of its intersection with AZ 179, cater to the tour-bus trade. There are several exceptions, though. The largest concentration of stores and galleries is in Central Sedona, along AZ 179, south of the "Y." West Sedona, the more residential area that stretches west of the "Y" along AZ 89A, doesn't have as concentrated areas of shops as Uptown and Central.

In central Sedona, a minute or two south of the Hozho Center on AZ 179 is the **Hillside Courtyard & Marketplace** (✉671 AZ 179, Central ☎928/282–4500). The **Hozho Center** (✉431 AZ 179, Central ☎928/204–2257) itself is a small, upscale complex in a beige Santa Fe–style building.

Inveterate bargain hunters will want to head south on AZ 179, 2 mi past Chapel of the Holy Cross, to the Village of Oak Creek. At the **Oak Creek Factory Outlets** (✉ 6601 S. AZ 179, Village of Oak Creek ☎ 928/284–2150) are stores such as Corning/Revere, Mikasa, Anne Klein, Bass, Jones New York, and Van Heusen. **Tlaquepaque Arts & Crafts Village** (✉ AZ 179, just south of "Y," Central ☎ 928/282–4838) gathers more than 100 artisans. The complex of red-tile-roof buildings arranged around a series of courtyards shares its name and architectural style with a crafts village just outside Guadalajara. It's a lovely place to browse, but prices tend to be high; locals joke that it's pronounced "to-lock-your-pocket."

Stores & Galleries

Gear up with maps, clothing, and camping equipment at **Canyon Outfitters** (✉ 2701 W. 89A, West ☎ 928/282–5294) before your outdoor adventures. **Clay Pigeon** (✉ Hillside Courtyard & Marketplace, 671 AZ 179, Central ☎ 928/282–2845) carries boldly designed dishes and sculptures with a Western accent. **Crystal Magic** (✉ 2978 W. 89A, West ☎ 928/282–1622) dabbles in the metaphysical with crystals, jewelry, and books for the new age. A good bet for Southwestern art is **El Prado Gallery by the Creek** (✉ Tlaquepaque, AZ 179, No. 101, Bldg. E, Central ☎ 928/282–7390). **Esteban's** (✉ Tlaquepaque, AZ 179, No. 103, Bldg. B, Central ☎ 928/282–4686) focuses on ceramics and Native American crafts. **Garland's Navajo Rugs** (✉ 411 AZ 179, Central ☎ 928/282–4070) has a collection of new and antique carpets, as well as Native American–katsina dolls, pottery, and baskets. **Isadora** (✉ Tlaquepaque, AZ 179, No. 120, Bldg. A, Central ☎ 928/282–6232) has beautiful handwoven jackets and shawls. **James Ratliff Gallery** (✉ 431 AZ 179, Central ☎ 928/282–1404) has fun and functional pieces by not-yet-established artists. **Kuivato** (✉ Tlaquepaque, AZ 179, No. 122, Bldg. B, Central ☎928/282–1212) carries gorgeous glassware. **Lanning Gallery** (✉ Hozho Center, 431 AZ 179, Central ☎ 928/282–6865) sells Southwestern art and jewelry. **Looking West** (✉ 242 N. AZ 89A, Uptown ☎ 928/282–4877) sells the spiffiest cowgirl-style getups in town. **Robert Shields Design** (✉ Sacajawea Plaza, 301 N. AZ 89A, Uptown ☎ 928/204–9253) carries colorful clay snakes and unusual silver jewelry. (If you still remember them, it's the same Shields who used to perform with Yarnell.) **Sedona Pottery** (✉ 411 AZ 179, Central ☎ 928/282–1192) sells unusual pieces, including flower-arranging bowls, egg separators, and life-size ceramic statues by shop owner Mary Margaret Sather.

THE VERDE VALLEY, JEROME & PRESCOTT

About 90 mi north of Phoenix, as you round a curve approaching Exit 285 of Interstate 17, the valley of the Verde River suddenly unfolds in a panorama of grayish-white cliffs, tinted red in the distance and dotted with desert scrub, cottonwood, and pine. For hundreds of years many Native American communities, especially those of the southern Sinagua people, lined the Verde River. Rumors of great mineral deposits brought Europeans to the Verde Valley as early as 1583, when Hopi Indians guided Antonio de Espejo here, but it wasn't until the second half of the 19th century that this wealth was commercially exploited. The discovery of silver and gold in the Black Hills, which border the valley on the southwest, gave rise to such boomtowns as Jerome—and to military installations such as Fort Verde, set up to protect the white settlers and wealth seekers from the Native American tribes they displaced. Mineral wealth was also the impetus behind the establishment of Prescott, as a territorial capital by President Lincoln and other Unionists who wanted to keep the riches out of Confederate hands.

Numbers in the text correspond to numbers in the margin and on the North-Central Arizona, Prescott, Sedona, and Flagstaff maps.

Camp Verde

94 mi north of Phoenix on Interstate 17.

26 The military post for which **Fort Verde State Historic Park** is named was built between 1871 and 1873 as the third of three fortifications in this part of the Arizona Territory. To protect the Verde Valley's farmers and miners from Tonto Apache and Yavapai raids, the fort's administrators oversaw the movement of nearly 1,500 Native Americans to the San Carlos and Fort Apache reservations. A museum details the history of the area's military installations, and three furnished officers' quarters show the day-to-day living conditions of the top brass. Signs from any of Interstate 17's three Camp Verde exits will direct you to the 10-acre park. ✉ *125 Hollomon St.* ☏ *928/567–3275* ⊕ *www.pr.state. az.us* ⌨ *$3* ☉ *Daily 8–5.*

27 The five-story 20-room cliff
Fodor'sChoice dwelling at **Montezuma Castle National Monument** was named by explorers who believed it had been erected by the Aztecs. Southern Sinagua Native Americans actually built the roughly 600-year-old structure, one of the best-preserved prehistoric ruins in North America—and one of the most accessi-

WORD OF MOUTH

"I love Montezuma's Castle. It is a very easy walk and quite impressive. But I like even more the section a few miles away called Montezuma's Well. This is a big sinkhole with a few small cliff dwellings on the cliff above the well. You can hike down into the well. You can also hike to where the water comes out of the well and see how they irrigated 800 years ago. These are short hikes, although climbing back out of the well is mildly strenuous."

–bigtyke

ble. An easy paved trail (⅓ mi round-trip) leads to the dwelling and to adjacent Castle A, a badly deteriorated 6-story living space with about 45 rooms. No one is permitted to enter the ruins, but the viewing area is close by. From Camp Verde, take Main Street to Montezuma Castle Road.

Somewhat less accessible than Montezuma's Castle—but equally striking—is the **Montezuma Well** (☎ 928/567–4521) unit of the national monument. Although there are some Sinagua and Hohokam ruins here, the limestone sinkhole with a limpid blue-green pool lying in the middle of the desert is the park's main attraction. This cavity—55 feet deep and 365 feet across—is all that's left of an ancient subterranean cavern; the water remains at a constant 76°F year-round. It's a short hike up here, but the peace, quiet, and the views of the Verde Valley reward the effort. To reach Montezuma Well from Montezuma Castle, return to Interstate 17 and go north to Exit 293; signs direct you to the well, which is 4 mi east of the freeway. The drive includes a short section of dirt road. ✉ *Montezuma Castle Rd., 7 mi northeast of Camp Verde* ☎ *928/567–3322 Montezuma Castle, 928/567–3322 Ext. 15 bookstore* ⊕ *www.nps. gov/moca* 🔁 *$5* ☉ *Labor Day–Memorial Day, daily 8–5; Memorial Day–Labor Day, daily 8–6.*

☾ ㉘ **Out of Africa Wildlife Park.** In this Serengeti-theme wildlife preserve, a giraffe or two might poke its head inside your guide-driven Mercedes Unimog jeep expecting a treat and delivering a glancing blow with its long tongue if you don't divvy up. Among dozens of other species splayed out across the 104 acres, zebra, ostrich, and wildebeest will also vie for their fair share, coming near enough for great photo ops on an hour-long guided tour of the lower preserve. The predators, including such rare species as white tigers, black African leopards, and arctic wolves live in separate fenced areas on a hill above. You can take a tram up, or walk, but the latter means you won't have the advantage of a guide, or much in the way of interpretive signs. ✉ *Verde Valley Justice Ct. Rd., 3 mi west of I 17 on AZ 260* ☎ *928/567–2840* ⊕ *www. outofafricapark.com* 🔁 *$28* ☉ *Wed.–Sun. 9:30–5 PM; last tour 4 PM.*

Sports & the Outdoors

The **Verde Ranger District** office of the **Prescott National Forest** (✉ 300 E. AZ 260, Camp Verde ☎ 928/567–4121 ⊕ www.fs.fed.us/r3/prescott) is a good resource for places to hike, fish, and boat along the Verde River.

The **Black Canyon Trail** (✉ AZ 260, 4 mi south of Cottonwood, west on FR 359 4½ mi) is a bit of a slog, rising more than 2,200 feet in 6 mi, but the reward is grand views from the gray cliffs of Verde Valley to the red buttes of Sedona to the blue range of the San Francisco Peaks.

Dead Horse Ranch State Park

㉙ *20 mi northwest of Montezuma Castle National Monument; 1 mi north of Cottonwood, off Main St.*

In the late 1940s, when Calvin "Cap" Ireys asked his family to help him choose among the ranches he was thinking about buying in the Verde Valley, his son immediately picked "the one with the dead horse on it."

Ireys sold the land to the state in 1973 at one-third of its value, with the stipulation that the park into which it was to be converted retain the ranch's colorful name.

The 423-acre spread, which combines high-desert and wetlands habitats, is a pleasant place to while away the day. You can fish in the Verde River or the well-stocked Park Lagoon, or hike on some 6 mi of trails that begin in a shaded picnic area and wind along the river; adjoining forest service pathways are available for those who enjoy longer treks. Birders can check off more than 100 species from the Arizona Audubon Society lists provided by the rangers. Bald eagles perch along the Verde River in winter, and the common black hawks—a misnomer for these threatened avians—nest here in summer. ⊠ *675 Dead Horse Ranch Rd., Cottonwood* ☎ *928/634-5283* ⊕ *www.pr.state.az.us* ⌨ *Day use $6 per car; camping without electricity $12, with electricity $19* ☉ *Daily 8–5.*

Sports & the Outdoors

FISHING The best time to fish the upper Verde River is from November through March, when selected pools are stocked with six species of fish, including catfish, bass, and trout. The trout fishing is especially good. Catches average about 10 inches. Access the river from either Dead Horse State Park or Tuzigoot National Monument. If you're lucky you'll be fishing alongside bald eagles that nest here in winter. In March, springtime runoff may make the river muddy. Be aware of the three endangered native species—the spikedace, razorback sucker, and Colorado pike minnow—and throw them back.

Despite all the good fishing, there are no tackle shops in the sparsely populated Verde Valley. The closest shop, **On the Creek Sedona Outfitters** (⊠ 274 Apple Ave., #C, Sedona ☎ 928/203–9973), is almost 20 mi up AZ 89A in Sedona.

Where to Eat

$$ × **Kramer's at the Manzanita Restaurant & Lounge.** You might not expect
Fodor'sChoice   to find sophisticated cooking in Cornville, 6 mi east of Cottonwood,
★   but a European-born chef prepares Continental fare here, using organic produce and locally raised meat whenever possible. Roast duckling à l'orange and rack of lamb are beautifully presented; try the mushroom soup if it's available. The hours are not as cosmopolitan as the food: dinner ends at 8 PM. ⊠ *11425 E. Cornville Rd., Cornville* ☎ *928/634–8851* ⊟ *MC, V* ☉ *Closed Mon. and Tues.*

¢–$$ × **Page Springs Restaurant.** Come to these two rustic, wood-paneled rooms in Cornville, on the loop to the town of Page Springs—off AZ 89A—for down-home Western chow: great chili, burgers, and steaks. You'll get an Oak Creek view for much less than you'd pay closer to Sedona. ⊠ *1975 N. Page Springs Rd., Cornville* ☎ *928/634–9954* ⊟ *No credit cards.*

¢   × **Gabriela's Mexican Food.** Off the main Camp Verde drag, this tiny eatery serves traditional Mexican food. Try the *carne asada* (marinated, grilled beef) tacos and the chicken *burros* (what burritos are often called in this part of Arizona). ⊠ *154 W. Holliman St., Camp Verde* ☎ *928/567–4484* ▭ *No credit cards* ⊗ *Closed Sun.*

Tuzigoot National Monument

⑳ *3 mi north of Cottonwood.*

Not as well preserved as Montezuma Castle but more impressive in scope, Tuzigoot is another complex of ruins of the Sinagua people, who lived on this land overlooking the Verde Valley from about AD 1000 to 1400. The pueblo, constructed of limestone and sandstone blocks, once rose three stories and housed 110 rooms. Inhabitants were skilled dry farmers and traded with peoples hundred of miles away. Items used for food preparation, as well as jewelry, weapons, and farming tools excavated from the site, are displayed in the visitor center. Within the ruins, you can step into a reconstructed room. ⊠ *Broadway Rd., between Cottonwood's Old Town and Clarkdale, Clarkdale* ☎ *928/634–5564* ⊕ *www.nps.gov/tuzi* ⊠ *$5* ⊗ *Labor Day–Memorial Day, daily 8–5; Memorial Day–Labor Day, daily 8–6.*

> ### WORD OF MOUTH
>
> "Tuzigoot was very small—it's a much smaller version of Wupatki. I'd only do it if you have extra time. It is fairly easy to reach, though, on the way to Sedona."
> —mykidssherpa

Clarkdale

㉛ *19 mi northwest of Camp Verde, via AZ 260 and AZ 89A, 23 mi southwest of Sedona on AZ 89A, 2 mi southwest of Tuzigoot National Monument.*

There's little to see in Clarkdale these days but it's the place to catch the Verde Canyon Railroad, which follows a dramatic route through the Verde Canyon, the remains of a copper smelter, and much unspoiled desert that is inaccessible by car. The destination might not be that impressive, but the ride is undeniable scenic. Clarkdale once provided the smelter for copper mines in nearby Jerome. Its current incarnation is said to have arisen from a colony of prostitutes and hard-core gamblers who were tossed out of a rowdy mining camp.

★ Train buffs come to catch the 22-mi **Verde Canyon Railroad** (⊠ Arizona Central Railroad, 300 N. Broadway, Clarkdale ☎ 800/320–0718 ⊕ www.verdecanyonrr.com), whose knowledgeable announcers regale riders with the area's colorful history and point out natural attractions along the way—in winter, you're likely to see bald eagles. This trip, which takes about four hours, is especially popular in fall-foliage season and in spring, when the desert wildflowers bloom; make reservations well in advance. Round-trip rides cost $54.95. For $79.95 you can ride the much more comfortable living-room-like first-class cars, where hot hors d'oeuvres, coffee, and a cocktail are included in the price. Reservations are required.

Jerome

★ *3½ mi southwest of Clarkdale, 20 mi northwest of Camp Verde, 33 mi northeast of Prescott, 25 mi southwest of Sedona on AZ 89A.*

Jerome was once known as the Billion Dollar Copper Camp, but after the last mines closed in 1953, the booming population of 15,000 dwindled to 50 determined souls, earning Jerome the "ghost town" designation it still holds, although its population has risen back to almost 500. It's hard to imagine this town was once the location of Arizona's largest JCPenney store and one of the state's first Safeway supermarkets. Jerome saw its first revival during the mid-1960s, when hippies arrived and turned it into an arts colony of sorts, and it has since become a tourist attraction. In addition to its shops and historic sites, Jerome is worth visiting for its scenery: it's built into the side of Cleopatra Hill, and from here you can see Sedona's red rocks, Flagstaff's San Francisco Peaks, and even eastern Arizona's Mogollon Rim country.

> ### WORD OF MOUTH
>
> "Jerome has the feeling of what Sedona used to be before it became a major tourist destination. Jerome was once a mining town; now it is full of small art galleries and funky shops; it's perched on the side of a mountain. Definitely within reach if you're doing Sedona. I stayed in the Grand Hotel there, which used to be the hospital for the miners, and is supposedly haunted. The restaurant is really wonderful."   –robhart

Jerome is about a mile above sea level, but structures within town sit at elevations that vary by as much as 1,500 feet, depending on whether they're on Cleopatra Hill or at its foot. Blasting at the United Verde (later Phelps Dodge) mine regularly shook buildings off their foundations—the town's jail slid across a road and down a hillside, where it sits today. And that's not all that was unsteady about Jerome. In 1903 a reporter from a New York newspaper called Jerome "the wickedest town in America," due to its abundance of drinking and gambling establishments; town records from 1880 list 24 saloons. Whether by divine retribution or drunken accidents, the town burned down several times.

Jerome currently has around 50 retail establishments (that's more than one for every 10 residents). You can get a map of the town's shops and its attractions at the visitor-information trailer on AZ 89A. Except for the state-run historic park, attractions and businesses don't always stay open as long as their stated hours if things are slow.

Of the three mining museums in town, the most inclusive is part of **Jerome State Historic Park.** Just outside town, signs on AZ 89A will direct you to the turnoff for the park, reached by a short, precipitous road. The museum occupies the 1917 mansion of Jerome's mining king, Dr. James "Rawhide Jimmy" Douglas Jr., who purchased Little Daisy Mine in 1912. You can see some of the tools and heavy equipment used to grind ore, but accounts of the town's wilder elements—such as the House of Joy brothel—are not so prominently displayed. ⊠ *State Park Rd.* ☎ *928/634–5381* ⊕ *www.pr.state.az.us* ⊠ *$4* ⊘ *Daily 8–5.*

The **Mine Museum** in downtown Jerome is staffed by the Jerome Historical Society. The museum's collection of mining stock certificates alone is worth the (small) price of admission—the amount of money that changed hands in this town 100 years ago boggles the mind. ⊠ *200 Main St.* ☎ *928/634–5477* ⊠ *$2* ⊘ *Daily 9–5.*

Where to Stay & Eat

$–$$ ✕ **Haunted Hamburger/Jerome Palace.** After the climb up the stairs from Main Street to this former boardinghouse, you'll be ready for the hearty burgers, chili, cheese steaks, and ribs that dominate the menu. Lighter fare, including such meatless selections as the guacamole quesadilla, is also available. An outdoor deck overlooks Verde Valley and offers the option of smoking. ⊠ *410 Clark St.* ☎ *928/634–0554* ⊟ *MC, V.*

¢ ✕ **Flatiron Cafe.** Ask where to have lunch or a late-afternoon snack, and nearly every Main Street–shop owner will direct you to a tiny eatery at the fork in the road. The menu includes healthful sandwiches, such as black-bean hummus with feta cheese, and many coffee drinks. Breakfast is also served. ⊠ *416 Main St.* ☎ *928/634–2733* ⊟ *No credit cards* ⊘ *Closed Wed. and Thurs. No dinner.*

¢ ✕ **Red Rooster Café.** The old Safeway is now a café with tin ceilings and country accents, yet the delicious meat-loaf sandwich is nontraditional, served on whole wheat bread with Dijon mustard *sans* mashed potatoes. A compact but eclectic lunch menu includes green-chile quiche and a turkey wrap topped with bacon, avocado, and chipotle mayonnaise. Leave room for the delicate bread pudding made from croissants. ⊠ *363 Main St.* ☎ *928/634–7087* ⊟ *MC, V* ⊘ *Closed Tues. No dinner.*

$–$$ ▦ **Ghost City Inn.** The outdoor veranda at this 1898 B&B affords sweeping views of the Verde Valley and Sedona. Most rooms are decorated in Victorian style, but one has contemporary Western touches and another has a rustic appeal. Afternoon tea with cookies is an unexpected luxury for this formerly rough-and-ready town. ⊠ *541 N. Main St., 86331* ☎ *928/634–4678 or 888/634–4678* ⊕ *www.ghostcityinn.com* ⇆ *6 rooms* ∆ *In-room VCRs, outdoor hot tub, some pets allowed (fee); no kids under 14, no smoking* ⊟ *AE, D, MC, V* ⦿l *BP.*

$–$$ ▦ **Jerome Grand Hotel.** This full-service hotel is housed in a former hospital built in 1927. The rooms are comfy, with homey furnishings that part with the institutional past. Many rooms have splendid views. ⊠ *200 Hill St., 86331* ☎ *928/634–8200 or 888/817–6788* ☎ *928/639–0299* ⊕ *www.jeromegrandhotel.net* ⇆ *22 rooms, 1 suite* ∆ *Restaurant, in-room VCRs, lounge* ⊟ *AE, D, MC, V.*

★ $–$$ ▦ **Surgeon's House.** Plants, knickknacks, bright colors, and plenty of sunlight make this Mediterranean-style home a welcoming place to stay. The friendly ministrations of innkeeper Andrea Prince enhance the experience. Multicourse breakfasts might include overstuffed burritos or a marinated fruit compote. There are two suites and two rooms, including a former chauffeur's quarters that has a skylight and private patio. All have private bathrooms. Knockout vistas can be seen from almost everywhere in the house. ⊠ *101 Hill St., 86331* ☎ *928/639–1452 or*

800/639–1452 ⊕ *www.surgeonshouse.com* ⇆ *2 rooms, 2 suites* ⟡ *Some kitchenettes, some pets allowed (fee); no room TVs* ▭ *MC, V* ¶⊙¶ *BP.*

WORD OF MOUTH

"I love Jerome! . . . it's a kind of artsy town breathtakingly set perched on a mountain. On a clear day you can see to the San Francisco Mtns. "   –cassidy2002

CAMPING   For information about camping near Jerome at Mingus Mountain, Playground, or Potato Patch—all open May through October—contact the Prescott National Forest's **Verde Ranger District** (⊠ 300 E. AZ 260, Camp Verde ☎ 928/567–4121 ⊕ www.fs.fed.us/r3/prescott).

Nightlife

Paul & Jerry's Saloon (⊠ Main St. ☎ 928/634–2603) attracts a rowdy crowd to its two pool tables and old wooden bar. On weekends there's live music and a lively scene at the **Spirit Room** (⊠ Main St. and AZ 89A ☎ 928/634–8809); the mural over the bar harks back to the days when it was a dining spot for the prostitutes of the red-light district.

Shopping

Jerome has its share of art galleries (some perched precariously on Cleopatra Hill), along with boutiques, and they're funkier than those in Sedona. Main Street and, just around the bend, Hull Avenue are Jerome's two primary shopping streets. Your eyes may begin to glaze over after browsing through one boutique after another, most offering tasteful Southwestern paraphernalia.

Aurum (⊠ 369 Main St. ☎ 928/634–3330) focuses on contemporary art jewelry in silver and gold; about 30 artists are represented. **Designs on You** (⊠ 233 Main St. ☎ 928/634–7879) carries attractively styled women's clothing. **Jerome Artists Cooperative Gallery** (⊠ 502 Main St. ☎ 928/639–4276) specializes in jewelry, sculpture, painting, and pottery by local artists. The **Jewel** (⊠ 420 Hull Ave. ☎ 928/639–0259) specializes in Australian opals. **Nellie Bly** (⊠ 136 Main St. ☎ 928/634–0255) stocks perfume bottles and outstanding kaleidoscopes. Among the work of 300 artists at the **Raku Gallery** (⊠ 250 Hull Ave. ☎ 928/634–2876) you'll find wrought-iron furniture, free-blown glass, and fountains. **Sky Fire** (⊠ 140 Main St. ☎ 928/634–8081), the most sophisticated shop in Jerome, has two floors of items to adorn your person and your house, from Southwestern-pattern dishes to handcrafted Mission-style hutches.

EN ROUTE   The drive down a mountainous section of AZ 89A from Jerome to Prescott is gorgeous (if somewhat harrowing in bad weather), filled with twists and turns through **Prescott National Forest.** A scenic turnoff near Jerome provides one last vista and a place to apply chains during surprise snowstorms. There's camping, picnicking, and hiking at the crest of Mingus Mountain. If you're coming from Phoenix, the route that crosses the Mogollon Rim, overlooking the Verde Valley, is scenic but less precipitous.

Prescott

33 mi southwest of Jerome on AZ 89A to U.S. 89, 100 mi northwest of Phoenix via Interstate 17 to AZ 69.

In a forested bowl 5,300 feet above sea level, Prescott is a prime summer refuge for Phoenix-area dwellers. It was proclaimed the first capital of the Arizona Territory in 1864 and settled by Yankees to ensure that gold-rich northern Arizona would remain a Union resource. (Tucson and southern Arizona were strongly pro-Confederacy.) Although early territorial settlers thought that ruins in the area were of Aztec origin, today it's believed that ancestors of the Yavapai, whose reservation is today on the outskirts of town, were the area's original inhabitants. You can see the results of this notion—inspired by *The History and Conquest of Mexico,* a popular book by historian William Hickling Prescott, for whom the town was named—in such street names as Montezuma, Cortez, and Alarcon.

Despite a devastating downtown fire in 1900, Prescott remains the Southwest's richest town of late-19th-century New England–style architecture (some have called it the "West's most Eastern town"). With two institutions of higher education, Yavapai College and Prescott College, Prescott could be called a college town, but it doesn't really feel like one, perhaps because so many retirees also reside here, drawn by the temperate climate and low cost of living.

The city's main drag is Gurley Street, named after John Addison Gurley, who was slated to be the first governor but died days before he was to move to the Arizona Territory. Those interested in architecture should get a map of the Victorian neighborhoods. Most are within walking distance of the chamber office. Many Queen Annes have been beautifully restored, and a number are now B&Bs. Antiques and collectibles shops line Cortez Street to the north of the courthouse.

TIMING Tourism in Prescott can be bustling but rarely overwhelming. Any day will do to tour the Victorian homes and antiques shops, but if you enjoy museums, avoid going on Sunday. The museum hours are stunted on this day, and you won't want to be rushed through the extensive grounds of the Sharlot Hall Museum. Devoting a full day to tour Prescott is plenty, with time left over, perhaps, to watch the sunset from Thumb Butte.

What to See

🕄 **Courthouse Plaza.** The 1916 Yavapai County Courthouse stands in the heart of Prescott, guarded by an equestrian bronze of turn-of-the-20th-century journalist and lawmaker Bucky O'Neill, who died while charging San Juan Hill in Cuba with Teddy Roosevelt during the Spanish-American War. ⊠ *Bounded by Gurley, Goodwin, Cortez, and Montezuma Sts., Downtown.*

🕄 **Phippen Museum of Western Art.** The paintings and bronze sculptures of George Phippen, along with works by other artists of the West, form the permanent collection of this museum, about 5 mi north of downtown. Phippen met with a group of prominent cowboy artists in 1965

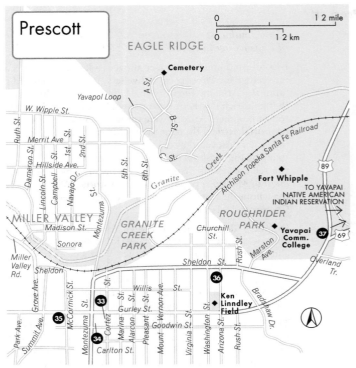

to form the Cowboy Artists of America, a group dedicated to preserving the Old West as they saw it, and he became the president but died the next year. A memorial foundation set up in his name opened the doors of this museum in 1984. ⊠ *4701 U.S. 89 N* ☎ *928/778–1385* ⊕ *www.phippenartmuseum.org* 🖃 *$5* ☉ *Tues.–Sat. 10–4, Sun. 1–4.*

👋 ③⑤ **Sharlot Hall Museum.** Local history is documented at this remarkable mu-
Fodor'sChoice seum. Along with the original ponderosa-pine log cabin, which housed
★ the territorial governor, and the museum, named for historian and poet Sharlot Hall, the parklike setting contains three fully restored period homes and a transportation museum. Territorial times are the focus, but natural history and artifacts of the area's prehistoric peoples are also on display. ⊠ *415 W. Gurley St., 2 blocks west of Courthouse Plaza, Downtown* ☎ *928/445–3122* ⊕ *www.sharlot.org* 🖃 *$5* ☉ *Mon.–Sat. 10–4, Sun. noon–4.*

③⑥ **Smoki Museum.** The 1935 stone-and-log building, which resembles an Indian pueblo, is almost as interesting as the Native American artifacts inside. Baskets, katsinas, pottery, rugs, and beadwork make up the collection, which represents Native American culture from the pre-Columbian period to the present. ⊠ *147 N. Arizona St., Downtown* ☎ *928/445–*

1230 ⊕ www.smokimuseum.org ✉ $4 ⊙ Apr.–Dec., Mon.–Sat. 10–4, Sun. 1–4; Jan.–Mar., Fri., Sat., and Mon. 10–4, Sun. 1–4.

❸❹ **Whiskey Row.** Twenty saloons and houses of pleasure once lined this stretch of Montezuma Street. Social activity is more subdued these days, and the historic bars provide an escape from the street's many boutiques. ⊠ *Montezuma St. along west side of Courthouse Plaza, Downtown.*

NEED A BREAK?

Caffe St. Michael is a great place to relax over a coffee or grab a bowl of black-bean chili and watch the people on Whiskey Row. The café and bar has been restored to its original 1901 style. The service at the counter is brisk and will leave you plenty of time for antiquing or museum browsing for the remainder of the day. ⊠ 205 W. Gurley St., Downtown ☎ 928/776–7318.

Sports & the Outdoors

HIKING & CAMPING   More than a million acres of national-forest land surround Prescott. Thumb Butte is a popular hiking spot, but there are lots of other trekking and overnighting options. Contact the **Bradshaw Ranger District** (⊠ 2230 E. AZ 69, Hwy. 69 ☎ 928/445–7253 ⊕ www.fs.fed.us/r3/prescott) for information about hiking trails and campgrounds in the Prescott National Forest south of town down to Horse Thief Basin. Campgrounds near Prescott are generally not crowded.

The **Thumb Butte Loop Trail** (⊠ Thumb Butte Rd., 3 mi west of Prescott following Gurley St.—which turns into Thumb Butte), a 2-mi trek on a paved yet steep loop, takes you 600 feet up near the crest of its namesake. The vistas are large, but you won't be alone on this popular trail.

HORSEBACK RIDING   **Granite Mountain Stables** (⊠ 2400 W. Shane Dr., 7 mi northeast of Prescott, Hwy. 89 ☎ 928/771–9551) has daily guided rides as well as group specials, such as hay-wagon outings.

Where to Stay & Eat

$$–$$$ ✕ **Murphy's.** Mesquite-grilled meats and beer brewed exclusively for the restaurant are the specialties. The baby back ribs, fresh steamed clams, and fresh fried catfish are your best bets. The bar has a good selection of microbrews as well. ⊠ *201 N. Cortez St., Downtown* ☎ *928/445–4044* ⊟ *AE, D, MC, V.*

$$ ✕ **The Palace.** Legend has it that the patrons who saved the Palace's ornately carved 1880s Brunswick bar from a Whiskey Row fire in 1900 continued drinking at it while the rest of the row burned across the street. Whatever the case, the bar remains the centerpiece of the beautifully restored turn-of-the-20th-century structure, with a high, pressed-tin ceiling. Steaks and chops are the stars here, but the grilled fish and hearty corn chowder are fine, too. ⊠ *120 S. Montezuma St., Downtown* ☎ *928/541–1996* ⊟ *AE, MC, V.*

$–$$ ✕ **Genovese.** Low-price, classic southern-Italian fare makes this restaurant near Courthouse Plaza a local favorite. Try the cannelloni stuffed with shrimp, crab, ricotta cheese, and spinach. ⊠ *217 W. Gurley St., Downtown* ☎ *928/541–9089* ⊟ *AE, MC, V.*

¢–$$ ✕ **Prescott Brewing Company.** Good beer, good food, good service, and good prices—for a casual meal, it's hard to beat this cheerful restaurant. In addition to chili, fish-and-chips, and British-style bangers and mash, vegetarian enchiladas made with tofu, and pasta salad are on the menu. Fresh-baked beer bread comes with many entrées. ⊠ *130 W. Gurley St., Downtown* ☎ *928/771–2795* ▭ *AE, D, DC, MC, V.*

¢–$ ✕ **El Charro Restaurant.** This is the best Mexican food in town: mostly heavy Sonoran food, and most of it homemade. The restaurant has been open since 1959, and the enchiladas, fajitas, and basic soft tacos are perennial customer favorites. The salsa has been tamed over the years, but ask for hot sauce and your wish will be granted. ⊠ *120 N. Montezuma St., Downtown* ☎ *928/445–7130* ▭ *AE, MC, V.*

¢ ✕ **Kendall's Famous Burgers and Ice Cream.** A great diner, replete with booths and a 1950s-style soda fountain, Kendall's serves hamburgers cooked to order with your choice of 14 condiments. Make sure you try the homemade french fries. ⊠ *113 S. Cortez St., Downtown* ☎ *928/778–3658* ▭ *D, MC, V.*

$$–$$$ ▦ **Prescott Resort Conference Center and Casino.** On a hill on the outskirts of town, this upscale property has views of the mountain ranges surrounding Prescott and the Valley. Many guests hardly notice, so riveted are they by the poker machines and slots in Arizona's only hotel casino. There are plenty of recreational facilities to occupy those able to resist the one-armed bandits. ⊠ *1500 AZ 69, Hwy. 69, 86301* ☎ *928/776–1666 or 800/967–4637* 🖷 *928/776–8544* ⊕ *www.prescottresort.com* ⤳ *161 rooms* ♤ *Restaurant, coffee shop, refrigerators, cable TV, 4 tennis courts, pool, gym, hot tub, sauna, racquetball, piano bar, casino, no-smoking rooms* ▭ *AE, D, DC, MC, V.*

★ $–$$$ ▦ **Hassayampa Inn.** Built in 1927 for early automobile travelers, the Hassayampa Inn oozes character. The ceiling in the lobby is hand-painted, and some rooms still have the original furnishings. A free full breakfast of your choice at the restaurant gilds the lily of reasonable rates. The Peacock Room, the hotel's pretty—if overly formal—dining room, has tapestried booths, dim lighting, and better than average Continental food. ⊠ *122 E. Gurley St., Downtown, 86301* ☎ *928/778–9434 or 800/322–1927* 🖷 *928/445–8590* ⊕ *www.hassayampainn.com* ⤳ *58 rooms, 10 suites* ♤ *Restaurant, cable TV, bar* ▭ *AE, D, DC, MC, V* ⦿ *BP.*

$–$$ ▦ **Marks House Victorian Bed and Breakfast.** Victoria still reigns at this B&B, once owned by the mayor of territorial Prescott. It now belongs to Beth Maitland, a star of the daytime soap *The Young and the Restless*, and is ably managed by her parents. Rooms are impeccably furnished with period antiques: the suite in the circular turret, overlooking Thumb Butte, is particularly impressive. Breakfast is served in the formal dining room. ⊠ *203 E. Union St., Downtown, 86303* ☎ *928/778–4632 or 800/370–6275* ✍ *markshouse@cableone.net* ⤳ *2 rooms, 2 suites* ♤ *Dining room; no room TVs* ▭ *D, MC, V* ⦿ *BP.*

$ ▦ **Hotel Vendome.** This World War I–era hostelry has seen miners, health seekers, and such celebrities as cowboy star Tom Mix walk through its doors. Old-fashioned touches, including the original claw-foot tubs, remain. Like many other historic hotels, the Vendome has its obligatory resident ghost (her room costs slightly more). Only a block from Courthouse Plaza, this is a good choice for those who want to combine sightseeing, modern comforts, and good value. ⊠ *230 Cortez St., Downtown, 86303* ☎ *928/776–0900 or 888/468–3583* 🖷 *928/771–0395*

CLOSE UP

Rodeo Lesson

COWBOYS VIED for the unofficial titles of best roper and rider at the end of the big cattle drives of the late 19th century. As their day jobs were curtailed in scope by the spread of railroads and the fencing-in of the West, they made the contests more formalized and the sport of rodeo was born.

The five standard events in contemporary rodeo are calf roping, bull riding, steer wrestling, saddle bronc-riding, and bareback bronc-riding. ("Bronc" is short for bronco, an unbroken range horse with a tendency to buck, or throw, a rider.) Two other events are recognized in championship competitions: single-steer roping and team roping. The barrel race, a saddle-horse race around a series of barrels, is a popular contest for women.

Participants pay entry fees, and the prize money won is their only compensation. More than half of all rodeos are independent of state and county fairs, livestock shows, or other attractions, and many are held in arenas devoted to the purpose. The equipment, however, is simple and may be improvised.

In 1929 the Rodeo Association of America was formed to regulate the sport. The contestants themselves took a hand in 1936 after a strike in Boston Garden and organized the Cowboy Turtles Association—"turtles" because they had been slow to act. This group was renamed the Rodeo Cowboys Association (RCA) in 1945 and became the Professional Rodeo Cowboys Association (PRCA) in 1975. Its rules became accepted by most rodeos.

Prescott's annual rodeo started in 1888 and is claimed to be the world's oldest. It's part of the popular Frontier Days during the week surrounding the 4th of July.

⊕ *www.vendomehotel.com* ↩ *16 rooms, 4 suites* ⅄ *Fans, cable TV, bar; no smoking* ⊟ *AE, D, DC, MC, V* ⦿ *CP.*

¢–$ 🔲 **Hotel St. Michael.** Don't expect serenity on the busiest corner of Courthouse Plaza, but for low rates and historic charm it's hard to beat this hotel in operation since 1900. Rooms have 1920s–40s-era antiques; some face the plaza and others look out on Thumb Butte. The first-floor Café St. Michael serves great coffee and croissants. ⊠ *205 W. Gurley St., Downtown, 86303* ☎ *928/776–1999 or 800/678–3757* 🖷 *928/776–7318* ↩ *71 rooms* ⅄ *Coffee shop, cable TV, shop* ⊟ *AE, D, MC, V.*

Nightlife & the Arts

Prescott's popular **Bluegrass Festival on the Square** takes place in June. The town, which had its first organized cowboy competition in 1888, lays claim to having the world's oldest rodeo: the annual **Frontier Days** roundup, held on July 4 weekend at the Yavapai County Fairgrounds. In August the **Cowboy Poets Gathering** brings together campfire bards from around the country.

The **Prescott Fine Arts Association** (⊠ 208 N. Marina St., Downtown ☎ 928/445–3286) sponsors musicals and dramas, plays for children, and a concert series. The association's gallery also presents rotating exhibits by local, regional, and national artists. The **Prescott Jazz Society** (✉ 129½ N. Cortez St., Downtown ☎ 928/925–1422) has an intimate storefront lounge. The **Yavapai Symphony Association** (✉ 228 N. Alarcon St., Suite B, Downtown ☎ 928/776–4255) hosts performances by the Phoenix and Flagstaff symphonies; call ahead for schedules and venues.

Montezuma Street's Whiskey Row, off Courthouse Plaza, is nowhere near as wild as it was in its historic heyday, but most bars have live music—and a lively collegiate crowd—on the weekends. The **Cadillac Bar and Grill** (✉ 216 W. Gurley St., Downtown ☎ 928/777–0018) offers live blues, jazz, rock, and pop Friday and Saturday at 9 PM. It also has happy-hour entertainment beginning at 5 PM. For a more refined experience, head over to the art nouveau–piano bar at the **Hassayampa Inn** (✉ 122 E. Gurley St., Downtown ☎ 928/778–9434); there's always someone tickling the ivories on the weekend. The Brunswick bar at **Lyzzard's Lounge** (✉ 120 N. Cortez St., Downtown ☎ 928/778–2244) was shipped from England via the Colorado River.

Shopping

Shops selling antiques and collectibles line Cortez Street, just north of Courthouse Plaza. There is fun stuff—especially Western kitsch—as well as some good buys on valuable pieces. Many of the stores gather together groups of retailers. Courthouse Plaza, especially along Montezuma Street, is lined with specialty and gift shops. Many match those in Sedona for quality and price. Be sure to check out **Arts Prescott** (✉ 134 S. Montezuma St., Downtown ☎ 928/776–7717), a cooperative gallery of talented local craftspeople and artists. **Bashford Courts** (✉ 130 Gurley St., Downtown ☎ 928/445–9798) has three floors of artsy stores. At 14,000 square feet, the **Merchandise Mart Antique Mall** (✉ 205 N. Cortez St., Downtown ☎ 928/776–1728) is the largest of the town's collections of collectors. To get your fill of Old West kitsch, stop at **Prescott Museum & Trading Company** (✉ 142 S. Montezuma St., Downtown ☎ 928/776–8498), which also displays vintage boots, saddles, and taxidermy. **Sun West Gallery** (✉ 152 S. Montezuma St., Downtown ☎ 928/778–1204) has artwork, furnishings, and Zapotec rugs.

NORTH-CENTRAL ARIZONA ESSENTIALS

To research prices, get advice from other travelers, and book travel arrangements, visit ⊕ www.fodors.com.

Transportation

BY AIR

Prescott Municipal Airport is 8 mi north of town on U.S. 89. Flagstaff Pulliam Airport is 3 mi south of town off Interstate 17 at Exit 337. Sedona Airport is in West Sedona.

America West flies frequently from Phoenix into Prescott Municipal Airport and to Flagstaff Pulliam Airport. Sedona Airport is a base for several air tours and has no regularly scheduled flights.

A taxi from the airport to downtown should cost about $8 to $10. Cabs are not regulated; some, but not all, have meters. It's wise to agree on a rate before you leave for your destination.

📳 Flagstaff Pulliam Airport ☎ 928/556–1234. **Prescott Municipal Airport** ☎ 928/445–7860. **Sedona Airport** ☎ 928/282–1046.

BY BUS

Greyhound Lines has daily connections from throughout the West to Flagstaff, but none to Sedona. Buses also run between Prescott and Phoenix Sky Harbor International Airport.

The Sedona/Phoenix Shuttle Service makes eight trips daily between those cities; the fare is $45 one-way, $85 round-trip. You can also get on or off at Camp Verde, Cottonwood, or the Village of Oak Creek. The bus leaves from three terminals of Sky Harbor International Airport in Phoenix. Reservations are required.

📳 Greyhound Lines ✉ 399 S. Malpais La., Flagstaff ☎ 928/774–4573 or 800/231–2222 ✉ 820 E. Sheldon Ave., Prescott ☎ 928/445–5470 ⊕ www.greyhound.com. **Sedona/Phoenix Shuttle Service** ☎ 928/282–2066, 800/448–7988 in Arizona ⊕ www.sedona-phoenix-shuttle.com.

BY CAR

It makes sense to rent a car in this region since trails and monuments stretch miles past city limits and many area towns cannot be reached by the major bus companies. The major rental agencies have offices in Flagstaff, Prescott, and Sedona. If you want to explore the red rocks of Sedona, you can rent a four-wheel drive from one of the local agencies like Canyon Jeep Rentals or Sedona Car Rental.

A Red Rock Pass is required to park anywhere in the Coconino National Forest from Oak Creek Canyon through Sedona. Passes cost $5 for the day, $15 for the week, or $20 for an entire year and can be purchased at four visitor centers surrounding and within Sedona. Passes are also available from vending machines at popular trailheads including Boynton Canyon, Bell Rock, and Huckaby. Locals widely resent the pass, feeling that free access to National Forests is a right. The Forest Service counters that it doesn't receive enough federal funds to maintain the land surrounding Sedona, trampled by 5 million visitors each year, and that a parking fee is the best way to raise revenue.

Flagstaff lies at the intersection of Interstate 40 (east–west) and Interstate 17 (running south from Flagstaff), 134 mi north of Phoenix via Interstate 17. The most direct route to Prescott from Phoenix is to take Interstate 17 north for 60 mi to Cordes Junction and then drive northwest on AZ 69 for 36 mi into town. Interstate 17, a four-lane divided highway, has several steep inclines and descents (complete with a number of runaway-truck ramps). However, it's generally an easy and scenic thoroughfare. If you want to take the more leisurely route through Verde Valley to Prescott, continue north on Interstate 17 another 25 mi past Cordes Junction until you see the turnoff for AZ 260, which will take you to Cottonwood in 12 mi. Here you can pick up AZ 89A, which leads southwest to Prescott (41 mi) or northeast to Sedona (19 mi).

Sedona stretches along AZ 89A, its main thoroughfare, which runs roughly east–west through town. AZ 89A is bisected by AZ 179. The more commercial section of AZ 89A east of AZ 179 is known as Uptown; locals tend to frequent the shops on the other side, called West Sedona. To the south of AZ 89A, AZ 179 is lined with upscale retailers for a couple of miles. To reach Sedona more directly from Phoenix, take Interstate 17 north for 113 mi until you come to AZ 179; it's another 15 mi on that road into town. The trip should take about 2½ hours. The 27-mi drive from Sedona to Flagstaff on AZ 89A, which winds its way through Oak Creek Canyon, is breathtaking.

Weekend traffic near Sedona, especially during the high season, can approach gridlock on the narrow highways. Leave for your destination at first light to bypass the day-trippers, late risers, and midday heat.
🚗 **Canyon Jeep Rentals** ⊠ Oak Creek Terrace Resort, 4548 AZ 89A, Sedona ☎ 928/282-6061 or 800/224-2229. **Red Rock Pass** ☎ 928/282-4119 information only ⊕ www.redrockcountry.org. **Sedona Car Rental** ⊠ Sedona Airport, Sedona ☎ 928/282-2227.

BY TAXI

In Sedona, try Bob's Sedona Taxi. A Friendly Cab and Sun Taxi are also options. A–1 Quick Cab & Tours in Flagstaff provides local and long-distance service.
🚗 **A–1 Quick Cab & Tours** ☎ 928/214-8294. **A Friendly Cab** ☎ 928/774-4444. **Bob's Sedona Taxi** ☎ 928/282-1234. **Sun Taxi** ☎ 928/774-7400.

BY TRAIN

Amtrak comes into the downtown Flagstaff station twice daily. There's no rail service into Prescott or Sedona.
🚆 **Amtrak** ⊠ 1 E. Rte. 66 ☎ 928/774-8679.

Contacts & Resources

EMERGENCIES

🚨 Ambulance, Fire & Police **Ambulance, Fire, and Police Emergencies** ☎ 911.
🏥 Hospitals **Columbia Northwest Medical Center** ⊠ 6200 N. La Cholla Blvd., Northwest ☎ 520/742-9000. **Flagstaff Medical Center** ⊠ 1200 N. Beaver St., Flagstaff ☎ 928/779-3366. **St. Joseph's Hospital** ⊠ 350 N. Wilmot Rd., Eastside ☎ 520/873-3000. **Tucson Medical Center** ⊠ 5301 E. Grant Rd., Central ☎ 520/327-5461. **University Medical Center** ⊠ 1501 N. Campbell Ave., University ☎ 520/694-0111, a teaching hospital with a first-rate trauma center. The **Verde Valley Medical Center Sedona Campus** ⊠ 3700 W. AZ 89A, Sedona ☎ 928/204-3000. **Yavapai Regional Medical Center** ⊠ 1003 Willow Creek Rd., Prescott ☎ 928/445-2700.
💊 Pharmacies in Flagstaff **Flagstaff Medical Center Pharmacy** ⊠ 1200 N. Beaver St., Flagstaff ☎ 928/779-3366. **Fry's Food and Drug** ⊠ 201 N. Switzer Canyon Dr., at Rte. 66, Flagstaff ☎ 928/774-3389. **Walgreens** ⊠ 1500 E. Cedar Ave., Flagstaff ☎ 928/773-1011.
💊 Pharmacy in Prescott **Goodwin Street Pharmacy** ⊠ 406 W. Goodwin St., Prescott ☎ 928/776-9939.
💊 Pharmacies in Sedona **Rite Aid** ⊠ 2350 W. AZ 89A, Sedona ☎ 928/282-9734. **Walgreens** ⊠ 1995 W. AZ 89A, Sedona ☎ 928/282-2528.
💊 Pharmacies **Walgreens 24-Hour Pharmacy** ⊠ 4685 E. Grant Rd., Central ☎ 520/326-4341 ⊠ 7114 N. Oracle Rd., Northwest ☎ 520/297-2826.

TOUR OPTIONS

IN FLAGSTAFF The Ventures program, run by the education department of the Museum of Northern Arizona, offers tours of the area led by local scientists, artists, and historians. Trips might include rafting excursions down the San Juan River, treks into the Grand Canyon or Colorado Plateau backcountry, or bus tours into the Navajo reservation to visit with Native American artists. Prices start at about $150 for cultural tours and go up to $1,500 for outdoor adventures, with most tours in the $900 to $1,100 range.

IN SEDONA Sedona Trolley offers two types of daily orientation tours, both departing from the main bus stop in Uptown and lasting less than an hour. One goes along AZ 179 to the Chapel of the Holy Cross, with stops at Tlaquepaque and some galleries; the other passes through West Sedona to Boynton Canyon (Enchantment Resort). Rates are $10 for one or $18 for both.

Several jeep-tour operators headquartered along Sedona's main Uptown drag conduct excursions, some focusing on geology, some on astronomy, some on vortices, some on all three. You can even find a combination jeep tour and horseback ride.

The ubiquitous Pink Jeep Tours are a popular choice. Sedona Red Rock Jeep Tours is also a reliable operator. Prices start at about $52 per person for two hours and go up to $102 per person for four hours. Although all the excursions are safe, many are not for those who dislike heights or bumps.

> ## WORD OF MOUTH
>
> "My husband and I were in Sedona last June and I would definitely recommend the Pink Jeep tour. It takes you on 'roads' that no car can travel on and you see some wonderful scenery. You also make a couple of stops to walk around and see breathtaking views. Plus the ride itself is great! It was a lot of fun and one of our best memories of that trip. I highly recommend it."   —teddysmom

Prices for hot-air-balloon tours generally start at $180 per person for one to two hours. The only two companies with permits to fly over Sedona are Northern Light Balloon Expeditions and Red Rock Balloon Adventures.

Sedona Photo Tours will take you to all the prime spots and help you take your best (photographic) shot. Rates are $35 per person for a basic two-hour tour.

Museum of Northern Arizona ☎ 928/774–5213 ⊕ www.musnaz.org. **Northern Light Balloon Expeditions** ☎ 928/282–2274 or 800/230–6222 ⊕ www.sedona.net/fun/balloon. **Pink Jeep Tours** ✉ 204 N. AZ 89A, Sedona ☎ 928/282–5000 or 800/873–3662 ⊕ www.pinkjeep.com. **Red Rock Balloon Adventures** ☎ 928/284–0040 or 800/258–3754 ⊕ www.redrockballoons.com. **Sedona Photo Tours** ✉ 252 N. AZ 89A, Sedona ☎ 928/282–4320 or 800/973–3662. **Sedona Red Rock Jeep Tours** ✉ 270 N. AZ 89A, Sedona ☎ 928/282–6826 or 800/848–7728 ⊕ www.redrockjeep.com. **Sedona Trolley** ☎ 928/282–6826 or 928/282–5400 ⊕ www.sedonatrolley.com.

VISITOR INFORMATION

🚹 **Camp Verde Chamber of Commerce** ☎ 928/567-9294 ⊕ www.campverde.org. **Clarkdale Chamber of Commerce** ☎ 928/634-3382 ⊕ www.clarkdalechamber.com. **Cottonwood/Verde Valley Chamber of Commerce** ☎ 928/634-7593 ⊕ http://cottonwood.verdevalley.com. **Flagstaff Visitors Center** ☎ 928/774-9541 or 800/842-7293 ⊕ www.flagstaffarizona.org. **Jerome Chamber of Commerce** ☎ 928/634-2900. **Prescott Chamber of Commerce** ☎ 928/445-2000 or 800/266-7534 ⊕ www.prescott.org. **Sedona-Oak Creek Canyon Chamber of Commerce** ☎ 928/282-7722 or 800/288-7336 ⊕ www.sedonachamber.com.

The Northeast

WORD OF MOUTH

"Canyon de Chelly and Moab were real highlights for me. We hiked de Chelly with a guide arranged through the visitor center . . . He was wonderful!!! We learned so much and saw the canyon intimately—hiking, climbing on the rocks, sometimes using footholds that had been carved out centuries before. The hike was filled with ruins, petroglyphs, vegetation and lore. Don't miss Canyon de Chelly, it's not just another canyon."

—thelmaandlouise

"If at all possible, I would try to take a tour of the Antelope Slot Canyons just outside of Page. They are incredibly beautiful and were a highlight of our trip. You have to go in on an organized tour which you can book in advance . . ."

—KathrynT

Updated by
Tom Carpenter

NORTHEAST ARIZONA IS a vast and magnificent land of lofty buttes, towering cliffs, and turquoise skies so clear that horizons appear endless. Most of the land in the area belongs to the Navajo and Hopi peoples, who cling to ancient traditions based on spiritual values, kinship, and an affinity for nature. In many respects life on the Hopi Mesas has changed little during the last two centuries, and visiting this land can feel like traveling to a foreign country. In such towns as Tuba City and Window Rock it's not uncommon to hear the gliding vowels and soft consonants of the Navajo language, a tongue as different from Hopi as English is from Chinese. As you drive in the vicinity, tune your AM radio to 660 KTNN, the Voice of the Navajo Nation. You'll quickly understand why the U.S. Marine Navajo "code talkers" communicating in their native tongue were able to devise a code within their language that was never broken by the Japanese.

The Navajo Nation encompasses more than 25,000 square mi, an area that would rank it larger than 10 of the 50 states. In its approximate center sits the 2,500-square-mi Hopi Reservation, a series of adobe villages built on high mesas overlooking the cultivated land. On Arizona's northern and eastern borders, where the Navajo Nation continues into Utah and New Mexico, the Navajo National Monument and Canyon de Chelly contain haunting cliff dwellings of ancient people who lived in the area 1,500 years ago. Glen Canyon Dam, which abuts the far northwestern corner of the reservation on U.S. 89, holds back more than 200 mi of emerald waters known as Lake Powell.

Most of northeast Arizona is desert country, but it's far from boring: eerie and spectacular rock formations as colorful as desert sunsets highlight immense mesas, canyons, and cliffs; towering stands of ponderosa pine cover the Chuska Mountains to the north and east of Canyon de Chelly. Navajo Mountain to the north and west in Utah soars more than 10,000 feet, and the San Francisco Peaks climb to similar heights to the south and west by Flagstaff. According to the Navajo creation myth, these are two of the four mountainous boundaries of the sacred land where the Navajo first emerged from the Earth's interior.

Top 5 Experiences in Northern Arizona

- **Canyon de Chelly:** This is one of the most spectacular natural wonders in the Southwest, rivaling the Grand Canyon for beauty—though on a smaller scale. The self-guided 2.5 mi White House Trail is the only hike you can take without a Navajo guide; follow the trail to the ruins at the bottom of the canyon and you'll understand what is so special about the region.

- **Glen Canyon Dam and National Recreation Area:** The best way to get to know the area is by taking a boat out on Lake Powell, amid the towering cliffs and secluded channels embroidering this huge reservoir. An excursion can take on the dimensions of an ocean voyage if you decide to explore the far reaches of the reservoir.

- **Hubbell Trading Post National Historic Site:** The self-guided tour is really an unforgettable glimpse into the past that reveals the interdependence of the Native people and the Indian traders.

GREAT ITINERARIES

IF YOU HAVE 2 DAYS

If you're just driving through the area on your way west, you might start off in 🖼 **Window Rock ❶** ☞. From there, it's an easy drive to some of the most interesting sights in northeastern Arizona. On your first day, visit **Canyon de Chelly ❷**. On the second, set out for the **Hopi Mesas ❺–❼**, stopping along the way at **Hubbell Trading Post National Historic Site ❸** and, perhaps, **Keams Canyon Trading Post ❹** for a mid-morning snack.

IF YOU HAVE 5 DAYS

If you plan to spend a bit more time exploring the region after a trip to the Grand Canyon, head north on U.S. 89 on your first day to 🖼 **Tuba City ❽** ☞. Along the way, you might wish to stop by **Cameron Trading Post ❾**. Explore the area, and relax for the night. On the second day, head east at Moenkopi

on AZ 264 for the **Hopi Mesas ❺–❼**. (And fill your tank before you leave since Tuba City is the last stop for gas before the mesas.) Have lunch at the **Hopi Cultural Center,** then return to Tuba City and head northeast on U.S. 160 toward 🖼 **Kayenta ❿**, where you can spend your second night. Get up early the next day to visit the **Navajo National Monument ⓮** and hike to Beta-Takin or Keet Seel pueblo (if you have made reservations in advance). Spend your third night at the lodge at 🖼 **Goulding's Trading Post ⓭** in Monument Valley. The next day, visit **Monument Valley Navajo Tribal Park ⓫**, and then take U.S. 160 north to where it connects with U.S. 191 near the town of Mexican Water. Head south for Chinle, a good base for touring 🖼 **Canyon de Chelly ❷**.

- **Hopi Mesas:** The Hopi sustain their culture through the continuous occupation of the ancient villages on these mesas—the spiritual center of their existence. A visit here won't be the stuff of glitz and glamour, but it will provide an unforgettable glimpse of a way of life that is deeply connected to the seasons and the elements.

- **Monument Valley Navajo Tribal Park:** Within its boundaries of this 92,000 acre area, you can see first hand the landscape that was the backdrop of such iconic western films as *Stagecoach, She Wore a Yellow Ribbon,* and *The Searchers*. Majestic sandstone buttes tower above the desert floor and overhead, clouds hang like white buttes, their shadows sweeping across a vastness that envelopes one of the most photographed places on earth.

Exploring the Northeast

The Navajo Nation, which encircles the Hopi Reservation, occupies most of northeastern Arizona. Canyon de Chelly is in the eastern part of the reservation. The Navajo National Monument and Monument Valley are in north–central "Navajoland" (a term used by the Navajo in promotional material). In the northwestern corner of the Arizona portion of the reservation are Lake Powell and Glen Canyon Dam.

Numbers in the margin correspond to numbers on the Northeast Arizona map.

> **FINDING YOUR WAY AROUND**
>
> Northeastern Arizona is sparsely inhabited, with few roads. Services and establishments rarely have numbered street addresses; even the post office operates on the basis of landmarks. And don't count on using your cell phone in most of the region—at least, not yet. Talks are under way with the Navajo Nation to install cell-phone towers in some areas.

About the Restaurants

Northeastern Arizona is a vast area with small hamlets and towns scattered miles apart, and there are few stores or restaurants along the highway. Most restaurants serve basic Native American and Southwestern cuisine, and are very casual. Navajo and Hopi food consists mainly of mutton stew, Hopi *piki* (paper-thin, blue-corn bread), and Navajo fry bread. Navajo tacos are fry bread piled with refried beans, ground beef, lettuce, tomato, scallions, cheese, avocado, sour cream, and salsa. When spread with butter, honey, and confectioner's sugar, Navajo fry bread becomes a delicious dessert. In the smaller reservation communities, only fast food may be available.

About the Hotels

One of the most important things to know when traveling in northeastern Arizona is which of the scattered communities have motels. Bed-and-breakfasts have begun to proliferate in Page. Contact the Page/Lake Powell Chamber of Commerce or the Navajo Nation Visitors Center for a list of area B&Bs, campgrounds, and RV facilities. Accommodations are also available in Native American hogans, eight-side domed houses made of mud, logs, or even contemporary building materials. During summer months, it's especially wise to make reservations. Most motels throughout this region are national chains and are clean, comfortable, and well maintained. Unless otherwise indicated, all rooms have air-conditioning, private baths, telephones, and TVs.

WHAT IT COSTS				
$$$$	**$$$**	**$$**	**$**	**¢**
RESTAURANTS over $30	$21–$30	$13–$20	$8–$12	under $8
HOTELS over $250	$176–$250	$121–$175	$70–$120	under $70

Restaurant prices are per person for a main course at dinner. Hotel prices are for a standard double in high season, excluding taxes and service charges.

Timing

Summer is a busy time around Lake Powell, and reservations for accommodations are suggested. Travelers seeking a quieter vacation should plan to visit between early November and late March, when the crowds—and the prices—ebb. The first weekend of September after Labor Day is a good time to be at Window Rock, when the Navajo Nation Annual Tribal Fair takes place. It's the world's largest Native American fair and includes a rodeo, traditional Navajo music and dances, food booths, and

IF YOU LIKE

FISHING

Lake Powell, known for its bass fishing, also holds other varieties including bluegill and pike, and the Colorado River below Glen Canyon Dam is known for its large trout. Keep in mind that Lake Powell stretches into Utah; a fishing license is required for each state. The eastern region of the Navajo Reservation has scattered lakes, most of them remote and small, but two of the more popular and accessible ones are near Canyon de Chelly: Wheatfields Lake, on Indian Highway 12 about 11 mi south of the community of Tsaile, and Many Farms Lake, near the community of Many Farms, on U.S. 191. Permits are required for fishing on the reservation.

HIKING

Some of the best hikes in this region are in Canyon de Chelly, up the streambed between the soaring orange-and-white sandstone cliffs, with the remains of the ancient ancestral Puebloan communities frequently in view. Mummy Cave is especially worth a look, its three-story watchtower nearly perfectly preserved. The more weathered Antelope House and White House stand against the sweeping canyon cliffs as impressive reminders of a bygone era. The Navajo National Monument offers impressive hikes to two ruins: Beta-Takin, a settlement dating back to AD 1250, and Keet Seel, which dates back as far as AD 950. Both are in alcoves at the base of gigantic overhanging cliffs. Remember, you cannot hike or camp on private property or tribal land without a backcountry permit; it's important to be respectful of this law.

HOPI CEREMONIES

The Hopi are well known for colorful ceremonial dances, many of which are supplications for rain, fertile crops, and harmony with nature. Most of these ceremonies take place in village plazas and kivas (underground ceremonial chambers) and last two days or longer; outsiders are sometimes permitted to watch segments of some ceremonies but are never allowed into kivas unless invited. Seasonal katsina dances performed at agricultural ceremonies may be restricted, so it's best to inquire upon arrival. Each clan has its own sacred rituals, starting times, and dates, which are determined by tribal elders.

SHOPPING

Most visitors to the area are tempted by the beautiful pottery, turquoise and sterling-silver jewelry, handwoven baskets, Navajo wool rugs, and other examples of Native American crafts. Many trading posts also carry the work of some New Mexico tribes, including exquisite inlaid Zuni jewelry and the world-acclaimed pottery of the Pueblo people. A vast majority of the products sold on the Hopi and Navajo Reservations are authentic, but the possibility of imitations does exist. Trading posts are very reliable, as are most roadside stands, which can offer some outstanding values, but be wary of solo vendors hanging around parking lots. If you're planning on shopping on the Hopi Reservation or elsewhere outside the Navajo trading posts, it's a good idea to carry cash or traveler's checks. Phone lines in the region are sometimes unreliable, which can make credit-card use impossible.

4

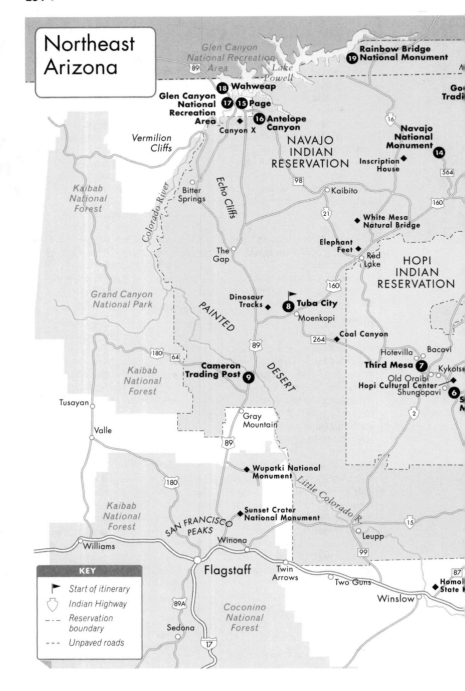

Northeast Arizona

Glen Canyon
National Recreation
Area ⑧⑨

Lake
Powell

⑲ Rainbow Bridge
National Monument

Go
Tradi

⑱ Wahweap

**Glen Canyon
National
Recreation
Area**

⑰⑮ Page

⑯ Antelope
Canyon

Canyon X

Vermilion
Cliffs

NAVAJO
INDIAN
RESERVATION

16

**Navajo
National
Monument** ⑭

Inscription
House

564

Kaibab
National
Forest

Bitter
Springs

98

Kaibito

Colorado River

Echo Cliffs

The
Gap

21

**White Mesa
Natural Bridge**

160

Elephant
Feet ♦
Red
Lake

HOPI
INDIAN
RESERVATION

Grand Canyon
National Park

PAINTED

Dinosaur
Tracks ♦

⑧ Tuba City

Moenkopi

160

180 64

**Cameron
Trading Post** ⑨

DESERT

89

264

Coal Canyon

Hotevilla   Bacovi

Third Mesa ⑦   Kykots

Old Oraibi
Hopi Cultural Center
Shungopavi

⑥

Kaibab
National
Forest

Tusayan

Valle

Gray
Mountain

89

2

89A

Williams

180

Kaibab
National
Forest

SAN FRANCISCO
PEAKS

Winona

♦ **Wupatki National
Monument**

♦ **Sunset Crater
National Monument**

Little Colorado R.

Leupp

15

99

Flagstaff

Twin
Arrows

Two Guns

87

Winslow

**Homo
State**

Sedona

17

Coconino
National
Forest

KEY	
▶	Start of itinerary
⌂	Indian Highway
- - -	Reservation boundary
- - -	Unpaved roads

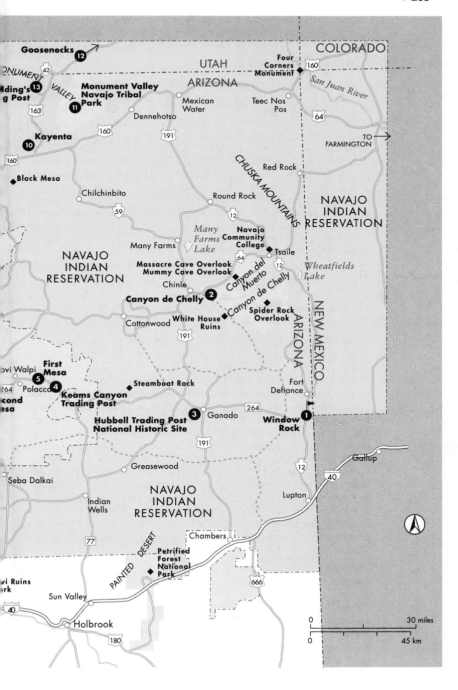

Goosenecks 12

COLORADO

UTAH

Four
Corners
Monument 160

San Juan River

ꓳNUMENꓕ 42

ꓲding's
g Post 13

VALLEY

ARIZONA

Monument Valley
Navajo Tribal
Park 11

Mexican
Water

Teec Nos
Pos

64

163

Dennehotso

TO
FARMINGTON

160

191

Kayenta 10

160

Black Mesa

Chilchinbito

Round Rock

Red Rock

CHUSKA MOUNTAINS

NAVAJO
INDIAN
RESERVATION

59

12

Many
Farms
Lake

Navajo
Community
College

NAVAJO
INDIAN
RESERVATION

Many Farms

Tsaile

Wheatfields
Lake

Massacre Cave Overlook
Mummy Cave Overlook

64

12

Chinle

Canyon del
Muerto

Canyon de Chelly 2

Canyon de Chelly

Cottonwood

White House
Ruins

Spider Rock
Overlook

ARIZONA

NEW MEXICO

191

ꓳvi Walpi

First
Mesa 5

Steamboat Rock

Fort
Defiance

264

Polacca 4

econd
esa

Keams Canyon
Trading Post

Hubbell Trading Post
National Historic Site 3

Ganado

264

Window
Rock 1

191

Seba Dalkai

NAVAJO
INDIAN
RESERVATION

Greasewood

12

Gallup

40

Lupton

Indian
Wells

77

PAINTED DESERT

Chambers

ꓥi Ruins
rk

40

Sun Valley

Petrified
Forest
National
Park

666

Holbrook

180

0   30 miles

0   45 km

an intertribal powwow. August and September bring the Hopi Harvest Festival, a celebration featuring Harvest and Butterfly social dances.

NAVAJO NATION EAST

Land has always been central to the history of the Navajo people: it's embedded in their very name. The Tewa were the first to call them *Navahu*—which means "large area of cultivated land." But according to the Navajo creation myth, they were given the name *ni'hookaa diyan diné*—"holy earth people"—by their creators. Today, among tribal members, they call themselves the Diné. The eastern portion of the Arizona Navajo Nation (in Navajo, *diné bikéyah*) is a dry but often surprisingly green land, especially in the vicinity of the aptly named Beautiful Valley, south of Canyon de Chelly along U.S. 191. A landscape of rolling hills, wide arroyos, and small canyons, the area is dotted with traditional Navajo hogans, sheepfolds, cattle tanks, and wood racks. The region's easternmost portion is marked by tall mountains and towering sandstone cliffs cut by primitive roads that are generally accessible only by horse or four-wheel-drive vehicles.

Window Rock

▶ ❶ *192 mi from Flagstaff, east on Interstate 40 and north on Indian Hwy. 12; 26 mi from Gallup, New Mexico, north on U.S. 191 and west on NM and AZ 264.*

Named for the immense arch-shape "window" in a massive sandstone ridge above the city, Window Rock is the capital of the Navajo Nation and the center of its Tribal Government. With a population of fewer than 5,000, this community serves as the business and social center for Navajo families throughout the reservation. Window Rock is a good place to stop for food, supplies, and gas. The **Navajo Nation Council Chambers** is a handsome structure that resembles a large ceremonial hogan. The murals on the walls depict scenes in the history of the tribe, and the bell beside the entrance was a gift to the tribe by the Santa Fe Railroad to commemorate the thousands of Navajos who worked to build the railroad. Visitors can observe sessions of the council, where 88 delegates representing 110 reservation chapters meet on the third Monday of January, April, July, and October. Turn east off Indian Highway 12, about ½ mi north of AZ 264, to reach the Council Chambers. **Window Rock Navajo Tribal Park,** near the Council Chambers, is a memorial park honoring Navajo veterans, including the famous World War II code talkers. ✉ *AZ 264* ☎ *928/871–6647.*

The **Navajo Nation Museum Library & Visitors Center,** on the grounds of the former Tse Bonito Park off AZ 264, is devoted to the art, culture, and history of the Navajo people and has an excellent selection of books on the Navajo Nation. The museum hosts exhibitions of native artists each season; call for a list of shows. In the same building as the Navajo Nation Museum is the **Navajo Nation Visitor Center,** a great resource for all sorts of information on reservation activities. Within walking distance of the Navajo Nation Museum, the **Navajo Arts and Crafts Enter-**

CLOSE UP

Reservation Rules

Visitors to the Navajo Nation and Hopi Reservation should observe several rules, as follows:

Alcohol & Drugs: The possession and consumption of alcoholic beverages or illicit drugs is illegal on Hopi and Navajo land. You can't purchase alcohol legally while you are on the reservations, and you shouldn't bring any with you.

Camping: No open fires are allowed in reservation campgrounds; you must use grills or fireplaces. You may not gather firewood on the reservation—bring your own. Camping areas have quiet hours from 11 PM to 6 AM. Pets must be kept on a leash or confined. Don't litter.

Hopi Shrines: Hopi spirituality is intertwined with daily life, and objects that seem ordinary to you may have deeper significance. If you come upon a collection of objects at or near the Hopi Mesas do not disturb them.

Permits & Permissions: No off-trail hiking, rock climbing, or other off-road travel is allowed unless you are accompanied by a local guide. A tribal permit is required for fishing.

Violations of fish and game laws are punishable by heavy fines, imprisonment, or both.

Photography: Always ask permission before taking photos of locals. Even if no money is requested, consider offering a dollar or two to the person whose photo you have taken. The Navajo are very open about photographs; the Hopi do not allow photographs at all, including videos, tape recordings, notes, or even sketches.

Religious Ceremonies: Should you see a ceremony in progress, look for posted signs indicating who is welcome. If there are no signs, check with local shops or the village community to see if the ceremony is open to the public. Unless you're specifically invited, stay out of kivas (ceremonial rooms) and stay on the periphery of dances or processions.

Respect for the Land: Do not wander through residential areas or disturb property. Do not disturb or remove animals, plants, rocks, petrified wood, or artifacts. They are protected by Tribal Antiquity and federal laws.

---

prises displays local artwork, including pottery, jewelry, and blankets. ⌂ *AZ 264, next to Navajo Nation Inn* ☏ *928/871–6673 museum, 928/871–7371 visitor center* 🎟 *Free* ☉ *Mon. and Sat. 8–5, Tues.–Fri. 8–8.*

Amid the sandstone monoliths on the border of Arizona and New Mexico, the **Navajo Nation Zoological and Botanical Park** displays domestic and native animals, birds, and amphibians that figure in Navajo legends, as well as examples of plants used by traditional people. It's the only Native American–owned-and-operated zoo in the United States. ⌂ *AZ 264, northeast of Navajo Nation Museum* ☏ *928/871–6573* 🎟 *Free* ☉ *Daily 10–5.*

Many all-Indian rodeos are held near the center of downtown at the **Navajo Tribal Fairgrounds.** The community hosts the annual Fourth of July celebration, with a major rodeo, ceremonial dances, and a parade. The

Navajo Nation Tribal Fair, much like a traditional state fair, is held in early September. It offers standard county-fair rides, midway booths, contests, powwow competitions, and an all-Indian rodeo. ⊠ *AZ 264* ☎ *928/871–6282 Navajo Nation Fair Office.*

Where to Stay

¢ ⌕ **Quality Inn Navajo Nation Capital.** Rooms in this two-story beam-and-stucco motel are decorated with a Navajo-style palette of tan, orange, and yellow that complements the basic pine furniture. The Haskeneini Restaurant ($–$$)serves Navajo cuisine and regular American fare (you can build your own Navajo tacos), and the gift shop sells authentic Navajo jewelry. ⊠ *48 W. AZ 264, at Indian Hwy. 12, 86515* ☎ *928/871–4108 or 800/ 662–6189* 📠 *928/871–5466* ⊕ *www.qualityinnwindowrock.com* 🛏 *56 rooms* ⌂ *Restaurant, cable TV, shop, meeting rooms, some pets allowed, Internet room, no-smoking rooms* ⊟ *AE, D, MC, V* Ⓞⵏ *CP.*

Shopping

An outlet of the **Navajo Arts and Crafts Enterprises** (⊠ AZ 264 at Indian Hwy. 12, next to Navajo Nation Inn ☎ 928/871–4090) stocks tribal art purchased from craftspeople across the reservation. Local artisans are occasionally at work here. Major credit cards are accepted.

Canyon de Chelly

❷ *25 mi west of Window Rock on AZ 264, then north on U.S. 191.*

Fodor'sChoice
★

Home to ancestral Puebloans from AD 350 to AD 1300, the nearly 84,000-acre Canyon de Chelly (pronounced d'*shay*) is one of the most spectacular natural wonders in the Southwest. On a smaller scale, it rivals the Grand Canyon for beauty. Its main gorges—the 26-mi-long Canyon de Chelly ("canyon in the rock") and the adjoining 35-mi Canyon del Muerto ("canyon of the dead")—have sheer, heavily eroded sandstone walls that rise to 1,100 feet. Ancient pictographs and petroglyphs decorate some of the cliffs, and within the canyon complex there are more than 7,000 archaeological sites. Stone walls rise hundreds of feet above streams, hogans, tilled fields, and sheep-grazing lands.

The first inhabitants of the canyons arrived more than 2,000 years ago—anthropologists call them the basket makers because baskets were the predominant artifacts the left behind. By AD 750, however, the basket makers had disappeared—their reason for leaving the region is unknown, but some speculate they were forced to leave because of encroaching cultures or climatic

> **WORD OF MOUTH**
>
> "Canyon de Chelly is wonderful to visit—almost a spiritual experience. We only did the half-day tour, but if you have time I would recommend a full day. Also, if you have time take the scenic drive along the brim of the canyon out to the last point overlooking Spider Rock. Plan on an extra 1-2 hours to do this depending on how many of the overlooks you want to stop at. When you get to the Spider Rock one, there's a short, easy path that you need to follow to get to the actual overlook—definitely worth it if you have time."   –Cher

changes—and they were replaced by Pueblo tribes who constructed stone cliff dwellings. The departure of the Pueblo people around AD 1300 is widely believed to have resulted from changing climatic conditions, soil erosion, dwindling local resources, disease, and internal conflict. Present-day Hopis see these people as their ancestors. Beginning around AD 780, Hopi farmers settled here, followed by the Navajo around 1300. The Navajo migrated from far northern Canada; no one is sure when they arrived in the Southwest. Despite evidence to the contrary, most Navajos hold that their people have always lived here and that the Diné passed through three previous underworlds before emerging into this, the fourth or Glittering World.

Prehistoric ruins can be found near the base of cliffs and perched on high, sheltering ledges. The dwellings and cultivated fields of the present-day Navajo lie in the flatlands between the cliffs, and those who inhabit the canyon today farm much the way their ancestors did. Most residents leave the canyon in winter but return in early spring to farm.

The **visitor center** has exhibits on the history of the cliff dwellers and provides information on scheduled hikes, tours, and National Park Service programs offered throughout the summer months.

Both Canyon de Chelly and Canyon del Muerto have a paved rim drive with turnoffs and parking areas. Each drive takes about two hours. Overlooks along the rim drives provide incredible views of the canyon; be sure to stay on trails and away from the canyon edge, and to control children and pets at all times.

The **South Rim Drive** (36 mi round-trip with seven overlooks) of Canyon de Chelly starts at the visitor center and ends at **Spider Rock Overlook,** where cliffs plunge 1,000 feet to the canyon floor. The view here is of two pinnacles, Speaking Rock and Spider Rock; the latter rises about 800 feet from the canyon floor and is considered a sacred place. Other highlights on the South Rim Drive are Junction Overlook, where Canyon del Muerto joins Canyon de Chelly; White House Overlook, from which a trail leads to the **White House Ruin,** with dwelling remains of nearly 60 rooms and several kivas; and Sliding House Overlook, where you can see ruins on a narrow, sloped ledge across the canyon. The carved and sometimes narrow trail down the canyon side to White House Ruin is the only access to Canyon de Chelly without a guide—but if you have a fear of heights, this may not be the hike for you.

The **North Rim Drive** (34 mi round-trip with four overlooks) of Canyon del Muerto also begins at the visitor center and continues northeast on Indian Highway 64 toward the town of Tsaile. Major stops include Antelope House Overlook, the site of a large ruin named for the animals painted on an adjacent cliff; the Mummy Cave Overlook, where two mummies were found inside a remarkably unspoiled pueblo dwelling, and Massacre Cave Overlook, which marks the spot where an estimated 115 Navajo were killed by the Spanish in 1805. (The rock walls of the cave are still pockmarked from the Spaniards' ricocheting bullets.)

✉ *Indian Hwy. 7, 3 mi east of U.S. 191, Chinle* ☎ *928/674–5500 visitor center* ⊕ *www.nps.gov/cach* 🖃 *Free* ☉ *Daily 8–5.*

In Tsaile, Navajo medicine men worked with architects to design the town's six-story **Diné College,** the first Native American–owned community college in the country. Because all important Navajo activities traditionally take place in a circle (a hogan is essentially circular), the campus was laid out in the round, with the buildings inside its perimeter and the reflective glass of the buildings mirror the piñon-covered landscape surrounding the campus. Diné College's **Hatathli Museum** is actually two museums in one: one concentrates on Navajo culture, the other contains intertribal exhibits from across the United States. ✉ *Indian Hwy. 12, south of Indian Hwy. 64, Tsaile* ☎ *928/724–3311 college, 928/724–6654 museum* 🖃 *By donation* ☉ *Museum weekdays 8:30–4.*

To the north of Tsaile are the impressive **Chuska Mountains,** covered with sprawling stands of ponderosa pine. There are no established hiking trails in the Chuska Mountains, but up-to-date hiking information and backcountry-use permits (rarely granted if a Navajo guide does not accompany the trip) can be obtained through the Navajo Nation. ✉ *Navajo Nation Parks and Recreation Department, Bldg. 36A, E. AZ 264, Window Rock* ♅ *Box 2520, 86515* ☎ *928/871–6647* ⊕ *www.navajonationparks.org.*

Sports & the Outdoors

HIKING From late May through early September, free three-hour ranger-led hikes depart from the visitor center at 9 AM. Also in summer, two four-hour hikes (about $10 per person) leave from the visitor center in the morning and afternoon. Some trails are strenuous and steep; others are easy or moderate. Those with health concerns or a fear of heights should proceed with caution. Call ahead: hikes are occasionally canceled due to local customs or events.

Only one hike within Canyon de Chelly National Monument—the **White House Ruin Trail** on the South Rim Drive—can be done without an authorized guide. The trail starts near White House Overlook and runs along sheer walls that drop about 550 feet. If you have concerns about height, be aware that the path gets narrow and somewhat slippery along the way. The hike is 2½ mi round-trip, and hikers should carry their own drinking water.

Private, guided hikes to the interior of the canyons cost about $20 per hour with a three-hour minimum for groups of up to four people. (Don't venture into the canyon without a guide or you'll face a stiff fine.) For overnights, you'll need a guide as well as permission to stay on private land. If you have a four-wheel-drive vehicle and want to drive yourself, guides will accompany you for a charge of about $20 an hour with a three-hour minimum for up to three vehicles. All Navajo guides are members of the **Tsegi Guide Association** (✉ Canyon de Chelly Visitor Center, Indian Hwy. 7, Chinle ☎ 928/674–5500 ⊕ www.nps.gov/cach). You can hire a guide on the spot at the visitor center, or you can call ahead and make a reservation.

HORSEBACK RIDING **Totsonii Ranch** (✉ South Rim Dr. ☎ Box 434, Chinle 86503 ☎ 928/755–6209 ⊕ www.totsoniiranch.com), 13 mi from the visitor center to the end of the paved road, offers four-hour round-trip horseback rides 1,000 feet down Bat Trail to Spider Rock. Rates are $10 per hour for each horse plus $15 per hour for a guide.

JEEP TOURS **Canyon de Chelly Tours** (☎ 928/674–3772) offers private jeep tours into Canyon de Chelly and arranges group tours and overnight camping in the canyon as well as late day and evening tours. Entertainment such as storytellers, music, and Navajo legends can be arranged with advance reservation. Treks with **Thunderbird Lodge Canyon Tours** (✉ Thunderbird Lodge Gift Shop, Indian Hwy. 7, Chinle ☎ 928/674–5841 or 800/679–2473), in six-wheel-drive vehicles, are available from late spring to early fall. Half-day tours are $39.95 and start at 9 AM and 2 PM daily; all-day tours cost $64.95 and include lunch.

WALKING TOURS **Footpath Journey Tours** (☎ 928/724–3366 ⊕ www.footpathjourneys. com) offers prearranged daylong hiking tours in the canyon for $85. Custom weeklong treks are $600 not including food.

Where to Stay & Eat

Chinle is the closest town to Canyon de Chelly. There are good lodgings with restaurants, as well as a supermarket and a campground. Be aware that you'll probably be approached by panhandlers in the grocery store parking lot, as well as hungry, forlorn, homeless dogs. In late August each year, Chinle is host to the Central Navajo Fair, a public celebration complete with a rodeo, carnival, and traditional dances.

> ### WORD OF MOUTH
>
> "Don't obsess too much over accommodations at Canyon de Chelly—they're all pretty basic without much ambience. The main experience is the Canyon itself."
> –Cher

★ **$–$$** ✕🏠 **Thunderbird Lodge.** In an ideal location within the national monument's borders, this pleasant establishment has stone-and-adobe units that match the site's original 1896 trading post. The cafeteria (¢–$) is in the original trading post and serves reasonably priced soups, salads, sandwiches, and entrées, including charbroiled steaks. The lodge also offers truck tours of Canyon de Chelly and Canyon del Muerto. ✉ *Indian Hwy. 7* ☎ *Box 548, Chinle 86503* ☎ *928/674–5841 or 800/679–2473* ⊕ *www.tbirdlodge.com* ⮑ *74 rooms* ☖ *Cafeteria, cable TV, shop, travel services* ▭ *AE, D, DC, V.*

$ ✕🏠 **Best Western Canyon de Chelly Inn.** This two-story motel about 3 mi from Canyon de Chelly has cheerful rooms with modern oak furnishings. All rooms have coffeemakers. The on-site Junction restaurant (¢–$$) opens for breakfast at 6:30 AM; traditional Navajo, Mexican, and American fare is served until 9 PM. ✉ *100 Main St.* ☎ *Box 295, Chinle 86503* ☎ *928/674–5288 or 800/327–0354* 🖷 *928/674–3715* ⊕ *www.canyondechelly.com* ⮑ *102 rooms* ☖ *Restaurant, cable TV, pool, some pets allowed, no-smoking rooms* ▭ *AE, D, DC, MC, V.*

$ ✕⊞ **Holiday Inn Canyon de Chelly.** Once Garcia's Trading Post, this motel near Canyon de Chelly is less generic than you might expect: the exterior is territorial fort in style although the rooms are predictably pastel and contemporary. The lobby restaurant (¢–$$), low-key by most standards, is the most upscale eatery in the area, serving well-prepared specialties such as mutton stew with fry bread and honey. The hotel restaurant offers a box picnic ($5.95) for guests and has a gift shop stocked with local Native American arts and crafts. ⊠ *Indian Hwy. 7* ⌖ *Box 1889, Chinle 86503* ☎ *928/674–5000* 🖷 *928/674–8264* ⊕ *www.sixcontinentshotels.com* ⇨ *108 rooms* ⌂ *Restaurant, cable TV, pool, shop, no-smoking rooms* ⊟ *AE, D, DC, MC, V.*

¢ ⊞ **Many Farms Inn.** Many Farms High School runs this facility, which is staffed by Navajo students of hotel management. It's not fancy, but rooms are pleasant and contain two single beds, which means single or double occupancy only. Bathrooms are shared, and you have to go to the first floor to use pay phones or watch TV. ⊠ *U.S. 191 and Indian Hwy. 59* ⌖ *Box 307, Many Farms 86538* ☎ *928/781–6362* 🖷 *928/781–6355* ⇨ *30 rooms* ⌂ *Refrigerators; no room phones, no room TVs* ⊟ *No credit cards* ☉ *Closed weekends Aug.–May.*

CAMPING ⛺ **Cottonwood Campground.** This sometimes cramped and noisy camp-
¢ ground has 52 RV sites (maximum length 35 feet; no hookups) and 95 tent sites that are available free, on a first-come, first-served basis. Cottonwood trees shade the sites. Although it's open year-round, there are limited facilities from November to March. No reservations. ⊠ *Indian Hwy. 7, near Canyon de Chelly visitor center, Chinle 86503* ☎ *928/674–5501* ⊕ *www.nps.gov/cach* ▦ *Free* ⇨ *52 RV sites, 95 tent sites* ⌂ *Grills, flush toilets, drinking water, picnic tables* ☉ *Open year-round.*

¢ ⛺ **Spider Rock Campground.** Cordial Navajo owner Howard Smith makes everyone feel comfortable at this informal campground nestled in low piñons within a few hundred yards of the canyon. The camp is just a short drive from the famous Spider Rock site and overlook. There's a 3-mi self-guided hike to the rim overlooking ancestral Puebloan ruins in Wild Cherry Canyon, and Howard will also customize guided hikes into the Canyon on such routes as Grandmother's Trail, which has ancestral Puebloan footholds and handholds worn into the sandstone. ⊠ *Indian Hwy. 7, 10 mi east of Canyon de Chelly Visitor Center* ⌖ *Box 2509, Chinle 86503* ☎ *928/674–8261 or 877/910–2267* ⊕ *www.home.earthlink.net/~spiderrock* ▦ *$10 tent site, $15 partial hookups, $25 hogans* ⇨ *30 camp sites, 2 hogans* ⌂ *Pit toilets, partial hookups (electricity), dump station, drinking water, showers, fire pits, picnic tables* ☉ *Open year-round.*

Hubbell Trading Post National Historic Site

❸ *40 mi south of Canyon de Chelly, off AZ 264; 32 mi west of Window Rock.*

John Lorenzo Hubbell, a merchant and friend of the Navajo, established this trading post in 1876. Hubbell taught, translated letters, settled family quarrels, and explained government policy to the Navajo, and during an 1886 smallpox epidemic, he turned his home into a hospital and ministered to the sick and dying. He died in 1930 and is buried near the trading post.

The National Park Service Visitor Center exhibits illustrate the post's history, and you can take a self-guided tour of the grounds and visit the Hubbell Trading Post, which contains a fine display of Native American artistry. The visitor center has a fairly comprehensive bookstore specializing in Navajo history, art, and culture; local weavers often demonstrate their craft on site.

The **Hubbell Trading Post Store** is famous for "Ganado red" Navajo rugs, which are sold at the store here. The quality is outstanding and prices are high but fair—rugs can cost anywhere from $100 to around $30,000. Considering the time that goes into weaving each one, the prices are quite reasonable. It's hard to resist the beautiful designs and colors, and it's a pleasure just to browse around this rustic spot, where Navajo artists frequently show their work. Documents of authenticity are provided for all works. Note: when photographing weavers, ask permission first. They expect a few dollars in return. ⊠ *AZ 264, 1 mi west of town, Ganado* ☎ *928/755–3475 park office, 928/755–3254 store* ⊕ *www.wnpa.org* ⧟ *Free* ☉ *May–Sept., daily 8–6; Oct.–Apr., daily 8–5.*

EN ROUTE About 20 mi west of Hubbell Trading Post on AZ 264 is **Steamboat Rock,** an immense, jutting peninsula of stone that resembles an early steamboat, complete with a geologically formed waterline. At Steamboat Rock you are only 5 mi from the eastern boundary of the Hopi Reservation.

THE HOPI MESAS

The Hopi occupy 10 villages in regions referred to as First Mesa, Second Mesa, and Third Mesa. Although these areas have similar languages and traditions, each has its own individual features. Generations of Hopitu, "the peaceful people," much like their Puebloan ancestors, have lived in these settlements of stone-and-adobe houses, which blend in with the earth so well that they appear to be natural formations. Television aerials, satellite dishes, and automobiles notwithstanding, these Hopi villages still impart the air of another time.

Descendants of the ancient Hisatsinom, the Hopi number about 10,000 people today. Their culture can be traced back 2,000 years, making them one of the oldest known tribes in North Amer-

KATSINA DOLLS

Katsina dolls are the spirits of the invisible life forces of the Hopi. They are carved not as toys but as tools to instruct children about the hundreds of katsina spirits. Today the finer carvings are collector's items. You may have heard them referred to as Kachina dolls, but because the Hopi have no "ch" sound in their language, they are more accurately known as "katsina."

ica. They successfully developed "dry farming" and grow many kinds of vegetables and corn—called maize—as their basic food—in fact the Hopi are often called the "corn people." They incorporate nature's cycles into most of their religious rituals. In the celebrated Snake Dance ceremony, dancers carry venomous snakes in their mouths to appease the gods and to bring rain. In addition to farming the land, the Hopi create fine pottery and basketwork and excel in wood carving of katsina dolls.

Although you do not need permission before entering the Hopi Reservation, you must obtain a permit to visit certain areas. Since all Hopi villages are separate and autonomous, each has its own governing policies, which are sometimes posted at the entrance to the village. Many villages don't allow cars, and some close to the public when they are participating in religious ceremonies. Lodging is available on Second Mesa and recommended if you wish to see the Hopi Mesas at a leisurely pace.

Keams Canyon Trading Post

❹ *48 mi west of Hubbell Trading Post on AZ 264.*

The trading post established by Thomas Keam in 1875 to do business with local tribes is now the area's main tourist attraction, offering a primitive campground, restaurant, service station, and shopping center. An administrative center for the Bureau of Indian Affairs, Keams Canyon also has a number of government buildings. A road, accessible by passenger car, winds northeast 3 mi into the 8-mi wooded canyon. At **Inscription Rock,** about 2 mi down the road, frontiersman Kit Carson engraved his name in stone. There are several picnic spots in the canyon.

Where to Eat

¢ ✕ **Keams Canyon Restaurant.** A typical roadside diner with Formica tabletops, Keams offers both American and Native American dishes, including Navajo tacos heaped with ground beef, chile, beans, lettuce, and grated cheese. Daily specials, offered at $1 to $2 off the regular price, may include anything from barbecued ribs to lamb chops to crab legs. ⊠ *Keams Canyon Shopping Center, AZ 264, Keams Canyon* ☎ *928/ 738–2296* ▤ *D, MC, V* ☺ *No dinner weekends.*

Shopping

Keams Canyon Arts and Crafts and McGee's Art Gallery (⊠ AZ 264, Keams Canyon ☎ 928/738–2295), upstairs from the Keams Canyon Restaurant, sells first-rate, high-quality Hopi crafts such as handcrafted jewelry, pottery, beautiful carvings, basketry, and artwork.

First Mesa

★ ❺ *11 mi west of Keams Canyon, on AZ 264.*

First Mesa villages are renowned for their polychrome pottery and katsina-doll carvings. The first village that you approach is Polacca; the older and more impressive villages of Hano, Sichomovi, and

Walpi are at the top of the mesa. From Polacca, a paved road (off AZ 264) angles up to a parking lot near the village of Sichomovi, and to the Punsi Hall Visitor Center. You must get permission at Punsi Hall to take the guided walking tour of Hano, Sichomovi, and Walpi. Admission is by tour only, so call ahead to find out when they're offered.

The older Hopi villages have structures built of rock and adobe mortar in simple architectural style. **Hano** actually belongs to the Tewa, a New Mexico Pueblo tribe. In 1696 the Tewa Indians sought refuge with the Hopi on First Mesa after an unsuccessful rebellion against the Spanish in the Rio Grande Valley. Today, the Tewa live close to the Hopi but maintain their own language and ceremonies. **Sichomovi** is built so close to Hano that only the residents can tell where one ends and the other begins. Constructed in the mid-1600s, this village is believed to have been built to ease overcrowding at Walpi, the highest point on the mesa. **Walpi,** built on solid rock and surrounded by steep cliffs, frequently hosts ceremonial dances. It's the most pristine of the Hopi villages, with cliff-edge houses and vast scenic vistas. Inhabited for more than 1,000 years (dating back to 900 AD), Walpi's cliff-edge houses seem to grow out of the nearby terrain. Today, only about 10 residents occupy this settlement, which has neither electricity nor running water. Note that Walpi's surroundings make it a less than ideal destination for acrophobes. ⊠ *Punsi Hall Visitor Center, First Mesa* ☎ *928/737–2262* ⊕ *www.hopi.nsn.us* ⊒ *Guided tours $8* ⊙ *Tours Nov.–mid-Mar., daily 9:30–4:30; mid-Mar.–Oct., daily 8:30–4:30, except when ceremonies are being held.*

Second Mesa

❻ *10 mi southwest of First Mesa, on AZ 264.*

The Mesas are the Hopi universe, and Second Mesa is the "Center of the Universe." **Shungopavi,** the largest and oldest village on Second Mesa, which was founded by the Bear Clan, is reached by a paved road angling south off AZ 264, between the junction of AZ 87 and the Hopi Cultural Center. The villagers here make silver overlay jewelry and coil plaques. Coil plaques are woven from galleta grass and yucca and are adorned with designs of katsinas, animals, and corn. The art of making the plaques has been passed from mother to daughter for generations, and fine coil plaques have become highly sought after collector's items. The famous Hopi snake dances (closed to the public) are held here in August during even-numbered years. Two smaller villages are off a paved road that runs north from AZ 264, about ⅕ mi east of the Hopi Cultural Center. **Mishongnovi,** the easternmost settlement, was built in the late 1600s. For permission to visit

Sipaulovi, which was originally at the base of the mesa before being moved to its present site in 1680, call the Sipaulovi Village Community Center (☎ 928/737–2570).

At the **Hopi Cultural Center,** you can stop for the night, learn about the people and their reservation, and eat authentic Hopi cuisine. The museum here is dedicated to preserving the Hopi traditions and to presenting those traditions to non-Hopi visitors. A gift shop sells works by local Hopi artisans at reasonable prices, and a modest picnic area on the west side of the building is a pleasant spot for lunch with a view of the San Francisco Peaks. ⊠ *AZ 264, Second Mesa* ☎ *928/734–6650* ⊕ *www. psv.com/hopi.html* ⊡ *Museum $3* ☉ *Mid-Mar.–Oct., weekdays 8–5 and weekends 9–3; Nov.–mid-Mar., weekdays 8–5.*

Where to Stay & Eat

¢–$ ✕⊡ **Hopi Cultural Center Restaurant and Motel.** This Hopi-run establishment is the only place to eat or sleep in the immediate area, but because of its remote location it almost always has vacant rooms. The motel offers clean, quiet, moderately priced rooms with coffeemakers. The restaurant (¢–$) serves traditional Hopi dishes, including Indian tacos, Hopi blue-corn pancakes, fry bread (delicious with honey or salsa), and *nok qui vi* (a tasty stew made with tender bits of lamb, hominy, and mild green chiles). ⊠ *5 mi west of AZ 87 on AZ 264, Second Mesa 86403* ☎ *928/734–2401* ⊕ *www.hopiculturalcenter.com* ⇥ *33 rooms* ᗞ *Cable TV; no smoking* ⊟ *DC, MC, V.*

Shopping

The **Hopi Arts and Crafts/Silvercrafts Cooperative Guild** (⊠ AZ 264, Second Mesa ☎ 928/734–2463), west of the Hopi Cultural Center, hosts craftspeople selling their wares; you might even see silversmiths at work here. Shops at the **Hopi Cultural Center** (⊠ AZ 264, Second Mesa ☎ 928/ 734–2401) carry the works of local artists and artisans. At **Hopi Fine Arts** (⊠ AZ 264 at AZ 87, Second Mesa ☎ 928/737–2222), proprietor Alph Secakuku is a native of the Hopi Pueblo and an authority on all arts and crafts of the Hopi people. He represents about 75 active artisans in his user-friendly gallery. **Tsakurshovi** (⊠ AZ 264, Second Mesa ☎ 928/ 734–2478), 1½ mi east of the Hopi Cultural Center, is a small shop where Hopi come to buy bundles of sweet grass and sage, deer hooves with which to make rattles, and ceremonial belts adorned with seashells. The proprietor's wife, Janice Day, is a renowned Hopi basket maker. The shop has one of the largest collections of Hopi baskets in the Southwest.

Third Mesa

➐ *10 mi northwest of Second Mesa, on AZ 264.*

Third Mesa villages are known for their agricultural accomplishments, textile weaving, wicker baskets, and plaques. You'll find crafts shops and art galleries, as well as occasional roadside vendors, along AZ 264. The Hopi Tribal Headquarters and Office of Public Relations in Kykotsmovi should be visited first for necessary permissions to visit the villages of Third Mesa.

Kykotsmovi, at the eastern base of Third Mesa, is literally translated as "ruins on the hills" for the many ruin sites on the valley floor and in the surrounding hills. Present-day Kykotsmovi was established by Hopi people from Oraibi—a few miles west—who either converted to Christianity or who wished to attend school and be educated. Kykotsmovi is the seat of the Hopi Tribal Government.

Old Oraibi, a few miles west and on top of Third Mesa, is believed to be the oldest continuously inhabited community in the United States, dating from around AD 1150. It was also the site of a rare, bloodless conflict between two groups of the Hopi people; in 1906, a dispute, settled uniquely by a "push of war" (a pushing contest), sent the losers off to establish the town of Hotevilla. Oraibi is a dusty spot, and, as an act of courtesy, tourists are asked to park their cars outside and approach the village on foot.

Hotevilla and **Bacavi** are about 4 mi west of Oraibi, and their inhabitants are descended from the former residents of that village. The men of Hotevilla continue to plant crops and beautiful gardens along the mesa slopes. ⊠ *Cultural Preservation Office, AZ 264* ☏ *Box 123, Kykotsmovi 86039* ☎ *928/734–3000 or 928/734–2441* ⊕ *www.hopi.nsn.us* ☉ *Weekdays 8–5.*

EN ROUTE

Beyond Hotevilla, AZ 264 descends from Third Mesa, exits the Hopi Reservation, and crosses into Navajo territory, past **Coal Canyon,** where Native Americans have long mined coal from the dark seam just below the rim. The colorful mudstone, dark lines of coal, and bleached white rock have an eerie appearance, especially by the light of the moon. Twenty miles west of Coal Canyon, at the junction of AZ 264 and U.S. 160, is the town of Moenkopi, the last Hopi outpost. Established as a farming community, it was settled by the descendants of former Oraibi residents.

NAVAJO NATION WEST

The Hopi Reservation is like a doughnut hole surrounded by the Navajo Nation. If you approach the Grand Canyon from U.S. 89, via Flagstaff, north of the Wupatki National Monument, you'll find two significant sites in the western portions of the Navajo Reservation, the Cameron Trading Post and Tuba City. Situated 45 mi west of the Hopi town of Hotevilla, Tuba City is a good stop over if you're traveling east to the Hopi Mesas or northeast to Page.

> **WHAT TIME IS IT?**
>
> Unlike the rest of Arizona (including the Hopi Reservation), the Navajo Reservation observes daylight saving time. Thus for half the year—April to October—it's an hour later on the Navajo Reservation than everywhere else in the state.

At Cameron, the turnoff point for the Grand Canyon South Rim, the Cameron Trading Post was built in 1916 and commemorates Ralph Cameron, a prestatehood territorial-legislative delegate. The sheer walls of the Little Colorado River Canyon about 10 mi west of U.S. 89 along AZ 64 are quite impressive and also worth a stop.

Tuba City

▶ ❽ *50 mi northwest of Third Mesa on AZ 264.*

Tuba City, named after a Hopi chief "Tuba," with about 12,000 permanent residents, is the administrative center for the western portion of the Navajo Nation. In addition to a motel, hostel, and a few restaurants, this small town has a hospital, a bank, a trading post, and a movie theater. In late October, Tuba City hosts the Western Navajo Fair, a celebration combining traditional Navajo song and dance with a parade, pageant, and countless arts-and-crafts exhibits. The octagonal **Tuba City Trading Post** (⊠ Main St. ☎ 928/283–5441), founded in the early 1870s, sells groceries and authentic, reasonably priced Navajo rugs, pottery, baskets, and jewelry.

About 5½ mi west of Tuba City, between mileposts 316 and 317 on U.S. 160, is a small sign for the **Dinosaur Tracks.** More than 200 million years ago, dilophosaurus—a carnivorous bipedal reptile more than 10 feet tall—left tracks in mud that turned to sandstone. There's no charge for a look. Ask the locals about guiding you to the nearby petroglyphs and freshwater springs. Four miles west of the dinosaur tracks on U.S. 160 is the junction with U.S. 89. This is one of the most colorful regions of the **Painted Desert,** with amphitheaters of maroon, orange, and red rocks facing west; it's especially glorious at sunset.

Where to Stay & Eat

$–$$ ✕ **Hogan Restaurant.** The fare at this spot is mostly Southwestern and Mexican, but the menu also lists basic American and Navajo dishes. The chicken enchiladas and beef tamales are as good as any south of the border. Breakfast is served, too. ⊠ *Main St. (AZ 264)* ☎ *928/283–5260* ▤ *AE, D, DC, MC, V.*

¢–$ ✕ **Kate's Cafe.** A favorite of locals, this all-American café serves breakfast—try the vegetarian omelet—lunch, and dinner. At lunch choose from hearty burgers, Kate's club sandwich, grilled chicken, or salads. Dinner selections include five daily pasta specials and a charbroiled New York–strip steak. There may be a wait, but for local color and fine food at reasonable prices, this is the place to be. ⊠ *Main St. (AZ 264)* ☎ *928/ 283–6773* ▤ No credit cards.

¢–$ ✕ **Tuba City Truck Stop Cafe.** Home cooking and fast service are the specialties at this small, convenient restaurant. The popular Navajo vegetarian taco, available for lunch and dinner, is a mix of beans, lettuce, sliced tomato, shredded cheese, and green chiles served open face on fry bread. Meatier options include mutton stew served with fry bread and hominy. It's open at 6 AM for breakfast and closes at 10 PM every day. ⊠ *Main St., AZ 264, at U.S. 160* ☎ *928/283–4975* ▤ *MC, V.*

$ ▥ **Quality Inn Navajo Nation.** This hotel has a trading post and shops for essentials, gifts, and souvenirs. Standard rooms are spacious and well maintained, fine for an overnight stop before or after a visit to the Hopi

Mesas. The on-site Hogan Restaurant serves basic fare. ⊠ *Main St. at Moenave Rd.* ☎ *Box 247, 86045* ☏ *928/283–4545 or 800/644–8383* 🖷 *928/283–4144* ⊕ *www.qualityinntubacity.com* ⇒ *78 rooms, 2 suites* ♿ *Restaurant, cable TV, some in-room data ports, shop, laundry facilities, no-smoking rooms* ⊟ *AE, D, DC, MC, V.*

¢ 🖵 **Grey Hills Inn.** Hotel management students at Grey Hills High School run this unusual lodging, a former dormitory with large, clean rooms and comfortable beds. Paintings and other touches add character to otherwise plain rooms. Bathrooms and showers are down the hall but the rates are reasonable. A share of the inn's profits helps support the students' class. ⊠ *Grey Hills High School, U.S. 160, ½ mi north of AZ 264* ☎ *Box 160, 86045* ☏ *928/283–6271 Ext. 142, 928/ 283–4450 weekends and after-school hrs* ⇒ *32 rooms with shared bath* ⊟ *MC, V.*

CAMPING   ⛺ **Quality Inn Tuba City Campground.** Adjacent to the Quality Inn, this
¢   park has some shade trees and is geared toward RVs. Several tent sites situated along the perimeter of the campground are little more than concrete slabs. Reservations are accepted through the hotel's 800 number and check-in is at the hotel's front desk. ⊠ *Main St., AZ 264* ☎ *Box 247, 86045* ☏ *928/283–4545 or 800/644–8383* 🖷 *928/283–4144* ⊠ *$13–$21* ⇒ *25 RV sites, 6 tent sites* ♿ *Grills, flush toilets, full hookups, dump station, drinking water, guest laundry, showers, picnic tables* ⊟ *AE, D, DC, MC, V* ☼ *Open year-round.*

Shopping

The **Native American swap meet** (⊠ Main St.), behind the community center and next to the baseball field, held every Friday from 8 AM on, has great deals on jewelry, jewelry-making supplies, semiprecious stones, rugs, pottery, and other arts and crafts; there are also food concessions and booths selling herbs. The **Toh Nanees Dizi Shopping Center** (⊠ U.S. 160), ½ mi northeast of town, has a pizza parlor, supermarket, and the Silver Screen Twin Theaters. **Van's Trading Company** (⊠ U.S. 160 ☎ 928/283–5343), on the outskirts of town, has a "dead-pawn" auction at 3 PM on the 15th of each month. Dead pawn means that the time limit for the original owner to repurchase a pawned item has expired. You can generally find some older pieces of Navajo turquoise and silver jewelry.

Cameron Trading Post

❾ *25 mi southwest of Tuba City on U.S. 89.*

Cameron Trading Post and Motel, established in 1916, is one of the few remaining authentic trading posts in the Southwest. A convenient stop if you're driving from the Hopi Mesas to the Grand Canyon, it has reasonably priced dining, lodging, camping, and shopping (⇨ *see* the listing *in* Chapter 3 for more detailed information). Fine authentic Navajo products are sold at an outlet of the **Navajo Arts and Crafts Enterprises** (⊠ U.S. 89 at AZ 64, Cameron ☎ 928/679–2244). ⊠ *U.S. 89, Cameron* ☏ *928/679–2231.*

EN ROUTE

As you proceed toward Kayenta, 22 mi northeast of Tuba City on U.S. 160, you'll come to the tiny community of Red Lake. Off to the left of the highway is a geologic phenomenon known as **Elephant Feet.** These massive eroded-sandstone buttes offer a great family photo opportunity: pose under the enormous columns. Northwest of here at the end of a graded dirt road in Navajo backcountry is **White Mesa Natural Bridge,** a massive arch of white sandstone that extends from the edge of White Mesa. The long **Black Mesa** plateau runs for about 15 mi along U.S. 160. Above the prominent escarpments of this land formation, mining operations—a major source of revenue for the Navajo Nation—delve into the more than 20 billion tons of coal deposited there.

MONUMENT VALLEY

The magnificent Monument Valley stretches to the northeast of Kayenta into Utah. At a base altitude of about 5,500 feet, the sprawling, arid expanse was once populated by ancestral Puebloan people (more popularly known by the Navajo word *Anasazi,* which means both "ancient ones" and "enemy ancestors") and in the last few centuries has been home to generations of Navajo farmers. The soaring red buttes, eroded mesas, deep canyons, and naturally sculpted rock formations of Monument Valley are easy to enjoy on a leisurely drive.

At U.S. 163 and the Monument Valley entrance is a street of disheveled buildings called Vendor Village. Here you can purchase trinkets and souvenirs without paying sales tax. Bartering is perfectly acceptable and expected.

> **IF IT LOOKS FAMILIAR . . .**
>
> If Monument Valley looks familiar it probably should. Scenes from many movies, including *National Lampoon's Vacation, How the West Was Won, Forrest Gump, Stagecoach, 2001: A Space Odyssey,* and *Wind Talkers*—have been filmed. It's also the world's most popular backdrop for TV and magazine advertisements.

Kayenta

 80 mi northeast of Tuba City, on U.S. 160, 25 mi south of Monument Valley.

Kayenta, a small town with a few grocery stores, a handful of chain motels, and a hospital, is a good base for exploring nearby Monument Valley Navajo Tribal Park and the Navajo National Monument. The Burger King in town has an excellent Navajo Code Talker exhibit with lots of memorabilia relative to this heroic World War II marine group.

Take a self-guided walking tour through the small outdoor cultural park, the **Navajo Cultural Center of Kayenta,** which describes the beliefs and traditions that have shaped North America's largest Native American tribe. ⊠ *U.S. 160 between Hampton Inn and Burger King* ☎ *928/697–3170* 🎟 *Free* ☉ *Daily 7 AM–sunset.*

The Navajo and the Hopi

BOTH THE NAVAJO AND HOPI base their culture on the land around them, but they are very different from on another. The Navajo refer to themselves as the Diné (pronounced din-*eh*)—"the people"—and live on 17 million acres in Arizona, New Mexico, Utah, and Colorado. The Hopi trace their roots back to the original settlers of the area, whom they call the *Hisatsinom,* or "people of long ago"—they are also known as Anasazi, meaning both "ancient ones" and "ancient enemies." Hopi culture is more formal and structured than that of the Navajo, and their religion has remained stronger and purer. For both tribes, unemployment is high on the reservation, and poverty a constant presence.

The Navajos use few words and possess a subtle sense of humor that can pass you by quickly if you're not a good listener. From childhood they are taught not to talk too much, be loud, or show off. Eye contact is considered impolite. If you're conversing with Navajos, some may look down or away even though they are paying attention to you. Likewise, touching is seen differently; handshaking may be the only physical contact that you see. When shaking hands, a light touch is preferred to a firm grip which is considered overbearing.

Although most Navajos speak English with varying degrees of mastery, listen closely to the language of the Diné. From the Athabascan family, the language is difficult for outsiders to learn because of subtle accentuation. The famous Marine Corps Navajo "Code Talkers" of World War II saved thousand of lives in the South Pacific by creating a code within their native Navajo language thereby mystifying the Japanese. Their unbreakable messages got safely through by radio to American troops quickly and accurately. These Native Americans are true patriots who today speak humbly of their accomplishments. Many of those still living reside in the area around Tuba City.

Hopi mythology holds that a white-skinned people will save the tribe from its difficult life. Long ago, however, in the face of brutal treatment by whites, most Hopi became convinced that salvation would originate elsewhere. (Some Hopi now look to the Dalai Lama for redemption.) Although not easy to witness, the disappointment of the Hopi and the despair of the Navajo are easy to understand after a visit to the reservation.

Most Navajo and Hopi disapprove of the practice, but some panhandlers cluster at shopping centers and view sites, hoping to glean a few tourist dollars. Visitors should respond to panhandlers with a polite but firm "no." If you wish to help, make a donation to a legitimate organization that raises funds at reservation grocery stores.

4

Where to Stay & Eat

¢–$ ✕ **Amigo Cafe.** The tables are packed with locals who frequent this small, clean establishment where everything is made from scratch. The delicious fry bread is the real drawing card. If you've never had a Navajo taco or Navajo hamburger, this is a good place to be initiated. ⊠ *North of Hwy. 160 on U.S. 163* ☎ *928/697–8448* ▭ *MC, V* ⊗ *Closed Sun.*

¢–$ ✕ **Golden Sands.** The decor and the service at this local café next to the Best Western Wetherill Inn are equally unrefined, but you can fuel up on hamburgers, Navajo tacos, and other regional specialties. It's also a good place to learn about the area from residents who stop in for coffee. ⊠ *U.S. 163* ☎ *928/697–3684* ▭ *No credit cards* ⊗ *Closed Mon.*

$–$$ ✕▦ **Hampton Inn of Kayenta.** Warm and inviting, this motel is a good spot for a night's rest. The simple rooms and lobby are tastefully decorated with Southwest textures, and the on-site restaurant (¢–$) is staffed by Native Americans wearing traditional Navajo garb. Stick with the Native American cuisine; a good choice is the Sheepherder's Taco. There's a free Continental-breakfast bar, a patio with a beehive fireplace, and a gift shop with top-quality Native American art and unique gifts. ⊠ *U.S. 160* ⌖ *Box 1219, 86033* ☎ *928/697–3170* ⎙ *928/697–3189* ⊕ *www.hamptoninn.com* ⟿ *73 rooms* ⌂ *Restaurant, cable TV, pool, shop, no-smoking rooms* ▭ *AE, D, DC, MC, V* ❙◎❙ *CP.*

$–$$ ✕▦ **Holiday Inn Monument Valley.** This contemporary motel has everything you would expect from a Holiday Inn. The on-site Wagonwheel Restaurant ($–$$) offers both standard and Native American fare, and the gift shop offers traditional local arts and crafts. ⊠ *U.S. 160 at U.S. 163* ⌖ *Box 307, 86033* ☎ *928/697–3221 or 800/465–4329* ⎙ *928/697–3349* ⊕ *www.holiday-inn.com* ⟿ *160 rooms* ⌂ *Restaurant, cable TV, pool, shop, no-smoking rooms* ▭ *AE, D, DC, MC, V.*

$ ▦ **Best Western Wetherill Inn.** This clean two-story motel has Southwestern decor and a well-stocked gift shop. ⊠ *U.S. 163* ⌖ *Box 175, 86033* ☎ *928/697–3231 or 800/528–1234* ⊕ *www.bestwestern.com* ⟿ *54 rooms* ⌂ *Cable TV, pool, shop, no-smoking rooms* ▭ *AE, D, DC, MC, V.*

Monument Valley Navajo Tribal Park

⟳ ⓫ *24 mi northeast of Kayenta, off U.S. 163.*

Fodor'sChoice
★

For generations, the Navajo have grown crops and herded sheep in Monument Valley, considered to be one of the most scenic and mesmerizing destinations in the Navajo Nation. Within Monument Valley lies the 30,000-acre Monument Valley Navajo Tribal Park where eons of wind and rain have carved the mammoth red-sandstone monoliths into memorable formations. The monoliths, which jut hundreds of feet above the desert floor, stand on the horizon like sentinels, frozen in time and unencumbered by electric wires, telephone poles, or fences . . . a scene virtually unchanged for centuries. These are the very same nostalgic images so familiar to movie buffs who recall the early Western films of John Wayne. A 17-mi self-guided driving tour on a dirt road (there's only one road, so you can't get lost) passes the memorable **Mittens** and **Totem Pole** formations, among others. Drive slowly, and be sure to walk (15 minutes round-trip) from North Window around the end of Cly Butte for the views. The park has a 99-site campground, which closes from early October through April. Call ahead for road conditions in winter.

The **Monument Valley Visitor Center** has a small crafts shop and exhibits devoted to ancient and modern Native American history. Most of the independent guided tours here use enclosed vans and charge about $20 for 2½ hours; you can generally find Navajo Native American guides in the center or through the booths in the parking lot. They will escort you to places that you are not allowed to visit on your own. ✉ *Visitor Center, off U.S. 163, 24 mi north of Kayenta, Monument Valley* ✆ *Box 2520, Window Rock 86515* ☎ *435/727–3353 park visitor center, 928/871–6647 Navajo Parks & Recreation Dept.* ⊕ *www.navajonationparks.org* ✉ *$5* ☉ *Visitor center May–Sept., daily 7–7; Oct.–Apr., daily 8–5.*

> ### WORD OF MOUTH
>
> "My wife and I visited Monument Valley. It was great. We decided to go on one of the tours offered by the native guides there. They have a booth in the middle of the parking lot and use large 4-wheel drive vehicles. It was great. The 2 ½ hour tour was well worth the $40 pp. In addition to not having to worry about the bad road the guide gave us all kinds of information on the land and native peoples. He took us into the beautiful back country to see several arches and rock formations which were far more breathtaking than anything off the public road."
>
> –nuggetboy

Sports & the Outdoors

HIKING, HORSEBACK RIDING & JEEP TOURS

Jeep tours of the valley, from hour-long to overnight, can be arranged through Roland Cody Dixon at **Roland's Navajoland Tours** (✆ Box 1542, Kayenta 86033 ☎ 928/697–3524); he offers cultural tours with crafts demonstrations, camping, and photography. **Sacred Monument Tours** (✆ Box 360530, Monument Valley 84536 ☎ 435/727–3218 or 928/380–4527 🖷 435/727–3355 ⊕ www.monumentvalley.net) has hiking, jeep, photography, and horseback riding tours into Monument Valley. **Simpson's Trailhandler Tours** (✆ Box 360–377, Monument Valley, UT 85436 ☎ 435/727–3362 ⊕ www.trailhandlertours.com) offers four-wheel-drive jeep tours as well as photography and hiking tours. **Totem Pole Tours** (✆ Box 360579, Monument Valley, UT 85436 ☎ 435/727–3313 or 800/345–8687 ⊕ www.moab-utah.com/totempole) offers jeep tours, some that include entertainment and outdoor barbecues.

Where to Stay

CAMPING
¢

🏕 **Mitten View Campground.** This RV and tent campground is within the Navajo Tribal Park, next to the park headquarters at an elevation of 5,500 feet. The sites are crowded together, but most offer spectacular views of Monument Valley. Restrooms and showers are open in summer only. Only group sites can be reserved. ✉ *Monument Valley Navajo*

Tribal Park, near visitor center, off U.S. 163, 25 mi north of Kayenta, 86003 ☎ 435/727–5870 or 435/727–5871 ☑ $5 Oct.–Apr., $10 May–Sept., $20 group site ⌖ 99 sites ⚑ Flush toilets, dump station, drinking water, showers, picnic tables ▭ No credit cards ⊘ May–Oct.; some sites open year-round.

OFF THE BEATEN PATH

FOUR CORNERS MONUMENT – An inlaid brass plaque marks the only point in the United States where four states meet: Arizona, New Mexico, Colorado, and Utah. Despite the Indian wares and booths selling greasy food, there's not much else to do here but pay a fee and stay long enough to snap a photo; you'll see many a twisted tourist trying to get an arm or a leg in each state. The monument is a 75-mi drive from Kayenta and is administered by the Navajo Nation Parks & Recreation Department. ⊠ *7 mi northwest of the U.S. 160 and U.S. 64 junction, Teec Nos Pos ⌖ Box 9000, Window Rock 86515 ☎ 928/871– 6647 Navajo Parks & Recreation Dept ⊕ www.navajonationparks. org ☑ $6 per car.*

Goosenecks Region, Utah

⑫ *33 mi north of Monument Valley Navajo Tribal Park, on UT 316.*

Fodor's Choice
★

Monument Valley's scenic route, U.S. 163, continues from Arizona into Utah, where the land is crossed, east to west, by a stretch of the San Juan River known as the Goosenecks—named for the myriad twists and curves it takes. This barren, erosion-blasted gorge has a stark beauty. This spot is a well-known take-out point for white-water runners on the San Juan, a river that vacationing sleuths will recognize as the setting of many of Tony Hillerman's Jim Chee mystery novels. The scenic overlook for the Goosenecks is reached by turning west from U.S. 163 onto UT 261, 4 mi north of the small community of **Mexican Hat,** then proceeding on UT 261 for 1 mi to a directional sign at the road's junction with UT 316. Turn left onto UT 316 and proceed 4 mi to the vista-point parking lot.

Where to Stay & Eat

★ ¢
✕▦ **San Juan Inn & Trading Post.** The inn's Southwestern-style, rustic rooms overlooking the river at Mexican Hat are clean and well maintained. Diners can watch the river at the Old Bridge Bar & Grill ($–$$), which serves great grilled steak and juicy hamburgers, fresh trout, and inexpensive Navajo dishes. ⊠ *U.S. 163 ⌖ Box 310276, Mexican Hat, UT 84531 ☎ 435/683–2220 or 800/447–2022 ⊟ 435/683–2210 ⊕ www. sanjuaninn.net ⌖ 36 rooms ⚑ Restaurant, cable TV, gym, laundry facilities, no-smoking rooms ▭ AE, D, DC, MC, V.*

Goulding's Trading Post

⑬ *1 mi west of Monument Valley Navajo Tribal Park, off U.S. 163 on Indian Hwy. 42.*

Established in 1924 by Harry Goulding and his wife "Mike," this trading post provided a place where Navajos could exchange livestock and handmade goods for necessities. Goulding's is probably best known, though, for being used as a headquarters by director John Ford when he filmed the Western classic *Stagecoach*. Today the compound has a lodge, restaurant, museum, gift shop, grocery store, and campground. The Goulding Museum displays Native American artifacts and Goulding family memorabilia as well as an excellent multimedia show about Monument Valley.

Where to Stay & Eat

$$ ✕⛺ **Goulding's Lodge.** There are spectacular views of Monument Valley from each room's private balcony and all the rooms have coffeemakers and hair dryers. The on-premises Stagecoach restaurant ($–$$$), serving American fare, is decorated with Western movie memorabilia. Goulding's also conducts custom guided tours of Monument Valley and provides Navajo guides into the backcountry. The lodge is 2 mi off U.S. 163, at the Monument Valley Navajo Tribal Park turnoff. ⊠ *Off U.S. 163, 24 mi north of Kayenta* ⬡ *Box 360001, Monument Valley, UT 84536* ☎ *435/727–3231* ⊕ *www.gouldings. com* ➷ *62 rooms* ⚒ *Restaurant, grocery, cable TV, in-room VCRs, pool, shop, laundry facilities, travel services* ⊟ *AE, D, DC, MC, V.*

> ### WORD OF MOUTH
>
> "The best way to start your Monument Valley experience is to stay overnight at Goulding's Lodge, wake up early, go out on your balcony and watch the sun rise over the monuments."   –HowardR

CAMPING **Goulding's Good Sam Campground.** Views of Monument Valley are
¢ the draw at this clean, modern campground. Check in at Goulding's grocery store (in Goulding's Trading Post). Campers have access—at no additional charge—to the 17-mi-loop drive around Monument Valley. Shuttle vans provide free transportation to Gouldings' restaurant and museum. ⊠ *Off U.S. 163, 24 mi north of Kayenta* ⬡ *Box 360001, Monument Valley, UT 84536* ☎ *435/727–3235* ➴ *$18 tent sites, $28 full hookups* ➷ *66 RV sites, 50 tent sites* ⚒ *Grills, flush toilets, full hookups, guest laundry, showers, general store, play area, swimming (indoor pool)* ⊟ *AE, D, DC, MC, V* ☺ *Open year-round; limited service Nov.–Mar. 15.*

Navajo National Monument

⑭ *53 mi southwest of Goulding's Trading Post. From Kayenta, take U.S.*
Fodor'sChoice *160 southwest to AZ 564, and follow signs 9 mi north to monument.*
★

At the Navajo National Monument, two unoccupied 13th-century cliff pueblos, Betatakin and Keet Seel, stand under the overhang cliffs of Tsegi Canyon. The largest ancient dwellings in Arizona, these stone-and-mortar complexes were built by ancestral Puebloans, obviously for permanent occupancy, but abandoned after less than half a century.

The well-preserved, 135-room **Betatakin** (Navajo for "ledge house") is a cluster of cliff dwellings that seem to hang in midair before a sheer sandstone wall. When discovered in 1907 by a passing American rancher, the apartments were full of baskets, pottery, and preserved grains and ears of corn—as if the occupants had been chased away in the middle of a meal. For an impressive view of Betatakin, walk to the rim overlook about ½ mi from the visitor center. Ranger-led tours (a 5-mi, four-hour, strenuous round-trip hike including a 700-foot descent into the canyon) leave once a day

---

WORD OF MOUTH

"If you get a chance, stop at Navajo National Monument . . . there's a wonderful little museum and an informative film . . . and you can walk to see cliff dwellings."
–desertduds

---

from late May to early September at 8 AM and return between 12–1 PM. No reservations are accepted; groups of no more than 25 form on a first-come, first-served basis.

Keet Seel (Navajo for "broken pottery") is also in good condition in a serene location, with 160 rooms and five kivas. Explorations of Keet Seel, which lies at an elevation of 7,000 feet and is 8½ mi from the visitor center by foot, are restricted: only 20 people are allowed to visit per day, and only between late May and early September, when a ranger is present at the site. A permit—which also allows campers to stay overnight near the ruins—is required. Trips to Keet Seel are very popular, so reservations are taken up to two months in advance. Anyone who suffers from vertigo might want to avoid this trip: the trail leads down a 1,100-foot near-vertical rock face.

The **visitor center** houses a small museum, exhibits of prehistoric pottery, and a good crafts shop. Free campground and picnic areas are nearby, and rangers sometimes present campfire programs in summer. No food, gasoline, or hotel lodging is available at the monument. AZ 564 turns north off U.S. 160 at the Black Mesa gas station and convenience store and leads to the visitor center. ⊠ *AZ 564, Black Mesa* ✆ *HC 71, Box 3, Tonalea 86044* ☎ *928/672–2700* 🖷 *928/672–2703* ⊕ *www.nps. gov/nava* 🖾 *Free* ☉ *Daily 8–5; tours late May–early Sept.*

Sports & the Outdoors

HIKING   Horseback tours have been suspended in the area so hiking is the best way for adventurous souls to see Keet Seel at the Navajo National Monument. It's a fairly strenuous hike to the ruins, but if you're fit and leave early enough, it's well worth it to visit some of the best-preserved ruins in the Southwest. It's free, but the trail is open only from late May through early September, and you need to call ahead to make a reservation, usually at least two months in advance. ✆ *Navajo National Monument, HC 71, Box 3, Tonalea 86044* ☎ *928/672–2366* 🖾 *Free* ☉ *Daily 8–5; tours late May–early Sept.*

Where to Stay & Eat

¢   ✕🏨 **Anasazi Inn–Tsegi Canyon.** On U.S. 160, 10 mi east of Black Mesa and 9 mi west of Kayenta, this is the closest lodging to Navajo National Monument. The one-story property offers basic, clean accommodations with exterior entrances and commanding views of Tsegi Canyon. There's also a well-stocked gift shop and a restaurant that serves sandwiches, burgers, and basic Navajo fare. ⊠ *Off U.S. 160, 9 mi w Kayenta* ⌂ *Box 1543, Kayenta, AZ 86033* ☎ *928/697–3793* ℻ *697–8249* ☞ *57 rooms* ⟐ *Restaurant, cable TV, shop, picnic tables* ⊟ *AE, D, MC, V.*

CAMPING ⛺ **Navajo National Monument Campground.** Beautiful and serene with
¢ no fee, this campground has no hookups, and open fires are not allowed (you must use camp stoves). Because of its remote locale, the campground, ¼ mi west of the visitor center, usually has available sites. Winter snows can block the road. ⊠ *AZ 564, Black Mesa* ☎ *928/672–2366* ☞ *Free* ☞ *30 sites* ⟐ *Flush toilets, drinking water* ⟐ *Reservations not accepted* ☉ *Open year-round, weather permitting.*

GLEN CANYON DAM & LAKE POWELL

Lake Powell is the heart of the huge 1,255,400-acre Glen Canyon National Recreation Area. Created by the barrier of Glen Canyon Dam in the Colorado River, Lake Powell is ringed by red cliffs that twist off into 96 major canyons and countless inlets (most accessible only by boat) with huge, red-sandstone buttes randomly jutting from the sapphire waters. It extends through terrain so rugged it was the last major area of the United States to be mapped. You could spend 30 years exploring the lake and still not experience everything there is to see. The Sierra Club has started a movement to drain the lake to restore water-filled Glen Canyon, which some believe was more spectacular than the Grand Canyon, but the lake is likely to be around for years to come.

> **LAKE POWELL FAST FACTS**
>
> ▪ Lake Powell is 185 mi long with 2,000 mi of shoreline—longer than America's Pacific coast.
>
> ▪ This is the second-largest man-made lake in the nation and it took 17 years to fill.
>
> ▪ The Glen Canyon Dam is a 710-foot-tall wall of concrete.

South of Lake Powell the landscape gives way to **Echo Cliffs,** orange-sandstone formations rising 1,000 feet and more above the highway in places. At **Bitter Springs,** the road ascends the cliffs and provides a spectacular view of the 9,000-square-mi Arizona Strip to the west and the 3,000-foot Vermilion Cliffs to the northwest.

Page

⓯ *96 mi west of the Navajo National Monument, 136 mi north of Flagstaff on U.S. 89.*

Built in 1957 as a Glen Canyon Dam construction camp, Page is now a tourist spot and a popular base for day trips to Lake Powell; it has also become a major point of entry to the Navajo Nation. The nearby Vermilion Cliffs are where the California condor, an endangered species, has been successfully reintroduced into the wild. The town's human population of 10,000 makes it the largest community in far-northern Arizona, and most of the motels, restaurants, and shopping centers are concentrated along **Lake Powell Boulevard,** the name given to U.S. 89 as it loops through the business district. Each year, more than 3 million people come to play at Lake Powell.

At the corner of North Navajo Drive and Lake Powell Boulevard is the **John Wesley Powell Memorial Museum,** whose namesake led the first known expeditions down the Green River and the rapids-choked Colorado through the Grand Canyon between 1869 and 1872. Powell mapped and kept detailed records of his trips, naming the Grand Canyon and many other geographic points of interest in northern Arizona. Artifacts from his expeditions are displayed in the museum. The museum also doubles as the town's visitor information center. A travel desk dispenses information and allows you to book boating tours, raft trips, scenic flights, accommodations in Page, or Antelope Canyon tours. When you sign up for tours here, concessionaires give a donation to the nonprofit museum with no extra charge to you. ☒ *6 N. Lake Powell Blvd.* ☏ *928/645–9496* ⊕ *www.powellmuseum.org* ☜ *$3* ⊗ *Weekdays 8:30–5:30, Memorial Day–Labor Day also open Sat., call for hrs.*

The **Navajo Village Heritage Center** imparts an understanding of life on the reservation. You can take a guided tour of a traditional Navajo hogan and bread oven. For $49.95, the village hosts a four-hour "Evening with the Navajo–Grand Tour," which includes two hours of cultural entertainment and a Navajo taco dinner around a campfire. ☒ *531 Haul Rd.* ☏ *928/660–0304* ⊕ *www.navajo-village.com* ☜ *$10* ⊗ *Apr.–Oct., daily 9–3.*

Sports & the Outdoors

For water sports on Lake Powell, *see* Wahweap *below.*

FLOAT TRIPS **Wilderness River Adventures** (☏ 928/645–3296 or 800/992–8022 ⊕ www.riveradventures.com) offers waterborne tours, including a 4½-hour guided rafting excursion down a calm portion of the Colorado River on comfortable, safe J boats ($52). The scenery—multicolor-sandstone cliffs adorned with Native American petroglyphs—is spectacular. The point of departure in Page is the Wilderness Outfitters Store at 50 South Lake Powell Boulevard, but transportation is furnished both to the launch site and back from Lees Ferry, where the trip ends.

GOLF **Lake Powell National Golf Course** (☒ 400 Clubhouse Dr., off U.S. 89 ☏ 928/645–2023 ⊕ www.lakepowellgolf.com) has wide fairways, tiered greens with some of the steepest holes in the Southwest, and a generous lack of hazards. A round at this 18-hole, par-72 course costs $45 (including cart); from the fairways you can enjoy vistas of Glen Canyon Dam and Lake Powell. There's a 9-hole, par-36 municipal course here as well.

HIKING The **Glen Canyon Hike** (☒ Off U.S. 89), a short walk from the parking lot down a flight of uneven rock steps, takes you to a viewpoint on the canyon rim high above the Colorado River and provides fantastic views of the Colorado as it flows through Glen Canyon. To reach the parking lot, turn west on Scenic View Drive, 1½ mi south of Carl Hayden Visitor Center.

The **Horse Shoe Bend Trail** (⊠ Off U.S. 89) has some steep up and down paths and a bit of deep sand to maneuver; however, the views are well worth the hike. The trail leads up to a bird's-eye view of Glen Canyon and the Colorado River downstream from Glen Canyon Dam. There are some sheer drop-offs here, so watch children. To reach the trail, drive 4 mi south of Page on U.S. 89 and turn west onto a blacktop road 2/10 mi south of mile marker 545. It's a ¾-mi hike from the parking area to the top of the canyon.

Where to Stay & Eat

$–$$$ ✕ **Dam Bar and Grille.** Although the Grille's decor more resembles a construction site than a restaurant, the food is good, well prepared, and imaginative for the all-purpose palate. It's general American with good steaks and a few touches that take you south of the border. ⊠ *644 N. Navajo Dr.* ☎ *928/645–2161* ⊕ *www.damplaza.com* ⊟ *AE, MC, V.*

$–$$ ✕ **Zapata's.** Specials include green chile and home-style enchiladas, not to mention very good margaritas. Everything is made from "scratch" using family recipes. The basic, clean restaurant is decorated with Mexican blankets, *ristras* (strings of dried red-chiles), and pottery. ⊠ *614 N. Navajo Dr.* ☎ *928/645–9006* ⊟ *AE, D, MC, V.*

$–$$ ▥ **Days Inn & Suites.** One of the newer hotels in the area has views of Lake Powell, the Vermilion Cliffs, and Glen Canyon Dam. Standard rooms are spacious, and 22 suites have wet bars, microwaves, refrigerators, and data ports. All are decorated in a pleasant Southwestern motif. ⊠ *961 N. U.S. 89, 86040* ☎ *928/645–2800* ⊟ *928/645–2604* ⊕ *www.daysinn. com* ⊷ *82 rooms* ⚬ *Some microwaves, some refrigerators, cable TV, some in-room data ports, pool, shop, laundry facilities, no-smoking rooms* ⊟ *AE, D, DC, MC, V* ⊚ *CP.*

¢–$$ ▥ **Courtyard by Marriott.** An attractive motel on the grounds of Lake Powell National Golf Course, the Courtyard has comfortable rooms decorated in a Southwestern motif, health and fitness facilities, and on-premises dining in Peppers ($1–$2), an eatery specializing in American fare. ⊠ *600 Clubhouse Dr.* ▱ *Box 4150, 86040* ☎ *928/645–5000* ⊕ *www.courtyard.com* ⊷ *153 rooms* ⚬ *Restaurant, cable TV, in-room data ports, pool, gym, sauna, bar, shop, laundry facilities, laundry service, business services, meeting rooms, no-smoking rooms* ⊟ *AE, D, DC, MC, V.*

$ ▥ **Best Western Arizonainn.** On a bluff at the northern end of Page, this modern, well-run motel has large rooms with queen-size beds and Southwestern-print bedspreads and has fantastic views of Lake Powell. Butterfield Steakhouse serves Southwestern and standard American fare. ⊠ *716 Rim View Dr.* ▱ *Box 250, 86040* ☎ *928/645–2466 or 800/826–2718* ⊕ *www.bestwestern.com* ⊷ *103 rooms* ⚬ *Restaurant, cable TV, in-room data ports, pool, hot tub, bar, laundry facilities, meeting rooms, no-smoking rooms* ⊟ *AE, D, DC, MC, V* ⊚ *CP.*

$ ▥ **Best Western at Lake Powell.** The newer of the two Best Westerns in town is a modern, three-story motel on a high bluff overlooking Glen

Tribes & Their Crafts

THERE ARE 21 NATIVE AMERICAN TRIBES inhabiting 20 reservations in Arizona, and many of them create types of arts and crafts that date back several centuries.

As the Spanish ventured northward from Mexico in the late 1500s and early 1600s, they taught the Native Americans their silvercrafting skills, while tribes specializing in pottery and weaving carry on a tradition that began hundreds of years ago. Generally, tribes used indigenous ingredients and supplies that were at hand. Tribes living along rivers and waterways were more apt to produce baskets since reeds were plentiful; tribes that required water to be carried to their village were most likely to create pottery.

Railroads were built and travelers came west by train, and Fred Harvey, who had established fine eating establishments at railroad stops along the route, realized that the easterners were looking for souvenir handicrafts to take home with them. He encouraged Navajo weavers to create large pieces, such as rugs and wall hangings.

Navajos wove blankets from wool using natural plant dyes for color. Each community is known for specific colors and designs that are often passed down within a family, from mother to daughter, for generations. A medium-size rug (5' x 7') with a complex pattern may require more than half a year to create. Don't be shocked if the price tag reads above $30,000.

Native beadwork traces its origins to trades with early trappers and explorers. Trade beads, as they were known, often came from Europe. The beads became popular adornments for clothing and everyday items. Beaded fetishes, drums, rattles, and dolls were often part of spiritual ceremonies.

Navajo silver and turquoise jewelry is one of the more alluring items to visitors. The famous squash blossom necklaces, if completely handmade, can run more than $1,000, especially if the silver beads are made as two separate hemispheres. Proud craftsmen have individual logos or personal marks that are put into each piece. Authentic pieces will also indicate that the silver is Sterling.

There are a number of Indian Art markets that take place throughout the state year round. Most often, the sellers are willing to bargain, if it's done in good faith. But be aware that there has always been a problem with counterfeit imported crafts that are passed off as genuine. They're usually, but not always, found at the cheaper souvenir-type shops and even at some roadside stands. If they're not Native made, they legally must be labeled as imported. Your best bet for big ticket items is to buy directly from the native craftsmen themselves or from a reputable dealer. If you're traveling in Navajoland, the Cameron Trading Post north of Flagstaff, or the Hubbell Trading Post south of Canyon de Chelly at Ganado are two spots where you can find exemplary rugs, jewelry, and craft items.

In Phoenix, the gift shop at the famed Heard Museum offers some of the finest Native American handicrafts at reasonable prices. You can be certain that each and every piece of jewelry and art sold there is 100% native crafted.

By Bob & Gloria Willis

Canyon Dam with dazzling views of the Vermilion Cliffs. The large rooms are functional, and the beds are comfortable. ✉ *208 N. Lake Powell Blvd., 86040* ☎ *928/645–5988 or 888/794–2888* ⊕ *www.bestwestern. com/atlakepowell* ⇌ *132 rooms* ⚹ *Some microwaves, some refrigerators, cable TV, pool, gym, hot tub, laundry facilities, meeting rooms, no-smoking rooms* ▤ *AE, D, DC, MC, V* ⦿l *CP.*

$ ⊡ **Canyon Colors B&B.** Run by New England transplants Bev and Rich Jones, this desert-country B&B offers travelers a personal touch. The Sunflower and Paisley rooms, which can accommodate up to five and four, respectively, have queen beds, futons, and wood-burning stoves. The B&B also has an extensive video library, including many videos of Lake Powell and the Navajo Nation. Reservations, necessary in summer, can be made up to a year in advance. ✉ *225 S. Navajo Dr.* ⊕ *Box 3657, 86040* ☎ *928/645–5979 or 800/536–2530* ☏☏ *928/ 645–5979* ⊕ *www.canyoncolors.com* ⇌ *2 rooms* ⚹ *BBQ, refrigerators, cable TV, in-room VCRs, pool; no smoking* ▤ *AE, D, DC, MC, V* ⦿l *BP.*

CAMPING ⛺ **Page–Lake Powell Campground.** Lake Powell is a popular destina-
¢ tion and very busy in summer months so make reservations if you're planning to stay at this in-town campground. The Antelope Point launch ramp on Lake Powell is 7 mi away. ✉ *849 S. Coppermine Rd., 86040* ☎ *928/645–3374* ⊕ *http://campground.page-lakepowell.com* ⊟ *$18 tent site, $23 partial hookup, $29 full hookups (with cable)* ⇌ *85 RV sites, 20 tent sites* ⚹ *Flush toilets, full hookups, partial hookups (electric and water), dump station, guest laundry, showers, picnic tables, general store, swimming (indoor pool)* ▤ *MC, V* ⊗ *Open year-round.*

Nightlife

The **Bowl** (✉ 24 N. Lake Powell Blvd. ☎ 928/645–2682) is a 10-lane bowling alley with an outdoor patio, billiards, and coffee shop. **Gunsmoke Saloon & Eatery** (✉ 644 N. Navajo Dr. ☎ 928/645–1888) is a spot where you can dance to live music, play billiards and video games, and munch on chicken wings until 1 AM. **Ken's Old West Restaurant & Lounge** (✉ 718 Vista Ave. ☎ 928/645–5160) has country-and-western music and dancing; you can also get good steak, prime rib, seafood, or a barbecued-chicken dinner.

Shopping

There are numerous gift shops and clothing stores in the downtown area along Lake Powell Boulevard. There's lots of junk, but you can find authentic Native American arts and crafts, too. **Big Lake Trading Post** (✉ 1501 AZ 98 ☎ 928/645–2404) has a gas station, convenience store, car wash, and coin laundry. **Blair's Dinnebito Trading Post** (✉ 626 Navajo Dr. ☎ 928/645–3008 ⊕ www.blairstradingpost.com) has been around for more than half a century. Authentic Native American arts and crafts are only a small part of what this store sells. Need tack equipment, rodeo ropes, rugs, saddlery, pottery? It's all here and reasonably priced. Wander upstairs and visit the Elijah Blair collection and memorabilia rooms. The gift shop at **Lake Powell Resort** (✉ 100 Lake Shore Dr., Wahweap

☎ 928/645–2433 ⊕ www.blairstradingpost.com) carries authentic Native American rugs, pottery, jewelry, and baskets as well as tourist T-shirts and postcards.

Antelope Canyon

★ ⑯ *4 mi east of Page on the Navajo Reservation, on AZ 98.*

You've probably seen dozens of photographs of Antelope Canyon, a narrow, red-sandstone slot canyon with convoluted corkscrew formations, dramatically illuminated by light streaming down from above. And you're likely to see assorted shutterbugs waiting patiently for just the right shot of these colorful, photogenic rocks, which are actually petrified-sand dunes of a prehistoric ocean that once filled this portion of North America. The best photos are taken at high noon, when light filters through "the slot" in the canyon surface. This is one place that you'll need to protect your camera equipment against blowing dust. Access to the canyon is limited to those on licensed tours. ⊠ *AZ 98, Page ⊕ Box 2520, Window Rock 86515 ☎ 928/871–6647 Navajo Parks & Recreation Dept. ⊕ www.navajonationparks.org ☜ $6, included in tour cost.*

Antelope Canyon Tours

Access to Antelope Canyon is restricted by the Navajo Tribe to licensed tour operators. The tribe charges a $6 per-person fee—included in the price of tours offered by the licensed concessionaires in Page. The easiest way to book a tour is in town at the John Wesley Powell Memorial Museum Visitor Center. You pay nothing extra for the museum's service; if you'd like to go directly to the tour operators, you can do that, too. Most companies offer 1½-hour sightseeing tours for about $30, or longer photography tours for $48. The best time to see the canyon is between 8 AM and 2 PM.

Antelope Canyon Adventures (⊠ 104 S. Lake Powell Blvd., Page ☎ 928/645–5501 ⊕ www.jeeptour.com) offers 1½-hour sightseeing tours. **John Wesley Powell Memorial Museum Visitor Center** (⊠ 6 N. Lake Powell Blvd., Page ☎ 928/645–9496 ⊕ www.powellmuseum.org) arranges and books 1½-hour tours and 5-hour photography tours. Photo tours leave from Page at 8 and 9:30 AM and return about 2 PM. The shorter sightseeing tours leave frequently between 8 AM and 4 PM. **Overland Canyon Tours** (⊠ 695 N.

> ### SLOT CANYONS
>
> Slot canyons are unique to the southwest. Carved through sandstone by wind and water, they are narrow at the top—some are only a foot wide on the surface—and wider at the bottom, which can be more than 100 feet below ground level. The play of light as it filters down through the slot onto the sandstone walls makes them remarkable subjects for photographs, but they are inherently dangerous, particularly during the summer rainy season when flash floods can rush through them and sweep away the unwary hiker who has no place to run. If you're considering a hike into a slot canyon, consult with locals and pay attention to weather forecasts.

Navajo Dr., Page ☎ 928/608–4072 ⊕ www.navajoindiantours.com) is the only Native American–operated tour company in Page. Tours include a narrative explaining the canyon's history and geology. **Antelope Canyon Tours** (✉ 22 S. Lake Powell Blvd., Page ☎ 928/645–9102 ⊕ www.antelopecanyon.com) offers several tours daily from 8 AM to 3 PM for sightseers and photographers. The photo tour gives serious and amateur photographers the opportunity to wait for the "right light" to photograph the canyon and get basic information on equipment setup. Tickets can be purchased at the John Wesley Powell Museum Visitor Center.

CANYON X TOURS   On private property, the isolated slot canyon known as Canyon X can be toured only by Navajo guide Harley Klemm and his company, Overland Canyon Tour, which also operates popular tours to Antelope Canyon. Tours depart from Page at approximately 8 AM and return at 3 PM, by advance reservation only. The six-hour tour for serious shutterbugs ($225 per person) offers treks to three different, off-the-beaten-track canyons and is guided by a professional slot-canyon photographer. The four-hour guided hiking tour ($85 per person) is limited to groups of 16. Because the area is rugged, children are not allowed, and participants should have good physical mobility to climb crevasses and some rough terrain.

Glen Canyon National Recreation Area

⑰ *2 mi west of Page on U.S. 89.*

Once you leave the Page business district heading northwest, the Glen Canyon Dam and Lake Powell behind it immediately become visible. This concrete-arch dam—all 5 million cubic feet of it—was completed in September 1963, its power plant an engineering feat that rivaled the Hoover Dam. The dam's crest is 1,560 feet across and rises 710 feet from bedrock and 583 feet above the waters of the Colorado River. When Lake Powell is full, it's 560 feet deep at the dam. The plant generates some 1.3 million kilowatts of electricity when each generator's 40-ton shaft is generating nearly 200,000 horsepower. Power from the dam serves a five-state grid consisting of Colorado, Arizona, Utah, California, and New Mexico and provides energy for some 1.5 million users.

With only 8 inches of annual rainfall, the Lake Powell area enjoys blue skies nearly year-round. Summer temperatures range from the 60s to the 90s. Fall and spring are usually balmy, with daytime temperatures often in the 70s and 80s, but chilly weather can set in. Nights are cool even in the summer, and in winter the risk of a cold spell increases, but all-weather houseboats and tour boats make for year-round cruising.

Boaters and campers should note that regulations require the use of portable toilets on the lake and lakeshore to prevent water pollution.

Just off the highway at the north end of the bridge is the **Carl Hayden Visitor Center,** where you can learn about the controversial creation of Glen Canyon Dam and Lake Powell and enjoy panoramic views of both. To enter the visitor center, you must go through a metal detector.

Absolutely no bags are allowed inside. ✉ *U.S. 89, 2 mi west of town, Page* ☎ *928/608–6404* ⊕ *www.nps.gov/glca* 💰 *$10 per vehicle, $10 per week boating fee* ☉ *Visitor Center Memorial Day–Labor Day, daily 8–6; Labor Day–Memorial Day, daily 8–5.*

Wahweap

⑱ *5 mi north of Glen Canyon Dam on U.S. 89.*

Most waterborne-recreational activity on the Arizona side of the lake is centered on this vacation village, where everything needed for a lakeside holiday is available: tour boats, fishing, boat rentals, dinner cruises, and more. The Lake Powell Resort has excellent views of the lake area and you can take a boat tour from the Wahweap Marina.

★ **⑲** A boat tour to **Rainbow Bridge National Monument** is a great way see the enormity of the lake and its incredible, rugged beauty. This 290-foot red-sandstone arch is the world's largest natural bridge and can be reached by boat or strenuous hiking (⇨ Hiking). The lake level is down due to the prolonged drought throughout the region, so expect a 1½ mi hike from the boat dock to the monument. The bridge can also be viewed by air. To the Navajos, this is a sacred area with deep religious and spiritual significance, so outsiders are asked not to hike underneath the arch itself.

> **WORD OF MOUTH**
>
> "Rainbow Bridge is really a great experience. The trip there and back on the tour boat really lets you see a lot of the lake, buttes and mesas you can't see from land."   –utahtea

Sports & the Outdoors

BOATING Lake Powell has been called "the most scenic lake on earth": the 186 mi of clear sapphire waters are edged with vast canyons of red and orange rock. Ninety-six major side canyons intricately twist and turn into the main channel of Lake Powell, into what was once the main artery of the Colorado River through Glen Canyon. In some places the lake is 500 feet deep, and by June the lake's waters begin to warm and stay that way well into October.

An $80 million project being built in four phases, with completion of 225 resort casitas planned for 2008, **Antelope Point Marina** (⌂ BIA Hwy. N22B, Mile Marker 4, Navajo Nation 86040 ☎ 602/952–0114 🖷 602/468–0084 ⊕ www.azmarinas.com) will include a Navajo Cultural Center, artist studios, more than 400 wet slips for houseboats and watercraft, a floating marina village, and an RV park and campground. At **Aramark's Lake Powell Resorts & Marinas** (⌂ Box 56909, Phoenix 85079 ☎ 800/528–6154 central reservations, 928/645–1004 direct to hotel 🖷 602/331–5258 ⊕ www.visitlakepowell.com) houseboat rentals range widely in size, amenities, and price, depending upon season. For more information on houseboats, *see* Houseboating *in* Where to Stay & Eat, *below.* You may want to rent a powerboat or personal water craft along with a houseboat for exploring the many narrow canyons and waterways on the lake. An 18-foot powerboat for eight passengers runs from approximately $139 to $232 per day.

State Line Marina (✉ U.S. 89, State Line, UT ☎ 928/645–1111), 1½ mi north of Lake Powell Resort, formerly Wahweap Lodge, is part of Aramark's Lake Powell Resorts & Marina concession and site of the boat-rental office. It's here that you pick up rental houseboats, powerboats, kayaks, Jet Skis, and personal water craft. There's also a public launch ramp if you're towing your own boat. **Wahweap Marina** (✉ 100 Lake Shore Dr., Wahweap ☎ 928/645–2433) is

> **WORD OF MOUTH**
>
> "I could not get enough of Lake Powell. We rented a houseboat, and then rented jet skis for a half day. On a jet ski, you can go way up all the little shallow crevices left by the drought. I understand there are petroglyphs back up in there that have only recently been uncovered with the receding waterline. And on a jet ski, you can go where ever you want and stop where ever you want."
>
> –waikikigirl

the largest of the four full-service Lake Powell marinas run by Aramark's Lake Powell Resorts & Marinas. There are 850 slips and the most facilities, including a decent diner, public launch ramp, fishing dock, and a marina store where you can buy fishing licenses and other necessities. It's the only full-service marina on the Arizona side of the lake (the other three marinas—Hite, Bullfrog, and Halls Crossing—are in Utah).

BOAT TOURS Excursions on double-decker scenic cruisers piloted by experienced guides leave from the dock of Lake Powell's **Lake Powell Resort** (✉ 100 Lake Shore Dr., Wahweap ☎ 928/645–2433 or 800/528–6154), formerly the Wahweap Lodge. The most popular tour is the half-day trip to Rainbow Bridge National Monument for $80 (lemonade, water, and coffee are included, and you can bring your own snacks or lunch). The full-day cruise visits several side canyons as well as Rainbow Bridge and costs about $109; this one includes a box. A 2½-hour sunset dinner cruise costs about $63: a prime-rib dinner—vegetarian lasagna dinners are available if ordered in advance—is served on the fully enclosed decks of the 95-foot *Canyon King* paddle wheeler, a reproduction of a 19th-century bay boat. The dinner cruise is a 2½-hour tour with the captain's choice of routes.

FISHING Anglers delight in the world-class bass fishing on Lake Powell. You'll hear over and over how the big fish are "biting in the canyons," so you'll need a small vessel if you plan on fishing for the big one. Landing a 20-pound striper isn't unusual (the locals' secret is to use anchovies for bait). Fishing licenses for both Arizona and Utah are available at the **Marina Store at Wahweap Marina** (✉ 100 Lake Shore Dr., Wahweap ☎ 928/645–1136). **Stix Market** (✉ 5 S. Lake Powell Blvd., Page ☎ 928/645–2891) can recommend local fishing guides.

HIKING Bring plenty of water and electrolyte-rich beverages such as Gatorade when hiking, and drink often. It's important to remember when hiking at Lake Powell to watch the sky for storms: it may not be raining where you are but flooding can occur in downstream canyons—particularly slot canyons—from a storm miles away.

Only seasoned hikers in good physical condition will want to try either of the trails leading to **Rainbow Bridge**; both are about 26 to 28 mi round-trip through challenging and rugged terrain. This site is considered sacred by the Navajo, and it's requested that visitors show respect by not walking under the bridge. Take Indian Highway 16 north toward the Utah state border. At the fork in the road, take either direction for about 5 mi to the trailhead leading to Rainbow Bridge. Excursion boats pull in at the dock at the arch, but no supplies are sold there.

Navajo Nation Parks and Recreation Department (✉ Bldg. 36A, E. AZ 264 🕾 Box 2520, Window Rock 86515 ☎ 928/871–6647 ⊕ www. navajonationparks.org) provides backcountry permits (a slight fee is charged), which must be obtained before hiking to Rainbow Bridge. Write to the office, and allow about a month to process the paperwork.

Where to Stay & Eat

$$ ✕☷ **Lake Powell Resort.** This sprawling one-story lodge, run by Aramark,
Fodor'sChoice sits on a promontory above Lake Powell and serves as the center for
★ recreational activities in the area. The brightly colored Southwestern-style suites in the newest building are particularly attractive. The Rainbow Room restaurant ($–$$) offers an extensive Southwestern, American, and Continental menu and breakfast buffet, all with panoramic views of Lake Powell. In season there are also decent pizzas from Itza Pizza. ✉ *100 Lake Shore Dr., 7 mi north of Page off U.S. 89, Wahweap 🕾 Box 1597, Page 86040* ☎ *928/645–2433 or 800/528–6154* ⊕ *www. aramarkparks.com* ➽ *350 rooms* ↻ *Restaurant, pizzeria, refrigerators, cable TV, 2 pools, boating, waterskiing, fishing, bar, travel services, some pets allowed* ⊟ *AE, D, DC, MC, V.*

CAMPING Beautiful campsites are abundant on Lake Powell, from large beaches to secluded coves, with the most desirable areas accessible only by boat. You're allowed to camp anywhere along the shores of the lake unless it's restricted by the National Park Service; however, camping within ¼ mi of the shoreline requires a portable toilet or bathroom facilities on your boat. Campfires are allowed on the shoreline, but since there's little firewood available around the lake, you'll need to bring your own.

¢ △ **Wahweap Campground.** This campground in the Wahweap Marina complex, which is run by the National Park Service Concessionaire, has views of the lake and serves both RVers and tent campers. There are showers and coin-laundry services at the nearby grocery store. ✉ *U.S. 89, 5 mi north of Page near shore of Lake Powell, Wahweap 86040* ☎ *928/645–1059* ➽ *112 tent sites, 94 full hookups* ↻ *Grills, flush toilets, full hookups, dump station, drinking water, fire pits, picnic tables* ☒ *$15 tent site, $28 full hookup* ⊟ *AE, D, DC, MC, V* ☉ *Open year-round.*

¢ ⛺ **Wahweap Trailer Village.** This Aramark-managed park for RVs has 120 full-service hookups, showers, and a coin laundry. It's open year-round, and reservations are accepted. ✉ *U.S. 89, 5 mi north of Page near shore of Lake Powell, Wahweap 86040* ☎ *928/645–1004 or 800/528–6154* 🖃 *$28* 🛏 *120 RV sites* ⚄ *Flush toilets, full hookups, dump station, drinking water, guest laundry, showers, picnic tables* 🖃 *AE, D, DC, MC, V* ☺ *Open year-round.*

HOUSEBOATING Without a doubt, the most popular and fun way to vacation on Lake Powell is to rent a houseboat. Houseboats, ranging in size from 36 to 59 feet and sleeping 6 to 12 people, come complete with marine radios, fully equipped kitchens, and bathrooms with hot showers; you need only bring sheets and towels. The larger, deluxe boats are a good choice in hot summer months since they have air-conditioning. **Aramark's Lake Powell Resorts & Marinas** (🖃 Box 56909, Phoenix 85079 ☎ 800/528–6154 ⊕ www.lakepowell.com 🖃 AE, D, DC, MC, V) is the only concessionaire that rents boats on Lake Powell. There are many vacation packages available. One houseboat that sleeps eight (four double beds) can run about $900 for three nights. Larger, 59-foot Admiral Class–luxury houseboats may cost as much as $3,200 for three nights. You receive hands-on instruction before you leave the marina.

NORTHEAST ARIZONA ESSENTIALS

To research prices, get advice from other travelers, and book travel arrangements, visit ⊕ *www.fodors.com.*

Transportation

BY AIR
No major airlines fly directly to northeastern Arizona. To get closer to this part of the state, you can fly into Sky Harbor International Airport in Phoenix and take a small plane operated by Denver-based Great Lakes Aviation to Page Municipal Airport.

🛫 **Great Lakes Aviation** ☎ 800/554–5111 ⊕ www.greatlakesav.com. **Page Municipal Airport** ☎ 928/645–4337 ⊕ www.cityofpage.org.

BY BUS
The Navajo Transit System has extensive, fixed routes throughout the Navajo Reservation as well as charter service; write or phone for schedules and bus station locations. The buses are modern, in good condition, and generally on time, but they do not make frequent runs, and when they do run they can be slow. Fares range from 50¢ for local rides to a high of $13.05 (Window Rock to Tuba City). This can be an up-close-and-personal way to travel the Navajo Nation and meet the people who live here as they go about their daily business.

🛫 **Navajo Transit System** 🖃 Drawer 1330, Window Rock 86515 ☎ 928/729–4002 ⊕ www.navajotransitsystem.com.

BY CAR

The only practical way to tour the Navajo and Hopi nations is by car. If you're arriving from southern California or southern Arizona, Flagstaff is the best jumping-off point into northeastern Arizona. If you're traveling from Utah or Nevada, you might come in from Utah on U.S. 89, starting your tour at Page. For those driving south from Colorado, logical entry points are Farmington and Shiprock, New Mexico, via U.S. 64 (what looks like a more direct route to Canyon de Chelly through Red Rock ends up crossing an unimproved road). Gallup, New Mexico, to the east, is also a convenient starting point for exploring.

A tour of Navajo-Hopi country involves driving long distances among widely scattered communities, so a detailed, up-to-date road map is essential. A wrong turn could send you many miles out of your way. Gas stations carry adequate state maps, but two other maps are particularly recommended: the AAA guide to Navajo-Hopi country or the excellent map of the northeast prepared by the Navajo Nation Tourism Office.

Most of the 25,000 square mi of the Navajo Reservation and other areas of northeastern Arizona are off the beaten track. Many travelers in northeastern Arizona generally stay on the well-maintained paved thoroughfares, which are patrolled by police officers. If you don't have the equipment for wilderness travel—including a four-wheel-drive vehicle and provisions—and do not have backcountry experience, stay off the dirt roads unless they are signed and graded and the skies are clear. Seek weather information if you see ominous rain clouds in summer or signs of snow in winter. Never drive into dips or low-lying road areas during a heavy rainstorm; they could be flooded or could flood suddenly. If you heed these simple precautions, car travel through the region will be as safe as anywhere else. While driving around the Navajo Nation, tune in to 660 AM (KTNN) for local news and weather.

Road service, auto repairs, and other automotive services are few and far between, so service your vehicle before venturing into the Navajo and Hopi reservations, and carry emergency equipment and supplies. If you need assistance, ask a local for the nearest auto-repair service. Diamond Towing offers a 24-hour emergency road service.

🚗 **Diamond Towing** ✉ Kayenta ☎ 928/697-8437.

BY TRAIN

No passenger trains enter the interior of the Navajo or Hopi Reservation or stop at any of the other towns along its perimeter. Amtrak serves Flagstaff.

Contacts & Resources

BANKS AND EXCHANGING SERVICES

Wells Fargo has branch offices with ATMs in Window Rock, Kayenta, and Tuba City on the Navajo Reservation. Near the reservation, Flagstaff, Page, Winslow, Chinle, and Holbrook have banks and ATMs.

EMERGENCIES

Dial 911 for emergencies on reservation lands.

🚨 Ambulance & Fire **Kayenta Ambulance** ☎ 928/697-4074. **Page Ambulance** ☎ 928/645-2461.

🚨 Hospitals **Monument Valley Health Center** ✉ 4 Rock Door Canyon, Monument Valley, UT 84536 ☎ 801/727-3241. **Page Hospital** ✉ 501 N. Navajo Ave., Page ☎ 928/645-2424. **Sage Memorial Hospital** ✉ Ganado ☎ 928/755-3411. **U.S. Public Health Service Indian Hospital** ✉ Chinle ☎ 928/674-7001 ✉ Fort Defiance ☎ 928/729-5741 ✉ Keams Canyon ☎ 928/738-2211 ✉ Tuba City ☎ 928/283-2501.

🚨 Pharmacies **Safeway Pharmacy** ✉ Page Plaza, Page ☎ 928/645-5714 or 928/645-5068. **Wal-Mart Pharmacy** ✉ Gateway Plaza, Page ☎ 928/645-2917.

🚨 Police **Canyon de Chelly Police** ☎ 928/674-2111 or 928/674-2112. **Hopi tribal police: Hopi Mesas** ☎ 928/738-2233 or 928/738-2234. **Navajo tribal police** ✉ Chinle ☎ 928/674-2111 or 928/674-2112 ✉ Tuba City ☎ 928/283-3111 or 928/283-3112 ✉ Window Rock ☎ 928/871-6111 or 928/871-6112 ✉ Kayenta ☎ 928/697-5600 ✉ **Page Police** ☎ 928/645-2463.

MEDIA

RADIO KTNN radio (660 AM), the Voice of the Navajo Nation, serves the Hopi and Navajo Reservations from studios in Window Rock. Some programming is in Navajo, but there are news and weather reports in English; its "sister" station is KWRK, at 106.1 on the FM dial. Another radio station you might tune to for news and weather is KOB (770 AM, 107.3 FM, or 97.9 FM). For the boater's emergency band, dial Channel 16 on the marine band.

TOUR OPTIONS

AIR TOURS American Aviation offers flightseeing tours of Monument Valley, Lake Powell, and Rainbow Bridge, and Bryce Gallup Flying Service offers photo and scenic aerial tours of Navajoland from Gallup, New Mexico.

🚨 **American Aviation** ✉ 238 10th Ave., Page, AZ 86040 ☎ 928/608-1060. **Gallup Flying Service** ✉ West Hwy. 66, Gallup, NM 87301 ☎ 505/863-6606.

VISITOR INFORMATION

🚨 **Glen Canyon Recreation Area** ☎ 928/608-6200 or 928/608-6404 ⊕ www.nps.gov/glca. **Hopi Tribe Office of Public Relations** ☎ 928/734-2441 ⊕ www.hopi.nsn.us. **Navajo Nation Tourism Office** ☎ 928/871-7371 ⊕ www.navajoland.com. **Page/Lake Powell Chamber of Commerce** ⊡ Box 727, 86040 ☎ 928/645-2741 ⊕ www.pagelakepowellchamber.org.

WORD OF MOUTH

Opinions on the Petrified Forest tend to be one extreme or the other:

"The Petrified Forest isn't worth a special trip—it's a lot of sand and rocks—the rocks being petrified wood scattered all over the landscape."

—USNR

"We went to the Petrified Forest and I would advise you not to miss it—it doesn't take long to drive through, along with some short hikes. We spent time at each Visitor Center to learn about geology, etc. Yes, you can see pieces of petrified wood at many local shops, but it is unbelievable to see these massive 'trees' laying around."

—BBEAR

Updated by
Janet Webb
Farnsworth

IN A STATE OF DRAMATIC NATURAL WONDERS, eastern Arizona is often overlooked—truly a tragedy, as it's one of Arizona's great outdoor playgrounds. In the White Mountains, northeast of Phoenix, you can hike amid the largest stand of ponderosa pine in the world, fish for trout in babbling brooks, swim in clear reservoirs fed by unsullied mountain streams, and, at night, camp under millions of twinkling stars. The region's winter sports are just as varied: you can ski downhill or cross country, snowboard, snowshoe, and snowmobile on hundreds of miles of designated trails. And although some regions were burned in the devastating Rodeo-Chediski wildfire of 2002, visitor services were disrupted only temporarily. Though the effects are still evident, new grass is starting to grow, and the burned trees are being harvested; they'll be burned to produce electricity.

The White Mountains are unspoiled high country at its best. Certain areas have been designated as primitive wilderness, removed from the touch of people. In these vast tracts, the air is rent with piercing cries of hawks and eagles, and majestic herds of elk graze in verdant, wildflower-laden meadows. Past volcanic activity has left the land strewn with cinder cones, and the whole region is bounded by the Mogollon Rim (pronounced *muh*-gee-on)—a 200-mi geologic upthrust that splits the state—made famous as the "Tonto Rim" in Zane Grey's books. Much of the plant life is unique to this region; this is one of the few places in the country where such desert plants as juniper and manzanita grow intermixed with mountain pines and aspen.

The human aspects of the landscape are equally appealing. Historic Western towns are friendly outposts of down-home hospitality, and the many prehistoric ruins are reminders of the native cultures that once flourished here. Native Americans are still a vital presence. The Fort Apache Reservation, home to the White Mountain Apache Tribe, is north of the Salt River, and the San Carlos Apache Tribal Reservation is south of the river. Visitors are welcome to explore most reservation lands. All that's required is a permit—easily obtained from tribal offices.

However, there's more to eastern Arizona than the White Mountains. To the north, along historic Route 66, are the Painted Desert and Petrified Forest National Park and Homolovi Ruins State Park—extraordinary attractions in their own right. The austere mesas of the Painted Desert are famous for their multihued sedimentary layers. Nature has also worked wonders on the great fallen logs of the Petrified Forest National Park. In Triassic times, the park was a great, steamy swampland; some 225 million years ago, seismic activity forced the swamp's decaying plant matter (and a number of deceased dinosaurs) deep underground, where it eventually turned to stone. Fifty miles west of these unusual geologic remains, Homolovi Ruins State Park marks the site of four major ancestral Hopi pueblos, two of which contain more than 1,000 rooms. Between these artifacts of times past and the recreational bounty of the White Mountains wilderness, eastern Arizona offers a cultural and outdoor experience that defines the pleasures of Arizona.

Top 5 Eastern Arizona Experiences

- **Drive through Salt River Canyon:** Drive U.S. 60 between Globe and Show Low at a leisurely pace; you'll pass through pines to desert then back to pines as you travel through the wildly eroded Salt River Canyon, where Arizona's geologic history is revealed in colorful rock strata.

- **Get outside:** Step out the back door of your cabin to fish for trout in the cold, clear Little Colorado River at Greer. Miles of trails are great for summer hiking or winter cross-country skiing.

- **Sunrise Park Resort:** High in the White Mountains, the winter skiing, cool summer temperatures, and golden fall foliage make this ski resort a great destination in any season.

- **Drive the Coronado Trail National Scenic Byway:** Plan on slow travel, high country meadows, and vistas of hazy mountain ranges as you follow the stunning Byway as it drops from 9,000 feet to 3,464 feet in 123 mi of twisting road.

- **Petrified Forest National Park:** Marvel at huge petrified logs scattered like giant jackstraws across open grasslands at Petrified Forest National Park; the colors are most vibrant in early morning or late afternoon.

Exploring Eastern Arizona

Eastern Arizona runs the gamut of high-desert wonders. In the northern part of the region is the Petrified Forest National Park, covering 93,000 acres and including a portion of the Painted Desert; a straight shot west on Interstate 40 leads to important ancestral Hopi pueblos at Homolovi Ruins State Park. South of here, on the western edge of the region, is Salt River Canyon, known to many as the mini–Grand Canyon, where the San Carlos and Fort Apache Reservations abut. Much of the White Mountains is National Forest land. The mountain town of Pinetop-Lakeside is on the northern edge of the Sitgreaves National Forest; Greer is in the middle of the forest. Springerville-Eagar is just north of the Apache National Forest boundary. All three towns are connected by AZ 260. At Springerville-Eagar, you can connect to U.S. 191, also known as the Coronado Trail Scenic Byway. Towering over this southern part of the White Mountains is Mount Baldy, an 11,590-foot extinct volcano considered sacred by the Apache. Of note—and definitely worth exploring—is the Mogollon Rim, a limestone escarpment that extends 200 mi from southwest of Flagstaff to the White Mountains in eastern Arizona. In the winter months, stick to major thoroughfares, as many Forest Service roads are closed, and be sure to call for a road and weather report before setting off during this time.

About the Restaurants

In the White Mountains, you might settle in for a relaxing evening at a candlelighted restaurant in the pines. "Formal dining" is almost unheard of in the mountains, and a laid-back feeling is preferred by residents and visitors alike. If cowboy-size steaks and Old West atmosphere are what you seek, choose a more rustic setting at one of the area's many West-

GREAT ITINERARIES

The itineraries below assume that you're traveling between March and October. Winter travelers may have to rearrange their trips to accommodate seasonal road closures and chain requirements.

IF YOU HAVE 3 DAYS

Drive up to 🖼 **Pinetop-Lakeside ❸** ➤, 🖼 **Greer ❺**, or 🖼 **Springerville-Eagar ❼** and take advantage of a day or two of hiking, fishing, or biking. In winter, snow enthusiasts commonly make the pilgrimage to **Sunrise Park Resort ❹** for just a day or two.

If your main priority is visiting the **Petrified Forest National Park ⑩-⑰** ➤ and the **Painted Desert,** spend the first night in 🖼 **Snowflake-Taylor ⑲**. On Day 2 tour the park; spend the night in nearby 🖼 **Holbrook ㉑**, or make the scenic 75-mi drive southeast into 🖼 **Springerville-Eagar ❼**. Another option is to retrace your route back on AZ 77 and head east for accommodations in 🖼 **Show Low ❷**. Spend your third day driving back to Phoenix. You can return via U.S. 60 or opt for the daylong trip down the **Coronado Trail,** one of the state's most scenic byways.

IF YOU HAVE 5 DAYS

After exploring the **Painted Desert** and **Petrified Forest National Park ⑩-⑰** ➤, head south to the White Mountains and spend the night in either 🖼 **Springerville-Eagar ❼** or 🖼 **Pinetop-Lakeside ❸**, depending on whether you take AZ 77 or U.S. 180. Indulge in a day of local sightseeing in either pair of twin towns, then spend the following day working your way across east–west AZ 260 through the Apache Sitgreaves National Forest and parts of the White Mountain Apache Reservation, stopping for the night in tiny 🖼 **Greer ❺**. On the last day, retrace your route back to Phoenix via U.S. 60 or, if departing from Springerville-Eagar, via the **Coronado Trail.** If you're looking for solitude and remote beauty, skip poking along AZ 260's towns and head straight from the Petrified Forest down U.S. 180 to **Hannagan Meadow ❾**, returning on the remainder of the Coronado Trail on Day 5.

5

ern-style cafés. In and around the Navajo and Hopi reservations, be sure to sample Indian tacos, an authentic treat made with scrumptious fry bread, beans, and chiles.

About the Hotels

The communities of Pinetop-Lakeside, Greer, Show Low, and Springerville-Eagar offer lodging choices including modern resorts, rustic cabins, and small bed-and-breakfasts. Note that air-conditioning is not a standard amenity in the high country, where the nights are cool enough for a blanket even in summer. Closer to the Navajo and Hopi reservations, many establishments are run by Native Americans, tribal enterprises intent on offering first-class service and hospitality.

WHAT IT COSTS				
$$$$	**$$$**	**$$**	**$**	**¢**
RESTAURANTS over $25	$19–$25	$13–$18	$7–$12	under $7
HOTELS over $175	$131–$175	$91–$130	$50–$90	under $50

Restaurant prices are per person for a main course at dinner. Hotel prices are for a standard double in high season, excluding taxes and service charges.

Numbers in the margin correspond to numbers on the Eastern Arizona and Petrified Forest National Park maps.

Timing

If you're a skier, winter is definitely the time to tour the White Mountains. The White Mountain Winter Games at Sunrise Park Resort bring real-life mushing to the region in January.

Spring is unpredictable, and snow sometimes lasts to May. Generally, the hotel and ski runs at Sunrise Park Resort close by mid-March, and forest roads are open in May. The hotel reopens Memorial Day Weekend through mid-October for summer visitors, then closes again until snow brings the ski season. In mid-May, the tiny hamlet of Greer celebrates Greer Days with a parade, crafts, dances, and a fishing derby. Crowds begin converging on the White Mountains in late June, when school is out and Valley of the Sun temperatures start to become uncomfortably warm.

Autumn is a splendid time for a drive down the Coronado Trail, with hairpin turns winding through the yellows and golds of aspen and oak. The Pinetop-Lakeside Fall Festival is held the last weekend of September, with a parade and crafts booths. The White Mountain Apache Tribal Fair is celebrated Labor Day weekend with a parade and professional Native American rodeo.

THE WHITE MOUNTAINS

With elevations climbing to more than 11,000 feet, the White Mountains of east-central Arizona are a winter wonderland and a summer haven from the desert heat. In the 1870s, U.S. soldier and diarist John Gregory Bourke labeled the White Mountain region "a strange upheaval, a freak of nature, a mountain canted up on one side; one rides along the edge and looks down two or three thousand feet into . . . a weird scene of grandeur and rugged beauty." The area is still grand and rugged, carved by deep river canyons and tall cliffs covered with ponderosa pine. It's also much less remote than it was in Bourke's time, with a full-scale real-estate boom now under way.

Winter travelers through the White Mountains should be aware that weather conditions can change without notice. Call for weather information before heading out to White Mountains highways.

IF YOU LIKE

HIKING & BICYCLING

Hikers and mountain bikers of all abilities enjoy the White Mountains' interconnecting loop trails, which are open to those on foot or on two nonmotorized wheels. Stop at ranger stations for maps and tips on trails and overnight hikes. Allow one hour for each 2 mi of trail covered, plus an additional hour for every 1,000 feet gained in altitude. Mountain bikers will thrill over the White Mountain Trail System's 225 mi of interconnecting multiuse trails though many bike routes follow narrow Forest Service roads, which carry heavy traffic during the logging season from April to November. Be cautious when biking on reservation roads as bicyclists are generally unexpected. Always carry ample water and be aware that poison ivy grows in White Mountain wilderness areas.

FISHING

Anglers flock to the more than 65 lakes, streams, and reservoirs in the White Mountains, where they hook German browns, rainbow, and brook trout, as well as the occasional arctic grayling or native Apache trout, the official state fish, which is unique to Arizona. High-country warm-water fishing consists mostly of largemouth bass, bluegill, catfish, and walleye, hailed as the tastiest catch in the region. During winter months only artificial lures and flies are permitted. An Arizona fishing license is required; on tribal land, an additional White Mountain Apache fishing license is required.

GOLF

The High Country's links draw golfers from the Valley of the Sun and Tucson. These mountain fairways, with their cool temperatures, angle through lush forests and wind past lakes, streams, and springs. Pinetop-Lakeside has three championship courses, and Alpine has the highest golf course in the Southwest, at 8,500 feet above sea level.

NATIVE AMERICAN RUINS

North of Springerville-Eagar, Casa Malpais Archaeological Park is a prehistoric pueblo site with construction characteristics of both the ancient Puebloan peoples to the north and the Mogollon peoples to the south. Nearby Lyman Lake State Park has petroglyph trails with some of the region's more accessible rock art. West of Holbrook, Homolovi Ruins State Park is home to a large complex of Hopi ancestral pueblos. Petroglyphs and pueblos dating back more than 600 years can be found at stops along the 28-mi park road in the Petrified Forest National Park.

SKIING

Famous regionally for winter skiing, the 11,000-foot White Mountains offer hilly, wooded landscapes that invite downhill and cross-country skiing adventurers. Greer is an ideal hub for cross-country skiers: The nearby Pole Knoll Trail System and surrounding Forest Service roads make for 33 mi of cross-country trails. No matter where you stay in the White Mountains, Sunrise Park Resort is never more than an hour's drive away, and there are equipment-rental facilities throughout the region.

5

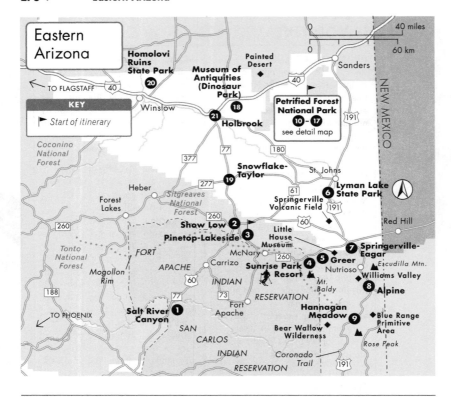

Salt River Canyon

❶ *40 mi north of Globe on U.S. 60.*

Fodor'sChoice
★

Exposing a time lapse of 500 million years, the multicolor spires, buttes, mesas, and walls of the **Salt River Canyon** have inspired its nickname, the mini–Grand Canyon. Approaching the Salt River Canyon from Phoenix, U.S. 60 climbs through rolling hills, and the terrain changes from high desert with cactus and mesquite trees to forests of ponderosa pine. After entering the San Carlos Indian Reservation, the highway drops 2,000 feet—from the Natanes Plateau into the canyon's vast gorge—and makes a series of hairpin turns down to cross the Salt River. Stop at the viewing and interpretive display area before crossing the bridge to stretch your legs. Wander along the banks below and enjoy the rock-strewn rapids. On hot days slip your shoes off and dip your feet into the chilly water. The river and canyon are open to hiking, camping, fishing,

> **WORD OF MOUTH**
>
> "The Salt River has rafting trips that are very mild. Note that the season is very short. Tubing the Salt River is another option during the summer—it's great fun, by the way." —jkgourmet

and white-water rafting, but you need a permit as this is tribal land. For information and recreational permits, contact the **San Carlos Apache Tribe** (☎ 928/475–2343) or the **White Mountain Apache Tribe** (☎ 928/338–4385).

The Apache people migrated to the Southwest around the 10th century. Divided into individual bands instead of existing as a unified tribe, they were a hunting and gathering culture, moving with the seasons to gather food, and their crafts—baskets, beadwork, and cradleboards—were compatible with their mobile lifestyle. The U.S. government didn't understand that different Apache bands might be hostile to each other and tried to gather separate tribes on one reservation, compounding relocation problems. Eventually, the government established San Carlos Apache Indian Reservation in 1871 and Fort Apache Indian Reservation in 1897. Both tribes hold fiercely to their cultures. The native language is still spoken and taught in schools and tribal ceremonies continue to be held. Both tribes have highly acclaimed "hot-shot" crews that immediately respond to forest fires throughout the West.

The Salt River forms the boundary between these two large Apache reservations of eastern Arizona. The **San Carlos Apache Indian Reservation** (☎ 928/475–2361 for tribal offices), established in 1871 for various Apache tribes, covers 1.8 million acres southeast of Salt River Canyon. One third of the reservation is covered with forest, and the rest is desert. The San Carlos Apaches number about 12,500 and are noted for their beadwork and basketry. Peridot, a beautiful yellow-green stone resembling the emerald, is mined near the town of Peridot and made into jewelry. The Apache Gold Casino and cattle ranching provide most of the tribal income.

The **Cultural Center** houses displays of Apache history and culture, along with explanations of cultural traditions like Changing Women Ceremony, a girls' puberty rite. Crafts are sold here. ⊠ *Hwy. 70, Milepost 272, Peridot* ☎ *928/475–2894* ⌕ *$3* ⊙ *Weekdays 9–5.*

The 1.6-million-acre **Fort Apache Indian Reservation** (☎ 928/338–1230 for tribal tourism) is the ancestral home of the White Mountain Apache Tribe. The elevation of the tribal lands ranges from 3,000 feet at the bottom of Salt River to 11,000 feet in the White Mountains and provides some of the best outdoor recreation area in the state. Most of the over 12,000 tribal members live in nine towns, with the largest, Whiteriver (population 2,500), serving as tribal headquarters. Tribal enterprises include Sunrise Ski Resort, Hon Dah Casino, cattle ranching, and lumber. The White Mountain region is famous for elk, bear, mountain lion, and mule deer hunting. The tribe sells hunting permits for trophy elk. Tribal permits are needed for all outdoor activities, but state licenses for hunting, fishing, and boating are not required.

Apache Cultural Museum. The entrance price buys access to three great places to visit on the Fort Apache Indian Reservation. The museum explains the history, culture, and artistic traditions of the Apaches, and sells local crafts and books. The **Fort Apache Historical Park** harks back to cavalry days with horse barns, parade grounds, log cabins, and officer's homes. **Kinishba Ruins,** 5 mi west of Fort Apache (get directions and map at the Cultural Center) is a partly restored sandstone pueblo and the only Native American ruin on the reservation that is open to visitors. ⊠ *½ mi east of junction of State Rte. 73 and Indian Rte. 46, 5 mi south of White River* ☎ *928/338–4625* 🖾 *$3* ☉ *Sept.–May, weekdays 8–5, June–Aug., Mon.–Sat. 8–5.*

EN ROUTE The road out of the Salt River Canyon climbs along the canyon's northern cliffs, providing views of this truly spectacular chasm, unfairly overlooked in a state full of world-famous gorges. The highway continues some 50 mi northward to the **Mogollon Rim**—a huge geologic ledge that bisects much of Arizona—and its cool upland pine woods.

Show Low

❷ *60 mi north of the Salt River Canyon on U.S. 60.*

Show Low has little of the charm of its neighboring White Mountains communities, but it's the main commercial center for the High Country. Additionally, the city is a crossing point for east–west traffic along the Mogollon Rim and traffic headed for Holbrook and points north. If you're heading up to the Painted Desert and Petrified Forest from Phoenix, you might want to spend the night here.

Fodor'sChoice ★ Look around the collectibles shop **Painted Nest** for antiques and unusual crafts. The owners turn used furniture into shabby chic, and you might pick up a some decorating ideas. ⊠ *1191 E. Duece of Clubs* ☎ *928/537–2755* ☉ *Closed Sun. and Mon.*

Sports & the Outdoors

FISHING ☾ **Fool Hollow Lake Recreational Area** (⊠ 2 mi north of U.S. 60 off AZ 260 ☎ 928/537–3680) is open year-round for camping, fishing, and boating. Set amid a piney 800 acres, the lake is stocked with rainbow trout, walleye, and bass, and the surrounding area provides wonderful opportunities for wildlife viewing. **Show Low Lake** (⊠ Show Low Lake Rd. ☎ 928/537–4126), south of town and 1 mi off AZ 260, holds the state record for the largest walleye catch and is well stocked with largemouth bass, bluegill, and catfish. Lucky anglers have pulled out 9-pound rainbow trout. Facilities include a bait shop, marina with boat

WHAT AN ODD NAME!

Yes, Show Low *is* an odd name for a town. Local legend has it that two partners, Clark and Cooley, homesteaded the surrounding 100,000 acres in 1870 but found themselves wanting to dissolve the partnership some years later after an argument. They decided to play cards, and the winner would buy out the loser. On the last hand of the night, Cooley was a point behind when Clark allegedly offered "show low and you win." Cooley cut the deck and came up with the deuce of clubs, thereby winning the game and the land. Part of the partners' then-ranch is now the town of Show Low, and the main drag through town is called Deuce of Clubs.

rentals, and campsites with bathrooms and showers. **Troutback Flyfishing** (⌖ Box 864, Show Low 85902 ☎ 928/532–3474 or 800/903–4092 ⊕ www.troutback.com) has access to some of the most scenic lakes and private waters in the region. From April through October, this fishing guide company specializes in fly-fishing instruction, guided walk-wades, and float tube and boating trips.

GOLF **Bison Golf & Country Club** (✉ 860 N. 36th Dr., at AZ 260 ☎ 928/537–4564) is a par-70 course with a back nine in the pines and a front nine in a more open meadow setting. Need to practice driving or putting? You can do it here. The course is open year-round. **Silver Creek Golf Club**

Fodor'sChoice ★
(✉ 2051 Silver Lake Blvd. ☎ 928/537–2744 ⊕ www.silvercreekgolfclub. com), 5 mi east of town on U.S. 60, then 7½ mi north on Bourdon Ranch Road, is an 18-hole championship golf course. Voted by the PGA as one of the top 10 golf courses in Arizona, it's also one of the more affordable. Given its lower elevation, this course is usually a few degrees warmer than Show Low and stays open year-round. Greens fees change seasonally; call for details.

Where to Stay & Eat

$–$$$$ ✕ **Native New Yorker.** If you want to catch your favorite sporting event, this restaurant has eight TVs in the dining room and nine TVs in the adjacent sports bar. Famous for their wings, the soup in the sourdough bread bowl is good, too. A steak dinner runs about $33. ✉ *391 W. Deuce of Clubs* ☎ *928/532–5100* ▭ *AE, D, MC, V* ☉ *Daily 11 AM–10 PM.*

¢–$$ ✕ **High in the Pines Deli.** Locals flock to this deli and coffeehouse for tasty specialty sandwiches—the roasted pork tenderloin sandwich is out of this world. European-style charcuterie boards include selections of pâtés, meats, and cheeses served with a fresh baguette. On a cold day, try the Show Low hot chocolate or steaming homemade soups. Box lunches are available. ✉ *1191 E. Hall St.* ☎ *928/537–1453* ▭ *AE, D, MC, V* ☉ *Closed Sun. No dinner.*

★ ¢–$$ ✕ **Licano's Mexican Food and Steakhouse.** Licano's serves what locals claim are the best enchiladas on the mountain, along with prime rib and lobster tail. The spacious lounge, with a weekday happy hour 4:30–6:30, stays open to 9:30 nightly. ✉ *573 W. Deuce of Clubs* ☎ *928/537–8220* ▭ *AE, D, DC, MC, V.*

$ 🏨 **Best Western Paint Pony Lodge.** Spacious rooms have wood accents and picture windows overlooking Arizona's pine-studded high country. Suites and some rooms include fireplaces, and use of an off-property gym is free for hotel guests. ✉ *581 W. Deuce of Clubs, 85901* ☎ *928/537–5773* ⊕ *www.bestwestern.com* ⥱ *46 rooms, 4 suites* ⌂ *Some microwaves, refrigerators, cable TV, Wi-Fi, some pets allowed (fee), no-smoking rooms* ▭ *AE, D, DC, MC, V* ⅋ *CP.*

¢–$ 🏨 **KC Motel.** Victorian decor, including four-poster beds, and large rooms make this a not-so-typical motel. All rooms have cable TV and refrigerators. ✉ *60 W. Deuce of Clubs, 85901* ☎ *928/537–4433 or 800/531–7152* ⥱ *37 rooms* ⌂ *Refrigerators, cable TV, in-room broadband, hot tub* ▭ *AE, D, DC, MC, V* ⅋ *CP.*

Pinetop-Lakeside

▶ ❸ *15 mi southeast of Show Low on AZ 260.*

At 7,200 feet, the community of Pinetop-Lakeside borders the world's largest stand of ponderosa pine. Two towns, Pinetop and Lakeside, were incorporated in 1984 to form this municipality—although they still retain separate post offices. The modest year-round population is 4,200, but in summer months it can jump as high as 30,000. Once popular only with the retirement and summer-home set, the city now lures thousands of "flatlanders" up from the Valley of the Sun with its gorgeous scenery, excellent multiuse trails, premier golf courses, and temperatures rarely exceeding 85°F. The main drag is known as both AZ 260 and White Mountain Boulevard.

Sports & the Outdoors

BICYCLING & HIKING

Ranked No. 3 in the country's "Top Ten Trail Towns" by the American Hiking Society, Pinetop-Lakeside is the primary trailhead for the White Mountains Trails System, roughly 200 mi of interconnecting multiuse loop trails spanning the White Mountains. All these trails are open to mountain bikers, horseback riders, and hikers.

Half a mile off AZ 260 on Woodland Road, **Big Springs Environmental Study Area** is a ½-mi loop trail that wanders by riparian meadows, two streams, and a spring-fed pond. A series of educational signs is devoted to the surrounding flora and fauna. The trailhead for **Country Club Trail** is at the junction of Forest Service roads 182 and 185; these 3½ mi of moderate-difficulty mountain-biking and hiking trails can be spiced up by following the spur-trail to the top of Pat Mullen Mountain and back. The well-traveled and very easy **Mogollon Rim Interpretive Trail** follows a small part of the 19th-century **Crook Trail** along the Mogollon Rim; the ¼-mi path, with a trailhead just west of the Pinetop-Lakeside city limits, is well marked with placards describing local wildlife and geography. The 8-mi **Panorama Trail**, rated moderate, affords astonishing views from the top of extinct double volcanoes known as the Twin Knolls and passes though a portion of designated wildlife habitat area; the trailhead is 6 mi east on Porter Mountain Road, off AZ 260.

You can get trail brochures or other information from the **Apache-Sitgreaves National Forest** (✉ Lakeside Ranger Station, 2022 W. White Mountain Blvd., Lakeside 85929 ☎ 928/368–5111 ⊕ www.fs.fed.us/r3/asnf), including a $2 booklet on the White Mountains Trail System.

FISHING

East of Pinetop-Lakeside and 9 mi south of AZ 260, 260-acre **Hawley Lake** (✉ AZ 473, Hawley Lake ☎ 928/338–4385) sits on Apache territory and yields mostly rainbow trout; rental boats are available in the marina. Tribal permits are required for all recreational activities: contact **Tribal Game and Fish** for details. **Bob's Bang Room Sporting Goods & Pawn Shop** (✉ 3973 AZ 260, Lakeside ☎ 928/368–5040 ⊕ www.bobsbangroom.com) deals in hunting, archery, and pawned fishing equipment.

GOLF **Pinetop Lakes Golf & Country Club** (⊠ 4643 Buck Springs Rd., Pinetop ☎ 928/369–4184 ⊕ www.pinetoplakesgolf.com) has fewer trees than other area courses, but it offers several water hazards by way of compensation. The shorter course is wonderful for public play. The club has a driving range, putting greens, and tennis courts, not to mention a restaurant and lounge. It's open April to October. Greens fees range from $26 to $36 for 18 holes.

HORSEBACK RIDING **Porter Mountain Stables** (⊠ 4048 Porter Mountain Rd., Lakeside ☎ 928/368–5306) offers one-hour to all-day horseback trips in the summer.

SKIING & SNOWBOARDING The **Skier's Edge** (⊠ 560 W. White Mountain Blvd., Pinetop ☎ 928/367–6200 or 800/231–3831 ⊕ www.skiersedgepinetop.com) has cross-country and downhill skis as well as snowboards and boots. At the same location, Paradise Creek Anglers sells fly-fishing and hiking supplies. **Snowriders** (⊠ 857 E. White Mountain Blvd., Pinetop ☎ 928/367–3373 ⊕ www.azsnowriders.com) sells and rents skis and snowboards and offers special seasonal rental packages for children 12 and under. It's open December through March 15, weather permitting.

Where to Stay & Eat

★ $$–$$$$ ✕ **Christmas Tree.** Year-round festive lights and displays of colorful ornaments inside this restaurant highlight a theme that's been at work here since 1977. Chicken and dumplings are the house specialty, but beef Stroganoff and honey duck served with fried apples are also highly recommended. Steaks, chops, lamb, and seafood are also available, as well as a children's menu. Save room for a piece of the Christmas Tree's famous fresh-baked fruit cobbler or Texas sheet cake à la mode. Reservations are a good idea. ⊠ *455 N. Woodland Rd., near AZ 260, Lakeside* ☎ *928/367–3107* ▤ *D, MC, V* ☉ *Closed 3rd wk in Oct.–Thanksgiving. Closed Mon. and Tues. No lunch.*

$$–$$$$ ✕ **Tuscan Glass.** With white tablecloths and red linen napkins, this is about as upscale as Pinetop gets, even though it's in a small shopping mall. Two wine bars serve 40 wines, and the menu varies from sandwiches to roast duck, or splurge on filet mignon for about $37. ⊠ *1450 E. White Mountain Blvd.* ☎ *928/367–5456* ▤ *AE, D, MC, V.*

¢–$$ ✕ **Los Corrales.** Bright yellows and oranges make for a cheerful family-style eatery. With Mexican seafood dishes such as *Camarones a la Crema* (shrimp and mushrooms in cream sauce) and luncheon specials, locals stop by often. Dessert specialties include fried ice cream and apple chimichanga. A small bar serves drinks. ⊠ *845 E. White Mountain Blvd.* ☎ *928/367–5585* ▤ *AE, D, DC, MC V.*

$$–$$$ 🏨 **Northwoods Resort.** Each of the 14 cabins at this mountain retreat has its own covered porch and barbecue. Inside, natural wood paneling, brick fireplaces, and wall-to-wall carpeting add to the homey feel. Full electric kitchens have full-size refrigerators, ovens, microwave ovens, and adjacent dinette sets. Proprietors here keep their promise to provide "meticulously maintained" accommodations, all the way down to a daily replenishment of firewood. The honeymoon cabin features an indoor spa, and the two-story cabins can accommodate up to 16 people. ⊠ *AZ 260, Milepost 352* ⊲ *Box 397N, Pinetop 85935* ☎ *928/367–2966 or 800/813–2966* 🖷 *928/367–2969* ⊕ *www.*

northwoodsaz.com ⇦ *14 cabins* ♨ *BBQs, kitchens, cable TV, outdoor hot tub, volleyball, playground, laundry facilities; no a/c, no smoking* ⊟ *D, MC, V.*

$–$$$ ⊡ **Whispering Pines Resort.** These well-maintained cabins have fireplaces (wood or natural gas), grills, and double sofa beds. One-, two-, and three-bedroom units—some with second bathrooms—have either handsome knotty-pine or more modern wood-panel interiors. The four log cabins, three of them studio units, have that cabiny-hideaway vibe. Couples may want to request one of the alpine suites, with whirlpool tubs. On 12 acres bordering the Apache-Sitgreaves National Forest, cabins are in walking distance of Woodland Lake and Walnut Creek. There's a four-night minimum in summer and during holidays. ⊠ *AZ 260, just beyond Milepost 352* ⬡ *Box 1043, Pinetop 85935* ☎ *928/367–4386 or 800/840–3867* ⊜ *928/367–3702* ⊕ *www.whisperingpinesaz.com* ⇦ *38 cabins* ♨ *Some in-room hot tubs, some kitchens, some kitchenettes, cable TV, hot tub, laundry facilities, some pets allowed (fee), no-smoking rooms; no a/c* ⊟ *AE, D, MC, V.*

$$ ⊡ **Pinetop Country B&B and Cottages.** This inn, on 4 acres surrounded by tall ponderosa pines, has three large guest rooms plus three lakeside cottages. A common room has a cozy fireplace, a library, and an extensive video selection; a 1950s-style game room is loaded with diversions, including a jukebox, pool table, large-screen TV, and Pac-Man game. Choose from 10 items at breakfast; homemade desserts are served in the evening. Some rooms have fireplaces and small balconies. ⊠ *2444 Jan La., Pinetop 85935* ☎ *928/367–0479 or 888/521–5044* ⊜ *928/367–0479* ⊕ *www.pinetopcountry.com* ⇦ *3 rooms, 3 cottages* ♨ *Refrigerators, cable TV, bicycles, billiards, recreation room, no-smoking rooms; no a/c* ⊟ *MC, V* ⦿ *BP.*

$–$$ ⊡ **Hon-Dah Resort Casino and Conference Center.** Stuffed high-country creatures atop a mountain of boulders welcome you to Apache Tribe–operated Hon Dah. The main draw is the casino, with hundreds of slot machines, live poker and blackjack, and weekend entertainment. Large rooms all have coffeemakers and wet bars. A high-roof atrium holds the pool and hot tub. The Indian Pine Restaurant serves three daily meals, and a small gift shop sells local Apache crafts. ⊠ *777 AZ 260, Pinetop 85935* ☎ *928/369–0299 or 800/929–8744* ⊜ *928/369–7405* ⊕ *www.hon-dah.com* ⇦ *126 rooms, 2 suites* ♨ *Restaurant, refrigerators, cable TV, indoor pool, hot tub, sauna, 2 bars, casino, nightclub, shop, meeting rooms, no-smoking rooms* ⊟ *AE, D, DC, MC, V.*

Nightlife

Charlie Clark's Steakhouse (⊠ 1701 E. White Mountain Blvd., Pinetop ☎ 928/367–4900) has been around since 1938; the cook knows how to produce a mouthwatering prime rib and other specialties over mesquite. The lounge, with a full bar, pool tables, and a bouncing jukebox, stays open until 1 AM on weekends, which is about as late as nightlife lasts in Pinetop. The **Orchard** (⊠ 1701 E. White Mountain Rd. Pinetop ☎ 928/367–4900), outside in a real apple orchard, has appetizers and a full bar from May to October.

Shopping

Antique Mercantile Company (✉ 2106 W. White Mountain Blvd., Lakeside ☎ 928/368–9090) has century-old collectibles ranging from first-edition law encyclopedias to working Victrolas. Upscale-quality glass, china, furniture, military items, and vintage sports and camera equipment are all for sale. In winter it's open by appointment only. The log-cabin **Harvest Moon Antiques** (✉ 392 W. White Mountain Blvd., Pinetop ☎ 928/367–6973), open Memorial Day through Thanksgiving weekend, specializes in Old West relics, ranging from buckskins and Apache wares to old guns and U.S. Cavalry items. This is an excellent place to find affordable Indian jewelry and Navajo rugs. **Orchard Antiques** (✉ 1664 W. White Mountain Blvd., Lakeside ☎ 928/368–6563), open from April to October and on all major holidays, is a reliable purveyor of high-quality furniture, glass, china, and sterling and deals in some quilts and vintage clothing.

5

Sunrise Park Resort

🕐 **❹** *17 mi southeast of McNary, 7 mi south of AZ 260 on AZ 273.*

In winter and early spring, skiers and other snow lovers flock to this ski area. There's plenty more than downhill and cross-country skiing here, including snowboarding, snowmobiling, snowshoeing, ice-fishing, and sleigh rides. The resort has 10 lifts and 65 trails on three mountains rising to 11,000 feet. Eighty percent of the downhill runs are for beginning or intermediate skiers, there's a "ski-wee" hill for youngsters, and many less-intense trails begin at the top so skiers of varying skill levels can enjoy riding the chairlifts together. The Sunrise Express high-speed chairlift anchors the 10 lifts and has an uphill skier capacity of 16,000 skiers per hour. One-day lift tickets are $41. Sunrise's Snowboard Park features jumps of all difficulty levels and its own sound system. Restricted to snowboarders only, the area can support enthusiasts' quests to "get a great ollie, hit the kicker, and go big," while simultaneously lessening tension on the hill between boarders and skiers. Cross-country skiers enjoy 13½ mi of interconnecting trails. You can rent equipment at the ski shop. In summer a marina is open for boat rentals on Sunrise Lake. ✉ *AZ 273, 7 mi south of AZ 260* 📪 *Box 117, Greer 85927* ☎ *928/735–7669, 800/772–7669 hotel reservations and snow reports* ⊕ *www.sunriseskipark.com* 🖃 *AE, D, MC, V.*

Where to Stay

$–$$ 🏨 **Sunrise Park Lodge.** Catering to those who want to be as close as possible to the lifts, this hotel runs a shuttle to the slopes every half hour, has comfortable rooms with ski racks, and offers lodging and lift-ticket packages. The VIP Suite, with its wet bar, refrigerator, microwave oven, and hot tub, comes with two lift tickets that grant the holders line-cutting privileges on the slopes. In summer you can enjoy boating on Sunrise Lake, "3-D" archery, scenic chairlift rides, horseback riding, and mountain biking on designated trails. Call ahead because the lodge closes from end of ski season until Memorial Day weekend in spring and then closes again in fall from mid-October until first heavy snowfall. ✉ *AZ 273, 7 mi south of AZ 260* ☎ *Box 117, Greer 85927* ☎ *928/735–7669 or 800/772–7669* 🖨 *928/735–7315* 🌐 *www. sunriseskipark.com* 🛏 *96 rooms, 1 suite* 🍴 *2 restaurants, some in-room hot tubs, some microwaves, some refrigerators, cable TV, indoor pool, lake, outdoor hot tub, sauna, boating, marina, volleyball, ski shop, lounge, recreation room, meeting rooms, no-smoking rooms; no a/c* 🖃 *AE, D, DC, MC, V.*

Greer

★ ❺ *35 mi southeast of Pinetop-Lakeside and 15 mi southwest of Eagar on AZ 260, 8 mi east of AZ 273 turnoff, via AZ 373 south.*

The charming community of Greer sits just south of AZ 260 among pine, spruce, willow, and aspen on the banks of the Little Colorado River. At an elevation of 8,500 feet, this portion of gently sloping national forest land is covered with meadows and reservoirs and is dominated by 11,590-foot Baldy Peak. Much of the surrounding area remains under the control of the Apache tribe, so visitors must take care to respect Apache law and land. AZ 373 is also Greer's "Main Street," which winds through the village and crosses the Little Colorado River, eventually coming to a dead end. It's affectionately called the Road to Nowhere.

Listed on the National Register of Historic Places, the **Butterfly Lodge Museum** was built as a hunting lodge in 1914 by John Butler, the husband of "Aunt Molly" (of Molly Butler Lodge fame), for author James Willard Schultz and his artist son, Lone Wolf, a prolific painter of Indian and Western scenes. There's a small gift shop. In spring and summer take time to watch the surrounding meadow come to life with beautiful butterflies, from which the lodge got its name. ✉ *AZ 373 at CR 1126* ☎ *928/735–7514* 🌐 *www.wmonline.com/butterflylodge.htm* 🎫 *$2* 🕐 *Memorial Day–Labor Day, Fri.–Sun. 10–5.*

Sports & the Outdoors

The **Tin Star Trading Post** (✉ 38940 AZ 373 ☎ 928/735–7540) sells sleds in winter and tackle the rest of the year. Fishing licenses, groceries, and camping supplies are also for sale.

FISHING The three Greer Lakes are actually the Bunch, River, and Tunnel reservoirs. Bait and fly-fishing options are scenic and plentiful, and there are several places to launch a boat. Winding through Greer, the Little Colorado River's West Fork is well stocked with brookies and rainbows and has 23 mi of fishable waters.

HIKING The difficult but accessible **Mount Baldy Trail** begins at **Sheeps Crossing,** southwest of Greer on AZ 273. In just under 8 mi (one-way), the trail climbs the northern flank of 11,590-foot Mount Baldy, the second-highest peak in Arizona. Note that the summit of Baldy is on the White Mountain Apache Reservation. Considered sacred land, this final ¼ mi is off-limits to non-Apaches. The boundary is clearly marked; please respect it, regardless of how much you might wish to continue to the peak.

SKIING Cross-country skiers find Greer an ideally situated hub for some of the mountain's best trails. About 2½ mi west of AZ 373 on AZ 260, a trailhead marks the starting point for the **Pole Knoll Trail System**, nearly 30 mi of well-marked, groomed cross-country trails interlacing through the Apache Sitgreaves National Forest and color-coded by experience level. Trail maps are available from the **Apache-Sitgreaves National Forest** (⊠ Springerville Ranger District, 165 S. Mountain Ave., Springerville 85938 ☎ 928/333–4372 ⊕ www.fs.fed.us/r3/asnf).

Where to Stay & Eat

¢–$$ ✕ **Rendezvous Diner.** Previous reincarnations of this cozy, colorful eatery include a family home as well as Greer's main post office. Rendezvous Diner has earned a reputation for serving up some of Greer's tastiest dishes, not to mention the area's best hot spiced cider. Of particular note are the pineapple teriyaki and green-chile burgers, 8-ounce sirloin steak with shrimp, and generous portions of homemade desserts. It's open year-round for breakfast and lunch, with dinner served Thursday through Sunday. ⊠ *117 Main St.* ☎ *928/735–7483* ⊟ *MC, V* ⊘ *Closed Tues.*

Fodor'sChoice ★

¢–$ ✕ **Greer Mountain Resort Country Cafe.** This plant-hung diner-café is open from 7 AM to 3 PM. Grab a seat by the fireplace and sample the homemade ranch beans, a signature grilled-cheese sandwich with green chiles and tomato, or fresh-baked cobbler. ⊠ *AZ 373, 1½ mi south of AZ 260* ☎ *928/735–7560* ⊟ *MC, V* ⊘ *Closed Wed. No dinner.*

¢–$ ✕▦ **Molly Butler Lodge.** Colorful quilts and wood furnishings fill the comfortable rooms at Arizona's oldest lodge. There are no phones or TVs in the rooms, but both are available in the main lodge. The menu in the Molly Butler Lodge restaurant ($–$$) is divided between entrées "upstream" (sautéed scallops, halibut, trout amandine) and "downstream" (prime rib au jus, "hot dang" chili), but it's the aged steaks that draw locals. Enjoy sweeping views of Greer's pristine wilderness amid the lodge's cozy, rustic decor, with kerosene lamps on the tables and mounted hunting trophies on the walls. There's a two-night minimum. ⊠ *109 Main St., 85927* ☎ *928/735–7226* ⊕ *www.mollybutlerlodge.com* ➥ *17 rooms* ⚬ *Bar, video game room, some pets allowed (fee); no a/c, no room phones, no room TVs* ⊟ *AE, D, MC, V.*

★ $$–$$$$ ▦ **Greer Lodge and Spa.** Perfect for those who want luxury with their outdoor experience, this three-story lodge originally built in 1948 as a church camp underwent a $1.8 million renovation in 2004. Guests can enjoy fly-fishing in three private trout ponds or fish along the Little Colorado River, and a dining room and bar, plus a spa, make it unnecessary to leave the property—but hiking, cross-country skiing, and opportunities for wildlife-viewing are close by. Children under 16 are welcomed in the cabins but not allowed in the lodge rooms. A three-day "girls getaway" package remakes the idea of the slumber party, with fly-fishing lessons, guided hikes, wine, and massages. ⊠ *44 Main St.* ⊕ *Box 244, 85927* ☎ *928/735–7216* ⊕ *www.greerlodgeaz.com* ➥ *10 rooms, 12 cabins* ⚬ *Restaurant, spa, fishing, bar; no a/c in some rooms, no TV in some rooms* ⊟ *AE, D, DC, MC, V* ⦿ *EP.*

$$–$$$$ ▦ **White Mountain Lodge.** On the banks of the Little Colorado River, this charming lodge is the oldest building in Greer. The lodge holds three suites and six cabins with kitchens/kitchenettes and gas fireplaces; most have whirlpool tubs. Wildlife-watching in Greer Meadow is a popular

pastime, as is just sitting on a bench next to the beaver pond. ✉ *140 Main St.* ☎ *928/735–7568 or 888/493–7568* 🖷 *928/735–7498* ⊕ *www. wmlodge.com* ⇆ *3 suites, 6 cabins* ⚑ *Some in-room hot tubs, kitchens, kitchenettes, satellite TV, VCRs, hiking; no a/c, no smoking* ▭ *AE, D, DC, MC, V* ¶◎¶ *BP.*

$$$ ▥ **Red Setter Inn.** From the vaulted ceiling in the breakfast room to the
Fodor'sChoice player piano in the gathering room, this hand-hewn-log inn is rich in
★ detail. Some rooms have fireplaces and private decks; the cottage rooms share a full kitchen. A spacious deck has Adirondack chairs and permits excellent wildlife viewing—don't be surprised to see mountain lions or black bear around the stream below, stopping to have a drink or to catch unsuspecting trout. Weekend guests who set out to hike or fish during the day are sent off with sack lunches. Weekends, there's a two-night minimum stay (three nights over holidays). If you're traveling with a group, consider the four-bedroom cottage ($600 a night). ✉ *8 Main St.* ⌂ *Box 133, 85927* ☎ *928/735–7441 or 888/994–7337* 🖷 *928/735–7425* ⊕ *www.redsetterinn.com* ⇆ *12 rooms, 3 cottages* ⚑ *Some in-room hot tubs, some kitchens, some in-room VCRs, fishing, hiking, cross-country skiing, recreation room; no a/c, no room phones, no TV in some rooms, no kids under 16, no smoking* ▭ *AE, D, MC, V* ¶◎¶ *BP.*

$–$$$ ▥ **Greer Mountain Resort.** Budget travelers and families appreciate these cabin-style accommodations. Each unit is different, but most can sleep up to six people and contain either a fireplace or a gas- or wood-burning stove. The smallest, one-bedroom, knotty-pine units have no fireplaces, but they're reasonably priced and good for couples. You may want to enjoy breakfast or lunch at the resort's roadside restaurant, or you can whip up your own feast in the fully equipped kitchens. ✉ *AZ 373, 1½ mi south of AZ 260* ⌂ *Box 145, Greer 85927* ☎☎ *928/735–7560* ⊕ *www.greermountainresort.com* ⇆ *8 units* ⚑ *Kitchens; no a/c, no room TVs* ▭ *MC, V.*

CAMPING ⚠ **Rolfe C. Hoyer Campgrounds.** Nestled among pristine stands of pon-
¢ derosa pine, these choice campsites in the Apache-Sitgreaves National Forest have no utility hookups but are proximate to equipment rentals, gas, groceries, and restaurants in the town of Greer. A $9 surcharge (per booking, not per night) is added by the company that handles the reservations. The abundant local wildlife is one of this site's draws, but remember to secure campsites from foraging four-legged friends. There's a $3 fee to use the dump stations or to take a shower. ✉ *AZ 373* ☎ *928/333–4372 or 877/444–6777* ⊕ *www.reserveusa.com* ⬚ *$14* ⇆ *100 sites* ⚑ *Grills, flush toilets, dump station, drinking water, showers, fire pits, picnic tables* ⊗ *Open May 15–Oct. 15.*

Nightlife

Tiny Greer's nightlife can be found in the bar and lounge of the **Molly Butler Lodge** (✉ 109 Main St. ☎ 928/735–7226), where you can listen to vintage tunes on the jukebox, sink into a cozy seat near the fireplace, play an arcade game, or challenge a local to a game of pool or darts.

CLOSE UP

The Writing on the Wall

THE ROCK ART OF EARLY NATIVE AMERICANS is carved or painted on basalt boulders, on canyon walls, and on the underside of overhangs throughout eastern Arizona. Designs pecked or scratched into the stone are called petroglyphs; those that are painted on the surface are pictographs. Few pictographs remain because of the deleterious effects of weathering, but the more durable petroglyphs number in the thousands. No one knows the exact meaning of these signs, and interpretations vary from use in shaman or hunting rituals to clan signs, maps, or even indications of visits by extra-terrestrials.

It's just as difficult to date a "glyph" as it is to understand it. Archaeologists try to determine a general time frame by judging the style, the date of the ruins and pottery in the vicinity, the amount of patination (formation of minerals) on the design, or the superimposition of newer images on top of older ones. Most of eastern Arizona's rock art is estimated to be at least 1,000 years old, and many of the glyphs were created even earlier.

Some glyphs depict animals like big horn sheep, deer, bear, and mountain lions; others are geometric patterns. The most unusual are the anthropomorphs, strange humanlike figures with elaborate headdresses. A concentric circle is a common design. A few of these circles served as solstice signs, indicating summer and winter solstice and other important dates. At a certain time in the year, when the angle of the sun is just right, a shaft of light shines through a crack in a nearby rock, illuminating the center of the circle. Archaeologists believe these solar calendars helped determine the time for ceremonies and planting. Many solstice signs are in remote regions, but you can visit the Petrified Forest National Park around June 20 to see a concentric circle illuminated during the summer solstice. The glyph, reached by paved trail just a few hundred yards from the parking area, is visible year-round, but a finger of light shines directly in the center during the week of the solstice. The phenomenon occurs at 9 AM, a reasonable hour for looking at the calendar.

Damaged by vandalism, many rock-art sites are not open to the public, but Hieroglyphic Point in Salt River Canyon, Five-Mile Canyon in Snowflake, Lyman Lake State Park, and Petrified Forest National Park are all good spots to view petroglyphs. Do not touch petroglyphs or pictographs—the oils from your hands can cause damage to the image.

—Janet Webb Farnsworth

Lyman Lake State Park

❻ *18 mi north of Springerville on U.S. 180/191, 55 mi southeast of National Park on U.S. 180.*

Created in 1915, when the Little Colorado River was dammed for irrigation purposes, the 3-mi-long **Lyman Lake** reservoir is popular for boating, waterskiing (a permit is required for the exclusive waterskiing course on the dam end), windsurfing, and sailing. Designated swimming beaches accommodate those who prefer to stick closer to shore.

A buoyed-off "no-wake" area at the lake's west end ensures that fishing efforts there won't be disturbed by passing speedboats and water-skiers. Bait your hook for largemouth bass as well as the good-size (6 to 8 pounds) channel catfish that can be pulled up from May to August. Locals recommend early spring for walleye—the tastiest catch of all; Lyman Lake also has lots of crawfish, aka "poor man's shrimp."

Between early May and late October, ranger-led pontoon-boat tours go across Lyman Lake to the **Ultimate Petroglyph Trail,** where some of the state's most wondrous and accessible Native American rock art lies chiseled in basalt. Check out the Rattlesnake Point Pueblo site, which dates to the 14th century and has three rooms and a kiva.

Other attractions in the 1,200-acre park include a volleyball court, horseshoe pits, and a water-ski slalom course. There's also a campground, along with several log cabins and yurts for rent, and a camping supply and boat rental store, but no gasoline for cars is sold here. In nearby St. Johns, there are lodging, restaurants, gasoline, and an airfield and fuel for planes. ✉ *U.S. 180/191, 18 mi north of Springerville/Eagar* ✆ *Box 1428, St. Johns 85936* ☎ *928/337–4441* ⊕ *www.pr.state.az.us.*

EN ROUTE The junction of U.S. 180/191 and U.S. 60, just north of Springerville, is the perfect jumping-off spot for a driving tour of the **Springerville Volcanic Field.** On the southern edge of the Colorado Plateau, it covers a total area larger than the state of Rhode Island and is spread across a high-elevation plain similar to the Tibetan Plateau. Six miles north of Springerville on U.S. 180/191 are sweeping westward views of the **Twin Knolls**—double volcanoes that erupted twice here about 700,000 years ago. As you travel west on U.S. 60, Green's Peak Road and various south-winding Forest Service roads make for a leisurely, hour-long drive past **St. Peter's Dome** and a stop for impressive views from **Green's Peak,** the topographic high point of the Springerville Field. A free detailed driving-tour brochure of the Springerville Volcanic Field is available from the **Springerville-Eagar Regional Chamber of Commerce** (✉ 318 Main St. ✆ Box 31, Springerville 85938 ☎ 928/333–2123).

Springerville-Eagar

❼ *45 mi east of Pinetop-Lakeside on AZ 260, 67 mi southeast of Petrified Forest National Park on U.S. 180.*

Sister cities Springerville and Eagar are tucked into a circular, high mountain basin christened "Valle Redondo," or Round Valley, by early Basque settlers of the late 1800s. Nestled on the back side of massive 10,912-foot Escudilla Mountain, this self-proclaimed "Gateway to the White Mountains" sits in a different climate belt from nearby Greer and Sunrise Resort; insulated by its unique geography, Springerville-Eagar has markedly less severe winter temperatures and lighter snowfall than neighboring mountain towns. Geographically, the Round Valley also served as a unique Old West haven for the lawless—a great place to conceal stolen cattle and hide out for a while. Butch Cassidy, the Clantons, and the Smith gang all spent time here. So did the late John Wayne, whose former 26-Bar Ranch lies just west of Eagar off AZ 260.

The Round Valley is the favorite of skiers in the know, who appreciate the location as they commute to the lifts at Sunrise with the sun always at their back—important when you consider the glare off those blanketed snowscapes between the resort and Pinetop-Lakeside—and the dramatically lighter traffic on this less-icy stretch of AZ 260.

The 14½-acre **Casa Malpais Archaeological Park** pueblo complex is piquing the interest of a growing number of anthropologists and astronomers. The "House of the Badlands" (a sobriquet for the rough-textured ground's effect on bare feet) has a series of narrow terraces lining eroded edges of basalt (hardened lava flow) cliff, as well as an extensive system of subterranean rooms nestled within Earth's fissures underneath. Strategically designed gateways in the walls of the complex allow streams of sunlight to precisely illuminate significant petroglyphs prior to the setting equinox or solstice sun. Casa Malpais's Great Kiva (any kiva over 30 feet is considered great) is square cornered instead of round, consistent with Ancestral Puebloan heritage. Some archaeologists believe the pueblo served as a regional ceremonial center for the Mogollon people. Both Hopi and Zuni tribes trace their history to Casa Malpais. The site has a small museum in town, with artifacts from the Casa Malpais ruin, a butterfly collection, and items from early day Springerville; a small gift shop offers Indian jewelry and local history books. The site itself may only be visited on a tour; these leave from the museum at 9, 11, and 2. ⊠ *318 E. Main St., Springerville* ☎ *928/333–5375* ⊠ *$7* ☉ *Museum open daily 8 AM–4 PM.*

This **Little House Museum** has a collection of local pioneer and ranching memorabilia, but it's the mesmerizing tones from a rare collection of automatic musical instruments that you remember—that, and the museum's colorful curator, Wink Crigler, with her lore of this region's lively past. Tours to archaeological digs and petroglyphs are available by appointment. To reach the ranch, go 10 mi southwest of Eagar on AZ 260, turn south onto South Fork Road, and go 3 mi. ⊠ *X Diamond Ranch, S. Fork Rd., 10 mi southwest of Eagar* ☎ *928/333–2286* ⊕ *www. xdiamondranch.com* ⊠ *$7* ☉ *By reservation only.*

Fodor's Choice
★

The **Renée Cushman Art Collection Museum** is open to the public only by special appointment, but a visit is worth the effort. Renée Cushman's extensive collection of objets d'art—some acquired on her travels, some collected with the accumulated resources of three wealthy husbands, some willed to her by her artistic father—is administered by the Church of Latter-day Saints. Her treasure includes a Rembrandt engraving, Tiepolo pen-and-inks, and an impressive collection of European antiques, some dating back to the 15th century. Call the **Springerville-Eagar Regional Chamber of Commerce** (☎ 928/333–2123) to arrange your visit.

Sports & the Outdoors

For your mountain-sport needs the **Sweat Shop** (⊠ 74 N. Main St., Eagar ☎ 928/333–2950) rents skis, snowboards, and mountain bikes.

FISHING **Becker Lake** (⊠ U.S. 60, 2 mi northwest of Springerville, Becker Lake ☎ 928/367–4281) is a "specialty lake" for trout fishing; call for seasonal bait requirements. **Big Lake** (⊠ AZ 273, 24 mi south of AZ 260, Big Lake ☎ 928/735–7313), known to many as the "queen of all trout lakes," is stocked each spring and fall with rainbow, brook, and cutthroat trout. **Nelson Reservoir** (⊠ U.S. 191, Nutrioso), between Springerville-Eagar and Alpine, is well stocked with rainbow, brown, and brook trout. The **Speckled Trout** (⊠ 224 E. Main St., Springerville ☎ 928/333–0852 ⊕ www.cybertrails.com/~cltrout) offers fishing guide services and sells Orvis-licensed fly-fishing equipment. A small gift shop features books, linens, and windchimes, along with nonalcoholic drinks like espresso and fruit smoothies. **Sport Shack** (⊠ 329 E. Main St., Springerville ☎ 928/333–2222) sells camping equipment, fishing tackle, and hunting and fishing licenses. **Troutback** (⌂ Box 864, Show Low 85901 ☎ 928/532–3474 ⊕ www.troutback.com) is a fly-fishing guide service that will create half- or full-day fishing trips for novices and seasoned anglers alike throughout the White Mountains. Equipment, including boats, waders, fly rods and reels, and float tubes, is available for rent. **Western United Drug** (⊠ 105 E. Main St., Springerville ☎ 928/333–4321) stays open 365 days a year and has a well-stocked sporting-goods and outdoor-equipment section.

Where to Stay & Eat

¢–$$ ✕ **Booga Reds.** The delicious home-style cooking, such as fish-and-chips and roast beef dinners, is worth a stop. Should your palate demand something spicier, try one of the many Mexican dishes—the enchiladas are wonderful. Save room for the daily fruit or cream pie. Booga Reds opens at 5:30 AM for an early breakfast but closes relatively early—at 9 PM—so make your dinner an early one, too. ⊠ *521 E. Main St., Springerville* ☎ *928/333–2640* ⊟ *AE, MC, V.*

¢–$ ✕ **Java Blues.** Not your typical mountain eatery, Java Blues oozes a coffeehouse vibe with its overstuffed couches and stained-glass windows. Salads, soups, sandwiches, and a Greek Board—a variety of Greek meats and cheeses served with toasted baguette—are on the menu. Locals swear by the grilled roast beef and Brie sandwich and the grilled chicken and bacon chef salad. The restaurant opens early and closes early (weekdays 5 AM–6 PM, Saturday 7 AM–6 PM, and Sunday 7 AM–3 PM), so plan accordingly. Hear live bluegrass every Sunday afternoon. ⊠ *341 E. Main St., Springerville* ☎ *928/333–5282* ⊟ *MC, V.*

★ $$–$$$$ ▦ ✕ **Diamond & MLY Ranch.** This magnificent ranch has log cabins complete with porches, fireplaces, and full kitchens. Most sleep two to six, but the Butler House sleeps eight and has an atrium and private yard. Activities include fly-fishing, horseback riding, and tours of Little Bear archaeological site—in June you can even participate in the excavation yourself. Nonguests are welcome to participate in activities. ⊠ *South Fork Rd., 10 mi southwest of Eagar off AZ 260* ⌂ *Box 791, Springerville 85938* ☎ *928/333–2286* ☒ *928/333–5009* ⊕ *www.xdiamondranch.com* ⇖ *7 cabins ⌂ Kitchens, cable TV, fishing, hiking, horseback riding, no-smoking rooms; no a/c* ⊟ *AE, D, MC, V.*

★ **$–$$** ⊡ **Paisley Corner B & B.** From embossed-tin ceilings and stained-glass windows in the parlor to an authentic soda shop re-creation replete with Wurlitzer jukebox, not a detail has been overlooked in this restored 1910 colonial revival–style home. Rooms have antique beds and armoires, old-fashioned showers, and pull-chain commodes. Lush terry robes, wine, baskets of fresh fruit, and homemade munchies are included. The owners operate a coffeehouse 2 mi away where guests can have breakfast (included in the room price). ⊠ *287 N. Main St., Springerville 85938* ☎ *928/333–4665* ↪ *4 rooms* ⚏ *Cable TV; no smoking* ⊟ *MC, V* ⦿⦿⧄ *BP.*

$ ⊡ **Rode Inn.** Don't let the John Wayne motif scare you away—two cardboard figures of "The Duke" in full cowboy regalia are perched on a walkway above the lobby, and his photos decorate the walls; the rooms and service here are excellent. John Wayne did in fact stay here (when it was a Ramada Inn), and the room in which he slept has been converted into a plush suite. ⊠ *242 E. Main St., Springerville 85938* ☎ *928/ 333–4365* ⊕ *www.rodeinn.com* ↪ *60 rooms, 3 suites* ⚏ *Some microwaves, some refrigerators, cable TV, Wi-Fi, hot tub, laundry facilities, no-smoking rooms* ⊟ *AE, D, DC, MC, V* ⦿⦿⧄ *CP.*

¢**–$** ⊡ **Reed's Lodge.** It's an older motel, but a town favorite. The rooms of this mostly single-story motel have Western accents such as knotty-pine paneling and Navajo-print bedspreads. Perks include a recreation room with pool table, video games, and a pinball machine; movie rentals for a nominal fee; a gift shop; and complimentary bicycles. Proprietor Roxanne Knight will arrange visits for guests on a working cowboy-style (not dude) ranch, cattle drives, horseback adventures, four-wheel-drive tours, wildlife and petroglyph-viewing trips, or fossil-hunting expeditions. ⊠ *514 E. Main St., Springerville 85938* ☎ *928/333–4323 or 800/814–6451* ⨮ *928/333–5191* ⊕ *www.k5reeds.com* ↪ *45 rooms, 5 suites* ⚏ *Some microwaves, some refrigerators, cable TV, in-room VCRs, outdoor hot tub, recreation room* ⊟ *AE, D, DC, MC, V.*

CAMPING ⛰ **Big Lake Campgrounds.** On the southeast shore of Big Lake, 30 mi
¢ southwest of the Round Valley, these campgrounds are along the shore of a popular White Mountains summer destination. The lake supplies more than 300,000 trout to anglers each year. The civilized Rainbow site offers paved loops to its more developed units. The lake's smaller sites—Grayling, Cutthroat, and Brookchar—are less swank but within walking distance of Rainbow's amenities. The lake has a marina where boats and motors are available for rent. ⊠ *AZ 273, 24 mi south of AZ 260, Big Lake* ☎ *928/735–7313* ⨮ *$12–$22* ↪ *152 sites at Rainbow* ⚏ *Flush toilets, dump station, drinking water, showers, general store, swimming (lake)* ⊙ *Open mid-May–early Sept.*

Nightlife

Out on the edge of town, where U.S. 60/180 enters Springerville, the bright yellow **Main Street Station** (⊠ *262 W. Main St., Springerville* ☎ *928/333–5790*) is a cowboy bar with pool tables, darts, and live music and dancing on the weekends. Behind Booga Reds restaurant, **Tequila Red's** (⊠ *521 E. Main St., Springerville* ☎ *928/333–5036*) is a popular watering hole and the best place to catch a televised sporting event.

Shopping

K-5 Western Gallery (✉ Reed's Lodge, 514 E. Main St., Springerville ☎ 928/333–4323) sells wares created by White Mountains artists and local craftspeople, including those from nearby reservations. The gallery teems with Western-theme paintings, books on local history, wildlife, and cowboy poetry, and even John Wayne paperdolls.

Coronado Trail

Fodor'sChoice ★ *The 127-mi stretch of U.S. 191 from Springerville to Clifton.*

Surely one of the world's curviest roads, this steep, winding portion of U.S. 191 was referred to as the Devil's Highway in its prior incarnation as U.S. 666. More significantly, the route parallels the one allegedly followed more than 450 years ago by Spanish explorer Francisco Vásquez de Coronado on his search for the legendary Seven Cities of Cíbola, where the streets were reputedly paved with gold and jewels.

This 127-mi stretch of highway is renowned for the transitions of its spectacular scenery over a dramatic 5,000-foot elevation change—from rolling meadows to spruce- and ponderosa pine–covered mountains, down into the Sonoran Desert's piñon pine, grassland savannas, juniper stands, and cacti. A trip down the Coronado Trail crosses through Apache Sitgreaves National Forest, as well as the White Mountain Apache and San Carlos Indian reservations.

■ TIP→ Allow a good four hours to make the drive, more if you plan to stop and leisurely explore—which you should.

Pause at **Blue Vista,** perched on the edge of the Mogollon Rim, about 30 mi outside Alpine, to take in views of the Blue Range Mountains to the east and the succession of tiered valleys dropping some 4,000 feet back down into the Sonoran Desert. Still above the rim, this is one of your last opportunities to enjoy the blue spruce, ponderosa pine, and high-country mountain meadows.

About 17 mi south of Blue Vista, the Coronado Trail continues twisting and turning, eventually crossing under 8,786-foot **Rose Peak.** Named for the wild roses growing on its mountainside, Rose Peak is also home to a fire lookout tower from which peaks more than 100 mi away can be seen on a clear day. This is a great picnic-lunch stop.

After Rose Peak, enjoy the remaining scenery some 70 more mi until reaching the less scenic towns of Clifton and Morenci, homes to a massive Phelps Dodge copper mine. U.S. 191 then swings back west, links up with U.S. 70, and provides a fairly straight shot to Globe. ✉ *U.S. 191 between Springerville and Clifton.*

Alpine

❽ *27 mi south of Springerville-Eagar on U.S. 191.*

Known as the Alps of Arizona, the tiny, scenic village of Alpine promotes its winter recreation opportunities, but outdoors enthusiasts will find that the town, sitting on the lush plains of the San Francisco River, is an ideal base for hiking, fishing, and mountain-biking excursions during the warmer months. With summer cabins tucked in the pines, campgrounds, 11 lakes, and 200 mi of trout streams within a 30-mi radius, outdoor recreation drives this mountain burg.

Sports & the Outdoors

BICYCLING The 8-mi **Luna Lake Trail** (⊠ U.S. 180, Alpine), 5 mi east of U.S. 191, is a good two-hour cruise for beginning and intermediate cyclists. The trailhead is on the north side of the lake, before the campground entrance.

FISHING A divergence of the San Francisco River's headwaters, 80-acre **Luna Lake** (⊠ U.S. 180, Alpine), 5 mi east of U.S. 191, is well stocked with rainbow trout. **Tackle Shop** (☎ 928/339–4338), at the junction of U.S. 180 and 191, carries trout and fly-fishing supplies. **Arizona Mountain Flyfishing** (☎ 928/339–4829 ⊕ www.azmtflyfishing.com) guides anglers to top fishing streams and teaches novices.

GOLF **Alpine Country Club** (⊠ 58 County Rd. 2122 ⌂ Box 526, Alpine 85920 ☎ 928/339–4944 ⊕ www.geocities.com/alpinecountryclub) is off U.S. 180, 3 mi east of U.S. 191. At 8,500 feet above sea level, it's one of the highest golf courses in the Southwest. Even if you don't play golf, stop in for New Mexican style food—enchiladas here are stacked, not rolled—and breathtaking scenery at the club's Aspen Room Restaurant. It's 1 mi south of Alpine on Blue River Road. The course is closed in winter.

HIKING The **Escudilla National Recreation Trail** (⊠ U.S. 191, Hulsey Lake) is more idyllic than arduous; the 3-mi trail wends through the Escudilla Wilderness to the summit of towering 10,912-foot **Escudilla Mountain,** Arizona's third-tallest peak. The trail climbs 1,300 feet to a fire tower ¼ mi from the summit. From Alpine, take U.S. 191 north and follow the signs to Hulsey Lake (about 5 mi).

SKIING **Williams Valley Winter Sports Area** (⊠ FSR 249, Alpine ☎ 928/339–4384), 2½ mi west of town, has 12½ mi of cross-country trails of varying difficulty maintained by the Alpine Ranger District. Toboggan Hill is a favorite for families, with sleds, toboggans, and tubes. Shelters, picnic facilities, and toilets are available.

SNOWMOBILING Trails begin just off Forest Service Road 249, on the west side of **Williams Valley Winter Sports Area** (⊠ FSR 249, Alpine ☎ 928/339–4384), and the network of snow-covered Forest Service roads extends for miles. Pick up an Apache Sitgreaves National Forest map and Winter Sports brochure from the Alpine Ranger District, and call for conditions prior to heading out, as weak links in longer routes sometimes "burn out."

Where to Stay & Eat

★ $–$$ ✕▣ **Tal-Wi-Wi Lodge.** This lodge draws many repeat visitors to its lush meadows, a favorite for bird-watchers. Motel-style rooms are simple and clean, with three of the most popular rooms offering woodburning fireplace-stoves, indoor hot tubs, or both. In the evening stroll the grounds and gaze at the Milky Way in the brilliant night sky. With satellite TV and live country music on weekends, the lodge saloon draws a loyal local following. The cozy, casual restaurant is open May through November and serves breakfast on weekends and dinner Thursday through Saturday. Prime rib is the house specialty at the restaurant, but they also serve pizza and homemade pies. ⊠ *U.S. 191* ⌁ *Box 169, Alpine 85920* ☎ *928/339–4319 or 800/476–2695* ⊟ *928/339–1962* ⊕ *www. talwiwilodge.com* ⌁ *20 rooms* ⌂ *Restaurant, some in-room hot tubs, bar, some pets allowed (fee); no a/c, no room TVs* ⊟ *MC, V.*

Hannagan Meadow

★ ❾ *50 mi south of Springerville-Eagar on U.S. 191, 23 mi south of Alpine on U.S. 191.*

Surely one of the state's most remote places, Hannagan Meadow is a pastorally mesmerizing location for several splendid camping areas. Lush and isolated at a 9,500-foot-plus elevation, the meadow is home to elk, deer, and range cattle, as well as blue grouse, wild turkey, and the occasional eagle. Adjacent to the meadow, the Blue Range Primitive Area gives access to miles of untouched wilderness and some beautiful rugged terrain, and it's a designated recovery area for the endangered Mexican gray wolf. It's believed that Francisco Vásquez de Coronado and his party came through the meadow on their famed expedition in 1540 to find the Seven Cities of Cibola.

OFF THE BEATEN PATH

BLUE RANGE PRIMITIVE AREA – Directly east of Hannagan Meadow, this unspoiled 170,000-acre area, lovingly referred to by locals as "The Blue," is the last designated primitive area in the United States. The area's diverse terrain surrounds the Blue River and is crossed by the Mogollon Rim from east to west. No motorized or mechanized equipment is allowed—including mountain bikes; passage is restricted to foot or horseback. Many trails interlace the Blue: prehistoric paths of the ancient native peoples, cowboy trails to move livestock between pastures and water sources, access routes to lookout towers and fire trails. Avid backpackers and campers may want to spend a few days exploring the dozens of hiking trails. Even though trail access is fairly good, hikers need to remember that this is primitive, rough country and to carry adequate water supplies. Contact **Apache-Sitgreaves National Forest** (⊠ Alpine Ranger District, U.S. 191 ⌁ Box 469, Alpine 85920 ☎ 928/339–4384 ⊕ www.fs.fed.us/r3/asnf) for trail maps and information.

Sports & the Outdoors

FISHING In the Blue Range, anglers will want to cast into KP Creek and Grant Creek, both of which rush through spectacular scenery. **Bear Wallow Wilderness Area** (⊠ West of U.S. 191 and bordered by FSR 25 and 54 ☎ 928/339–4384 Alpine Ranger District office ⊕ www.fs.fed.us/r3/asnf) has a network of cool, flowing streams stocked with native Apache trout.

HIKING Twenty-one miles of trail wind through the 11,000 acres of the **Bear Wallow Wilderness Area** (⊠ West of U.S. 191 and bordered by FSR 25 and

54 ☎ 928/339–4384 Alpine Ranger District office ⊕ www.fs.fed.us/r3/asnf). The **Rose Spring Trail** is a pleasant 5½-mi hike with a moderate gradient and magnificent views from the Mogollon Rim's edge; the trailhead is at the end of Forest Service Road 54. **Reno Trail** and **Gobbler Trail** both drop into the main canyon from well-marked trailheads off Forest Service Road 25. Reno Trail meanders 2 mi through conifer forest and aspen, while Gobbler Trail is 2½ mi long with views overlooking the Black River and Fort Apache Indian Reservation. This designated wilderness (and some of its trails) borders the San Carlos Indian Reservation, where an advance permit is required for entry.

SKIING   The 8½ mi of groomed cross-country trails of the **Hannagan Meadow Winter Recreation Area** (⊠ U.S. 191, Hannagan Meadow ☎ 928/339–4384 Alpine Ranger District office ⊕ www.fs.fed.us/r3/asnf) are narrower than the trails of neighboring Williams Valley. The 4½-mi **Clell Lee Loop** is an easy route; the advanced-level, ungroomed **KP Rim Loop** traverses upper elevations of the Blue Primitive Range and provides some of the most varied (and tranquil) remote skiing in the state. There are no rental shops nearby, so bring your own equipment.

SNOWMOBILING   The area just northeast of U.S. 191 is a snowmobile playground. Trailheads are at U.S. 191 and Forest Service Road 576. Snowmobile trail maps are available at the Alpine Ranger District office and Hannagan Meadow Lodge.

Where to Stay

★ $–$$ 🏠 **Hannagan Meadow Lodge.** Antiques and floral prints impart a genteel, Victorian feel to this lodge. The dining room has hewn-log beams and a glass wall that overlooks a pristine meadow; room rates include breakfast (unless you stay in the cabins). Log cabins are more rustic; some have full kitchens and fireplaces, whereas others are equipped with microwaves, stove tops, and wood-burning stoves. The solitude of the area is enhanced by the absence of phones and TVs in rooms and cabins. The general store sells sundries as well as fishing supplies and rents snowshoes, cross-country skis, and mountain bikes. ⊠ *U.S. 191, 22 mi south of Alpine, Hannagan Meadow* ⌂ *HC 61, Box 335, Alpine 85920* ☎ *928/339–4370* ⊕ *www.hannaganmeadow.com* ⇴ *8 rooms, 10 cabins* ⌂ *Restaurant, some kitchens, some kitchenettes, bicycles, hiking, horseback riding, cross-country skiing, snowmobiling, some pets allowed; no a/c, no room phones, no room TVs* ▭ *MC, V* ⍾ *CP.*

CAMPING   △ **Hannagan Campground.** This collection of tent campsites sits under
¢   a canopy of spruce, fir, and aspen trees and is surrounded by tall, mature forest. ⌂ *Grills, pit toilets, drinking water, fire pits, picnic tables* ⍿ *Free* ⇴ *8 campsites* ⊠ *U.S. 191, ¼ mi past Hannagan Meadow Lodge, Hannagan Meadow* ⊕ *www.fs.fed.us/r3/asnf* ⍾ *Open May–Oct.*

THE PETRIFIED FOREST & THE PAINTED DESERT

Only about 1½ hours from Show Low and the lush, verdant forests of the White Mountains, Arizona's diverse and dramatic landscape changes from pine-crested mountains to the sunbaked terrain of the Petrified Forest and lunarlike landscape of the Painted Desert.

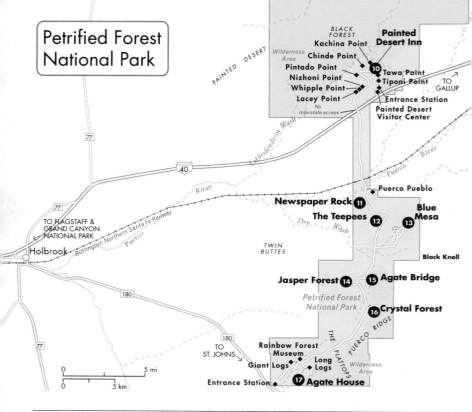

Petrified Forest
National Park

Petrified Forest National Park

Numbers in the text correspond to numbers on the Petrified Forest National Park map.

Fodor's Choice ★

Northern Entrance: 54 mi east of Homolovi Ruins State Park and 27 mi east of Holbrook on Interstate 40; Southern Entrance: 18 mi east of Holbrook on U.S. 180.

A visit to the Petrified Forest is a trip back in geological time. In 1984 the fossil remains of one of the oldest dinosaurs ever unearthed—dating from the Triassic period of the Mesozoic era 225 million years ago—were discovered here; other plant and animal fossils in the park date from the same period. Remnants of ancient human beings and their artifacts, dating back 10,000 years, have been recovered at more than 500 sites in this national park.

The park derives its name from the grounds that are covered with petrified tree trunks whose wood cells were replaced over centuries by brightly hued mineral deposits—silica, iron oxide, manganese, aluminum, copper, lithium, and carbon. In many places, petrified logs scattered about the landscape resemble a fairy-tale forest turned to stone. The park's 93,000 acres doubled to nearly 186,000 acres with new land acquisition in 2005, but most of this new area will remain as backcountry. Included in the park are portions of the vast, pink-hue lunarlike landscape known as the **Painted Desert.** In the northern area of the park, this colorful but essentially barren series of windswept plains, hills, and mesas is considered by geologists to be part of the Chinle formation, deposited at an early stage of the Triassic period. At midday the park may seem bland; to appreciate the colors visit before 10 AM and after 2 PM.

You can easily spend most of a day on the park's 28 mi of paved roads and walking trails. Lookouts on the north end of the park provide beautiful Painted Desert vistas. Originally built in 1924, ❿ **Painted Desert Inn,** 2-mi south of the north entrance, is a museum and gift shop. Its colorful murals by Hopi artist

> ## CAREFUL WITH THAT ROCK
>
> Because so many looters hauled away large quantities of petrified wood in the early 20th century, President Roosevelt made the area a national monument in 1906. Since then, it has been illegal (bad karma) to remove even a sliver of petrified wood from the park, although souvenir pieces are available at the gift shop and surrounding trading posts. Don't miss the "Guilt Books" in each entrance's museum. These preserve letters from guilt-riddled former visitors anxiously returning their purloined souvenirs and detailing directly attributable hexes—from runs of bad luck to husbands turning into "hard-drinking strangers."

5

Fred Kabotie were commissioned by the well-known architect Mary Jane Colter, and painted in the 1940s. Completely remodeled in 2006, it also houses cultural history exhibits and Native American crafts. Native American petroglyphs survive on boulders at ⓫ **Newspaper Rock** and Puerco Ruins, which also has a partially stabilized 100-room pueblo more than 600 years old. A spiral symbol near Puerco Ruins marks the summer solstice. The interaction of light and shadow is visible about a week before and a week after the solstice. You can observe the solstice marker by yourself, but to find out when a ranger will be there to answer your questions call 928/524–6228. Approximately 2 mi on down the road, a cone-shape rock formation called ⓬ **The Teepees** shows layers of blues, purples, and grays. Picnicking is allowed in the park, so pull out your lunch and enjoy the vast expanse of ⓭ **Blue Mesa.** ⓮ **Jasper Forest** and ⓰ **Crystal Forest** contain stunning hunks of petrified trees scattered on the desert floor. The 100-foot petrified log spanning a 40-foot arroyo at ⓯ **Agate Bridge** still intrigues visitors. Near the southern end of the park, ⓱ **Agate House** is a pueblo structure assembled from pieces of petrified wood.

At the north entrance of the park, the **Painted Desert Visitor Center** shows a 20-minute movie entitled *Timeless Impressions,* tracing the natural history of the area. The **Rainbow Forest Museum and Visitor Center** (✉ Near south entrance, off U.S. 180, 18 mi southeast of Holbrook) displays skeletons from the Triassic period, including that of "Gertie"—the ferocious phytosaur, a crocodilelike carnivore. The museum has numerous exhibits relating to the world of cycads (tropical plants), ferns, fish, and other early life, as well as artifacts and tools of ancient humans. Exhibits were updated and a theater added in 2006. Within the park's boundaries, visitors also have access to a seasonal snack bar at the north end of the park. Those interested in purchasing books or slides should know that many of the same titles are offered at the gift shops (there's one at each end of the park) and at the Painted Desert Visitor Center (at the north end of the park). Only those books purchased from the visitor center will fund the continued research and interpretive activities for the park.

Hiking is the best way to see the Petrified Forest National Park. Stretch your legs on any of the short walks in the park or load on the backpack and head out for several days in the Wilderness Area. All trails start from the main road and vary in length up to 3 mi. The 1-mi **Painted Desert Rim Trail** is at its best in early morning or late afternoon, when the sun accentuates the brilliant colors. Paved and handicapped accessible, **Puerco Pueblo Trail,** an easy 0.3-mi walk, leads to a 100-room pueblo and petroglyphs. Moderately strenuous, **Blue Mesa Trail** follows a 1-mi loop among badland hills. An easy 7.5-mi walk along **Crystal Forest Trail** passes logs that were "mined" for crystals in the early 1900s. Combine **Long Logs Trail** and **Agate House Trail** for a 3-mi round-trip past a small pueblo and one of the largest concentration of petrified wood in the park. Right behind the museum at the south entrance, the popular 0.4-mi **Giant Logs Trail** features "Old Faithful," a petrified log almost 10 feet across.

Kachina Point, on the northwest side of the Painted Desert Inn Museum, is the trailhead for wilderness hiking. A 1-mi trail leads to the Wilderness Area but from there you're on your own. With no developed trails, hiking here is cross-country style, but expect to see strange formations, beautifully colored landscape, and if you're lucky, a pronghorn antelope. Remember to take plenty of water and appropriate clothing. Summer temperatures can reach over 100°F with very little shade available. Winter nighttime temperatures plunge to near zero. A permit isn't needed for a day hike, but plan to be back to your vehicle by the park's closing time.

The only camping allowed in the park is minimal-impact camping in a designated zone north of Lithodendron Wash in the Wilderness Area. A free permit must be obtained and group size is limited to eight. There's no shade available and if it rains, that pretty Painted Desert formation turns to sticky clay. For those not interested in hiking several miles to find a sleeping spot, try **Homolovi State Park** campgrounds, 4 mi northeast of Winslow off AZ 87. If you're headed south to the White Mountains, check out **Fool Hollow Lake Recreation Area** in Show Low.

There's a small restaurant at the northern visitor center, and a seasonal snack bar with sandwiches is available at the southern entrance. No lodging is available at the Petrified Forest National Park, but there are motels in Holbrook, which is 27 mi west of the park's northern entrance on Interstate 40.

Visitors can begin the 28-mi drive through the park either from the northern Interstate 40 entrance or the southern entrance off U.S. 180. Those continuing on to New Mexico should enter from the park's south entrance, ending up with Interstate 40's straight shot over the border toward Albuquerque. Visitors with accommodations in Holbrook should tour the park from south end to north end, saving dramatic sunset vistas of the Painted Desert for last. As you leave the park, rangers will question you to be certain you haven't been tempted to collect a souvenir of petrified wood. *North Entrance ⊠ I–40, Milepost 311, 27 mi east of Holbrook, Petrified Forest ☎ 928/524–6228 ⊕ www.nps.gov/ pefo ⊕ Box 2217, Petrified Forest 86028 ⊠ $10 per vehicle, valid for 1 wk ⊙ Mid-Oct.–May, daily 8–5; June–mid-Oct., daily 7–7.*

⑱ Museum of Antiquities (Dinosaur Park). No you're not seeing things, that *was* a dinosaur you just passed along I–40 between the Petrified Forest National Park and Holbrook. The fearsome-looking beasts are advertisement for this unusual museum-park that houses one of the best collections of Ancestral Puebloan (Anasazi) pottery in the region. Fossils, oddities, and a gift shop with jewelry, petrified wood, and souvenirs are a draw. Visitors can drive through or hike the trails. Watch out—a total of 19 life-size dinosaurs are on the property. Fees are reasonable: $10 per car no matter how many dinosaur-loving kids you have tucked in the back seat. *⊠ I–40, Exit 292, 1001 Petrified Forest Dr., Holbrook ☎ 928/524–9198 ⊙ Mid-May–Oct., daily 8–6; Nov.–mid-May, daily 9–5.*

FodorsChoice
★

5

Snowflake-Taylor

⑲ *15 mi north of Show Low on AZ 77.*

Snowflake-Taylor is a good jumping-off point for exploring eastern Arizona; it's an easy day trip to the Homolovi Ruins or the Petrified Forest. The towns are also a less-crowded alternative for summer excursions in the nearby White Mountains. Most Phoenix weekenders head for the higher towns, so Snowflake and Taylor avoid the crush of summer visitors that results in higher prices at hotels and restaurants. Sandwiched between the White Mountains and the Colorado Plateau, the communities enjoy year-round pleasant weather with summer highs in the 90s. Yes, it snows in Snowflake, but it seldom lasts more than a day.

Snowflake and Taylor were settled by Mormons in the 1870s and named for Mormon church leaders. Snowflake's unusual name is a combination of Mr. Snow, an apostle in the early Mormon church of Salt Lake City, Utah, and Mr. Flake, one of the town founders. One of only two Mormon temples in Arizona sits on Temple Hill west of Snowflake, and the towns still have a large Mormon contingent in their combined population of 9,000. Snowflake's historical district features a walking tour, antiques store, and pioneer homes.

The **Stinson Museum** once served as a schoolhouse. James Stinson, the first rancher in the valley, was the original resident of the small adobe home. William J. Flake bought out Stinson's holdings and founded the town of Snowflake. Flake added on to the structure, which today is a museum containing pioneer memorabilia, quilts, Indian artifacts, and a small gift shop. Check with the Chamber of Commerce (☎ 928/536–

4331) for seasonal winter hours. ⊠ *102 N. 1st St.* ☎ *928/536–4881* 📠 *$1* ⊙ *Mon.–Sat. 10–2.*

The **Taylor Museum,** a small local museum with pioneer and Native American exhibits, celebrates July 4 by "firing the anvil" at sunrise. At 4 AM, revelers place an anvil on the ground, a newspaper and gun powder on top, then another anvil. When the gunpowder is lit, the anvil flies 3 feet into the air with a deafening bang. The rest of the year, the anvil resides at the museum along with the Jennings drum, which was brought to town by early Mormon settlers. ⊠ *2 N. Main St.* ☎ *928/536–6649* 📠 *$2 donation suggested* ⊙ *Mon., Tues., and Thurs.–Sat. 10–2.*

Sports & Outdoor Activities

GOLF   One of the least expensive golf courses in the White Mountains, the 27-hole **Snowflake Municipal Golf Course** (⊠ 90 N. Country Club Dr. ☎ 928/536–7233) is open year-round. Especially scenic with red rocks and waterfalls, the course includes a driving range and water hazard. The restaurant is open May through October. Greens fees are $12 for 9 holes plus $6 for a cart, and $24 for 18 holes plus $14 for a cart; rates are lower November through April.

HIKING   At the junction of Silver Creek Canyon and Five-Mile Canyon, 5 mi north of Snowflake, ancient peoples left petroglyphs carved through the dark desert varnish revealing the light sandstone of the canyon walls. **Petroglyph Hike** (⊠ Silver Creek Canyon), the trail from canyon top down to the petroglyphs, is short but steep. Trail access is regulated by the city of Snowflake. To check-in and get directions, contact the **Snowflake-Taylor Chamber of Commerce** (☎ 928/536–4331 or 928/536–4881).

Where to Stay & Eat

¢–$$ ✕ **Enzo's Ristorante Italiano.** Behind Heritage Antiques, in the historic district of Snowflake, is the only Italian restaurant in town. Sauces and breads are homemade, and although they may take a while, the minestrone soup, baked pastas, and shrimp Alfredo are worth the wait. ⊠ *50 E. 1st St. N, Snowflake* ☎ *928/243–0450* 🗔 *No credit cards* ⊙ *Closed Mon. and Tues. No lunch.*

★ ¢–$$ ✕ **La Cocina de Eva.** If you like Mexican food, stop here. The green-corn tamales and enchiladas are delicious, and locals go for the bean burro smothered in green chile sauce. Portions are large and service is friendly. A combination of Mexican knickknacks and Western paintings gives this popular spot a homey feel. ⊠ *101 S. Main St., Snowflake* ☎ *928/536–7683* 🗔 *MC, V* ⊙ *Closed Sun.*

¢–$$ ✕ **Trapper's.** Opened in 1973 by "Trapper" Hatch and still family-owned, this hometown diner is decorated with Hatch's old trapping equipment and animal paintings by local artists. Chicken-fried steak and homemade barbecue sauce draw a loyal crowd. People drive out of their way just to stop for a piece of Trapper's pies, especially banana cream. Have a slice at the counter with a cup of coffee. ⊠ *9 S. Main St., Taylor* ☎ *928/536–7758* 🗔 *MC, V* ⊙ *Closed Sun.*

$–$$ 🏠 **Osmer D. Heritage Inn.** Elegantly furnished with period antiques, this
FodorśChoice   redbrick home with a white-picket fence was built in 1890 by Mormon
★   pioneer Osmer D. Flake. Filled with pioneer style, Osmer D's is next door to Heritage Antiques and between two restaurants—making it the

best place to start Snowflake's historic walking tour. ✉ *161 N. Main St., Snowflake 85937* ☎ *928/536–3322 or 866/486–5947* ⊕ *www. heritage-inn.net* ⌂ *9 rooms, 2 suites* ♨ *Cable TV, Wi-Fi, hot tub; no smoking* ⊟ *AE, D, MC, V* ⏀ *BP.*

$ ▥ **Comfort Inn.** The Comfort Inn is the only hotel in either Snowflake or Taylor with a pool. The pool, the large rooms, and the complimentary Continental breakfast make the inn a great deal for families. A large river-rock fireplace and rustic furniture adorn the comfortable lobby. ✉ *2055 S. Main St., Snowflake 85937* ☎ *928/536–3888 or 877/505– 3888* ☎ *928/536–3888* ⊕ *www.comfortinn.com* ⌂ *64 rooms* ♨ *Some refrigerators, cable TV, Wi-Fi, pool, exercise equipment, laundry facilities, meeting rooms, no-smoking rooms* ⊟ *AE, D, MC, V* ⏀ *CP.*

$ ▥ **Rodeway Silver Creek Inn.** Simply furnished, clean, and near fast-food restaurants, Silver Creek sees many "regulars" who travel through the area often. There's ample parking for RVs and trailers, and it's close to Taylor's only grocery store. ✉ *825 N. Main St., Taylor 85939* ☎ *928/ 536–2600* ⌂ *42 rooms* ♨ *Microwaves, refrigerators, cable TV, hot tub* ⊟ *AE, D, DC, MC, V* ⏀ *CP.*

Homolovi Ruins State Park

★ ❷ *53 mi east of Flagstaff, 33 mi west of Holbrook. Exit 257 off Interstate 40.*

Homolovi is a Hopi word meaning "place of the little hills." The pueblo sites here are thought to have been occupied between AD 1200 and 1425 and include 40 ceremonial kivas and two pueblos containing more than 1,000 rooms each. The Hopi believe their immediate ancestors inhabited this place and still hold the site to be sacred. Many rooms have been excavated and recovered for protection. Weekdays in June and July you can see archaeologists working the site. Mobility-impaired persons should check with the ranger station for alternate access information; rangers conduct guided tours. The Homolovi Visitor Center has a small museum with Hopi pottery and ancestral Puebloan artifacts; it also hosts workshops on native art, ethnobotany, and traditional foods. ✉ *AZ 87, 5 mi northeast of Winslow* ⌂ *HCR 63, Box 5, Winslow 86047* ☎ *928/ 289–4106* ⊕ *www.pr.state.az.us.*

Fodor's Choice ★ The Ancestral Puebloan petroglyphs of **Rock Art Ranch,** in Chevelon Canyon, are startling vivid after over 1,000 years. Brantly Baird, owner of this working cattle ranch, will guide you along the ¼-mi trail, explaining western and archaeological history. It's mostly easy walking, except for the climb in and out of Chevelon Canyon, where there are hand rails. Baird houses his Indian artifacts and pioneer farming items in his own private museum. It's out of the way and on a dirt road, but you'll see some of the best rock art in northern Arizona. Reservations are required. ✉ *Off AZ 87, 13 mi southeast of Winslow* ⌂ *Box 224, Joseph City 85032* ☎ *928/288–3260* ⊠ *$20* ☉ *May–Oct. by appointment only.*

Where to Stay

Homolovi Ruins State Park is 5 mi northeast of the town of Winslow. Frequent flooding on the Little Colorado River frustrated the attempts of Mormon pioneers to settle here, but, with the coming of the railroad, the town roared into life. Later, Route 66 sustained the community until Interstate 40 passed north of town. New motels and restaurants sprouted near the interstate exits, and downtown was all but abandoned. Downtown Winslow is now revitalizing, with La Posada Hotel as its showpiece, but dining options are still scarce.

$–$$ ☲ **La Posada Winslow.** One of the great railroad hotels, La Posada (it
FodorsChoice means "resting place") exudes the charm of an 18th-century Spanish
★ hacienda. Architect Mary Colter, famous for her work at the Grand Canyon, designed and decorated the 68,000-square-foot hotel. Spanish and Native American furniture, antiques, and art permeate her designs. The lobby is a gallery for paintings by Tina Mion, one of the owners. Individually decorated rooms are restored to 1930s style and the lush gardens are a swathe of green in the red-rock Colorado Plateau. If you can't spend the night, take the self-guided tour ($2 donation). ⊠ *303 E. 2nd St., Winslow 86047* ☎ *928/289–4366* 🖶 *928/289–3873* ⊕ *www. laposada.org* ⇝ *37 rooms* ⚍ *Restaurant, cable TV, lounge; no room phones, no smoking* ⊟ *AE, D, DC, MC, V.*

Camping

¢ ⚠ **Homolovi Ruins State Park Campground.** At an elevation of 4,900 feet, this campsite for tents and RVs is a short walk from Homolovi I pueblo and close to several other archaeological sites and trails leading to petroglyphs and evidence of prehistoric habitations. Bring a sun umbrella, as there are no shade trees. ⊠ *AZ 87, 5 mi northeast of Winslow* ☎ *928/289–4106* 🖾 *$10–$15* ⚍ *Grills, flush toilets, partial hookups (electric and water), dump station, drinking water, showers, fire pits, picnic tables* ⇝ *53 campsites.*

Holbrook

㉑ *35 mi east of Homolovi State Park via Interstate 40.*

Downtown Holbrook is a monument to Route 66 kitsch. The famous "Mother Road" traveled through the center of Holbrook before Interstate 40 replaced it as the area's major east–west artery, and remnants of the "good ole days" can be found all over town.

Route 66 itself still runs through Holbrook, following Navajo Boulevard and Hopi Drive. It made a sharp corner at the intersection of these two roads, causing traffic jams. The Downtowner, a popular coffee shop on this corner, served simple meals and coffee to sleepy truck drivers. As if traffic weren't already scrambled enough, crowds from the movie theater at what is today East Hopi Drive brought Route 66 to a standstill. Moviegoers, who thronged into the streets at the end of the show, considered it their right to block traffic; after all, many had traveled over 100 mi to see the movie.

Before Route 66 rolled into Holbrook, the town was a notorious hangout for cowboys from the vast Aztec Land and Cattle Company, better known as the Hashknife Outfit after the shape of their brand. Pick up a walking tour at the Chamber of Commerce and see the sites, including the infamous Bucket of Blood Saloon.

★ The **Old Courthouse Museum** (☎ 800/524–2459 ⊕ www.ci.holbrook. az.us ☒ Free ☉ Weekdays 8–5, weekends 8–4), at the corner of Arizona Street and Navajo Boulevard, holds memorabilia from the Route 66 heyday along with Old West and railroad records. Near the railroad tracks you'll be surprised by models of bright green dinosaurs glaring down at you. The Indian Rock Shop makes dinosaurs, and their wares are stored outside. The shop isn't open to the public, but it's hard to find a place to store a dinosaur.

Where to Stay & Eat

$–$$ ✕ **Mesa Italiana Restaurant.** The chef here uses the finest herbs, spices, and other ingredients to create an authentic taste of old Italy. Locals recommend the fresh pastas, calzones, spaghetti with Italian mushrooms, and homemade salads. A dinner of steak and shrimp will run you $21. Don't forget the spumoni for dessert. ☒ *2318 E. Navajo Blvd.* ☎ *928/524–6696* ☐ *AE, D, MC, V* ☉ *No weekend lunch.*

$ ⊞ **Holbrook Days Inn.** This modern Southwestern-style structure of stucco walls and Spanish-tile roofs stands amid petrified-wood landscaping. Free Continental breakfast and local phone calls, a heated indoor pool and hot tub, plus nearby restaurants make this a pleasant, convenient choice. ☒ *2601 Navajo Blvd., Holbrook 86025* ☎ *928/524–6949* ⊕ *www.daysinn.com* ↩ *51 rooms, 3 suites* ⚬ *Some microwaves, some refrigerators, cable TV, indoor pool, hot tub* ☐ *AE, D, DC, MC, V* ⦿ *CP.*

★ ¢ ⊞ **Wigwam Motel.** Classic Route 66, the Wigwam consists of 15 bright white concrete tepees where you can sleep inexpensively, in a quirky environment. As you might expect, wigwams are phoneless, but—ode to Mother Progress—these have cable TV. A small lobby museum exhibits Mexican, Native American, and military relics collected by the owner's family. The 180-pound, polished petrified wood sphere is one of the largest in the Southwest. All of the classic cars parked by the tepees also belong to the owners. ☒ *711 W. Hopi Dr., Holbrook 86025* ☎ *928/524–3048* ↩ *15 rooms* ⚬ *Cable TV; no room phones* ☐ *MC, V.*

Shopping

Fodor'sChoice **McGees Beyond Native Tradition** (☒ 2114 E. Navajo Blvd., Holbrook
★ ☎ 928/524–1977 ⊕ www.hopiart.com or www.mcgeeshopitraders. com) is the area's premier source of high-quality Native American jewelry, rugs, Hopi baskets, and katsina dolls. The owners have long-standing relationships with reservation artisans and a knowledgeable staff that adroitly assists first-time buyers and seasoned collectors.

EASTERN ARIZONA ESSENTIALS

To research prices, get advice from other travelers, and book travel arrangements, visit ⊕ *www.fodors.com.*

BY BUS
White Mountain Passenger Lines has service between Phoenix and Show Low; one-way fares are around $44. Greyhound Lines travels from

Phoenix to Winslow, 50 mi west of Petrified Forest National Park, for around $40.

🚌 **Greyhound Lines** ⊠ 2201 N. Park Dr., Winslow ☎ 928/289-2171. **White Mountain Passenger Lines** ⊠ 1041 E. Hall St., Show Low ☎ 928/537-4539 ⊠ 319 S. 24th St., Phoenix ☎ 602/275-4245.

BY CAR

A car is essential for touring eastern Arizona, especially because most of the region's top scenic attractions are between towns. Rental facilities are few and far between in these parts, so rent a car from your departure point, whether it's Phoenix, Flagstaff, or Albuquerque.

If you're arriving from points west via Flagstaff, Interstate 40 leads directly to Holbrook, where drivers can take AZ 77 south into Show Low or U.S. 180 southeast to Springerville-Eagar. Those departing from the metropolitan Phoenix area should take the scenic drive northeast on U.S. 60, or the only slightly faster AZ 87 north to AZ 260 east, both of which lead to Show Low. From Tucson, AZ 77 connects with U.S. 60 at Globe and continues through Show Low up to Holbrook. From New Mexico, drivers can enter the state on Interstate 40 and take U.S. 191 south into Springerville-Eagar, or continue on to Holbrook and reach the White Mountains via AZ 77. For those who want to drive the Coronado Trail south-to-north, U.S. 70 and AZ 78 link up with U.S. 191 from Globe to the west and New Mexico to the east, respectively.

ROAD CONDITIONS
In winter, motorists should travel prepared, with jumper cables, a shovel, tire chains, and—for tire traction on icy roads—a bag of cat litter. Chain requirements apply to all vehicles, including those with four-wheel drive. Bridges and overpasses freeze first and are often slicker than normal road surfaces; never assume sufficient traction simply because a road appears to be sanded. Drivers who must travel in poor visibility conditions should turn on the headlights and always keep the highway's white reflectors to their right. For road conditions throughout the region, call the White Mountains Road and Weather Information Line.

🚗 **White Mountains Road and Weather Information Line** ☎ 928/537-7623.

BY TRAIN

Amtrak trains depart daily at 6:15 AM from Flagstaff to Winslow. There's no train service to Phoenix; those traveling from Phoenix will need to take the Amtrak shuttle—which departs Phoenix-area bus stations four times daily bound for Flagstaff—and stay overnight in Flagstaff to catch the early-morning train to Winslow. From Albuquerque, Winslow is only a three-hour ride, leaving daily at 5:28 PM.

🚆 **Amtrak** ☎ 928/774-8679 in Flagstaff.

CAMPING

Call or write the Apache-Sitgreaves National Forest for a brochure listing all public camping facilities in the region, most of which operate from April to November. To ensure a site at a fee campground, call the National Recreation Reservation Service, which charges a reservation fee of $10 per transaction. Book your campground site well in advance with the Game and Fish Division of the White Mountain Apache Tribe.

ℹ **Apache-Sitgreaves National Forest** ☎ 928/368-5111 ⊕ www.fs.fed.us/r3/asnf. **National Recreation Reservation Service** ☎ 877/444-6777 ⊕ www.reserveusa.com. **White Mountain Apache Tribe** ☎ 928/338-4385 ⊕ www.wmat.nsn.us.

EMERGENCIES

ℹ Ambulance & Fire **Ambulance and Fire Emergencies** ☎ 911.

ℹ Hospitals **Navapache Regional Medical Center** ✉ 2200 E. Show Low Lake Rd., Show Low ☎ 928/537-4375 ⊕ www.nrmc.org. **White Mountain Regional Medical Center** ✉ 118 S. Mountain Ave., Springerville ☎ 928/333-4368.

ℹ Police **Police Emergencies** ☎ 911.

VISITOR INFORMATION

ℹ **Alpine Chamber of Commerce** ☎ 928/339-4330. **Holbrook Chamber of Commerce** ☎ 928/524-6558 or 800/524-2459 ⊕ www.ci.holbrook.az.us. **Pinetop-Lakeside Chamber of Commerce** ☎ 928/367-4290 or 800/573-4031 ⊕ www.pinetoplakesidechamber.com. **Show Low Chamber of Commerce** ☎ 928/537-2326 or 888/746-9569 ⊕ www.showlowchamberofcommerce.com. **Snowflake/Taylor Chamber of Commerce** ☎ 928/536-4331 ⊕ www.snowflaketaylorchamber.org. **Springerville-Eagar Regional Chamber of Commerce** ☎ 928/333-2123 ⊕ www.az-tourist.com. **White Mountain Apache Office of Tourism** ☎ 928/338-1230 ⊕ www.wmat.nsn.us.

LAND-MANAGEMENT AGENCIES ℹ **Apache Sitgreaves National Forest** ☎ 928/333–4301 ⊕ www.fs.fed.us/r3/asnf ☎ 928/339–4384 ✉ Lakeside Ranger District ☎ 928/368–5111 ☎ 928/333–4372. **Arizona Game & Fish Department** ☎ 928/367–4281 ⊕ www.gf.state.az.us. **San Carlos Apache Tribe** ☎ 928/475–2361. **White Mountain Apache Fish & Game Department** ☎ 928/338–4385.

Tucson

WORD OF MOUTH

"If you want nightlife and shopping, go to Phoenix. If you want quiet, laid-back, beautiful surroundings with fabulous hiking opportunities, try Tucson."
                                    —tucsonartist

"Tucson is a city, but you can be in the foothills quickly . . . you can hike and encounter nature, too. The foothills offer a different kind of desert scenery—no red rocks—but lots of giant saguaro cacti (Saguaro National Park East and West) and Sabino Canyon in Coronado National Forest— a beautiful place to hike. Inspiring views. Tucson offers lots of other attractions, too, like Mission San Xavier del Bac and Kitt Peak National Observatory (actually not in Tucson, but within easy travel distance)."
                                    —MlWinnie

Updated by
Mara Levin

THE OLD PUEBLO, AS TUCSON is affectionately known, is built upon a deep Native American, Spanish, Mexican, and Old West foundation. Arizona's second-largest city is both a bustling center of business and a relaxed university and resort town. Metropolitan Tucson has more than 850,000 residents, including thousands of snowbirds who flee colder climes to enjoy the warm sun that shines on the city more than 340 days a year (Tucson averages only 12 inches of rain a year). Winter temperatures hover around 65°F during the day and 38°F at night. Summers are unquestionably hot—July averages 104°F during the day and 75°F at night—but, as Tucsonans are fond of saying, "it's a dry heat."

Native Americans have lived along the waterways in this valley for thousands of years. During the 1500s, Spanish explorers arrived to find Pima Indians growing crops in the area. Father Eusebio Francisco Kino, a Jesuit missionary whose influence is still strongly felt throughout the region, first visited the area in 1687 and returned a few years later to build missions.

The name Tucson came from the Native American word *stjukshon* (pronounced *stook*-shahn), meaning "spring at the foot of a black mountain." (The springs at the foot of Sentinel Peak, made of black volcanic rock, are now dry.) The name became Tucson (originally pronounced *tuk*-son) by the Spanish explorers who built a wall around the city in 1776 to keep Native Americans from reclaiming it. At the time, this *presidio* (fortified city), called San Augustin del Tuguison, was the northernmost Spanish settlement in the area, and current-day Main Avenue is a quiet reminder of the former Camino Real ("royal road") that stretched from this tiny walled fort all the way to Mexico City.

Four flags have flown over Tucson—Spanish, Mexican, Confederate, and, finally, the Stars and Stripes. Tucson's allegiance changed in 1820 when Mexico declared independence from Spain, and again in 1853 when the Gadsden purchase made it part of the United States, though Arizona didn't become a state until 1912. In the 1850s the Butterfield stage line was extended to Tucson, bringing adventurers, a few settlers, and more than a handful of outlaws. The arrival of the railroad in 1880 marked another spurt of growth, as did the opening of the University of Arizona in 1891.

Tucson's 20th-century growth occurred after World War I, when veterans with damaged lungs sought the dry air and healing power of the sun, and again during World War II with the opening of Davis-Monthan Air Force Base and the rise of local aeronautical industries. It was also around this time that air-conditioning made the desert climate hospitable year-round.

Today many transplants come from the Midwest and nearby California because of the lower housing costs, cleaner environment, and spectacular scenery. And despite the ubiquitous strip malls and tract-home developments, this college town has Mexican and Native American–cultural influences, a striking landscape, and all the amenities of a resort town. High-tech industries have moved into the area, but the economy still relies heavily on tourism and the university—although, come summer, you'd never guess; when the snowbirds and students depart, Tucson can be a sleepy place.

Top 5 Experiences in Tucson

- **Commune with cacti:** Unique to this region, the saguaro cactus is the quintessential symbol of the Southwest. The best places to check out saguaros up close are at Saguaro National Park East or West and Sabino Canyon, where you can enjoy the desert landscape on foot, bicycle, horseback, or from an open-air tram.

- **Eat Mexican food:** Tucson boasts that it's the "Mexican Food Capital," and you won't be disappointed at any of the Mexican restaurants listed in this chapter.

- **Spend a morning at the Arizona Sonora Desert Museum:** Anyone who thinks that museums are boring hasn't been to this one, where you can learn about the wildlife, plants, and geology of the region in a gorgeous, mostly outdoors, setting. Don't miss one of the daily hawk- or falcon-flying demonstrations.

- **Tour Mission San Xavier del Bac:** The "White Dove of the Desert" is the oldest building in Tucson, and arguably the best example of Mission Architecture in the U.S. Ornate carvings and frescoes inside the brilliant white church set against the Tucson Mountains add to the mystical quality of this active parish on the Tohono O'odham reservation.

- **Strolling the U of A campus:** Stop in at one or two of the five museums here, then stroll down University Boulevard and 4th Avenue, where you'll get a sense of Tucson's hipper element.

EXPLORING TUCSON

Tucson has a tri-cultural (Hispanic, Anglo, Native American) population, and the chance to see how these cultures interact—and to sample their cuisines—is one of the pleasures of a visit. The city is particularly popular among golfers, but the area's many hiking trails will keep non-duffers busy, too. If the weather is too hot to stay outdoors comfortably, museums like the Arizona State Museum offer a cooler alternative. An influx of both new residents and visitors has given the city some growing pains, but city planners are addressing the issues of development and pollution control.

Getting Your Bearings

The metropolitan Tucson area covers more than 500 square mi in a valley ringed by mountains—the Santa Catalinas to the north, the Santa Ritas to the south, the Rincons to the east, and the Tucson Mountains to the west. A car is essential to explore the valley. The central portion of town—which has most of the shops, restaurants, and businesses—is roughly bounded by Craycroft Road on the east, Oracle Road on the west, River Road to the north, and 22nd Street to the south. The older downtown section, east of I–10 off the Broadway-Congress exit, is much smaller and easy to navigate on foot. Streets downtown don't run true to any sort of grid, however, and many are one-way, so it's best to get a good, detailed map. The city's Westside area is the vast region west of I–10 and I–19, which includes the western section of Saguaro National Park and the San Xavier Indian Reservation.

GREAT ITINERARIES

IF YOU HAVE 1 DAY
With only one day and a great deal of ground to cover, you would be better off experiencing a taste of both the wild and developed parts of Tucson. Head out to the **Arizona–Sonora Desert Museum** ㉚. Children may enjoy a stop at the **Old Tucson Studios** ㉙, nearby. On your way back, drive through downtown's **Barrio Historico** neighborhood and **El Presidio Historic District** for a glimpse into the city's past, but with just a day, you won't have time to do much stopping.

IF YOU HAVE 3 DAYS
Follow the first day's itinerary, through Old Tucson Studios. The next morning, drive out to the **Mission San Xavier del Bac** ㉛ and have some Native American–fry

bread for lunch in the plaza. You might wish to continue south to the **Titan Missile Museum** ㉟ and then continue on to **Tubac** ㊲ for some shopping. On the third day, head **Downtown** ❶–⓫ to explore Tucson's early history and, in the afternoon, visit one of the several museums at the **University of Arizona** ⑫–⑱. While near the U of A, you might also want to consider heading to 4th Avenue between 2nd and 9th streets, where boutiques and used-book stores await.

IF YOU HAVE 4 DAYS
What you do on the fourth day depends on the weather: if it's hot, visit **Mt. Lemmon** ㉓ to cool off; if it's not, you might enjoy breakfast at **Tohono Chul Park** ㉔ followed by a visit to beautiful **Sabino Canyon** ㉒.

Remember, too, that the old cliché is reversed here: it's not the humidity—it's the heat. If you're accustomed to humid conditions, then chances are you'll be unprepared for Tucson's dry climate, so use lip balm and skin moisturizer, and drink water or other noncaffeinated fluids frequently, whether you're active or not. Also, the strong solar radiation here (Tucson is second only to Cape Town, South Africa, in skin cancer incidence) makes sunscreen a must.

Downtown

The area bordered by Franklin Street on the north, Cushing Street on the south, Church Avenue on the east, and Main Avenue on the west encompasses more than two centuries of the city's architectural history, dating from the original walled El Presidio de Tucson, a Spanish fortress built in 1776, when Arizona was still part of New Spain. A good deal of Tucson's history was destroyed in the 1960s, when large sections of the downtown's barrio were bulldozed to make way for the Tucson Convention Center, high-rises, and parking lots. However, within the areas' three small historic districts it's still possible to explore parts of the original Spanish settlement and to see a number of the posh residences that accompanied the arrival of the railroad.

El Presidio Historic District, north of the Convention Center and the government buildings that dominate downtown, is a representative mixture of Tucson's historic architecture, a thumbnail of the city's former self. The north–south streets Court, Meyer, and Main are sprinkled with traditional Mexican adobe houses sitting cheek by jowl with territorial-style houses, with wide attics and porches. Paseo Redondo, once called Snob Hollow, is the wide road along which wealthy merchants built their homes.

The area most closely resembling 19th-century Tucson is the **Barrio Historico**, also known as Barrio Viejo. The narrow streets of this neighborhood, including Convent Avenue, have a good sampling of thick-wall adobe houses. The houses are close to the street, hiding the yards and gardens within.

> ### LONG LIVE ADOBE!
>
> Adobe—brick made of mud and straw, cured in the hot sun—was used widely as a building material in early Tucson because it provides a natural insulation from the heat and cold and because it's durable in Tucson's dry climate. When these buildings are properly made and maintained, they can last for centuries! Driving around Tucson, you'll see adobe houses painted in vibrant hues such as bright pink and canary yellow.

To the east of the Barrio Historico, across Stone Avenue, is the **Armory Park** neighborhood, mostly constructed by and for the railroad workers who settled here after the 1880s. The brick or wood territorial-style homes here were the Victorian era's adaptation to the desert climate.

Numbers in the text correspond to numbers in the margin and on the What to See in Downtown Tucson map.

A GOOD TOUR

Drive up to **"A" Mountain** (Sentinel Peak) ❶ ▶ for a great perspective of downtown Tucson (if you're squeamish about heights, be aware that the narrow, winding road has no guard rails). Come down from on high and head east along Congress Street, stopping at Santa Cruz River Park to view the religious sculptures and mosaics by local artists, before crossing the **Santa Cruz River** ❷. Continue east along Congress, and turn right (heading south) on Granada, passing the new Federal Court Building. The **Sosa-Carillo-Fremont House** ❸ is on the left (park at the adjacent convention center lot if no events are in progress). Continuing south on Granada, turn left onto Cushing Street and then right onto Main, to see the shrine of **El Tiradito (The Castaway)** ❹, next to El Minuto Restaurant's parking lot. As you make your way through the Barrio Historico neighborhood, you'll pass adobe houses being restored and painted in bright colors.

Turn right onto Simpson, left onto Samaniego, left onto 17th Street, and left onto Convent, which becomes Church. One-way streets require you to drive north on Church, east on Broadway Boulevard, and then south on Stone Avenue to see **St. Augustine Cathedral** ❺. Head east on McCormick to 6th Avenue, where your kids may want to check out the hands-on activities at the **Tucson Children's Museum** ❻. To get to the **Tucson Museum of Art and Historic Block** ❼, take 6th Avenue north to Congress Street, where you'll see the historic Hotel Congress on the right. This stretch of Congress was once Tucson's bustling center, before suburban growth supplanted it. Drive west on Congress to Church Avenue,

IF YOU LIKE

MEXICAN- & NATIVE-AMERICAN CULTURE

Mexican Americans make up about 30% of Tucson's population and play a major role in all aspects of daily life. The city's south-of-the-border soul is visible in its tile-roof architecture, mariachi festivals, and abundance of Mexican restaurants. Native Americans have a strong presence in the area as well: the Tohono O'odham—the name means "desert people who have come from the Earth"—reservation borders Tucson, and the Pascua Yaqui have their villages within the city limits. Local events, especially religious festivals around Christmas and Easter, celebrate the culture of these and other Arizona tribes. Native American crafts encompass exquisite jewelry and basketry as well as the more pedestrian (but still authentic) tourist trinkets.

GETTING OUTDOORS

A warm, dry climate and varied terrain make the Tucson area wonderful for outdoor sports throughout the year. The city has miles of bike paths (shared by joggers and walkers) and plenty of open spaces with memorable desert views. Those same expanses contain some of the best golf courses in the country, with options ranging from well-manicured links at posh resorts to reasonably priced, excellent municipal courses. In winter, hikers enjoy the myriad desert trails; in summer, they go on cooler treks in nearby mountain ranges: Saguaro (pronounced suh-war-oh) National Park (both east and west), Sabino Canyon, and Catalina State Park are all within 20 minutes of central Tucson. Both equestrians and ersatz cowboys and cowgirls will find scenic trails and horseback riding options to suit them at one of the many area stables. City ordinances against "light pollution"—laws designed to minimize the amount of man-made light emitted into the atmosphere—allow viewing of the usually clear desert skies, even in the city center.

6

head north to Alameda, then west to Main, where you'll enter the El Presidio neighborhood and find convenient public parking. The museum and historic complex include **La Casa Cordova** ❽, the **J. Knox Corbett House** ❾, and the **Stevens Home** ❿. After your museum tour, walk east on Alameda and then south on Church to reach the **Pima County Courthouse** ⓫, downtown's architectural jewel.

TIMING You can see most of the highlights of downtown, including the Tucson Museum of Art, in about four hours. Although it's all accessible by car, the one-way streets can be frustrating and time-consuming, so you might consider parking and walking between destinations if the weather is not too hot. On weekends, the area is less crowded and parking is easier, but some businesses and restaurants are closed.

What to See

▶ ❶ **"A" Mountain** (Sentinel Peak). The original name of this mountain west of downtown was derived from its function as a lookout point for the Spanish. In 1915 fans of the University of Arizona football team white-

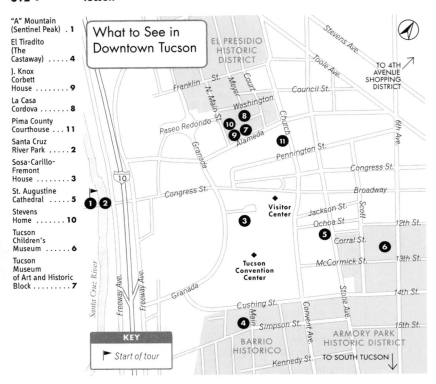

washed a large "A" on its side to celebrate a victory, and the tradition has been kept up ever since—the permanent "A" is now red, white, and blue. The Pima village and cultivated fields that once lay at the base of the peak are long gone. During the day, the peak's a great place to get an overview of the town's layout; at night the city lights below form a dazzling carpet, but the teenage hangout–make-out scene may make some uncomfortable. ⊠ *Congress St. on Sentinel Peak Rd., Downtown.*

❹ **El Tiradito** (The Castaway). No one seems to know the details of the story behind this little shrine, but everyone agrees a tragic love triangle was involved. A bronze plaque indicates only that it's dedicated to a sinner who is buried here on unconsecrated ground. The candles that line the cactus-shrouded spot attest to its continuing importance in local Catholic lore. People light candles and leave *milagros* (literally, "miracles"; little icons used in prayers for healing) for loved ones. A modern-day miracle: the shrine's inclusion on the National Register of Historic Places helped prevent a freeway from plowing through this section of the Barrio Historico. ⊠ *Main Ave. south of Cushing St., Downtown.*

❾ **J. Knox Corbett House.** Built in 1906–07, this house was occupied by members of the Corbett family until 1963. The original occupants were J. Knox Corbett, successful businessman, postmaster, and mayor of Tucson, and his wife Elizabeth Hughes Corbett, an accomplished musician and daughter of Tucson pioneer Sam Hughes. Tucson's Hi Corbett field (the spring training field for the Colorado Rockies) is named for their grandnephew, Hiram. The two-story, Mission Revival–style residence has been furnished with Arts and Crafts pieces: Stickley, Roycroft, Tiffany, and Morris are among the more famous manufacturers represented. ⊠ *180 N. Main Ave., Downtown* ☎ *520/624–2333* ⊕ *www.TucsonMuseumofArt.org* ⌸ *Included in $8 admission to Tucson Museum of Art* ☉ *Tues.–Sat. 10–4, Sun. noon–4. Free guided tour Tues. at 11.*

❽ La Casa Cordova. One of the oldest buildings in Tucson is also one of the best local examples of a Sonoran row house. This simple but elegant design is a Spanish style adapted to adobe construction. The oldest section of La Casa Cordova, constructed around 1848, has been restored to its original appearance and is now the Mexican Heritage Museum. Furnishings of the Native American and pioneer settlers and an exhibit on the presidio's history are inside. ⊠ *175 N. Meyer Ave., Downtown* ☎ *520/ 624–2333* ⊕ *www.TucsonMuseumofArt.org* ⌸ *Included in $8 admission to Tucson Museum of Art* ☉ *Tues.–Sat. 10–4, Sun. noon–4.*

NEED A BREAK?

On the patio of Stevens Home, a 19th-century adobe building adjacent to the Tucson Museum of Art, **Cafe A La C'Arte** (⊠ 150 N. Main Ave., Downtown ☎ 520/ 628–8533) serves fanciful salads, soups, and sandwiches on weekdays. For a tasty frittata or panini (pressed sandwich), try **Caffé Milano** (⊠ 46 W. Congress St., Downtown ☎ 520/628–1601), an Italian deli open weekdays until 2 PM.

★ ⓫ Pima County Courthouse. This Spanish colonial–style building with a mosaic-tile dome is among Tucson's most beautiful historic structures. It was built in 1927 on the site of the original single-story adobe court of 1869; a portion of the old presidio wall can be seen in the south wing of the courthouse's second floor. To the side of the building, the county assessor's office has a diorama depicting the area's early days. The courthouse, still in use, is on the eastern side of El Presidio Park. ⊠ *115 N. Church Ave., between Alameda and Pennington Sts., Downtown* ⊕ *www.jp.co.pima.az.us* ⌸ *Free* ☉ *Weekdays 8–4:30, Sat. 8–noon.*

❷ Santa Cruz River & River Park. The Santa Cruz is a dry wash, or arroyo, most of the year, but sudden summer thunderstorms and rainwater from upper elevations can turn it into a raging river in a matter of hours. The river has been the location of a settlement for thousands of years, and most archaeological finds in the valley are along its banks. When Europeans arrived, the Santa Cruz was a river with wide banks suitable for irrigation. Over time its banks have been narrowed and contained and are now lined by River Park. A favorite spot for walkers, joggers, bicyclists, and horseback riders, the park has a bike path, restrooms, drinking fountains, and sculptures created by local artists.

❸ Sosa-Carillo-Fremont House. One of Tucson's oldest adobe residences, this was the only building spared when the surrounding barrio was torn down to build the Tucson Convention Center. Originally purchased by José Maria Sosa in 1860, it was owned by the Carillo family for 80 years and leased at one time to territorial governor John C. Fremont. The restored house, now a branch of the Arizona Historical Society, is furnished in 1880s fashion and has changing displays of territorial life. The house is in the Convention Center complex. ⊠ *151 S. Granada Ave., Downtown* ☎ *520/622–0956* ⊕ *www.arizonahistoricalsociety.org* ✑ *$3 guided walking tours of Presidio and Tucson Historic District $10* ⊙ *Wed.–Sat. 10–4; walking tours Nov.–Apr., Thurs. and Sat. at 10.*

❺   St. Augustine Cathedral. Construction began in 1896 on this striking structure. Although the imposing white-and-beige Spanish-style building was modeled after the Cathedral of Queretaro in Mexico, a number of its details reflect the desert setting: above the entryway, next to a bronze statue of St. Augustine, are carvings of local desert scenes with saguaro cacti, yucca, and prickly pears—look closely and you'll find the horned toad. Compared with the magnificent facade, the modernized interior is a bit disappointing. ■ **TIP→ For a distinctly Southwestern experience, attend the mariachi mass celebrated Sunday at 8 AM.** ⊠ *192 S. Stone Ave., Downtown* ☎ *520/623–6351* ✑ *Free* ⊙ *Daily 7–6.*

❿   Stevens Home. It was here that wealthy politician and cattle rancher Hiram Stevens and his Mexican wife, Petra Santa Cruz, entertained many of Tucson's leaders during the 1800s. A drought brought the Stevens's cattle ranching to a halt in 1893, and Stevens killed himself in despair, after unsuccessfully attempting to shoot his wife (the bullet was deflected by the comb she wore in her hair). The 1865 house was restored in 1980 and now houses the Tucson Museum of Art's permanent collections of pre-Columbian, Spanish colonial, and Latin American folk art. A café on the porch serves sandwiches, soups, and pastries weekdays 11 to 3. It's a great place to fortify yourself against museum fatigue. ⊠ *150 N. Main Ave., Downtown* ⊕ *www.TucsonMuseumofArt.org* ✑ *Included in $8 admission to Tucson Museum of Art* ⊙ *Tues.–Sat. 10–4, Sun. noon–4* ⊙ *Closed Mon.*

☾ ❻   Tucson Children's Museum. Youngsters are encouraged to touch and explore the science, language, and history exhibits here. They can key in on Little Tikes IBM computers or turn on the electricity in the streets of a model town. There's Dinosaur Canyon, with mechanical prehistoric creatures, and a bubble room where children can place themselves in the middle of a large vertical soap bubble. For smaller fry there's a toddler's playroom. ⊠ *200 S. 6th Ave., Downtown* ☎ *520/792–9985* ⊕ *www.tucsonchildrensmuseum.org* ✑ *$5.50* ⊙ *Tues.–Sat. 10–5, Sun. noon–5.*

★ ❼   Tucson Museum of Art and Historic Block. The five historic buildings on this block are listed in the National Register of Historic Places and you can enter La Casa Cordova, the Stevens Home, the J. Knox Corbett House, and the Edward Nye Fish House. The Romero House, believed to incorporate a section of the presidio wall, is not open to the public. In the center of the museum complex is the Plaza of the Pioneers, honoring Tucson's early citizens.

The museum building, the only modern structure of the complex, houses a permanent collection of modern and contemporary art and hosts traveling shows. It's permanent and changing exhibitions of Western art fill the Edward Nye Fish House. This 1868 adobe belonged to an early merchant, entrepreneur, and politician and to his wife, Maria Wakefield Fish, a prominent educator. The building is notable for its 15-foot beamed ceilings and saguaro cactus–rib supports. There are free docent tours of the museum, and you can pick up a self-guided tour map of the El Presidio district. Free parking is in a lot behind the museum at Washington and Meyer streets. ⊠ *140 N. Main Ave., Downtown* ☎ *520/624–2333* ⊕ *www.TucsonMuseumofArt.org* ✉ *$8 free 1st Sun. of every month; tours free* ⊘ *Tues.–Sat. 10–4, Sun. noon–4. Guided tours Tues.–Sun. No guided tours June–Sept.* ⊘ *Closed Mon.*

The University of Arizona

A university might not seem to be the most likely spot for a vacation visit, but this one is unusual. The campus itself is an arboretum, and there are several museums, with exhibitions ranging from astronomy to photography, on the grounds.

The U of A (as opposed to ASU, its rival state university in Tempe) covers 353 acres and is a major economic influence with a student population of more than 34,000. The land for the university was "donated" by a couple of gamblers and a saloon owner in 1891 (their benevolence was reputed to have been inspired by a bad hand of cards), and $25,000 of territorial (Arizona was still a territory back in 1891) money was used to build Old Main (the original building) and hire six faculty members. Money ran out before Old Main's roof was placed, but a few enlightened citizens pitched in funds to finish it. Most of the city's populace was less enthusiastic about the institution: they were disgruntled when the 13th Territorial Legislature granted the University of Arizona to Tucson and awarded Phoenix with what was considered the real prize—an insane asylum and a prison.

The university's flora is impressive—it represents a collection of plants from arid and semiarid regions around the world. An extremely rare mutated, or "crested," saguaro grows at the northeast corner of the Old Main building. The long, grassy Mall in the heart of campus—itself once a vast cactus garden—sits atop a huge underground student activity center, and makes for a pleasant stroll on a balmy evening.

Numbers in the text correspond to numbers in the margin and on the What to See at the University of Arizona map.

A GOOD WALK

Start your tour near the northwest corner of campus, at Euclid and 2nd streets, at the public parking garage. Walk a half-block east on 2nd Street to the **Arizona Historical Society's Museum** ⑫ ⌐, and see how far the Old Pueblo has come in 100 years. One block south on Park Avenue, just inside the main gate of the university, is the **Arizona State Museum** ⑬, the place to explore Native American culture. Heading east on University Boulevard and deeper into the campus, you'll pass Old Main and the crested saguaro. As the road curves to the left, University Boulevard turns into the campus mall. The Student Union and University Bookstore are on your left; the sculpture in front of the complex depicts Arizona–Mexico border struggles. Cross over to the south side of the mall (watch out for Frisbees) and take a peek inside the old Gymnasium, where Wildcats fans cheered their team before the construction of McKale Center.

6

Continue east, passing the steps leading down to the underground activity center, and you'll come to the **Flandrau Science Center and Planetarium ⓮**, at the intersection of N. Cherry Avenue. Check telescope-viewing schedules, see a light show, or stock up on science-oriented gifts here.

Walk north on Cherry, then turn left onto 2nd Street, passing several fairly tame fraternity and sorority houses. Turn right on Olive Road to find the **Center for Creative Photography ⓯**, home to most of photographer Ansel Adams's negatives and a slew of other exhibits in this medium. Across from the center is the **University of Arizona Museum of Art ⓰**. From here it's a short walk west on Speedway Boulevard to Park Avenue, where you can go south to 2nd Street and return to the Arizona Historical Society's Museum and the parking lot.

To soak up more college culture, continue down Park to University Boulevard and turn right. This section of University is the hub of off-campus activity, packing restaurants, cafés, and trendy boutiques into a few blocks. At this point, you can walk—or on weekends ride aboard the **Old Pueblo Trolley ⓱**—along University to **4th Avenue ⓲**, Tucson's last bastion of bohemia, for shopping and people-watching.

TIMING To see this huge university campus in less than a full day takes careful planning. Call ahead to verify hours for the university's museums, as yearly budget revisions often cause schedule changes. If you drive, leave your car in a university garage or lot; those on 2nd Street at Mountain Avenue, on Speedway Boulevard at Park Avenue, on Tyndall Avenue south of University Boulevard, and on 2nd Street at Euclid Avenue are the most convenient. Parking costs $2 for the first hour and $1 for each additional hour, with free parking on weekends and holidays. During school semesters, you're better off visiting on the weekend when parking is free and plentiful; there's no problem in summer when most of the students leave campus. Visit the Web site **University of Arizona** (⊕ www.arizona. edu), for parking maps and the latest visitor information.

What to See

✆ ▶ ⓬ **Arizona Historical Society's Museum.** Flanking the entrance to the museum are statues of two men: Father Kino, the Jesuit who established San Xavier del Bac and a string of other missions, and John Greenaway, indelibly linked to Phelps Dodge, the copper-mining company that helped Arizona earn statehood in 1912. The museum houses the headquarters of the state Historical Society and has exhibits exploring the history of southern Arizona, the Southwest United States, and northern Mexico, starting with the Hohokam Indians and Spanish explorers. Check out the harrowing "Life on the Edge: A History of Medicine in Arizona" exhibit to gain a new appreciation of modern drugstores in present-day Tucson. Children enjoy the exhibit on copper mining (complete with an atmospheric replica of a mine shaft and camp) and the stagecoaches in the transportation area. The library houses an extensive collection of historic Arizona photographs and sells inexpensive reprints. You can park your car in the garage at the corner of 2nd and Euclid streets and get a free parking pass in the museum. ⊠ *949 E. 2nd St., University* ☎ *520/ 628-5774* ⊕ *www.arizonahistoricalsociety.org* ⌧ *$5 free 1st Sat. of every month* ☉ *Mon.–Sat. 10–4; library weekdays 10–3, Sat. 10–1.*

What to See at the University of Arizona

⓭ Arizona State Museum. Inside the main gate of the university is Arizona's oldest museum, dating from territorial days (1893) and recognized as one of the world's most important resources for the study of Southwestern cultures. Exhibits in the original (south) building focus on the state's ancient history, including fossils and a fascinating sample of tree-ring dating. "Paths of Life: American Indians of the Southwest" is a permanent exhibit that explores the cultural traditions, origins, and contemporary lives of 10 native tribes of Arizona and Sonora, Mexico. ⊠ *Park Ave. at University Blvd., University* ☎ *520/621–6302* ⊕ *www. statemuseum.arizona.edu* ⊠ *Free* ☉ *Mon.–Sat. 10–5, Sun. noon–5.*

NEED A BREAK?

Just outside the west campus gate, University Boulevard is lined with student-oriented eateries. **Sinbad's** (⊠ 810 E. University Blvd., University ☎ 520/623–4010) nestled in the verdant Geronimo Plaza, serves felafel and other Middle-Eastern fare, and has a great patio where you can watch the passing university scene. The Chinese and Thai fast food at **Pei Wei** (⊠ 845 E. University Blvd., University ☎ 520/884–7413) is flavorful, healthful, and affordable. For custom-made burritos and tacos, try the branch of the **Chipotle** (⊠ 905 E. University Blvd., University ☎ 520/628–7967) chain.

Beer lovers should head over to **Gentle Ben's** (✉ 865 E. University Blvd., University ☎ 520/624–4177), a burger-and-brew pub. The deck upstairs affords a good view of the sunset.

★ ⑮ **Center for Creative Photography.** Ansel Adams conceived the idea of a photographer's archive and donated the majority of his negatives to this museum. In addition to its superb collection of his work, the center has works by other major photographers including Paul Strand, W. Eugene Smith, Edward Weston, and Louise Dahl-Wolfe. Changing exhibits in the main gallery display selected pieces from the collection, but if you'd like to see the work of a particular photographer in the archives, call to arrange an appointment. ✉ *1030 N. Olive Rd., north of 2nd St., University* ☎ *520/621–7968* ⊕ *www.creativephotography.org* ⊠ *Free* ☉ *Weekdays 9–5, weekends noon–5.*

🐾 ⑭ **Flandrau Science Center and Planetarium.** Attractions include a 16-inch public telescope; the impressive Star Theatre, where a multimedia show brings astronomy to life; an interactive meteor exhibit; and a Mineral Museum, which exhibits more than 2,000 rocks and gems, some rather rare. Bring a camera—special adapters allow you to take pictures through the telescopes. ✉ *Cherry Ave. and University Blvd., University* ☎ *520/621–4515, 520/621–7827 recorded message* ⊕ *www.flandrau.org* ⊠ *Exhibits $3; planetarium shows $5.50; observatory free* ☉ *Exhibits Mon.–Wed. 9–5, Thurs.–Sat. 9–5 and 7 PM–9 PM, Sun. 1–5. Planetarium show times vary. Observatory 7:30 PM–10 PM.*

⑱ **4th Avenue.** Students and counterculturists favor this ½-mi strip of 4th Avenue. Vintage-clothing stores rub shoulders with ethnic eateries from Guatemalan to Greek. After dark, 4th Avenue bars pulse with live and recorded music. ✉ *Between University and 9th Sts.*

⑰ **Old Pueblo Trolley.** You can ride historic electric trolleys through the streets of Tucson along University Boulevard and 4th Avenue past shops and restaurants. The route passes restored historic buildings on part of the original 1898 streetcar track and terminates near the Arizona Historical Society. ✉ *360 E. 8th St., University* ☎ *520/792–1802* ⊕ *www.oldpueblotrolley.org* ⊠ *Fri. and Sat. $1, Sun. 25¢* ☉ *Fri. 6 PM–10 PM, Sat. noon–midnight, Sun. noon–6.*

⑯ **University of Arizona Museum of Art.** This small museum houses a collection of European paintings from the Renaissance through the 17th century. A highlight is the Kress Collection's Retablo from Ciudad Rodrigo: 26 panels of an altarpiece made in 1488 by Fernando Gallego. ✉ *Fine Arts Complex, Bldg. 2, southeast corner of Speedway Blvd. and Park Ave., University* ☎ *520/621–7567* ⊕ *www.artmuseum.arizona.edu* ⊠ *Free* ☉ *Tues.–Fri. 9–5, weekends noon–4.*

Central Tucson, the Santa Catalinas & East

The U of A, built in 1891, determined the direction in which the city would grow: most residential areas and major attractions are east of the main freeway, I–10. Tucson has continued to sprawl east and north into the foothills of the Santa Catalina Mountains.

Numbers in the text correspond to numbers in the margin and on the What to See in Greater Tucson map.

A GOOD TOUR

In Central Tucson the sights worth seeing include the **Tucson Botanical Gardens** ⑲ ➤ at the corner of Grant Road and North Alvernon Way; the small **Reid Park Zoo** ⑳; and the **Fort Lowell Park and Museum** ㉑, where the museum has artifacts from territorial days and the park has a playground and a pond.

Venturing farther afield, you can head north into the Santa Catalinas, stopping off at your choice of **Sabino Canyon** ㉒, **De Grazia's Gallery in the Sun** ㉓, **Tohono Chul Park** ㉔, or **Mount Lemmon** ㉕. Sabino Canyon has hiking trails, a tram, and loads of saguaros and vistas, making it a rewarding destination close to town. Mount Lemmon, although more time-consuming (it's a one-hour drive each way), is a good alternative on a warm day because of its high elevation and cooler temperatures.

If caves or aviation are your fancy, you may want to head east instead, driving to **Colossal Cave Mountain Park** ㉖, then south to **Pima Air and Space Museum** ㉗.

TIMING

If it's warm, visit outdoor attractions such as the Tucson Botanical Gardens and Sabino Canyon in the morning. Mount Lemmon, high up and cooler, makes an excellent midday destination in summer. Colossal Cave stays at a constant, comfortable temperature.

6

What to See

☾ ㉖ **Colossal Cave Mountain Park.** This limestone grotto 20 mi east of Tucson (take Broadway Boulevard or 22nd Street East to Colossal Cave Road) is the largest dry cavern in the world. Guides discuss the fascinating crystal formations and relate the many romantic tales surrounding the cave, including the legend that an enormous sum of money stolen in a stagecoach robbery is hidden here. Forty-five-minute cave tours begin every 30 minutes and require a ½-mi walk and 363 stairs. The park includes a ranch area with trail rides ($27 per hour), a gemstone-sluicing area, a small museum, nature trails, a butterfly garden, a snack bar, and a gift shop. ⊠ *Colossal Cave Rd. at Old Spanish Trail Rd., Eastside* ☎ *520/647–7275* ⊕ *www.colossalcave.com* ⊠ *Park $5 per car; cave tour $8.50 per person* ☽ *Oct.–mid-Mar., Mon.–Sat. 9–5, Sun. 9–6; mid-Mar.–Sept., Mon.–Sat. 8–6, Sun. 8–7.*

㉓ **De Grazia's Gallery in the Sun.** Arizonan artist Ted De Grazia, who depicted Southwest Native American and Mexican life in a manner some find kitschy and others adore, built this sprawling, spacious single-story museum with the assistance of Native American friends, using only natural material from the surrounding desert. You can visit De Grazia's workshop, former home, and grave. Although the original works are not for sale, the museum's gift shop has a wide selection of prints, ceramics, and books by and about the colorful artist. ⊠ *6300 N. Swan Rd., Foothills* ☎ *520/299–9191* ⊕ *www.degrazia.org* ⊠ *Free* ☽ *Daily 10–4.*

☾ ㉑ **Fort Lowell Park and Museum.** Fertile soil and proximity to the Rillito River once enticed the Hohokam to construct a village on this site. Centuries later, a fort was built here to protect the fledgling city of Tucson against

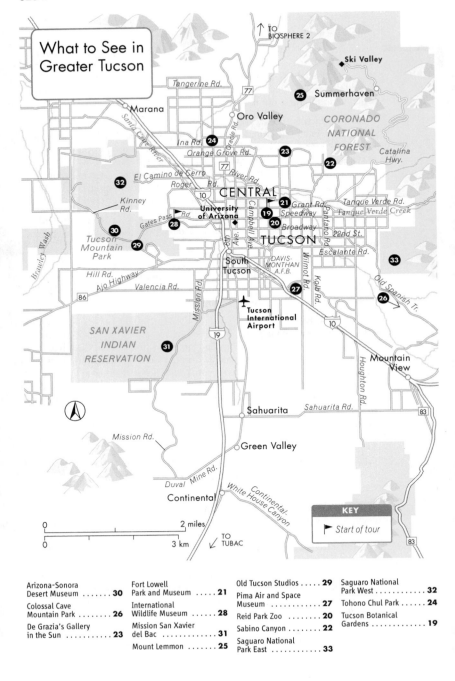

What to See in Greater Tucson

↑ TO BIOSPHERE 2

Ski Valley

Tangerine Rd. 77

25 Summerhaven

Marana Oro Valley CORONADO
NATIONAL
FOREST Catalina
Hwy.

Ina Rd. 24 23
Orange Grove Rd. 22
77 River Rd.

El Camino de Cerro
32 Roger Rd.
10 CENTRAL Tanque Verde Rd.

Kinney
Rd. University
of Arizona 21 Grant Rd. Tanque Verde Creek
19 Speedway
20 Broadway
Gates Pass Rd. 28 TUCSON
30 29 22nd St.
Tucson
Mountain
Park Escalante Rd.
South 33
Hill Rd. Tucson DAVIS-
MONTHAN
A.F.B.
86 Ajo Highway
Valencia Rd. 27 Old Spanish Tr.
26

10

SAN XAVIER Tucson
INDIAN International
RESERVATION Airport 19
31
Mountain
View

Sahuarita Sahuarita Rd.
83

Mission Rd.
Green Valley

Duval Mine Rd.
Continental
Continental-
White House Canyon
Continental

0   2 miles
0   3 km TO
TUBAC

the Apaches (1873–91). The former commanding officer's quarters display artifacts from military life in territorial days. Some of the descendants of the inhabitants of El Fuerte, a Mexican village that arose among the abandoned fort buildings in the 1890s, live in El Callejón, an alley off Fort Lowell Road just west of the museum. The park has a playground, ball fields, tennis courts, and a duck pond. ⊠ *2900 N. Craycroft Rd., Central* ☎ *520/885–3832* ▧ *Free* ☼ *Wed.–Sat. 10–4.*

㉕ Mount Lemmon. In 1881 Sara Lemmon became the first woman to reach the peak of this mountain, part of the Santa Catalina range. Mount Lemmon is the southernmost ski slope in the continental United States, but you don't have to be a skier to enjoy it. You can picnic and hike among the 150 mi of marked and well-maintained trails and the mountain's 9,157-foot elevation brings relief from summer heat.

Mount Lemmon Highway twists its way for 28 mi up the mountainside. Every 1,000-foot climb in elevation is equivalent, in terms of climate, to traveling 300 mi north: you'll move from typical Sonoran Desert plants in the foothills to vegetation similar to that found in southern Canada at the top. Rock formations along the way look as though they were carefully balanced against each other by sculptors from another planet.

At milepost 18 of your ascent, on the left-hand side of the road, is the Palisades Ranger Station of **Coronado National Forest** (☎ 520/749–8700). Rangers have information on the mountain's campgrounds, hiking trails, and picnic spots. It's open weekends 8:30 to 4:30 in winter, daily 9 to 6 in summer. Even if you don't make it to the top of the mountain, you'll find stunning views of Tucson at Windy Point, about halfway up. Look for a road on your left between the Windy Point and San Pedro lookouts; it leads to Rose Canyon Lake, a lovely reservoir.

Just before you reach the ski area, you'll pass through the tiny alpine-style village of **Summerhaven,** which has some casual restaurants, gift shops, and pleasant lodges. Though much of Summerhaven was destroyed by a forest fire in summer 2003, rebuilding is well underway. An excursion up the mountain can be capped off with breakfast, lunch, or a slice of home-made pie at **Mount Lemmon Café** (☎ 520/576–1234), the first building on the left as you enter the village.

Mount Lemmon Highway ends at **Mount Lemmon Ski Valley** (☎ 520/576–1321). Skiing depends on natural conditions—there's no artificial snow, so call ahead. There are 16 runs, open daily in winter, ranging from beginner to advanced. Lift tickets cost $35 for an all-day pass and

$30 for a half-day pass (starting at 1 PM). Equipment rentals and instruction are available. In off-season you can take a ride ($9) on the chairlift, which whisks you to the top of the slope—some 9,100 feet above sea level. Many ride the lift, then head out hiking on one of several trails that crisscross the summit. There are some concessions at the ski lift.

There are no gas stations on Mount Lemmon Highway, so be sure to check the road conditions in winter and to gas up before you leave town any time of year. To reach the highway, take Tanque Verde Road to Catalina Highway, which becomes Mount Lemmon Highway as you head north. ⊠ *Mount Lemmon Hwy., Northeast* ☎ *520/576–1400 recorded snow report, 520/547–7510 winter road conditions* ⌨ *$5 per vehicle per day or $20 for an annual pass; includes Sabino Canyon* ⊙ *Daily, depending on snow in ski season.*

㉗ Pima Air and Space Museum. This huge facility ranks among the largest private collections of aircraft in the world. More than 200 airplanes are on display, including a presidential plane used by both John F. Kennedy and Lyndon B. Johnson, a full-scale replica of the Wright brothers' 1903 Wright Flyer, and a mock-up of the X-15, the world's fastest aircraft. World War II planes are particularly well-represented. Hour-long van tours of Aerospace Maintenance and Regeneration Center (AMARC)—affectionately called "The Boneyard"—at Davis-Monthan Air Force Base provide an eerie glimpse of hundreds of mothballed aircraft lined up in rows on a vast tract of desert; you must reserve in advance for this tour. ⊠ *6000 E. Valencia Rd., I–10, Exit 267, South* ☎ *520/ 574–0462* ⊕ *www.pimaair.org* ⌨ *$11.75, tram $4, AMARC tour $6* ⊙ *Daily 9–5, last admission at 4; AMARC tours weekdays only.*

㊳ ㉚ Reid Park Zoo. This small but well-designed zoo won't tax the children's—or your—patience. There are plenty of shady places to sit, a wonderful gift shop, and a snack bar to rev you up when your energy flags. The youngsters will love the zoo's adorable newborns and the South American enclosure with its rain forest and exotic birds. If you're visiting in summer, go early in the day when the animals are active. The park surrounding the zoo has playground structures and a lake where you can feed ducks and rent paddleboats. ⊠ *Reid Park, Randolph Way off 22nd St. between Alvernon Way and Country Club Rd., Central* ☎ *520/ 791–3204* ⊕ *www.tucsonzoo.org* ⌨ *$5* ⊙ *Daily 9–4.*

★ ㉒ Sabino Canyon. Year-round, but especially in summer, locals flock to Coronado National Forest to hike, picnic, and enjoy the waterfalls, streams, swimming holes, and shade trees. No cars are allowed, but a narrated tram ride (about 45 minutes round-trip) takes you up a WPA-built road to the top of the canyon; you can hop off and on at any of the nine stops or hike any of the numerous trails. There's also a shorter tram ride to adjacent Bear Canyon, where a much more rigorous but rewarding hike leads to the popular Seven Falls (it'll take about 1½ hours each way from the drop-off point, so carry plenty

> **WORD OF MOUTH**
>
> "Sabino Canyon is pretty much a favorite of locals and tourists alike." –lori

CLOSE UP

The Desert's Fragile Giant

EASY TO ANTHROPOMORPHIZE BECAUSE THEY HAVE "ARMS," saguaros are thought to be the descendants of tropical trees that lost their leaves and became dormant during drought. *Carnegiea gigantea* (the saguaro's scientific name) grows nowhere else on Earth than the Sonoran Basin, an area that includes southern Arizona and northern Mexico.

Tourists are often amazed to find that these odd-looking plants actually bloom each May or June. Each bloom opens only for a few evening hours after sunset. The next afternoon, the creamy-white chalice closes forever. An adult saguaro produces six or seven flowers a day for about a month. They are cross-pollinated by bees, Mexican white-winged doves, and brown bats.

Because the saguaro stores massive quantities of water (enough to

conceivably last two years), it's often called the "cactus camel." New saguaros are born when the seeds of the flower take root, an arduous process. Late freezes and even high heat can kill a seedling in its first days. Once a seed is established, it grows up under the protection of a "nurse" tree, such as a paloverde. Fully grown, a saguaro can weigh as much as 7 tons.

The saguaro, like many other wild plants, is protected by Arizona law. Without an Arizona Department of Agriculture permit, it's illegal to move a saguaro or sell one from private property.

Some say the saguaro has its own means of protecting itself from would-be poachers or vandals: in the early 1980s a hunter fired a shotgun at a large saguaro near Phoenix. It collapsed onto him, killing him instantly!

6

of water). If you're in Tucson near a full moon, take the special night tram and watch the desert come alive with nocturnal critters. ⊠ *Sabino Canyon Rd. at Sunrise Dr., Foothills* ☎ *520/749–2861 recorded tram information, 520/749–8700 visitor center* ⊕ *www.fs.fed.us/r3/coronado* ⊠ *$5 per vehicle per day or $20 for an annual pass, includes Mount Lemmon, tram $7.50, Bear Canyon tram $3* ☉ *Visitor center weekdays 8–4:30, weekends 8:30–4:30; call for tram schedules.*

㉔ Tohono Chul Park. A 48-acre retreat designed to promote the conservation of arid regions, Tohono Chul—the name means "desert corner" in the language of the Tohono O'odham—uses a demonstration garden, greenhouse, and geology wall to explain this unique desert area. Enjoy the shady nooks, nature trails, small art gallery, great gift shop, and tearoom at this peaceful spot. ⊠ *7366 N. Paseo del Norte, Northwest* ☎ *520/742–6455* ⊕ *www.tohonochulpark.org* ⊠ *$5; free 1st Tues. of each month* ☉ *Park daily 8 AM–sunset; buildings daily 9–5.*

▶ ⑲ Tucson Botanical Gardens. On 5 acres are a tropical greenhouse; a sensory garden, where you can touch and smell the plants and listen to the abundant bird life; historical gardens, which display the Mediterranean landscaping that the property's original owners planted in the 1930s; a garden designed to attract birds; and a cactus garden. Other special gardens showcase wildflowers, Australian plants, and Native American crops and herbs. Call ahead to find out what's blooming. All of the paths are wheelchair accessible, and there's a little gift shop near the entrance. ✉ *2150 N. Alvernon Way, Central* 📞 *520/326–9686* 🌐 *www.tucsonbotanical.org* 🎫 *$5* ⊙ *Daily 8:30–4:30.*

OFF THE
BEATEN
PATH

BIOSPHERE 2 CENTER – In the town of Oracle, some 30 minutes north of Tucson, eight scientists walked into a self-contained, sealed ecosystem in 1992, and remained inside for two years. The experiment wasn't a complete success, but the structure remains an interesting phenomenon.

The miniature world within Biosphere includes tropical rain forest, savanna, desert, thorn scrub, marsh, ocean, and agricultural areas, including almost 3,000 plant and animal species. A film and a large, rotating cutaway model in the visitor center explain the project. Guided walking tours, which last about two hours and cover ¾ mi, take you inside some of the biomes, and observation areas let you peer in at the rest. A snack bar overlooks the Santa Catalina Mountains. Biosphere 2 Center is now managed by Columbia University's Earth Institute, which directs all of the current scientific, educational, and visitor-center operations. At this writing the biosphere is still open to the public, but word is that its future is up in the air; call ahead to confirm it's still open before you go. ✉ *AZ 77, Milepost 96.5, Oracle* 📞 *520/838–6200* 🌐 *www.bio2. com* 🎫 *$19.95* ⊙ *Daily 9–4.*

Westside & the Sonoran Desert

If you're interested in the flora and fauna of the Sonoran Desert—as well as some of its appearances in the cinema—heed the same advice given the pioneers: go west.

TIMING   Although the attractions in this area are not close together, it's possible to tour all the sights in one very busy day, as they're on a fairly direct route to one another. If you're going to skip something, you might consider saving the Wildlife Museum for another trip. You could start the morning at Saguaro National Park and then head over to the Arizona–Sonora Desert Museum, where you can lunch at the Ironwood Terrace or the more upscale Ocotillo Café. How long you spend at Saguaro National Park depends on whether you choose a short walk to see petroglyphs at Signal Hill on the Loop Drive (an hour should suffice), or hike a longer mountain trail. Allow at least two hours for your visit at the Desert Museum. The hottest time of the afternoon can be spent ducking in and out of attractions at Old Tucson, visiting the air-conditioned International Wildlife Museum, or enjoying the indoor sanctuary of San Xavier mission. You could save the Mission for another day as it's on the road to Tubac, Tumacácori, and Nogales.

What to See

🟢 ㉚   **Arizona–Sonora Desert Museum.** The name "museum" is misleading; this
Fodor'sChoice   delightful site is a beautifully planned zoo and botanical garden featur-
★   ing the animals and plants of the Sonoran Desert. Hummingbirds, cac-

tus wrens, rattlesnakes, scorpions, bighorn sheep, and prairie dogs all busy themselves in ingeniously designed habitats. An Earth Sciences Center has an artificial limestone cave and a hands-on meteor and mineral display. The coyote and javelina exhibits have "invisible" fencing that separates humans from animals, and the Riparian Corridor section affords great underwater views of otters and beavers. The gift shop carries books about Arizona and the desert, plus jewelry and crafts. ✉ *2021 N. Kinney Rd., Westside* ☎ *520/883–2702* ⊕ *www.desertmuseum.org* ✍ *$12* ☉ *Mar.–Sept., daily 7:30–5; Oct.–Feb., daily 8:30–5.*

6

🖐 ▶ **㉘ International Wildlife Museum.** This imposing structure has no real wildlife in it at all: almost 400 species of animals are stuffed and mounted in re-creations of their natural habitats. A "petting" menagerie allows children to touch different animal skins; they can also learn about birds and mammals from all over the world via interactive computers. ✉ *4800 W. Speedway, Westside* ☎ *520/629–0100* ⊕ *www.thewildlifemuseum. org* ✍ *$7* ☉ *Weekdays 9–5, weekends 9–6.*

㉛ **Mission San Xavier del Bac.** The oldest Catholic church in the United States

Fodor'sChoice still serving the community for which it was built, San Xavier was

★ founded in 1692 by Father Eusebio Francisco Kino, who established 22 missions in northern Mexico and southern Arizona. The current structure was made out of native materials by Franciscan missionaries between 1777 and 1797 and is owned by the Tohono O'odham tribe.

The beauty of the mission, with elements of Spanish, baroque, and Moorish architectural styles, is highlighted by the stark landscape against which it is set, inspiring an early-20th-century poet to dub it the White Dove of the Desert. Inside, there's a wealth of painted statues, carvings, and frescoes. Paul Schwartzbaum, who helped restore Michelangelo's masterwork in Rome, supervised Tohono O'odham artisans in the restoration of the mission's artwork, completed in 1997; Schwartzbaum has called the mission the Sistine Chapel of the United States. Mass is celebrated at 8:30 AM weekdays in the church and three times on Sunday morning. Call ahead for information about special celebrations.

Across the parking lot from the mission, San Xavier Plaza has a number of crafts shops selling the handiwork of the Tohono O'odham tribe, including jewelry, pottery, friendship bowls, and baskets with man-in-the-maze designs. ⊠ *San Xavier Rd., 9 mi southwest of Tucson on I-19, South* ☎ *520/294-2624* ⊕ *www.sanxaviermission.org* ⊠ *Free* ⊙ *Church daily 7–5, gift shop daily 8–5.*

NEED A BREAK?	For wonderful Indian fry bread—large, round pieces of dough taken fresh from the hot oil and served with sweet or savory toppings like honey, powdered sugar, beans, meats, or green chiles—stop in the **Wa:k Snack Shop** (☎ No phone) at the back of San Xavier Plaza. You can also have breakfast or a lunch of Mexican food here, and if you're lucky, local dancers will be performing for one of the many tour groups that stop here.

☺ ㉙ **Old Tucson Studios.** This film studio–cum–theme park, originally built for the 1940 motion picture *Arizona,* has been used to shoot countless movies, such as *Rio Bravo* (1959) and *The Quick and the Dead* (1994), and the TV shows *Gunsmoke, Bonanza,* and *Highway to Heaven.* Actors in Western garb perform and roam the streets talking to visitors. Youngsters enjoy the simulated gunfights, rides, stunt shows, and petting farm, while adults might appreciate the screenings of old Westerns and the little-bit-bawdy Grand Palace Hotel's Dance Hall Revue. There are plenty of places to chow down and to buy souvenirs. ⊠ *Tucson Mountain Park, 201 S. Kinney Rd., Westside* ☎ *520/883–0100* ⊕ *www. oldtucson.com* ⊠ *$14.95* ⊙ *Sun.–Fri. 10–3, Sat. 10–4.*

Saguaro National Park

Tucson Mountain District (west section): off I–10 Exit 242 (Avra Valley Rd.) or Exit 257, then Speedway Blvd. west to Kinney Rd. and turn right. Rincon Mountain District (east section): off I–10 Exit 275 (Houghton Rd.), then north to Old Spanish Trail.

The towering saguaro cactus, standing sentinel in the desert, might be the most familiar emblem of the American Southwest. A native to the Sonoran Desert, the saguaro is known for its towering height (often 50 feet) and arms that reach out in weird configurations. The cactus is ribbed vertically with accordionlike pleats that expand to store water gathered through its shallow roots during infrequent desert rains. At any time of year, the sight of these kings of the desert is awe-inspiring but in late spring (usually May), the giant succulent's top is covered with tiny white blooms. The slow-growing cacti (they can take up to 15 years to grow a foot and 75 years to grow their first arm) are protected by state and federal laws, so enjoy but don't disturb them. The worlds' largest concentration of saguaros is in Saguaro National Park.

The park is made up of two sections that bookend Tucson. The western section is the smaller—at 24,000 acres—more heavily visited area. The eastern section covers more than 67,000 acres and climbs through five climate zones, which makes for dramatic hikes. Both sections have scenic drives and hiking and biking options as well. Pack a lunch before setting off for either section of the park and bring plenty of water: there's no food sold at the park and not only are you likely to get de-

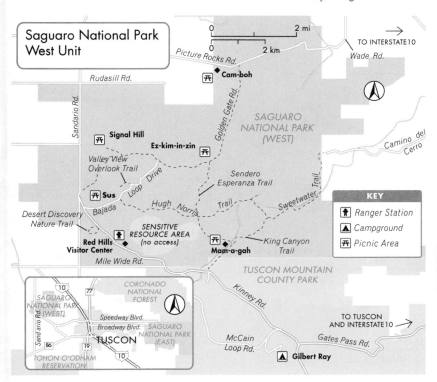

Saguaro National Park West Unit

hydrated in the hot, dry landscape, but you can't depend on finding water should you run out. The best plan is to set out in the early morning—it's cooler and the best time to see the wildlife at its liveliest.

32 **Saguaro National Park West.** Before you venture into the desert, it's Fodor'sChoice worth stopping at the impressive **Red Hills Visitor Center.** A slide show ★ (given every half hour from 9 to 4:30) offers a Native American perspective of the saguaro cactus, and a lifelike display simulates the flora and fauna of the region.

A drive through the park on a 6-mi unpaved loop through dense saguaro forest takes ½–2 hours depending on how many stops you make. At **Signal Hill,** you can inspect ancient petroglyphs left by the Hohokam Indians centuries ago. For bird-watching focus your binoculars on the saguaro limbs, where many different birds make their homes. Volunteer-led birding walks (November–April) and wildflower hikes (March–May) begin at the visitor center. Ask for a list of activities. ☒ 2700 N. Kinney Rd., 2 mi north of Arizona–Sonora Desert Museum entrance, Westside ☎ 520/733–5158 ⊕ www.nps.gov/sagu ☒ $10 per vehicle or $5 per person on foot or bike ☺ Visitor center daily 9–5, park roads daily sunrise–sunset.

Hiking. The accessible Desert Discovery Nature Trail is a pleasant ½-mi stroll through desert flora for old and young, with benches thoughtfully

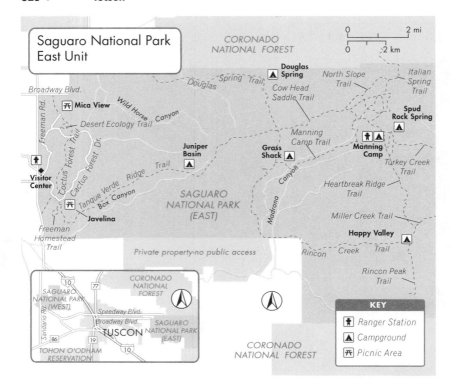

Saguaro National Park East Unit

CORONADO NATIONAL FOREST

0   2 mi
0   2 km

Broadway Blvd.

Douglas Spring Trail

Douglas Spring ▲

North Slope Trail

Italian Spring Trail

Cow Head Saddle Trail

Spud Rock Spring ▲

Mica View ㋡

Wild Horse Canyon

Desert Ecology Trail

Freeman Rd.

Coctus Forest Trail

Cactus Forest Dr.

Juniper Basin ▲

Manning Camp Trail

Grass Shack ▲

Manning Camp 👤▲

Turkey Creek Trail

Tanque Verde Ridge Trail

Visitor Center ♦

Box Canyon

SAGUARO NATIONAL PARK (EAST)

Madrona Canyon

Heartbreak Ridge Trail

Miller Creek Trail

㋡ Javelina

Freeman Homestead Trail

Happy Valley ▲

Private property—no public access

Rincon Creek Trail

Rincon Peak Trail

CORONADO NATIONAL FOREST

SAGUARO NATIONAL PARK (WEST)

Sandario Rd.

10
77

Speedway Blvd.
Broadway Blvd.

TUCSON

SAGUARO NATIONAL PARK (EAST)

86
19
10

TOHON O'ODHAM RESERVATION

CORONADO NATIONAL FOREST

KEY
👤 Ranger Station
▲ Campground
㋡ Picnic Area

placed under shade trees. Another short but rewarding trail is the 1-mi Valley View Overlook, where you'll be treated to splendid mountain vistas. The 9.8-mi Hugh Norris Trail, named after a Tohono O'odham police chief, is one of the most impressive in the Southwest. With switchbacks and some moderately steep sections, it leads hikers through the Tucson Mountains to the top of Wasson Peak.

Camping. There's no camping inside Saguaro's west district, but **Gilbert Ray Campground** is only 3 mi south (⇨ *see* Where to Stay).

㉝ Saguaro National Park East. You can explore by car, bicycle, horseback, or on foot. The 8-mi paved Cactus Forest Drive loops around the park and leads to trailheads and picnic areas. From October through April, naturalists give talks on the wildlife, geology, and archaeology of the area. Take a ranger-led moonlight hike (scheduled monthly) for a different perspective. Beginning and experienced mountain bikers enjoy the 2½-mi Cactus Forest Trail, a sandy single track with varied terrain. Here you'll see plenty of wildlife, as well as older, larger saguaro, alongside palo verde and mesquite trees. At the visitor center, ask for a detailed map and a schedule of activities. To get here from town, take Speedway Boulevard to Houghton and go south to Old Spanish Trail. ✉ *3693 S. Old Span-*

ish Trail, Eastside ☎ *520/733–5153* ⊕ *www.nps.gov/sagu* 🎫 *$10 per vehicle, $5 per person on foot or bike* ☉ *Visitor center daily 9–5, park roads daily 7 AM–sunset.*

Hiking. To really experience the majesty of the saguaros, wander among these silent sentinels. **The Desert Ecology Trail,** a wheelchair-accessible, ¼-mi loop near the **Mica View** Picnic Area, has exhibits explaining how local plants and animals subsist on a limited supply of water. The Freeman Homestead Trail gives a bit of the history of homesteading in the region. Look for owls living in the cliffs above you along this 1-mi loop. The 14-mi Tanque Verde Ridge Trail takes you from desert scrub to oak, juniper, and pine trees at the 6,000-foot peak. The elevation gain also makes for spectacular views of the surrounding mountain ranges.

Camping. The only camping permitted in the park is at the six designated primitive campgrounds, which are open all year. **Manning Camp** is the only one of these backcountry sites with water, which must be treated. Camping fees are $6 per night.

> ### WORD OF MOUTH
>
> "Our first trip was to the eastern Saguaro National Park, which features magnificent mountain/desert scenery populated with gazillions of tall, branched Saguaro cactus, along with more kinds of colorful and oddly shaped cactus than we Easterners knew existed. It was a fascinating place, and we vastly enjoyed the slow 8-mile drive through. There are lots of trails, which younger people would do well to explore. We old folks were quite content to drive and occasionally get out to stroll around."
> –ckwald

WHERE TO EAT

Tucson boldly proclaims itself to be the "Mexican Food Capital of the U.S." Most of the Mexican food in town is Sonoran style—native to the adjoining Mexican state of Sonora—using cheese, mild peppers, corn tortillas, pinto beans, and beef or chicken. Tucson is the birthplace of the *chimichanga* (Spanish for "whatchamacallit"), a flour tortilla filled with meat or cheese, rolled and deep-fried. The majority of the best Mexican restaurants are concentrated in South Tucson and Downtown.

Up in the Foothills, at resorts along Sunrise Drive, upscale, Southwestern cuisine flourishes at such destination restaurants as Janos at the Westin La Paloma, the Grill at Hacienda del Sol Resort, and the Ventana Room at Loews Ventana Canyon. Cheaper but no less tasty fare as varied as Chinese, Guatemalan, and Greek can be enjoyed on the west side of U of A's campus, along University Boulevard and 4th Avenue. Tucson also has good sushi, Indian, Italian, and Cajun food at reasonable prices, scattered around town.

Although the city's selection of restaurants is impressive, Tucson doesn't offer much in the way of late-night dining. Most restaurants in town are shuttered by 10 PM; some spots that keep later hours are noted below.

Costs

	WHAT IT COSTS				
	$$$$	**$$$**	**$$**	**$**	**¢**
AT DINNER	over $30	$21–$30	$13–$20	$8–$12	under $8

Prices are per person for a main course.

Downtown Tucson

Contemporary

$–$$$ ✕ **Barrio.** Lively at lunchtime, this trendy grill serves the most innovative cuisine in the downtown area. Try a "little plate" of black tiger shrimp rubbed with tamarind paste, or stuffed Anaheim chile in red bell–pepper cream. Entrées are as varied as the simple but delicious fish tacos and the linguine with chicken, dried papaya, and mango in a chipotle-chardonnay cream sauce. Save room for an elegant dessert of fresh berries drenched in crème anglaise or a chilled chocolate custard topped with caramel. ☒ *135 S. 6th Ave., Downtown* ☏ *520/629–0191* ▤ *AE, D, DC, MC, V* ☺ *Closed Mon. No lunch weekends.*

¢–$$ ✕ **Cup Café.** This charming spot off the lobby of Hotel Congress is at the epicenter of Tucson's hippest downtown scene, but it's also a down-home, friendly place. Try the Gunpowder (eggs, potatoes, chorizo, and cheese) for breakfast or the Queer Steer Burger (a veggie burger) for lunch. The Heartbreaker appetizer (Brie melted over artichoke hearts and apple slices on a baguette) complements such entrées as chicken satay or "Tornados" of Beef. Open until 11 PM, it becomes interestingly crowded in the evening with patrons from the Club Congress, the hotel nightclub. ☒ *Hotel Congress, 311 E. Congress St., Downtown* ☏ *520/ 798–1618* ▤ *AE, D, MC, V.*

Mexican

$$ ✕ **Café Poca Cosa.** In what is arguably Tucson's most creative Mexican
Fodor's Choice restaurant, the chef prepares recipes inspired by different regions of her
★ native Mexico. The menu, which changes daily, might include chicken mole or pork *pibil* (made with a tangy Yucatán barbecue seasoning). Servings are plentiful, and each table gets a stack of warm corn tortillas and a bowl of beans to share. Order the daily Plato Poca Cosa, and the chef will select one beef, one chicken, and one vegetarian entrée for you to sample. The bold-color walls are hung with Latin Ameri-can art. ☒ *110 E. Pennington St., Downtown* ☏ *520/622–6400* ▤ *MC, V* ☺ *Closed Sun. and Mon.*

> **WORD OF MOUTH**
>
> "Café Poca Cosa is an absolutely terrific Mexican (but not typical enchilada/taco stuff) restaurant downtown."   –lori

¢–$$ ✕ **El Charro Café.** Started by Monica Flin in 1922, El Charro still serves splendid versions of the Mexican-American staples Flin claims to have originated, most notably chimichangas (deep-fried flour tortillas filled with seasoned beef or chicken) and cheese crisps. The *carne seca* chimichanga, made with beef dried on the premises—on the roof—is delicious. ✉ *311 N. Court Ave., Downtown* ☎ *520/622–1922* ⊟ *AE, D, DC, MC, V.*

¢–$ ✕ **El Minuto Café.** Popular with local families and the business crowd at lunch, this bustling restaurant is in Tucson's Barrio Historico neighborhood and open until midnight Friday and Saturday and until 10 PM the rest of the week. For more than 50 years, El Minuto has served up *topopo* salads (a crispy tortilla shell heaped with beans, guacamole, and many other ingredients), huge burritos, and green-corn tamales (in season) made just right. The spicy *menudo* (tripe soup) is reputed to be a great hangover remedy. ✉ *354 S. Main Ave., Downtown* ☎ *520/882–4145* ⊟ *AE, D, DC, MC, V.*

University of Arizona

American

¢ ✕ **B Line.** In the heart of 4th Avenue's amalgam of antique clothing stores, pubs, and natural food grocers, this casual café attracts a blend of students, professors, downtown professionals, and artists with its simple but refined meals and desserts. Homemade biscuit sandwiches and excellent coffee start the day. The lunch–dinner menu features soups, salads, pastas, and burritos. The converted 1920s bungalow has small tables tucked into a hardwood floor dining room. ✉ *621 N. 4th Ave., University* ☎ *520/882–7575* ⊟ *MC, V.*

Continental

$$$–$$$$ ✕ **Arizona Inn Restaurant.** Executive chef Odell Baskerville presides over one of Tucson's most elegant restaurants. Dine on the patio overlooking the lush grounds of this inn, or enjoy the view from the dining room, which has Southwestern details from the 1930s. The culinary range is broad, from bouillabaisse to a vegetarian corn–and–butternut squash cannelloni. Locals come for weekday power-breakfast meetings, Sunday brunch, or afternoon high tea in the library. ✉ *Arizona Inn, 2200 E. Elm St., University* ☎ *520/325–1541* ⊟ *AE, MC, V.*

Greek

$–$$ ✕ **Athens.** The tranquil dining room in this Greek spot off 4th Avenue is furnished with lace curtains, white stucco walls, and potted plants. Enjoy classics like *kotopoulo stin pita* (grilled chicken breast with a yogurt-cucumber sauce on fresh pita), moussaka, or the *pastitsio* (a casserole made with pasta, meat, and béchamel). The house favorite is braised lamb shoulder in a light tomato sauce over pasta—call to reserve your order ahead of time. ✉ *500 N. 4th Ave., at 6th St., University* ☎ *520/624–6886* ⊟ *AE, D, DC, MC, V* ⊘ *Closed Sun.*

Central Tucson

American

$–$$$ ✕ **Kingfisher Bar and Grill.** Kingfisher is a standout for American cuisine. The emphasis is on fresh seafood, but the kitchen does baby back ribs and steak with equal success. Try the delicately battered fish-and-chips or the clam chowder on the late-night menu, served from 10 PM to midnight. Bright panels of turquoise and terra-cotta, black banquettes, and

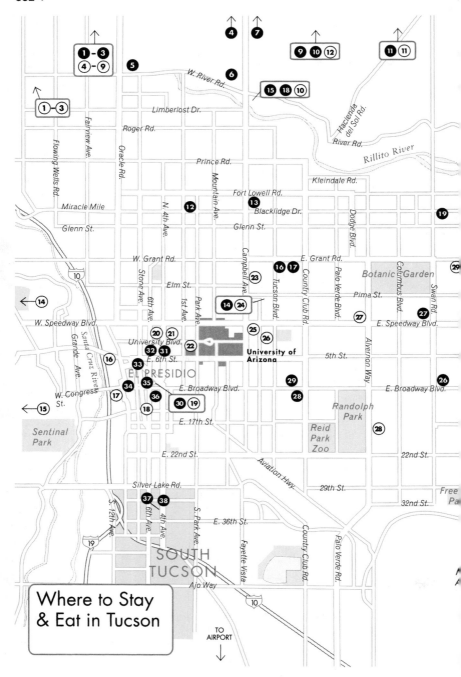

Where to Stay
& Eat in Tucson

neon lighting make for a chic space. ⊠ *2564 E. Grant Rd., Central* ☎ *520/323-7739* ▤ *AE, D, DC, MC, V* ☉ *No lunch weekends.*

American–Casual

¢ ✕ **Beyond Bread.** Twenty-seven varieties of bread are crafted at this bustling bakery. Highlights from the huge sandwich menu include Annie's Addiction (hummus, tomato, sprouts, red onion, and cucumber) and Brad's Beef (roast beef, provolone, onion, green chiles, and Russian dressing); soups and salads are equally scrumptious. Eat inside or on the patio, or order takeout. Be sure to splurge on at least one of the incredible desserts. ⊠ *3026 N. Campbell Ave., Central* ☎ *520/322-9965* ⊠ *6260 E. Speedway Blvd.* ☎ *520/747-7477* ▤ *AE, D, MC, V.*

¢ ✕ **Marlene's Hungry Fox.** Marlene's hungry customers have been coming here for good ol' fashioned breakfasts, served until 2 PM, since 1962. It's the home of the "double yoke," meaning when you order one egg, you'll get two (and so on). You'll also get a real slice of Tucson life at this cheerful, unpretentious place decorated with cow and farm photos, and a spoon collection that lines the walls. ⊠ *4637 E. Broadway Blvd., Central* ☎ *520/326-2835* ▤ *AE, D, MC, V* ☉ *No dinner.*

Cajun–Creole

$–$$ ✕ **Nonie.** Combine the flamboyant style of a New Orleans bistro with good food, fast service, and a hopping dose of Cajun music, and you get the idea. Try the Blue Cheese Oysters (dipped in cornmeal, fried, and topped with a blue cheese sauce), and you might think you're in Louisiana. Save room for pecan pie or bread pudding. ⊠ *2526 E. Grant Rd., Central* ☎ *520/319-1965* ▤ *AE, MC, V* ☉ *Closed Mon. No lunch weekends.*

Contemporary

$–$$$ ✕ **Elle.** Northern Californian, French, and Italian cuisines influence Elle's menu. Choose from pasta and risotto dishes, including squash ravioli with spinach, mushrooms, and sage butter, or try the grilled venison in roasted-garlic sauce with rosemary polenta. Servers provide expert assistance in selecting the perfect wine—from the nearly 90 vintages available (all from California, Oregon, and Washington), 45 can be ordered by the glass. The dining area is open and expansive. ⊠ *3048 E. Broadway Blvd., Central* ☎ *520/327-0500* ▤ *AE, DC, MC, V.*

$$ ✕ **Red Sky Cafe.** Trained in Paris, chef-owner Steve Schultz returned to Tucson to create his own contemporary cuisine, a fusion of French, Californian, and Southwestern flavors; the result is well-prepared, exquisitely presented meals. For a starter, try the foie gras with a potato pancake. Main courses include soup or salad made with fresh (and often exotic) produce from the U of A's greenhouses. ⊠ *Plaza Palomino, 2910 N. Swan Rd., Central* ☎ *520/326-5454* ▤ *AE, MC, V* ☉ *Closed Sun.*

Ethiopian

¢–$ ✕ **Zemam.** It can be hard to get a table in this small eatery—except in summer, when the lack of air-conditioning presents a challenge. The sampler plate of any three items allows you to try dishes like *yesimir wat* (a spicy lentil dish) and *lega tibs* (a milder beef dish with a tomato sauce). Most of the food has a stewlike consistency, so don't come if you feel the need to crunch. Everything is served on a communal platter with *injera*, a spongy bread, and eaten with the hands. ⊠ *2731 E. Broadway Blvd., Central* ☎ *520/323–9928* ⌲ *Reservations not accepted* ☱ *MC, V* ⊘ *Closed Mon.* ⛄ *BYOB.*

Italian

★ **$–$$** ✕ **Zona 78.** Fresh food takes on a whole new meaning at this contemporary bistro emphasizing inventive pizzas, pastas, and salads. The casual interior's focal point is a huge stone oven, where the pies are fired with toppings like Australian blue cheese, kalamata olives, sausage, and even chicken with peanut sauce. Whole wheat crust is an option. For those avoiding carbs, there are baked salmon and chicken entrées. The housemade mozzarella is delectable, either on top of a pizza or in a salad with organic tomatoes. ⊠ *78 W. River Rd., Central* ☎ *520/888–7878* ☱ *AE, D, MC, V* ⊘ *No lunch Sun.*

Mexican

¢–$ ✕ **Molina's Midway.** Tucked into a side street just north of Speedway, this unassuming restaurant holds its own against any in South Tucson. Specialties include Sinchiladas (chicken or beef with chiles, cheese, and a cream sauce) and *carne asada* (chunks of mildly spiced steak) wrapped in soft corn or flour tortillas. Seating is plentiful and the service is friendly. ⊠ *1138 N. Belvedere, Central* ☎ *520/325–9957* ☱ *AE, D, MC, V* ⊘ *Closed Mon.*

Vegetarian

¢–$ ✕ **Govinda.** One of the few places in town with a strictly meatless menu, this Hare Krishna–run restaurant has reasonably priced all-you-can-eat lunch and dinner buffets, which include vegan options. Hot and cold dishes vary daily, but ingredients are consistently fresh, and the food is tasty if not spicy. Choose from three seating areas, including an outdoor patio with a koi pond and an aviary, where you can hear the calls of the resident peacocks. No alcohol is served or permitted. ⊠ *711 E. Blacklidge Dr., Central* ☎ *520/792–0630* ⌲ *Reservations not accepted* ☱ *MC, V* ⊘ *Closed Mon. No lunch Tues. No dinner Sun.*

Eastside

Indian

$–$$ ✕ **New Delhi Palace: Cuisine of India.** Vegetarians, carnivores, and seafood lovers will all find something to enjoy at this savory Indian restaurant. The congenial staff is helpful in explaining the menu, which includes lots of tandoori dishes, curries, rice, and breads. The "heat" of each dish can be adjusted to individual preference by the chef. ⊠ *6751 E. Broadway Blvd., Eastside* ☎ *520/296–8585* ☱ *AE, MC, V.*

Japanese

¢–$$ ✕ **Sachiko Sushi.** Perfectly prepared sushi, generous combinations of tempura and teriyaki, and friendly service greet you at what many locals consider the best Japanese restaurant in Tucson. Try a bowl of udon noodles, served in broth with assorted meat, seafood, or vegetables. The dish is a satisfying meal in itself. ⊠ *1101 Wilmot Rd., Eastside* ☎ *520/886–7000* ☱ *AE, DC, MC, V* ⊘ *No lunch Sun.*

Steak

⊕ ¢–$$ ✕ **Pinnacle Peak Steakhouse.** Anybody caught eating newfangled foods like fish tacos here would probably be hanged from the rafters—along with the ties snipped from city slickers who overdressed. This cowboy steak house serves basic cowboy fare: mesquite-broiled steak, chicken, and grilled fish with salad and pinto beans. The restaurant is part of Trail Dust Town, a re-creation of a turn-of-the-20th-century town, complete with a working antique carousel and a narrow-gauge train. Gunfights are staged outside nightly at 7, 8, and 9. Expect a long wait on weekends. ⊠ *6541 E. Tanque Verde Rd., Eastside* ☎ *520/296–0911* ⌦ *Reservations not accepted* ▭ *AE, D, DC, MC, V* ⊗ *No lunch.*

Northeast Tucson

Continental

★ $$$$ ✕ **Ventana Room.** This formal restaurant—the only one in Tucson to receive Mobil's 5 stars—is a triumph of dining elegance: muted colors, a fireplace, grand views of the city lights, and waiters who attend to every detail. The contemporary Continental menu contains such entrées as a mixed grill of game (venison, quail, and buffalo) with black barley and huckleberries, and potato-wrapped striped sea bass with spinach, tomato, and sweet-basil wine sauce. There's also a spa tasting menu for those watching fat and calories. ⊠ *Loews Ventana Canyon Resort, 7000 N. Resort Dr., Northeast* ☎ *520/299–2020 Ext. 5194* ⌂ *Jacket required* ▭ *AE, D, DC, MC, V* ⊗ *No lunch.*

Greek

$$–$$$ ✕ **Olive Tree.** In a modern Santa Fe–style building, the Olive Tree serves fine versions of such Greek standards as moussaka, shish kebab, and stuffed grape leaves, but it also has more unusual dishes on its menu. The Lamb Bandit is baked in foil with cheese, potatoes, and vegetables. Leg of lamb is roasted in wine and served with a well-prepared orzo. Daily fresh-fish specials are broiled or sautéed in garlic, oregano, and olive oil. If you don't have room for baklava, a cup of strong Greek coffee makes a satisfying finish. ⊠ *7000 E. Tanque Verde Rd., Northeast* ☎ *520/298–1845* ▭ *AE, DC, MC, V* ⊗ *No lunch weekends.*

Southwestern

$$ ✕ **Fuego.** The "fire" of Alan Zeman's cooking refers not so much to hot, spicy fare but to the flambéed chorizo and tequila shrimp appetizer, which can start your meal off with tableside pyrotechnics. Fresh oysters and seafood, prickly pear pork tenderloin, and ostrich are all tasty selections at this comfortable bar and grill with knotty-pine floors and a brick fireplace. Most children like the kids' menu, with tacos and pastas as well as the usual burger and chicken-finger fare. ⊠ *6958 E. Tanque Verde Rd., Northeast* ☎ *520/886–1745* ▭ *AE, MC, V* ⊗ *No lunch.*

Catalina Foothills (North)

Contemporary

★ $$$–$$$$ ✕ **The Grill at Hacienda del Sol.** Tucked into the foothills and surrounded by flowering gardens, this special-occasion restaurant, a favorite for locals to take out-of-town visitors, provides an alternative to the chile-laden dishes of most Southwestern nouvelle cuisine. Wild mushroom bisque, pecan-grilled buffalo, and pan-seared sea bass are among the menu choices. Tapas (and most items on the full menu) can be enjoyed on the more casual outdoor patio, accented by live Flamenco guitar music. The lavish Sunday brunch buffet is worth a splurge. ⊠ *Hacienda del Sol Guest Ranch Resort, 5601 N. Hacienda del Sol Rd., Foothills* ☎ 520/529–3500 ⊟ *AE, DC, MC, V.*

$$–$$$ ✕**Acacia.** One of Tucson's premier chefs, Albert Hall, has opened a restaurant in one of its most artistic settings. A glass waterfall sculpture by local artist Tom Philabaum graces one wall, and bold red-and-blue glass plates and stemware seem to float atop the tables. Roasted plum tomato and basil soup, a recipe from Albert's mom, is a favorite starter. Creative dishes like wild salmon with a pecan honey-mustard glaze and wood-fired quail filled with pancetta, mozzarella, roasted tomatoes, and Oaxacan risotto are among the many tempting entrées. Weekend evenings bring live jazz to their patio, which overlooks the pretty, flower-filled St. Phillip's Plaza. ⊠ *4340 N. Campbell Ave., St. Phillip's Plaza, Foothills* ☎ 520/232–0101 ⊟ *AE, D, MC, V.*

$$–$$$ ✕ **Bistro Zin.** French cooking meets American comfort food at this high-energy (and somewhat noisy) hip sister restaurant to Wildflower Grill and North. Indulge in delicately flaky chicken potpie and french fries, a bistro steak, or scallops a l'orange. A hundred wines are available by the glass or "flight"—three tastes of the same type of wine from different vintners. Although lunch hums with the business crowd, at night it's a place to see and be seen. ⊠ *1865 E. River Rd., Foothills* ☎ 520/ 299–7799 ⊟ *AE, D, DC, MC, V* ⊙ *No lunch weekends.*

★ **$$–$$$** ✕**Soleil.** Watch the sun set over the Tucson Mountains from either the outdoor terrace or the panoramic picture window inside—then gaze at the twinkling city lights below as you feast on contemporary fare like caramelized sea scallops or filet mignon with sweet corn and shiitake mushrooms. A full vegetarian menu with vegan options also shines. Try a selection from the unique and well-stocked champagne bar, even if you don't usually indulge in bubbly. After dinner, stroll the fine art galleries in the imaginatively designed El Cortijo shopping complex. ⊠ *El Cortijo, 3001 E. Skyline Dr., Foothills* ☎ 520/299–3345 ⊟ *AE, D, MC, V* ⊙ *Closed Mon.*

Italian

★ **$$–$$$** ✕ **North.** This trendy newcomer in the upscale La Encantada Shopping Center sports an urban loft look with exposed pipe ceiling, white leather booths, dark concrete floors, and an open kitchen, and draws crowds for its excellent thin crust pizzas, pastas, fish, and steak. Alfresco dining on plush lounge furniture affords views of the city and quieter dining; on most evenings, the expansive bar area inside buzzes with Tucson's young professionals. ⊠ *2995 E. Skyline Dr., La Encantada, Foothills* ☎ 520/299–1600 ⊟ *AE, D, MC, V.*

$$–$$$ ✕ **Vivace.** A nouvelle Italian bistro in the lovely St. Philip's Plaza, Vivace has long been a favorite with Tucsonans. Wild mushrooms and goat cheese in puff pastry is hard to resist as a starter. For a lighter alternative to such entrées as a rich osso buco, try the fettuccine with grilled salmon. For dessert, the molten chocolate cake with spumoni ice cream is worth the 20 minutes it takes to create. Patio seating is especially invit-

6

ing on warm evenings. ✉ *4310 N. Campbell Ave., Foothills* ☎ *520/795–7221* ▭ *AE, D, MC, V* ✆ *Closed Sun.*

Southwestern

$$$–$$$$
Fodor's Choice
★
✕ **Janos.** Chef Janos Wilder was one of the first to reinvent Southwestern cuisine, and the menu, wine list, and service place this restaurant among the finest in the West. The hillside location on the grounds of the Westin La Paloma is a stunning backdrop for such dishes as sweet and spicy glazed quail with butternut-squash cannelloni, salmon with a scallop mousse served on polenta, and venison loin with chile-lime paste and pecans. Have a drink or a more casual meal of Caribbean fare next door at J Bar, a lively and lower-priced venue for sampling Janos's innovative cuisine. ✉ *Westin La Paloma, 3770 E. Sunrise Dr., Foothills* ☎ *520/615–6100* ▭ *AE, DC, MC, V* ✆ *Closed Sun. No lunch.*

$–$$$
✕ **Café Terra Cotta.** Everything about this restaurant says Southwest—from the bright orange and purple walls, large windows, and exposed beams to the contemporary art—but especially the food. Specialties include tortilla soup, maple leaf duck in a drunken cherry sauce, and creative pizzas with toppings like grilled shrimp and chiles or goat cheese and artichokes. This is the ultimate casual and lively yet classy place to dine in town. ✉ *3500 E. Sunrise Dr., Foothills* ☎ *520/577–8100* ▭ *AE, D, DC, MC, V.*

Northwest Tucson

Contemporary

$$–$$$
✕ **Wildflower Grill.** A glass wall separates the bar from the dining area, where an open kitchen, high ceiling with painted clouds, and rose-color banquettes complete the light and airy effect. Wildflower Grill is well known for its creative American fare and stunning presentation and the menu has compelling choices like warm Maine lobster salad; bow-tie pasta with grilled chicken, tomatoes, spinach, and pine nuts; and rack of lamb with a Dijon crust. The decadently huge desserts are equally top-notch. Request a banquette in the evening if you want quiet conversation; the table seating can be noisy. ✉ *7037 N. Oracle Rd., Northwest* ☎ *520/219–4230* ▭ *AE, D, DC, MC, V* ✆ *No lunch Sun.*

Southwestern

$$–$$$$
✕ **The Gold Room.** Every seat in this casually elegant and quiet dining room at the Westward Look Resort, high in the Catalina Foothills, has a spectacular view of the city below. The fare includes classics like sautéed halibut and roasted rack of lamb in truffle port sauce, as well as regional specialties such as mesquite-grilled buffalo sirloin. ✉ *Westward Look Resort, 245 E. Ina Rd., Northwest* ☎ *520/297–1151* ▭ *AE, DC, MC, V.*

¢–$
✕ **Tohono Chul Tea Room.** The food is fine, but what stands out here is the location—inside a wildlife sanctuary and surrounded by desert gardens. The Southwestern interior has Mexican tile, light wood, and a cobblestone patio. Dine outside to watch hummingbirds and butterflies. House favorites include tortilla soup with avocado, served with bread and scones baked on the premises, and grilled raspberry chipotle chicken. Open daily 8 to 5, the Tea Room is popular for Sunday brunch—which can mean long waits in high season. ✉ *Tohono Chul Park, 7366 N. Paseo del Norte, Northwest* ☎ *520/797–1222* ▭ *AE, MC, V* ✆ *No dinner.*

South Tucson

Mexican

¢–$ ✕**Mi Nidito.** A perennial favorite among locals (be prepared to wait
Fodor'sChoice awhile), Mi Nidito—"my little nest"—has also hosted its share of vis-
★ iting celebrities. Following President Clinton's lunch here, the rather hefty
"Presidential Plate" (bean tostada, taco with barbecued meat, chile relleno, chicken enchilada, and beef tamale with rice and beans) was added
to the menu. Top that off with the mango chimichangas for dessert, and
you're talkin' executive privilege. ⊠ *1813 S. 4th Ave., South* ☎ *520/
622–5081* ⊟ *AE, DC, MC, V* ⊘ *Closed Mon. and Tues.*

¢–$ ✕**Micha's.** Family-owned for 24 years, this local institution is a nonde-
script Mexican diner serving some of the best Sonoran classics this side
of the border. House specialties include *machaca* (shredded beef) enchiladas and chimichangas, and *cocido*, a hearty vegetable beef soup.
Homemade chorizo spices up breakfast, which is served daily. A second location now brings this great food close to the University. ⊠ *2908
S. 4th Ave., South* ☎ *520/623–5307* ⊠ *1220 E. Prince Rd.* ☎ *520/293–
0375* ⊟ *AE, DC, MC, V* ⊘ *No dinner Mon.*

WHERE TO STAY

In Tucson you can choose from luxurious desert resorts, basic accommodations offered by small to medium-size hotels and motels, or area
bed-and-breakfasts ranging from bedrooms in modest homes to private
cottages nestled on wildlife preserves. Southwestern-style "dude"
ranches—some of them former cattle ranches from the 1800s—are on
the outskirts of town. Unless otherwise indicated, price categories for
guest ranches include all meals and most activities.

If you like being able to walk to sights, shops, and restaurants, plan on
staying in the Downtown, University, or Central Tucson neighborhoods.
The posh resorts in the Foothills and Northwest areas, while farther away
from town, have many activities on-site, including some of the town's
top-rated restaurants, and can arrange transportation to shopping and
sights. Resorts here typically charge an additional daily resort fee for
"use of facilities," such as pools, tennis courts, and exercise classes and
equipment. Be sure to ask what is included when you book a room.

Summer rates (late May–September) are up to 60% lower than those
in the winter. Note that unless you book months in advance, you'll be
hard-pressed to find a Tucson hotel room at any price the week before
and during the huge gem and mineral show, which is usually held the
first two weeks in February.

Costs

WHAT IT COSTS				
$$$$	**$$$**	**$$**	**$**	**¢**
FOR 2 PEOPLE over $250	$176–$250	$101–$175	$80–$100	under $80

Prices are for a standard double in high season.

Downtown Tucson

$$ 🏨 **The Hotel Arizona.** If you want to be based at a full-service hotel in the heart of downtown, this former Radisson property near the Convention Center and El Presidio Historic District will suffice. The renovated rooms are pretty standard; passes to use the gym at the modern YMCA across the street are included. ✉ *181 W. Broadway, Downtown, 85701* 🕿 *520/624–8711 or 800/845–4596* 🖷 *520/624–9963* ⊕ *www.thehotelaz.com* ⟳ *300 rooms, 8 suites* ⟡ *Restaurant, some refrigerators, cable TV, in-room data ports, pool, bar, shop, laundry facilities, concierge floor, business services, meeting rooms, parking (fee), no-smoking rooms* 🖃 *AE, D, MC, V.*

$$ 🏨 **The Royal Elizabeth Bed and Breakfast Inn.** Fans of Victoriana will adore this B&B built in 1878. The inn, part of the Armory Park historic district, is beautifully furnished with period antiques. The six spacious rooms are outfitted with ceiling fans, and two of the larger rooms have separate sitting areas with pull-out sofa beds. Gracious hosts Jeff and Charles take turns in the kitchen, preparing two-course breakfasts that might include chiles rellenos, a wild mushroom frittata, or a fresh fruit soufflé. ✉ *204 S. Scott Ave., Downtown, 85701* 🕿 *520/670–9022* 🖷 *928/833–9974* ⊕ *www.royalelizabeth.com* ⟳ *6 rooms* ⟡ *Cable TV, in-room VCRs, pool, hot tub, Wi-Fi; no smoking* 🖃 *AE, D, MC, V* 🍴 *BP.*

$–$$ 🏨 **Inn Suites Hotel & Resort.** Just north of downtown, this hotel is next to I–10 but quiet nevertheless. The large, peach-and-green Southwestern-theme rooms, circa 1980, face an interior courtyard with a sparkling pool and *palapas* (thatched open gazebos). Free daily extras such as a breakfast buffet, newspaper, and happy-hour cocktails make this a haven in the center of the city. ✉ *475 N. Granada Ave., Downtown, 85701* 🕿 *520/622–3000 or 877/446–6589* 🖷 *520/623–8922* ⊕ *www.innsuites.com* ⟳ *265 rooms, 35 suites* ⟡ *Restaurant, room service, microwaves, refrigerators, cable TV with movies and video games, pool, hot tub, bar, business services, meeting rooms, no-smoking rooms* 🖃 *AE, D, DC, MC, V* 🍴 *BP.*

¢ 🏨 **Hotel Congress.** This hotel built in 1919 has been artfully restored to
Fodor$Choice its original Western version of art deco. The gangster John Dillinger was
★ almost caught here in 1934 (his luggage, filled with guns and ammo, was suspiciously heavy; he was captured later near the university). Each room has black-and-white tile baths and the original iron bed frames. The convenient location downtown means it can be noisy: don't get a room over the popular Club Congress or you'll be up until the wee hours. A great place to stay for younger or more adventurous visitors, it's the center of Tucson's hippest scene. ✉ *311 E. Congress St., Downtown, 85701* 🕿 *520/622–8848 or 800/722–8848* 🖷 *520/792–6366* ⊕ *www.hotelcongress.com* ⟳ *40 rooms* ⟡ *Restaurant, bar, lobby lounge, nightclub, no-smoking rooms; no room TVs* 🖃 *AE, D, MC, V.*

University of Arizona

$$$ 🏨 **Arizona Inn.** Although close to the university and many sights, the
Fodor$Choice beautifully landscaped lawns and gardens of this 1930 inn seem far away
★ from the hustle and bustle. The spacious rooms are spread over 14 acres

in pink adobe-style casitas—most have private patios and some have fireplaces. The resort also has two luxurious two-story houses with their own heated pools and full hotel service. The main building houses a library, a fine restaurant, and a cocktail lounge where a jazz pianist plays. ⊠ *2200 E. Elm St., University, 85719* ☏ *520/325–1541 or 800/933–1093* 🖶 *520/881–5830* ⊕ *www.arizonainn.com* ✈ *70 rooms, 16 suites, 3 casitas* ♺ *2 restaurants, room service, cable TV, 2 tennis courts, pool, gym, sauna, bar, library, dry cleaning, business services, meeting rooms, no-smoking rooms* 🖃 *AE, DC, MC, V.*

★ **$$$** 🏨 **Tucson Marriott University Park.** With the University of Arizona less than a block from the front door, the Marriott is an ideal place to stay when visiting the campus. This clean, contemporary hotel has a lush atrium lobby area that can be enjoyed from the restaurant and bar. The university shopping district's cafés, pubs, and short stores are all within a short stroll. ⊠ *880 E. 2nd St., University, 85719* ☏ *520/792–4100 or 888/236–2427* 🖶 *520/882–4100* ⊕ *www.marriott.com* ✈ *234 rooms, 16 suites* ♺ *Restaurant, room service, some refrigerators, cable TV with movies, in-room data ports, pool, gym, outdoor hot tub, sauna, lounge, laundry service, concierge floor, business services, meeting rooms, no-smoking rooms* 🖃 *AE, D, DC, MC, V.*

$$ 🏨 **Adobe Rose Inn.** This 1933 adobe home offers six rooms of varying sizes and amenities. Two have beehive fireplaces and stained-glass windows, two have kitchenettes, and one is an upstairs suite with its own balcony. In the historic Sam Hughes neighborhood just east of the university, the well-maintained inn is within easy walking distance of shops, restaurants, and two major bus lines. Breakfast dishes like Southwestern soufflés or blueberry pancakes, always served with fruit and muffins, are enjoyed in a dining room overlooking the bougainvillea-draped pool area. ⊠ *940 N. Olsen Ave., University, 85719* ☏ *520/318–4644 or 800/328–4122* 🖶 *520/318–4644* ⊕ *www.aroseinn.com* ✈ *6 rooms* ♺ *Dining room, cable TV, pool, outdoor hot tub, Wi-Fi; no kids under 10, no smoking* 🖃 *AE, MC, V* 🍴 *BP.*

$$ 🏨 **Catalina Park Inn.** Classical music plays softly in the living room of this beautifully restored 1927 neoclassical house behind a gate. The original art nouveau–tile work and a butler's pantry are among many charming architectural details. All rooms are spacious and quite private, and include robes, irons, and hair dryers. You may be tempted to fill your suitcase with the papaya and lime scones that are part of breakfast. ⊠ *309 E. 1st St., University, 85705* ☏ *520/792–4541 or 800/792–4885* ⊕ *www.catalinaparkinn.com* ✈ *6 rooms* ♺ *Cable TV, Wi-Fi; no kids under 10, no smoking* 🖃 *AE, D, MC, V* 🍴 *BP.*

$$ 🏨 **Four Points Sheraton Tucson University Plaza.** Formerly the Plaza Hotel, this older high-rise has a prime location, across from the University of Arizona, two blocks from the University Medical Center, and at the intersection of two major bus routes. A favorite of visiting faculty, prospective students, and parents, and the spring training home of the Chicago White Sox, this is a no-nonsense hotel with somewhat dreary corridors and an average restaurant. There are, however, many other places to eat within walking or driving distance. ⊠ *1900 E. Speedway Blvd., University, 85719* ☏ *520/327–7341 or 888/625–5144* 🖶 *520/327–0276*

⊕ *www.starwood.com* ⊏⊅ *150 rooms* ⌂ *Restaurant, room service, cable TV with movies and video games, in-room data ports, pool, gym, bar, lounge, free parking, no-smoking rooms* ▭ *AE, D, MC, V.*

$$ ☷ **La Posada del Valle.** Noted Swiss architect Josias Joesler designed this gracious B&B in the Spanish colonial–Territorial style he popularized in the Tucson area. Breezeways and gentle arches characterize the soothing pink-adobe structure across from the University Medical Center. High pink walls keep out the noise of traffic. Guest rooms, furnished with Victorian antiques, each have private entrances off the courtyard and gardens as well as from the interior hallway. Breakfasts are delicious, as are the cookies freshly baked every afternoon. ⊠ *1640 N. Campbell Ave., University, 85719* ☎ *520/795–3840 or 888/404–7113* ⊕ *www.bbonline.com/az/laposada* ⊏⊅ *6 rooms* ⌂ *Some kitchenettes, cable TV, Wi-Fi, massage; no smoking* ▭ *AE, MC, V* ⊺⊘⌿ *BP.*

★ **$$** ☷ **Peppertrees B&B Inn.** This restored 1905 Victorian just west of the U of A campus affords privacy along with B&B camaraderie. Two contemporary-style guesthouses at the rear of the tree-shaded main house have full kitchens, separate phone lines, private patios, and washers and dryers (for guesthouse guests only). The antiques-filled main house (furnished with pieces from innkeeper Jill Light's family in England) has several guest rooms, as well as a separate one-bedroom apartment. Light prepares elaborate breakfasts, and dinner and room service are available on request. ⊠ *724 E. University Blvd., University, 85719* ☎ *520/622–7167 or 800/348–5763* ⊕ *www.peppertreesinn.com* ⊏⊅ *3 rooms, 1 suite, 2 guest houses* ⌂ *Some kitchens, massage; no smoking* ▭ *D, MC, V* ⊺⊘⌿ *BP.*

Central Tucson

$$–$$$ ☷ **Doubletree Hotel at Reid Park.** The municipal golf course at Randolph Park hosts the LPGA tournament every year, and most of the participants stay across the street at this hotel and conference center. Reid Park (adjacent to Randolph Park) has a pleasant jogging trail and a zoo. This sprawling, contemporary hotel is also convenient to the airport, the center of town, and the El Con shopping mall. ⊠ *445 S. Alvernon Way, Central, 85711* ☎ *520/881–4200 or 800/222–8733* 🖷 *520/323–5225* ⊕ *www.doubletree.com* ⊏⊅ *295 rooms* ⌂ *2 restaurants, room service, cable TV with movies, in-room data ports, 3 tennis courts, pool, gym, hot tub, bar, video game room, dry cleaning, laundry service, business services, no-smoking rooms* ▭ *AE, D, DC, MC, V* ⊺⊘⌿ *BP.*

$$ ☷ **Embassy Suites Tucson–Broadway.** Towering palms, red-tile roofs, and a bold orange-red exterior greet you from the front of this central property. The older, spacious two-room suites open onto a plant-filled atrium. Among the extras are a free cooked-to-order breakfast and nightly happy hour, passes to a local gym, and shuttle service to anywhere within 5 mi. The lounge has a large-screen television and billiard tables. ⊠ *5335 E. Broadway Blvd., Central, 85711* ☎ *520/745–2700 or 800/362–2779* 🖷 *520/790–9232* ⊕ *www.embassysuites.com* ⊏⊅ *142 suites* ⌂ *Kitchenettes, cable TV with movies, in-room data ports, pool, hot tub, billiards, recreation room, laundry facilities, business services, meeting rooms, no-smoking rooms* ▭ *AE, D, DC, MC, V* ⊺⊘⌿ *BP.*

$$ ⊞ **Varsity Clubs of America.** This sports-theme time-share facility also doubles as a hotel, so it may have any or all of its suites available for rental at any given time. Home to the Diamondbacks and the Rockies teams during spring training, its handy location is surprisingly quiet. One- and two-bedroom suites have whirlpool tubs and full kitchens; alternatives to cooking include the Stadium Sports Grill downstairs or any of the several restaurants within walking distance. There's a billiard room, a putting green, and a cozy library with a fireplace. ⊠ *3855 E. Speedway Blvd., Central, 85716* ☎ *520/318–3777 or 888/594–2287* 🖷 *888/410–9770* ⊕ *www.ilxresorts.com* ⟿ *59 suites* ⟳ *Restaurant, kitchens, cable TV with movies and video games, pool, gym, hot tub, billiards, library, business services, no-smoking rooms* ⊟ *AE, D, MC, V.*

¢   ⊞ **Extended StayAmerica.** If you're seeking convenience and value (and don't mind a certain blandness), this modern chain property will suffice. All rooms have kitchenettes, queen-size beds, and recliner chairs. Don't expect a view or coffee in the lobby, but local calls are free, and you're two blocks from the Crossroads Shopping Center, where there are restaurants, a Starbucks, a grocery store, shops, and a cinema. ⊠ *5050 E. Grant Rd., Central, 85712* ☎ *520/795–9510 or 800/398–7829* 🖷 *520/795–9504* ⊕ *www.extendedstay.com* ⟿ *120 rooms* ⟳ *Kitchens, microwaves, refrigerators, cable TV, Wi-Fi, laundry facilities, no-smoking rooms* ⊟ *AE, D, MC, V.*

Eastside

★ $$$$ ⊞ **Tanque Verde Ranch.** The most upscale of Tucson's guest ranches and one of the oldest in the country, the Tanque Verde sits on 640 beautiful acres in the Rincon Mountains next to Saguaro National Park East. Rooms in one-story casitas have tasteful Western-style furnishings, fireplaces, and picture-window views of the desert. Breakfast and lunch buffets are huge, and barbecues add variety to the daily dinner menu. Horseback excursions are offered for every skill level (lessons are included in rates), and children can participate in daylong activity programs, from riding to tennis to crafts, leaving parents to their leisure. ⊠ *14301 E. Speedway Blvd., Eastside, 85748* ☎ *520/296–6275 or 800/234–3833* 🖷 *520/721–9426* ⊕ *www.tanqueverderanch.com* ⟿ *49 rooms, 23 suites, 2 casitas* ⟳ *5 tennis courts, 2 pools (1 indoor), gym, hot tub, fishing, bicycles, basketball, hiking, horseback riding, children's programs (ages 4–11), no-smoking rooms; no room TVs* ⊟ *AE, D, MC, V* ❖| *FAP.*

$$–$$$ ⊞ **The SunCatcher.** The four rooms in this B&B are decorated in honor of four groups who settled the Old West: Cowboys, Native Americans, Spanish, and Oriental. Some have fireplaces and Jacuzzi tubs, and can be reconfigured as suites for families. Focal points in the spacious living room are a sunken seating area facing a copper-hooded fireplace and a mesquite wood bar where happy-hour snacks are served. It's a comfortable retreat after a day of sightseeing or hiking. ⊠ *105 N. Avda. Javelina, Eastside, 85748* ☎ *520/885–0883* ⊕ *www.thesuncatcher.com* ⟿ *4 rooms* ⟳ *Cable TV, in-room DVDs, in-room data ports, pool, hot tub; no smoking* ⊟ *AE, D, MC, V* ❖| *BP.*

$$ ⊞ **Tucson Hilton East.** This high-rise hotel and conference center is set comfortably back off a main road on the suburban east side of town. An airy atrium lobby takes full advantage of the view of the Santa Catalina Mountains; better yet, push "6" in the glass elevator and ascend for a spectacular vista. The rooms are spacious and well tended but not particularly distinctive. ⊠ *7600 E. Broadway Blvd., Eastside, 85710* ☎ *520/721–5600 or 800/774–1500* 🖷 *520/721–5696* ⊕ *www.hilton. com* ⇄ *225 rooms, 8 suites* ⚭ *Restaurant, cable TV, Wi-Fi, pool, gym, outdoor hot tub, bar, business services, meeting rooms, no-smoking rooms* ⊟ *AE, D, DC, MC, V.*

$ 🖪 **Smuggler's Inn.** At the corner of Wilmot Street and Speedway Boulevard, this comfortable hotel, where you can park by your door, has easy access to Eastside activities and restaurants. A lushly landscaped central courtyard is the focus for the serviceable rooms, which have either a balcony or patio. A full, hot breakfast is included; you might also want to stock up on treats from the Trader Joe's Market and Beyond Bread Bakery across the street. ⊠ *6350 E. Speedway Blvd., Eastside, 85710* ☎ *520/296–3292 or 800/525–8852* 🖷 *520/722–3713* ⊕ *www. smugglersinn.com* ⇄ *150 rooms* ⚭ *Restaurant, cable TV with movies and video games, in-room data ports, pool, outdoor hot tub, bar, laundry facilities, no-smoking rooms* ⊟ *AE, D, MC, V* ⍟⎮ *BP.*

Northeast Tucson

★ $$$$ 🖪 **Canyon Ranch.** The Canyon Ranch draws an international crowd of well-to-do health seekers to its superb spa facilities on 70 acres in the desert foothills. Two activity centers include an enormous spa complex and a Health and Healing Center, where dietitians, exercise physiologists, behavioral-health professionals, and medical staff attend to body and soul. Just about every type of physical activity is possible, from Pilates to guided hiking, and the food is plentiful and healthy. Rates include all meals, activities, taxes, and gratuities. There's a four-night minimum. ⊠ *8600 E. Rockcliff Rd., Northeast, 85750* ☎ *520/749–9000 or 800/742–9000* 🖷 *520/749–1646* ⊕ *www.canyonranch.com* ⇄ *240 rooms* ⚭ *Dining room, cable TV, golf privileges, 8 tennis courts, 4 pools (1 indoor), health club, hair salon, sauna, spa, steam room, basketball, racquetball, squash, library, laundry facilities, business services, airport shuttle; no kids under 12, no smoking* ⊟ *AE, D, MC, V* ⍟⎮ *FAP.*

★ $$$$ 🖪 **Loews Ventana Canyon Resort.** This is one of the most luxurious of the big resorts, with dramatic stone architecture and an 80-foot waterfall cascading down the mountains. Rooms, facing either the Catalinas or the golf course and city, are modern and elegantly furnished in muted earth tones and light woods; each bath has a miniature TV, a double-wide tub, and bubble bath. Dining options include everything from poolside snacks at Bill's Grill to fine Continental cuisine at the Ventana Room. The scenic Ventana Canyon trailhead is steps away, and there's a free shuttle to nearby Sabino Canyon. ⊠ *7000 N. Resort Dr., Northeast, 85750* ☎ *520/299–2020 or 800/234–5117* 🖷 *520/299–6832* ⊕ *www. loewshotels.com* ⇄ *384 rooms, 14 suites* ⚭ *4 restaurants, room service, minibars, cable TV with movies, in-room data ports, 2 18-hole golf courses, 8 tennis courts, pro shop, 2 pools, health club, hot tub, sauna, spa, steam room, mountain bikes, hiking, bar, lobby lounge, shops, chil-*

dren's programs (ages 4–12), business services, meeting rooms, no-smoking rooms ⊟ *AE, D, DC, MC, V.*

$–$$ ▥ **Ramada Inn Foothills.** Families and business travelers stay in this Ramada on the northeastern side of town, close to many restaurants and Sabino Canyon. An attractive stucco building with a Spanish tile roof and a fake bell tower, the serviceable, if generic, rooms and small suites all have pillowtop mattresses. Complimentary beer, wine, and appetizers are served in the afternoon. The Southwestern restaurant next door, Fuego, provides room service. Free passes to a local health club are available; tennis facilities are nearby. ⊠ *6944 E. Tanque Verde Rd., Northeast, 85715* ☎ *520/886–9595 or 800/228–2828* 🖷 *520/721–8466* ⊕ *www.ramadafoothillstucson.com* ⥱ *52 rooms, 61 suites* ⚘ *Room service, microwaves, refrigerators, cable TV, in-room data ports, pool, sauna, laundry facilities, business services, meeting rooms; no smoking* ⊟ *AE, D, DC, MC, V* ⦿ *CP.*

Catalina Foothills (North)

★ $$$$ ▥ **Westin La Paloma.** Vying with the Hilton El Conquistador and Loews Ventana for convention business, this sprawling, pale pink resort offers views of the Santa Catalina Mountains above and the city below. It specializes in relaxation with an emphasis on fun: the golf, tennis, and spa facilities are top-notch, and the huge pool complex has an impressively long water slide, as well as a swim-up bar and grill for those who can't bear to leave the water. On-site kids' programs, including weekly "dive-in movies," make for a vacation the whole family can enjoy. Janos, one of Tucson's top restaurants, is also here. ⊠ *3800 E. Sunrise Dr., Foothills, 85718* ☎ *520/742–6000 or 888/625–5144* 🖷 *520/577–5878* ⊕ *www.starwood.com* ⥱ *455 rooms, 32 suites* ⚘ *4 restaurants, room service, cable TV with movies and video games, in-room data ports, 3 9-hole golf courses, 12 tennis courts, 3 pools, gym, 3 outdoor hot tubs, spa, racquetball, volleyball, 2 bars, shops, children's programs (ages 6 mo–12 yrs), business services, meeting rooms, no-smoking rooms* ⊟ *AE, D, DC, MC, V.*

★ $$–$$$ ▥ **Hacienda del Sol Guest Ranch Resort.** This 32-acre hideaway in the Santa Catalina foothills is part guest ranch, part resort, and entirely gracious. It's a charming and lower-price alternative to the larger resorts. Designed in classic Mexican hacienda style, this former finishing school for girls attracted stars like Clark Gable, Katharine Hepburn, and Spencer Tracy when it was converted to a guest ranch during World War II. Some of the one- and two-bedroom casitas have fireplaces and private porches, where you can watch the sun set over the Tucson Mountains. The superb Grill at Hacienda del Sol is part of the resort. ⊠ *5601 N. Hacienda del Sol Rd., Foothills, 85718* ☎ *520/299–1501 or 800/728–6514* 🖷 *520/299–5554* ⊕ *www.haciendadelsol.com* ⥱ *22 rooms, 8 suites* ⚘ *Restaurant, cable TV, pool, outdoor hot tub, horseback riding, library, business services, meeting rooms; no smoking* ⊟ *AE, D, MC, V.*

$$ ▥ **Windmill Inn at St. Philip's Plaza.** This all-suites hotel is in a chic shopping plaza filled with glitzy boutiques and good restaurants. Each 500-square-foot suite has a small sitting area, wet bar, two TVs, and three telephones (local calls are free). A few dollars extra will buy you a view

Where the West Is Still Wild

IF YOU THINK TUCSON HAS GONE THE WAY of sprawling suburban development like Phoenix to the north . . . well, you're partly right. Many of the wide-open spaces that once inspired the lyrics of old cowboy songs have become housing tracts, golf courses, and shopping malls. But a sliver of the rugged and free-spirited ranching life that shaped the American West is alive and well on the outskirts of town, where urban cowboys and cowgirls come to fulfill their dreams at dude ranches, also called guest ranches.

Riding is the preferred activity on the ranch. Slow, fast, mountain, and all-day rides are offered daily, and some ranches allow you to help groom and feed the horses. As you ride up into Saguaro National Park or the Coronado National Forest, wranglers give sage advice on horsemanship and tell tales (some tall) of their most harrowing cattle drives. Afterwards, you can soak in the hot tub, get a massage, or laugh with new friends about the day's adventures over a pitcher of margaritas.

These lodgings are much more than resorts that offer horseback riding, however. Guests who don't saddle up can choose from birding and nature walks, mountain hikes, tennis, and swimming.

After a day of riding or hiking, or perhaps simply sitting outside enjoying a good book, guests find a warm welcome at happy hour, dinner, and around the campfire. Lodges are outfitted with comfortable couches, crackling fireplaces, board games, and Western saloon-type bars (one even has saddles for barstools). TVs, and

the anti-social habits they encourage, are banned from guest rooms (for those who must catch an occasional news- or sportscast, there's usually a set in the common area). Ranch stays are popular for family vacations—parents relax while the kids make new friends. The ranch experience also draws many single travelers who can easily find camaraderie in this setting.

Though accommodations are a bit more rustic than resort hotels, there are arguably more comforts: you're served three hearty meals every day. The dude ranch experience eliminates many stresses often associated with more traditional vacations. Since all meals and activities are included, you have fewer decisions about structuring your day (will it be the mountain ride or team penning?), and no anxiety about choosing a restaurant or dealing with crowds.

Three ranches are in the Tucson area. The large and luxurious **Tanque Verde Guest Ranch,** on the eastern edge of town, has two swimming pools (one indoor), a tennis pro, and lavish buffet meals. Children are separated from adults for rides and activities. The **White Stallion Ranch,** adjacent to Saguaro National Park's west unit, has challenging riding as well as massages and a fitness center. The owners live and work on this 3,000-acre cattle ranch, the setting for *High Chaparral.* The smaller and more rustic **Lazy K Bar Ranch,** also in the Northwest, has two hilltop banquet rooms with patios for special events.

By Mara Levin

of the pool and fountain rather than the parking lot. Complimentary coffee, muffins, juice, and a newspaper are delivered to your door; additional breakfast goodies are set up in the lobby. There are bicycles available for excursions along the nearby Rillito River, and free passes to a nearby gym are included in the rate. ⊠ *4250 N. Campbell Ave., Foothills, 85718* ☎ *520/577–0007 or 800/547–4747* 🖷 *520/577–0045* ⊕ *www. windmillinns.com* ⇨ *122 suites* ⚘ *Minibars, microwaves, refrigerators, cable TV, Wi-Fi, pool, hot tub, bicycles, library, laundry facilities, business services; no smoking* ▤ *AE, D, DC, MC, V* ⦿*l BP.*

Northwest Tucson

$$$$ 🏨 **Hilton Tucson El Conquistador.** A huge copper mural of cowboys and cacti and a wide view of the rugged Santa Catalina Mountains grace the lobby of the Hilton's golf and tennis resort. This friendly upscale property draws families and conventioneers, some taking advantage of lower summer rates for the excellent sports facilities, the spa, and the pool complex with a 140-foot waterslide and children's play pool. Rooms, either in private one-bedroom casitas or the main hotel building, are decorated in desert tones of taupe, sand, and gold, and more than half of them have kiva-style fireplaces. ⊠ *10000 N. Oracle Rd., Northwest, 85737* ☎ *520/544–5000 or 800/325–3525* 🖷 *520/544–1224* ⊕ *www.hiltonelconquistador.com* ⇨ *328 rooms, 57 suites, 43 casitas* ⚘ *5 restaurants, minibars, cable TV with movies and video games, in-room data ports, 2 18-hole golf courses, 31 tennis courts, 3 pro shops, 4 pools, 2 gyms, spa, bicycles, basketball, horseback riding, racquetball, volleyball, piano bar, shops, children's programs (ages 4–12), business services, meeting rooms, no-smoking rooms* ▤ *AE, D, DC, MC, V.*

$$$$ 🏨 **Lazy K Bar Guest Ranch.** Though new housing subdivisions are encroaching on this family-oriented guest ranch in the Tucson Mountains northwest of town, greenhorns can feel like they've escaped to a slower, simpler vacation here. Guest rooms are in eight casitas. Those in the older structures, made of Mexican stucco, have fireplaces and wood-beam ceilings; rooms in the newer, adobe-brick buildings are larger and more modern. In addition to horseback riding offered twice daily, you can enjoy cookouts, hayrides, and evening entertainment such as squaredancing and cowboy roping tricks. There are also hammocks, a heated pool, and a hot tub to relax those post-equestrian muscles. ⊠ *8401 N. Scenic Dr., Northwest, 85743* ☎ *520/744–3050 or 800/321–7018* 🖷 *520/744–7628* ⊕ *www.lazykbar.com* ⇨ *19 rooms, 4 suites* ⚘ *Picnic area, pool, outdoor hot tub, hiking, horseback riding, library, meeting rooms, airport shuttle, no-smoking rooms; no room phones, no room TVs* ▤ *AE, D, MC, V* ⊘ *Closed June–Aug.* ⦿*l FAP.*

★ **$$$$** 🏨 **Miraval.** Giving Canyon Ranch a run for its money, this New Age health spa 30 mi north of Tucson has a secluded desert setting and beautiful Southwestern rooms. Most of the spa services and wellness programs, based primarily on Eastern philosophies, help you get in touch with your inner self. Whether you prefer to be pampered with a hot stone massage or seaweed body mask, partake in fitness and nature activities; or just do yoga, it's all here. All gratuities and meals, including tasty buffets (with calories and fat content noted), are included. ⊠ *5000 E.*

6

Via Estancia Miraval, Catalina 85739 ☎ 520/825–4000 or 800/825–4000 📠 520/825–5163 🌐 www.miravalresort.com ⇄ 106 rooms ♁ 2 restaurants, in-room safes, refrigerators, cable TV, in-room data ports, 2 tennis courts, 3 pools, health club, hot tub, sauna, spa, steam room, bicycles, horseback riding, bar, laundry facilities, laundry service; no smoking ▭ AE, D, DC, MC, V 🍽 FAP.

$$$$ **Omni Tucson National Golf Resort & Spa.** Perfect for couples with differing ideas on how to spend a vacation, Tucson National is both a premier golf resort (it hosts the Tucson Open) and a full-service European-style spa, where you can be coiffed, waxed, wrapped, and worked over to your heart's content. Most of the rooms, although not technically suites, are spacious with separate sitting areas. Some casitas have full kitchens and dining rooms. Although this resort is a little farther from central Tucson than others, it's still convenient to shopping and restaurants in the thriving Northwest area. ✉ *2727 W. Club Dr., Northwest 85742 ☎ 520/297–2271 or 800/528–4856 📠 520/297–7544 🌐 www.omnihotels.com ⇄ 143 rooms, 24 suites ♁ 3 restaurants, cable TV with movies, some in-room data ports, some Wi-Fi, 3 9-hole golf courses, 4 tennis courts, 2 pools, gym, hot tub, spa, basketball, billiards, volleyball, 2 bars, shop, concierge, business services, meeting rooms, no-smoking rooms ▭ AE, D, DC, MC, V.*

$$$$ Fodor's Choice ★ **White Stallion Ranch.** A 3,000-acre working cattle ranch run by the hospitable True family since 1965, this place is the real deal. You can ride up to four times daily, hike in the mountains, enjoy a hayride cookout, and compete in team cattle penning. Most rooms retain their original Western furniture, and newer deluxe rooms have whirlpool baths or fireplaces. A recently completed spa and fitness center bring even more comforts to this well-endowed but authentic setting. Rates include all meals, riding, and daily entertainment such as weekend rodeos, country line dancing, telescopic stargazing, and campfire sing-alongs. ✉ *9251 W. Twin Peaks Rd., Northwest, 85743 ☎ 520/297–0252 or 888/977–2624 📠 520/744–2786 🌐 www.wsranch.com ⇄ 24 rooms, 17 suites ♁ 2 tennis courts, pool, gym, hot tub, massage, basketball, billiards, horseback riding, shuffleboard, volleyball, bar, library, piano, recreation room, business services, meeting rooms, airport shuttle; no room phones, no room TVs ▭ No credit cards ⊙ Closed June–Aug. 🍽 FAP.*

$$$–$$$$ **Westward Look Resort.** Originally the 1912 homestead of William and Mary Watson, this laid-back lodging offers Southwestern character, attentive service, and all the amenities you expect at a major resort. The Watsons' original living room, with beautiful, dried ocotillo branches draped along the ceiling and antique furnishings, is now a comfortable lounge off the main lobby. The couple probably never envisioned anything like the Sonoran Spa, offering hot desert-stone massages and three-mud body masks. Spacious rooms have wrought-iron beds and Mission-style furniture. Borrow a bike or take a stroll along the beautiful and well-marked nature trails. ✉ *245 E. Ina Rd., Northwest, 85704 ☎ 520/297–1151 or 800/722–2500 📠 520/297–9023 🌐 www.westwardlook.com ⇄ 244 rooms ♁ 2 restaurants, minibars, cable TV with movies, 8 tennis courts, 3 pools, gym, spa, mountain bikes, horseback riding, shop, concierge, business services, meeting rooms, no-smoking rooms ▭ AE, D, DC, MC, V.*

$$ 🏨 **Marriott TownePlace Suites.** With full kitchens in all of its studio, one-bedroom, and two-bedroom suites, this newer property is suitable for short or extended stays. In fact, the longer you stay, the lower your nightly rate. Its location is handy, yet the interior hallways and the way the buildings are set back from the road making for a quiet retreat. Some suites have a view of the neighboring golf course, and a half-dozen are designed for wheelchair access. ✉ *405 W. Rudasill Rd., Northwest, 85704* ☎ *520/292–9697 or 800/257–3000* 🖷 *520/292–9884* ⊕ *www.towneplacesuites.com* 🛏 *77 suites ☼ Kitchens, cable TV, in-room data ports, pool, exercise equipment, laundry facilities, no-smoking rooms* ▭ *AE, MC, V* ⦿⊢ *CP.*

$–$$ 🏨 **La Posada Lodge and Casitas.** This 1960s motor lodge has been re-born as a charming Santa Fe–style boutique hotel. Though most rooms in the three-story lodge have Saltillo-tile floors and hand-painted Mexican headboards, a few are whimsically decorated with blue-and-lime-green–checkered bedspreads and curtains, along with kitschy furniture and lava lamps, as a tribute to the hotel's past life. Upper-floor rooms have balconies with mountain and city views, and the one-story casitas have sofa sleepers, kitchenettes, and private patios. The restaurant, Miguel's ($$–$$$), is an upscale Latin-theme jewel, specializing in seafood. ✉ *5900 N. Oracle Rd., Northwest, 85704* ☎ *520/887–4800 or 800/810–2808* 🖷 *520/293–7543* ⊕ *www.laposadalodge.com* 🛏 *72 rooms ☼ Restaurant, room service, some kitchenettes, microwaves, refrigerators, cable TV, in-room data ports, pool, gym, hot tub, bar, meeting rooms; no smoking* ▭ *AE, MC, V* ⦿⊢ *CP.*

¢–$ 🏨 **Quail's Vista Bed and Breakfast.** Innkeeper and former concierge Barbara Bauer and her husband, Richard, can direct you to all the best things to see and do in Tucson; some activities, like bird-watching or soaking in a hot tub that faces the dramatic west side of the Santa Catalina Mountains, can be done right in the inn's backyard. Inside, peeled spruce columns support the beamed ceiling and thick, rounded walls of this adobe home. Fiesta dinnerware, Native American pottery, and bright Mexican blankets decorate the common area, which has cozy nooks for reading or watching the wildlife out the windows. ✉ *826 E. Palisades Rd., Northwest, 85737* ☎ *520/297–5980* ⊕ *www.quails-vista-bb.com* 🛏 *3 rooms, 1 with bath ☼ In-room data ports, hot tub, laundry facilities; no TV in some rooms, no smoking* ▭ *No credit cards* ⊗ *Closed May–Sept.* ⦿⊢ *CP.*

West of Tucson

$$$–$$$$ 🏨 **JW Marriott Starr Pass Resort & Spa.** Set amid saguaro forests and mesquite groves in the Tucson Mountains (yet only 15 minutes to downtown), the city's newest—and largest—resort opened in early 2005. Massive sun-bleached stone walls blend rather than compete with the natural surroundings, and there are stunning views from interior dining areas and lounges. Outside terraces, with chairs and sofas clustered around kiva fireplaces, overlook the pools and golf course and provide views of the city. Resort amenities include an on-site Starbucks and a full-service spa. ✉ *3800 W. Starr Pass Blvd., Westside, 85701* ☎ *520/792–3500* 🖷 *520/792–3351* ⊕ *www.starrpassmarriott.com* 🛏 *538 rooms, 37 suites ☼ 4 restaurants, room service, cable TV with movies,* *in-room data ports, 3 9-hole golf courses, 2 pools, gym, 2 hot tubs, spa, bar, shops, concierge, business services, meeting rooms, no-smoking rooms* 🖃 *AE, D, MC, V.*

$$ 🖼 **Casa Tierra.** For a real desert experience, head to this B&B on 5 acres
Fodor'sChoice near the Desert Museum and Saguaro National Park West. The last 1½
★ mi are on a dirt road. All rooms have private patio entrances and look out onto a lovely central courtyard. The Southwestern-style furnishings include Mexican *equipales* (chairs with pigskin seats), tile floors, and beamed ceilings. A full vegetarian breakfast served on fine china is included, and there's a media room for those who can't stand the quiet. There's a minimum stay of two nights. 🖃 *11155 W. Calle Pima, Westside, 85743* ☎ *520/578–3058 or 866/254–0006* 🖷 *520/578–8445* 🌐 *www.casatierratucson.com* 🛏 *3 rooms, 1 suite* 🛆 *Microwaves, refrigerators, gym, hot tub, recreation room; no room TVs, no smoking* 🖃 *AE, MC, V* ⊘ *Closed mid-June–mid-Aug.* ¶◎¶ *BP.*

NIGHTLIFE & THE ARTS

The Arts

For a city of its size, Tucson is abuzz with cultural activity. It's one of only 14 cities in the United States with a symphony as well as opera, theater, and ballet companies. Wintertime, when Tucson's population swells with vacationers, is the high season, but the arts are alive and well year-round. The low cost of Tucson's cultural events comes as a pleasant surprise to those accustomed to paying East or West Coast prices: symphony tickets are as little as $10 for some performances, and touring Broadway musicals can often be seen for $24. Parking is plentiful and frequently free.

The free *Tucson Weekly* (🌐 www.tucsonweekly.com) and the "Caliente" section of the *Arizona Daily Star* (🌐 www.azstarnet.com) both hit the stands on Thursday and have listings of what's going on in town.

Much of the city's cultural activity takes place at or near the **Tucson Convention Center** (🖃 260 S. Church St., Downtown ☎ 520/791–4101, 520/791–4266 box office 🌐 www.ci.tucson.az.us/tcc). Dance, music, and other kinds of performances take place at the University of Arizona's **Centennial Hall** (🖃 1020 E. University Blvd., University ☎ 520/621–3341 🌐 www.uapresents.org).

One of Tucson's hottest rock-music venues, the **Rialto Theatre** (🖃 318 E. Congress St., Downtown ☎ 520/798–3333 🌐 www.rialtotheatre.com), was once a silent-movie theater but now reverberates with the sounds of jazz, folk, and world-music concerts, although the emphasis is on hard rock. The Rialto hosts dance and dramatic productions as well.

Each season brings visiting opera, theater, and dance companies to Tucson. Tickets to many events can be purchased through **Ticketmaster** (☎ 520/321–1000 🌐 www.ticketmaster.com 🖂 Robinsons-May, El Con Mall, 3435 E. Broadway Blvd., Central ☎ 520/795–3950 🖂 Robinsons-May, Tucson Mall, 4470 N. Oracle Rd., Central ☎ 520/292–0345).

Dance

Tucson shares its professional-ballet company, **Ballet Arizona** (☎ 888/ 322–5538 ⊕ www.balletaz.org), with Phoenix. Performances, from classical to contemporary, are held at the Music Hall in the Tucson Convention Center. Tucson's most established modern dance company, **Orts Theatre of Dance** (✉ 930 N. Stone Ave., Downtown ☎ 520/624–3799 ⊕ www.orts.org), incorporates trapeze flying into the dances. Outdoor and indoor performances are staged throughout the year.

Music

A Wednesday-night chamber-music series is hosted by the **Arizona Friends of Chamber Music** (☎ 520/577–3769 ⊕ arizonachambermusic.org) at the Leo Rich Theater in the Tucson Convention Center from October through April. It also presents a festival the first week of March. The **Arizona Opera Company** (☎ 520/293–4336 ⊕ www.azopera.com), based in Tucson, puts on five major productions each year at the Tucson Convention Center's Music Hall. The **Arizona Symphonic Winds** (✉ Tanque Verde and Sabino Canyon Rds., Northeast ⊕ www.azsymwinds.org) has both a winter and spring–summer schedule of performances. Many of the spring–summer performances are in Morris T. Udall Park. Performances are usually at 7 PM, but you need to arrive at least an hour early. From late February through late June, the **Tucson Pops Orchestra** (✉ Lake Shore La. off 22nd St. between Alvernon Way and Country Club Rd., Central ⊕ www.tucsonpops.org) gives free concerts each Saturday evening at the De Meester Outdoor Performance Center in Reid Park. Arrive about an hour before the music starts (usually at 7 PM) to stake your claim on a viewing spot.

The **Tucson Symphony Orchestra** (✉ 443 S. Stone Ave., Downtown ☎ 520/ 882–8585 box office, 520/792–9155 main office ⊕ www.tucsonsymphony. org), part of Tucson's cultural scene since 1929, holds concerts in the Music Hall in the Tucson Convention Center and at sites in the Foothills and the northwest as well.

Tucson's small but vibrant jazz scene encompasses everything from afternoon jam sessions in the park to Sunday jazz brunches at resorts in the Foothills. Call the **Tucson Jazz Society Hot Line** (☎ 520/903–1265) for information.

Poetry

The first weekend in April brings the **Tucson Poetry Festival** (☎ 520/620– 2045 ⊕ www.tucsonpoetryfestival.org) and its four days of readings and related events, including workshops, panel discussions, and a poetry slam. Such internationally acclaimed poets as Jorie Graham and Sherman Alexie have participated.

The **University of Arizona Poetry Center** (✉ 1600 E. 1st St., University ☎ 520/626–3765 ⊕ www.poetrycenter.arizona.edu) runs a free series open to the public. Check during fall and spring semesters for information on scheduled readings.

Theater

Arizona's state theater, the **Arizona Theatre Company** (✉ Temple of Music and Art, 330 S. Scott Ave., Downtown ☎ 520/622–2823 box office, 520/

884–8210 company office ⊕ www.aztheatreco.org), performs classical pieces, contemporary drama, and musical comedy at the historic Temple of Music and Art from September through May. It's worth coming just to see the beautifully restored historic Spanish colonial–Moorish-style theater; dinner at the adjoining Temple Café is a tasty prelude.

The University of Arizona's **Arizona Repertory Theatre** (✉ Speedway Blvd. and Olive St., University ☎ 520/621–1162 ⊕ www.uatheatre.org) has performances during the academic year. **Borderlands Theater** (✉ 40 W. Broadway, Downtown ☎ 520/882–7406) presents new plays about Southwest border issues—often multicultural and bilingual—at venues throughout Tucson, usually from late June through April. Children of all ages love the clever melodramas at the **Gaslight Theatre** (✉ 7010 E. Broadway Blvd., Eastside ☎ 520/886–9428 box office), where hissing at the villain and cheering the hero are part of the audience's duty. **Invisible Theatre** (✉ 1400 N. 1st Ave., Central ☎ 520/882–9721) presents contemporary plays and musicals.

Nightlife

Bars & Clubs

In addition to the places listed below, most of the major resorts have late spots for drinks or dancing. The Westward Look Resort's Lookout Bar, with its expansive view and classic rock band on Friday and Saturday nights, is a popular spot for dancing. The bars at Westin La Paloma, Hacienda del Sol, and Loews Ventana have live acoustic music on weekends.

BLUES & JAZZ **Boondocks** (✉ 3306 N. 1st Ave., Central ☎ 520/690–0991) is the unofficial home of the Blues Heritage Foundation, hosting local and touring singer-songwriters.

A jazz combo plays Wednesday–Saturday nights on the lovely patio of **Acacia** (✉ 4340 N. Campbell Ave., St. Phillip's Plaza, Central ☎ 520/232–0101). **Old Pueblo Grille** (✉ 60 N. Alvernon Way, Central ☎ 520/326–6000) has live jazz on Sunday nights. **Ric's Café** (✉ 5605 E. River Rd., Northeast ☎ 520/577–7272) features jazz musicians in the courtyard on Friday and Saturday nights.

COUNTRY & WESTERN An excellent house band gets the crowd two-stepping on Tuesday, Thursday, Friday, and Saturday nights at the **Maverick** (✉ 6622 E. Tanque Verde Rd., Eastside ☎ 520/298–0430).

GAY & LESBIAN BARS **Ain't Nobody's Bizness** (✉ 2900 E. Broadway Blvd., Central ☎ 520/318–4838) is the most popular lesbian bar in town. It has a karaoke night where you may hear more than your fair share of Melissa Etheridge. **IBT's (It's 'Bout Time)** (✉ 616 N. 4th Ave., University ☎ 520/882–3053) is Tucson's most popular gay men's bar, with a patio, rock and disco DJ music, and Sunday-night drag shows. Expect long lines on weekends.

ROCK & MORE **Berky's** (✉ 5769 E. Speedway Blvd., Central ☎ 520/296–1981) has live R&B and rock and roll every night, though mostly cover songs rather than original music. The **Cactus Moon Café** (✉ 5470 E. Broadway Blvd., Central ☎ 520/748–0049), catering to a mostly yuppie crowd, offers a standard mix of Top 40, hip-hop, and modern country, often with free appetizer buffets during happy hour. The **Chicago Bar** (✉ 5954 E. Speedway Blvd., Central ☎ 520/748–8169) is a good place to catch Tucson blues legend Sam Taylor; other nightly shows include reggae and rock.

Club Congress (✉ Hotel Congress, 311 E. Congress St., Downtown ☎ 520/622–8848) is the main Friday venue for cutting-edge rock bands, with a mixed-bag crowd of alternative rockers, international travelers, and college kids. Saturday brings a more outrageous crowd dancing to an electronic beat. **El Parador** (✉ 2744 E. Broadway, Central ☎ 520/881–2808) has a live salsa band Friday and Saturday nights, with dance lessons at 10 PM. The **Nimbus Brewing Company** (✉ 3850 E. 44th St., Southeast ☎ 520/745–9175) is the place for acoustic blues, folk, and bluegrass, not to mention good, cheap food and microbrew beer.

Plush (✉ 340 E. 6th St., University ☎ 520/798–1298) hosts bands like Camp Courageous and Greyhound Soul, as well as local performers with a loyal following. You can go totally retro at the **Shelter** (✉ 4155 E. Grant Rd., Central ☎ 520/326–1345), a former bomb shelter decked out in plastic 1960s kitsch, lava lamps, and JFK memorabilia, which plays Elvis videos and music by the likes of Burt Bacharach and Martin Denny.

Casinos

After a long struggle with the state of Arizona, two Native American tribes now operate casinos on their Tucson-area reservations west of the airport. The casinos are virtually the same, and quite unlike their distant and much grander cousins in Las Vegas and Atlantic City. Don't expect much glamour, ersatz or otherwise; these casinos are more like glorified video arcades, although you can lose money much faster. You'll be greeted by a wall of cigarette smoke (the reservation is exempt from the city's antismoking laws) and the wail of hundreds of slot machines and video poker, blackjack, roulette, and craps machines. The only "live" gaming is keno, bingo, blackjack, and certain types of poker. The crowd is mostly older smokers, and no one under age 21 is permitted.

The Pascua Yaqui tribe's **Casino of the Sun** (✉ 7406 S. Camino de Oeste, off W. Valencia Rd. about 5 mi west of I–19, South ☎ 520/883–1700 or 800/344–9435 ⊕ www.casinosun.com) has slot and video-gambling machines, high-stakes bingo, and live poker. Food selections include an all-you-can-eat prime rib buffet. A few miles farther west is their newer, larger facility, **Casino del Sol** (✉ 5655 W. Valencia, Southwest ☎ 520/883–1700 or 800/344–9435 ⊕ www.casinodelsol.com), with live poker and blackjack, bingo, slots, and an above-average Italian restaurant. An adjacent 4,600-seat outdoor amphitheater books entertainers like Bob Dylan and James Taylor. Free shuttle buses operate from points all over Tucson; call for a schedule. The Tohono O'odham tribe operates the **Desert Diamond Bingo and Casino** (✉ 7350 S. Old Nogales Hwy., 1 mi south of Valencia, just west of the airport, South ☎ 520/294–7777 ⊕ www.desertdiamondcasino.com), which has 500 one-arm bandits and video poker in addition to live keno, bingo, and Stud High, Texas Hold'em, Omaha, and Stud Lo poker. Players are served free nonalcoholic beverages (you have to pay for alcoholic ones), and can order tacos, burritos, sandwiches, and several varieties of Native American fry bread.

SPORTS & THE OUTDOORS

Ballooning

Three companies in Tucson offer hot-air-balloon flights from September through May, flown by FAA-certified pilots. Passengers toast with champagne on tours by **Balloon America** (✆ Box 31255, Tucson 85751 ☎ 520/299–7744 ⊕ www.balloonrideusa.com). Tours depart from the east side of Tucson. **Fleur de Tucson Balloon Tours** (✆ 4635 N. Caida Pl., Tucson 85718 ☎ 520/529–1025 ⊕ www.fleurdetucson.net) has two flight options: over the Tucson Mountains and Sagaro National Park West, or over the Avra Valley. **Southern Arizona Balloon Excursions** (✆ 537 W. Grant Rd., Tucson 85705 ☎ 520/624–3599 ⊕ www.vanity.qwestdex. com/tucsoncomefly) offers daily sunrise flights over northwest Tucson.

Baseball

It doesn't have as many teams as Phoenix, but Tucson does have its share of baseball spring training action: the Arizona Diamondbacks, the Chicago White Sox, and the Colorado Rockies are in the Tucson area from mid-February until the end of March. The Diamondbacks and White Sox play at Tucson Electric Park, south of town near the airport. The Rockies play at Hi Corbett Field, which is adjacent to Reid Park and most easily reached by driving south at the junction of East Broadway Boulevard and Randolph Way; parking is tight at Hi Corbett, so arrive early to enjoy a picnic lunch at one of the many nearby ramadas (wooden shelters that supply shade for your table). Not surprisingly, some people plan vacations around scheduled training dates; there are plenty of local fans, too. The **Pacific Coast League** (⊕ www.pclbaseball.com) includes the Tucson Sidewinders, the AAA team of the Arizona Diamondbacks, who play in Tucson Electric Park from April through July.

Arizona Diamondbacks (✉ Tucson Electric Park, 2400 E. Ajo Way, South ☎ 520/434–1367 or 866/672–1343 ⊕ www.tucsonbaseball.com). **Chicago White Sox** (✉ Tucson Electric Park, 2400 E. Ajo Way, South ☎ 520/434–1367 or 866/672–1343 ⊕ www.tucsonbaseball.com). **Colorado Rockies** (✉ Hi Corbett Field, 3400 E. Camino Campestre, Central ☎ 520/327–9467 or 800/388–7625 ⊕ www.coloradorockies.com). **Tucson Sidewinders** (☎ 520/434–1021 ⊕ www.tucsonsidewinders.com).

Bicycling

Tucson, ranked among America's top five bicycling cities by *Bicycling* magazine, has well-maintained bikeways, routes, lanes, and paths all over the city. Scenic-loop roads in both sections of Saguaro National Park offer rewarding rides for all levels of cyclists. Most bike stores in Tucson carry the monthly newsletter of the Tucson chapter of **GABA** (Greater Arizona Bicycling Association; ✆ Box 43273, Tucson 85733 ⊕ www. bikegaba.org), which lists rated group rides. You can pick up a map of Tucson-area bike routes at the **Pima Association of Governments** (✉ 177 N. Church St., Suite 405, Downtown ☎ 520/792–1093).

Mountain bikes, comfort bikes, and road bikes can be rented by the day or week at **Fair Wheel Bikes** (✉ 1110 E. 6th St., University ☎ 520/884–9018). **Tucson Bicycles** (✉ 4743 E. Sunrise Dr., Foothills ☎ 520/577–7374) rents a selection of road and mountain bikes and organizes group rides of varying difficulty.

Bird-Watching

The naturalist and illustrator Roger Tory Peterson (1908–96) considered Tucson one of the country's top birding spots, and avid "life listers"—birders who keep a list of all the birds they've sighted and identified—soon see why. In the early morning and early evening, Sabino Canyon is alive with cactus and canyon wrens, hawks, and quail. Spring and summer, when species of migrants come in from Mexico, are great hummingbird seasons. In the nearby Santa Rita Mountains and Madera Canyon, you can see elegant trogons nesting in early spring. The area also supports species usually found only in higher elevations.

You can get the latest word on the bird on the 24-hour line at the **Tucson Audubon Society** (☎ 520/798–1005 ⊕ www.tucsonaudubon.org); sightings of rare or interesting birds in the area are recorded regularly.

The society's **Audubon Nature Shop** (⊠ 300 E. University Blvd., Suite 120, University ☎ 520/629–0510) carries field guides, bird feeders, binoculars, and natural-history books. The **Wild Bird Store** (⊠ 3526 E. Grant Rd., Central ☎ 520/322–9466) is an excellent resource for bird-watching books, maps, and trail guides.

Several companies offer birding tours in the Tucson area. **Borderland Tours** (⊠ 2550 W. Calle Padilla, Northwest, Tucson 85745 ☎ 520/882–7650 or 800/525–7753 ⊕ www.borderland-tours.com) leads bird-watching tours in Arizona and all over the world. **Wings** (⊠ 1643 N. Alvernon Way, Suite 105, Central, Tucson 85712 ☎ 520/320–9868 ⊕ www.wingsbirds.com), a Tucson-based company, leads ornithological expeditions locally and worldwide.

Golf

For a detailed listing of the state's courses, contact the **Arizona Golf Association** (⊠ 7226 N. 16th St., Phoenix 85020 ☎ 602/944–3035 or 800/458–8484 ⊕ www.azgolf.org). The **Golf Stop Inc.** (⊠ 1830 S. Alvernon Way, South ☎ 520/790–0941), a shop owned and run by two LPGA pros, can fit you with custom clubs, repair your old irons, or give you lessons. If you're planning to stay a week or more, **Tucson's Resort Golf Card** (☎ 520/886–8800), offering discounts at 13 of the area's best courses, is a good deal. Tee off after 1 PM at many of these courses, and you can shave off nearly half the greens fees. Some courses also have slightly lower fees Monday through Thursday.

MUNICIPAL COURSES One of Tucson's best-kept secrets is that the city's five low-price, municipal courses are maintained to standards usually found only at the best country clubs. To reserve a tee time at one of the city's courses, call the **Tucson Parks and Recreation Department** (☎ 520/791–4653 general golf information, 520/791–4336 automated tee-time reservations ⊕ www.tucsoncitygolf.com) at least a week in advance.

Dell Urich Golf Course (⊠ 600 S. Alvernon Way, Central ☎ 520/791–4161), ($39 to walk, $49 with a cart), adjacent to Randolph and formerly known as Randolph South, is a par-70, 18-hole course with tall trees and dramatic elevation changes.

El Rio Golf Course (✉ 1400 W. Speedway Blvd., Westside ☎ 520/791–4229), ($34 to walk, $44 with a cart), has 18 holes of tight fairways, small greens, and two lakes on fairly flat terrain.

Fred Enke Golf Course (✉ 8251 E. Irvington, Eastside ☎ 520/791–2539), ($34 to walk, $44 with a cart), is a hilly, semi-arid (less grass and more native vegetation) 18-hole course. It's southeast of town.

Fodor'sChoice ★ **Randolph Park Golf Course–North Course** (✉ 600 S. Alvernon Way, Central ☎ 520/791–4161), ($39 to walk, $49 with a cart), a long, scenic 18-hole course that has hosted the LPGA Tour for many years, is the flagship of Tucson's municipal courses.

Silverbell Golf Course (✉ 3600 N. Silverbell Rd., Northwest ☎ 520/791–5235), ($30 to walk, $40 with a cart), with spacious fairways and ample greens, has an 18-hole layout set along the west bank of the Santa Cruz River.

PUBLIC COURSES **Arizona National Golf Club** (✉ 9777 E. Sabino Greens Dr., Eastside ☎ 520/749–3636 ⊕ www.arizonanationalgolfclub.com), ($165), is a gorgeous 18-hole, par-71 course.

Dorado Golf Course (✉ 6601 E. Speedway Blvd., Eastside ☎ 520/885–6751), ($20 to walk, $29 with a cart), has an 18-hole executive course good for those who want to play just a few short rounds.

Esplendor Resort & Country Club (✉ 1069 Camino Carampi, Rio Rico ☎ 800/288–4746 ⊕ www.esplendor-resort.com), ($65), south of Tucson, near Nogales, was designed by Robert Trent Jones, Sr. This 18-hole course is one of Arizona's lesser-known gems.

San Ignacio Golf Club (✉ 4201 S. Camino del Sol, Green Valley ☎ 520/648–3468 ⊕www.irigolfgroup.com), ($65), was designed by Arthur Hills and is a challenging 18-hole desert course.

Tubac Golf Resort (✉ 1 Otero Rd., Tubac ☎ 520/398–2021 ⊕ www.tubacgolfresort.com), ($89), an 18-hole course 45 minutes south of Tucson, will look familiar to you if you've seen the movie *Tin Cup*.

RESORTS Avid golfers check into one of Tucson's many tony resorts and head straight for the links. The resort courses listed below are open to the public; resort guests pay slightly lower greens fees. Those who don't mind getting up early to beat the heat will find some excellent golf packages at these places in the summer.

Hilton Tucson El Conquistador (✉ 10000 N. Oracle Rd., Northwest ☎ 520/544–5000 ⊕ www.hiltonelconquistador.com), ($120), has 45 holes of golf in the Santa Catalina foothills with panoramic views of the city.

Fodor'sChoice ★ **Lodge at Ventana Canyon** (✉ 6200 N. Clubhouse La., Northeast ☎ 520/577–1400 or 800/828–5701), ($209), has two 18-hole Tom Fazio–designed courses. Their signature hole, No. 3 on the mountain course, is a favorite of golf photographers. Guests staying up the road at Loews Ventana Resort also have privileges here.

Omni Tucson National Golf Resort (✉ 2727 W. Club Dr., Northwest ☎ 520/575–7540 ⊕ www.tucsonnational.com), ($180), cohost of an annual PGA winter open, offers 27 holes and beautiful, long par 4s. The resort's orange and gold courses were designed by Robert Van Hagge and Bruce Devlin.

Starr Pass Golf Resort (✉ 3645 W. Starr Pass Blvd., Westside ☎ 520/670–0400 ⊕ www.starrpasstucson.com), ($185), with 18 magnificent holes in the Tucson Mountains, was developed as a Tournament Player's Course. Managed by Arnold Palmer, Starr Pass has become a favorite of visiting pros; playing its No. 15 signature hole has been likened to threading a moving needle. Guests at the JW Marriott Starr Pass Resort also have privileges here.

Westin La Paloma (✉ 3800 E. Sunrise Dr., Foothills, 85718 ☎ 520/742–6000 ⊕ www.westinlapalomaresort.com), ($185), in the Tucson foothills, is rated among the top resort courses by *Golf Digest*. The 27-hole layout was designed by Jack Nicklaus.

Hiking

For hiking inside Tucson city limits, you can test your skills climbing trails up Sentinel Peak ("A" Mountain), but there are also hundreds of other trails in the immediate Tucson area. The Santa Catalina Mountains, Sabino Canyon, and Saguaro National Park East and West beckon hikers with waterfalls, birds, critters, and huge saguaro cacti.

Catalina State Park (✉ 11570 N. Oracle Rd., Northwest ☎ 520/628–5798 ⊕ www.pr.state.az.us) is crisscrossed by hiking trails. One of them, the relatively easy, two-hour (5.5-mi round-trip) Romero Canyon Trail, leads to Romero Pools, a series of natural *tinajas,* or stone "jars," filled with water much of the year. The trailhead is on the park's entrance road, past the restrooms on the right side.

The Bear Canyon Trail in **Sabino Canyon** (✉ Sabino Canyon Rd. at Sunrise Dr., Foothills ☎ 520/749–8700 ⊕ www.fs.fed.us/r3/coronado), also known as Seven Falls Trail, is a three-hour, 7.8-mi round-trip that is moderately easy and fun, crisscrossing the stream several times on the way up the canyon. Kids enjoy the boulder-hopping and all are rewarded with pools and waterfalls as well as views at the top. The trailhead can be reached from the parking area by either taking a five-minute Bear Canyon Tram ride or walking the 1.8-mi tram route.

In the west unit of **Saguaro National Park** (✉ 2700 N. Kinney Rd., Westside ☎ 520/733–5158 ⊕ www.nps.gov/sagu) a favorite hike is the Hugh Norris Trail. Named after a Tohono O'odham police chief, this moderately difficult trail makes a gradual climb to Wasson Peak, affording wonderful views of the Tucson valley, surrounding mountain ranges, and saguaro forests below. The 9.8-mi round-trip begins on Hohokam Road, about 1 mi past the Red Hills Visitor Center.

The local chapter of the **Sierra Club** (✉ 738 N. 5th Ave., University, Tucson ☎ 520/620–6401) welcomes out-of-towners on weekend hikes around Tucson. The **Southern Arizona Hiking Club** (☎ 520/751–4513 ⊕ www.sahcinfo.org) leads weekend hikes of varying difficulty. For hiking on your own, a good source is **Summit Hut** (✉ 5045 E. Speedway Blvd., Central ☎ 520/325–1554), which has a collection of hiking reference materials and a friendly staff who will help you plan and outfit your trip. Packs, tents, bags, and climbing shoes can be rented here.

Horseback Riding

Colossal Cave Stables (✉ 16600 Colossal Cave Rd., Eastside ☎ 520/647–3450) takes riders into Saguaro National Park East on one-hour or longer trail rides. Wranglers at **Corcoraque Ranch** (✉ Mile Wide Rd., Westside ☎ 520/682–8594) lead riders through their working cattle ranch into Saguaro National Park's west district. **Pusch Ridge Stables** (✉ 13700 N. Oracle Rd., Northwest ☎ 520/825–1664), adjacent to Catalina State Park, can serve up a cowboy-style breakfast on your trail ride; gentle children's horse walks, one-hour, and overnight rides are available.

Rodeo

In the last week of February, Tucson hosts **Fiesta de Los Vaqueros**, the largest annual winter rodeo in the United States, a five-day extravaganza with more than 600 events and a crowd of more than 44,000 spectators a day at the **Tucson Rodeo Grounds** (✉ 4823 S. 6th Ave., South ☎ 520/294–8896 ⊕ www.tucsonrodeo.com). The rodeo kicks off with a 2-mi parade of horseback riders (Western and fancy-dress Mexican *charro*), wagons, stagecoaches, and horse-drawn floats; it's touted as the largest nonmotorized parade in the world. Local schoolkids especially love the celebration—they get a two-day holiday from school. Daily seats at the rodeo vary from $8 to $14.

Tennis

Excellent tennis facilities can be found at area resorts, among them Loews Ventana Canyon (8 courts), Hilton Tucson El Conquistador (31 courts), Westin La Paloma (12 courts), Westward Look (8 courts), and Canyon Ranch (8 courts). **Catalina High School** (✉ 3645 E. Pima, Central), singer Linda Ronstadt's alma mater, is a favorite among local tennis enthusiasts for its well-lighted, no-charge courts, which are open to the public when school's out. **Fort Lowell Park** (✉ 2900 N. Craycroft Rd., Central ☎ 520/791–2584) has eight lighted courts and tennis instruction for all ages. **Himmel Park** (✉ 1000 N. Tucson Blvd., University ☎ 520/791–3276), 1 mi east of the university, has eight lighted tennis courts and low prices. The **Randolph Tennis Center** (✉ 50 S. Alvernon Way, Central ☎ 520/791–4896) has 24 tennis courts (and 10 racquetball courts), all of them lighted, at very reasonable rates.

SHOPPING

Much of Tucson's retail activity is focused around malls, but shops with more character and some unique wares are in the city's open plazas: St. Philip's Plaza (River Road and Campbell Avenue), Plaza Palomino (Swan and Fort Lowell roads), Casas Adobes Plaza (Oracle and Ina roads), and La Encantada (Skyline Drive and Campbell Avenue).

The 4th Avenue neighborhood near the University of Arizona—especially 4th Avenue between 2nd and 9th streets—is fertile ground for unusual items in the artsy boutiques, galleries, and secondhand-clothing stores. Be forewarned: you may experience aggressive panhandling here.

Hard-core bargain hunters usually head south to the Mexican border town of Nogales, for jewelry, liquor, home furnishings, and leather goods. For in-town deals, the outlet stores at the Foothills Mall in northwest Tucson score high marks.

Malls & Shopping Centers

Casas Adobes Plaza (✉ Oracle and Ina Rds., southwest corner, Northwest ⊕ www.casasadobesplaza.com) originally served the ranchers and orange grove owners in this once remote part of town, which is now the fastest-growing area. It's an outdoor, Mediterranean-style shopping center with a full-service grocery with organic meats and produce, the superb Wildflower Grill, Sauce (for upscale flat-crust pizzas and salads), a bagel shop, and several boutiques and gift shops.

Foothills Mall (✉ 7401 N. La Cholla Blvd. at Ina Rd., Northwest ☎ 520/742–7191 ⊕ www.shopfoothillsmall.com) has a Barnes & Noble Superstore, a Saks Fifth Avenue outlet store, and many other outlets including Samsonite, Nike, and Adidas. A 16-screen cineplex, video arcade, and several restaurants round out the place.

Historic Broadway Village (✉ Country Club Rd. and Broadway Blvd., Central), Tucson's first shopping center, was designed by esteemed local architect Josias Joesler and built in 1939. Although small by today's standards, this outdoor complex with a courtyard houses interesting shops such as the Clues Unlimited mystery bookstore, Zocalo for colonial Mexican furniture, Yikes! for off-the-wall toys, and Picante for Mexican clothing and crafts.

La Encantada (✉ Skyline Dr. and Campbell Ave., Foothills ☎ 520/299–3566), the newest outdoor mall, has close to 50 stores (plus four restaurants) decidedly aimed at affluent consumers. North, a nouvelle Italian bistro, is definitely the standout eatery. Trendy tenants Crate & Barrel and Pottery Barn, plus a huge gourmet grocery that also serves casual meals, anchor the shopping center.

The Lost Barrio (✉ Park Ave. and 12th St., south of Broadway, Central ☎ No phone) is a cluster of 10 shops in an old warehouse district; Southwestern and ethnic art, furniture, and gifts (both antique and modern) are specialties.

Old Town Artisans Complex (✉ 186 N. Meyer Ave., Downtown ☎ 520/623–6024), across from the Tucson Museum of Art, has a large selection of Southwestern wares, including Native American jewelry, baskets, Mexican handicrafts, pottery, and textiles.

Park Place (✉ 5870 E. Broadway Blvd., Eastside ☎ 520/747–7575) is the busiest enclosed mall, with plush chairs and couches throughout, a toddler play area, an extensive food court, a 20-screen cineplex, and more than 120 stores, including Dillard's, Macy's, and Borders.

Plaza Palomino (✉ 2980 N. Swan Rd., at Fort Lowell Rd., Central ☎ 520/795–1177), an outdoor mall, has unique shops, galleries, and clothing boutiques including Enchanted Earthworks Jewelry and Culinary Concepts. On Saturday, you can sample locally grown produce, baked goods, salsas, and tamales at the farmers' market. The Red Sky Cafe is also here.

St. Philip's Plaza (✉ 4280 N. Campbell Ave., at River Rd., Foothills ☎ 520/886–7485) arranges its chic shops around a series of Spanish-style outdoor patios. You can shop at more than a dozen boutiques and eye outstanding art at Obsidian Gallery and Philabaum Contemporary Glass. The restaurants Vivace and Acacia can provide chic sustenance.

6

Tucson Mall (✉ 4500 N. Oracle Rd., at Wetmore Rd., Central ☎ 520/ 293–7330), an indoor mall on the west side, has Dillard's, Macy's, Mervyn's, Sears Roebuck, JCPenney, and more than 200 specialty shops. For tasteful Southwestern-style T-shirts, belts, jewelry, and prickly pear candies, check out the shops on "Arizona Avenue," a section of the first floor that's devoted to regional items.

Specialty Shops

ART GALLERIES If you're seeking out work by regional artists, you might want to drive down to Tubac, a community 45 mi south of Tucson (⇨ Sidetrips Near Tucson). *Art Life in Southern Arizona* (🖉 Box 36777, Tucson 85740 ☎ 520/797–1271 ⊕ artlifearizona.com), published annually, lists galleries and artists statewide.

Dinnerware Contemporary Arts (✉ 210 N. 4th Ave., Downtown ☎ 520/ 792–4503), a nonprofit, membership gallery, focuses on artists of Southern Arizona in various media, including painting, sculpture, digital art, and furniture.
Etherton Gallery (✉ 135 S. 6th Ave., Downtown ☎ 520/624–7370) specializes in photography but also represents artists in other media.
Gallery Row at El Cortijo (✉ 3001 E. Skyline Dr., Foothills ☎ 520/298– 0390) is a complex of nine galleries that collectively represent regional and national artists working in all media, including Native American, Western, and contemporary painting, crafts, and jewelry. The highly regarded **Rosequist Galleries** (☎ 520/577–8107) is the oldest in town.
Obsidian Gallery (✉ St. Phillip's Plaza, 4340 N. Campbell Ave., Suite 90, Central ☎ 520/577–3598) has exquisite glass, ceramic, and jewelry pieces.
Philabaum Contemporary Glass (✉ St. Phillip's Plaza, 4280 N. Campbell Ave., Suite 105, Foothills ☎ 520/299–1939) sells magnificent handblown vases, artwork, table settings, and jewelry.

BOOKS **Antigone** (✉ 411 N. 4th Ave., University ☎ 520/792–3715) specializes in books by and about women and also sells creative feminist cards and T-shirts.
Barnes & Noble (✉ 5130 E. Broadway Blvd., Eastside ☎ 520/512–1166 🖉 Foothills Mall, 7325 N. La Cholla Blvd., Northwest ☎ 520/742– 6402) is capacious but comfortable, with a well-stocked children's section and bustling café.
Bookman's (✉ 1930 E. Grant Rd., Central ☎ 520/325–5767 🖉 3733 W. Ina Rd., Northwest ☎ 520/579–0303 🖉 6230 E. Speedway Blvd., Eastside ☎ 520/748–9555) carries an eclectic selection of used and new books, music, magazines, and software in three spacious locations.
Book Stop (✉ 2504 N. Campbell Ave., Central ☎ 520/326–6661) is a wonderful browsing place for used and out-of-print books.
Borders Books and Music (✉ Park Place Mall, 5870 E. Broadway Blvd., Eastside ☎ 520/584–0111 🖉 4235 N. Oracle Rd., Northwest ☎ 520/ 292–1331) has a vast selection of books, music, and DVDs.
Clues Unlimited (✉ Historic Broadway Village, 3000 E. Broadway Blvd., Central ☎ 520/326–8533) specializes in mysteries.
Crescent Tobacco and Newsstand (✉ 200 E. Congress St., Downtown ☎ 520/622–1559 🖉 7037 E. Tanque Verde Rd., Northeast ☎ 520/296–

3102) carries hundreds of daily newspapers and magazines from around the world, not to mention imported cigars and cigarettes.

Tucson's Map and Flag Center (⊠ 3239 N. 1st Ave., Central ☎ 520/887–4234) is the place to pick up your topographical maps and specialty guides to Arizona.

Waldenbooks (⊠ Tucson Mall, 4500 N. Oracle Rd., Central ☎ 520/293–6799) is handy if you need to take a break from souvenir shopping at the mall.

CACTI **B&B Cactus Farm** (⊠11550 E. Speedway Blvd., Eastside ☎520/721–4687), which you'll pass en route to Saguaro National Park East, has a huge selection of cacti and succulents. They ship anywhere in the country.

Native Seeds/Search (⊠ 526 N. 4th Ave., University ☎ 520/622–5561), dedicated to preserving native crops and traditional farming methods, sells 350 kinds of seeds as well as Native American crafts.

GIFTS **Del Sol** (⊠ 435 N. 4th Ave., University ☎ 520/628–8765) specializes in Mexican folk art, jewelry, and Southwest-style clothing.

Mrs. Tiggy Winkle's Toys (⊠4811 E. Grant Rd., Central ☎520/326–0188) will probably remind you of the toy shops of the past—only better—with many items that are hard to find in the big-box toy stores.

United Nations Center (⊠ 6242 E. Speedway Blvd., Central ☎ 520/881–7060) sells reasonably priced ethnic jewelry, apparel, and crafts from all over the world.

JEWELRY **Abbott Taylor** (⊠ 6383 E. Grant Rd., Eastside ☎ 520/745–5080) creates custom designs in diamonds and other precious stones.

Beth Friedman (⊠ Joesler Village, 1865 E. River Rd., Suite 121, Foothills ☎ 520/577–6858) sells unsurpassed designs in silver and semiprecious stones. Her store also carries an eclectic selection of ladies' apparel, fine art, and home furnishings.

Patania's Originals (⊠3000 E. Broadway Blvd., Central ☎520/795–0086), formerly the Thunderbird Shop, is one of the best-known jewelers in the Southwest. The Patania family has been creating unique designs in silver, gold, and platinum here and in Santa Fe for three generations. The shop is 1 mi east of the El Con mall.

Turquoise Door (⊠ St. Phillip's Plaza, 4340 N. Campbell Ave., Foothills ☎ 520/299–7787) creates innovative jewelry that amounts to a modern take on classic Southwestern designs.

MEXICAN FURNISHINGS **Antigua de Mexico** (⊠ 3235 W. Orange Grove Rd., Northwest ☎ 520/742–7114) sells well-made furniture and crafts that you are not likely to find elsewhere in town.

NATIVE AMERICAN ARTS & CRAFTS San Xavier Plaza, across from San Xavier mission and also part of the Tohono O'odham reservation, is a good place to find vendors and stores selling the work of this and other area tribes.

Bahti Indian Arts (⊠ St. Philip's Plaza, 4300 N. Campbell Ave., Foothills ☎ 520/577–0290) is owned and run by Mark Bahti, whose father, Tom, literally wrote the book on Native American art, including an early definitive work on katsinas. The store sells high-quality jewelry, pottery, rugs, art, and more.

Grey Dog Trading Company (⊠ Plaza Palomino, 2970 N. Swan Rd., Central ☎ 520/881–6888) has an ample selection of jewelry, katsinas, weaving, pottery, and Zuni fetishes.

Kaibab Courtyard Shops (⊠ 2837 N. Campbell Ave., Central ☎ 520/795–6905) sells traditional Native American arts, along with Mexican imports and Nambé dinnerware.

Silverbell Trading (⊠ Casa Adobes Plaza, 7007 N. Oracle Rd., Northwest ☎ 520/797–6852) carries the work of local and regional artists.

WESTERN WEAR　Tucsonans who wear Western gear keep it simple for the most part—jeans, a Western shirt, maybe boots. This ain't Santa Fe.

Arizona Hatters (⊠ 3600 N. 1st Ave., Central ☎ 520/292–1320) can fit you for that Stetson you've always wanted.

Corral Western Wear (⊠ 4525 E. Broadway Blvd., Eastside ☎ 520/322–6001) sells shirts, hats, belts, jewelry, and boots, catering to both urban and authentic cowboys and cowgirls.

Stewart Boot Manufacturing (⊠ 30 W. 28th St., South ☎ 520/622–2706) has been making handmade leather boots since the 1940s.

Western Warehouse (⊠ 3719 N. Oracle Rd., Northwest ☎ 520/293–1808 ⊠ 6701 E. Broadway Blvd., Eastside ☎ 520/885–4385) is the place if you want to go where native Tucsonans shop for their everyday Western duds.

SIDE TRIPS NEAR TUCSON

Interstate 19 heads south from Tucson to Tubac, carrying with it history buffs, bird-watchers, hikers, art enthusiasts, duffers, and shoppers. The road roughly follows the Camino Real (King's Road), which the conquistadors and missionaries traveled from Mexico up to what was once the northernmost portion of New Spain.

The Asarco Mineral Discovery Center

❸❹ *15 mi south of Tucson off I–19.*

Operated by the American Smelting and Refining Co. (ASARCO), this facility is designed to elucidate the importance of mining to your everyday life. Exhibits include a walk-through model of an ore crusher, video stations that explain refining processes, and a film on extraction of minerals from the earth. The big draw, however, is the yawning open pit of the Mission Mine, some 2 mi long and 1¾ mi wide because so much earth has to be torn up to extract the 1% that is copper. It's impressive, but doesn't bolster the case the center tries to make about how environmentally conscious mining has become. Tours of the pit, which take about one hour, leave the center on the half hour; the last one starts at 3:30. ⊠ *1421 W. Pima Mine Rd.* ⊕ *www.mineraldiscovery.com* ☎ *520/625–0879* ⊠ *$6* ☉ *Tues.–Sat. 9–5.*

Titan Missile Museum

❸❺ *25 mi south of Tucson, off I–19.*

During the cold war, Tucson was ringed by 18 of the 54 Titan II missiles that existed in the United States. After the SALT II treaty with the

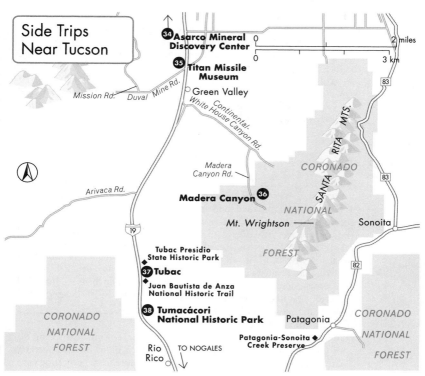

Side Trips Near Tucson

34 **Asarco Mineral Discovery Center**
35 **Titan Missile Museum**
○ Green Valley
Mission Rd. Duval Mine Rd.
Continental-White House Canyon Rd.
Madera Canyon Rd.
Arivaca Rd.
Madera Canyon 36
Mt. Wrightson
Tubac Presidio State Historic Park ◆
37 **Tubac**
◆ **Juan Bautista de Anza National Historic Trail**
38 **Tumacácori National Historic Park** Patagonia
Patagonia-Sonoita Creek Preserve ◆
Rio Rico ○ TO NOGALES
CORONADO NATIONAL FOREST
SANTA RITA MTS.
CORONADO NATIONAL FOREST
Sonoita
CORONADO NATIONAL FOREST

6

Soviet Union was signed in 1979, this was the only missile-launch site left intact. Now a National Historic Landmark, the Titan Missile Museum makes for a sobering visit. Guided tours, running every half hour, last about an hour and take you down 55 steps into the command post, where a ground crew of four lived and waited. Among the sights is the 103-foot, 165-ton, two-stage liquid-fuel rocket. Now empty, it originally held a nuclear warhead with 214 times the explosive power of the bomb that destroyed Hiroshima. This museum is operated by the Pima Air and Space Museum and combination tickets are available. ✉ *1580 W. Duval Mine Rd., I–19, Exit 69* ☎ *520/625–7736* ⊕ *www.pimaair.org* 🎟 *$8.50* ☉ *Daily 9–5; last tour departs at 4.*

Madera Canyon

36 *61½ mi southeast of Tucson; Exit 63 off I–19, then east on White House Canyon Rd. for 12½ mi, it turns into Madera Canyon Rd.*

This is where the Coronado National Forest meets the Santa Rita Mountains—among them Mount Wrightson, the highest peak in southern Arizona, at 9,453 feet. With approximately 200 mi of scenic trails, the Madera Canyon recreation area is a favorite destination for hikers. Higher elevations and thick pine cover make it especially popular with Tucsonans looking to escape the summer heat. Trails vary from a steep trek up Mount Baldy to a paved, wheelchair-accessible path. Birders flock here year-round; about 400 avian species have been spotted in the area. The small, volunteer-run visitor center is open only on weekends. Nearby, the Bog Springs Campground has 13 sites, with toilets, potable water, and grills, available on a first-come, first-served basis. The cost is $10 per vehicle per night. ⊠ *Madera Canyon Rd., Madera Canyon* ☎ *520/ 281–2296 Nogales Ranger District office* ⊕ *www.fs.fed.us/r3/coronado* ⊡ *Donation requested* ☉ *Daily.*

Tubac

★ ③⑦ *45 mi south of Tucson at Exit 40 off I-19.*

Established in 1726, Tubac is the site of the first European settlement in Arizona. A year after the Pima Indian uprising in 1751, a military garrison was established here to protect Spanish settlers, missionaries, and peaceful Native American converts of the nearby Tumacácori Mission. It was from here that Juan Bautista de Anza led 240 colonists across the desert—the expedition resulted in the founding of San Francisco in 1776. In 1860 Tubac was the largest town in Arizona. Today, the quiet little town is a popular art colony. More than 80 shops sell such crafts as carved wooden furniture, hand-thrown pottery, delicately painted tiles, and silk-screen fabrics (note that many shops are closed on Monday). You can also find Mexican pottery and trinkets without having to cross the border. The annual **Tubac Festival of the Arts** has been held in February for more than 30 years.

> **WORD OF MOUTH**
>
> "Tubac is one of our very favorite places and I would definitely recommend staying there . . . That area is gorgeous."   –desertduds

There's an archaeological display of portions of the original 1752 fort at the **Tubac Presidio State Historic Park and Museum** in the center of town. In addition to the visitor center and the adjoining museum, which has detailed the history of the early colony, the park includes Tubac's 1885 schoolhouse and a pleasant picnic area. ⊠ *Presidio Dr.* ☎ *520/ 398–2252* ⊕ *www.pr.state.az.us* ⊡ *$3* ☉ *Daily 8–5.*

Where to Stay & Eat

¢ ✕ **Tubac Deli & Coffee Co.** Smack in the middle of Tubac village, this pleasant little eatery serves generous sandwiches, salads, and soups—as well as cappuccinos and pastries—every day until 5:30 PM. ⊠ *6 Plaza Rd.* ☎ *520/398–3330* ☷ *No credit cards* ☉ *No dinner.*

$$ ✕⊡ **Amado Territory Inn and Cafe.** Although this quiet, friendly B&B is directly off the highway frontage road, it feels worlds away. The inn resembles a late-19th-century ranch house, its soaring ceiling and contemporary Southwestern art make the interior distinctly modern. Rooms are furnished with handcrafted Mexican pieces, and some have a view of the garden and the Santa Rita Mountains. Breakfast is included (try the huevos rancheros); next door, the Amado Cafe serves savory Greek-style pasta, chicken, and fish specialties for lunch and dinner. ⊠ *3001*

E. Frontage Rd., off Exit 48 of I–19 ⌂ *Box 81, Amado 85645* ☎ *520/398–8684 or 888/398–8684* ☐ *520/398–8186* ⊕ *www.amado-territory-inn.com* ⌑ *9 rooms, 2 suites* ⚬ *Restaurant, putting green, meeting rooms; no room phones, no room TVs, no smoking* ▭ *MC, V* ⎜⊙⎟ *BP.*

$–$$ ⊡ **Tubac Country Inn.** Down the lane from the shops and eateries of Tubac village, you'll find this charming two-story inn. Tastefully decorated in contemporary Southwest style, all rooms and suites have kitchenettes. The common outdoor space is a tranquil desert flower garden with willow chairs, a Mexican fireplace, and a barbecue for guest use. Each morning a breakfast basket of muffins, cheeses, fruits, and juice is brought to your door. ⊠ *13 Burruel St., Tubac 85646* ☎ *520/398–3178* ☐ *520/398–3178* ⊕ *www.tubaccountryinn.com* ⌑ *3 rooms, 2 suites* ⚬ *Microwaves, refrigerators, cable TV, Wi-Fi; no room phones, no smoking* ▭ *AE, D, MC, V* ⎜⊙⎟ *BP.*

EN ROUTE You can tread the same road as the conquistadors: the first 4½ mi of the **Juan Bautista de Anza National Historic Trail** (⊕ www.nps.gov/juba) from Tumacácori to Tubac were dedicated in 1992. You'll have to cross the Santa Cruz River (which is usually low) three times to complete the hike, and the path is rather sandy, but it's a pleasant journey along the tree-shaded banks of the river.

Tumacácori National Historic Park

㊳ *3 mi south of Tubac, Exit 29 off I–19.*

The site where Tumacácori National Historic Park now stands was visited by missionary Father Eusebio Francisco Kino in 1691, but the Jesuits didn't build a church here until 1751. You can still see some ruins of this simple structure, but the main attraction is the mission of San José de Tumacácori, built by the Franciscans around 1799–1803. A combination of circumstances—Apache attacks, a bad winter, and Mexico's withdrawal of funds and priests—caused the remaining inhabitants to flee in 1848. Persistent rumors of wealth left behind by both the Franciscans and the Jesuits led treasure seekers to pillage the site; it still bears those scars. The site was finally protected in 1908, when it became a national monument.

Information about the mission and the Anza trail is available at the visitor center, and guided tours are offered daily (more in winter than in summer). A small museum displays some of the mission's artifacts, and sometimes fresh tortillas are made on a wood-fire stove in the courtyard. In addition to a Christmas Eve celebration, costumed historical high masses are held at Tumacácori in spring and fall. An annual fiesta the first weekend of December has arts and crafts and food booths. ⊠ *I–19, Exit 29, Tumacácori* ☎ *520/398–2341* ⊕ *www.nps.gov/tuma* ⛶ *$3* ⊙ *Daily 8–5.*

Where to Stay

$$ ⊡ **Esplendor Resort.** Too close to Tucson to be a real getaway, this ridgetop hotel and conference center languished for many years before finally coming into its own. Renovated in 2004, the three-story complex has a historic Western theme, with a blacksmith, a tinsmith, and

6

a saloon. Some rooms continue the theme, with whimsical bordello furnishings and tepee bed canopies. Most people come for the golf course designed by Robert Trent Jones, the splendid views, and the isolation. Nogales, Mexico, is a short drive south. ✉ *1069 Camino Caralampi, off I–19 at Rio Rico Rd. (Exit 17), Rio Rico 85648* ☎ *520/281–1901 or 800/288–4746* 🖷 *520/281–7132* ⊕ *www.esplendor-resort.com* 📟 *166 rooms, 14 suites* ♨ *Restaurant, refrigerators, cable TV with movies, Wi-Fi, 18-hole golf course, 4 tennis courts, pool, gym, outdoor hot tub, sauna, hiking, horseback riding, bar, laundry service, business services, meeting rooms, no-smoking rooms* ▤ *AE, D, MC, V.*

TUCSON ESSENTIALS

To research prices, get advice from other travelers, and book travel arrangements, visit ⊕ *www.fodors.com.*

Transportation

BY AIR

Tucson International Airport is 8½ mi south of downtown, west of I–10 off the Valencia exit.

Check plane fares carefully when planning your trip. Although you may not want to spend time in Phoenix, sometimes it's cheaper to fly there and take a scenic 2½-hour drive down the Pinal Pioneer Parkway (U.S. 79), or a speedier (by ½-hour) trip on I–10, to Tucson.

Many hotels provide courtesy airport shuttle service; inquire when making reservations.

To get to and from the airport, Arizona Stagecoach takes groups and individuals to all parts of Tucson and Green Valley, for $9 to $38, depending on the location. If you're traveling light and aren't in a hurry, you can take a city Sun Tran bus to central Tucson. Bus 11, which leaves every half hour from a stop at the left of the lower level as you come out of the terminal, goes north on Alvernon Way, and you can transfer to most of the east–west bus lines from this main north–south road; ask the bus driver which one would take you closest to the location you need. You can also transfer to several lines from Bus 6, which leaves less frequently from the same airport location and heads to the Roy Laos center at the south of town.

🚐 Arizona Stagecoach ☎ 520/889-1000. Sun Tran ☎ 520/792-9222. Tucson International Airport (TUS) ☎ 520/573-8000 ⊕ www.tucsonairport.org. Aerocalifornia ☎ 800/237-6225.

BY BUS

Within the city limits, public transportation, which is geared primarily to commuters, is available through Sun Tran, Tucson's bus system. On weekdays, bus service starts around 5 AM; some lines operate until 10 PM, but most go only until 7 or 8 PM, and weekend service is limited. A one-way ride costs $1; transfers are free, but be sure to request them when you pay your fare, for which exact change is required. An all-day pass costs $2. Those with valid Medicare cards can ride for 40¢. Call for information on Sun Tran bus routes.

The city-run Van Tran has specially outfitted vans for riders with disabilities. Call for information and reservations.

Buses to Los Angeles, El Paso, Phoenix, Flagstaff, Douglas, and Nogales (Arizona) depart and arrive regularly from Tucson's Greyhound Lines terminal. For travel to Phoenix, Arizona Shuttle Service, Inc., runs express service from three locations in Tucson every hour on the hour, 4 AM to 9 PM every day; the trip takes about 2¼ hours. One-way fare is $24. Call 24 hours in advance for reservations.

🛈 **Arizona Shuttle Service, Inc.** ☎ 520/795-6771. **Greyhound Lines terminal** ✉ 2 S. 4th Ave., at E. Broadway Blvd., Downtown ☎ 520/792-3475 or 800/229-9424 ⊕ www. greyhound.com. **Sun Tran** ☎ 520/792-9222. **Van Tran** ☎ 520/620-1234.

BY CAR

You will need a car to get around Tucson and the surrounding area. It makes sense to rent a car at the airport; all the major rental-car agencies—Avis, Budget, Hertz, and National—are represented, along with Alamo, Dollar, and Thrifty. The driving time from the airport to the center of town varies, but it's usually less than a half hour; add 15 minutes during rush hours (7:30 AM–9 AM and 4:30 PM–6 PM). Parking is not a problem in most parts of town.

If you haven't rented a car at the Tucson International Airport, or if you want to save the 10% "airport concession fee" the airport imposes on renters there, several car-rental agencies also have pick-up and drop-off locations in the central, northwest, and east areas of town. In addition, Carefree Rent-a-Car rents reliable used cars at good rates. If you think you might be interested in driving farther into Mexico than Nogales (where you can park on the U.S. side of the border), check in advance to make sure that the rental company will allow this and that you are covered on your rental-insurance policy: many rental-insurance agreements do not cover accidents or thefts that occur outside the United States.

From Phoenix, 111 mi northwest, I–10 east is the road that will take you to Tucson. Also a major north–south traffic artery along the west side of town, I–10 has well-marked exits all along the route. At Casa Grande, 70 mi north of Tucson, I–8 connects with I–10, bringing travelers into the area from Yuma and San Diego. From Nogales, 63 mi south on the Mexican border, take I–19 into Tucson.

Much of the year, traffic in Tucson isn't especially heavy, but during the busiest winter months (December through March) streets in town can get congested during rush hour, between 4 and 6 PM.

🛈 **Alamo** ☎ 520/573-4740. **Avis** ☎ 520/294-1494. **Budget** ☎ 520/889-8800. **Carefree Rent-a-Car** ☎ 520/790-2655. **Dollar** ☎ 520/573-8486. **Enterprise** ☎ 520/792-1602. **Hertz** ☎ 520/294-7616. **National** ☎ 520/573-8050. **Thrifty** ☎ 520/790-2277.

BY TAXI

Taxi rates vary widely; they're unregulated in Arizona. It's always wise to inquire about the cost of a trip before getting into a cab. It should be about $24 from the airport to central Tucson. Two of the more reliable Tucson cab companies are Allstate Taxi and Yellow Cab, which also operates Fiesta Taxi, whose drivers speak English and Spanish.

🚩 **Allstate Taxi** ☎ 520/798-1111. **Fiesta Taxi** ☎ 520/622-7777. **Yellow Cab** ☎ 520/624-6611.

BY TRAIN

Amtrak serves the city with westbound and eastbound trains six times a week.

🚩 **Amtrak** ✉ 400 E. Toole Ave., Downtown ☎ 520/623-4442 or 800/872-7245 ⊕ www.amtrak.com.

Contacts & Resources

EMERGENCIES

🚩 Hospitals **Columbia Northwest Medical Center** ✉ 6200 N. La Cholla Blvd., Northwest ☎ 520/742-9000. **St. Joseph's Hospital** ✉ 350 N. Wilmot Rd., Eastside ☎ 520/873-3000. **Tucson Medical Center** ✉ 5301 E. Grant Rd., Central ☎ 520/327-5461. **University Medical Center** ✉ 1501 N. Campbell Ave., University ☎ 520/694-0111; a teaching hospital with a first-rate trauma center.

🚩 Pharmacies **Walgreens 24-Hour Pharmacy** ✉ 4685 E. Grant Rd., Central ☎ 520/326-4341 ✉ 7114 N. Oracle Rd., Northwest ☎ 520/297-2826.

TOUR OPTIONS

ADVENTURE & ECOTOURS Sunshine Jeep Tours and Trail Dust Adventures arrange trips into the Sonoran Desert outside Tucson in open-air, four-wheel-drive vehicles. Baja's Frontier Tours explores the natural history of Tucson and the surrounding area.

MISSION TOURS In the spring and fall, those interested in visiting the area's historic missions can contact Kino Mission Tours, which has professional historians and bilingual guides on staff.

ORIENTATION TOURS Great Western Tours takes individuals and groups to such popular sights as Old Tucson, Sabino Canyon, and the Arizona–Sonora Desert Museum; in-depth tours of the city and its neighborhoods are also available. Tour operators are on limited schedules (or close altogether) in summer.

WALKING TOURS The friendly, knowledgeable docents of the Arizona Historical Society conduct walking tours of the downtown historic districts (departing from the Sosa-Carillo-Fremont House) every Thursday and Saturday at 10 from November through mid-April the cost is $5.

🚩 **Arizona Historical Society** ☎ 520/622-0956. **Baja's Frontier Tours** ☎ 520/887-2340 or 888/297-2508 ⊕ www.bajasfrontiertours.com. **Great Western Tours** ☎ 520/572-1660 ⊕ www.gwtours.net. **Kino Mission Tours** ☎ 520/628-1269. **Sunshine Jeep Tours** ☎ 520/742-1943 ⊕ www.sunshinejeeptours.com. **Trail Dust Adventures** ☎ 520/747-0323 ⊕ www.traildustadventures.com.

VISITOR INFORMATION

🚩 **Metropolitan Tucson Convention and Visitors Bureau** ☎ 520/624-1817 or 800/638-8350 ⊕ www.visittucson.org.

Southern Arizona

WORD OF MOUTH

"I would suggest Tubac, Patagonia, and San Rafael Valley to Sonoita, a wonderful drive, different from any other part of Arizona, with grassy, rolling hills . . . Southern Arizona has a lot to offer and is well worth a trip; winter is usually absolutely wonderful, sunny, warmish during the day, cool at night."
—desertduds

"We spent a week in Tucson and drove to Bisbee and Tombstone for a day . . . one of those times where the drive was as much of a pleasure as the destination. We toured the mine, ate at the Bisbee Grille and walked around, then drove back to Tombstone . . . It's very touristy but that's OK. (Get it, OK, like corral.) I bought a nice pair of Navajo earrings at the Cochise Trading Post; seemed like the best place for quality and value." —elizabeth reed

Updated by
Mara Levin

SOUTHERN ARIZONA CAN DO little to escape its cliché-ridden image as a landscape of cow skulls, tumbleweeds, dried-up riverbeds, and mother lodes—but it doesn't need to. The area that evokes such American dime-novel notions as Indian wars, vast land grants, and savage shoot-'em-ups is not simply another part of the Wild West drunk on romanticized images of its former self; local farmers and ranchers here evoke the self-sufficiency and ruggedness of their pioneer ancestors and revel in the area's rowdy past. Abandoned mining towns and sleepy Western hamlets dot a lonely landscape of rugged rock formations, deep pine forests, dense mountain ranges, and scrubby grasslands.

South of Sierra Vista, just above the Mexican border, a stone marker commemorates the spot where the first Europeans set foot in what is now the United States. In 1540, 80 years before the pilgrims landed at Plymouth Rock, Spanish conquistador Don Francisco Vásquez de Coronado led one of Spain's largest expeditions from Mexico along the fertile San Pedro River valley, where the little towns of Benson and St. David are found today. They had come north to seek the legendary Seven Cities of Cíbola, where Native American pueblos were rumored to have doors of polished turquoise and streets of solid gold. The wealth of the region, however, lay in its rich veins of copper and silver, not tapped until more than 300 years after the Spanish marched on in disappointment. Once word of this cache spread, these parts of the West quickly became much wilder: fortune seekers who rushed to the region came face-to-face with the Chiricahua Apaches, led by Cochise and Geronimo, while Indian warriors battled encroaching settlers and the U.S. Cavalry sent to protect them.

Although the search for mineral booty in southeastern Arizona is more notorious, the western side of the state wasn't untouched by the rage to plunder. The leaching plant built by the New Cornelia Copper Company in 1917 transformed the sleepy desert community of Ajo into one of the most important mining districts in the state. Interest in going for the gold in California gave rise to the town of Yuma: the Colorado River had to be crossed to get to the West Coast, and Fort Yuma was established in part to protect the Anglo ferry business at a good fording point of the river from Indian competitors. The Yuma tribe lost that battle, but another group of Native Americans, the Tohono O'odham, fared better in this part of the state. Known for a long time as the Papago—or "bean eaters"—they were deeded a large portion of their ancestral homeland by the U.S. Bureau of Indian Affairs. The largest of their three reservations, stretching across an almost completely undeveloped section of southwestern Arizona, encompasses 2,774,370 acres.

Top 5 Experiences in Southern Arizona

- **Tour Karchner Caverns:** The underground world of a living, "wet" cave system is a rare and wonderful sensory experience. You'll see a multicolor limestone kingdom and probably feel "cave kiss" droplets grace your head; just *don't touch anything.*

- **Hike in the Chiricahuas:** Stunning "upside-down" rock formations, flourishing wildlife, and relatively easy trails make for great hiking in this unspoiled region. If you must choose only one, the 3.4 mi Echo Canyon Loop Trail is a winner.

GREAT ITINERARIES

Numbers in the text correspond to numbers in the margin and on the Southeast Arizona and Southwest Arizona maps.

IF YOU HAVE 2 DAYS

If you only have a short time to explore this region, choose whether to tour the eastern or western section of southern Arizona. If you're headed east from Tucson, head to ⬚ **Tombstone ❶** ▶ to experience the Wild West. After strolling the shoot-'em-up capital, head south to ⬚ **Bisbee ❷**, a good place to spend the night. Take the mine tour the next morning and devote the afternoon to exploring the shops on Main Street. Another option is to explore **Sonoita ❹** and **Patagonia ❺** in the morning before heading to ⬚ **Nogales ⓭** for a late lunch and an afternoon of shopping in Mexico.

If you're going west, take a leisurely drive to **Kitt Peak National Observatory ⓯**. Stop at the Tohono O'odham Reservation capital, **Sells ⓰**, en route to ⬚ **Ajo ⓱**, to sleep. Plan to spend most of the next day hiking or driving around **Organ Pipe Cactus National Monument ⓲**, but set aside a little time to explore the pleasant mining town.

IF YOU HAVE 4 DAYS

Head out early for **Tombstone ❶** ▶ so you can spend the morning exploring the town; in the afternoon head south to see the sights of ⬚ **Bisbee ❷** and stay overnight. Head north the next day to **Chiricahua National Monument ❼**, hike or drive through the magnificent rock formations, and spend the night in the area. On your way back toward Tucson, stop in Dragoon at **Texas Canyon ❿** and visit the Amerind Foundation's gallery and museum. A few miles farther west on I-10 is **Benson ⓫**, where you can have lunch and then tour the huge underground world of stalactites and stalagmites in **Kartchner Caverns State Park ⓬**. If you're still feeling adventurous drop down to explore Arizona's wine country by visiting the vineyards around ⬚ **Sonoita ❹** and Elgin. Stay overnight here or in ⬚ **Sierra Vista ❻** near Ramsey Canyon, where you're likely to be greeted by hummingbirds in the morning.

7

- **Explore Bisbee:** Put on a yellow rain slicker and hardhat, then board the Queen Mine Train and venture into the life of a copper miner at the turn of the last century. Afterward, check out the narrow, hilly town's Victorian houses and thriving shops.

- **Bargain hunting in Nogales, Mexico:** Shop for glassware, silver, leather, and pottery—and bargain with the sellers for 30%, 40%, or 50% off the marked price. Park on the Arizona side, and walk across the border to enjoy a different culture and delicious Mexican food.

- **Stargaze at Kitt Peak:** Clear skies, very dry air, and the abundance of mountains here provide ideal conditions for stargazing. The evening observation program, with top-notch telescopes and enthusiastic guides, is an excellent introduction to astronomy.

Exploring Southern Arizona

The diverse geography of this region and the driving distances between sights require that you strategize when planning your trip. With Tucson as a starting point, the rolling hills and grasslands of Sonoita and Patagonia are little more than an hour away, as are the underground marvels in Kartchner Caverns (to the southeast) and the starry skies above Kitt Peak Observatory (to the southwest). You can explore the Old West of Tombstone, Bisbee, and the surrounding ghost towns in one day, or more leisurely in two. To see hillsides covered with Organ Pipe Cactus National Monument, however, you'll need to drive about three hours southwest to reach the national monument and then take at least a full day to hike or drive around it and the town of Ajo. A trek through the stunning Chiricahua rock formations calls for an overnight stay, since the area is a 2½-hour drive southeast of Tucson.

About the Restaurants

In southern Arizona, cowboy fare is more common than haute cuisine. There are exceptions to the rule, though, especially in the wine-growing area of Sonoita and in Bisbee, both popular for weekend outings from Tucson. And a region that shares its border with Mexico is bound to have a fair number of good taquerias.

About the Hotels

From historic hotels, bed-and-breakfasts, and guest ranches to Nature Conservancy casitas, southern Arizona has an increasing array of properties that let you lay down your head surrounded by nature and history. Still, it's easy to find the park-your-car-outside-the-room chain-variety lodgings. Prices for the high season (winter and spring) tend to be a bit higher than for the low season (summer to early fall).

WHAT IT COSTS					
	$$$$	**$$$**	**$$**	**$**	**¢**
RESTAURANTS	over $30	$21–$30	$13–$20	$8–$12	under $8
HOTELS	over $250	$176–$250	$121–$175	$70–$120	under $70

Restaurant prices are per person for a main course at dinner. Hotel prices are for a standard double in high season, excluding taxes and service charges.

Timing

As you might expect, the desert areas are popular in winter, and the cooler mountain areas are more heavily visited in summer. Southern Arizona has developed seasonal travel, causing area hotels to adopt high-season (winter and spring) and low-season (summer and early fall) prices. In general, however, prices tend to be lower here than in the north.

SOUTHEAST ARIZONA

From the rugged mountain forests to the desert grasslands of Sierra Vista, the southeast corner of Arizona is one of the state's most scenic regions. Much of this area is part of Cochise County, named in 1881 in honor of

IF YOU LIKE

BIRD-WATCHING

Southern Arizona is one of the best areas for bird-watching in the United States; nearly 500 species have been spotted in the area. To the east, birders flock to the Patagonia-Sonoita Creek and Ramsey Canyon preserves, the San Pedro Riparian National Conservation Area, the ponds and dry lake beds south of Willcox, and the Portal-Cave Creek area in the Chiricahua Mountains near the New Mexico border. To the west, the Buenos Aires and Imperial national wildlife refuges are among the many places famed for their abundance of avian visitors.

CAMPING

Sleeping under the vast, starry desert sky reminds you that there are still huge swaths of undeveloped wilderness in the untrammeled southwest. Though it can get chilly at night in the desert, the weather is usually good enough year-round to make sleeping out an appealing option. Summer is the time to camp in the state's cooler, higher-altitude campgrounds. Campgrounds in the rural areas of southern Arizona rarely come close to getting full except on holiday weekends, and even then, campers tend to stay close to major cities and towns. Keep in mind that the camping conditions are fairly primitive (RV hookups are rare). It's advisable to bring your own fresh drinking water and be prepared to carry out what trash you bring in.

GHOST TOWNS

A number of the smaller mining communities in Cochise County died when their veins of ore ran out, and their adobe buildings gradually melted back into the desert. Some of what are termed ghost towns in the area are only heaps of rubble, but others show strong evidence of better days. In addition to Gleeson and Fairbank, a few holdouts remain—with enough residents to keep the post office open—in the town of Dos Cabezas, 15 mi southeast of Willcox, where you'll see the 1885 Wells Fargo station still standing. A tunnel through the mountaintop connects the eastern and western halves of the abandoned town of Hilltop, farther southeast of Willcox. Six miles northwest of Portal in the Chiricahua Mountains, Paradise was active in the 1900s, and a few old-timers still live here. Look for the old town jail among the ruined buildings. To get a good sense of the historical, you can sign up for a tour based out of Bisbee or Tombstone.

WINERIES

The term "Arizona wine country" may sound odd, but the soil and climate in the Santa Cruz Valley southeast of Tucson are ideal for growing grapes. Wine grapes first took root in the region 400 years ago, when the Spanish missionaries planted the first vines of "mission" grapes for the production of sacramental wine. However, it wasn't until the 1970s that the first commercial vinifera grapes were planted in the region as part of an agricultural experiment. Connoisseurs have debated the merits of the wines produced in this area since 1974, but if you want to decide for yourself, tour some of the region's wineries.

7

CLOSE UP

The Legend of Wyatt Earp

Popularized in dime novels and on the silver screen, the legend of Wyatt Earp follows the American tradition of the tall tale. This larger-than-life hero of the Wild West is cloaked with romance and derring-do. Stripped of the glamour, though, Earp emerges as a man with a checkered past who switched from fugitive to lawman several times over his long life.

Born in 1848, Wyatt Berry Stapp Earp earned renown as the assistant city marshal of Dodge City. Wyatt and his brothers James, Virgil, and Morgan moved to Tombstone with their wives in 1879 and it was here that they, along with Wyatt's friend Doc Holliday, made their mark in history. Wyatt ran a gambling concession at the Oriental Saloon and Virgil became the city marshal of Tombstone. When trouble began to brew with the Clanton gang, Virgil recruited Wyatt and Morgan as deputy policemen. The escalating animosity between the "cowboys" and the Earps peaked on October 26, 1881, at the O.K. Corral—a 30-second gunfight that left three of the Clanton gang dead and Morgan and Virgil wounded. Doc Holliday was creased, but Wyatt walked away from the fight uninjured. And then the real trouble for the Earps began.

In December, Virgil was shot and crippled by unknown assailants and on March 18, 1882, Morgan was shot to death in a pool hall. In retribution, Wyatt went on a bloody vendetta. After the smoke had settled, the remaining "cowboys" were dead and Wyatt had left Tombstone for good. He made the rounds of mining camps in the West and up into Alaska, then settled in California. He died on January 13, 1929. His legend lives on in recent movies such as *Tombstone* and *Wyatt Earp*.

---

the chief of the Chiricahua Apache. Cochise waged war against troops and settlers for 11 years, and was respected by Indian and non-Indian alike for his integrity and leadership. Today Cochise County is dotted with small towns, many of them smaller—and tamer—than they were in their heyday. Cochise County encompasses 6 and part of the 7th of the 12 mountain ranges that compose the 1.7-million-acre Coronado National Forest.

In the valleys between Southeastern Arizona's jagged mountain ranges you'll discover the 19th-century charm of Bisbee—Queen of the Copper Camps. You can explore the eerie hoodoos and spires of Chiricahua National Monument and walk in the footsteps of the legendary Apaches, who valiantly stood against the U.S. Army until Geronimo's final surrender in 1886. This is also where you can travel through the grassy plains surrounding Sonoita and Elgin—the heart of Arizona's wine country.

A trip to this historically and ecologically important corner of the state will also take you to Fort Huachuca, the oldest continuously operating military installation in the Southwest; to the Southeastern Arizona's "sky islands," the lush microclimates in the Huachuca and Chiricahua Mountains, where jaguars roam and migratory tropical birds flit through the canopy; and to historic mining and military towns, the tenacious survivors of the Old West—including Bisbee, Sierra Vista, and Tombstone.

Southeast Arizona

CORONADO
NATIONAL
FOREST

TO
TUCSON

Vail

Benson ⑪

**Kartchner
Caverns** ⑫
State Park

Sonoita ④

Elgin

Patagonia ⑤

**Sierra
Vista** ⑥

Nicksville

Fairbank

SAN PEDRO
RIPARIAN NAT'L
CONSERVATION
AREA

CORONADO
NATIONAL
FOREST

Palominas

① Tombstone

Gleeson

**Texas
Canyon** ⑩

Pearce

Sunizona

Sunsites

Dragoon

Cochise

⑨ Willcox

DOS CABEZAS MTS.

DRAGOON MTS.

Bowie

San
Simon

**⑧ Fort Bowie
National Historical
Site**

**Chiricahua
National
Monument** ⑦

Portal

CORONADO
NATIONAL
FOREST

SWISSHELM MTS.

PEDREGOSA
MTS.

Elfrida

McNeal

Pirtleville

Bisbee

Lavender
Pit

Douglas ③

KEY

▶ *Start of itinerary*

NEW MEXICO

MEXICO

0 ——— 20 miles
0 ——— 30 km

Shoot, just mention Tombstone and you'll hear the dime store treatment of Wyatt Earp and the O.K. Corral. That's what Tombstone is all about, right? Wrong.

This 30-second gunfight is virtually synonymous with Tombstone, but the 1880s boomtown holds much more history than that vengeful street fight. In its heyday, Tombstone not only claimed more than 100 saloons, some of the prettiest shady ladies in the state, and gunslingers galore— it was also home to the Cochise County seat and several churches and dining establishments. Today, a trip down the boardwalks on Allen Street will take you back in time.

Tombstone

❶ *28 mi northeast of Sierra Vista via AZ 90, 24 mi south of Benson via AZ 80.*

It's hard to imagine now but Tombstone, headquarters for most of the area's gamblers and gunfighters, was once bigger than San Francisco. The legendary headquarters of Wild West rowdies, Tombstone was part of an area called Goose Flats in the late 1800s and was prone to attack by nearby Apache tribesmen. Ed Schieffelin, an intrepid prospector, wasn't discouraged by those who cautioned that "all you'll find there is your tombstone," and in 1877 he struck one of the West's richest veins of silver in the tough old hills. He gave the town its name as an ironic "I told you so," and called the silver mine Lucky Cuss, figuring that he fit the description himself.

The promise of riches attracted all types of folks, including outlaws. Soon gambling halls, saloons, and houses of prostitution sprang up all along Allen Street. In 1881 the Earp family and Doc Holliday battled to the death with the Clanton boys at the famous shoot-out at the OK Corral. Over the past century, scriptwriters and storytellers have done much to rewrite the exact details of the confrontation, but it's a fact that the town was the scene of several gunfights in the 1880s. On Sunday you can witness replays of some of these on Allen Street.

Tombstone's rough-and-ready heyday was popularized by Hollywood in the 1930s and capitalized on by the local tourist industry in the decades that followed. "The town too tough to die" (it survived two major fires, an earthquake, the closing of the silver mines, and the moving of the county seat to Bisbee) was also a cultural center, and many of its original buildings remain intact.

Allen Street, the main drag, is lined with restaurants and curio shops. Many of the street's buildings still bear bullet holes from livelier days.

Start your tour of this tiny town at **Tombstone Visitor Center** (✉ 4th and Allen Sts. ☎ 520/457–3929 ⊕ www.tombstone.org). There's a self-guided walking tour, but the best way to get the lay of the land is to take the 15-minute **stagecoach ride** ($10, $5 for kids) around downtown. Drivers relate a condensed version of Tombstone's notorious past. You'll also pass the Tombstone Courthouse and travel down Toughnut Street, once called Rotten Row—because of the lawyers that lived there.

Boot Hill Graveyard, where the victims of the OK Corral shoot-out are buried, is on the northwest corner of town, facing U.S. 80. Chinese names in one section of the "bone orchard" bear testament to the laundry and

---

WORD OF MOUTH

"Tombstone isn't very impressive, IMO. I always say that someone who is truly fascinated by the history of the place, a real buff, would probably enjoy just being there. Anyone else would be bored. It's a small, dusty, not at all picturesque place graced by a kitschy saloon where you can dress up in period clothes and have your picture taken and printed onto a Wanted poster. Food is standard, not awful. Any special reason you thought of Tombstone? I hope I didn't rain on your parade—it's just my take on it."   –E

"I'm one of those history buffs the previous poster spoke of and I have enjoyed my two visits to Tombstone. While it has become somewhat touristy, it is less so than many of the other western towns where history was made. You'll be surprised at the small space in which the gunfight occurred (which was not actually at the OK Corral but behind it, next to Fry's Photo Studio)."
                                    –dwooddon

restaurant workers who came from San Francisco during the height of Tombstone's mining fever. One of the more amusing epitaphs at the cemetery, however, is engraved on the headstone of Wells Fargo agent Lester Moore, which poetically lists the cause of his untimely demise: "Here lies Lester Moore, four slugs from a .44, no less, no more." If you're put off by the commercialism of the place—you enter through a gift shop that sells novelty items in the shape of tombstones—remember that Tombstone itself is the result of crass acquisition. ⊠ *U.S. 80* ☎ *520/457–9344 or 800/457–9344* 🖅 *Free* ⊘ *Daily 7:30–6.*

For an introduction to the town's—and the area's—past, visit the **Tombstone Courthouse State Historic Park.** This redbrick 1882 county courthouse offers exhibits of the area's mining and ranching history; pioneer lifestyles, the 1882 judge's chambers, and the 1904 district attorney's office. The two-story building housed the Cochise County jail, a courtroom, and public offices until the county seat was moved to Bisbee in 1929. The stately building became the cornerstone of Tombstone's historic preservation efforts in the 1950s and was Arizona's first operational state park. Today, you can relax with an outdoor lunch at the park's tree-shaded picnic tables. ⊠ *219 E. Toughnut St., at 3rd St.* ☎ *520/457–3311* ⊕ *www.pr.state.az.us* 🖅 *$4* ⊘ *Daily 8–5.*

Originally a boardinghouse for the Vizina Mining Company and later a popular hotel, the **Rose Tree Inn Museum** has 1880s period rooms. Covering more than 8,600-square-feet, the Lady Banksia rose tree, planted by a homesick bride in 1885, is reported to be the largest of its kind in the world. The best time to see the tree is in April when its tiny white roses bloom. Romantics can purchase a healthy clipping from the tree ($10.95 plus tax) to plant in their own yard. The museum might not look like much from the outside, but the collectibles and tree make this one of the best places to visit in town. ⊠ *116 S. 4th St., at Toughnut St.* ☎ *520/457–3326* 🖅 *$3* ⊘ *Daily 9–5.*

☺ Vincent Price narrates the dramatic version of the town's past in the **Historama**—a 26-minute multimedia presentation. At the adjoining **OK Corral,** a recorded voice-over details the town's famous shoot-out, while life-size figures of the gunfight's participants stand poised to shoot. A reenactment of the gunfight at the OK Corral is held daily at 2 PM. Photographer C. S. Fly, whose studio was next door to the corral, didn't record this bit of history, but Geronimo and his pursuers were among the historic figures he did capture with his camera. Many of his fascinating Old West images may be viewed at the **Fly Exhibition Gallery.** ⊠ *Allen St. between 3rd and 4th Sts.* ☎ *520/457–3456* ⊕ *www.ok-corral. com* 🖅 *Historama, OK Corral, and Fly Exhibition Gallery $5.50, gunfight $2* ⊘ *Daily 9–5, Historama shows on the half hr 9:30–4:30.*

You can see the original printing presses for the town's newspaper at the **Tombstone Epitaph Museum** (⊠ 9 S. 5th St. ☎ 520/457–2211 🖅 Free ⊘ Daily 9:30–5). The newspaper was founded in 1880 by John P. Clum and is still publishing today. You can purchase one of the newspaper's special editions—*The Life and Times of Wyatt Earp, The Life and Times of Doc Holliday,* or *Tombstone's Pioneering Prostitutes.*

A Tombstone institution, known as the wildest, wickedest night spot between Basin Street and the Barbary Coast, the **Bird Cage Theater** is a former music hall where Enrico Caruso, Sarah Bernhardt, and Lillian Russell—among others—performed. It was also the site of the longest continuous poker game recorded: the game started when the Bird Cage opened in 1881 and lasted eight years, five months, and three days. Some of the better-known players included Diamond Jim Brady, Adolphus Busch (of brewery fame), and William Randolph Hearst's father. The cards were dealt round the clock; players had to give a 20-minute notice when they were planning to vacate their seats, because there was always a waiting list of at least 10 people ready to shell out $1,000 (the equivalent of about $30,000 today) to get in. In all, some $10 million changed hands.

When the mines closed in 1889, the Bird Cage was abandoned but the building has remained in the hands of the same family, who threw nothing out. You can walk on the stage visited by some of the top traveling performers of the time, see the faro table once touched by the legendary gambler Doc Holliday, and pass by the hearse that carried Tombstone's deceased to Boot Hill. The basement, which served as an upscale bordello and gambling hall, still has all the original furnishings and fixtures intact, and you can see the personal belongings left behind by the ladies of the night when the mines closed and they, and their clients, headed for California. The $22 family special admission admits two parents and all children under the age of 18. ⊠ *308 E. Allen St., at 6th St.* ☎ *520/457–3421* ⊠ *$8* ☉ *Daily 8–6.*

At the **Tombstone Western Heritage Museum,** owner Steve Elliott shares his eclectic collection of Tombstone artifacts and other relics of the Old West including 1880s dentist tools, clay poker chips, historic photographs, vintage firearms, and a stagecoach strongbox. ⊠ *515 Fremont St., at 6th St.* ☎ *520/457–3800* ⊠ *$5* ☉ *Mon.–Sat. 9–6, Sun. noon–6.*

Where to Stay & Eat

$–$$ ✕ **Lamplight Room.** Part of the Tombstone Boarding House B&B, this 1880 restaurant uses 1880s recipes from a period cookbook. Selections include Parmesan-encrusted salmon, chicken cordon bleu, roast pork loin, and a full Mexican menu. ⊠ *108 N. 4th St.* ☎ *520/457–3716 or 877/225–1319* ⊟ *AE, D, MC, V.*

¢–$$ ✕ **Longhorn Restaurant.** Across the street from Big Nose Kate's Saloon, named for Doc Holliday's girlfriend, the Longhorn Restaurant was originally the Bucket of Blood Saloon. Today it's noisier and definitely for the whole family, with burgers, steaks, ribs, tacos, and enchiladas. It may not be haute cuisine, but the huge helpings are filling and the restaurant is open for three meals a day. ⊠ *501 E. Allen St.* ☎ *520/457–3405* ⊟ *MC, V.*

¢–$ ✕ **Nellie Cashman's.** You can order anything from a burger to a hearty dinner of juicy pork chops or chicken-fried steak in this homey spot, named for the original owner, a Tombstone pioneer who opened a hotel and restaurant in 1882. Old photographs and postcards decorate the walls. Nellie's is also a great place for a country breakfast complete with biscuits and gravy. ⊠ *117 5th St.* ☎ *520/457–2212* ⊟ *AE, D, MC, V.*

$–$$ ▦ **Curly Bill's Bed & Breakfast.** Though named for one of the baddest outlaws in Tombstone Territory, this B&B is quite serene. Five blocks from Allen Street, the hacienda has views of the Dragoon Mountains from the sunporch and hot tub. Two rooms furnished with Victorian antiques share a bath, and two larger rooms with fireplaces have private baths. Hosts Curly and Sally, both historians, can inform and advise you about Tombstone highlights; or (for an extra fee) you may want to hop into their jeep for a customized tour of area sights and ghost towns. ☒ *210 N. 9th St., 85638* ☎ *520/457–3858* ⊕ *www.curlybillsbandb.com* ➾ *4 rooms, 2 with shared bath* ☽ *Fans, some in-room VCRs, hot tub; no TV in some rooms, no smoking* ⊟ *MC, V* ⫶⃝⃒ *BP.*

$ ⊡ **Holiday Inn Express.** Nestled into a hill just outside of town, this newer two-story property has spectacular views of the mountains and desert valley. The rooms are Western-theme, of course, and every night an old Western movie is screened in the dining room (with free popcorn). ☒ *1001 N. Highway 80, 85638* ☎ *520/457–9507 or 888/465–4329* ⊞ *520/457–9506* ⊕ *www.hitombstone.com* ➾ *60 rooms, 7 suites* ☽ *Refrigerators, cable TV with movies, in-room broadband, pool, hot tub, laundry, business services, no-smoking rooms* ⊟ *AE, D, MC, V.*

★ $ ⊡ **Tombstone Boarding House Bed & Breakfast.** This friendly B&B is actually two meticulously restored 1880s adobes that sit side by side: guests sleep in one house and go next door for a hearty country breakfast. The spotless rooms, all with private entrances, have period furnishings collected from around Cochise County. Even if you don't stay here, a visit to the Lamplight Room restaurant is worth a visit. ☒ *108 N. 4th St.* ⊡ *Box 906, 85638* ☎ *520/457–3716 or 877/225–1319* ⊕ *www. tombstoneboardinghouse.com* ➾ *6 rooms* ☽ *Restaurant, some pets allowed; no room phones, no room TVs, no smoking* ⊟ *AE, D, MC, V* ⫶⃝⃒ *BP.*

¢–$ ⊡ **Tombstone Motel.** Catercorner from the offices of the *Tombstone Epitaph,* on the town's main street, this comfortable and well-run motel will remind you of the motor courts of years past. The major attractions of Allen Street are less than a block away and the renovated rooms are neat and spacious. If you want peace and quiet, your best bet is to book a room on the courtyard. ☒ *502 E. Fremont St.* ⊡ *Box 837, 85638* ☎ *520/457–3478 or 888/455–3478* ⊞ *520/457–9017* ⊕ *www. tombstonemotel.com* ➾ *31 rooms, 6 suites* ☽ *Some refrigerators, cable TV with movies, in-room data ports, laundry facilities, some pets allowed (fee)* ⊟ *AE, D, MC, V* ⫶⃝⃒ *CP.*

Nightlife

★   If you're looking to wet your whistle, stop by the **Crystal Palace** (☒ 420 E. Allen St., at 5th St. ☎ 520/457–3611), where a beautiful mirrored mahogany bar, wrought-iron chandeliers, and tinwork ceilings date back to Tombstone's heyday. Locals come here on weekends to dance to live country-and-western music. Another hopping bar on Allen Street is **Big Nose Kate's Saloon** (☒ On Allen St. between 4th and 5th Sts. ☎ 520/457–3107 ⊕ www.bignosekate.com). Occasionally an acoustic concert livens things up even more at this popular pub, once part of the original Grand Hotel built in 1881. Saloon girls encourage visitors to get into the 1880s spirit by dressing up in red feather boas and dusters.

Shopping

Several curio shops and old-time photo emporiums await in the kitschy collection of stores lining Allen Street. Given the town's bloody history, it's not surprising that guns aren't permitted in most of the establishments but it's worth a visit to **G. F. Spangenberg Pioneer Gun Shop** (⌧ 17 S. 4th St., at Allen St. ☎ 520/457–3227), established in 1880. Wyatt Earp, Virgil Earp, Doc Holliday, the Clantons, and the McLowrys all purchased weapons at this shop, which still sells period firearms. Get into the spirit of the Old West by renting or purchasing 1880s-style costumes at the **Oriental Saloon** (⌧ 500 E. Allen St., at 5th St. ☎ 520/457–3922), which originally opened in 1880 and was touted as one of the fanciest bars in town. **Silver Hills Trading Co** (⌧ 504 E. Allen St. ☎ 520/457–3335) offers everything from Native American jewelry to kitschy southwestern souvenirs. Well-stocked **Tombstone Old West Books** (⌧ 401 E. Allen St. ☎ 520/457–2252) has a wide selection of books about Cochise County and the Old West.

Bisbee

❷ *24 mi south of Tombstone.*

★ Like Tombstone, Bisbee was a mining boomtown, but its wealth was in copper, not silver, and its success was much longer lived. The gnarled Mule Mountains aren't as impressive as some of the other mountain ranges in southern Arizona, but their rocky canyons concealed one of the richest mineral sites in the world.

Jack Dunn, a scout with Company C from Fort Huachuca chasing hostile Apaches in the area, first discovered an outcropping of rich ore here in 1877. By 1900 more than 20,000 people lived in the crowded canyons around the Bisbee mines. Phelps Dodge purchased all of the major mines by the time the Great Depression rolled around and mining continued until 1975, when the mines were closed for good. In less than 100 years of mining, the area surrounding Bisbee yielded more than 6.1 billion dollars of mineral wealth.

Once known as the Queen of the Copper Camps, Bisbee is no longer one of the biggest cities between New Orleans and San Francisco. It was rediscovered in the early 1980s by burned-out city dwellers and revived as a kind of Woodstock West. The population is a mix of retired miners and their families, aging hippie jewelry makers, and enterprising restaurateurs and boutique owners from all over the country.

If you want to head straight into town from U.S. 80, get off at the Brewery Gulch interchange. You can park and cross under the highway, taking Main, Commerce, or Brewery Gulch Street, all of which meet here.

Bisbee Visitors Center. This is a good place to start your visit of this historic mining town. It offers up-to-date information on attractions,

> ### WORD OF MOUTH
>
> "I loved Bisbee . . . it is so quaint and charming . . . surrounded by beautiful hills and mountains . . . the Copper Queen Hotel is in the center of town and it dates back to the turn of the century . . . there's a Southeastern Arizona Bird Observatory based in Bisbee . . . my kids loved the Bisbee Mining and Historical Museum . . . you can actually go for a ride in a mine . . . Bisbee gets my vote."   –Merilee

dining, lodging, and special events. ⊠ *2 Copper Queen Plaza* ☎ *520/ 432–3554* ⊕ *www.discoverbisbee.com.*

About ¼ mi after AZ 80 intersects with AZ 92, you can pull off the highway into a gravel parking lot, where a short, typewritten history of the **Lavender Pit Mine** (⊠ AZ 80) is attached to the hurricane fence surrounding the area (Bisbee isn't big on formal exhibits). The hole left by the copper miners is huge, with piles of lavender-hue "tailings," or waste, creating mountains around it. Arizona's largest pit mine yielded some 94 million tons of copper ore before mining activity came to a halt.

For a lesson in mining history, take the **Copper Queen Mine Underground Tour.** The mine is less than ½ mi to the east of the Lavender Pit, across AZ 80 from downtown at the Brewery Gulch interchange. Tours are led by Bisbee's retired copper miners, who are wont to embellish their spiel with tales from their mining days.

The 75-minute tours (you can't enter the mine at any other time) go into the shaft via a small open train, like those the miners rode when the mine was active. Before you climb aboard, you're outfitted in miner's garb— a yellow slicker and a hard hat with a light that runs off a battery pack. You may want to wear a sweater or light coat under your slicker because temperatures inside are cool. You'll travel thousands of feet into the mine, up a grade of 30 feet (not down, as many visitors expect). Those who are a bit claustrophobic might instead consider taking one of the van tours of the surface mines and historic district that depart from the building at the same times as the mine tours (excluding 9 AM). Reservations suggested. ⊠ *478 N. Dart Rd.* ☎ *520/432–2071 or 866/432– 2071* ⊕ *www.cityofbisbee.com/queenminetours.htm* ⊑ *Mine tour $12, van tour $10* ☉ *Tours daily at 9, 10:30, noon, 2, and 3:30.*

The **Bisbee Mining and Historical Museum** is in a redbrick structure built in 1897 to serve as the Copper Queen Consolidated Mining Offices. The rooms today are filled with exhibits, photographs, and artifacts that offer a glimpse into the everyday life of Bisbee's early mining community. This was the first rural museum in the United States to become a member of the Smithsonian Institution Affiliations Program. If you plan to visit the Bisbee Mining and Historical Museum and the Copper Queen Mine during the summer months from May through October, consider purchasing a Bisbee Visitor Passport. It costs $17, includes admission to both attractions, and is packed with discounts redeemable at more than 15 local restaurants, hotels, and attractions. ⊠ *5 Copper Queen Plaza* ☎ *520/432–7071* ⊕ *www.bisbeemuseum.org* ⊑ *$5* ☉ *Daily 10–4.*

The **Copper Queen Hotel** (⊠ 11 Howell Ave.), built a century ago and still in operation (⇨ *see* Where to Stay & Eat), is behind the Mining and Historical Museum. It has housed the famous as well as the infamous: General John "Black Jack" Pershing, John Wayne, Theodore Roosevelt, and mining executives from all over the world made this their home away from home. The hotel also hosts three resident ghosts. Take a minute to look through the ghost journal at the front desk where guests have described their haunted encounters.

Brewery Gulch, a short street running north and south, is adjacent to the Copper Queen Hotel. In the old days, the brewery housed here allowed the dregs of the beer that was being brewed to flow down the street and into the gutter.

Bisbee's **Main Street** is alive and retailing. This hilly commercial thoroughfare is lined with appealing art galleries, antiques stores, crafts shops, boutiques, and restaurants—many in well-preserved turn-of-the-20th-century brick buildings.

Tom Mosier, a native of Bisbee, gives the **Lavender Jeep Tours** (⊠ 45 Gila Dr. ☎ 520/432–5369) for $25 to $49. He regales locals and visitors with tales of the town and its buildings.

Where to Stay & Eat

★ **$$–$$$** ✕ **Café Roka.** This is the deserved darling of the hip Bisbee crowd. The constantly changing northern Italian–style evening menu is not extensive, but you can count on whatever you order—gulf shrimp tossed with lobster ravioli, roasted quail, New Zealand rack of lamb—to be wonderful. Portions are generous, and entrées include soup, salad, and sorbet. Exposed-brick walls and soft lighting form the backdrop for original artwork, and the 1875 bar hearkens to Bisbee's glory days. There's live jazz on Friday nights. ⊠ *35 Main St.* ☎ *520/432–5153* ⊕ *www.caferoka. com* ⊟ *AE, MC, V* ⊘ *Closed Sun.–Wed. No lunch.*

$–$$ ✕ **The Bisbee Grille.** You might not expect diversity at a place with a reputation for having the best burger in town, but this restaurant delivers with salads, sandwiches, fajitas, pasta, salmon, steaks, and ribs. The dining room, built to resemble an old train depot, fills up fast on the weekends. ⊠ *#2 Copper Queen Plaza* ☎ *520/432–6788* ⊟ *AE, D, MC, V.*

★ **$–$$$** ▥ **Canyon Rose Suites.** Steps from the heart of downtown, this all-suites B&B is in the 1905 Allen Block Building, formerly a furniture store and miner's rooming house. Upstairs are six spacious units, all with hardwood floors, 10-foot ceilings, and fully equipped kitchens. Local art (for sale) adorns the walls. In the spa downstairs you can get pampered with a hot-stone massage or herbal body wrap after a day in the mines. ⊠ *27 Subway St.* ⌖ *Box 1915, 85603* ☎ *520/432–5098 or 866/296–7673* ⊕ *www.canyonrose.com* ⇴ *6 suites* ⌂ *Kitchens, cable TV, in-room VCRs, spa, library, laundry facilities* ⊟ *D, MC, V.*

$–$$ ▥ **Copper Queen Hotel.** Built by the Copper Queen Mining Company when Bisbee was the biggest copper-mining town in the world, this hotel has been operating since 1902. Some rooms are small or oddly laid out, and walls are thin, but all have a Victorian charm. You might want to request room 211, where John Wayne once stayed; room 315, which is said to be inhabited by the ghost of former employee Julia Lowell; or room 406, which was once occupied by President Teddy Roosevelt. ⊠ *11 Howell Ave.* ⌖ *Drawer CQ, 85603* ☎ *520/432–2216 or 800/247–5829* ⎙ *520/432–4298* ⊕ *www.copperqueen.com* ⇴ *48 rooms* ⌂ *Restaurant, coffee shop, cable TV, pool, bar* ⊟ *AE, MC, V.*

¢–$$ ▥ **Shady Dell Vintage Trailer Park.** For a blast to the past, stay in one of

Fodor'sChoice the funky, vintage aluminum trailers at this trailer park off the beaten
★ path. Choices include a 1952, 10-foot homemade unit and a 1951, 33-

foot Royal Mansion. The entire collection is decked out 1950s style. Not all of the trailers have private bathrooms and none is equipped with a shower, but park restrooms are clean and have hot showers. Full RV hookups and camp sites are also available. In keeping with the theme, on-site Dot's Diner serves up burgers, fries, and milk shakes. ⊠ *1 Old Douglas Rd., 85603* ☎ *520/432–3567* ⊕ *www.theshadydell.com* ⤺ *11 trailers* ⟁ *Restaurant, BBQs, kitchens, laundry facilities; no a/c, no room phones, no room TVs, no kids under 10, no smoking* ▤ *MC, V.*

¢–$ 🏠 **School House Inn Bed & Breakfast.** You might flash back to your classroom days at this B&B, a schoolhouse built in 1918 at the height of Bisbee's mining days. Perched on the side of a hill, the two-story brick building has a pleasant outdoor patio shaded by an oak tree. The inn's rooms all have a theme—history, music, library, reading, arithmetic, art, geography, and the principal's office—reflected in the decor. The upstairs deck and a comfy TV room provide two places to lounge after a day's adventures. ⊠ *818 Tombstone Canyon Rd.* ⌂ *Box 32, 85603* ☎ *800/ 537–4333* 📠 *520/432–2996* ⊕ *www.virtualcities.com/ons/az/ b/azb4501.htm* ⤺ *6 rooms, 3 suites* ⟁ *Wi-Fi; no a/c, no room phones, no room TVs, no kids under 14, no smoking* ▤ *AE, D, MC, V* ⦿ *BP.*

Fodor'sChoice ★

Nightlife

Once known for shady ladies and saloons, Brewery Gulch retains a few shadows of its rowdy past. Established in 1902, **St. Elmo Bar** (⊠ 36 Brewery Gulch ☎ 520/432–5578) is decorated with an assortment of the past and present—a 1922 official map of Cochise County hangs next to a neon beer sign. The jukebox plays during the week but on weekends Buzz and the Soul Senders rock the house with rhythm and blues. **The Stock Exchange Bar** (⊠ 15 Brewery Gulch ☎ 520/432–3317), in the historic Muheim building, has shuffleboard, a pool table, and off-track betting. The 1914 stock board still hangs on the wall.

Shopping

Artist studios, galleries, and boutiques in historic buildings line Main Street, which runs though Tombstone Canyon. **55 Main Street** (⊠ 55 Main St. ☎ 520/432–4694) is just one of many art galleries selling contemporary work along the main drag. **Belleza Fine Arts Gallery** (⊠ 29 Main St. ☎ 520/432–5877 ⊕ www.bellezagallery.org) is owned and operated by Bisbee's Women's Transition Project, which aids homeless women and their children. This unusual gallery features the artwork of local and national artists as well as Adirondack chairs and birdhouses made by women receiving assistance from the program. The gallery's 50% commission goes directly into funding the Transition project. A trip to Bisbee wouldn't be complete without a stop at **The Killer Bee Guy** (⊠ 15 Main St. ☎ 877/227–9338 ⊕ www.killerbeeguy.com). Bee-keeper Reed Booth has appeared on the Discovery Channel and the Food Network; you can sample his honey butters and mustards and pick up some killer honey recipes. **Optimo Custom Panama Hatworks** (⊠ 47 Main St. ☎ 520/ 432–4544 ⊕ www.optimohatworks.com) is nationally renowned, popular for its custom, hand-woven Panama hats. It also sells works of beaver, cashmere, hare, and rabbit felt.

7

Douglas

❸ *23 mi southeast of Bisbee.*

This town on the U.S.–Mexico border was founded in 1902 by James Douglas to serve as the copper-smelting center for the mines in Bisbee. Be aware of your surroundings when wandering; the area is no stranger to drug traffickers and illegal border crossings. If you're here, the interior of the Gadsden Hotel is an architectural gem, but otherwise, there's not much reason to come to Douglas.

The must-see historic landmark in town and still the center of much of Douglas's activity is the **Gadsden Hotel** (✉ 1046 G Ave. ☎ 520/364–4481 ⊕ www.hotelgadsden.com), built in 1907. The lobby contains a solid-white Italian-marble staircase, two authentic Tiffany-vaulted skylights, and a 42-foot-long stained-glass mural. One thousand ounces of 14-karat gold leaf were used to decorate the capitals. The bar is lively all day and still serves as a meeting place for local ranchers. The guest rooms are less impressive. Most of the rugs and drapes look weary, and the old plumbing and fixtures aren't always well maintained.

Where to Eat

$–$$ ✕ **Grand Café.** The Marilyn Monroe tribute wall and red velvet–draped dining niche may be kitschy, but the Mexican cooking here is taken very seriously. Among the soups, the soothing *caldo de queso* is laced with cheese and chunks of fresh potato, and the bracing *menudo* is nicely spiced. The refried beans served on the side of such well-prepared Sonoran specialties as chiles rellenos are wonderful. ✉ *1119 G Ave.* ☎ *520/364–2344* ▤ *MC, V* ☽ *Closed Sun.*

Sonoita

❹ *34 mi southeast of Tucson on I–10 to AZ 83, 57 mi west of Tombstone on AZ 82.*

The grasslands surrounding modern-day Sonoita captured the attention of early Spanish explorers, including Father Eusebio Francisco Kino, who mapped and claimed the area in 1701. The Tuscan-like beauty of the rolling, often green hills framed by jutting mountain ranges has been noticed by Hollywood filmmakers. As you drive along AZ 83 and AZ 82 you might recognize the scenery from movies filmed here, including *Oklahoma* and *Tin Cup*.

Today, this region is known for its vineyards and wineries as well as for its ranching history. Sonoita, at the junction of AZ 83 and AZ 82, offers several restaurants and upscale B&Bs, but it's the nearby wineries that draw the crowds. There are several events at the wineries, including the Blessing of the Vines in the spring and the Harvest Festivals in fall. Summer is also a good time to visit, where you can sample some of Arizona's vintages and chat with a wine master or local vintner.

To explore the wineries of southern Arizona, head south on AZ 83 from Sonoita and then east on Elgin Road. Most of the growers are in and around the tiny village of Elgin, 9 mi southeast of Sonoita.

Fodor'sChoice **Callaghan Vineyards** (✉ 336 Elgin Rd., Elgin ☎ 520/455–5322 ⊕ www.
★ callaghanvineyards.com), open Friday through Sunday, 11 to 3, produces
the best wine in Arizona. Its Buena Suerte ("good luck" in Spanish) Cuvee
was named as one of the top wines in the U.S. by the *Wall Street Journal.* In Elgin, stop for tastings daily from 10 to 5 at **Village of Elgin Winery** (✉ The Elgin Complex, Upper Elgin Rd., Elgin ☎ 520/455–9309
⊕ www.elginwines.com), one of the largest producers of wines in the
state and the home to Tombstone Red, which the winemaker claims is
"great with scorpion, tarantula, and rattlesnake meat." **Sonoita Vineyards**
(✉ Canelo Rd., 3 mi south of town, Elgin ☎ 520/455–5893 ⊕ www.
sonoitavineyards.com), known for its high-quality reds, offers tours
and tastings daily 10 to 4. Originally planted in the early 1970s as an
experiment by Dr. Gordon Dutt, former agriculture professor at the University of Arizona, this was the first commercial vineyard in Arizona.

Where to Stay & Eat

¢–$$$$ ✕ **Steak Out Restaurant & Saloon.** A frontier-style design and a weath-
ered-wood exterior help to create the mood at this Western restaurant
and bar known for its tasty margaritas and live country music played
on weekend evenings. Built and owned by the same family that operates the Sonoita Inn next door, the restaurant serves cowboy fare:
mesquite-grilled steaks, ribs, chicken, and fish. ✉ *3235 AZ 82* ☎ *520/
455–5205* ▭ *AE, D, DC, MC, V* ☽ *No lunch weekdays.*

★ ¢–$$ ✕ **Café Sonoita.** Like Sonoita itself, the Café Sonoita combines city so-
phistication with small-town charm. A local favorite, the restaurant also
draws day-trippers from Tucson and tourists from afar. The dinner
menu, which changes daily, incorporates locally grown produce, local
wines, and beers. Some of the specialties here include prickly pear bar-
becue ribs, buffalo burgers, and the tequila shrimp chile relleno. Save
room for the café's homemade pies, cheesecakes, and brownies. ✉ *3280
AZ 82* ☎ *520/455–5278* ▭ *MC, V* ☽ *Closed Sun.–Tues.*

$–$$ ▥ **Sonoita Inn.** The owner of the Sonoita also owned the Triple
Crown–winning racehorse Secretariat and the walls of the inn celebrate
the horse's career with photos, racing programs, and press clippings.
Hardwood floors, colorful woven rugs, and retro-cowboy bedspreads
distinguish the spacious rooms, some of which have views of the Santa
Rita mountains. The inn is near the intersection of AZ 82 and AZ 83
and is adjacent to the Steak Out Restaurant & Saloon. ✉ *3243 AZ 82*
🖂 *Box 99, 85637* ☎ *520/455–5935 or 800/696–1006* 🖷 *520/455–5069*
⊕ *www.sonoitainn.com* 🛏 *18 rooms* ♨ *Cable TV, in-room VCRs,
some pets allowed (fee)* ▭ *AE, D, MC, V* ❍ *CP.*

$ ▥ **Rainbow's End.** An old ranch manager's house on a horse farm over-
looking the Sonoita countryside is now a B&B furnished in period antiques. Four bedrooms, each with a modern bathroom, share a great room
with fireplace and a big kitchen, where guests can assemble their own
Continental breakfast and organic snacks (supplied by the hosts, who
live just down the hill). ✉ *3088 AZ 83* 🖂 *Box 717, 85637* ☎ *520/455–
0202* 🖷 *520/455–0303* ⊕ *www.rainbowsendbandb.com* 🛏 *4 rooms*
♨ *Dining room, library, pets allowed; no room TVs, no smoking* ▭ *AE,
D, MC, V* ❍ *CP.*

Patagonia

⑤ *12 mi southwest of Sonoita via AZ 82.*

Served by a spur of the Atchison, Topeka & Santa Fe Railroad, Patagonia was a shipping center for cattle and ore. The town declined after the railroad departed in 1962, and the old depot is now the town hall. Today, with the migration of artists here in recent years, art galleries and boutiques coexist with real Western saloons in this tiny, tree-lined village in the Patagonia Mountains. The surrounding region is a prime birding destination with more than 275 species of birds found around Sonoita Creek.

The **Patagonia Visitors Center** (317 McKeown Ave. ☎ 520/394–0060 or 888/794–0060 ⊕ www.patagoniaaz.com) is a good first stop for an overview. Sharing quarters with the visitors center are **Mariposa Books & More** (✉ 317 McKeown Ave. ☎ 520/394–9186) and **Creative Spirit Co-op** (✉ 317 McKeown Ave. ☎ 520/394–9186), where the jewelry, paintings, quilts, and pottery of more than 40 local artists are displayed.

At the Nature Conservancy's **Patagonia–Sonoita Creek Preserve,** 1,350 acres of cottonwood-willow riparian habitat are protected along the Patagonia–Sonoita Creek watershed. More than 275 bird species have been sighted here, along with white-tailed deer, javelina, coati mundi (raccoon-like animals native to the region), desert tortoise, and snakes. There's a self-guided nature trail; guided walks are given every Saturday at 9 AM along 2 mi of loop trails. Three concrete structures near an elevated berm of the Railroad Trail serve as reminders of the land's former life as a truck farm. To reach the preserve from Patagonia, make a right on 4th Avenue; at the stop sign, turn left onto Blue Haven Road. This paved road soon becomes dirt and leads to the preserve in about 1¼ mi. The admission fee is good for seven days. ✉ *150 Blue Haven Rd.* ☎ *520/394–2400* ⊕ *www.nature.org* ✒ *$5* ☉ *Apr.–Sept., Wed.–Sun. 6:30–4; Oct.–Mar., Wed.–Sun. 7:30–4.*

Ⓒ Eleven miles south of town, **Patagonia Lake State Park** is the spot for water sports, picnicking, and camping. Formed by the damming of Sonoita Creek, the 265-acre reservoir lures anglers with its largemouth bass, crappie, bluegill, and catfish; it's stocked with rainbow trout in the wintertime. You can rent rowboats, paddleboats, canoes, and camping and fishing gear at the marina. Most swimmers head for Boulder Beach. The entrance fee is good for both Patagonia Lake State Park and for the Sonoita Creek State Natural Area. ✉ *400 Lake Patagonia Rd.* ☎ *520/287–6965* ⊕ *www.pr.state.az.us* ✒ *$7 per vehicle* ☉ *Visitor center daily 9–4:30, gates closed 10 PM–4 AM.*

Arizona State Parks has designated almost 5,000 acres surrounding Patagonia Lake as **Sonoita Creek State Natural Area.** This project, funded by the Arizona State Parks Heritage Fund (lottery monies) and the State Lake Improvement Fund, offers environmental educational programs and university-level research opportunities. The riparian area is home to giant cottonwoods, willows, sycamores, and mesquites; nesting black hawks; and endangered species. Rangers offer guided birding tours (fee) every Tuesday, Saturday, and Sunday at 9, 10:15, and 11:30 AM. The entrance fee is good for both Patagonia Lake State Park and for the Sonoita Creek State Natural Area. ✉ *AZ 82, 5 mi south of town* ☎ *520/287–2791 or 800/285–3703* ⊕ *www.pr.state.az.us* ⚍ *$7 per vehicle.*

Where to Stay & Eat

$–$$ ✕ **Velvet Elvis Pizza Co.** There can't be too many places where you can enjoy a pizza heaped with organic veggies, a crisp salad of organic greens tossed with homemade dressing, and freshly pressed juice (try the beet, apple, and lime juice concoction), organic wine, and microbrewed and imported beer while surrounded by images of Elvis *and* the Virgin Mary. Owner Cecilia San Miguel uses a 1930s dough recipe for the restaurant's delightful crust, and you can pick up some pizza sauce in the gift shop if you want to try your hand at pizza-making at home. They also have fabulous fruit pies for dessert. ✉ *292 Naugle Ave.* ☎ *520/394–2102* ⊕ *www.velvetelvispizza.com* ⊟ *MC, V* ⊙ *Closed Mon.–Wed.*

$ ✕ **Wagon Wheel Saloon.** The Wagon Wheel's restaurant, serving ribs, steaks, and burgers, is a more recent development, but the cowboy bar, with its neon beer signs and mounted moose head, has been around since the early 1900s. This is where every Stetson-wearing ranch hand in the area comes to listen to the country jukebox and down a long-neck, maybe accompanied by some jalapeño poppers. ✉ *400 W. Naugle Ave.* ☎ *520/394–2433* ⊟ *AE, MC, V.*

¢–$ ✕ **Gathering Grounds.** This colorful café and espresso bar serves healthful breakfasts and imaginative soups, salads, and sandwiches through the late afternoon during the week, with extended hours on the weekend. It also doubles as an art gallery showcasing local artists and offers live entertainment on Saturday nights. ✉ *319 McKeown Ave.* ☎ *520/394–2097* ⊟ *MC, V* ⊙ *No dinner Sun.–Thurs.*

$$$$ ☖ **Circle Z Ranch.** Rimmed by giant sycamore, ash, and cottonwood trees and surrounded by the Patagonia–Sonoita Creek Preserve, this guest ranch served as a setting in the movie *Red River* and in several episodes of *Gunsmoke*. Rooms in the adobe-style buildings have hardwood floors and area rugs, king-size or twin beds, and antique Monterrey wooden chests. Riders from beginners through advanced can be accommodated on adventurous, scenic trails. All meals, riding, and amenities are included. There are discounted rates for children ages 5–17; children under 5 are not allowed to ride. The ranch requires a three-day minimum stay. ✉ *AZ 82, 4 mi southwest of town* ☖ *Box 194, 85624* ☎ *520/394–2525 or 888/854–2525* ⊕ *www.circlez.com* ⇖ *24 rooms* ☖ *Dining room, tennis court, pool, billiards, hiking, horseback riding, Ping-Pong, no-smoking rooms; no a/c, no room phones, no room TVs* ⊟ *MC, V* ⊙ *Closed mid-May–Oct.* ❮◯❯ *FAP.*

★ $ ☖ **Duquesne House Bed & Breakfast/Gallery.** Built as a miner's boardinghouse at the turn of the 20th century, the rooms of this adobe home are painted in pastel Southwest colors, lovingly and whimsically detailed by a local artist, and decorated with Mexican folk art. Breakfast is served in your room or in the Santa Fe–style great room. A tiered backyard garden with hammocks adds to the tranquillity. ✉ *357 Duquesne Ave.* ☖ *Box 772, 85624* ☎ *520/394–2732* ⇖ *4 suites* ☖ *Wi-Fi; no TV in some rooms* ⊟ *No credit cards* ❮◯❯ *BP.*

$ ▦ **Stage Stop Inn.** Old territorial appearance notwithstanding, the building isn't historic and the rooms are standard motel issue, but this is still a decent place to lay your head for the night. The center-of-town location is prime and the price is right. ✉ *303 W. McKeown Ave.* ✏ *Box 777, 85624* ☎ *520/394–2211 or 800/923–2211* 📠 *520/394–2212* ⟿ *43 rooms* ⚘ *Restaurant, some kitchenettes, cable TV, pool, bar, some pets allowed (fee)* ☰ *MC, V.*

CAMPING   ⚠ **Patagonia Lake Campground.** This civilized campground in Patagonia Lake State Park has a marina and even some boat-camping sites.
¢   Campsites fill up quickly though—and you can't make reservations. ⚘ *Grills, flush toilets, partial hookups (electric and water), dump station, drinking water, showers, picnic tables, public telephone, general store, swimming (lake)* ⟿ *72 tent sites, 34 RV sites, 12 boat sites* ✉ *AZ 82, 4 mi southeast of town* ☎ *602/542–4174* ⊕ *www.pr.state.az.us* ✉ *$12–$15 tent site, $19–$22 RV site* ⚘ *Reservations not accepted* ☰ *MC, V* ⊙ *Open year-round.*

Nightlife

If you're looking for some weekend rock-n-roll fun in this sleepy section of the state, stop by the **La Mision de San Miguel** (✉ 335 McKeown ☎ 520/394–0123 ⊙ Closed Mon.–Thurs.). Inside a replica of a Spanish Colonial church, this tongue-in-cheek venue offers a smoke-free environment, live music, and dancing into the wee hours.

Shopping

Patagonia is quickly turning into a shopping destination in its own right. Unlike the trendy shops in nearby Tubac, the stores here have reasonable prices in addition to small-town charm. Some of the artist spaces are open only by appointment. **Global Arts Gallery** (✉ 315 McKeown Ave. ☎ 520/394–0077) showcases everything from local art and antiques to Native American jewelry, Middle Eastern rugs, and exotic musical instruments. At **High Spirits, Inc** (✉ 714 Red Rock Ave. ☎ 520/394–2900 or 800/394–1523 ⊕ www.highspirits.com), you can pick up Odell Borg Native American flutes. Shirley and Bill Ambrose sell decorative gourds and horseshoe art at their studio **Lil' Bit of Everything** (✉ 567 Harshaw ☎ 520/394–2923) by appointment only. **Painted House Studio** (✉ 355 McKeown Ave. ☎ 520/394–2740) has an intriguing collection of hand-painted pieces including chairs, hutches, bowls, pillows, and birdhouses. The studio is open by appointment on weekdays. The **Shooting Star Pottery** (✉ 370 Smelter Ave. ☎ 520/394–2752) displays clay pieces created by the village potter Martha Kelly by appointment only—or you can check out the mosaics Kelly and her students completed at the Patagonia Community Arts Center just off Highway 82.

Sierra Vista

❻ *42 mi southeast of Patagonia via AZ 82 to AZ 90.*

Sierra Vista grew up as a characterless military town on the outskirts of Fort Huachuca and although there isn't much to do in town, it's a good base from which to explore the more scenic areas that surround it—and at 4,620 feet above sea level, the whole area has a year-round temperate climate. There are a few fast-food and chain restaurants for your basic dining needs, and any of the more than 1,100 rooms in area hotels, motels, and B&Bs can shelter you for the night.

Fort Huachuca, headquarters of the army's Global Information Systems Command, is the last of the great Western forts still in operation. It dates back to 1877, when the Buffalo Soldiers (yes, Bob Marley fans—*those* Buffalo Soldiers), the first all-black regiment in the U.S. forces, came to aid settlers battling invaders from Mexico, Indian tribes reluctant to give up their homelands, and assorted American desperadoes on the lam from the law back East. Three miles from the fort's main gate are the **Fort Huachuca museums.** The late-19th-century bachelor officers' quarters and the annex across the street provide a record of military life on the frontier. Another half block south, the **U.S. Army Intelligence Museum** focuses on America intelligence operations from the Apache Scouts through Desert Storm. Code machines, code books, decoding devices, and other intelligence gathering equipment are on display. Enter the main gate of Fort Huachuca on AZ 90, west of Sierra Vista. You need a driver's license, vehicle registration, and proof of insurance to get on base. ⊠ *Grierson St., off AZ 90, west of Sierra Vista, Fort Huachuca* ☎ *520/533–5736* ⊕ *huachuca-www.army.mil* ☜ *Free* ☉ *Weekdays 9–4, weekends 1–4.*

Those driving to **Coronado National Memorial,** dedicated to Francisco Vásquez de Coronado, will see many of the same stunning vistas of Arizona and Mexico the conquistador saw when he trod this route in 1540 seeking the mythical Seven Cities of Cíbola. It's a little more than 3 mi via a dirt road from the visitor center to Montezuma Pass, and another ½ mi on foot to the top of the nearly 7,000-foot Coronado Peak, where the views are best. Other trails include Joe's Canyon Trail, a steep 3-mi route (one-way) down to the visitor center, and Miller Peak Trail, 12 mi round-trip to the highest point in the Huachuca Mountains (Miller Peak is 9,466 feet). Kids ages 5 to 12 can participate in the memorial's Junior Ranger program, explore Coronado Cave, and dress up in replica Spanish armor or missionary robes. The turnoff for the monument is 16 mi south of Sierra Vista on AZ 92; the visitor center is 5 mi. ⊠ *4101 E. Montezuma Canyon Rd., Hereford* ☎ *520/366–5515* ⊕ *www.nps. gov/coro* ☜ *Free* ☉ *Visitor center daily 9–5.*

FodorśChoice
★

Ramsey Canyon Preserve, managed by the Nature Conservancy, marks the convergence of two mountain and desert systems: this spot is the northernmost limit of the Sierra Madre and the southernmost limit of the Rockies, and it's at the edge of the Chihuahuan and Sonoran deserts. The diverse terrain and the presence of the fresh water San Pedro River, fosters birdlife. Rare avian species, including the elegant trogon, nest here between April and October, and 14 species of hummingbird come to the area—more varieties than anywhere else in the United States. Stop at the visitor center for maps and books on the area's natural history, flora, and fauna. To get here, take AZ 92 south from Sierra Vista for 6 mi, turn right on Ramsey Canyon Road, and then go 4 mi to the preserve entrance. Admission is good for seven days. ⊠ *27 Ramsey Canyon Rd., Hereford* ☎ *520/378–2785* ⊕ *www.nature.org* ☜ *$5* ☉ *Mar.–Oct., daily 8–5; Nov.–Feb., daily 9–4.*

7

OFF THE
BEATEN
PATH

SAN PEDRO RIPARIAN NATIONAL CONSERVATION AREA – The San Pedro River, partially rerouted underground by an 1887 earthquake, may not look like much for most of the year, but it sustains an impressive array of flora and fauna. To maintain this fragile creek-side ecosystem, a 56,000-acre area along the river was designated a protected riparian area in 1988. More than 350 species of birds come here, as well as 82 mammal species and 45 reptiles and amphibians. Forty thousand years ago, this was the domain of woolly mammoths and mastodons: many of the huge skeletons in Washington's Smithsonian Institute and New York's Museum of Natural History came from the massive fossil pits in the area. As evidenced by a number of small, unexcavated ruins, the migratory Indian tribes who passed through centuries later also found this valley hospitable, in part because of its many useful plants. Information, guided tours, books, and gifts are available from the volunteer staff at San Pedro House, a visitor center operated by Friends of the San Pedro River. ⊠ *San Pedro House, 9800 AZ 90* ☎ *520/508–4445, 520/439–6400 Sierra Vista BLM Office* ⊕ *www.az.blm.gov* ☜ *Free* ☉ *Visitor center daily 9:30–4:30, conservation area daily sunrise–sunset.*

Where to Stay & Eat

$–$$$ ✕ **The Outside Inn.** The Outside Inn serves salads, sandwiches, and burgers for lunch and steak, chicken, seafood, veal, and lamb for dinner. The prime rib is delicious, but available only on Friday and Saturday nights. Meals are served with a casual flair in an airy dining room. ⊠ *4907 S. AZ 92* ☎ *520/378–4645* ▤ *AE, MC, V* ☉ *Closed Sun. No lunch Sat.*

★ **$$** ▥ **Ramsey Canyon Inn Bed & Breakfast.** The Ramsey Canyon Preserve is a bird haven, and the nearby Ramsey Canyon Inn is a bird-watcher's delight. Antique furnishings and original watercolors of hummingbirds adorn the Inn's rooms and apartment suites. The innkeepers serve a rotating menu of 14 breakfast treats, such as French toast stuffed with cream cheese and nuts and topped with a cranberry sauce, as well as homemade pie in the afternoon. Reserve in advance during the busy spring season. ⊠ *29 Ramsey Canyon Rd., Hereford 85615* ☎ *520/378–3010* 🖷 *520/378–0487* ⊕ *www.ramseycanyoninn.com* ☜ *6 rooms, 3 suites* ⚶ *Some kitchens; no a/c in some rooms, no phones in some rooms, no room TVs, no smoking* ▤ *D, MC, V* ⫣ *BP.*

$$ ▥ **Casa de San Pedro.** Bird-watchers are drawn to this contemporary hacienda-style B&B abutting the San Pedro Riparian National Conservation Area, and the hosts do everything they can to accommodate them. Hiking trails pass behind the property, and guided birding tours can be arranged. Each of the bright and modern rooms has handcrafted wooden furnishings from northern Mexico. A labyrinth for meditation and butterfly gardens surround the house. ⊠ *8933 S. Yell La., Hereford 85615* ☎ *520/366–1300 or 888/257–2050* 🖷 *520/366–0701* ⊕ *www. bedandbirds.com* ☜ *10 rooms* ⚶ *BBQs, Wi-Fi, horseshoes, library; no room phones, no room TVs, no kids under 12* ▤ *AE, D, MC, V* ⫣ *BP.*

$ ▥ **Windemere Hotel & Conference Center.** This hotel complex, across from the area's shopping mall, is on AZ 92 in what used to be the eastern outskirts of Sierra Vista but is now a rapidly growing commercial corridor. Despite all this development, it's not uncommon to see roadrunners dashing about the hotel grounds. The three-story hotel has large, comfortable rooms, and most offer sweeping views of the nearby Huachuca Mountains. Rates include access to a nearby health club and evening cocktails. ✉ *2047 S. AZ 92, 85635* ☎ *520/459–5900 or 800/ 825–4656* 🖷 *520/458–1347* ⊕ *www.windemerehotel.com* ⇨ *149 rooms, 3 suites* ♿ *Restaurant, microwaves, refrigerators, cable TV with movies and video games, Wi-Fi, pool, hot tub, lounge, dry cleaning, laundry facilities, laundry service, business services, meeting rooms, some pets allowed, no-smoking rooms* ▤ *AE, D, DC, MC, V* ¶◯¶ *BP.*

CAMPING   ⛺ **Ramsey Vista.** Though not easy to reach—you drive up the side of a
  ¢   mountain on an unpaved and winding road to an elevation of 7,400 feet— this National Forest Service campground is never crowded and is well worth the trip. The birding is excellent, and you're likely to see coati mundi, javelina, and deer. Go 7 mi south of Sierra Vista on AZ 92, then turn on Carr Canyon Road, and go 10 mi farther west. RVs are not allowed on this road. ♿ *Pit toilets, fire pits, picnic tables* ⇨ *8 sites* ✉ *Carr Canyon Rd.* ☎ *520/378–0311* ⊕ *www.fs.fed.us/r3/coronado* 🖃 *$10 per night* ♿ *Reservations not accepted* ☉ *Open year-round, weather permitting.*

Chiricahua National Monument

🅒 **❼**   *58 mi northeast of Douglas on U.S. 191 to AZ 181, 36 mi southeast of*
Fodor'sChoice   *Willcox via AZ 186 to AZ 181.*
  ★

Vast fields of desert grass are suddenly transformed into a landscape of forest, mountains, and striking rock formations as you enter the 12,000-acre Chiricahua National Monument. The Chiricahua Apache—who lived in the mountains for centuries and, led by Cochise and Geronimo, tried for 25 years to prevent white pioneers from settling here—dubbed it the Land of the Standing-Up Rocks. Enormous outcroppings of volcanic rock worn by erosion and fractured by uplift into strange pinnacles and spires in a forest where autumn and spring seem to occur at the same time. Because of the particular balance of sunshine and rain in the area, in April and May visitors will see brown, yellow, and red leaves coexisting with new green foliage. Summer in Chiricahua National Monument is exceptionally wet: from July through September there are thunderstorms nearly every afternoon. Few other areas in the United States have such varied plant, bird, and animal life. Deer, coatimundis, peccaries, and lizards live among the aspen, ponderosa pine, Douglas fir, oak, and cypress trees— to name just a few. Well worth the driving distance, this is an excellent area for bird-watchers, and hikers have more than 17 mi of scenic trails. The admission fee is good for seven days. Some of the most beautiful and untouched camping areas in Arizona are nearby, in the Chiricahua Mountains. ✉ *AZ 181, 36 mi southeast of Willcox* ☎ *520/824–3560* ⊕ *www. nps.gov/chir* 🖃 *$5* ☉ *Visitor center daily 8–4:30.*

Where to Stay

★ **$$$**   🏠 **Grapevine Canyon Ranch.** This guest ranch on the west side of the Chiricahuas adjoins a working cattle ranch. Visitors get the chance to watch—and, in some cases, participate in—day-to-day cowboy activities. Riders of all levels of experience are welcome, and hiking trails crisscross this quintessentially Western terrain. Rooms are decorated in a mix of country and Southwestern-style furnishings—and all have spacious decks and porches. Rates include meals and all activities. There's a three-night minimum. ⊠ *Highland Rd.* ☎ *Box 302, Pearce 85625* ☎ *520/826–3185 or 800/245–9202* 🖷 *520/826–3636* ⊕ *www.gcranch. com* 🛏 *12 rooms* ⚒ *Refrigerators, pool, hot tub, hiking, horseback riding, library, laundry facilities; no a/c, no room phones, no room TVs, no kids under 12* ⊟ *AE, D, MC, V* ⦿ *FAP.*

$$$ 🏨 **Sunglow Guest Ranch.** Named after the ghost town of Sunglow, this ranch consists of nine casitas decked out in Southwestern style with fireplaces. Breakfast, afternoon tea, and dinner are served in a cozy dining room with a wraparound porch. You can borrow mountain bikes to explore the trails in the Coronado National Forest, which borders the property on three sides. Birding and hiking are popular, and "star parties" attract astronomers, as this remote region offers some of the blackest skies around and perfect conditions for stargazing. Additional attractions include scheduled art exhibits, writing workshops, and yoga retreats. ⊠ *Turkey Creek Rd.* ☎ *HCR 1, Box 385, Pearce 85625* ☎ *520/824–3334 or 866/786–4569* 🖷 *520/824–3176* ⊕ *www.sunglowranch.com* 🛏 *4 1-room casitas, 4 2-room casitas, 1 2-bedroom casita* ⚒ *Café, microwaves, refrigerators, bicycles, hiking, library, meeting room, some pets allowed (fee); no room phones, no room TVs, no smoking* ⊟ *AE, MC, V* ⦿ *MAP* ⊙ *Closed July and Aug.*

$ 🏨 **Portal Peak Lodge.** This barracks-style structure, just east of Chiricahua National Monument near the New Mexico border, is notable less for its rooms (clean and pleasant but nondescript) than for its winged visitors: the elegant trogon, 14 types of hummingbird, and 10 species of owl are among the 330 varieties of birds that flock to nearby Cave Creek Canyon. Decks outside each room provide a good vantage point. ⊠ *1215 Main St.* ☎ *Box 364, Portal 85632* ☎ *520/558–2223* 🖷 *520/558–2473* ⊕ *www.portalpeaklodge.com* 🛏 *16 rooms* ⚒ *Restaurant, grocery, cable TV, no-smoking rooms; no room phones* ⊟ *AE, D, MC, V.*

WORD OF MOUTH

"I think our biggest thrill came on the day we traveled to the Chiricahua National Monument, homeland of the Chiricahua Apache Indians and a stunningly beautiful mountain landscape that we reached after a mind-numbing couple of hours driving through desert grasslands. It rises up dramatically from the valley floor to over nine thousand feet, cresting in a series of uneven, volcanic looking peaks. As you drive up and into them you discover areas of spectacular pinnacles, columns, spires and precariously balanced boulders that are simply breathtakingly beautiful—and you are in an area of actual green trees and shrubs, for which we were pitifully grateful. There are, of course, trails and a campsite, and waysides offering one stunning scenic view after another. We simply loved it, but oh boy, getting there without stopping is sooo boring."

–ckwald

Fort Bowie National Historical Site

8 *8 mi northwest of Chiricahua National Monument. Take AZ 186 east from Chiricahua National Monument; 5 mi north of junction with AZ 181, signs direct you to road leading to fort.*

It's a bit of an outing to the site of Arizona's last battle between Native Americans and U.S. troops in the Dos Cabezas (Two-Headed) Mountains, but history buffs will find it interesting and scenic. Once a focal point for military operations—the fort was built here because Apache Pass was an important travel route for Native Americans and wagon trains—it now serves as a reminder of the brutal clashes between the two cultures.

Upon entering the site, you'll drive down a winding gravel road to a parking lot where a challenging trail leads 1½ mi to the historic site. The fort itself is virtually in ruins, but there's a small ranger-staffed visitor center with historical displays, restrooms, and books for sale.

Points of interest along the trail, indicated by historic markers, include the remnants of an Apache wickiup (hut), the fort cemetery, Apache Springs (their water source), and the **Butterfield stage stop,** a crucial link in the journey from east to west in the mid-19th century that happened to be in the heart of Chiricahua Apache land. Chief Cochise and the stagecoach operators ignored one another until sometime in 1861, when hostilities broke out between U.S. Cavalry troops and the Apache. After an ambush by the chief's warriors at Apache Pass in 1862, U.S. troops decided a fort was needed in the area, and Fort Bowie was built within weeks. There were skirmishes for the next 10 years, followed by a peaceful decade. Renewed fighting broke out in 1881. Geronimo, the new leader of the Indian warriors, finally surrendered in 1886. ⊠ *Apache Pass Rd., 26 mi southeast of Willcox* ☎ *520/847–2500* ⊕ *www.nps.gov/fobo* ☜ *Free* ☉ *Daily 8–4:30.*

Willcox

9 *26 mi northwest of Fort Bowie National Historical Site on AZ 186.*

The small town of Willcox, in the heart of Arizona ranching country, began in the late 1870s as a railroad construction camp called Maley. When the Southern Pacific Railroad line arrived in 1880, the town was renamed in honor of the highly regarded Fort Bowie commander, General Orlando B. Willcox. Once a major shipping center for cattle ranchers and mining companies, the town has preserved its rustic charm; the downtown area looks like an Old West movie set. An elevation of 4,167 feet means moderate summers and chilly winters, ideal for growing apples, and apple pie fans from as far away as Phoenix make pilgrimages to sample the harvest. Don't miss the mile-high apple pies and hand-pressed cider at **Stout's Cider Mill** (⊠ 1510 N. Circle I Rd. ☎ 520/384–3696). Pick your own apples from late August to mid-September.

If you visit in winter, you can see some of the more than 10,000 sandhill cranes that roost at the **Willcox Playa,** a 37,000-acre area resembling a dry lake bed 12 mi south of Willcox. They migrate in late fall and head north to nesting sites in February, and bird-watchers migrate to Willcox the third week in January for the annual Wings over Willcox birdwatching event held in their honor.

Outside Willcox is the headquarters for the **Muleshoe Ranch Cooperative Management Area** (✉ 6502 N. Muleshoe Ranch Rd. ☎ 520/507–5229 ⊕ www. nature.org), nearly 50,000 acres of riparian desert land in the foothills of the Galiuro Mountains that are jointly owned and managed by the Nature Conservancy, the U.S. Forest Service, and the U.S. Bureau of Land Management. It's a 30-mi drive on a dirt road to the ranch—it takes about an hour—but the scenery, wildlife, and hiking are worth the bumps. Backcountry hiking and mountain-biking trips can be arranged by the ranch, and overnight accommodations are available. To reach the ranch, take Exit 340 off I–10, turn right on Bisbee Avenue and continue to Airport Road, turn right again, and after 15 mi take the right fork at a junction just past a group of mailboxes and continue to the end of the road.

The **Rex Allen Arizona Cowboy Museum,** in Willcox's historic district, is a tribute to Willcox's most famous native son, cowboy singer Rex Allen. He starred in several rather average cowboy movies during the 1940s and '50s for Republic Pictures, but he's probably most famous as the friendly voice that narrated Walt Disney nature films of the 1960s. Check out the glittery suits the star wore on tour—they'd do Liberace proud. If you're visiting this museum as a family, you can all get in for the special family rate of $5. ✉ *150 N. Railroad Ave.* ☎ *520/384–4583 or 877/234–4111* ⊕ *www.rexallenmuseum.org* 🎫 *$2* ⊙ *Daily 10–4.*

The **Chiricahua Regional Museum and Research Center** is in downtown Willcox. Exhibits relating to Native American and military history and culture, including a separate Geronimo exhibit, were created by the Sulphur Springs Valley Historical Society. One oddity the museum points out is that the memoirs of Civil War general Orlando Willcox, for whom the town was named, don't even mention a visit to Arizona. ✉ *127 E. Maley St.* ☎ *520/384–3971* 🎫 *$2* ⊙ *Mon.–Sat. 10–4.*

Where to Stay & Eat

$–$$$ ✕ **Desert Rose Café.** Enjoy breakfast, lunch, dinner, or the Sunday buffet with the locals at this family-owned, family-friendly restaurant in Willcox. The food is as down-home as the atmosphere—mostly burgers, chicken, steak, and seafood standards—so it's just the place to go when you want a meal that's predictable, unpretentious, but also good. ✉ *706 S. Haskell Ave.* ☎ *520/384–0514* ▭ *AE, MC, V.*

¢–$ ✕ **Salsa Fiesta Mexican Restaurant.** You can't miss the bright neon lights of this little restaurant, just south of I–10 at Exit 340 in Willcox. The interior is cheerful and clean, with tables, chairs, and walls painted in a spicy medley of hot pink, purple, turquoise, green, and orange. The menu consists of Mexican standards, and the salsa bar runs the gamut from mild to super-hot. There is a modest selection of domestic and Mexican beers, and takeout is available. ✉ *1201 W. Rex Allen Dr.* ☎ *520/ 384–4233* ▭ *AE, D, MC, V* ⊙ *Closed Tues.*

$–$$ 🏠 **Muleshoe Ranch.** This turn-of-the-20th-century ranch is run by the Arizona chapter of the Nature Conservancy. Five casitas with kitchens sit in a pristine setting in the grassland foothills of the Galiuro Mountains.

Four of the casitas are around a courtyard setting hacienda-style. The fifth, a stone cabin, is off by itself affording more privacy to its guests and is the only unit open to families with children. There are a visitor center, 22 mi of hiking trails, a guided, ¾-mi nature walk on Saturday at 9 AM, and private natural hot springs. There's a two-night minimum from September to May, and a three-night minimum on holiday weekends. ⊠ *6502 N. Muleshoe Ranch Rd.* ✑ *R.R. 1, Box 1542, 85643* ☎ *520/507–5229* ⊕ *www.muleshoelodging.org* ⤳ *5 units* ⚇ *Kitchens, hiking, library, piano; no a/c in some rooms, no room phones, no room TVs* ⊟ *AE, MC, V* ☯ *Closed June–Aug.*

Texas Canyon

⑩ *16 mi west of Willcox off I–10.*

Fodor's Choice
★

A dramatic change of scenery along I–10 will signal that you're entering Texas Canyon. The rock formations here are exceptional—huge boulders appear to be delicately balanced against each other.

Texas Canyon is the home of the **Amerind Foundation** (a contraction of "American" and "Indian"), founded by amateur archaeologist William Fulton in 1937 to foster understanding about Native American cultures. The research facility and museum are housed in a Spanish colonial revival–style structure designed by noted Tucson architect H. M. Starkweather. The museum's rotating displays of archaeological materials, crafts, and photographs give an overview of Native American cultures of the Southwest and Mexico. The adjacent Fulton–Hayden Memorial Art Gallery displays an assortment of art collected by William Fulton. The museum's gift shop has a superlative selection of Native American art, crafts, and jewelry. ⊠ *2100 N. Amerind Rd., 1 mi southeast of I–10, Exit 318, Dragoon* ☎ *520/586–3666* ⊕ *www.amerind.org* ✉ *$5* ☯ *Tues.–Sun. 10–4.*

Benson

⑪ *12 mi west of Texas Canyon and 50 mi east of Tucson via I–10.*

Back in its historic heyday as a Butterfield stagecoach station, and later as the hub of the Southern Pacific Railroad, Benson was just a place to stop on the way to somewhere else. That started to change with the 1974 discovery of a pristine cave beneath the Whetstone Mountains west of Benson, culminating 25 years later with the opening of Kartchner Caverns State Park, one of the most remarkable living cave systems in the world.

Though the city is undergoing dramatic changes, you can see the story of Benson's past at the little **San Pedro Valley Arts and Historical Society Museum** (⊠ S. San Pedro Ave. at E. 5th St. ☎ 520/586–3070), a free museum that is closed in August.

As you pass Benson on I–10, watch for Ocotillo Avenue, Exit 304. Take a left and drive about 2¼ mi, where a mailbox with a backward SW signals that you've come to the turnoff for **Singing Wind Bookshop.** Make a right at the mailbox and drive ¼ mi until you see a green gate. Let yourself in, close the gate, and go another ¼ mi to the shop. If you don't

Fodor's Choice
★

7

see Winifred Bundy, who also runs the ranch, ring the gong out front. This unique bookshop-on-a-ranch has a good selection of books on Arizona wildlife, history, and geology, as well poetry and psychology. She doesn't take credit cards, though. ⊠ *700 W. Singing Wind Rd.* ☎ *520/ 586–2425* ☉ *Daily 9–5.*

Where to Stay & Eat

$–$$$ ✕ **Chute-Out Steakhouse & Saloon.** Don't be deceived by the unassuming exterior of this stucco steak house a block from Benson's main street. Once inside this warm and welcoming place, you'll understand why it's so popular. The food is excellent, and the service is efficient and friendly. Mesquite-grilled steaks, ribs, chicken, and seafood, fresh-baked breads and desserts, and salads (the house dressing is superb) make this spot well worth the visit. It's open for dinner only. ⊠ *161 S. Huachuca St.* ☎ *520/586–7297* ▭ *AE, D, MC, V.*

$–$$ ✕ **Galleano's.** The kitchen at this upscale roadhouse, a local favorite, turns out traditional diner fare—including great burgers and fries—as well as pastas and salads. There's a big salad bar, too—unusual in these parts. ⊠ *601 W. 4th St.* ☎ *520/586–3523* ▭ *MC, V* ☉ *No dinner Sun.*

¢–$$ ✕ **Horseshoe Steakhouse & Cantina.** For a good green-chile burrito or a patty melt, stop at this eclectic eatery, which has graced Benson's main street for more than 60 years. You'll know you're in cowboy country when you see the neon horseshoe on the ceiling, the macramés of local cattle brands, and the large jukebox with its selection of country-and-western ballads. ⊠ *154 E. 4th St.* ☎ *520/586–3303* ▭ *MC, V.*

¢ ✕ **Ruiz's Mexican Food & Cantina.** In this part of the world, the name is
Fodor'sChoice pronounced "Reese." This tiny spot on the main drag has been in op-
★ eration since 1959, serving a daily stream of customers, morning to night, hungry for green-corn tamales, chiles rellenos, *topopo* (deep-fried tortilla) salads, and other specialties. The adjoining bar serves beer, wine, and cocktails. ⊠ *687 W. 4th St.* ☎ *520/586–2707* ▭ *MC, V.*

★ ☾ **$–$$** ⊞ **Astronomers Inn.** You don't have to be an astronomer to enjoy this hilltop lodging on the grounds of the private Vega-Bray Observatory, but eight powerful telescopes are available for your universe-viewing pleasure. The B&B reflects the owners' delight in science: the comfortable rooms have such gadgets as lamps that simulate lightning and decorations (visible in black light) that resemble constellations painted on the ceiling. A special section in the science room is dedicated to kids. Astronomers travel from Tucson to the observatory on clear evenings to lead an evening of observation and science classes. The inn also provides a classroom complete with computers and hands-on-science projects, a 2-mi nature trail, and two ponds for relaxed boating. ⊠ *1311 Astronomers Rd., 2 mi southeast of I–10, Exit 306* ☎ *520/586–7906* ⊞ *520/586–1123* ⊕ *www. astronomersinn.com* ⇆ *5 rooms* ▭ *MC, V* ❍❙ *BP.*

★ **$–$$** ⊞ **Holiday Inn Express.** The closest lodging to Kartchner Caverns State Park, this motel sits just off I–10 at the "Kartchner Corridor," a few miles west of Benson. It has the comfort and amenities you'd expect but with a Southwestern elegance rarely found in chain motels around the area. Rooms have coffeemakers and hair dryers, and a Continental breakfast is included. ⊠ *630 S. Village Loop* ☍ *Box 2252, 85602* ☎ *520/586–8800 or 888/ 263–2283* ⊞ *520/586–1370* ⊕ *www.hiexpress.com/bensonaz* ⇆ *62* *rooms* ♿ *Microwaves, refrigerators, cable TV, Wi-Fi, pool, gym, laundry facilities, business services, meeting room* ▭ *AE, D, DC, MC, V* ⭘⏐ *CP.*

$ ▦ **Days Inn of Benson.** Like other businesses in the Benson area, this motel has seized the opportunity to capitalize on its proximity to Kartchner Caverns State Park, offering special package rates that include tickets for the cavern tour. The rooms are standard issue, large, clean, and comfortable, and a deluxe Continental breakfast is included in your stay. ✉ *621 Commerce Dr., 85602* ☏ *520/586–3000 or 800/329–7466* ⊕ *www.daysinn.com* ↬ *75 rooms* ♿ *Some microwaves, some refrigerators, cable TV with movies, in-room data ports, pool, hot tub, laundry facilities* ▭ *AE, MC, V* ⭘⏐ *CP.*

Kartchner Caverns State Park

⓬   *9 mi south of Benson on AZ 90.*

Fodor'sChoice
★

The publicity that surrounded the official opening of the Kartchner Caverns in November 1999 was in marked contrast to the secrecy that shrouded their discovery 25 years earlier and concealed their existence for 14 years. The two young men who stumbled into what is now considered one of the most spectacular cave systems anywhere played a fundamental role in its protection and eventual development. Great precautions have been taken to protect the wet-cave system—which comprises 13,000 feet of passages and two chambers as long as football fields—from damage by light and dryness.

The Discovery Center introduces visitors to the cave and its formations, and hour-long guided tours take small groups into the upper cave. Spectacular formations include the longest soda straw stalactite in the United States at 21 feet and 2 inches. The Big Room is viewed on a separate tour: it holds the world's most extensive formation of brushite moonmilk, the first reported occurrence of turnip shields, and the first noted occurrence of birdsnest needle formations. It's also the nursery roost for female cave myotis bats from April through September, during which time the lower cave is closed in an effort to foster the cave's unique ecosystem. Kartchner Caverns is a wet, "live" cave, meaning that water still rises up from the surface to increase the multicolored calcium carbonate formations already visible.

The total cavern size is 2⅖ mi long, but the explored areas cover only 1,600 feet by 1,100 feet. The average relative humidity inside is 99%, so visitors are often graced with "cave kisses," water droplets from above. Because the climate outside the caves is so dry, it is estimated that if air got inside, it could deplete the moisture in only a few days, halting the

> ### WORD OF MOUTH
>
> "If you haven't been to Kartchner Caverns, just outside of Tucson, it's awesome! . . . If you want to see Kartchner, you'll need to either pre-book or take a chance on the 100 or so tickets they reserve for first come, first served each day. It is well worth the wait. It's a living cave and they've gone to great lengths to preserve it that way while allowing those of us who don't like crawling through tiny spaces to see it."   –casugi

7

growth of the speleothems that decorate its walls. To prevent this, there are 22 environmental monitoring stations that measure air and soil temperature, relative humidity, evaporation rates, air trace gases, and airflow inside the caverns. Tour reservations are required and should be made several months in advance; hiking trails, picnic areas, and campsites are available on the park's 550 acres. If you're here and didn't make a reservation, you may be in luck: the park reserves 100 walk-up tickets, available on a first-come, first-served basis, for the Rotunda/Throne Room tour. ⊠ *AZ 90, 9 mi south of Exit 302 off I–10* ☎ *520/586–4100 information, 520/586–2283 tour reservations* ⊕ *www.pr.state.az.us* ▧ *$5 per vehicle up to 4 people, $1 each additional person; Rotunda/Throne Room tours $18.95, Big Room tours $22.95* ⊙ *Daily 7:30–6, cave tours, by reservation, daily 8:40–4:40.*

SOUTHWEST ARIZONA

The turbulent history of the West is writ large in this now-sleepy part of Arizona. It's home to the Tohono O'odham Indian Reservation (the largest in the country after the Navajo Nation's) and towns such as Ajo, created—and almost undone—by the copper-mining industry and Nogales, a vital entry point on the U.S.–Mexico border. Yuma, abutting the California border, was a major crossing point of the Colorado River as far back as the time of the conquistadors.

These days, people mostly travel *through* Sells, Ajo, and Yuma en route to the closest beaches: during the school year, especially on warm weekends and semester breaks, the 130-mi route from Tucson to Ajo is busy with traffic headed southwest to Puerto Penasco (Rocky Point), Mexico, the closest outlet to the sea for Arizonans. All summer long, I–8 takes heat-weary Tucsonans and Phoenicians to San Diego, California, and Yuma is the mid-point.

Natural attractions are a lure in this starkly scenic region: Organ Pipe Cactus National Monument provides trails for desert hikers, and Buenos Aires and Imperial wildlife refuges—homes to many unusual species—are important destinations for birders and other nature watchers. Much of the time, however, your only companions will be the low-lying scrub and cactus and the mesquite, ironwood, and paloverde trees.

Nogales

⓭ *15 mi south of Tumacácori, 63 mi south of Tucson on I–19 at the Mexican border.*

Nogales, named for the walnut trees that grew along the river here, is actually two towns: the somewhat bland, industrial American city and the smaller Mexican town over the border. The American side was once a focal point for cattle shipping between Sonora and the United States. Today, Nogales reaps the benefits of NAFTA, with warehouses and trucking firms dedicated to the distribution of Mexican produce, making it one of the world's busiest produce ports. The American side depends on the health of the peso and the shoppers who cross the border from Mexico to buy American goods that they can't get in their country. The

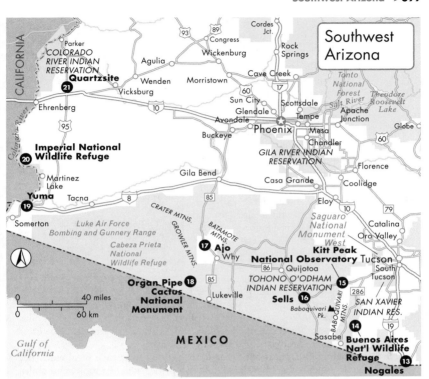

Southwest
Arizona

CALIFORNIA

Parker
COLORADO
RIVER INDIAN
RESERVATION
Quartzsite **21**
Agulia
Wenden
Vicksburg
Morristown
Congress
Wickenburg
Cordes
Jct.
Rock
Springs
Cave Creek
Tonto
National
Forest
Theodore
Roosevelt
Lake
Salt River
Ehrenberg
Sun City
Scottsdale
Glendale
Tempe
Apache
Junction
Globe
Buckeye
Phoenix
Mesa
Chandler
GILA RIVER INDIAN
RESERVATION
Florence

Imperial National
Wildlife Refuge **20**

Martinez
Lake
Yuma **19**
Tacna
Gila Bend
Casa Grande
Coolidge
Eloy

Somerton
Luke Air Force
Bombing and Gunnery Range
CRATER MTNS.
GROWLER MTNS.
BATAMOTE MTNS.
Ajo **17**
Why
Saguaro
National
Monument
West
Kitt Peak
National Observatory
Catalina
Oro Valley
Tucson
South
Tucson

Cabeza Prieta
National
Wildlife Refuge

Organ Pipe **18**
Cactus
National
Monument
Lukeville
Quijotoa
TOHONO O'ODHAM
INDIAN RESERVATION **15**
Sells **16**
Baboquivari
Pk.
SAN XAVIER
INDIAN RES. **14**

Gulf of
California
MEXICO
Sasabe
Buenos Aires
Nat'l Wildlife
Refuge **13**
Nogales

0 40 miles
0 60 km

Mexican side has grown with the economic success of *maquiladoras,* factories that manufacture goods destined for the United States. There's a great deal of commerce between the two sides of Nogales.

Some of this trade is in narcotics and undocumented workers, giving this border town a more edgy quality than other parts of Mexico. Bustling Nogales, Mexico can become fairly rowdy on weekend evenings, when underage Tucsonans head south of the border to drink. It has some good restaurants, however, and fine-quality crafts in addition to the usual souvenirs—and tourists as well as locals from Tucson and Phoenix enjoy a day trip of shopping and dining on the Mexico side. Security on the American side of the border is very tight; don't even think about taking a firearm near the border. You'll also do better not to drive your car into Mexico: not only is there a very real possibility it may be stolen, but you'll face significant delays because of the thorough search you and your vehicle will receive upon returning. This hassle is unnecessary, though, because you can cover Nogales in a day trip, and most of the good shopping is within easy walking distance of the border crossing. Park on the Arizona side, either on the street or, better yet, in one of many guarded lots that cost about $8 for the day (use restrooms on the U.S. side before you cross). Keep in mind that as of January 1, 2008, all travelers must have a passport or other accepted secure document to enter or reenter the United States.

Don't bother trading your dollars for pesos. Merchants prefer dollars and always have change on hand. Be prepared for aggressive selling tactics and sometimes-disorienting hubbub, but locals are always glad to point you in the right direction, and almost all speak some English.

Where to Stay & Eat

★ **$-$$$** ✕ **La Roca.** East of the railroad tracks and off the beaten tourist path, La Roca is a favorite of Tucsonans. It isn't difficult to find, just look for the towering black sign to the east of the border entrance. The setting—a series of tiled rooms and courtyards in a stately old stone house, with a balcony overlooking a charming patio—is lovely. Try the *carne tampiqueña*, an assortment of grilled meats that comes with chiles rellenos and an enchilada. Chicken mole is also a favorite. ✉ *Calle Elias 91, Nogales, Mexico* ☎ *631/312–0891* ▭ *MC, V.*

$-$$ ✕ **Elvira.** The free shot of tequila that comes with each meal will whet your appetite for Elvira's reliable fish dishes, chicken mole, and chiles rellenos. This large, friendly restaurant (divided into intimate dining areas) is at the foot of Avenida Obregón just south of the border and popular with those who visit Nogales often. ✉ *Avda. Obregón 1, Nogales, Mexico* ☎ *631/312–4773* ▭ *MC, V.*

¢-$ ✕ **Zula's.** Standard, old-fashioned border restaurant fare is served with Greek flair on the Arizona side of the border, with Sonoran food (tortillas, cheese, refried beans) alongside gyros and American selections, such as burgers, steaks, and seafood entrées. It's not as glitzy as the south-of-the-border places, but the food is just as tasty. ✉ *982 N. Grand Ave., Nogales* ☎ *520/287–2892* ▭ *MC, V.*

¢ ▦ **Americana Motor Hotel.** A serviceable place that has seen better days, the Americana has large, Aztec-style stone sculptures scattered around the grounds. Decorated in a Southwest motif, rooms are comfortable but worn. The restaurant and lounge are casual places to eat American food. ✉ *639 N. Grand Ave., 85621* ☎ *520/287–7211 or 800/874–8079* ⤶ *97 rooms* ⌂ *Restaurant, cable TV, pool, bar* ▭ *AE, MC, V.*

¢ ▦ **El Dorado Motel.** This typical motel offers casual, unpretentious border flavor. The small-town service, although friendly, is not particularly quick. ✉ *884 N. Grand Ave., 85621* ☎ *520/287–4611* ▤ *520/287–0101* ⤶ *100 rooms* ⌂ *Cable TV, pool, outdoor hot tub* ▭ *AE, MC, V.*

Shopping

The main shopping area is on the Mexican side, on Avenida Obregón, which begins a few blocks west (to your right) of the border entrance and runs north–south; just follow the crowds. You'll find handicrafts, furnishings, and jewelry here, but if you go off on some of the side streets, you might come across more interesting finds at better prices. Except at shops that indicate otherwise, bargaining is not only acceptable but expected. Playing this customary game can save you, on average, 50%, so don't be shy. The shops listed below tend to have fixed prices, so either buy here if you don't want to bargain at all, or note their prices and see if you can do better elsewhere.

Casa Bonita (⊠ Avda. Obregón 134, Nogales, Mexico ☎ 631/312–3059) carries jewelry, tinwork mirrors, carved wooden chests, and household items. **El Changarro** (⊠ Calle Elias 93, Nogales, Mexico ☎ 631/312–0545) sells high-quality (and high-price) furniture, antiques, pottery, and handwoven rugs. It's next door to La Roca Restaurant. **El Sarape** (⊠ Avda. Obregón 161, Nogales, Mexico ☎ 631/312–0309) specializes in sterling silver jewelry from Taxco and women's designer clothing. **Maya de México** (⊠ Avda. Obregón 150, Nogales, Mexico ☎ No phone) is the place to come for smaller folk-art items, including Day of the Dead displays, blue glass, painted dishes, and clothing.

Buenos Aires National Wildlife Refuge

⑭ *66 mi southwest of Tucson; from Tucson, take AZ 86 west 22 mi to AZ 286; go south 40 mi to Milepost 8, and it's another 3 mi east to the preserve headquarters.*

This remote nature preserve, in the Altar Valley and encircled by seven mountain ranges, is the only place in the United States where the Sonoran–savanna grasslands that once spread over the entire region can still be seen. The fragile ecosystem was almost completely destroyed by overgrazing, and a program to restore native grasses is currently in progress. In 1985 the U.S. Fish and Wildlife Service purchased the Buenos Aires Ranch—now headquarters for the 115,000-acre preserve—to establish a reintroduction program for the endangered masked bobwhite quail. Bird-watchers consider Buenos Aires unique because it's the only place in the United States where they can see a "grand slam" (four species) of quail: Montezuma quail, Gambel's quail, scaled quail, and masked bobwhite. If it rains, the 100-acre Aguirre Lake, 1½ mi north of the headquarters, attracts wading birds, shorebirds, and waterfowl—in all, more than 250 avian species have been spotted here. They share the turf with deer, antelope, coati mundi, badgers, bobcats, and mountain lions. Touring options include a 10-mi auto tour through the area, nature trails, a boardwalk through the marshes at Arivaca Cienega, and, by reservation only, weekend guided tours. ⊠ *AZ 286, Box 109, Sasabe 85633* ☎ *520/823–4251* 🖶 *520/823–4247* ⊕ *http://refuges.fws.gov* 🎫 *Free* ☉ *Refuge headquarters and visitor center daily sunrise–sunset.*

7

Snap "Shot" of Tequila

AGAVE, the plant from which fine tequila is made, flourishes in southern Arizona. Many people think the agave is a cactus, but it isn't. It's a succulent, closely related to the lily or amaryllis. Only blue agave—just one of 136 species—is used to make true tequila, but other species are used to make mezcal, the more generic type of liquor. Tequila is a specific type of mezcal, just as bourbon or scotch are specific types of whiskey. Many of the cheap brands are actually *mixtos,* which means they aren't 100% agave; true tequila isn't cheap, and you can pay more than $50 per bottle for a premium brand.

Aross the border in Mexico, there are more than 50 tequila producers, so it's understandable that tequila is a popular drink in Arizona. In fact, more tequila is consumed in the United States than anywhere else, including Mexico. The heart of the tequila-making region is Tequila itself, 30 mi west of Guadalajara, in the state of Jalisco. The hills around the town are responsible for its name, "tel" meaning "hill," and "quilla," a kind of lava around the dead volcanoes in the area.

To produce tequila, the bulb of the blue agave plant is harvested (it may weigh up to 150 pounds), heated to break down the sugars, and fermented. The best brands, Herradura and El Tesoro, are fermented with wild yeasts that add distinctive flavors to the final product. The fermented tequila is then placed into pot stills, where it is double-distilled to 90 proof or higher. Bottles designated "añejo" have been aged for a minimum of a year in oak barrels—these tequilas are the most expensive.

Where to Stay

$$$$ 🏨 **Rancho de la Osa.** This ranch, set on 250 eucalyptus-shaded acres near the Mexican border and Buenos Aires preserve, was built in 1889, and two adobe structures were added in the 1920s to accommodate guests. The rooms have modern plumbing and fixtures, wood-burning fireplaces, and porches with Adirondack chairs. Bread baked on the premises, salads made with ingredients grown in the garden, and water drawn from the well all contribute to the back-to-basics serenity. Rates include all meals and horseback riding, and guests are expected to dress for dinner. ⊠ *AZ 286* 🏠 *Box 1, Sasabe 85633* ☎ *520/823–4257 or 800/ 872–6240* 🖨 *520/823–4238* ⊕ *www.ranchodelaosa.com* 📇 *19 rooms* 🍽 *Dining room, pool, hot tub, massage, bicycles, billiards, hiking, horseback riding, bar, lounge, library, meeting rooms, Internet room; no room TVs, no kids under 6, no smoking* ⊟ *MC, V* 🍴 *FAP.*

Kitt Peak National Observatory

⑮ *56 mi southwest of Tucson; to reach Kitt Peak from Tucson, take I–10 to I–19 south, and then AZ 86. After 44 mi on AZ 86, turn left at AZ 386 junction and follow winding mountain road 12 mi up to observatory. In inclement weather, contact the highway department to confirm that the road is open.*

Funded by the National Science Foundation and managed by a group of more than 20 universities, Kitt Peak National Observatory is part of the Tohono O'odham Reservation. After much discussion back in the late 1950s, tribal leaders agreed to share a small section of their 4,400 square mi with the observatory's telescopes. Among these is the McMath, the world's largest solar telescope, which uses piped-in liquid coolant. From the visitors' gallery you can see into the telescope's light-path tunnel, which goes down hundreds of feet into the mountain. Kitt Peak scientists use these high-power telescopes to conduct vital solar research and observe distant galaxies.

The visitor center has exhibits on astronomy, information about the telescopes, and hour-long guided tours ($2 per person) that depart daily at 10, 11:30, and 1:30. Complimentary brochures enable you to take self-guided tours of the grounds, and there's a picnic area about 1½ mi below the observatory. The observatory buildings have vending machines, but there are no restaurants or gas stations within 20 mi of Kitt Peak. The observatory offers a nightly observing program ($36 per person) except from July 15 to September 1; reservations are necessary. ⊠ *AZ 386, Pan Tak* ☎ *520/318–8726, 520/318–7200 recorded message* ⊕ *www.noao.edu/kpno* ⊠ *$2 suggested donation* ☉ *Visitor center daily 9–3:45.*

Sells

⑯ *32 mi southwest of Kitt Peak via AZ 386 to AZ 86.*

The Tohono O'odham Reservation, the second-largest in the United States, covers 4,400 square mi between Tucson and Ajo, stretching south to the Mexican border and north almost to the city of Casa Grande. To the south of Kitt Peak, the 7,730-foot Baboquivari Peak is considered sacred by the Tohono O'odham as the home of their deity, I'itoi ("elder brother"). Less than halfway between Tucson and Ajo, Sells—the tribal capital of the Tohono O'odham—is a good place to stop for gas or a soft drink. Much of the time there's little to see or do in Sells, but in winter an annual rodeo and fair attract thousands of visitors. If you want something more substantial than a snack, head for the Sells Shopping Center, where you'll see **Basha's Deli & Bakery** (⊠ Topawa Rd. ☎ 520/383–2546). It's a good-size market and can supply all the makings for a picnic. For traditional Indian and Mexican food like fry bread, tacos, and chili, try the **Papago Cafe** (⊠ AZ 86, near Chevron Station ☎ 520/383–3510). The **Turquoise Turtle** (⊠ AZ 86 ☎ 520/383–2411) sells baskets and other crafts made on the reservation and beyond.

Ajo

⑰ *90 mi northwest of Sells.*

"Ajo" (pronounced *ah*-ho) is Spanish for garlic, and some say the town got its name from the wild garlic that grows in the area. Others claim the word is a bastardization of the Indian word *au-auho,* referring to red paint derived from a local pigment.

For many years Ajo, like Bisbee, was a thriving Phelps Dodge Company town. Copper mining had been attempted in the area in the late 19th century, but it wasn't until the 1911 arrival of the Calumet & Arizona Mining Company that the region began to be developed profitably. Calumet and Phelps Dodge merged in 1935, and the huge pit mine produced millions of tons of copper until it closed in 1985. Nowadays, Ajo is pretty sleepy; the town's population of 4,000 has a median age of 51, and most visitors are on their way to or from Rocky Point, Mexico.

At the center of town is a sparkling white Spanish-style plaza. The shops and restaurants that line the plaza's covered arcade today are rather modest. Unlike Bisbee, Ajo hasn't yet drawn an artistic crowd—or the upscale boutiques and eateries that tend to follow. Chain stores and fast-food haven't made a bee line here either–you'll find only one Dairy Queen and a Pizza Hut in this remote desert hamlet.

You get a panoramic view of Ajo's huge open-pit mine, almost 2 mi wide, from the **New Cornelia Open Pit Mine Lookout Point.** Some of the abandoned equipment remains in the pit, and mining operations are diagrammed at the visitors' shelter, where there's a 30-minute film about mining. ⊠ *Indian Village Rd.* ☎ *520/387–7742* ⊠ *Free* ✆ *Call for hrs.*

The **Ajo Historical Society Museum** has collected a mélange of articles related to Ajo's past from local townspeople. The displays are rather disorganized, but the historical photographs and artifacts are fascinating, and the museum is inside the territorial-style St. Catherine's Indian Mission, built around 1942. ⊠ *160 Mission St.* ☎ *520/387–7105* ⊠ *Donations requested* ✆ *Mon.–Sat. 10–4, Sun. noon–4.*

The 860,000-acre **Cabeza Prieta National Wildlife Refuge,** about 10 minutes from Ajo, was established in 1939 as a preserve for endangered bighorn sheep and other Sonoran Desert wildlife. A permit is required to enter, and only those with four-wheel-drive vehicles, needed to traverse the rugged terrain, can obtain one from the refuge's office. ⊠ *1611 N. 2nd Ave., Ajo 85321* ☎ *520/387–6483* ⊕ *http://refuges.fws.gov* ⊠ *Free* ✆ *Office weekdays 9–5, refuge daily dawn–dusk.*

Where to Stay & Eat

¢–$ ✕ **Señor Sancho.** Just about everybody in Ajo comes to this unprepossessing roadhouse at the north end of town for generous portions of Mexican food, well prepared and very reasonably priced. This friendly spot has light-wood booths and colorful murals with a Mexican motif. All the standard favorites are on the menu—hearty combination platters, tacos, enchiladas, chiles rellenos, flautas, and good chicken mole. ⊠ *663 N. 2nd Ave.* ☎ *520/387–6226* ▭ *No credit cards.*

$ ▦ **Guest House Inn Bed & Breakfast.** Built in 1925 to accommodate visiting Phelps Dodge VIPs, this lodging is a favorite for birders: guests can head out early to nearby Organ Pipe National Monument or just sit on the patio and watch the quail, cactus wrens, and other warblers that fly in to visit. Rooms are furnished in various Southwestern styles, from light Santa Fe to rich Spanish colonial. A full breakfast is served. ⊠ *700 Guest House Rd., 85321* ☎ *520/387–6133* ⊕ *www.guesthouseinn.biz*

🛏 *4 rooms* ♿ *Refrigerators, microwaves, Wi-Fi; no room phones, no room TVs, no smoking* 🖃 *DC, MC, V* ⚫ *BP.*

Organ Pipe Cactus National Monument

🔞 *32 mi southwest of Ajo; from Ajo, backtrack to Why and take AZ 85 south for 22 mi to reach the visitor center.*

Organ Pipe Cactus National Monument, abutting Cabeza Prieta National Wildlife Refuge but much more accessible to visitors, is the largest habitat north of the border for organ-pipe cacti. These multiarmed cousins of the saguaro are fairly common in Mexico but rare in the United States. Because they

WORD OF MOUTH

"Another often overlooked NP but highly recommended—Organ Pipe National Park, on the Arizona-Mexico border. Amazing cacti with such 'character,' and [I] only ran into a few other visitors."

—ellen_griswold

tend to grow on south-facing slopes, you won't be able to see many of them unless you take one of the two scenic loop drives: the 21-mi **Ajo Mountain Drive** or the 53-mi **Puerto Blanco Drive,** both on winding, graded one-way dirt roads.

⚠ Be aware that Organ Pipe has become an illegal border crossing hot spot. Migrant workers and drug traffickers cross from Mexico under cover of darkness. At this writing Puerto Blanco Drive was closed to the public. A two-way road that only travels 5 of the 53 mi on Puerto Blanco Drive is open, but the rest of the road will remain closed until further notice due to the construction of barriers along the Mexican border. Until the project is completed, there are still safety concerns at the monument. Even so, park officials emphasize that tourists have only occasionally been the victims of isolated property crimes—primarily theft of personal items from parked cars. Visitors are advised by rangers to keep valuables locked and out of plain view and not to initiate contact with groups of strangers whom they may encounter on hiking trails. A campground at the monument has 208 RV (no hookups) and tent sites. Facilities include a dump station, flush toilets, grills, and picnic tables. ✉ *AZ 85* ☎ *520/387–6849* ⊕ *www.nps.gov/orpi* 🖃 *$8 per vehicle* ⊙ *Visitor center daily 8–5.*

Yuma

🔞 *170 mi northwest of Ajo.*

Today, many people think of Yuma as a convenient stop between Phoenix or Tucson and San Diego—and this was equally true in the relatively recent past. It's difficult to imagine the lower Colorado River, now dammed and bridged, as either a barrier or a means of transportation, but until the early part of the 20th century, this section of the great waterway was a force to contend with. Records show that since at least 1540 the Spanish were using Yuma (then the site of a Quechan Indian village) as a ford across a relatively shallow juncture of the Colorado.

Three centuries later, the advent of the shallow-draft steamboat made the settlement a point of entry for fortune seekers heading through the Gulf of California to mining sites in eastern Arizona. Fort Yuma was established in 1850 to guard against Indian attacks, and by 1873 the town was a county seat, a U.S. port of entry, and an army depot.

The steamboat shipping business, undermined by the completion of the Southern Pacific Railroad line in 1877, was finished off by the building of Laguna Dam in 1909. In World War II, Yuma Proving Ground was used to train bomber pilots, and General Patton readied some of his desert war forces for battle at classified areas near the city. Many who served here during the war returned to Yuma to retire, and the city's economy now relies largely on tourism. The population swells during the winter months with retirees from cold climates who park their homes on wheels at one of the many RV communities on the outskirts of town. One fact may shed some light on why: according to National Weather Service statistics, Yuma is the sunniest city in the United States.

Most of the interesting sights in Yuma are at the north end of town. Stop in at the **Yuma Convention and Visitors Bureau** (⊠ 377 S. Main St. ☎ 928/783–0071 or 800/293–0071 ⊕ www.visityuma.com) and pick up a walking-tour guide to the historic downtown area. The adobe-style **Sanguinetti House Museum,** run by the Arizona Historical Society, was built around 1870 by merchant E. F. Sanguinetti and exhibits artifacts from Yuma's territorial days and details the military presence in the area. ⊠ *240 S. Madison Ave.* ☎ *928/782–1841* ⌨ *$3* ☉ *Tues.–Sat. 10–4.*

If you cross the railroad tracks at the northernmost part of town, you'll come to **Yuma Crossing National Historic Landmark,** which consists of the Quartermaster Depot and Fort Yuma, on the California side of the Colorado River. The mess hall of Fort Yuma, later used as a school for Native American children, now serves as the small **Fort Yuma Quechan Indian Museum.** Historical photographs, archaeological items, and Quechan arts and crafts are on display. ⊠ *CA 24* ☎ *760/572–0661* ⌨ *$1* ☉ *Daily 8–noon and 1–5.*

On the other side of the river from Fort Yuma, the Civil War–period quartermaster depot resupplied army posts to the north and east and served as a distribution point for steamboat freight headed overland to Arizona forts. The 1853 home of riverboat captain G. A. Johnson is the depot's earliest building and the centerpiece of the **Yuma Crossing State Historic Park.** The residence also served as a weather bureau and home for customs agents, among other functions, and the guided tour through the house provides a complete history. The Transportation Museum has stagecoaches, Wells Fargo wagons, and antique surreys, as well as more "modern" modes of transportation like the 1931 Model A pickup. You can also visit a re-creation of the Commanding Officer's Quarters, complete with period furnishings. ⊠ *201 N. 4th Ave., between 1st St. and Colorado River Bridge* ☎ *928/329–0471* ⊕ *www.pr.state.az.us* ⌨ *$3* ☉ *Daily 9–5.*

The most notorious tourist sight in town, **Yuma Territorial Prison,** now an Arizona state historic park, was built for the most part by the convicts who were incarcerated here from 1876 until 1909, when the prison outgrew its location. The hilly site on the Colorado River, chosen for security purposes, precluded further expansion.

Visitors gazing today at the tiny cells that held six inmates each, often in 115°F heat, are likely to be appalled, but the prison—dubbed the Country Club of the Colorado by locals—was considered a model of enlightenment by turn-of-the-20th-century standards: in an era when beatings were common, the only punishments meted out here were solitary confinement and assignment to a dark cell. The complex housed a hospital as well as Yuma's only public library, where the 25¢ that visitors paid for a prison tour financed the acquisition of new books.

The 3,069 prisoners who served time at what was then the territory's only prison included men and women from 21 different countries. They came from all social classes and were sent up for everything from armed robbery and murder to polygamy. R. L. McDonald, incarcerated for forgery, had been the superintendent of the Phoenix public school system. Chosen as the prison bookkeeper, he absconded with $130 of the inmates' money when he left.

The mess hall opened as a museum in 1940, and the entire prison complex was designated a state historic park in 1961. ⊠ *1 Prison Hill Rd., near Exit 1 off I–8* ☏ *928/783–4771* ⊕ *www.pr.state.az.us* ⊟ *$4* ⊘ *Daily 8–5.*

Where to Stay & Eat

$–$$$ ✕ **River City Grill.** This hip downtown restaurant is a favorite dining spot for locals and visitors. It gets a bit loud on weekend nights, but the camaraderie of diners is well worth it. Owners Nan and Tony Bain dish out a melody of flavors drawing on Mediterranean, Pacific Rim, Indian, and Caribbean influences. For starters you can sample everything from Vietnamese spring rolls to curried mussels. Entrées include delicacies like grilled wild salmon, rack of lamb, and such vegetarian dishes as ricotta and spinach ravioli. ⊠ *600 W. 3rd St.* ☏ *928/782–7988* ⊟ *AE, D, DC, MC, V* ⊘ *No lunch weekends.*

¢–$$ ✕ **Chretin's Mexican Food.** A Yuma institution, Chretin's opened as a dance hall in the 1930s before it became one of the first Mexican restaurants in town in 1946. Don't be put off by the nondescript exterior or the entryway, which leads back past the kitchen and cashier's stand into three large dining areas. The food is all made on the premises, right down to the chips and tortillas. Try anything that features *machaca* (shredded spiced beef or chicken). ⊠ *485 S. 15th Ave.* ☏ *928/782–1291* ⊟ *D, MC, V* ⊘ *Closed Sun.*

¢–$ ✕ **The Garden Café.** After a visit to the Sanguinetti House Museum, this adjoining café is a good place to stop for breakfast or lunch. This charming dining spot features lush gardens and aviaries on the outdoor patio, historical photos on the walls, and a menu of homemade salads, soups, and sandwiches. Favorites include the quiche, served with homemade fruit bread, and the tortilla soup. ⊠ *248 S. Madison Ave.* ☏ *928/ 783–1491* ⊟ *AE, MC, V* ⊘ *Closed Mon.*

¢–$ ✕ **Lutes Casino.** Almost always packed with locals at lunchtime, this large, funky restaurant and bar claims to be the oldest pool hall and domino parlor in Arizona. It's a great place for a burger and a brew. ⊠ *221 S. Main St.* ☎ *928/782–2192* ▭ *No credit cards.*

☾ **$$–$$$** ▦ **Shilo Inn.** This is an excellent family place to stay because of in-room facilities that come as close to a kitchen as you might want on a trip. Rooms are spacious and most have views of the courtyard and pool. A full breakfast is included in the rates and served in the restaurant. ⊠ *1550 S. Castle Dome Rd., 85365* ☎ *928/782–9511 or 800/222–2244* 🖷 *928/783–1538* ⊕ *www.shiloinns.com* ⬳ *131 rooms, 15 suites* ⚘ *Restaurant, microwaves, refrigerators, cable TV with video games, pool, gym, hot tub, sauna, lounge, business services, some pets allowed (fee)* ▭ *AE, D, DC, MC, V* ⚶ *BP.*

★ **$–$$** ▦ **Best Western Coronado Motor Hotel.** This Spanish tile–roofed motor hotel, convenient to the freeway and downtown, was built in 1938. Bob Hope used to stay here during World War II, when he entertained the gunnery troops training in Yuma. Yuma Landing Restaurant & Lounge is on-site with an impressive collection of historical photos. ⊠ *233 4th Ave., 85364* ☎ *928/783–4453 or 800/528–1234* 🖷 *928/782–7487* ⊕ *www.bestwestern.com* ⬳ *86 rooms* ⚘ *Restaurant, microwaves, refrigerators, cable TV, in-room VCRs, in-room data ports, pool, lobby lounge, laundry facilities* ▭ *AE, D, DC, MC, V* ⚶ *BP.*

$–$$ ▦ **Clarion Suites.** One wing of this sprawling hotel surrounds a well-manicured courtyard with a fountain and several orange trees; another faces the pool and Cabana Club, where the complimentary Continental breakfast and happy-hour drinks are served. This is an all-suites property, and each accommodation has a coffeemaker and a separate sitting area with a desk. ⊠ *2600 S. 4th Ave., 85364* ☎ *928/726–4830 or 800/333–3333* 🖷 *928/341–1152* ⊕ *www.choicehotels.com* ⬳ *164 suites* ⚘ *Microwaves, refrigerators, cable TV, pool, hot tub, lobby lounge, laundry facilities, airport shuttle* ▭ *AE, D, DC, MC, V* ⚶ *CP.*

Imperial National Wildlife Refuge

☾ ❷⓿ *40 mi north of Yuma; from Yuma, take U.S. 95 north past the Proving Ground and follow the signs to the refuge.*

A guided tour is the best way to visit the 25,765-acre Imperial National Wildlife Refuge, created by backwaters formed when the Imperial Dam was built. Something of an anomaly, the refuge is home both to species indigenous to marshy rivers and to creatures that inhabit the adjacent Sonoran Desert—desert tortoises, coyotes, bobcats, and bighorn sheep. Mostly, though, this is a major bird habitat. Thousands of waterfowl and shorebirds live here year-round, and migrating flocks of swallows pass through in spring and fall. During those seasons, expect to see everything from pelicans and cormorants to Canada geese, snowy egrets, and some rarer species. Canoes can be rented at Martinez Lake Marina, 3½ mi southeast of the refuge headquarters. It's best to visit from mid-October through May, when it's cooler and the ever-present mosquitoes are least active. Kids especially enjoy the 1.3-mi Painted Desert Nature Trail, which winds through the different levels of the Sonoran Desert. From an observation tower at the visitor center you can see the river, as well as the fields being planted with rye and millet, on which the migrating birds like to feed. ⊠ *Martinez Lake Rd., Box 72217 Martinez*

Lake 85365 ☎ *928/783–3371* 🖷 *928/783–0652* ⊕ *http://refuges.fws. gov* 🖾 *Free* ☉ *Visitor center mid-Apr.–mid-Oct., weekdays 7:30–4; mid-Oct.–mid-Apr., weekdays 7:30–4, weekends 9–4.*

Quartzsite

㉑ *84 mi north of Yuma; from Yuma, take U.S. 95 north.*

Most folks just pass right by this sleepy desert town, originally a mining camp around the Tyson's Well stage station. At the intersection of I–10 and U.S. Highway 95 near the Colorado River, Quartzsite is home to only 3,000 year-round residents. In the cooler winter months, though, nearly 1 million visitors stop over to check out the major gem and mineral shows, which are scheduled November through February. Most visitors to Quartzsite arrive in RVs, and with good cause: only a handful of motels are available, which inevitably fill up fast during high season.

If you're here, check out "Hi Jolly's Last Camp," a memorial to Hadji Ali or "Hi Jolly" as the soldiers called him. This Greek camel driver came to the United States in 1857 with a shipment of camels, which were ordered by the U.S. Army for an experiment in using them as pack animals in the arid Southwestern deserts. The camels, however, were not compatible with the Army's mules and were unsuited to the rocky terrain. When the U.S. Camel Corps. experiment was abandoned, Hi Jolly turned to prospecting and spent the rest of his days searching for riches along the Colorado River in western Arizona. He died in 1903 and today his memorial is the town's only major attraction.

SOUTHERN ARIZONA ESSENTIALS

To research prices, get advice from other travelers, and book travel arrangements, visit ⊕ *www.fodors.com.*

Transportation

BY AIR

Great Lakes Airlines flies direct from Phoenix to Sierra Vista. America West Express has direct flights to Yuma from Phoenix. Sky West, a United subsidiary, flies nonstop from Los Angeles to Yuma.

🎦 **America West Express** ☎ 800/235-9292 ⊕ www.americawest.com. **Great Lakes Airlines** ☎ 800/554-5111 ⊕ www.greatlakesav.com. **Sierra Vista Municipal Airport/ Fort Huachuca** ⊠2100 Airport Ave. ☎520/458-5775 ⊕www.ci.sierra-vista.az.us/Airport/ index.htm. **Sky West** ☎ 435/634-3000 ⊕ www.skywest.com. **Yuma International Airport (YUM)** ⊠ 2191 32nd St. ☎ 928/726-5882 ⊕ www.yumainternationalairport.com.

BY BUS

Greyhound Lines has service from Tucson to the stations in Benson, Willcox, and Yuma. The Ajo Stage Line offers regular shuttle van service from Tucson to Ajo.

🎦 **Ajo Transportation** ☎ 520/387-6467 or 800/942-1981. **Greyhound Lines** ☎ 800/ 454-2487 ⊕ www.greyhound.com ⊠ 680 E. 4th St., Benson ☎ 520/586-3141 ⊠ 622 N. Haskell Ave., Willcox ☎ 520/384-2183 ⊠ 170 E. 17th Pl., Yuma ☎ 928/783-4403.

BY CAR

A car is essential in southern Arizona. The best plan is to fly into Tucson, which is the hub of the area, or Phoenix, which has the most flights, and pick up a car at the airport.

You can rent a car from several national companies at Yuma International Airport. Most agencies allow you to take your rental into Mexico only if you buy their Mexican insurance packages. Be aware that road conditions in Mexico can be poor and that signs are in Spanish.

To get to Southeastern Arizona from Tucson, take I–10 east. AZ 90 is the turnoff for Kartchner Caverns. When you get to Benson, take AZ 80 south to reach Tombstone, Bisbee, and Douglas. If you want to go to Sonoita and Patagonia, or just take a pretty drive, turn off I–10 earlier, at the exit for AZ 83 south; you'll come to Sonoita, where this road intersects AZ 82. From here you can either continue south to Sierra Vista, head southwest on AZ 82 to Patagonia, or head east to Tombstone.

If you're driving to Southwestern Arizona, Ajo lies on AZ 85 (north–south) and Yuma is at the junction of I–8 and U.S. 95. For a scenic route to Ajo from Tucson (126 mi), take AZ 86 west to Why and turn north on AZ 85. Yuma is 170 mi from San Diego on I–8, and it is 300 mi from Las Vegas on U.S. 95.

🚗 **Avis** ☎ 928/726–5737 or 800/230–4898 ⊕ www.avis.com. **Budget** ☎ 928/344–1822 or 800/404–8033 ⊕ www.budget.com. **Dollar** ☎ 928/344–2097 or 800/800–4000 ⊕ www.dollar.com. **Hertz** ☎ 928/726–5160 or 800/654–3131 ⊕ www.hertz.com.

BY TAXI

Benson Taxi offers transport services in the Benson area. In Sierra Vista, ABC Cab Co. provides both local and regional transport. Yuma City Cab has the best taxi service in Yuma.

🚕 **ABC Cab Co.** ☎ 520/458–8429. **Benson Taxi** ☎ 520/586–1294. **Yuma City Cab** ☎ 928/782–4444.

BY TRAIN

Amtrak trains run three times a week from Tucson east to the Benson depot and west to Yuma. Both stations are unstaffed with Amtrak personnel; however, the Benson Visitor Center is in the train depot.

🚆 **Amtrak** ☎ 800/872–7245 ⊕ www.amtrak.com. **Benson train station** ✉ 4th St. at San Pedro Ave., Benson. **Yuma train station** ✉ 281 Gila St., Yuma.

Contacts & Resources

EMERGENCIES

In the U.S., call 911 for fire or police emergencies, or for an ambulance. If you're in Mexco, call 060.

There are local hospitals in many of the larger cities of Southern Arizona, and many of the chain drugstores have locations in the area.

🏥 **Benson Hospital** ✉ 350 S. Ocotillo St., Benson ☎ 520/586–2261. **Bisbee Copper Queen Hospital** ✉ 101 Cole St., Bisbee ☎ 520/432–5383. **Bob's IGA Pharmacy** ✉ 900 W. Rex Allen Dr., Willcox ☎ 520/384–2502. **Carondelet Health Network/Holy Cross**

Hospital ✉ 1171 W. Target Range Rd., Nogales ☎ 520/285-3000. **Desert Senita Community Health Center** ✉ 410 Malacate St., Ajo ☎ 520/387-5651. **Medicine Shoppe Pharmacy** ✉ 795 W. 4th St., Benson ☎ 520/586-1299. **Northern Cochise Community Hospital** ✉ 901 W. Rex Allen Dr., Willcox ☎ 520/384-3541 or 800/696-3541. **Rite Aid Pharmacy** ✉ 600 W. Catalina Dr., Yuma ☎ 928/726-7810. **Safeway Pharmacy** ✉ 101 Naco Hwy., Bisbee ☎ 520/432-3038. **Sierra Vista Regional Health Center** ✉ 300 El Camino Real, Sierra Vista ☎ 520/458-4641 or 800/880-0088. **Tom's Pharmacy** ✉ 40 W. Plaza St., Ajo ☎ 520/387-7080. **Walgreens** ✉ 1150 W. 8th St., Yuma ☎ 928/783-6834 ✉ 3121 S. 4th Ave., Yuma ☎ 928/344-0453 ✉ 21 W. Park St., Nogales ☎ 520/287-6521. **Yuma Regional Medical Center** ✉ 2400 S. Ave. A, Yuma ☎ 928/344-2000

SPORTS & THE OUTDOORS

CAMPING & HIKING
Douglas Ranger District and the Sierra Vista Ranger Station of the National Forest Service can give you information about camping and hiking in the Coronado National Forest, which covers most of the mountain ranges in southeastern Arizona. The Bureau of Land Management Yuma Field Office can give you details about outdoor recreational activities in that area.

🏢 **Bureau of Land Management Yuma Field Office** ✉ 2555 E. Gila Ridge Rd., Yuma 85365 ☎ 928/317-3200 ⊕ www.az.blm.gov. **Coronado National Forest** Douglas Ranger District ✉ 3081 N. Leslie Canyon Rd., Douglas ☎ 520/364-3468 ⊕ www.fs.fed.us/r3/coronado ✉ Sierra Vista Ranger Station ✉ 5990 S. AZ 92, Hereford 85615 ☎ 520/378-0311 ⊕ www.fs.fed.us/r3/coronado.

TOUR OPTIONS

BIRD-WATCHING TOURS
The Southeastern Arizona Bird Observatory is a nonprofit organization that offers guided tours, educational programs, and informational materials for bird-watchers visiting, or living in, Arizona. As an aid to birders, SABO offers a map of the best bird-watching sites along the Southeastern Arizona Birding Trail, which was created in collaboration with several private and public organizations. Write to the SABO or go on their Web site for a copy of the map. High Lonesome Ecotours offers birding tours with lodging.

BOAT TOURS
You can take a boat ride up the Colorado with Yuma River Tours. You can book 12- to 45-person jet-boat excursions through Smokey Knowlton, who has been exploring the area for more than 36 years.

GHOST TOWN TOURS
Lavender Jeep Tours (out of Bisbee) and Curly Bill's Jeep Tours (out of Tombstone) offer ghost town tours from a historical perspective.

GUIDED TOURS
Southern Arizona Adventures offers ecotours, hiking, backpacking, mountain biking, and historical/cultural expeditions from its base in Bisbee.

TRAIN EXCURSIONS
On weekends from October through June, you can take a two-hour round-trip jaunt on the Yuma Valley Railway. The 1922 coach, pulled by one of two historic diesel engines, departs at 1 PM from the 8th Street station in Yuma and runs south alongside the Colorado River for about 11 mi. Tickets cost $10.

🏢 **Curly Bill's Jeep Tours** ✉ 210 N. 9th St., Tombstone ☎ 520/457-3858. **High Lonesome Ecotours** ✉ 570 S. Little Bear Trail, Sierra Vista ☎ 520/458-9446, 800/743-2668 toll-free ⊕ www.hilonesome.com. **Lavender Jeep Tours** ✉ 45 Gila Dr., Bisbee ☎ 520/

7

432–5369. **Southern Arizona Adventures** ✉ 22 Main St., Bisbee ☎ 520/432–9058 or 800/319–7377 ⊕ www.arizonatour.com. **Southeastern Arizona Bird Observatory** ✉ Box 5521, Bisbee 85603 ☎ 520/432–1388 ⊕ www.sabo.org. **Yuma River Tours** ✉ 1920 Arizona Ave., Yuma 85364 ☎ 928/783–4400 ⊕ www.yumarivertours.com. **Yuma Valley Railway** ✉ 2nd Ave. and 1st St., behind City Hall, Yuma ☎ 928/783–3456.

VISITOR INFORMATION

🚩 In Southeastern Arizona **Benson Railroad Depot and Visitor Center** ☎ 520/586–4293 or 520/586–2245 ⊕ www.cityofbenson.com. **Bisbee Visitor Center** ☎ 520/432–3554 ⊕ www.discoverbisbee.com. **Douglas Visitor Center** ☎ 520/364–2478 or 888/315–9999. **Patagonia Visitors Center** ☎ 520/394–0060 or 888/794–0060 ⊕ www.patagoniaaz.com. **Sierra Vista Convention and Visitors Bureau** ☎ 520/458–6940 or 800/288–3861 ⊕ www.visitsierravista.com. **Tombstone Chamber of Commerce and Visitor Center** ☎ 520/457–3929, 520/457–9317, or 888/457–3929 ⊕ www.cityoftombstone.com. **Willcox Chamber of Commerce & Agriculture** ☎ 520/384–2272 or 800/200–2272 ⊕ www.willcoxchamber.com.

🚩 In Southwestern Arizona **Ajo Chamber of Commerce** ✉ 400 Taladro St., Ajo 85321 ☎ 520/387–7742. **Nogales-Santa Cruz Chamber of Commerce** ✉ 123 W. Kino Rd., Nogales 85621 ☎ 520/287–3685 ⊕ www.nogaleschamber.com. **Quartzsite Chamber of Commerce** ✉ 100 E. Main St., Quartzsite 85346 ☎ 928/927–5600. **Yuma Convention and Visitors Bureau** ✉ 377 S. Main St., Yuma 85364 ☎ 928/783–0071 or 800/293–0071 ⊕ www.visityuma.com.

Northwest Arizona & Southeast Nevada

WORD OF MOUTH

"I think Oatman is my favorite Route 66 stop. Make sure you are there in late afternoon for the gunfight on the main street. Take carrots for the burros."

—utahtea

"Bullhead City is essentially a bedroom community for Laughlin, NV, on the other side of the Colorado River. It is also one of the hottest places in the country during the summer (115-120F is not uncommon). There really is nothing to see or do in Bullhead City per se, but if you are into water sports or enjoy casino gambling it can be enjoyable. (Just don't expect Vegas . . .). I'd also recommend staying in Laughlin as the accommodation is better. If you are interested in water sports but not casinos Lake Havasu City would be a better choice."

—bonesaz

Updated by
Tom Carpenter

WESTERN ARIZONA AND SOUTHEASTERN NEVADA COMPRISE a unique blend of deserts, mountains, and 1,000 mi of shoreline. From its highest elevation, Hualapai Peak at 8,417 feet, to its lowest along the Colorado River at approximately 630 feet, this wide-open region of the Southwest offers a diverse topography ranging from aspen- and pine-covered glades to the austere and soft-spoken grandeur of the Mojave Desert. Despite the superficial aridity of much of the landscape, the region bubbles with an abundance of springs and artesian wells. Without these water sources weeping from the rocks and sand, western Arizona and southeastern Nevada would never have developed into the major crossroad it is today.

The defining feature of the region is the Colorado River. Since the late Pleistocene epoch when Paleo-Indians first set foot in the river that was once described as "too thick to drink and too thin to plow," the Colorado has been a blessing and a barrier. Prehistoric traders from the Pacific Coast crossed the river at Willow Beach on their way to trade shells for pelts with the Hopi Indians and other Pueblo tribes farther east. Although the Spanish claimed the region, they showed little interest in it. Fur trappers arrived in 1826 looking for beaver. When gold was discovered in California in 1848, entrepreneurs built ferries up and down the river to accommodate the miners drawn to the area by what Cortez described as "a disease of the heart for which the only cure is gold." The influx of miners brought them in conflict with the indigenous peoples of the area, the Mojave and Hualapai tribes.

By 1883 construction of the Atchison, Topeka, and Santa Fe railroad had been completed as far as the Colorado River. No longer would the mineral wealth extracted from the area need to be shipped overland to ports in California. The precious metals could be sent back east and, along with it, cattle and hogs raised in the area. Prosperity followed, particularly for Kingman. While mining towns in the surrounding hills boomed then busted, Kingman prospered as a mercantile and distribution center.

Every spring the snowmelt of the Rocky Mountain watershed of the Colorado River pulsed through high basaltic canyons like water through a garden hose and washed away crops and livestock. Harnessing such a powerful river required no ordinary dam. In 1935, notched into the steep and narrow confines of Black Canyon on the border separating Arizona and Nevada, 727-foot high Hoover Dam took control of the Colorado River and turned its power into electricity and its floodwaters into the largest man-made reservoir in the world: Lake Mead.

World War II brought a different kind of boom to the region. Between the numerous mountain ranges running more or less north–south and parallel to the river, wide valleys offered the Army Air Corps an excellent location to train bomber crews. More than 36,000 airmen were trained at the Kingman Army Air Field. After the war, many of the men and women who served at the airfield, returned to the area to build lives and raise families.

Today, interstate commerce brings hundreds of thousands of vehicles through western Arizona and southeastern Nevada every day. For many who view the area through the glass of their air-conditioned vehicles,

GREAT ITINERARIES

IF YOU HAVE 3 DAYS

🖼 **Kingman ❶** ⮞ is a good place to start. Spend the morning at the Mohave County Museum of History and Arts and take a walking tour of downtown. In the afternoon, drive to Grand Canyon Caverns for some underground touring. Plan to spend the second day in Hualapai Mountain Park. Pack a picnic and go hiking on the trails. On your third day, take a day excursion to Chloride or Oatman. Both historic mining towns have plenty to fill your day.

IF YOU HAVE 5 DAYS

Follow the suggested three-day itinerary, but make your way to Oatman rather than Chloride on the third day via Historic Route 66. Spend the morning visiting the shops and the Oatman Hotel, then take Route 66 west to AZ 95 and head south to 🖼 **Lake Havasu City ❷**. Use the remainder of the day to visit the London Bridge. In the morning make arrangements to spend the day on the lake. You'll want to relax after a day on the water, so consider taking in a dinner-theater performance at the London Arms Pub and Restaurant in the evening. In the morning grab your binoculars and spend a few hours looking for birds in the Havasu National Wildlife Refuge before you head back to Kingman.

the landscape is a daunting vision of opaque and distant mountains shimmering in the heat rising from sun-baked pavement. But for those who stop their vehicles and step into the clean open air, western Arizona and southeastern Nevada offer an enchanting blend of past and present, earth and sky, river and wind.

Top 5 Northwest Arizona & Southeast Nevada Experiences

- **Hoover Dam Tour:** Tour this engineering marvel and you'll learn not only the history of the dam's construction but also about the natural history of the region. You'll also get to explore the turbine room where eight giant turbines generate a electricity that provides power to the Southwest.

- **The Colorado River and her lakes:** There are more than 1,000 mi of shoreline in western Arizona; whether you want to paddle a canoe through the Topock Gorge on the Colorado River, take a houseboat holiday on Lake Havasu, race a Jet Ski across Lake Mohave, water ski for hours across the vastness of Lake Mead, or watch the big horn sheep traverse the cliffs of Black Canyon above Willow Beach, you can find it here.

- **London Bridge:** The bridge and the English Village beside it are the centerpieces of culture and tourism in the area; you can spend a pleasant day here wandering among the shops and pubs, or lazing about the beaches watching the boats go by.

- **Hualapai Mountains:** The tallest "sky island" in western Arizona provides a cool climate for hiking, camping, and watching wildlife.

8

- **Route 66:** This scenic drive over the Black Mountains to the Colorado River, from Kingman through Oatman to Topock, is the last remnant of the emigrant route that led Dust Bowl farmers to the verdant fields of California. This winding, narrow stretch of blacktop is the icon of road trips, road music, and road literature.

Exploring Northwest Arizona & Southeast Nevada

Western Arizona is a wedge of paradise for any outdoors enthusiast. The Colorado River, and the lakes that take shape along it like blue beads on a brown string, provides 1,000 mi of opportunities for fishing and water sports of all kinds. The valleys and mountains offer the curious traveler a topography replete with reasons for exploration and discovery. The three major communities of the area are Kingman, Bullhead City, and Lake Havasu City. Interstate 40, Historic Route 66, and U.S. 93 intersect in Kingman, which is also the seat of Mohave County. Bullhead City is on the Colorado River across from Laughlin, Nevada, and Lake Havasu City is farther south on the Colorado River and home to the famous London Bridge. With more than 2,100 mi of county roads in western Arizona, there are ample opportunities to strike out on your own to explore. It bears repeating that driving in the desert requires extra preparation. Make certain you are well stocked with radiator coolant, and be sure to carry plenty of water, a spare tire, a jack, and emergency supplies.

About the Restaurants

Whether you're looking for that cozy local café that smells of fresh soup and hot coffee, or the glamour of soft lighting and tablecloths complementing elegant cuisine, such dining choices are available in western Arizona. Casual dining establishments can be found in most of the communities in the region while the river communities of Lake Havasu City and Bullhead City provide opportunities for formal dining. Many of the finest dining establishments are in the casinos across the Colorado River from Bullhead City.

About the Hotels

A by-product of the major highways that stretch across western Arizona is the plethora of lodging choices. Most of the major chain motels and hotels have rooms available in each of the three major communities, with the added appeal of casino-hotels in Laughlin, Nevada.

WHAT IT COSTS					
	$$$$	$$$	$$	$	¢
RESTAURANTS	over $30	$21–$30	$13–$20	$8–$12	under $8
HOTELS	over $250	$176–$250	$121–$175	$70–$120	under $70

Restaurant prices are per person for a main course at dinner. Hotel prices are for a standard double in high season, excluding taxes and service charges.

Timing

The "H" word ("hot") isn't spoken by locals: the days start "warming up" in May and grow increasingly "warm" (exceeding 100°F) until Sep-

IF YOU LIKE

When you plan your trip to Arizona, it might not occur to you to include the western portion in your itinerary. With so many other interesting and well-known places to visit elsewhere in the state, it's easy to forget there are over 2½ million acres of land and 1,000 mi of shoreline waiting for you to discover in western Arizona. It's the best-kept secret in the state.

DRIVING

There's a lot of distance between things out here. Getting to them can require some significant windshield time. A soothing quality attends a leisurely drive to a new place, especially in spring. The desert air is moist with the subsiding breath of winter and the wildflowers are spilling from the earth like pastels from a tube. Roll down the windows and take it slow. Stop often. See how far you can see. Breathe in the scented desert air and you'll know forever what the desert really means.

WATER SPORTS

In this austere landscape, the first glimpse of water is always a thrill. Out here, the roads to all water are downhill and a momentum gathers the closer you get to it. Around a bend and suddenly a big beautiful lake or a thick brown river comes into view, and all you can think about is getting in it or on it, or finding a fishing rod.

tember, when things start to cool off. The mild winters mean temperatures in the mid-70s along the river, low precipitation, and abundant sunshine. It's no wonder Lake Havasu has become a popular destination for college students on spring break, so expect crowds in and around Lake Havasu City in March. April and May are the best months for enjoying the brief and beautiful appearance of desert wild flowers but September and October are considered the perfect-weather months, with temperatures in the 70s and just a hint of autumn in the air. Andy Devine Days festivities, usually scheduled for the first weekend in October, celebrate Kingman's most famous citizen. The Route 66 Fun Run takes place the first weekend in May and starts in Seligman. Saturday morning, cars of all makes and vintages travel in a caravan to Kingman where there's a big barbecue and dance. In the morning the caravan continues another 60 mi on "old 66" over the Black Mountains and through Oatman to Topock, where the road ends at the Colorado River.

Numbers in the text correspond to numbers in the margin and on the Northwest Arizona & Southeast Nevada map.

NORTHWEST ARIZONA

Towns like Kingman hark back to the glory days of the old Route 66, and the ghost towns of Chloride and Oatman bear testament to the mining madness that once reigned in the region. Water-sports fans, or those who just want to laze on a houseboat, will enjoy Lake Havasu, where you'll find the misplaced English icon London Bridge.

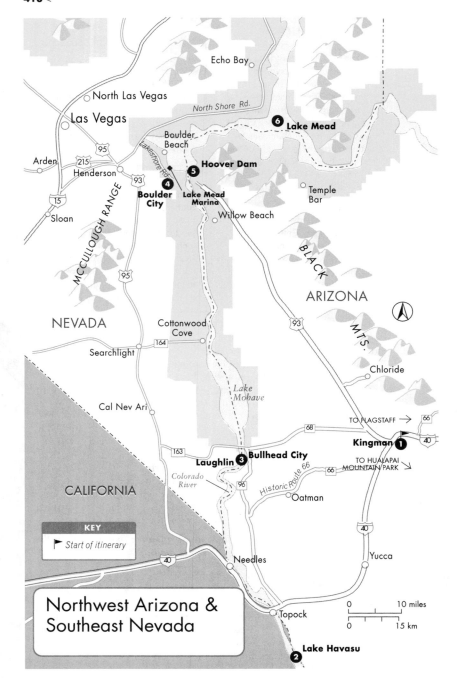

Echo Bay

North Las Vegas

Las Vegas

North Shore Rd.

6 Lake Mead

Boulder
Beach

Arden 95
215
Henderson 93

5 Hoover Dam

4 Boulder
City

Lake Mead
Marina

Temple
Bar

MCCULLOUGH RANGE

Sloan

15

95

Willow Beach

BLACK

ARIZONA

NEVADA

Cottonwood
Cove

164

93

MTS.

Searchlight

Chloride

*Lake
Mohave*

Cal Nev Ari

TO FLAGSTAFF →
66

68

Kingman **1**
40

163

3 Bullhead City

TO HUALAPAI
MOUNTAIN PARK ↘

Laughlin

96

Historic Route 66
66

CALIFORNIA

*Colorado
River*

Oatman

40

KEY
▶ *Start of itinerary*

Yucca

Needles

**Northwest Arizona &
Southeast Nevada**

40

Topock

2 Lake Havasu

0   10 miles
0   15 km

Kingman

▶ ❶ *188 mi northwest of Phoenix, 149 mi west of Flagstaff via I–40.*

The highway past Kingman may seem desolate, but the mountains that surround the area offer outdoor activities in abundance, especially along the Kingman and Colorado rivers. Water sports play a big part in the area's recreation simply because about 1,000 mi of freshwater shoreline lies within the county along the Colorado River and around Lakes Havasu, Mohave, and Mead. Fishing and boating are very popular activities here. Kingman is 35 mi from the river, whereas Bullhead and Lake Havasu cities are right next to water. A little exploring uncovers some scattered "ghost" towns in the area, including Chloride.

The **Historic Route 66 Museum** in the Powerhouse Visitor Center provides a nostalgic look at the evolution of the famous route that started as a footpath followed by prehistoric Indians and evolved into a length of pavement that reached from Chicago, Illinois, to Santa Monica, California. ✉ *120 W. Andy Devine Ave.* ☎ *928/753–9889* ⊕ *www.kingmantourism. org/to-do-and-see/museums/route-66-museum/links.php* ▧ *$3* ⊙ *Mar.–Nov., daily 9–6; Dec.–Feb., daily 9–5.*

The **Bonelli House** (✉ 430 E. Spring St. ☎ 928/753–1413), an excellent example of the Anglo-Territorial architecture popular in the early 1900s, is one of 62 buildings in the Kingman business district listed on the National Register of Historic Places. The **Kingman Area Chamber of Commerce** (✉ 333 W. Andy Devine Ave. ☎ 928/753–6106 ⊕ www. kingmanchamber.org) carries T-shirts, postcards, and the usual brochures to acquaint you with local attractions.

The **Mohave County Museum of History and Arts** includes an Andy Devine Room with memorabilia from Devine's Hollywood years and, incongruously, a portrait collection of every president and first lady. The museum has been expanded to add space for an exceptional library collection of research materials related to the region. There's also an exhibit of carved Kingman turquoise and a diorama depicting the expedition of Lt. Edward Beale, who led his camel-cavalry unit to the area in search of a wagon road along the 35th parallel (⇨ *General Jesup* and the Camels, *below*). Follow the White Cliffs Trail from downtown to see the deep ruts cut into the desert floor by the wagons that eventually came to Kingman after Beale's time. ✉ *400 W. Beale St.* ☎ *928/ 753–3195* ⊕ *www.ctaz.com/~mocohist/museum/index.htm* ▧ *$3* ⊙ *Weekdays 9–5, weekends 1–5.*

A 15-mi drive from town up Hualapai Mountain Road will take you **Fodor's**Choice to **Hualapai Mountain Park** (☎ 928/757–3859, 877/757–0915 for cabin ★ reservations), where more than 2,300 wooded acres at elevations ranging from 4,984 to 8,417 feet hold 10 mi of hiking trails as well as picnic areas, rustic cabins, and RV and tenting areas. You haven't truly hiked in western Arizona until you've hiked in Hualapai Mountain Park. There are dozens of fine trails throughout the region, but the trail system in the higher elevations of the park offers a striking variety of plant life such as prickly pear cactus and Arizona walnut. There are abun-

8

A Brief History of Old Route 66

IN 1938 the 2,400 mi of roadway connecting Chicago and Los Angeles was declared "continuously paved." U.S. Route 66 was transformed from a hodge-podge string of local roads—most of them dirt in summer and mud in winter—connecting one isolated small town to another, into an "all-weather" highway that would enable commerce and the military to travel the route. And just as the road crews changed the landscape to accommodate the roadbed, Route 66 changed the social landscape as communities adapted to the new road.

The needs of the traveler were met by the new ideas of the gas station, the diner, and the motel—and nostalgic glimpses of those icons and that culture can still be found. In Seligman, for example, you can stop at Delgadillo's Snow Cap Drive-in for a "small soda" and a chance to admire vintage automobiles. If you take Exit 139 from I-40, 5 mi west of Ash Fork, you'll find yourself at the beginning of the longest remaining continuous stretch of Route 66. It will take you almost 160 mi through Seligman, Peach Springs, Truxton, Valentine, Hackberry, Kingman, and Oatman, and on to the Colorado River near Topock.

dant species of birds and mammals such as the piñon jay and the Abert squirrel, and at the higher elevations, there are pristine stands of unmarred aspen and cool temperatures. Any of the trails can be hiked in about three hours. If you can only visit one place and do one thing in western Arizona, hiking in Hualapai Mountain Park should be it. A $5 per day use fee has been implemented to help defray the costs of maintaining the park.

OFF THE
BEATEN
PATH

CHLORIDE – The ghost town of Chloride, Arizona's oldest silver mining camp, takes its name from a type of silver ore mined in the area. During its heyday, from 1900 to 1920, there were some 75 mines operating in the area: silver, gold, lead, zinc, molybdenum, and even turquoise were mined here. About 500 folks live in Chloride today; there are three cafés, two saloons, a grocery store, a B&B, and two RV parks. Some of the residents are artists and craftspeople who have small studios and shops in the historic buildings. Sights include the old jail, Chloride Baptist Church, Silverbelle Playhouse, and the Jim Fritz Museum. Western artist Roy Purcell painted the large murals on the rocks on the edge of town. The murals, 10 feet high and almost 30 feet across, cover several granite boulders with depictions of a goddess figure, intertwined snakes, and numerous eastern and Native American symbols. The marked turnoff for Chloride is about 12 mi north of Kingman on U.S. 93.

★ **GRAND CANYON WEST RANCH –** This guest and working cattle ranch offers a slice of the Old West. Once the home of Tap Duncan, a member of the Hole-in-the-Wall Gang (⇨ The Man Who Died Twice box), the ranch now offers rustic cabins, home-cooked meals, horseback riding, and a stagecoach excursion. Take U.S. 93 north from Kingman 25 mi and turn right onto Pearce Ferry Road. Follow the paved road for 27 mi, then turn right onto the unpaved Diamond Bar Road. The Grand Canyon West Ranch is 7 mi farther on the right side of the road. Reservations are required. ⊠ *3785 E. Diamond Bar Ranch Rd., Meadview 86444* ☎ *702/736–8787 or 800/359–8727* ⊕ *www.grandcanyonwestranch.com.*

☺ **GRAND CANYON CAVERNS AND INN –** Nestled among rolling, juniper-covered hills 60 mi east of Kingman on Historic Route 66, the Grand Canyon Caverns and Inn have been a diversion for travelers for decades. Daily tours begin on the hour with an elevator descent to the main floor of the caverns, 210 feet below ground. These caves were formed in the limestone bed of a sea that covered northern Arizona more than 37 million years ago. The caverns are considered a dry cave, or one that no longer grows, but the full extent of the caverns is still unknown. The ¾-mi walking tour takes 45 minutes to complete. In the rodeo arena behind the 48-room hotel, area cowboys often hold calf-roping competitions that are a hoot to watch, and free to boot. ⊠ *Rte. 66* ☎ *928/422–3223* ☞ *$12.95* ☼ *Mar.–Oct., daily 8–6; Nov.–Feb., daily 10–5.*

Sports & the Outdoors

HIKING The **Hayden Peak Trail** is a branch of a 10-mi trail system within Hualapai Mountain Park. The hike begins at location No. 4, elevation 6,750 feet, shown on the trail-system map available at the ranger station. Markers along the trail coincide with the map. This is a strenuous, 5½-mi round-trip hike and a hiking stick is a valuable companion. There are benches and storm shelters along the trail. Along the way you climb through a narrow and shallow canyon that botanists call an Interior Riparian Deciduous Forest. A forest fire scorched this part of the mountains more than 50 years ago and today that scar has been replaced with pristine aspens, their thick, unmarred trunks white as parchment. The ground is covered with ungrazed grasses and soft foliage called deer's ears. At the end of the trail, elevation 8,050 feet, 200 feet below the summit of Hayden Peak, there's a bench with a view to the west that includes the gleaming surface of the Colorado River, some 60 mi away.

Where to Stay & Eat

Kingman has several decent places to eat and about three dozen motels, most of them along Andy Devine Avenue. Most of the major chains are represented, including Days Inn, Motel 6, and Super 8.

$–$$ ✕ **Hubb's Bistro.** The bustling eatery in the Brunswick Hotel caters to most tastes and does a wonderful job with everything from burgers to seafood, including some traditional French dishes. The owner is from France and very proud of his café. ⊠ *315 E. Andy Devine Ave.* ☎ *928/718–1800* ☰ *AE, D, MC, V* ☼ *Closed Sun.*

$–$$ ✕ **Yesterdays Restaurant.** This casual restaurant in Chloride is a popular destination for locals who find Oatman too commercial. ⊠ *9827 N. 2nd St.* ☎ *928/465–4251* ☰ *AE, D, MC, V.*

$ ✕ **El Palacio of Kingman Mexican Restaurant.** Out of the way but worth the effort, this casual restaurant with a Mexican motif is at the north end of town, near the intersection of Bank Street and Northern Avenue. It's a local gem and serves Mexican and American cuisine, and seafood—and what many believe are the best chiles rellenos in the county. ⊠ *401*

E. Andy Devine Ave. ☎ *928/718–0018* ☰ *AE, D, MC, V.*

¢–$ ⌂ **Brunswick Hotel.** This hotel opened its doors in 1909 and was the first three-story building in town. Rooms have antique furnishings and the early-1900s ambience is coupled with courtesy and today's amenities. ✉ *315 E. Andy Devine Ave., 86401* ☎ *928/718–1800* ⊕ *www.hotel-brunswick.com* ⤳*18 rooms, 9 with shared bath, 6 suites* �ᗜ *Restaurant, massage, bar, business services, no-smoking rooms, Internet room; no TV in some rooms* ☰ *AE, D, MC, V* ⦿ *CP.*

¢ ⌂ **Best Western-Kings Inn.** These are the nicest rooms in Kingman. ✉ *2930 E. Andy Devine Ave., 86401* ☎ *928/753–6101 or 800/750–6101* ⤳ *101 rooms* ᗜ *Microwaves, refrigerators, cable TV, in-room data ports, pool, hot tub; no-smoking rooms* ☰ *AE, D, DC, MC, V* ⦿ *CP.*

> ## HOW DEVINE
>
> Andy Devine (1905–77) is Kingman's most famous citizen. Born in Flagstaff, his family moved to Kingman when he was a year old. He was a raspy-voiced Western character actor who appeared in more than 400 films, most notably as the comic cowboy sidekick "Cookie," to Roy Rogers in 10 films, and several appearances with John Wayne, including *Stagecoach, Island in the Sky,* and as the hapless sheriff Linc Appleyard in *The Man Who Shot Liberty Valance.* He also played "the Cheerful Soldier" in *The Red Badge of Courage.*

▮ EN ROUTE A worthwhile stop on your way from Kingman to Lake Havasu, the ghost town of **Oatman** is reached via old Route 66. It's a straight shot across the Mojave Desert valley for a while, but then the road narrows and winds precipitously for about 15 mi through the Black Mountains. This road is public, but beyond a narrow shoulder, the land is privately owned and heavily patrolled by private security thanks to still-active gold mines throughout these low but rugged hills.

Oatman's main street is right out of the Old West; scenes from a number of films, including *How the West Was Won,* were shot here. It still has a remote, old-time feel: many of the natives carry side arms, and they're not acting. You can wander into one of the three saloons or visit the **Oatman Hotel,** where Clark Gable and Carole Lombard honeymooned in 1939 after they were secretly married in Kingman. The burros that often come in from nearby hills and meander down the street, however, are the town's real draw. A couple of stores sell hay to folks who want to feed these "wild" beasts, which at last count numbered about a dozen and which leave plenty of evidence of their visits in the form of "road apples"—so watch your step. For information about the town and its attractions, contact the **Oatman Chamber of Commerce** (☎ 928/768–6222 ⊕ www.oatmangoldroad.com).

Two miles east of Oatman is the **Gold Road Mine,** an active operation that dates back to 1900. A one-hour tour goes underground for a demonstration of drilling equipment and a visit to the "Glory Hole," where the vein structures in the rock are highlighted with a black light to show the gold. ✉ *AZ 66* ☎ *928/768–1600* ⊕ *www.goldroadmine.com* ⬛ *$12* ⊙ *Daily 10 AM–5 PM.*

Lake Havasu City

❷ *60 mi southwest of Kingman.*

Remember the old nursery rhyme "London Bridge Is Falling Down"? Well, it was. After about 150 years of constant use, the 294-foot-long landmark was sinking into the Thames. When Lake Havasu City founder, Robert McCullough, heard about this predicament, he set about actu-**Fodor'sChoice** ally to buy **London Bridge** and have it disassembled, shipped 10,000 mi ★ to western Arizona, and rebuilt, stone by stone. The bridge was reconstructed on mounds of sand and took three years to complete. When it was finished, a mile-long channel was dredged under the bridge and water was diverted from Lake Havasu through the Bridgewater Channel. Today, the entire city is centered on this unusual attraction.

If there's an Arizona Riviera, this is it. Lake Havasu has more than 45 mi of lake shoreline, and the area gets less than 4 inches of rain annually, which means it's almost always sunny. Spring, winter, and fall are the best times to visit in summer, temperatures often exceed 100°F. You can rent everything from water skis to Jet Skis, small fishing boats to large houseboats. There are no fewer than 13 RV parks and campgrounds, about 125 boat-in campsites, and hundreds of hotel and motel rooms for additional creature comforts. There are golf and tennis facilities, as well as fishing guides who'll help you find, and catch, the big ones.

If you're interested in exploring nearby old mines, a wildlife sanctuary, and the desert in general, join a four-wheel driving tour created by **Outback Adventures** (☎ 928/680–6151 ⊕ www.outbackadventures.com).

★ The **Havasu National Wildlife Refuge** (⊠ Off I–40 south of Needles, CA ☎ 760/326–3853 ⊕ southwest.fws.gov), between Needles and Lake Havasu City, is a 44,371-acre refuge for wintering Canada geese and other waterfowl, such as the snowy egret and the great blue heron. The largest surviving cottonwood-willow woodland in the region is part of the **Bill Williams River National Wildlife Refuge** (⊠ AZ 95, 23 mi south of Lake Havasu City ☎ 928/667–4144), south of Lake Havasu City. To reach the 6,000-acre refuge, travel south on AZ 95; the entrance is between mileposts 160 and 161.

OFF THE BEATEN PATH

'AHAKHAV TRIBAL PRESERVE – The 2,500-acre preserve is on the Colorado Indian Tribes Reservation and is a top spot in the area for bird-watching and hiking. There are several campgrounds, parks, and recreation areas along the Colorado River. Rent a canoe ($10 an hour or $25 a day) and bird-watch along the shoreline of the backwater area branching off the Colorado River. Some 350 species of migratory and native birds live around the region or visit on their annual migrations. The 3-mi hiking trail has exercise stations along the way, and a trail extension will lead you to the tribal historical museum and gift shop. From AZ 95 in Parker, which is at the southern end of Lake Havasu, head west on Mohave Road for about 2 mi. When you reach the PARKER INDIAN RODEO ASSOCIATION sign, continue ½ mi farther and turn left at the TRIBAL PRESERVE sign at Rodeo Drive. ⊠ 25401 Rodeo Dr., Parker ☎ 928/669–2664 🖶 928/669–8024.

Sports & the Outdoors

GOLF The semi-private **London Bridge Golf Club** (✉ 2400 Clubhouse Dr., Lake Havasu City ☎ 928/855–2719) has two regulation 18-hole courses. Greens fees are $50 for the East course and $69 for the West course. The West course is the championship caliber.

BACKCOUNTRY **Outback Off-Road Adventures** (✉ 362 London Bridge Rd., #2, Lake
EXPLORATION Havasu City ☎ 928/680–6151) has several tour packages. One option is traveling in a six-wheel-drive Pinzguaer through the Sonoran Desert and Mohave Mountains. For adults, a full-day tour costs $165; for children the rate is $135.

WATER SPORTS When construction of Parker Dam was completed in 1938, the reservoir it created to supply water to southern California and Arizona became Lake Havasu. The lake is a 45-mi-long playground for water sports of all kinds. Whether it's waterskiing, jet skiing, power boating, houseboating, swimming, fishing, or you name it, if water is required, it's happening on Lake Havasu.

Lake Havasu State Park (✉ 699 London Bridge Rd. ☎ 928/855–2784 ⊕ www.pr.state.az.us) is near the London Bridge. With four boat ramps and 42 campsites, it's an extremely popular spot in summer. On the eastern shore of the lake 15 mi south of Lake Havasu City is **Cattail Cove State Park** (✉ AZ 95, 15 mi south of Lake Havasu ☎ 928/855–1223 ⊕ www.pr.state.az.us). There are 62 campsites with access to electricity and water, and public restrooms with showers. Both parks charge $8 per vehicle for entry and are open from sunrise to 10.

If you have a boat, you have more options. You can find a quiet, secluded cove or beach to tie up and enjoy swimming or fishing or just resting. If you have a need for speed, you can plane up and down the lake with or without a skier in tow.

If you don't have the equipment or the vessel necessary to enjoy your water sport, they're available for rent from a number of reputable merchants. You can rent everything from Jet Skis to pontoon boats, by the day or by the week, at **Sand Point Marina and RV Park** (✉ 17952 S. Sand Point Resort Rd. ☎ 928/855–0549 ⊕ www.sandpointresort.com). You can rent more than just a Jet Ski at **Arizona Jet Ski Rentals** (✉ 655 Kiowa Ave. ☎ 800/393–5558 ⊕ www.arizonawatersports.com)—jet boats, ski boats, and pontoon boats are also available.

Where to Stay & Eat

Many tourists make this stop a day trip on their way to Laughlin or Las Vegas, but there are plenty of accommodations if you'd like to stay more than a night. Of the chain hotels in town, the Best Western and the Holiday Inn are your best bets.

★ $–$$$ ✕ **London Arms Pub and Restaurant.** With dinner theater on the weekends, this traditional-looking pub offers more than the standard fish-and-chips. Along with the salads and burgers, you can order Cornish game hen, lobster ravioli, or prime rib. If you opt for an evening in the Theatre Banquet Room, you'll be served a four-course feast for $19.95, prior to the performances held at 5:30 and 7 on Friday and Saturday and at noon Sunday. The popular theatrical musical *I Do! I Do!* is typical of the shows performed. The cost of the show is additional and varies. ⊠ *422 English Village* ☎ *928/855–8782* ▤ *AE, D, MC, V.*

★ **$–$$$** ✕ **Shugrue's.** If you've dined at the Sedona branch of this restaurant, you know what to expect here. Shugrue's features hand-cut steaks, very fresh seafood, salads, and other well-prepared American fare. The baked desserts are worth saving room for. Most tables have good bridge views. ⊠ *1425 McCulloch Blvd.* ☎ *928/453–1400* ▤ *AE, MC, V.*

$–$$ ✕ **Barley Brothers Brewery and Grill.** In the Island Mall adjacent to the English Village and the London Bridge, Barley Brothers offers casual dining and a microbrewery specializing in hefeweizen and a variety of ales. ⊠ *1425 McCulloch Blvd.* ☎ *928/505–7837* ⊕ *www.barleybrothers.com* ▤ *D, MC, V.*

$–$$ ✕ **Juicy's River Café.** This is a favorite hangout for the local folks who know good food when they taste it. The Sunday breakfast is especially popular. The restaurant is small (14 tables inside, 4 more outside) with a varied menu that includes corned beef and cabbage, smoked prime rib, meat loaf, pot roast and vegetables, and homemade soups and desserts. ⊠ *25 N. Acoma Blvd.* ☎ *928/855–8429* ▤ *AE, D, MC, V.*

¢ ✕ **Chico's Tacos.** The salsa bar at this decent Mexican fast-food joint offers fresh salsa in varying degrees of spiciness. ⊠ *1641 McCulloch Blvd.* ☎ *928/680–7010* ▤ *D, MC, V.*

★ **$–$$** ▥ **London Bridge Resort.** If you want to be close to the bridge, this hotel is a dependable choice. The decor is a strange mix of Tudor and Southwestern; other than that, studios are standard motel rooms with kitchenettes. One-bedroom condos have separate living and dining areas as well as full kitchens; two-bedroom condos have balconies. There's a serviceable restaurant. ⊠ *1477 Queen's Bay, 86403* ☎ *928/855–0888 or 800/624–7939* 🖷 *928/855–9209* ⊕ *www.londonbridgeresort.com* ⇨ *4 studios, 72 1-bedroom condos, 46 2-bedroom condos* ⬧ *Restaurant, some kitchens, some kitchenettes, cable TV, golf privileges, 3 pools, beach, no-smoking rooms* ▤ *AE, D, MC, V.*

$ ▥ **Havasu Springs Resort.** On a low peninsula reaching into Lake Havasu, the four hotels of this resort maximize your options. In addition to standard hotel rooms, the resort also offers suites and apartments. ⊠ *2581 AZ 95, Parker 85344* ☎ *928/667–3361* 🖷 *928/667–1098* ⊕ *www.havasusprings.com* ⇨ *38 rooms, 4 suites, 3 apartments* ⬧ *Restaurant, cable TV, beach, lounge* ▤ *AE, D, MC, V.*

¢–$ ▥ **Island Inn.** Fido is welcome here—if he's small, that is. And together, you can walk to London Bridge and London Bridge Beach. There are 117 rooms, a pool, hot tub, and meeting rooms. Rooms are large and basic. ⊠ *1300 W. McCulloch Blvd., 86403* ☎ *928/680–0606 or 800/243–9955* 🖷 *928/680–4218* ⇨ *117 rooms* ⬧ *Cable TV, pool, hot tub, meeting rooms, some pets allowed (fee)* ▤ *AE, D, MC, V.*

HOUSEBOATING **Club Nautical Houseboats.** What houseboats lack in speed and maneuverability, they make up for in comfort and shade. A day on the lake can be a scorching and dehydrating experience, even with plenty of sunscreen and lots of beverages on hand. Seeing the lake, any lake, from the sheltered deck of a houseboat is a safe and enjoyable alternative to

8

overexposure to the desert sun. ✉ *1000 McCulloch Blvd.* ☎ *800/843–9218* ⊕ *www.lakehavasuhouseboatrental.com.*

SOUTHEAST NEVADA

The tandem grandeur of Hoover Dam and Lake Mead will soon have another engineering marvel for company as work continues less than a ½ mi downstream on a bridge that will span the river canyon and link western Arizona to southeastern Nevada, dramatically reducing traffic across Hoover Dam. The chance to see a bridge of this size and complexity under construction is rare, and makes it worth the trip to the dam if for no other reason than to stand there and watch the bridge grow. Downstream 60 mi, the casino lights of Laughlin, Nevada, sparkle across the river from Bullhead City.

Bullhead City, Arizona & Laughlin, Nevada

❸ *35 mi northwest of Kingman.*

AZ 68 is the highway from Kingman to Bullhead City and Laughlin, Nevada. It crosses the Sacramento Valley and climbs over the Black Mountains through Union Pass and down the other side to the Colorado River valley. At night, across the river from Bullhead City, the lights of Laughlin glitter. Bullhead City has its small-town charms, but the lights of Laughlin are difficult to ignore.

Laughlin's founder, Don Laughlin, bought an eight-room motel here in 1966 and basically built the town from scratch. By the early 1980s Laughlin's Riverside Hotel-Casino was drawing gamblers and river rats from northwestern Arizona, southeastern California, and even southern Nevada, and his success attracted other casino operators. Today Laughlin is Nevada's third major resort area, attracting more than 5 million visitors annually. The city fills up, especially in winter, with retired travelers who spend at least part of the winter in Arizona and a younger resort-loving crowd. The big picture windows overlooking the Colorado River lend a bright, airy, and open feeling unique to Laughlin casinos. Take a stroll along the river walk, then make the return trip by water taxi ($3 round-trip; $2 one-way). Boating, Jet Skis, and plain old wading are other options for enjoying the water.

★ Across the Laughlin Bridge, ¼ mi to the north, the **Colorado River Museum** displays the rich past of the region where Nevada, Arizona, and California converge. There are artifacts from the Mojave Indian Tribe, models and photographs of steamboats that once plied the river, rock and fossil specimens, and the first telephone switchboard used in neighboring Bullhead City. ✉ *2201 AZ 68* ☎ *928/754–3399* ⊕ *www.bullheadcity.com/tourism/hismuseum.asp* ▨ *$2* ⊙ *Sept.–June, Tues.–Sun. 10–4.*

Where to Stay & Eat

★ ¢–$ ✕▨ **Avi Resort & Casino.** The only tribally-owned casino in Nevada is run by the Fort Mojave Tribe. The 25,000-square-foot casino houses nearly 1,000 slot and video-poker machines. The biggest draw, how-

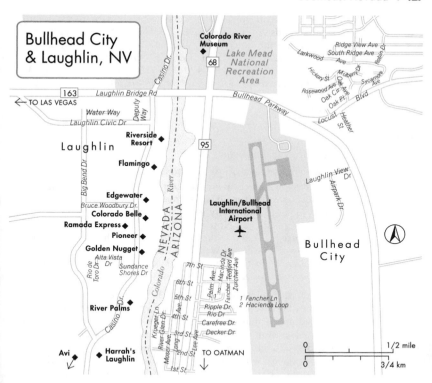

Bullhead City & Laughlin, NV

ever, is the private white-sand beach where you can lounge or rent a watercraft. Be sure to visit the **Moonshadow Grille,** preferably for the finest Sunday champagne brunch in the tri-state area. ⊠ *10000 Aha Macav Pkwy., Laughlin 89029* ☎ *702/535–5555 or 800/284–2946* ⊕ *www. avicasino.com* ⇱ *455 rooms, 29 spa suites* ⚒ *5 restaurants, cable TV, 18-hole golf course, pool, gym, spa, beach, marina, bar, lounge, casino, cinema, children's programs (ages 6 wks–12 yrs), no-smoking rooms* ⊟ *AE, D, DC, MC, V.*

¢–$ ✕▣ **Harrah's.** This is the classiest joint in Laughlin, and it has a private sand beach and two casinos (one is no-smoking). Big-name entertainers perform in the Fiesta Showroom and at the 3,000-seat Rio Vista Outdoor Amphitheater. **The Range Steakhouse** ($–$$$) serves Continental fare. ⊠ *2900 S. Casino Dr., Laughlin 89029* ☎ *702/298–4600 or 800/ 427–7247* 🖷 *702/298–6802* ⊕ *www.harrahs.com* ⇱ *1,561 rooms* ⚒ *5 restaurants, cable TV, some in-room data ports, 2 pools, gym, hair salon, hot tub, spa, beach, 3 bars, lounge, casino, showroom, shops, meeting rooms, no-smoking floors* ⊟ *AE, D, DC, MC, V.*

★ ¢–$ ✕▣ **Riverside Resort.** Town founder Don Laughlin still runs this northernmost joint himself. Check out the Loser's Lounge, with its graphic homage to famous losers, such as the *Hindenburg,* the *Titanic,* and the like. And don't pass up Don's two free classic-car showrooms with more than 80 rods, roadsters, and tin lizzies. The **Gourmet Room** restaurant serves Continental and American cuisine. ✉ *1650 S. Casino Dr., Laughlin 89029* ☎ *702/298–2535 or 800/227–3849* 🖷 *702/298–2614* 🌐 *www.riversideresort.com* 🛏 *1,400 rooms* 🔧 *6 restaurants, cable TV, 2 pools, hot tub, bowling, lounge, casino, nightclub, showroom, children's programs (ages 3 months–12 yrs), no-smoking rooms* 🖃 *AE, D, DC, MC, V.*

Boulder City, Nevada

❹ *76 mi northwest of Kingman.*

In the early 1930s Boulder City was built by the federal government to house 5,000 construction workers on the Hoover Dam project. A strict moral code was enforced to ensure timely completion of the dam, and to this day, the model city is the only community in Nevada in which gambling is illegal. Note that the two casinos at either end of Boulder City are just outside the city limits. After the dam was completed, the town shrank but was kept alive by the management and maintenance crews of the dam and Lake Mead. Today it's a vibrant little Southwestern town.

Built in 1933, the **Boulder Dam Hotel** (✉ 1305 Arizona St. ☎ 702/293–3510 🌐 www.boulderdamhotel.com) was a favorite getaway for notables, including the man who became Pope Pius XII and actors Will Rogers, Bette Davis, and Shirley Temple. The **Boulder City/Hoover Dam Museum** (☎ 702/294–1988 🌐 www.bcmha.org 🎟 $2 ⊙ Mon.–Sat. 10–5, Sun. noon–5), which preserves and displays artifacts relating to the workers and construction of Boulder City and Hoover Dam, occupies the second floor of the Boulder Dam Hotel. The **Boulder City Chamber of Commerce** (✉ 465 Nevada Way ☎ 702/293–2034 🌐 www. bouldercitychamber.com ⊙ weekdays, 9–5) is a good place to gather information on the history of Hoover Dam and other historic sights around town.

Hoover Dam

❺ *67 mi northwest of Kingman via U.S. 93.*

Fodor's Choice
★
Humanity's ability to reshape the natural world—for good or ill, depending on your viewpoint—is powerfully evident in the Hoover Dam. Completed in 1935, the dam is 726 feet high (the equivalent of a 70-story building) and 660 feet thick at the base (more than the length of two football fields). Its construction required 4.4 million cubic yards of concrete, enough to build a two-lane highway from San Francisco to New York. Originally referred to as Boulder Dam, the structure was later officially named Hoover Dam in recognition of President Herbert Hoover's role in the project. Look for artist Oskar Hansen's plaza sculptures, which include the 30-foot-tall *Winged Figures of the Republic*. Many people walk right over Hansen's most intriguing work: the plaza's terrazzo floor, inlaid with a celestial map.

The **Discovery Tour** allows you to see the power plant generators and other features. Guide staffers give talks every 15 minutes at each stopping point from 9 to 4:30 (early tours are less crowded). Cameras, pagers, tote bags, and cell phones are subject to X-ray screening. More than a million people take this tour annually. January and February are the slowest months.

The top of the dam is open to pedestrians during daylight hours only; approved vehicles can cross the dam 24/7. Note: all specified hours are Pacific time. ⊠ *U.S. 93 east of Boulder City* ☎ *702/494–2517* 🖨 *702/494–2587* ⊕ *www.usbr.gov/lc/hooverdam* ▤ *Discovery Tour $11, parking $7* ☉ *Daily 9–5* ☞ *Security, road, and Hoover Dam crossing information: 888/248–1259.*

> **WORD OF MOUTH**
>
> "The Hoover Dam tour is definitely worth it. We took the tour—you get a movie/slide show about the building of the Dam, then they bring you all the way down to the generators inside, up to the observation deck to get those postcard photos, downstairs to the exhibits, across the street to the dedication monument and then to the gift shop . . ."   –Rachpilaw

Lake Mead

6 *67 mi northwest of Kingman on U.S. 93.*

Fodor's Choice ★

Lake Mead, which is actually the Colorado River backed up behind the Hoover Dam, is the nation's largest man-made reservoir: it covers 229 square mi, is 110 mi long, and has an irregular shoreline that extends for 550 mi. You can get information about the lake's history, ecology, recreational opportunities, and the accommodations available along its shore at the **Alan Bible Visitors Center** (☎ 702/293–8990 ☉ Daily 8:30–4:30). People come to Lake Mead to swim: **Boulder Beach** on the Nevada side of the lake is the closest swimming beach to Arizona and only about a mile from the visitor center.

> **WORD OF MOUTH**
>
> "I love Lake Mead. The water is warm and crystal clear. You can swim in it and look down and see your feet treading water beneath you."   –kit

Angling and houseboating are favorite pastimes; marinas strung along the Nevada shore rent houseboats, personal watercraft, and ski boats. The lake is regularly stocked with a half-million rainbow trout, and at least a million fish are harvested every year. You can fish here 24 hours a day, year-round (except for posted closings). If you plan to catch and keep trout, be mindful that a trout stamp is required. Divers can explore the murk beneath, including the usually submerged foundations of St. Thomas, a farming community that was inundated in 1938. Other activities abound, including waterskiing, sailboating, and snorkeling. ⊕ *www.nps.gov/lame* ▤ *$5 per vehicle, good for 5 days; lake use fees $10 first vessel, $5 additional vessel, good for 1–5 days.*

Sports & the Outdoors

BOATING Rental options include houseboats, patio boats, fishing boats, and ski boats—pick up a list of marinas at the Alan Bible Visitors Center. Power-boats as well as houseboats are available at **Callville Bay Resort and Marina** (⊠ Callville Bay ☎ 702/565–8958 or 800/255–5561). **Echo Bay Resort** (⊠ Echo Bay ☎ 702/394–4000 or 800/752–9669) is a popular choice for Lake Mead houseboat rentals; the company also rents ski boats, fishing boats, and other personal watercraft. **Lake Mead Marina** (⊠ Boulder Beach, Boulder City ☎ 702/293–3484) has boat rentals, a beach, camping facilities, a gift shop, and a floating restaurant.

CRUISES **Lake Mead Cruises** (⊠ Lake Mead Marina, near Boulder Beach, Boulder City ☎ 702/293–6180 ⊕ www.lakemeadcruises.com) offers 1½-hr cruises of the Hoover Dam area on the 300-passenger *Desert Princess*. Also offered are breakfast-buffet cruises and early dinner and dinner-dance cruises. **Gray Line Tours** (☎ 702/384–1234 or 800/634–6579 ⊕ www.pcap.com/grayline.htm) has several sightseeing options.

Where to Stay

¢–$ ⊞ **Temple Bar Resort.** This motel right on the Arizona shore of the lake is a good choice if you want a quiet room; the hotel's remote location ensures peace. The restaurant, which serves typical American fare, has outdoor seating overlooking the water. ⊠ *Temple Bar, AZ 86643* ☎ *928/767–3211 or 800/752–9669* ⊃ *18 rooms, 4 cabins* ⊖ *Restaurant* ⊟ *D, MC, V.*

¢ ⊞ **Hacienda Resort.** Sitting just outside city limits, this large, Vegas-style casino eludes the Boulder City ban on gambling. Close to Lake Mead and Hoover Dam, the resort has seven restaurants, live entertainment, and more than 800 slot machines. ⊠ *U.S. 93, Boulder City, NV 89005* ☎ *702/293–5000* ⊕ *www.haciendaonline.com* ⊃ *375 rooms* ⊖ *7 restaurants, casino* ⊟ *D, MC, V.*

CAMPING ⊿ **Temple Bar Campground.** Space is available on a first-come, first-
¢ served basis at this 153-site campground on the Arizona shore of the lake, but there are usually plenty of unoccupied sites on all but the busiest holiday weekends. The nightly fee is $10. ⊠ *Temple Bar, AZ 86643* ☎ *928/767–3401 or 800/752–9669* ⊠ *$10* ⊃ *153 sites* ⊖ *Flush toilets, dump station, running water (non-potable), fire grates, picnic tables* ⊗ *Open year-round.*

HOUSEBOATING ⊞ **Seven Crown Resorts.** The beauty of renting a houseboat is that you
$$$$ can cruise down the lake and park where you please for as long as you like. It's an increasingly popular vacation option, especially for large groups. Seven Crown Resorts is a good resource for rentals. The boats come equipped with full kitchens and air-conditioning, and they can sleep up to 13 people. The minimum rental is for three days, two nights; you get the best rates on a one-week rental. Some boats have no air-conditioning. ⊂ *Box 16247 Irvine, CA 92623* ☎ *800/752–9669 or 928/767–3211* ⊕ *www.sevencrown.com* ⊖ *Kitchens; no room TVs* ⊟ *D, MC, V.*

NORTHWEST ARIZONA & SOUTHEAST NEVADA ESSENTIALS

To research prices, get advice from other travelers, and book travel arrangements, visit ⊕ www.fodors.com.

Transportation

BY AIR

Great Lakes Airlines has daily flights between Kingman and Phoenix; America West Express flies daily between Lake Havasu City and Phoenix and Lake Havasu City and Bullhead City. Sun Country flies to Laughlin/Bullhead City from 50 cities in 18 states, including Seattle, Portland, Denver, Minneapolis/St. Paul, San Francisco, Phoenix, and Dallas/Fort Worth. Several hotel-casinos also sponsor charter flights.

🛪 **Allegiant Charters** ☎ 800/221-1306. **America West Express** ☎ 800/235-9292. **Great Lakes Airlines** ☎ 800/554-5111. **Sun Country Airlines** ☎ 800/359-6786 ⊕ www. suncountry.com. **Kingman Airport** ☎ 928/757-5444. **Lake Havasu City Municipal Airport** ☎ 928/764-3330. **Laughlin/Bullhead International Airport** ☎ 928/754-2134.

BY BUS

Greyhound serves Kingman, Lake Havasu City, and Bullhead City. The Bullhead City bus stops at the Airport Chevron at 600 AZ 95. To get to Laughlin, Nevada, walk to the boat dock across the highway and take a free ride to a Nevada hotel river landing.

🛪 **Greyhound** ☎ 800/231-2222 ⊕ www.greyhound.com.

BY CAR

The best way to get your "kicks on Route 66" is to travel by automobile. This holds true for travel throughout western Arizona. Historic Route 66 crosses east–west and lies north of I–40, which also crosses the region. U.S. 93 is the main route for north–south travel. All of these roads are in excellent condition. On I–40 high winds occasionally raise enough blowing dust to restrict visibility. In winter, ice may be present on the stretch of I–40 between Kingman and Seligman, as well as on sections of Route 66. When signage warns of ice ahead, heed the warnings and slow down. Most of the county roads are improved dirt roads, but washboard sections may surprise you, so take your time and drive no faster than prudence dictates. Roll down the windows and enjoy the scent of desert air.

Fuel up while you're in this part of Arizona—all grades of gasoline can be as much as 30¢ to 50¢ per gallon less in Kingman and Bullhead City than in Laughlin.

BY TRAIN

Amtrak's *Southwest Chief* stops in Kingman and in Needles, California, which is 25 mi south of Bullhead City/Laughlin. An Amtrak Thruway bus shuttles passengers to the Ramada Express in Laughlin.

🛪 **Amtrak** ☎ 800/872-7245 ⊕ www.amtrak.com.

Contacts & Resources

EMERGENCIES

🚹 Ambulance, Fire & Police **Emergency services** ☎ 911.

🚹 Hospitals **Havasu Regional Medical Center** ✉ 101 Civic Center La., Lake Havasu City ☎ 928/855-8185. **Kingman Regional Medical Center** ✉ 3269 Stockton Hill Rd., Kingman ☎ 928/757-2101. **Western Arizona Regional Medical Center** ✉ 2735 Silver Creek Rd., Bullhead City ☎ 928/763-2273.

TOURS

BOATING & RAFTING TOURS There is no white water to be found on the Colorado River below Hoover Dam. Instead, the river and its lakes offer you many opportunities to explore the gorges and marshes that line the shores. If you prefer to do it yourself, look into the canoe and kayak rentals available on lakes Mead, Mohave, and Havasu. Raft adventures will take you through the Topock Gorge near Lake Havasu, or you can take a trip upriver from Willow Beach 12 mi to the base of Hoover Dam. Along the way, chances are good you'll see big horn sheep moving along the steep basaltic cliffs. Expect to spend $35 to $40 for half a day, and twice that for a full-day adventure.

🚹 **Black Canyon Adventures** ☎ 800/455-3490 ⊕ www.blackcanyonadventures.com. **Desert River Outfitters** ☎ 888/529-2533 ⊕ www.desertriveroutfitters.com. **Western Arizona Canoe & Kayak Outfitter** ☎ 888/881-5038 ⊕ www.azwacko.com.

VISITOR INFORMATION

🚹 **Boulder City Chamber of Commerce** ☎ 702/293-2034 ⊕ www.bouldercitychamber.com. **Bullhead City Area Chamber of Commerce** ☎ 928/754-4121 ⊕ www.bullheadchamber.com. **Kingman Area Chamber of Commerce** ☎ 928/753-6106 ⊕ www.kingmanchamber.org. **Lake Havasu Tourism Bureau** ☎ 928/453-3444 or 800/242-8278 ⊕ www.golakehavasu.com. **Laughlin Chamber of Commerce** ☎ 702/298-2214 or 800/227-5245 🖷 702/298-5708 ⊕ www.laughlinchamber.com. **Laughlin Visitors Bureau** ☎ 702/298-3321 or 800/452-8445 ⊕ www.visitlaughlin.com.

UNDERSTANDING ARIZONA

ARIZONA AT A GLANCE

THE NATIVE SOUTHWEST

BOOKS & MOVIES

ARIZONA AT A GLANCE

Fast Facts

Nickname: Grand Canyon State
Capital: Phoenix
Motto: Ditat Deus (God enriches)
State song: *Arizona*
State bird: Cactus Wren
State flower: Saguaro cactus blossom
(carnegiea gigantea)
State tree: Palo verde (cercidium)
Administrative divisions: 15 counties
Entered the Union: February 14, 1912
(48th state)
Population: 5.8 million
Population density: 46.9 people per
square mi
Median age: 34.2
Infant mortality rate: 6.9 deaths per
1,000 births
Literacy: 18% had trouble with basic
reading. Twenty-six percent spoke a
language other than English at home,
usually Spanish. Forty percent reported
that they did not speak English "very
well."
Ethnic groups: White 62%; Latino 27%;
Native American 4%; African American
3%; Asian 2%; other 2%
Religion: Unaffiliated 60%; Catholic
19%; Christian 12%; Mormon 5%;
Jewish 2%; other 2%

*Come to this land of sunshine
To this land where life is young.
Where the wide, wide world is
waiting,
The songs that will now be sung.*
    —opening lines of state song,
   Arizona, by Margaret Rowe Clifford

*The great pines stand at a
considerable distance from each
other. Each tree grows alone,
murmurs alone, thinks alone. They do
not intrude upon each other. The
Navajos are not much in the habit of
giving or of asking help. Their
language is not a communicative
one, and they never attempt an
interchange of personality in speech.
Over their forests there is the same
inexorable reserve. Each tree has its
exalted power to bear.*
   —Willa Cather (1873–1947), U.S.
   novelist, describing Navajo pine
      forests in northern Arizona.

Geography & Environment

Land area: 113,909 square mi
Terrain: Desert, with rocky mountains
stretching across the southern area of
the state. Along the Mogollon Rim that
reaches in a crescent across the eastern
third of the state, stands the largest
ponderosa-pine forest in the world. The
White Mountains of eastern Arizona
receive over 150 inches of snow
annually and the run-off provides much
of the water that enables the desert
communities to survive. Erosion by
rivers has formed much of the state's
geography, including the Grand Canyon
and the Painted Desert

Highest point: Humphreys Peak, 12,655
feet
Natural resources: Cement, copper
(Arizona leads the nation in
production), gravel, molybdenum, pine
and fir forests, sand
Natural hazards: Drought, earthquakes,
floods, severe storms, wildfires
Environmental issues: Especially around
Phoenix, air quality is bad enough that
year-round monitoring is done for
ground-level ozone pollution, carbon
monoxide, and particulate matter;
concern over how logging should be
done in Arizona's pine forests; soil

erosion from overgrazing, industrial development, urbanization, and poor farming practices; most of the state suffers from limited natural freshwater resources

Desert rains are usually so definitely demarked that the story of the man who washed his hands in the edge of an Arizona thunder shower without wetting his cuffs seems almost credible.

—Arizona: A State Guide (The WPA Guide to Arizona)

Economy

GSP: $160.6 billion
Per-capita income: $33,704
Unemployment: 4.5%
Work force: 2.7 million; financial/management 21%; trade, transportation, and utilities 19%; government 18%; educational and health services 11%; leisure/hospitality 10%; construction 8%; manufacturing 7%; other 4%; publishing/telecom 2%
Major industries: Cattle, dairy goods, manufacturing, electronics, printing and publishing, processed foods, aerospace, transportation, high-tech research and development, communications, construction, tourism, military
Agricultural products: Broccoli, cattle, cauliflowers, cotton, dairy goods, lettuce, sorghum
Exports: $10.7 billion
Major export products: Electronic and electric equipment, fabricated metal products, industrial machinery and computers, scientific and measuring instruments, transportation equipment

Did You Know?

• Yuma, Arizona, holds the world record for most sunshine. It gets an average of 4,055 hours, or more than 90%, of the 4,456 hours of sunshine possible in a year.

• The Arizona or "Apache" Trout can only be found in the White Mountains of Arizona.

• One of Arizona's most plentiful natural resources is molybdenum, an element linked with copper production. Molybdenum is used to make steel, as well as electrodes and catalysts.

• During daylight saving time, it's possible to drive in and out of time zones in Arizona in less than an hour. While the rest of the state sticks to Mountain Standard Time year-round, the state's Navajo Nation observes daylight saving, but the Hopi Reservation inside the Navajo goes along with the rest of Arizona.

• Cesar Chavez, who organized agricultural laborers across America, was born near Yuma, Arizona.

• In 1930, Pluto was discovered by Clyde Tombaugh at Lowell Observatory in Flagstaff.

• The Central Arizona Project Canal is 336 mi long and annually brings 1.5 million gallons of Colorado River water from Lake Havasu City, through the Phoenix metropolitan area, to Tucson.

• The Hohokam, Arizona's earliest known inhabitants, were good at something crucial to Arizona today: irrigation. They built canals more than 10 mi long that channeled water to fields in the southern part of the state in about AD 300.

• More than 10% of the nation's Native Americans live in Arizona.

THE NATIVE SOUTHWEST

CONSIDERING THE ARIDITY of the Southwest, the tremendous cultural productivity of its native civilizations is a fascinating case of people turning the challenges of nature into a meaningful existence. Within the compass of the state of Arizona, Native American pottery and cliff dwellings are the most apparent evidence of this. In fact, they are isolated phenomena on a vast trade route that spanned the continent from the Pacific coast all the way to Mesoamerica, an area in which not only goods but pottery-making techniques, agricultural technologies, and spiritual beliefs were transmitted. Some 4,000 years ago—at least 8,000 years after humans crossed the Bering Strait land bridge that once allowed passage on foot between Asia and North America—a major transition in cultures around the world saw people shifting from nomadic hunting-and-gathering lifestyles to more settled agricultural existence. In the Southwest, ancient pioneers brought the practice of cultivating corn, squash, and beans north from Mesoamerica. One group in particular, the Hohokam, is believed to have fostered this. In an area straddling the Arizona–New Mexico border, the Hohokam developed a highly productive system. Some archaeologists believe that they migrated from northwestern Mexico with knowledge of planting, growing, and irrigating. Others picture an evolution of Archaic peoples who gradually took on Mesoamerican practices. Either way, they had great success and in turn influenced their northern and eastern neighbors for more than a thousand years. Their artisans produced ritual objects, jewelry, and stone and ceramic wares with great skill. They regularly traded with Mesoamerican tribes, and Pacific coast exchange brought in raw materials for their own and other regional artisans.

The flowering of Hohokam culture began around 2,300 years ago. The period of their growth, expansion, and eventual decline, when they began to take new ideas in from the north, lasted about 1,500 years—twice as long as the Roman Empire. During that time, they cultivated corn, beans, squash, agave, and cotton, using remarkable irrigation methods. Some of their networks of canals stretched 3 mi from the Salt and Gila rivers to planted fields. Their contact with Mesoamerican cultures periodically brought new strains of corn to the Southwest, along with religious beliefs, ritual practices, and the ball game and ball courts well known from the Maya. The Hohokam culturally fertilized the region, providing a base for the Pueblo culture that has survived into the modern era.

The Mogollon (pronounced *muh*-gee-on) were another group, occupying an area stretching from eastern-central Arizona into New Mexico from 2,000 to 500 years ago. They took on Hohokam and so-called Anasazi-cultural patterns, but they never fully embraced an agricultural lifestyle. They became skillful potters, especially those living near the Mimbres River. Their contact with the Anasazi resulted in the production of some of the Southwest's most outstanding pottery. The principle Mimbres Mogollon site is now the Gila Cliff Dwellings National Monument in New Mexico.

Romanticized, mythicized, and perhaps misunderstood, the so-called Anasazi left wondrous architectural remains, most notably at Mesa Verde in Colorado; Chaco Canyon in New Mexico; and Canyon de Chelly, Betatakin, and Keet Seel in Arizona. Composed of various groups living around the Four Corners area, they have generated the most intense interest. For centuries they lived semi-nomadically, hunting, gathering, and marginally cultivating corn, squash, and beans. They eventually settled into villages and adopted much of the Hohokam culture, more than their Mogollon neighbors did.

These various Ancestral Pueblo peoples were not pueblo dwellers yet, however. They were slow to establish year-round communities. Perhaps they weren't convinced that the Hohokam model would work in their rugged, dry canyonlands. With fewer and smaller rivers, they couldn't irrigate on the Hohokam scale. About 1,500 years ago the Pueblo-cultural pattern called Anasazi began to take shape, owing, perhaps, to the introduction of a new, more productive strain of corn.

Ancestral Pueblo peoples made a significant contribution to Southwestern culture with their architecture. Their remarkable stone masonry evolved out of a pithouse style used by Archaic peoples. A precursor of the kiva, the pithouse was constructed around a shallow, circular dugout with mud walls packed around vertical pole supports. The new stone-and-mortar houses, on the other hand, were very often rectangular in plan. In small communities they were built on a scale to house groups of a few families. These groups would have individual clan *kivas* (the Hopi word for underground ceremonial chambers) or single great kivas.

The soaring cliff dwellings of Canyon de Chelly, Betatakin, Keet Seel, and Mesa Verde represented another type of settlement, more protected from the elements and, perhaps, from raiders. Villagers cultivated the land around them. All of these communities had kivas, ritual spaces central to the lives of deeply spiritual people.

Ancestral Pueblo culture reached its height about 1,000 years ago. Hitherto Puebloans had continued to refine their use of water, not actually irrigating but using sporadic rainfall to the greatest advantage. They would line stones across slopes and cut ditches to distribute rainfall and limit erosion. Occasionally they dug canals in order to channel rainwater into planted fields. Unquestionably, they were expert dry farmers, coaxing abundance out of a harsh environment.

At the time of this climax, some people began moving from smaller, widespread communities into larger, denser settlements—perhaps like today's migrations to cities. The volume of trade in nearly all directions was tremendous, and Pueblo artisans were making superb pottery. Decorative techniques varied from region to region: black-on-white, black-on-red, black-on-orange, red-on-orange, and expressive combinations of these. People also etched petroglyphs into, and painted pictograms onto, rock faces. Rock art is found at almost all Anasazi and Sinagua sites. The quantity of artifacts that they left behind—utility and ceremonial items alike—is unparalleled among native North American groups.

* * *

AROUND 850 YEARS AGO, a cultural decline began. Drought and climatic change put pressure on the Pueblos' settled, agricultural lifestyles. Longer winters shortened growing seasons in which less rain fell. Villagers continued to move to more productive areas. By the late 1200s, Canyon de Chelly was unoccupied. Chaco Canyon had been vacant for 100 years. Settlements at Wupatki continued a little longer, into the 1300s. The Hopi Mesas, on the other hand, first built in the 1100s, were growing. They absorbed some of their migrating neighbors, and their traditions testify to their assimilation of ancient Pueblo culture.

There are also a great number of transitional settlements, many yet to be excavated, that accommodated groups leaving the immediate Four Corners area. Some of them are quite substantial. Considering these transitional settlements, what used to be a question of a culture's simply disappearing can now take a more human shape. The Anasazi didn't vanish—they chose to move. Over a couple of centuries they gradually migrated to new locations, slightly altering their lifestyles. (For some of them, that may have been part of a centuries-old practice.) In the process they passed on their knowledge to the people they joined: the Hopi, the New Mexican Zuñi, the Acoma, and other Pueblos. The Zuñi perspective on this migration is telling. As opposed to archaeologists' causes—drought, climatic change, deforestation, disease, warfare—they see it as a process of searching for "the center place," a place of spiritual rightness. And that center place is where present-day Pueblos are living.

The Sinagua, their name meaning "without water" in Spanish, belonged to a diverse group called the Hakataya, spread out across central Arizona. Wupatki, Walnut Canyon, Tuzigoot, and the inappropriately named Montezuma Castle are all Sinagua sites. These people absorbed Hohokam, Mogollon, and Anasazi cultural patterns: agriculture, village life, and the Mesoamerican ball game; stone masonry and cliff-dwelling architecture; and pottery. Situated in the middle of these three groups, they became a composite but separate culture.

As the so-called Anasazi waned, Hopi and Navajo cultures grew. The Navajo, an Apachean group from the north, gradually migrated southward along the Rocky Mountains about 5,000 years ago and settled in unoccupied places around Pueblo villages. Hunting and gathering were just about all that the land would support for them. Over time they learned farming techniques from the Pueblos and traded with them and as a result took on a character distinct from other Apachean groups, such as the 19th-century Chiracahua and Mescalero Apache. Living in small, dispersed groups, Navajos also raided Pueblo farms and villages—a practice in retrospect notoriously Apachean.

Soon after the Navajo came the Spanish, invading the Southwest early in the 16th century. Unlike Anglo-European conquerors, they allowed elements of native cultures to survive, provided that they accept a transfusion of Catholicism and alien governance. Of course, their intrusion into Southwestern life was far from cordial. Their first contact was with New Mexican Pueblos, whose understandable lack of interest in accepting Spanish rule met with the sword. Pueblo retaliation brought further hostility from the invaders, who murdered hundreds of natives and destroyed villages.

The Spanish didn't have the chance to overrun the Apacheans, whose scattered settlements were more difficult to locate than were pueblos. After the Pueblo Revolt of 1680, which drove the Spanish away, only to have them return 12 years later, the Navajo periodically housed Pueblos seeking refuge from reprisals. In return, the Pueblos taught them rituals, customs, agricultural techniques, and arts—in some of which, like weaving, they eventually surpassed their teachers. In the 1700s, drought led many Hopis to seek refuge among the Navajo in the formerly vacated Canyon de Chelly—a poignant example of the longstanding cooperative relationship of the two groups.

The Navajo also picked up European skills, some of them from the Pueblos. Directly from the Spanish they learned about silversmithing, raising cattle, and riding horses—and they became superior horsemen. Horses extended their gathering range and gave them greater mobility for trading and raiding. The Navajo were not nomadic, however. Many of them had different seasonal residences, log-and-earth hogans, as they continue to do today. These are maintained as permanent dwellings.

After independent Mexico ceded New Mexico to the United States in 1848, the Southwest's new proprietors decided to put an end to Indian raids. Over the next 16 years U.S. troops and the Navajo clashed repeatedly. The United States set up army posts within Navajo territory. They attempted to impose treaties, but U.S. agents often arranged treaties with individual headmen who had no authority that the Navajo as a whole could accept.

This misunderstanding of Navajo organization had tragic results. When raids continued, the U.S. territorial governor believed he had been betrayed. In order to safeguard the so-called frontier, he called in Colonel Kit Carson to destroy Navajo crops and livestock. Over the next few months, the People, as the Navajo call themselves, began to give themselves up. In 1864, as many as 8,000 Navajo made the forced Long Walk to captivity in Fort Sumner, 300 mi to the southeast.

The People were allowed to return to their land after four years of concentration-camp life. Fewer in number and greatly demoralized, they had to reconstruct their lives from scratch, rebuilding customs and lifestyles that had been impossible, if not forbidden, in the camps. Since then, Navajo ingenuity and an impressive ability to seize opportunities have gained them a measure of success in modern America. Their democratically governed community— Navajo Nation—numbers more than 250,000.

* * *

THE HOPI DIDN'T SUFFER SUCH BRUTALITY. After conflicts with the Spanish—at the end of which they destroyed their own Christianized village of Awatovi in order to maintain the purity of Hopi ritual—their largely noncombative stance with the U.S. government afforded the Hopi more or less hands-off treatment.

In their proper observance of tradition and ritual, the Hopi are unique even among traditional Native Americans. In fact it was to Hopi spiritual leaders that many Native American traditionalists turned in the 1950s in what eventually became the Indian Unity Movement. Hopi beliefs focus on the relationship between the people, the land, and the Creator. In this strict moral order, prayer and ritual—which include the katsina rain power being

dances—are necessary to keep the natural cycle in motion and to ensure the flow of life-sustaining forces. The Earth is sacred, and they are its keepers.

The Hopi may well be the best dry farmers on the planet, successfully harvesting crops on a precarious 8 to 15 inches of rain per year—and no irrigation. Doubtless they manage this because they have perfected ancient Ancestral Pueblo techniques. The mesas on which they chose to live contain precious aquifers, particularly essential to life in such an arid territory. These vast water sources no doubt sustained them and their migrant guests when Pueblo peoples left places like Wupatki and Walnut Canyon and Canyon de Chelly 700 years ago. Unfortunately, the Hopi Tribal Council, which represents the progressive Christianized members of the Hopi, has sold sacred land to strip miners who in turn have destroyed parts of Black Mesa and depleted the aquifer. This is one indication of the rift between modernizers and those who continue to practice traditional ways. The traditionalists reside in the villages of Oraibi, Hotevilla, and Shungapovi. They are, understandably, intolerant of whites. They follow the Hopi Way even as contemporary life and the Tribal Council pose ever greater threats to it.

The present-day Tohono O'odham (called Papago by the Spanish) and the Pima, in central-southern Arizona, are descendants of the Hohokam. The Spanish first encountered them in the 17th century cultivating former Hohokam territory, using some of the ancient irrigation canals. Both tribes are Pimans, and both continue some Hohokam practices: living in rancherías along canals and performing costume dances and other rituals that link them to Uto-Aztecan language groups nearby in Mexico. The Pima live on the Salt River Reservation south of Phoenix, and the Tohono O'odham reservation stretches north from the Mexican border.

Like the Southwest's history, perspectives on Native American cultures are complex and fascinating—and have become confused in the clash of Euro-American and Native American ways. Take, for example, the enchanting and mysterious word *Anasazi,* which enters into almost any discussion of native Arizonans. This Navajo word, meaning both "ancient ones" and "enemy ancestors," automatically implies a Navajo perspective. Another of equal value is that of the Hopi, whose name for the ancient culture, *Hisatsinom,* means "people of long ago." Yet another perspective is that of the New Mexican Zuñi, who prefer the word *Enote:que,* "our ancient ones, our ancestors."

To scientifically trained Euro-American archaeologists, the term Anasazi conveniently groups together a variety of ancient Pueblo peoples who had similar lifestyles but often divergent adaptations to Southwestern conditions. In past decades researchers encouraged the myth of a lost Anasazi civilization and posed virtually unanswerable questions about who the people were and how and why they "vanished" from the scene. Had they taken the beliefs and statements of the Hopi and of New Mexican Pueblos seriously—acting as both archaeologists and anthropologists—the Hisatsinom–Enote:que–Anasazi would have fit seamlessly into the continuity of Native American life.

The perspective we can never know is that of the Ancestral Pueblos themselves—we don't even know what language they spoke. Yet we can try to get a sense of their world view by listening to contemporary Pueblos. If we project their uniquely American customs into the past, aspects of their ancestral culture come to life. And while Western tradition has its own ancient echoes, such as "know yourself" and "love your neighbor," traditional Pueblo ways speak of a life balanced in its relationship with the Earth.

Sources

What Happened to the Anasazi? Why Did They Leave? Where Did They Go?" A Panel Discussion at the Anasazi Heritage Center. Jerold G. Widdison, ed. Albuquerque: Southwest Natural and Cultural Heritage Association, 1990.

—Stephen Wolf

Stephen Wolf is a former Fodor's editor.

BOOKS & MOVIES

Books

Essays & Fiction. *Going Back to Bisbee,* by Richard Shelton, *Frog Mountain Blues,* by Charles Bowden, and *The Mountains Next Day,* by Janice Emily Bowers, are all fine personal accounts of life in southern Arizona. The hipster fiction classic *The Monkey Wrench Gang,* by Edward Abbey, details an eco-anarchist plot to blow up Glen Canyon Dam. *Stolen Gods,* a thriller by Jake Page, is set largely on Arizona's Hopi reservation and in Tucson. Fiction and essays by Tucson-based writers skillfully evoke the interplay between Native American culture and contemporary Southwest life: *Pigs in Heaven* and *High Tide in Tucson: Essays from Now or Never* by Barbara Kingsolver, *Almanac of the Dead,* by Leslie Marmon Silko, and *Yes Is Better Than No* by Byrd Baylor. Wild West adventure, with all of the mythological glory that Hollywood has tried to capture, abounds in Zane Grey's novels—buy a new copy or look for any of the charming illustrated hardcover editions in used- or out-of-print-book stores. Tony Hillerman's mysteries will put you in an equally Southwestern mood.

General History. *Arizona: A History,* by Thomas E. Sheridan, chronicles the Anglo, Mexican, and Native American frontier and details its transformation into the modern-day Sunbelt. *Arizona Cowboys,* by Dane Coolidge, is an illustrated account of the cowboys, Native Americans, settlers, and explorers of the early 1900s. Buried-treasure hunters will be inspired by *Lost Mines of the Great Southwest,* by John D. Mitchell, which is just enough of a nibble to start you sketching maps and planning strategy. First printed back in 1891, *Some Strange Corners of Our Country,* by Charles F. Lummis, takes readers on a century-old journey to the Grand Canyon, Montezuma Castle, the Petrified Forest, and other Arizonan "strange cor-

ners." For a dip into the back roads of the past, try *Arizona Good Roads Association Illustrated Road Maps and Tour Book,* a 1913 volume, replete with hotel ads, reprinted by *Arizona Highways* magazine. *Roadside History of Arizona,* by Marshall Trimble, will bring you up-to-date on many of the same thoroughfares. *Ghost Towns of Arizona,* by James E. and Barbara H. Sherman, gives historical details on the abandoned mining towns that dot the state and provides maps to find them. *The Great Arizona Orphan Abduction* by Linda Gordon tells the true story of the fate of 40 Irish orphans who were brought to the mining camps of Clifton and Morenci in 1904 and *Raising Arizona's Dams: Daily Life, Danger, and Discrimination in the Dam Construction Camps of Central Arizona, 1890s–1940s* by A. E. Rogge, D. Lorne McWatters, Melissa Keane, and Richard P. Emanuel, is an excellent history of the taming of the Salt River. *The Lunch Tree,* by Irene Cornwall Cofer, presents an intimate glimpse into the lives of pioneer women who settled along the Big Sandy River in western Arizona. For an anthology that covers the entire state's literature, consult *Named in Stone and Sky: An Arizona Anthology* edited by Gregory McNamee. For a sense of the Grand Canyon's mystery and allure, read *Sunk Without a Sound: The Tragic Colorado River Honeymoon of Glen and Bessie Hyde* by Brad Dimock.

Native American History. Two books provide excellent surveys of the ancient and more recent Native American past and cover in more depth sites mentioned in this guidebook. *Those Who Came Before: Southwestern Archaeology in the National Park System,* by Robert Lister and Florence Lister, provides a well-researched and completely accessible summary of centuries of life in the region informed by both contemporary Indian and archaeological perspectives. David G. Noble's *Ancient Ruins of the Southwest* covers similar territory more briefly and portably and includes directions for driving to sites. *Hohokam Indians of the Tucson Basin,* by Linda Gregonis, offers an in-depth look at this prehistoric tribe. In *Hopi,* by Susanne Page and Jake Page, the daily, ceremonial, and spiritual life of the tribe is explored in detail. Study up on the history of Hopi silversmithing techniques in *Hopi Silver,* by Margaret Wright. The beautifully illustrated *Hopi Indian Kachina Dolls,* by Oscar T. Branson, details the different ceremonial roles of the colorful Native American figurines. Navajo homes, ceremonies, crafts, and tribal traditions are kept alive in *The Enduring Navajo,* by Laura Gilpin. Navajo legends and trends from early days to the present are collected in *The Book of the Navajo,* by Raymond F. Locke.

A superb collection of Native American stories, songs, and poems, *Coming to Light,* edited by Brian Swann, includes material from all over the country, not only the Southwest. *Paths of Life: American Indians of the Southwest and Northern Mexico,* edited by Thomas E. Sheridan and Nancy J. Parezo, offers both contemporary and historical portraits of Native Americans.

Natural History. *The Arizona Sonora Desert Museum Book of Answers,* by David Lazaroff, covers hundreds of frequently asked natural-history questions. *Gathering the Desert,* by Gary Paul Nabhan, explores the Southwest from an ethnobotanist's viewpoint. *A Guide to Exploring Oak Creek and the Sedona Area,* by Stewart Aitchison, provides natural-history driving tours of this very scenic district. In *100 Desert Wildflowers in Natural Color,* by Natt N. Dodge, you'll find a color photo and brief description of each of the flowers included. Also written by Natt N. Dodge, *Poisonous Dwellers of the Desert* gives precise information on both venomous and nonvenomous creatures of the Southwest. *Venomous Animals of Arizona,* by Robert L. Smith, offers detailed information on venomous creatures of the Southwest. *Cacti of the Southwest,* by W. Hubert Earle, depicts some of the best-known species of the region with color photos and descriptive material. For comprehensive information on Grand Canyon geology, history, flora, and fauna, plus hiking suggestions, pick up *A Field Guide to the Grand Canyon,* by Steve Whitney. *Grand Canyon Country: Its Majesty and Lore,* by Seymour L. Fishbein, published by National Geographic Books, describes the Grand Canyon through photographs, maps, and firsthand accounts. *Common Edible and Useful Plants of the West,* by Muriel Sweet, gives the layperson descriptions of medicinal and other plants and shrubs, most of which were first discovered by Native Americans. *Roadside Geology of Arizona,* by Halka Chronic, is a good resource for finding the causes of the striking natural formations you'll see throughout the state. The *Arizona Breeding Bird Atlas,* edited by Troy E. Corman and Cathryn Wise-Gervais is a marvelous addition to the reference collection of any serious birder who visits Arizona.

Crafts. *The Traveler's Guide to American Crafts: West of the Mississippi,* by Suzanne Carmichael, gives browsers and buyers alike a useful overview of Arizona's traditional and contemporary handiwork.

General Interest. *Arizona Highways,* a monthly magazine, features exquisite color photography of this versatile state. Useful general travel information, fine pictures, and well-written historical essays all make the book *Arizona,* by Larry Cheek, a good pretrip resource.

Movies
The Arizona landscape has starred in a slew of films either as itself or as a stand-in for similar terrain—the Sahara, for instance—around the world. *The Postman* (1997), starring Kevin Costner, and *Buffalo Soldiers* (1997), starring Danny Glover, were filmed around Tucson. The Titan Missile Base near Green Valley was the locale for filming parts of *Star Trek:*

First Contact (1996). *Mars Attacks!* (1997), starring Jack Nicholson, Glenn Close, and Michael J. Fox was filmed on the dry plain of Red Lake near Kingman. Sun Devil Stadium in Tempe and Lost Dutchman State Park were featured in the blockbuster hit *Jerry Maguire* (1996). Parts of the Kevin Costner comedy *Tin Cup* (1996) were shot in Tubac. Much of director John Woo's bombastic *Broken Arrow* (1996), starring John Travolta and Christian Slater, was shot around Marble Canyon, which was also used, along with the Page–Lake Powell area, in the Mel Gibson–Jodie Foster vehicle *Maverick* (1994). Tom Hanks trotted through Monument Valley and Flagstaff in *Forrest Gump* (1994). Parts of Casa Grande were a stand-in Iraq in *Three Kings* (1999). The Tucson area served as the backdrop for much of *Boys on the Side* (1995), starring Whoopi Goldberg, Drew Barrymore, and Mary-Louise Parker. The nouveau Westerns *Tombstone* (1993), starring Val Kilmer and Kurt Russell, and Sharon Stone's *The Quick and the Dead* (1995) both made use of various sites in Mescal. Woody Harrelson and Juliette Lewis raged through Holbrook, Winslow, and other towns in *Natural Born Killers* (1994), and the Yuma area was used to otherworldly effect in the science-fiction film *Stargate* (1994). The remake of *The Getaway* (1994) was filmed in several Arizona locations including Phoenix, Yuma, and Prescott. Yuma stands in for a lot of places, including Morocco in Joseph von Sternberg's *Morocco* (1930), starring the sultry Marlene Dietrich, and the Bob Hope comedy *Road to Morocco* (1942). Buster Keaton wrote, directed, and starred in *Go West* (1925), a charming early western filmed on what is now Grand Canyon West Ranch.

The famous canyon loomed large in *Grand Canyon* (1991), starring Kevin Kline, Steve Martin, and Danny Glover. The independent cult hit *Red Rock West* (1991), directed by John Dahl and starring Nicolas Cage, was filmed in Willcox and other southeastern Arizona locales. Cage also starred, with Holly Hunter, in *Raising Arizona* (1987). Footage for the Joel Coen–directed film was shot in Scottsdale, Phoenix, and other locations. Chevy Chase frolicked through the Grand Canyon, Monument Valley, and Flagstaff in *National Lampoon's Vacation* (1983). Clint Eastwood stared down all comers in *The Outlaw Josey Wales* (1976), which showcases Patagonia and Mescal. Italian director Michelangelo Antonioni's *Zabriskie Point* (1968) includes scenes of Carefree and Phoenix. Marilyn Monroe dropped in on Phoenix in *Bus Stop* (1956). Gerd Oswald's noirish *A Kiss Before Dying* (1955), starring Robert Wagner and Joanne Woodward, filmed in Tucson. Parts of *The Bells of St. Mary's* (1954) take place in Old Tucson. Some Arizona locations worked better than the real thing in Fred Zinnemann's *Oklahoma!* (1954). Jean Harlow whooped it up as a harried movie superstar in Victor Fleming's very funny *Bombshell* (1933), which has scenes shot in Tucson proper.

Among the many classic Westerns shot in Arizona are *How the West Was Won* (1962), directed by John Ford and others and with an all-star cast that included Henry Fonda, Gregory Peck, and James Stewart; *The Searchers* (1956), *She Wore a Yellow Ribbon* (1949), *Fort Apache* (1948), and *Stagecoach* (1939), all directed by John Ford and starring John Wayne, both of whom spent a lot of time filming in the state over the years; *Gunfight at the OK Corral* (1957), starring Burt Lancaster and Kirk Douglas; *Hombre* (1967), starring Paul Newman and Richard Boone; *Junior Bonner* (1972), directed by Sam Peckinpah and starring Steve McQueen; *Johnny Guitar* (1954), director Nicholas Ray's Freudian take on the Old West that features Joan Crawford in a gender-bending performance as a tough-gal gunslinger; director Howard Hawks's moody *Red River* (1948), which stars John Wayne and Montgomery Clift; and Ford's *My Darling Clementine* (1946), in which Henry Fonda plays a reluctant sheriff.

SMART TRAVEL TIPS

There are planners and there are those who, excuse the pun, fly by the seat of their pants. We happily place ourselves among the planners. Our writers and editors try to anticipate all the issues you may face before and during any journey, and then they do their research. This section is the product of their efforts. Use it to get excited about your trip to Arizona, to inform your travel planning, or to guide you on the road should the seat of your pants start to feel threadbare.

AIR TRAVEL

CARRIERS

Phoenix is a hub for Southwest Airlines. America West and US Airways have merged and Phoenix is a hub for the combined companies. These carriers offer the most direct flights in and out of Phoenix. Most of the country's other major airlines fly into Phoenix and have a few flights into Tucson as well; US Airways flies only to Phoenix.

Among the smaller airlines, ATA flies only to Phoenix. Frontier connects Phoenix to Denver and points beyond. Great Lakes Airlines flies to Phoenix and Page. Midwest Express connects Phoenix and Milwaukee.

Flying time to Phoenix or Tucson is 5½ hours from New York, 3½ hours from Chicago, 1¼ hours from Los Angeles, and 11 hours from London.

Within Arizona, America West Express/ Mesa Airlines (part of America Express) flies from Phoenix to Flagstaff, Prescott, Lake Havasu, Kingman, and Yuma. Great Lakes Airlines connects Phoenix and Page. Scenic Airlines flies from Las Vegas to the Grand Canyon.

🛫 Major Airlines **Alaska Airlines** ☎ 800/252-7522 or 206/433-3100 ⊕ www.alaskaair.com. **American Airlines** ☎ 800/433-7300 ⊕ www.aa.com. **America West** ☎ 800/235-9292 or 480/693-6701 ⊕ www.americawest.com. **ATA** ☎ 800/435-9282 or 317/282-8308 ⊕ www.ata.com. **Continental Airlines** ☎ 800/523-3273 for U.S. and Mexico reservations, 800/231-0856 for international reservations ⊕ www.continental.com. **Delta Airlines** ☎ 800/221-1212 for U.S. reservations, 800/241-4141 for international reservations ⊕ www.delta.com. **JetBlue** ☎ 800/538-2583 ⊕ www.jetblue.com. **Northwest Airlines** ☎ 800/225-2525 for U.S. reservations, 800/447-4747 for international destinations ⊕ www.nwa.com. **Southwest Airlines** ☎ 800/435-9792 ⊕ www.southwest.com. **United Airlines** ☎ 800/864-8331 for U.S. reservations, 800/538-2929 for international reservations ⊕ www.united.com. **USAirways** ☎ 800/428-4322 for U.S. and Canada reservations, 800/622-1015 for international reservations ⊕ www.usairways.com.

🎵 **Smaller Airlines AeroMexico** ☎ 800/800-9999 ⊕ www.aeromexico.com. **Frontier Airlines** ☎ 800/432-1359 ⊕ www.frontierairlines.com. **Great Lakes Airlines** ☎ 800/554-5111 ⊕ www.greatlakesav.com. **Midwest Express** ☎ 800/452-2022 ⊕ www.midwestexpress.com. **Scenic Airlines** ☎ 800/535-4448.

CHECK-IN & BOARDING

Despite its daily passenger volume, lengthy lines at the check-in counters and security checkpoints at Phoenix Sky Harbor are rarely a problem.

Double-check your flight times, especially if you made your reservations far in advance. Airlines change their schedules, and alerts may not reach you. Always **bring a government-issued photo ID to the airport** (even when it's not required, a passport is best), and **arrive when you need to and not before.** Check-in usually at least an hour before domestic flights and two to three hours for international flights. But many airlines have more stringent advance check-in requirements at some busy airports. The TSA estimates the waiting time for security at most major airports and publishes the information on its Web site. Note that if you aren't at your gate at least 10 minutes before your flight is scheduled to take off (sometimes earlier), you won't be allowed to board.

Don't stand in a line if you don't have to. Buy an e-ticket, check in at an electronic kiosk, or—even better—check in on your airline's Web site before you leave home. If you don't need to check luggage, you could bypass all but the security lines. These days, most domestic airline tickets are electronic; international tickets may be either electronic or paper.

You usually pay a surcharge (usually at least $25) to get a paper ticket, and its sole advantage is that it may be easier to endorse over to another airline if your flight is cancelled and the airline with which you booked can't accommodate you on another flight. With an e-ticket, the only thing you receive is an e-mailed receipt citing your itinerary and reservation and ticket numbers. Be sure to carry this with you as you'll need it to get past security. If you lose you receipt, though, you can simply print out another copy or ask the airline to do it for you at check-in.

Particularly during busy travel seasons and around holiday periods, if a flight is oversold, the gate agent will usually ask for volunteers and will offer some sort of compensation if you're willing to take a different flight. **Know your rights.** If you're bumped from a flight *involuntarily,* the airline must give you some kind of compensation if an alternate flight can't be found within one hour. If your flight is delayed because of something within the airline's control (so bad weather doesn't count), then the airline has a responsibility to get you to your destination on the same day, even if they have to book you on another airline and in an upgraded class if necessary. Read your airline's Contract of Carriage; it's usually buried somewhere on the airline's Web site.

Be prepared to quickly adjust your plans by programming a few numbers into your cell: your airline, an airport hotel or two, your destination hotel, your car service, and/or your travel agent. Bring snacks, water, and sufficient diversions, and you'll be covered if you get stuck in the airport, on the tarmac, or even in the air during turbulence.

CUTTING COSTS

It's always good to **comparison shop.** Web sites (aka consolidators) and travel agents can have different arrangements with the airlines and offer different prices for exactly the same flight and day. Certain Web sites have tracking features that will e-mail you immediately when good deals are posted. Other people prefer to stick with one or two frequent-flier programs, racking up free trips and accumulating perks that can make trips easier. On some airlines, perks include a special reservations number, early boarding, access to upgrades, and more roomy economy-class seating.

Check early and often. Start looking for cheap fares up to a year in advance, and keep looking until you see something you can live with; you never know when a good deal may pop up. That said, **jump on the good deals.** Waiting even a few minutes might mean paying more. For most people, saving money is more important than flexibility, so the more affordable nonrefundable tickets work. Just remember that you'll pay dearly (often as much as $100) if you must change your travel plans. Check on prices for departures at different times of the day and to and from alternate airports, and look for departures on Tuesday, Wednesday, and Thursday, typically the cheapest days to travel. Remember to **weigh your options,** though. A cheaper flight might have a long layover rather than being nonstop, or landing at a secondary airport might substantially increase your ground transportation costs.

Note that many airline Web sites—and most ads—show prices *without* taxes and surcharges. Don't buy until you know the full price. Government taxes add up quickly. Also **watch those ticketing fees.** Surcharges are usually added when you buy your ticket anywhere but on an airline's own Web site. (By the way, that includes on the phone—even if you call the airline directly—and for paper tickets regardless of how you book).

📶 **Online Consolidators AirlineConsolidator.com** ⊕ www.airlineconsolidator.com, for international tickets. **Best Fares** ⊕ www.bestfares.com; $59.90 annual membership. **Cheap Tickets** ⊕ www. cheaptickets.com. **Expedia** ⊕ www.expedia.com. **Hotwire** ⊕ www.hotwire.com. **lastminute.com** ⊕ www.lastminute.com specializes in last-minute travel; the main site is for the U.K., but it has a link to a U.S. site. **Luxury Link** ⊕ www.luxurylink.com has auctions (surprisingly good deals) as well as offers at the high-end side of travel. **Orbitz** ⊕ www.

orbitz.com. **Onetravel.com** ⊕ www.onetravel.com. **Priceline.com** ⊕ www.priceline.com. **Travelocity** ⊕ www.travelocity.com.

ENJOYING THE FLIGHT

Get the seat you want. Avoid those on the aisle directly across from the lavatories. Most frequent fliers say those are even worse than the seats that don't recline (e.g., those in the back row and those in front of a bulkhead). For more legroom, you can request emergency-aisle seats, but only do so if you're capable of moving the 35- to 60-pound airplane exit door—a Federal Aviation Administration requirement of passengers in these seats. Seats behind a bulkhead also offer more legroom, but they don't have under-seat storage. Often you can pick a seat when you buy your ticket on an airline's Web site. But it's not always a guarantee, particularly if the airline changes the plane after you book your ticket; check back before you leave. Seat-Guru.com has more information about specific seat configurations, which vary by aircraft.

Fewer airlines are providing free food for passengers in economy class. **Don't go hungry.** If you're scheduled to fly during meal times, verify if your airline offers anything to eat; even when it does, be prepared to pay. If you have dietary concerns, request special meals. These can be vegetarian, low-cholesterol, or kosher, for example. It's a good idea to pack some healthful snacks and a small (plastic) bottle of water in your carry-on bag.

Ask the airline about its children's menus, activities, and fares. On some lines infants and toddlers fly for free if they sit on a parent's lap, and older children fly for half price in their own seats. Also ask about policies involving car seats; having one may limit where you can sit. While you're at it, ask about seatbelt extenders for carseats. And note that you can't count on a flight attendant to automatically produce an extender; you may have to inquire about it again when you board.

HOW TO COMPLAIN

If your baggage goes astray or your flight goes awry, complain right away. Most carriers require that you **file a claim immediately.** The Aviation Consumer Protection Division of the Department of Transportation publishes *Fly-Rights,* which discusses airlines and consumer issues and is available online. You can also find articles and information on ⊕ mytravelrights.com, the Web site of the nonprofit Consumer Travel Rights Center.

🔃 Airline Complaints **Office of Aviation Enforcement and Proceedings** (Aviation Consumer Protection Division) ☎ 202/366–2220 ⊕ airconsumer.ost. dot.gov. **Federal Aviation Administration Consumer Hotline** ☎ 866/835–5322 ⊕ www.faa.gov.

AIRPORTS

Major gateways to Arizona include Phoenix Sky Harbor International (PHX), about 3 mi east of Phoenix city center, and Tucson International Air Terminal (TUS), about 8½ mi south of the central business area.

Phoenix Sky Harbor International Airport is the fifth-busiest airport in the world for takeoffs and landings but rarely gives way to congestion or lengthy lines, and its spacious, modern terminals are easily navigable. Sky Harbor's three passenger terminals are connected by inter-terminal buses, which run regularly throughout the day. Tucson International Airport has one terminal, and although it services far fewer passengers per day than Sky Harbor, it does offer nonstop flights to major metropolitan areas around the country.

Long layovers don't have to be only about sitting around or shopping. These days they can be about burning off vacation calories. Check out ⊕ www.airportgyms. com for lists of health clubs that are in or near many U.S. and Canadian airports.

🔃 Airlines & Airports **Airline and Airport Links. com** ⊕ www.airlineandairportlinks.com has links to many of the world's airlines and airports. **Phoenix Sky Harbor International** ☎ 602/273–3300 ⊕ www.phxskyharbor.com. **Tucson International Airport** ☎ 520/573–8000 ⊕ www. tucsonairport.org.

🔃 Airline Security Issues **Transportation Security Agency** ⊕ www.tsa.gov/public has answers for almost every question that might come up.

BUS TRAVEL

Greyhound serves many Arizona destinations from most parts of the United States but does not serve any destinations on the Navajo and Hopi reservations in northeastern Arizona.

🔃 Bus Information **Greyhound Lines** ☎ 800/231–2222 ⊕ www.greyhound.com.

BUSINESS HOURS

MUSEUMS & SIGHTS

Most museums in Arizona's larger cities are open daily. A few are closed on Monday, and hours may vary between May and September (off-season in the major tourist centers of Phoenix and Tucson). Call ahead when planning a visit to lesser-known museums or attractions, whose hours may vary considerably. Major attractions are open daily.

SHOPS

Most retail stores are open 10 AM to 6 PM, although stores in malls tend to stay open until 9 PM. Those in the less-populated areas are likely to have shorter hours and may be closed on Sunday. Shopping centers, especially in larger cities, are also often open Sunday from noon to 5 or later.

CAR RENTAL

Rates in Phoenix begin around $25 a day and $165 a week for an economy car with air-conditioning, automatic transmission, and unlimited mileage. This does not include taxes and fees on car rentals, which can range from 16% to 46%, depending on pickup location. The base tax rate at Sky Harbor Airport is about 30%. When you add the daily fees (which are about $5 a day), the taxes and fees can add up to almost half the cost of the car rental. You may be able to save by taking a cab to a retail location nearby, where you avoid the airport tax and additional daily fees. Taxes outside of the airport are typically around 25% or less.

Request car seats and extras such as GPS when you book, and make sure that a confirmed reservation guarantees you a car. Agencies sometimes overbook, particularly for busy weekends and holiday periods. Rates are sometimes—but not always—better if you book in advance or reserve through a rental agency's Web site. There are other reasons to book ahead, though: for popular destinations, during busy times of the year, or to ensure that you get a certain type of car (vans, SUVs, exotic sports cars).

Rates in Phoenix may be higher during the winter months, which is considered the high tourist season. Check the Internet or local papers for discounts and deals, as they can significantly lower rental rates. Local rental agencies may also offer lower rates.

In Arizona most agencies won't rent to you if you're under the age of 21, and several major agencies will not rent to anyone under 25.

CUTTING COSTS

Really weigh your options. Find out if a credit card you carry or organization or frequent-renter program to which you belong has a discount program. And check that such discounts really are the best deal. You can often do better with special weekend or weekly rates offered by a rental agency. (And even if you only want to rent for five or six days, ask if you can get the weekly rate; it may very well be cheaper than the daily rate for that period of time.)

Price local car-rental companies as well as the majors. Also investigate wholesalers, which don't own fleets but rent in bulk from those that do and often offer better rates (note you must usually pay for such rentals before leaving home). Consider adding a car rental onto your air/hotel vacation package; the cost will often be cheaper than if you had rented the car separately on your own.

When traveling abroad, **look for guaranteed exchange rates,** which protect you against a falling dollar. With your rate locked in, you won't pay more, even if the price goes up in the local currency. (Note to self: not the best thing if the dollar is surging rather than plunging.)

Beware of hidden charges. Those great rental rates may not be so great when you add in taxes, surcharges, cancellation penalties, taxes, drop-off charges (if you're planning to pick up the car in one city and

leave it in another), and surcharges (for being under or over a certain age, for additional drivers, or for driving over state or country borders or out of a specific radius from your point of rental).

Note that airport rental offices often add supplementary surcharges that you may avoid by renting from an agency whose office is just off airport property. Don't buy the tank of gas that's in the car when you rent it unless you plan to do a lot of driving. Avoid hefty refueling fees by filling the tank at a station well away from the rental agency (those nearby are often more expensive) just before you turn in the car.

🔢 Local Agencies **ABC Rent-A-Car** ☎ 602/681-9000 or 888/899-9997 ⊕ www.abc-rentacar.com. **Airport Rent-A-Car** ☎ 602/267-9100 or 800/347-4030. **Arizona Auto Rental** ☎ 520/624-4548. **American Roadrunner Car Rental** ☎ 520/747-3825. **Tucson Auto Rental** ☎ 520/622-7700. 🔢 Major Agencies **Alamo** ☎ 800/462-5266 ⊕ www.alamo.com. **Avis** ☎ 800/230-4898 ⊕ www.avis.com. **Budget** ☎ 800/527-0700 ⊕ www.budget.com. **Hertz** ☎ 800/654-3131 ⊕ www.hertz.com. **National Car Rental** ☎ 800/227-7368 ⊕ www.nationalcar.com.

INSURANCE

Everyone who rents a car wonders about whether the insurance that the rental companies offer is worth the expense. No one—not even us—has a simple answer. It all depends on how much regular insurance you have, how comfortable you are with risk, and whether or not money is an issue.

If you own a car and carry comprehensive car insurance for both collision and liability, your personal auto insurance will probably cover a rental, but read your policy's fine print to be sure. If you don't have auto insurance, then you should probably buy the collision- or loss-damage waiver (CDW or LDW) from the rental company. This eliminates your liability for damage to the car. Some credit cards offer CDW coverage, but it's usually supplemental to your own insurance and rarely covers SUVs, minivans, luxury models and the like. If your coverage is secondary, you may still be liable for loss-of-use costs from the car-rental company (again, read the fine print). But no credit-card insurance is valid unless you use that card for *all* transactions, from reserving to paying the final bill.

You may also be offered supplemental liability coverage; the car-rental company is required to carry a minimal level of liability coverage that covers all renters, but it's rarely enough to cover claims in a really serious accident if you're at fault. Your own auto insurance policy will protect you if you own a car; if you don't, you have to decide if you're willing to take the risk.

U.S. rental companies sell CDWs and LDWs for about $15 to $25 a day; supplemental liability is usually over $10 a day. The car-rental company may offer you all sorts of other policies, but they're rarely worth the cost. Personal accident insurance, which is basic hospitalization coverage, is an especially egregious rip-off if you already have health insurance.

Note that you can decline the insurance from the rental company and purchase it through a third-party provider such as Travel Guard (www.travelguard.com)—$9 per day for $35,000 of coverage, which is sometimes just under half the price of the CDW offered by some car-rental companies. Also, Diners Club offers primary CDW coverage on all rentals reserved and paid for with the card. This means that Diners Club's company—not your own car insurance—pays in case of an accident. It *doesn't* mean your car-insurance company won't raise your rates once it discovers you had an accident.

In Arizona the car-rental agency's insurance is primary; therefore, the company must pay for damage to third parties up to a preset legal limit, beyond which your own liability insurance kicks in.

CAR TRAVEL

The highways in Arizona are well maintained, but there are some natural conditions to keep in mind.

Desert heat. Vehicles and passengers should be well equipped for searing summer heat in the low desert. If you're planning to drive through the desert, make sure you are well stocked with radiator coolant, and **carry plenty of water, a good spare tire, a jack, a cell phone, and emergency supplies.** If you get stranded, stay with your vehicle and wait for help to arrive.

Dust storms. These usually occur from May to mid-September, causing extremely low visibility. Dust storms are more common on the highways and interstates that traverse the open desert (Interstate 10 between Phoenix and Tucson, Interstate 10 between Benson and the New Mexico state line, and Interstate 8 between Casa Grande and Yuma). If you're on the highway, **pull as far off the road as possible, turn off your headlights to avoid being hit, and wait for the storm to subside.**

Flash floods. Warnings about flash floods should not be taken lightly. Sudden downpours send torrents of water racing into low-lying areas so dry that they are unable to absorb such a huge quantity of water quickly. The result can be powerful walls of water suddenly descending upon these low-lying areas, devastating anything in their paths. If you see rain clouds or thunderstorms in the area, stay away from dry riverbeds (also called arroyos or washes). If you find yourself in one, get out quickly. If you're with a car in a long gully, leave your car and climb out of the gully. You simply won't be able to outdrive a speeding wave. The idea is to **get to higher ground immediately when it rains.** Major highways are mostly flood-proof, but some smaller roads dip through washes; most roads that traverse through these low-lying areas will have flood warning signs, which should be seriously heeded during rainstorms. Washes filled with water should not be crossed until you can see the bottom. By all means, don't camp in these areas at any time, interesting as they may seem.

Fragile desert life. The dry and easily desecrated desert floor takes centuries to overcome human damage. Consequently, it's illegal for four-wheel-drive and all-terrain vehicles and motorcycles to travel off established roadways.

Many stretches on Arizona interstates have 75 mph speed limits. In cities, freeway limits are between 55 mph and 65 mph. Seat belts are required at all times. Tickets can be given for failing to comply. Driving with a blood-alcohol level higher than 0.08 will result in arrest and seizure of your driver's license. Fines are severe.

At some point you will probably pass through one or more of the state's 23 Indian reservations. Roads and other areas within reservation boundaries are under the jurisdiction of reservation police and governed by separate rules and regulations. **Observe all signs and respect Native Americans' privacy.** Be careful not to hit any animals, which often wander onto the roads; the penalties can be very high.

Always **strap children under age five into approved child-safety seats.** In Arizona, children must wear seat belts regardless of where they're seated. In Arizona, you may turn right at a red light after stopping if there's no oncoming traffic. When in doubt, wait for the green.

Arizona Department of Public Safety 602/223-2000, 602/223-2163 Highway Patrol. **Arizona Department of Transportation** 511 Arizona road information from within Arizona, 888/411-7623 Arizona road information from outside state www.az511.com.

EATING OUT

Two distinct cultures—Native American and Sonoran—have had the greatest influence on native Arizona cuisine. Chiles, beans, corn, tortillas, and squash are common ingredients for those restaurants that specialize in regional cuisine (cactus is just as tasty but less common). Mom-and-pop *taquerias* are abundant, especially in the southern part of the state.

MEALS & MEALTIMES

Unless otherwise noted, the restaurants listed in this guide are open daily for lunch and dinner.

PAYING

For guidelines on tipping, *see* Tipping *below.*

RESERVATIONS & DRESS

Regardless of where you are, it's a good idea to make a reservation if you can. In some places (Hong Kong, for example), it's expected. We only mention specifically when reservations are essential (there's no other way you'll ever get a table) or when they are not accepted. For popular restaurants, book as far ahead as you can (often 30 days), and reconfirm as soon as you arrive. (Large parties should always call ahead to check the reservations policy.) We mention dress only when men are required to wear a jacket or a jacket and tie.

WINE, BEER & SPIRITS

Although Arizona is not typically associated with viticulture, the region southeast of Tucson, stretching to the Mexico border, has several microclimates ideal for wine growing. The iron- and calcium-rich soil is similar to that of the Burgundy region in France and, when combined with the temperate weather and lower-key atmosphere, has enticed several independent and family-run wineries to open in the past few decades in the Elgin, Sonoita, and Nogales areas.

In Arizona, you must be 21 to buy any alcohol. Liquor stores are open daily, including Sunday, but must stop selling alcohol at 2 AM; bars also stop serving alcohol at this time. In many municipalities, including Phoenix and Flagstaff, smoking is prohibited in restaurants and bars. You'll find beer, wine, and alcohol at most supermarkets. Possession and consumption of alcoholic beverages is illegal on Indian reservations.

Was the service stellar or not up to snuff? Did the food give you shivers of delight or leave you cold? Did the prices and portions make you happy or sad? Rate restaurants and write your own reviews in Travel Ratings or start a discussion about your favorite places in Travel Talk on www.fodors.com. Your comments might even appear in our books. Yes, you, too, can be a correspondent!

Arizona Wine Growers Association www.arizonawine.org. **Callaghan Vineyards** 520/455-5322 www.callaghanvineyards.com. **Sonoita Vineyards** 520/455-5893 www.sonoitavineyards.com. **The Village of Elgin Winery** 520/455-9309 www.elginwines.com.

HEALTH
ANIMAL BITES
Wherever you're walking in desert areas, particularly between April and October, **keep a lookout for rattlesnakes.** You're likely not to have any problems if you maintain distance from snakes that you see—they can strike only half of their length, so a 6-foot clearance should allow you to stay unharmed, especially if you don't provoke them. If you are bitten by a rattler, don't panic. Get to a hospital within two to three hours of the bite. Try to keep the area that has been bitten below heart level, and stay calm, as increased heart rate can spread venom more quickly. Keep in mind that 30% to 40% of bites are dry bites, where the snake uses no venom (still, get thee to a hospital). **Avoid night hikes without rangers,** when snakes are on the prowl and less visible.

Scorpions and Gila monsters are really less of a concern, since they strike only when provoked. To avoid scorpion encounters, don't put your hands where you can't see with your eyes, such as under rocks and in holes. Likewise, if you move a rock to sit down, make sure that scorpions haven't been exposed. Campers should shake out shoes in the morning, since scorpions like warm, moist places. If you're bitten, see a ranger about symptoms that may develop. Chances are good that you won't need to go to a hospital. Children are a different case, however: scorpion stings can be fatal for them. Always try to keep an eye on what they may be getting their hands into to avoid the scorpion's sting. Gila monsters are relatively rare and bites are even rarer, but bear in mind that the reptiles are most active between April and June, when they do most of their hunting. Should a member of your party be bitten, it is most important to release the Gila monster's jaws as soon as possible to minimize the amount of venom released. This can usually be achieved with a stick, an open flame, or immersion of the animal in water.

DEHYDRATION
This underestimated danger can be very serious, especially considering that one of the first major symptoms is the inability to swallow. It may be the easiest hazard to avoid, however; simply **drink every 10–15 minutes,** up to a gallon of water per day in summer. Always carry a water bottle, and replenish frequently, whether hiking, walking in the city, or at an outdoor sports or arts event.

HYPOTHERMIA
Temperatures in Arizona can vary widely from day to night—as much as 40°F. Be sure to **bring enough warm clothing for hiking and camping, along with wet-weather gear.** It's always a good idea to pack an extra set of clothes in a large, waterproof plastic bag (a large resealable bag will do) that would stay dry in any situation. Exposure to the degree that body temperature dips below 95°F produces the following symptoms: chills, tiredness, then uncontrollable shivering and irrational behavior, with the victim not always recognizing that he or she is cold. If someone in your party is suffering from any of this, wrap him or her in blankets and/or a warm sleeping bag immediately and try to keep him or her awake. The fastest way to raise body temperature is through skin-to-skin contact in a sleeping bag. Drinking warm liquids also helps.

SUN EXPOSURE
Wear a hat and sunglasses and put on sunblock to protect against the burning Arizona sun. And **watch out for heatstroke.** Symptoms include headache, dizziness, and fatigue, which can turn into convulsions and unconsciousness and can lead to death. If someone in your party develops any of these conditions, have one person seek emergency help while others move the victim into the shade and wrap him or her in wet clothing (is a stream nearby?) to cool him or her down.

INSURANCE
What kind of coverage do you honestly need? Do you even need trip insurance at all? Take a deep breath and read on.

We believe that comprehensive trip insurance is especially valuable if you're booking a very expensive or complicated trip (particularly to an isolated region) or if you're booking far in advance. Who knows what could happen six months down the road? But whether you get insurance has more to do with how comfortable you are assuming all that risk yourself.

Comprehensive travel policies typically cover trip-cancellation and interruption, letting you cancel or cut your trip short because of a personal emergency, illness, or, in some cases, acts of terrorism in your destination. Such policies also cover evacuation and medical care. Some also cover you for trip delays because of bad weather or mechanical problems as well as for lost or delayed baggage. Another type of coverage to look for is financial default—that is, when your trip is disrupted because a tour operator, airline, or cruise line goes out of business. Generally you must buy this when you book your trip or shortly thereafter, and it's only available to you if your operator isn't on a list of excluded companies.

If you're going abroad, consider buying medical-only coverage at the very least. Neither Medicare nor some private insurers cover medical expenses anywhere outside of the United States besides Mexico and Canada (including time aboard a cruise ship, even if it leaves from a U.S. port). Medical-only policies typically reimburse you for medical care (excluding that related to preexisting conditions) and hospitalization abroad and provide for evacuation. You still have to pay the bills and await reimbursement from the insurer, though.

Expect comprehensive travel insurance policies to cost about 4% to 7% of the total price of your trip (it's more like 12% if you're over age 70). A medical-only policy may or may not be cheaper than a comprehensive policy. Always read the fine print of your policy to make sure that you're covered for the risks that are of the most concern to you. Compare several policies to make sure you're getting the best price and range of coverage available.

Just as an aside: you know you can save a bundle on trips to warm-weather destinations by traveling in rainy season. But there's also a chance that a severe storm will disrupt your plans. The solution? Look for hotels and resorts that offer storm/hurricane guarantees. Although they rarely allow refunds, most guarantees do let you rebook later if a storm strikes.

🔊 Insurance Comparison Sites **Insure My Trip. com** ⊕ www.insuremytrip.com. **Square Mouth.com** ⊕ www.quotetravelinsurance.com.

🔊 Comprehensive Travel Insurers **Access America** ☎ 866/807-3982 ⊕ www.accessamerica.com. **CSA Travel Protection** ☎ 800/729-6021 ⊕ www. csatravelprotection.com. **HTH Worldwide** ☎ 610/ 254-8700 or 888/243-2358 ⊕ www.hthworldwide. com. **Travelex Insurance** ☎ 888/457-4602 ⊕ www.travelex-insurance.com. **Travel Guard International** ☎ 715/345-0505 or 800/826-4919 ⊕ www.travelguard.com. **Travel Insured International** ☎ 800/243-3174 ⊕ www.travelinsured.com.

🔊 Medical-Only Insurers **Wallach & Company** ☎ 800/237-6615 or 504/687-3166 ⊕ www.wallach. com. **International Medical Group** ☎ 800/628-4664 ⊕ www.imglobal.com. **International SOS** ☎ 215/942-8000 or 713/521-7611 ⊕ www. internationalsos.com.

FOR INTERNATIONAL TRAVELERS

CURRENCY

The dollar is the basic unit of U.S. currency. It has 100 cents. Coins are the penny (1¢); the nickel (5¢), dime (10¢), quarter (25¢), and half-dollar (50¢); and the very rare golden $1 coin and even rarer silver $1. Bills are denominated $1, $5, $10, $20, $50, and $100, all mostly green and identical in size; designs and background tints vary. You may come across a $2 bill, but the chances are slim.

CUSTOMS

🔊 U.S. Customs and Border Protection ⊕ www. cbp.gov.

DRIVING

Driving in the United States is on the right. Speed limits are posted in miles per hour along roads and highways (usually between 55 mph and 70 mph). Watch for lower limits in small towns and on back roads (usually 30 mph to 40 mph). Most states require front-seat passengers to wear seat belts; many states require children to sit in the back seat and to wear seat belts. In major cities, rush hour is between 7 and

10 AM; afternoon rush hour is between between 4 and 7 PM expect heavy traffic. To encourage carpooling, some freeways have special lanes for so-called high-occupancy vehicles (HOV)—cars carrying more than one passenger, ordinarily marked with a diamond.

Highways are well paved. Interstate highways—limited-access, multilane highways whose numbers are prefixed by "I–"—are the fastest routes. Interstates with three-digit numbers encircle urban areas, which may have other limited-access expressways, freeways, and parkways as well. Tolls may be levied on limited-access highways. So-called U.S. highways and state highways are not necessarily limited-access but may have several lanes.

Gas stations are plentiful. Most stay open late (24 hours along large highways and in big cities), except in rural areas, where Sunday hours are limited and where you may drive long stretches without a refueling opportunity. Along larger highways, roadside stops with restrooms, fast-food restaurants, and sundries stores are well spaced. State police and tow trucks patrol major highways and lend assistance. If your car breaks down on an interstate, pull onto the shoulder and wait for help, or have your passengers wait while you walk to an emergency phone (available in most states). If you carry a cell phone, dial *55, noting your location on the small green roadside mileage markers.

To encourage carpooling, some freeways have special lanes for so-called high-occupancy vehicles (HOV)—cars carrying more than one passenger.

Bookstores, gas stations, convenience stores, and rest stops sell maps (about $3) and multiregion road atlases (about $10).

ELECTRICITY

The U.S. standard is AC, 110 volts/60 cycles. Plugs have two flat pins set parallel to each other.

EMERGENCIES

For police, fire, or ambulance dial 911 (0 in rural areas).

HOLIDAYS

Major national holidays are New Year's Day (Jan. 1); Martin Luther King Day (3rd Mon. in Jan.); Presidents' Day (3rd Mon. in Feb.); Memorial Day (last Mon. in May); Independence Day (July 4); Labor Day (1st Mon. in Sept.); Columbus Day (2nd Mon. in Oct.); Thanksgiving Day (4th Thurs. in Nov.); Christmas Eve and Christmas Day (Dec. 24 and 25); and New Year's Eve (Dec. 31).

MAIL

You can buy stamps and aerograms and send letters and parcels in post offices. Stamp-dispensing machines can occasionally be found in airports, bus and train stations, office buildings, drugstores, and the like. U.S. mail boxes are stout, dark blue, steel bins at strategic locations in major cities; pickup schedules are posted inside the bin (pull down the handle to see them). Parcels more than 1 pound must be mailed at a post office or at a private mailing center.

Within the United States, a first-class letter weighing 1 ounce or less costs 39¢, and each additional ounce costs 24¢; postcards cost 24¢. A 1-ounce airmail letter to most countries costs 84¢, an airmail postcard costs 75¢; to Canada and Mexico, a 1-ounce letter costs 63¢, a postcard 55¢. An aerogram—a single sheet of lightweight blue paper that folds into its own envelope, stamped for overseas airmail—costs 75¢ regardless of its destination.

To receive mail on the road, have it sent c/o General Delivery at your destination's main post office (use the correct five-digit ZIP code). You must pick up mail in person within 30 days and show a driver's license or passport.

DHL ☎ 800/225-5345 ⊕ www.dhl.com. **Federal Express** ☎ 800/463-3339 ⊕ www.fedex.com. **Mail Boxes, Etc.** (The UPS Store) ⊕ www.mbe.com. **United States Postal Service** ⊕ www.usps.com.

PASSPORTS & VISAS

Visitor visas aren't necessary for citizens of Australia, Canada, the United Kingdom, as well as for most citizens of European Union countries if you're coming for tourism and staying for fewer than 90 days. If you require a visa, the cost is $100 and, depending on where you live, the waiting time can be substantial. Apply for a visa at the U.S. consulate in your place of residence; look at the U.S. State Department's special Visa Web site for further information.

🛅 Visa Information **Destination USA** ⊕ www.unitedstatesvisas.gov.

PHONES

All U.S. telephone numbers consist of a three-digit area code and a seven-digit local number. Within many local calling areas, you dial only the seven-digit number; in others, you must dial "1" first and then the area code. To call between area-code regions, dial "1" then all 10 digits; the same goes for calls to numbers prefixed by "800," "888," "866," and "877"—all toll free. For calls to numbers preceded by "900" you must pay—usually dearly.

For international calls, dial "011" followed by the country code and the local number. For help, dial "0" and ask for an overseas operator. The country code is 61 for Australia, 64 for New Zealand, 44 for the United Kingdom. Calling Canada is the same as calling within the United States. Most phone books list country codes and U.S. area codes. The country code for the United States is 1.

For operator assistance, dial "0." To obtain someone's phone number, call directory assistance at 555–1212 or occasionally 411 (free at many public phones). You can reverse the charges on a long-distance call if phone "collect"; dial "0" instead of "1" before the 10-digit number.

At pay phones, instructions often are posted. Usually you insert coins in a slot (usually 25¢–50¢ for local calls) and wait for a steady tone before dialing. When you call long-distance, the operator tells you how much to insert; prepaid phone cards, widely available in various denominations, can be used from any phone. Follow the directions to activate the card (there is usually an access number and then an activation code for the card), then dial your number.

The United States has several GSM (Global System for Mobile Communications) networks, so multiband mobile phones from most countries (except for Japan) work here. Unfortunately, it's almost impossible to buy a pay-as-you-go mobile SIM card in the U.S.—which allows you to avoid roaming charges—without a phone. That said, cell phones with pay-as-you-go plans are available for well under $100. The cheapest ones with decent national coverage are the GoPhone from Cingular and Virgin Mobile, which only offers pay-as-you-go service.

🛅 Cell Phone Contacts **Cingular** ☎ 888/333–6651 ⊕ www.cingular.com. **Virgin Mobile** ☎ No phone ⊕ www.virginmobileusa.com.

LODGING

Arizona's hotels and motels run the gamut from world-class resorts to budget chains and from historic inns, bed-and-breakfasts, and mountain lodges to dude ranches, campgrounds, and RV parks. **Make reservations well in advance for the high season**—winter in the desert south and summer in the high country. Tremendous bargains can be found off-season, when even the most exclusive establishments can cut their rates by half.

Phoenix and Tucson have the greatest variety of accommodations in the state. Resorts in Sedona and in some of the smaller, more exclusive desert communities can be pricey, but there are cheap chains in (or near) just about every resort-oriented destination in the state. Even the budget chains in these areas can have rates in the upper double-digits, however, especially on holidays and high-season weekends. The Grand Canyon area is equally pricey, but camping options, cabins, and dorm-style resorts on or near the national park grounds can be more affordable. If you plan to stay at the Grand Canyon, make lodging reservations far in advance. You might have a more relaxing visit, and find better prices, if you stay at one of the gateway cities; Tusayan, Williams, and Flagstaff to the south, and Jacob Lake, Fredonia, and Kanab, Utah, to the north.

The lodgings we list are the cream of the crop in each price category. We always list the facilities that are available, but we don't specify whether they cost extra; when pricing accommodations, always ask what's included and what costs extra. Properties are assigned price categories based on the range from their least-expensive standard double room at high season (excluding holidays) to the most expensive. Properties marked ✕ 🗔 are lodging establishments whose restaurants warrant a special trip.

Did the resort look as good in real life as it did in the photos? Did you sleep like a baby, or were the walls paper thin? Did you get your money's worth? Rate hotels and write your own reviews in Travel Ratings or start a discussion about your favorite places in Travel Talk on ⊕ www.fodors.com. Your comments might even appear in our books. Yes, you, too, can be a correspondent!

Most hotels and other lodgings require you to give your credit card details before they will confirm your reservation. If you don't feel comfortable e-mailing this information, ask if you can fax it (some places even prefer faxes). However you book, get confirmation in writing and have a copy of it handy when you check in.

Be sure you understand the hotel's cancellation policy. Some places allow you to cancel without any kind of penalty—even if you prepaid to secure a discounted rate—if you cancel at least 24 hours in advance. Others require you to cancel a week in advance or penalize you for the cost of one night. Small inns and B&Bs are most likely to require you to cancel far in advance. Most hotels allow children under a certain age to stay in their parents' room at no extra charge, but others charge for them as extra adults; find out the cutoff age for discounts.

Assume that hotels operate on the European Plan (**EP**, no meals) unless we specify that they use the Breakfast Plan (**BP**, with full breakfast), Continental Plan (**CP**, Continental breakfast), Full American Plan (**FAP**, all meals), Modified American Plan (**MAP**, breakfast and dinner) or are **all-inclusive** (all meals and most activities).

APARTMENT & HOUSE RENTALS

🏠 **Interhome** ☎ 305/940-2299 or 800/882-6864 ⊕ www.interhome.us. **Vacation Home Rentals Worldwide** ☎ 201/767-9393 or 800/633-3284 ⊕ www.vhrww.com. **Villas International** ☎ 415/499-9490 or 800/221-2260 ⊕ www.villasintl.com.

BED & BREAKFASTS

The Arizona Association of Bed and Breakfast Inns has member inns in most of the popular destinations in the state. The Arizona Trails Reservation Service has an extensive list of B&B and other lodging rentals throughout the state and can also help with vacation packages, tours, and golf vacations. Intimate lodgings in Arizona boast a range of styles, from Southwestern adobe haciendas in areas like Sedona and Tucson to pine cabins in the White Mountains. The Arizona Office of Tourism (⇨ Visitor Information) has a statewide list of B&Bs.

🏠 Reservation Services **Arizona Association of Bed and Breakfast Inns** ☎ 800/284-2589 ⊕ www.arizona-bed-breakfast.com. **Arizona Trails Reservation Service** ☎ 480/837-4284 or 888/799-4284 ⊕ www.arizonatrails.com. **Mi Casa Su Casa** ☎ 480/990-0682 or 800/456-0682 🖷 480/990-3390 ⊕ www.azres.com.

Bed & Breakfast.com ☎ 512/322-2710 or 800/462-2632 ⊕ www.bedandbreakfast.com also sends out an online newsletter. **Bed & Breakfast Inns Online** ☎ 615/868-1946 ⊕ www.bbonline.com. **BnB Finder.com** ☎ 212/432-7693 or 888/469-6663 ⊕ www.bnbfinder.com.

CAMPING

You can choose from among federal, state, Native American, and private campgrounds in virtually all parts of the state. Most state parks have a 14-day maximum-stay limit. Camping is also permitted in Arizona's seven national forests, but be forewarned that they often have no facilities whatsoever; in most cases, backcountry camping permits must be reserved.

Pack according to season, region, and length of trip. Basics include a sleeping bag, a tent (optional, and forbidden in some RV parks), a camp stove, cooking utensils, food and water supplies, a first-aid kit, insect repellent, sunscreen, a lantern, trash bags, a rope, and a tarp.

🔢 **Arizona State Parks Department** ☎ 602/542-4174 ⊕ www.azstateparks.com. **Apache Sitgreaves National Forest** ☎ 928/333-4301 ⊕ www.fs.fed.us/r3/asnf. **Bureau of Land Management** ☎ 602/417-9528 ⊕ www.az.blm.gov. **Coconino National Forest** ☎ 928/527-3600 ⊕ www.fs.fed.us/r3/coconino. **Coronado National Forest** ☎ 520/670-4552 ⊕ www.fs.fed.us/r3/coronado. **National Park Service** ☎ 602/640-5250 or 202/208-6843 🖶 602/640-5265 ⊕ www.nps.gov. **Prescott National Forest** ☎ 928/443-8000 ⊕ www.fs.fed.us/r3/prescott. **Tonto National Forest** ☎ 602/225-5200 ⊕ www.fs.fed.us/r3/tonto. **Williams-Forest Service Visitor Center** ☎ 928/635-4061 ⊕ www.williamschamber.com.

DUDE-GUEST RANCHES

Down-home Western lifestyle, cooking, and activities are the focus of guest ranches, situated primarily in Tucson and southern Arizona and Wickenburg northwest of Phoenix. Some are resortlike properties where guests are pampered, whereas smaller, family-run ranches expect *everyone* to join in the chores. Horseback riding and other outdoor recreational activities are emphasized. Many dude ranches are closed in summer. The Arizona Dude Ranch Association can give you the names and addresses of its member ranches and their facilities and policies. Contact the Arizona Office of Tourism (⇨ Visitor Information) for the names and addresses of dude ranches throughout the state.

🔢 **The Arizona Dude Ranch Association** 🖶 No phone ⊕ www.azdra.com.

HOME EXCHANGES

With a direct home exchange, you stay in someone else's home while they stay in yours. Some outfits also deal with vacation homes, so you're not actually staying in someone's full-time residence, just their vacant weekend place.

🔢 **Exchange Clubs HomeLink International** ☎ 813/975-9825 or 800/638-3841 ⊕ www.homelink.org; $80 yearly for Web-only membership; $125 with Web access and two directories. **Home Exchange.com** ☎ 800/877-8723 ⊕ www.homeexchange.com charges; $49.95 yearly for a 1-year online listing; this is a Web-based company with no catalog. **Intervac U.S.** ☎ 800/756-4663 ⊕ www.intervacus.com; $128.88 yearly for a list-

ing, online access, and a catalog; $78.88 without catalog.

HOSTELS

Hostels offer barebones lodging at low, low prices—often in shared dorm rooms with shared baths—to people of all ages, though the primary market is young travelers, especially students. Most hostels serve breakfast; dinner and/or shared cooking facilities may also be available. In some hostels, you aren't allowed to be in your room during the day, and there may be a curfew at night. Nevertheless, hostels provide a sense of community, with public rooms where travelers often gather to share stories. Many hostels are affiliated with Hostelling International (HI), an umbrella group of hostel associations with some 4,500 member properties in more than 70 countries. Other hostels are completely independent and may be nothing more than a really cheap hotel.

Membership in any HI association, open to travelers of all ages, allows you to stay in HI-affiliated hostels at member rates. One-year membership is about $28 for adults; hostels charge about $10–$30 per night. Members have priority if the hostel is full; they're also eligible for discounts around the world, even on rail and bus travel in some countries.

🔢 **Hostelling International–USA** ☎ 301/495-1240 ⊕ www.hiusa.org. **Hostelling International Phoenix** ✉ ☎ 602/254-9803 ⊕ www.hiayh.org.

HOTELS

Weigh all your options (we can't say this enough). Join "frequent guest" programs. You may get preferential treatment in room choice and/or upgrades in your favorite chains. Check general travel sites and hotel Web sites as not all chains are represented on all travel sites. Always research or inquire about special packages and corporate rates. If you prefer to book by phone, note you can sometimes get a better price if you call the hotel's local toll-free number (if one is available) rather than the central reservations number.

If your destination's high season is December through April and you're trying to book, say, in late April, you might save considerably by changing your dates by a week or two. Note, though, that many properties charge peak-season rates for your entire stay even if your travel dates straddle peak and nonpeak seasons. High-end chains catering to businesspeople are often busy only on weekdays and often drop rates dramatically on weekends to fill up rooms. **Ask when rates go down.**

Watch out for hidden costs, including re-sort fees, energy surcharges, and "convenience" fees for such things as unlimited local phone service you won't use and a free newspaper—possibly written in a language you can't read. Always verify whether local hotel taxes are or are not included in the rates you're quoted, so that you'll know the real price of your stay. In some places, taxes can add 20% or more to your bill. If you're traveling overseas **look for price guarantees,** which protect you against a falling dollar. With your rate locked in, you won't pay more, even if the price goes up in the local currency.

All hotels listed have private bath unless otherwise noted. **Discount Hotel Rooms Accommodations Express** ☎ 800/444-7666 or 800/277-1064. **Hotels. com** ☎ 800/219-4606 or 800/364-0291 ⊕ www. hotels.com. **Quikbook** ☎ 800/789-9887 ⊕ www. quikbook.com. **Turbotrip.com** ☎ 800/473-7829 ⊕ w3.turbotrip.com.

MONEY MATTERS

Prices throughout this guide are given for adults. Substantially reduced fees are almost always available for children, students, and senior citizens. For information on taxes, *see* Taxes.

CREDIT CARDS

Throughout this guide, the following abbreviations are used: **AE,** American Express; **D,** Discover; **DC,** Diners Club; **MC,** MasterCard; and **V,** Visa.

It's a good idea to inform your credit card company before you travel, especially if you're going abroad and don't travel internationally very often. Otherwise, the credit-card company might put a hold on your card owing to unusual activity—not a good thing halfway through your trip. Record all your credit card numbers—as well as the phone numbers to call in the event your cards are lost or stolen—in a safe place so you're prepared should something go wrong. Both MasterCard and Visa have general numbers you can call (collect if you're abroad) if your card is lost, but you're better off calling the number of your issuing bank since MasterCard and Visa usually just transfer you to your bank; your bank's number is usually printed on your card.

Reporting Lost Cards American Express ☎ 800/992-3404 in U.S., 336/393-1111 collect from abroad ⊕ www.americanexpress.com. **Diners Club** ☎ 800/234-6377 in U.S., 303/799-1504 collect from abroad ⊕ www.dinersclub.com. **Discover** ☎ 800/347-2683 in U.S., 801/902-3100 collect from abroad ⊕ www.discovercard.com. **Master-Card** ☎ 800/622-7747 in U.S., 636/722-7111 collect from abroad ⊕ www.mastercard.com. **Visa** ☎ 800/847-2911 in U.S., 410/581-9994 collect from abroad ⊕ www.visa.com.

TRAVELER'S CHECKS & CARDS

Some consider this the currency of the cave man, and it's true that fewer establishments accept traveler's checks these days. Nevertheless, they're a cheap and secure way to carry extra money, particularly on trips to urban areas. Both Citibank (under the Visa brand) and American Express issue traveler's checks in the United States, but Amex is better known and more widely accepted; you can also avoid hefty surcharges by cashing Amex checks at Amex offices. Whatever you do, keep track of all the serial numbers in case the checks are lost or stolen.

American Express now offers a stored-value card called a Travelers Cheque Card, which you can use wherever American Express credit cards are accepted, including ATMs. The card can carry a minimum of $300 and a maximum of $2,700, and it's a safe way to carry your funds. Although you can get replacement funds in 24 hours if your card is lost or stolen, it doesn't really strike us as a very good deal. In addition to a high initial cost ($14.95 to set up the card, plus $5 each time you "reload"), you still have to pay a 2% fee for each purchase in a foreign currency (similar to that of any credit card). Further, each time you use the card in an ATM you pay a transaction fee of $2.50 on top of the 2% transaction fee for the conversion—add it all up and it can be considerably more than you would pay for simply using your own ATM card. Regular traveler's checks are just as secure and cost less.

🛈 **American Express** ☎ 888/412-6945 in U.S., 801/945-9450 collect outside of the U.S. to add value or speak to customer service ⊕ www.americanexpress.com.

NATIONAL PARKS

Look into discount passes to save money on park entrance fees. For $50, the National Parks Pass admits you (and any passengers in your private vehicle) to all national parks, monuments, and recreation areas, as well as other sites run by the National Park Service, for a year. (In parks that charge per person, the pass admits you, your spouse and children, and your parents, when you arrive together.) Camping and parking are extra. The $15 Golden Eagle Pass, a hologram you affix to your National Parks Pass, functions as an upgrade, granting entry to all sites run by the NPS, the U.S. Fish and Wildlife Service, the U.S. Forest Service, and the Bureau of Land Management. The upgrade, which expires with the parks pass, is sold by most national-park, Fish-and-Wildlife, and BLM fee stations. A major percentage of the proceeds from pass sales funds National Parks projects.

Both the Golden Age Passport ($10), for U.S. citizens or permanent residents who are 62 and older, and the Golden Access Passport (free), for persons with disabilities, entitle holders (and any passengers in their private vehicles) to lifetime free entry to all national parks, plus 50% off fees for the use of many park facilities and services. (The discount doesn't always apply to companions.) To obtain them, you must show proof of age and of U.S. citizenship or permanent residency—such as a U.S. passport, driver's license, or birth certificate—and, if requesting Golden Access, proof of disability. The Golden Age and Golden Access passes are available only at NPS-run sites that charge an entrance fee.

The National Parks Pass is also available by mail and phone and via the Internet.

🛈 **National Park Foundation** ☎ 202/238-4200, 888/467-2757 for National Parks Pass info ⊕ www.nationalparks.org. **National Park Service** ☎ 202/208-6843 ⊕ www.nps.gov. **National Parks Conservation Association** ☎ 202/223-6722 or 800/628-7275 ⊕ www.npca.org.

PACKING

Why do some people travel with a convoy of suitcases the size of large-screen TVs and yet never have a thing to wear? How do others pack a toaster-oven-size duffle with a week's worth of outfits *and* supplies for every possible contingency? We realize that packing is a matter of style—a very personal thing—but there's a lot to be said for traveling light. The tips in this section will help you win the battle of the bulging bag.

Make a list. In a recent Fodor's survey, 29% of respondents said they make lists (and often pack) at least a week before a trip. Lists can be used at least twice—once to pack and once to repack at the end of your trip. You'll also have a record of the contents of your suitcase, just in case it disappears in transit.

Think it through. What's the weather like? Is this a business trip or a cruise or resort vacation? Going abroad? In some places and/or sights, traditions of dress may be more or less conservative than you're used to. As your itinerary comes together, jot activities down and note possible outfits next to each (don't forget those shoes and accessories).

Edit your wardrobe. Plan to wear everything twice (better yet, thrice) and to do laundry along the way. Stick to one basic look—urban chic, sporty casual, etc. Build around one or two neutrals and an accent (e.g., black, white, and olive green). Women can freshen looks by changing scarves or jewelry. For a week's trip, you can look smashing with three bottoms, four or five tops, a sweater, and a jacket you can wear alone or over the sweater.

Be practical. Put comfortable shoes at the top of your list. (Did we need to tell you this?) Pack items that are lightweight, wrinkle resistant, compact, and washable. (Or this?) Try a simple wrinkling test: intentionally fold a piece of fabric between your fingers for a couple minutes. If it refuses to crease, it will probably come out of your suitcase looking fresh. That said if you stack and then roll your clothes when packing, they'll wrinkle less.

Check weight and size limitations. In the United States you may be charged extra for checked bags weighing more than 50 pounds. Abroad some airlines don't allow you to check bags weighing more than 60 to 70 pounds, or they charge outrageous fees for every pound your luggage is over. Carry-on size limitations can be stringent, too.

Be prepared to lug it yourself. If there's one thing that can turn a pack rat into a minimalist, it's a vacation spent lugging heavy bags over long distances. Unless you're on a guided tour or a cruise, select luggage that you can readily carry. Porters, like good butlers, are hard to find these days.

Lock it up. Several companies sell locks (about $10) approved by the Transportation Safety Administration that can be unlocked by all U.S. security personnel should they decide to search your bags. Alternatively, you can use simple plastic cable ties, which are sold at hardware stores in bundles.

Tag it. Always put tags on your luggage with some kind of contact information; use your business address if you don't want people to know your home address. Put the same information (and a copy of your itinerary) inside your luggage, too.

Don't check valuables. On U.S. flights, airlines are only liable for about $2,800 per person for bags. On international flights, the liability limit is around $635 per bag. But just try collecting from the airline for items like computers, cameras, and jewelry. It isn't going to happen; they aren't covered. And though comprehensive travel policies may cover luggage, the liability limit is often a pittance. Your homeowners' policy may cover you sufficiently when you travel—or not. You're really better off stashing baubles and gizmos in your carry-on—right near those prescription meds.

Report problems immediately. If your bags—or things in them—are damaged or go astray, file a written claim with your airline *before you leave the airport.* If the airline is at fault, it may give you money for essentials until your luggage arrives. Most lost bags are found within 48 hours, so alert the airline to your whereabouts for two or three days. If your bag was opened for security reasons in the United States and something is missing, file a claim with the TSA.

WHAT YOU'LL NEED IN ARIZONA

Pack casual clothing and resort wear for a trip to Arizona. Stay cool in cotton fabrics and light colors. T-shirts, polo shirts, sundresses, and lightweight shorts, trousers, skirts, and blouses are useful year-round in the southwest. Bring sun hats, swimsuits, sandals, and sunscreen—mandatory warm-weather items. Bring a sweater and a warm jacket in winter, necessary during December and January throughout the state, particularly in the high-country—anywhere around Flagstaff and north of it, and in the White Mountains east of Payson. And don't forget jeans and sneakers or sturdy walking shoes; they're important year-round.

SAFETY

Distribute your cash, credit cards, IDs, and other valuables between a deep front pocket, an inside jacket or vest pocket, and a hidden money pouch. Don't reach for the money pouch once you're in public.

If you travel frequently also look into the Registered Traveler program of the Transportation Security Administration (TSA; ⊕ www.tsa.gov). The program, which is still being tested in five U.S. airports, is designed to cut down on gridlock at security checkpoints by allowing prescreened travelers to pass quickly through kiosks that scan an iris and/or a fingerprint. How sci-fi is that?

STATE PARKS

Arizona state park day-use fees range from $5 to $8 per private vehicle. Campsites on park grounds range between $12 and $15, and are available on a first-come, first-served basis. If you plan on visiting several parks during your stay, consider the $45 Arizona State Parks Annual Pass. The pass admits you and the passengers in your vehicle (up to four adults) to most state parks in Arizona for a year; it also includes free museum admission for the holder of the pass. The pass does not include camping, nor does it include parks in the Colorado River area (Lake Havasu, Cattail Cove, Buckskin Mountain, and River Island, all of which are included in the $100 Colorado River State Parks Annual Pass). Passes can be purchased at any Arizona State Parks office.

🚩 **Arizona State Parks Department** ☎ 602/542-4174 ⊕ www.azstateparks.com.

TAXES
Arizona state sales tax (called a transaction privilege tax), which applies to all purchases except food in grocery stores, is 5.6%. Phoenix and Tucson levy city sales taxes of 1.8% and 2%, respectively, and Flagstaff taxes purchases at a rate of 1.51%. When added to county taxes, the total sales tax in Phoenix goes up to 8.1%; in Tucson, to 7.6%; and in Flagstaff, to 7.91%. Total sales taxes throughout the state range from 7.3% to 10.1%. Sales taxes do not apply on Indian reservations.

TIME
Arizona is in the Mountain Time Zone but Nevada, next door, is in the Pacific Time Zone. Arizona does not use Daylight Saving Time, though, and as a result, from late spring to early fall, Nevada and Arizona observe the same hours.

TIPPING
At restaurants, a 15% tip is standard for waiters; up to 20% may be appropriate at more expensive establishments or for excellent service at any restaurant. The same goes for taxi drivers, bartenders, and hairdressers. Coat-check operators usually expect $1; bellhops and porters should get $1 per bag; hotel maids should get about $2 per day of your stay, and as much as $5 per day at some smaller, upscale B&Bs and inns. On package tours, conductors and drivers usually get $10 per day from the group as a whole; check whether this has already been figured into your cost. For local sightseeing tours, you may individually tip the driver-guide a few dollars if he or she has been helpful or informative. Ushers in theaters do not expect tips.

TOURS & PACKAGES

GUIDED TOURS
Guided tours are a good option when you don't want to do it all yourself. You travel along with a group (sometimes large, sometimes small), stay in prebooked hotels, eat with your fellow travelers (sometimes included in the price of your tour, sometimes not), and follow a schedule. But not all guided tours are a "If This Is Tuesday, It Must Be Belgium" kind of experience. A knowledgable guide can take you places that you might never discover on your own, and you may be pushed to see more than you would have otherwise. Tours aren't for everyone, but they can be just the thing for trips to places where making travel arrangements is difficult or time-consuming (particularly when you don't speak the language). Whenever you book a guided tour, find out what's included and what isn't. A "land-only" tour includes all your travel (by bus, in most cases) in the destination, but not necessarily your flights to or even within it. Also, in most cases, prices in tour brochures don't include fees and taxes. And remember that you'll be expected to tip your guide (in cash) at the end of the tour.

A useful option for touring northern Arizona is the series of Walkabout Audio Tours, which has been produced and marketed by an anthropologist and former teacher in Sedona. The driving and walking tours cover popular historic and natural areas in northern and north-central Arizona, including several tours of the Grand Canyon, the Sedona area, the Petrified Forest, and other areas of the state. They can be purchased directly from the company and are also sold in some bookstores and gift shops in Sedona and the region. CDs are $16, cassettes

$9, or you can purchase a package of three tours at a discount.

🔃 Recommended Generalists **Walkabout Audio Tours** ☎ 877/530-1030 ⊕ www. walkaboutaudiotours.com.

🔃 Archaeology **Archaeological Conservancy** ☎ 505/266-1540 ⊕ www.americanarchaeology. org. **Crow Canyon Archaeological Center** ☎ 970/565-8975 or 800/422-8975 🖷 970/565-4859 ⊕ www.crowcanyon.org. **Southwest Ed-Ventures** ☎ 435/587-2156 or 800/525-4456 🖷 435/587-2193 ⊕ www.sw-adventures.org.

🔃 Bicycling **Backroads** ☎ 510/527-1555 or 800/462-2848 🖷 510/527-1444 ⊕ www.backroads.com. **Cycle America** ☎ 507/263-2665 or 800/245-3263 🖷 507/263-0873 ⊕ www.cycleamerica.com. **Timberline Adventures** ☎ 303/368-4418 or 800/417-2453 🖷 303/368-1651 ⊕ www.timbertours.com.

🔃 Environment **Earthwatch Institute** ☎ 978/461-0081 or 800/776-0188 🖷 978/461-2332 ⊕ www.earthwatch.org.

🔃 Golf **Golfpac** ☎ 407/260-2288 or 800/327-0878 🖷 407/260-8989 ⊕ www.golfpactravel.com.

🔃 Native American History **Journeys into American Indian Territory** ☎ 631/878-8655 or 800/458-2632 🖷 631/878-4518 ⊕ www.indianjourneys.com.

🔃 Natural History **Smithsonian Journeys** ☎ 202/357-4700 or 877/338-8687 🖷 202/633-9250 ⊕ www.smithsonianjourneys.org. **Victor Emanuel Nature Tours** ☎ 512/328-5221 or 800/328-8368 🖷 512/328-2919 ⊕ www.ventbird.com.

🔃 River Rafting For trips on the Colorado River: **Action Whitewater Adventures** ☎ 801/375-4111 or 800/453-1482 🖷 801/375-4175 ⊕ www.riverguide.com. **Grand Canyon Dories** ☎ 800/877-3679 🖷 209/736-2902 ⊕ www.grandcanyondories.com. **OARS** ☎ 209/736-4677 or 800/346-6277 🖷 209/736-2902 ⊕ www.oars.com. **World Wide River Expeditions** ☎ 435/259-7515 or 800/231-2769 🖷 435/259-7512 ⊕ www.worldwideriver.com.

🔃 Self-Drive **Off the Beaten Path** ☎ 406/586-1311 or 800/445-2995 🖷 406/587-4147 ⊕ www.offthebeatenpath.com.

🔃 Spas **Spafinder** ☎ 212/924-6800 or 800/255-7727 ⊕ www.spafinder.com represents numerous day and stay spas in Arizona.

VACATION PACKAGES

Packages *are not* guided tours. Packages combine airfare, accommodations, and perhaps a rental car or other extras (theater tickets, guided excursions, boat trips, reserved entry to popular museums, transit passes), but they let you do your own thing. During busy periods, packages may be your only option because flights and rooms may be otherwise sold out. Packages will definitely save you time. They can also save you money, particularly in peak seasons, but—and this is a really big "but"—you should price each part of the package separately to be sure. And be aware that prices advertised on Web sites and in newspapers rarely include service charges or taxes, which can up your costs by hundreds of dollars.

Note that local tourism boards can provide information about lesser-known and small-niche operators that sell packages to just a few destinations. And don't always assume that you can get the best deal by booking everything yourself. Some packages and cruises are sold only through travel agents.

Each year consumers are stranded or lose their money when packagers—even large ones with excellent reputations—go out of business. How can you protect yourself? First, always pay with a credit card; if you have a problem, your credit-card company may help you resolve it. Second, buy trip insurance that covers default. Third, choose a company that belongs to the U.S. Tour Operators Association, whose members must set aside funds ($1 million) to cover defaults. Finally choose a company that also participates in the Tour Operator Program of the American Society of Travel Agents (ASTA), which will act as mediator in any disputes. You can also check on the tour operator's reputation among travelers by posting an inquiry on one of the Fodors.com forums.

🔃 Organizations **American Society of Travel Agents (ASTA)** ☎ 703/739-2782, 800/965-2782 24-hr hotline ⊕ www.astanet.com. **U.S. Tour Operators Association (USTOA)** ☎ 212/599-6599 ⊕ www.ustoa.com.

🔃 Package Tours 🔃 Air/Hotel/Car **America West Vacations** ☎ 800/356-6611 ⊕ www. americawestvacations.com. **Delta Vacations** ☎ 800/872-7786 ⊕ www.deltavacations.com. **Southwest Airlines Vacations** ☎ 800/243-8372 ⊕ www.swavacations.com. **United Vacations** ☎ 800/328-6877 ⊕ www.unitedvacations.com. **US**

Airways Vacations ☎ 800/455-0123 ⊕ www. usairwaysvacations.com.
🗗 Custom Packages **Amtrak Vacations** ☎ 800/321-8684 ⊕ www.amtrak.com/savings/amtrakvacations.html.

TRAIN TRAVEL

Amtrak's *Southwest Chief* operates daily between Los Angeles and Chicago, stopping in Kingman, Flagstaff, and Winslow. The *Sunset Limited* travels three times each week between Los Angeles and Orlando, with stops at Yuma, Tucson, and Benson. There's a connecting bus (a 2½-hour trip) between Flagstaff and Phoenix.
🗗 Train Information **Amtrak** ☎ 800/872-7245 ⊕ www.amtrak.com.

TRAVEL AGENCIES

If you use an agent—brick-and-mortar or virtual—you'll pay a fee for the service. And know that the service you get from some online agents isn't comprehensive. For example Expedia or Travelocity don't search for prices on budget airlines like JetBlue, Southwest, or small foreign carriers. That said, some agents (online or not) *do* have access to fares that are difficult to find otherwise, and the savings can more than make up for any surcharge.

A knowledgeable brick-and-mortar travel agent can be a godsend if you're booking a cruise, a package trip that's not available to you directly, an air pass, or a complicated itinerary including several overseas flights. What's more travel agents that specialize in a destination may have exclusive access to certain deals and insider information on things such as charter flights. Agents who specialize in types of travelers (senior citizens, gays and lesbians, naturists) or types of trips (cruises, luxury travel, safaris) can also be invaluable.

A top-notch agent planning your trip to Russia will make sure you get the correct visa application and complete it on time; the one booking your cruise may get you a cabin upgrade or arrange to have bottle of champagne chilling in your cabin when you embark. And complain about the surcharges all you like, but when things don't work out the way you'd hoped, it's nice to have an agent to put things right.

🗗 Agent Resources **American Society of Travel Agents** ☎ 703/739-2782 ⊕ www.travelsense.org.
🗗 Online Agents **Expedia** ⊕ www.expedia.com. **Onetravel.com** ⊕ www.onetravel.com. **Orbitz** ⊕ www.orbitz.com. **Priceline.com** ⊕ www. priceline.com. **Travelocity** ⊕ www.travelocity.com.

VISITOR INFORMATION

🗗 Tourist Information **Arizona Office of Tourism** ☎ 602/364-3700 or 866/275-5816 🖷 602/364-3702 ⊕ www.arizonaguide.com.
🗗 Native American Attractions **Gila River Indian Community** ✑ Box 97, Sacaton, 85247 ☎ 520/562-6000 🖷 520/562-6010 ⊕ www.gric.nsn.us. **Hopi Tribe Office of the Chairman** ✑ Box 123, Kykotsmovi 86039 ☎ 928/734-2441 🖷 928/734-2435 ⊕ www.hopi.nsn.us. **Navajo Nation Tourism Office** ✑ Box 663, Window Rock 86515 ☎ 928/871-6436 or 928/871-7371 🖷 928/810-8500 ⊕ www.discovernavajo.com. **Salt River Pima-Maricopa Indian Community** ✉ 10005 E. Osborn Rd., Scottsdale, 85256 ☎ 480/850-8000 🖷 480/850-8014 ⊕ www.saltriver.pima-maricopa.nsn.us. **Tohono O'odham Nation** ✑ Box 837, Sells 85634 ☎ 520/383-2028 🖷 520/383-3379 ⊕ www.itcaonline.com/tribes_tohono.html. **White Mountain Apache Nation** ✑ Box 700, Whiteriver 85941 ☎ 877/338-9628 🖷 928/338-4778 ⊕ www.wmat.nsn.us.

WEB SITES

We're really proud of our Web site: Fodors.com is a great place to begin any journey. Scan Travel Wire for suggested itineraries, travel deals, restaurant and hotel openings, and other up-to-the-minute info. Check out Booking to research prices and book plane tickets, hotel rooms, rental cars, and vacation packages. Head to Talk for on-the-ground pointers from travelers who frequent our message boards. You can also link to loads of other travel-related resources.

After your trip, be sure to rate the places you visited and share your experiences and travel tips with us and other Fodorites in Travel Ratings and Talk on ⊕ www.fodors.com.

For more specific information on Arizona, visit the following:
🗗 All About Arizona 🗗 Grand Canyon **The Canyon** ⊕ www.thecanyon.com. **Grand Canyon National Park** ⊕ www.nps.gov/grca.

The Great Outdoors **Arizona State Parks Web Site** ⊕ www.azstateparks.com. **Great Outdoor Recreation Page** ⊕ www.gorp.com. **National Park Service Site** ⊕ www.nps.gov.

Newsweeklies *Phoenix New Times* ⊕ www.phoenixnewtimes.com. *Tucson Weekly* ⊕ www.tucsonweekly.com.

Time Zones **Timeanddate.com** ⊕ www.timeanddate.com/worldclock can help you figure out the correct time anywhere in the world.

Weather **Accuweather.com** ⊕ www.accuweather.com is an independent weather-forecasting service with especially good coverage of hurricanes. **Weather.com** ⊕ www.weather.com is the Web site for the Weather Channel.

INDEX

PHOTO CREDITS

NOTES

NOTES

NOTES

NOTES

ABOUT OUR WRITERS

Rebecca I. Allen moved to Arizona nine years ago to attend Arizona State University. She, husband Larry, and daughter Emily are proud to call the Valley of the Sun home. An award-winning freelance journalist, Rebecca writes for a variety of print and online publications, including *The Arizona Republic*, *In & Out*, *The Arizona Business Gazette*, *Arizona Highways*, and *Knowledge@WPCarey*.

Flagstaff resident Matt Baatz spends most free moments mountain biking and hiking the trails near Flagstaff and Sedona. He has traversed hundreds of miles of forest, desert, and canyon, but what remains unexplored may occupy him for years to come.

Newspaper columnist Tom Carpenter is a frequent contributor to *Arizona Highways* and *True West*. He enjoys telling people about the treasures and delights to be found throughout northwest Arizona.

Janet Webb Farnsworth is a true Native Arizonian; her family has been in the state for six generations. She's explored Arizona from one end to the other and is a frequent contributor to *Arizona Highways* and other southwestern travel magazines. She lives in Snowflake in Arizona's beautiful White Mountains.

On hiatus from traveling the globe, JoBeth Jamison recently decided to spend more time trotting around her home state of Arizona. The thirty-something Flagstaff native is a graduate of the University of Arizona and now lives in Phoenix where she works for *Arizona Highways* magazine, contributes to several local and national publications, and tours as a back-up singer for a rock band.

Tucson and Southern Arizona updater Mara Levin divides her time among travel writing, social work, and her role as mom to two daughters. A native of California, Mara now lives in Tucson, where the grass may not be greener but the mountains, tranquility, and slower pace of desert life have their own appeal.